THIRD WORLD IMPACT

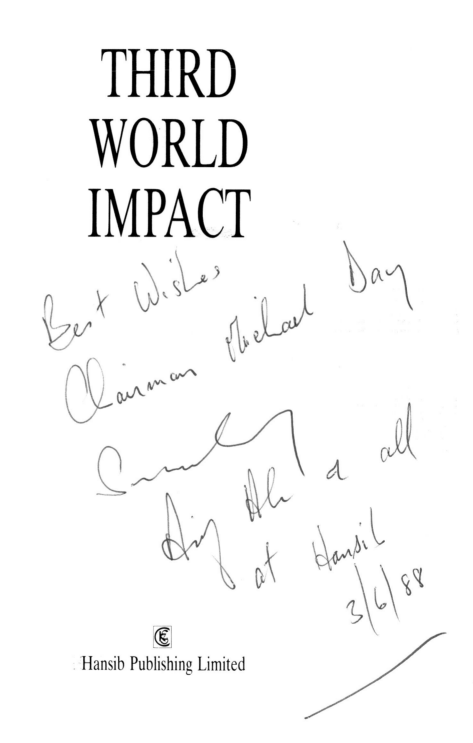

Best Wishes
Chairman Michael Day
Sincerely
Arif Ali & all
at Hansib
3/6/88

Hansib Publishing Limited

First published in Great Britain in 1973 by Hansib Publishing Limited, Tower House, 139/149 Fonthill Road, London N4 3HF.

First Edition 1973
Second Edition 1974
Third Edition 1975
Fourth Edition 1979
Fifth Edition 1982
Sixth Edition 1984
Seventh Edition 1986

Typesetting and Design by Hansib Publishing Limited
Printed in England by Camelot Press, Southampton

ISBN 1 870518 04 7

THIRD WORLD IMPACT

Eighth Edition
Edited by Arif Ali

Hansib Publishing Limited

Acknowledgments to

Those who have contributed their time and effort and who have helped in other ways – often without thought of self;
Our advertisers whose support remains invaluable;
Others who would not wish to be named but whose support is sometimes all the more essential for that;
To bulk writer/researcher/colleague/friend Keith Bennett, Political Editor of Hansib Publishing;
To Jenny Lawther, whose sterling drive and commitment made it possible to meet this schedule and many others;
To Roy Sawh whose efforts kept other departments afloat during the production period;
To John St. Lewis and Jackie Keizer who were responsible for marketing and advertising;
To John Hughes, Head of Hansib's Special Projects, who compiled the Reference and other sections;
To Sharon Atkin for her work on 'Who's Who', her articles and assistance;
To all those who contributed or helped with articles, both those published and those we were unable to use;
To Rolando Vitale who compiled the Sports section and to those who contributed the photographs including Malcolm MacKay, Terry Weir, the *Irish Times*, David Munden, Zahid Ali, Circle Photography, Chris Tofalos, Alan Pascoe Associates and Kevin Small;
To Amina Hussein and her colleagues in the typesetting department – Janice Moore, Paula Edgar, Drucilla Daley, Lesley Hallett, Shawn Martin, Lorna Clerice, Jackie Hughes and Oma Sawh;
To Michelle Wilson, who pushed herself and her team beyond our expectations. To the members of her design and lay-out studio – Salvatore M. Zuccarello, Chris Hill, Nikki Vounoridis, Kerry Thornton, Tim England, Harry Levene, Shireen Bocas and Joanna Reid;
and to Kevin Saul and Calvin Adams of the advertising design section;
To Mansukh Shah and all who assisted with proof reading, including Philip Straker, Julie Roberts, Sam Springer, Yvonne Chew, Bridgette Lawrence, David Roussel-Milner, Catherine Hogben and Brian Moyo;
To Rod Leon and members of the photographic department, Humphrey Nemar and Elvis Donaldson;
To other members of the team who assisted including Stephanie Dews and Abiola Awojobi;
To Michael Clerice, Derek Sansellus and Ricky Christopher who provided steadfast support;
To the numerous agencies, organisations and individuals, from Britain and many other countries, who assisted with research and to Hazel Smith;
To my son Kash and other members of the Ali family;
To those who helped and have been carelessly overlooked –
A very special Thank You. A.A.

Foreword

By Sir Peter Newsam

In his foreword to the 1986 edition of *Third World Impact*, Arif Ali expressed a hope. That hope was for less tokenism in employment, housing allocation, training, promotion and so on.

In 1988 how far has that hope been realised? It is difficult to give a cheerful answer to that question but crucial not to accept a despairing one.

Third World Impact points to some of the good news. There has been political progress. Four black MPs have taken their seats and have made their voices heard both in and out of parliament. They have kicked a door down for others to walk through.

Much the same has happened within local authorities. In the last two years a new group of black mayors and political leaders has emerged. They have not always been fully supported by their colleagues and have found themselves at the wrong end of hostile media coverage too often for this to be mere coincidence. But their struggle will make it easier for others to follow.

In the world of commerce, art, sport and enterprise, this edition of *Third World Impact* celebrates fresh and widespread achievement. Given half a chance, black Britons can do as well as and often better than any other citizens of this country.

But are black Britons given half a chance? Here the news is not good. The great weight of indifference remains. So too does the sudden sharp edge of active racial discrimination. Both need to be vigorously and unitedly opposed by official agencies, such as the Commission for Racial Equality, and by voluntary organisations and committed individuals.

It goes without saying that Hansib will remain in the forefront of the struggle for a fairer society. *Third World Impact* shows what has been achieved. It is also a beacon lighting the way to a better future. It deserves all possible support.

(Sir Peter Newsam is the Chief Executive of the Association of County Councils. He was Chair of the Commission for Racial Equality, 1982-87)

Dedication

To John Chapman, without whose support it would have probably been impossible to sustain our work, particularly in the early days. We might have managed without you – but it would have been something like climbing Mount Everest without a supply of oxygen. We thank you, John Chapman, for your help, efforts and friendship, and trust that you take as compensation the fact that you were pivotal in giving Britain's visible minorities a public presence and profile.

Contents

Advertisers

Introduction

This is the last edition of *Third World Impact* that will be published in the 1980s. Our ninth edition will be launched in 1990 – in the last decade of the twentieth century and of the second millenium.

We are living in disturbing and ominous times. There are more than passing similarities with the 1930s – with the incalculably greater danger that any conflict today cannot simply assume global proportions – it can destroy the globe. The destruction of humanity and its common home may also arise not only from military conflict – there are other dangers too, such as that posed by AIDS and the destruction of the environment.

World War II was fought in the name of liberty and the rights of peoples – their right to nationhood, freedom of religion and culture and the right to a decent standard of living, to health care and education. So many millions of lives were lost in that struggle, yet at times it tragically seems that those lives were wasted.

As in the 1930s, the end of the 1980s sees a trend towards fascism and authoritarianism in a number of countries. It comes in relatively blatant forms, such as the strong showing of the ultra-right National Front in France. It comes more discreetly in the form of Thatcherite and Reaganite creeping counter-revolution. It is flaunted in all its brutal ugliness in the form of state terrorism, usurpation of the land and the dispossession of the people in South Africa and in Palestine, where the victims of Nazism today play the role of Nazi.

The arms race between the great powers – if it is not checked – is leading the world to disaster. Every bomber and submarine built is a school or hospital that does not arise. For the developing countries to become self-sufficient in food – that is for the spectre of famine and hunger to be abolished for ever – would cost just 0.5 per cent of today's global military expenditure.

Yet, although the material means exist to banish poverty almost at a stroke, the governments of the United States, Western Europe and Japan are continuing to use food as a political weapon against states that do not meet with their approval; operating more and more as a closed shop they shut the door to the products of Third World countries in the name of protectionism whilst increasing the prices of their exports, thereby stifling any hope of independent development.

It is not to over-prettify the governments of the 1960s and 1970s to state that those of the 1980s have set new standards in grinding down the countries and peoples of the Third World, in being oblivious to the spread of disease and the destruction of the environment – to the shameless promotion of a crass ideology of selfishness. The crashes on the world's stockmarkets last autumn and the continued volatility of the markets are all – as with the events on Wall Street in 1929 – a warning signal calling for urgent action by those who control the destinies of hundreds of millions on our planet. We need to agitate constantly not merely for partial concessions but for new political thinking that can seize the chance to eliminate drought, disease, hunger, and all the evils that flow from the curse of underdevelopment and the subordination of one nation and people to another. Unless the developed countries accept the need for new political thinking they will in time reap the whirlwind – for the domination of the wealth and resources of the world by the less than 20 per cent of its population that is of European origin cannot last for ever.

Whilst being indifferent to the plight of the Third World and increasingly even to the ordinary people of their own countries, the governments of the USA and Western Europe (the Thatcher government in particular) spare nothing to prop up the odious and evil apartheid regime in South Africa. Without neglecting the pressing need to heal the other bleeding wounds in the world and to resolve outstanding conflicts, we can but express our regret over the fact that the Soviet Union has apparently not succeeded in extracting significant and visible concessions on South Africa from the West in exchange for their co-operation and goodwill in other areas.

The great powers – and we must include their peoples in this consideration – have developed a certain complacency with regard to the suffering and misery that is encapsulated in the word 'war'. They have been involved in war every year since 1945, but these wars have almost invariably been fought on the soil of Third World countries whose peoples have perished in their millions, whilst, with a few notable exceptions, such as Korea and Vietnam, the real aggressors have remained practically unscathed. But if people are blinded to the perils of war by this relative insulation, the realities of the nuclear age make this the height of suicidal folly.

Despite the dangerous situation in the world and the ravages of Thatcherism at home, there have been some positive developments for our community in Britain, not least regarding the political sphere. Never again may we expect to see an all-white House of Commons, and following the next general election we hope to see several more representatives of our communities joining Diane Abbott, Paul Boateng, Bernie Grant and Keith Vaz, as elected tribunes.

Despite this and other achievements scored by our community it remains a sad fact that we have to claw every inch of the way in order to achieve our rights. The degree of positive discrimination reserved for white people is still so extensive and so all-pervasive that any achievement by members of the visible minorities requires a Herculean effort – which by definition means that only a few can progress and advance.

There is a real need for a national effort in terms of positive measures to correct the crying injustices that have been meted out to the community, particularly in the 1980s under the Prime Ministership of Margaret Thatcher. Some hope must be given to the tens of thousands of children and young people from the visible minorities, who see the future solely in terms of a bleak and meaningless struggle for survival. No society, and especially a developed and multifaceted society such as Britain, is able to make real progress if it insists on holding the heads of a large and vibrant section of the community under water until they are able only to gasp and struggle for the very oxygen of survival. Anything built on such a foundation will be as durable as a sand castle – the incoming tide will certainly sweep it away.

The towns and cities of Britain have known riots and disturbances throughout the 1980s – ie. throughout the Prime Ministership of Mrs Margaret Thatcher. Riots are the voice of the unheard and the voiceless – and a warning to the society that provokes them. But it seems that the people in authority have learnt nothing – despite, like the ill-fated Bourbon dynasty, having clearly forgotten nothing. Such is the inescapable conclusion to be drawn from the legislative package that is currently ruining our cities and stripping us of all our democratic rights.

The days when Britain was one of the truly "great" countries in the world have long since passed – and to the extent that such "greatness" was tied to the oppression and occupation of countless nations in Africa, the Caribbean, Asia and elsewhere, we certainly do not regret it.

But there needs to be an alternative to destruction – there has to be a positive plan that can enable people to retain their dignity and hope. Without that we shall all be the losers.

With this Eighth edition, *Third World Impact* has once again expanded its scope and its breadth. We hope that it will find its way to an increasing number of readers who, in turn, will inspire us with their ideas to enhance our subsequent editions.

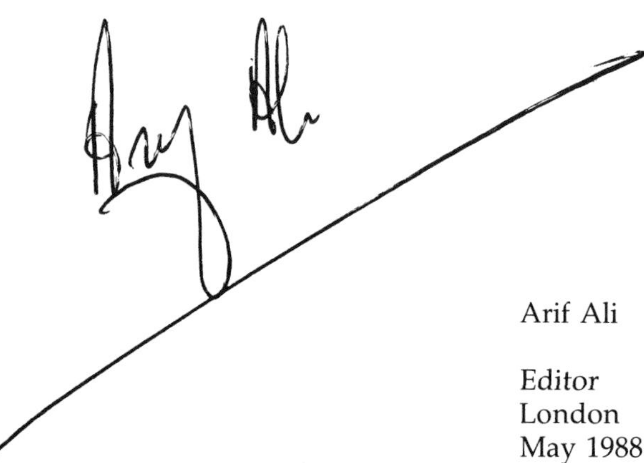

Arif Ali

Editor
London
May 1988

"BYE BYE."

US
"BYE BYE."

"BUY BUY."

First steps to peace

by Altaf Gauhar

The relaxation of superpower tensions following the signing of the Intermediate Nuclear Forces (INF) treaty in Washington, opens the way for solutions to regional conflicts. From Nicaragua to Kampuchea, Lebanon to Angola, Afghanistan, the Gulf and in the occupied territories, things are on the move. The Third World is on notice that a radical change in the state of the world is underway. Can its leaders take advantage of it?

The few months following the signing of the INF treaty have brought a remarkable flurry of diplomatic activity. First the United Nations Secretary-General Javier Perez de Cuellar's special envoy on Afghanistan, Diego Cordovez, rushes off to Rome to meet Zahir Shah, the former King of Afghanistan, without so much as giving a copy of his itinerary to the Pakistanis. The Soviet foreign minister, Eduard Shevardnadze, then proceeds to Kabul, while a senior United States State Department official makes a hurried trip to Islamabad. The withdrawal of Soviet forces from Afghanistan becomes a possibility. And then General Secretary Mikhail Gorbachov announces that the withdrawal could commence from May 15 or possibly even sooner.

In the Middle East, the brutality unleashed by Israel in the West Bank and Gaza invites universal condemnation. But the uprising in the Occupied Territories creates an irresistible impetus towards a Middle East peace settlement. For the first time in years, the US casts a vote in the UN security council which is critical of Israel. The Egyptian President, Hosni Mubarak, travels to Bonn, London, Washington and Paris with his peace proposals. Following on his heels, King Hussein of Jordan visits several European capitals.

Perez de Cuellar publishes a report on the Occupied Territories which condemns Israeli actions in the West Bank and Gaza and announces that the long-postponed international conference on the Middle East must be convened. Shevardnadze endorses this in a letter to the Secretary-General, saying: "It is our conviction that the UN has the prestige and possibilities to dynamise the process of a Near East settlement".

Prince Saud al-Faisal, Saudi Arabia's foreign minister, goes to Moscow and praises the principled position of the Soviet Union on the Palestinian issue. The Saudi minister also conveys the Arab League council's assessment of the Iran-Iraq conflict; Shevardnadze informs him of "the Soviet Union's determination to work for a radical change in world affairs".

Moscow, the Saudis are assured, is working for the resolution of regional conflicts through political means, taking into account the interests of all states and peoples. The Saudi minister learns from Andrei Gromyko, Chair of the Presidium of the Supreme Soviet, i.e. head of state, that the time has come to set up a preparatory committee to convene an international conference to establish peace in the Middle East. The need is recognised for a fresh UN initiative to end the Iran-Iraq war. The possible presence of a UN naval force in the Gulf is seen as a stabilising factor.

Simultaneously, things start moving in Central America. Nicaragua's President Daniel Ortega abandons his earlier refusal to engage in any form of dialogue with the right-wing 'Contra' rebels. He lifts the national emergency and invites the leaders of the 'Contras' to direct talks on a ceasefire and the terms of an amnesty.

This is his way of demonstrating his commitment to the peace process set out in Esquipulas II. The US House of Representatives shows its commitment to peace by rejecting President Reagan's assertion that continued financial support for the 'Contras' is required to keep the Sandinista government involved in peace negotiations.

Visible progress is made in Kampuchea, where the Soviet Union and China have been locked in a

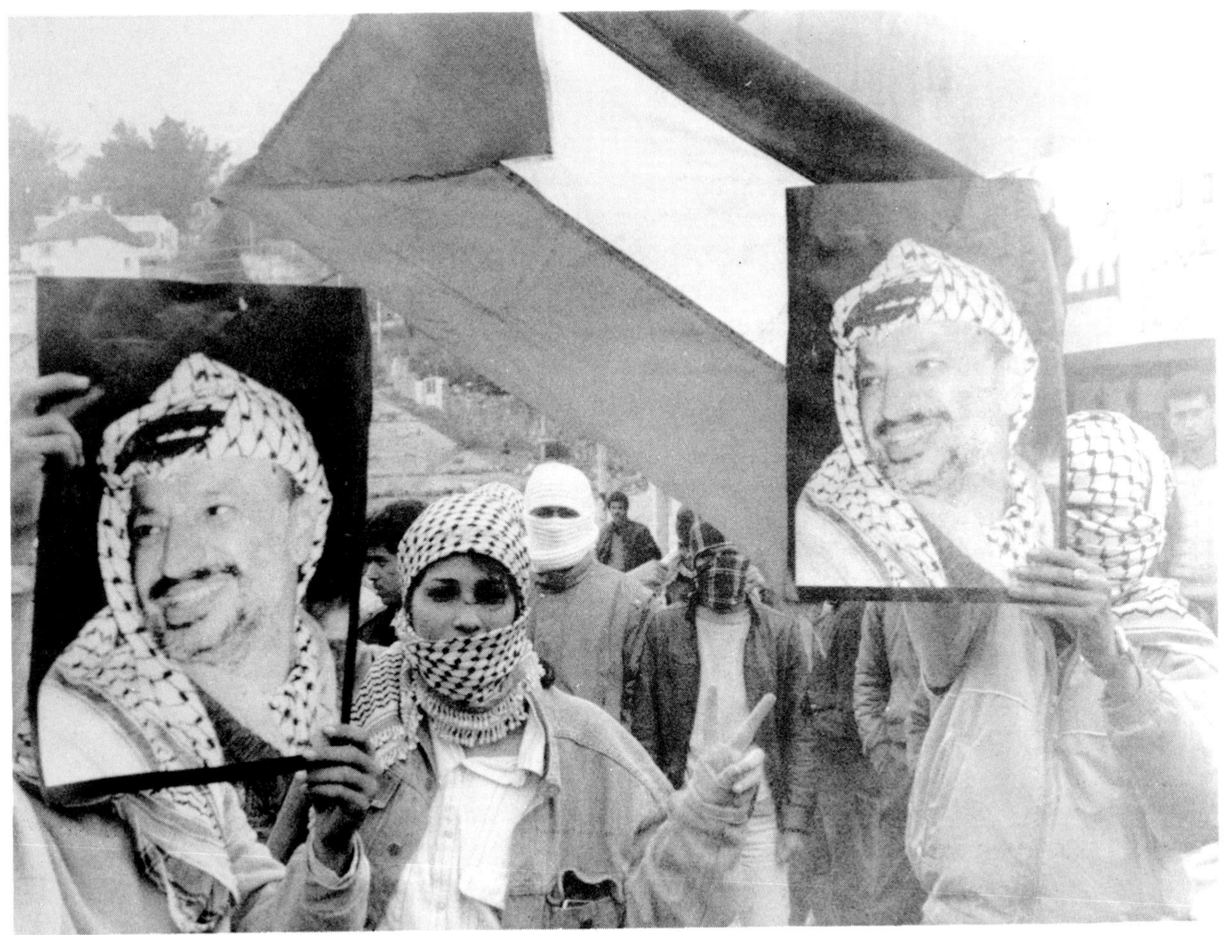

No force can stop the Palestinian people rallying around their revolutionary leadership.

stalemate. The Heng Samrin/Hun Sen government in Phnom Penh and Prince Norodom Sihanouk agree that the Kampuchean question must be resolved among the Kampuchean parties and that Kampuchea's independent, neutral and non-aligned status should be guaranteed by an international conference. The possibility emerges that a coalition government may be formed without the participation of the Khmer Rouge and with Sihanouk as constitutional president.

Next comes the proposal by Mikhail Gorbachov for a summit with China's Deng Xiaoping. When the suggestion is politely rejected by Beijing, the Soviet daily *Pravda* argues that a summit between the two leaders is a "necessity".

A leading Chinese commentator, Professor Huan Xiang, welcomes the INF treaty, saying: "The relaxation in superpower relations following the treaty would be different from the detente of the 1960s and early 1970s because the conditions leading up to it are not the same." Though he does not forsee any "drastic change" in Sino-US and Sino-Soviet relations, he suggests that "some regional military conflicts in which the superpowers are involved – directly or indirectly – are likely to gradually ease."

Drastic or not, there is progress in Sino-Soviet relations. The Soviets have recognised the Chinese claim that the common border lies in the middle of the Amur and Ussuri rivers, so resolving a major dispute between the two countries. Ten thousand Soviet troops have been withdrawn from Mongolia; both sides have reduced the number of troops along their 7,500km border. The withdrawal of Soviet troops from Afghanistan has now begun and if tensions in Kampuchea also start to ease, the prospects for a genuine reconciliation between China and the USSR are bound to improve.

Angola was a surprise development. US

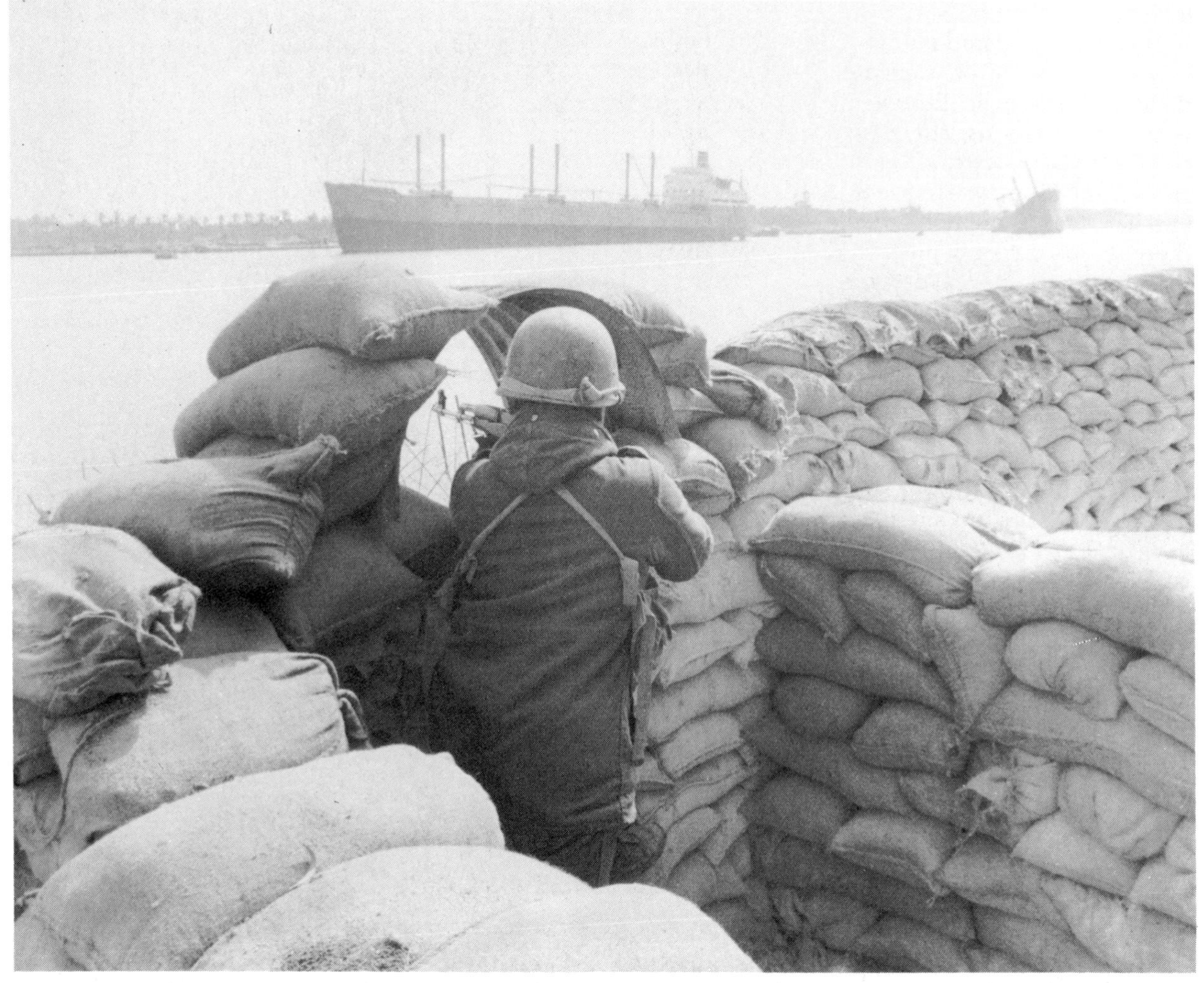

The Gulf War's spillover into the realms of international shipping is fraught with grave dangers for world peace.

Assistant Secretary of State Chester Crocker went to Luanda and met an Angolan delegation which included a member of the Cuban politbureau. The withdrawal of Cuban troops from Angola can take place only if the US stops providing assistance to the South African-backed Unita rebels. This raises another question. Is Washington about to dump the apartheid regime in Pretoria?

If regional issues were on the two leaders' agenda, Washington and Moscow must have come to some understanding about resolving them before they signed the INF treaty. The imminent summit meeting in Moscow between Ronald Reagan and Mikhail Gorbachov will no doubt shed further light on this matter.

There is a revealing sentence in the joint communique issued in Washington on December 8. This says that the talks reflected "both the continuing differences between the two sides, and their understanding that these differences are not insurmountable obstacles to progress in areas of mutual interest". Even though the two sides listed their differences and separated those which they thought were manageable from those they considered insurmountable, they agreed that progress in areas of mutual interest was possible.

This has now been confirmed by Gorbachov's statement that regional conflicts are being discussed and settled as further steps towards disarmament are being planned. If the agreement on medium-range missiles is to be followed by reductions in strategic missiles, so must the settlement in Afghanistan be followed by the settlement of other regional conflicts. He asks: "Which conflict will be settled next?" And he answers: "It is certain that there will be others to follow."

The two sides could not have agreed to eliminate a whole category of arms which has bedevilled their relationship in Europe for the last 20 years without reviewing their position on regional conflicts. The words "mutual interests" are significant because they are different from the familiar "vital national interests". The choice of these words can only mean that in some areas, at least, the two sides are willing to recognise and respect each other's interests on a reciprocal basis.

The stage is set for "a radical change in world affairs", and this change will come about in the new environment of superpower trust. The INF treaty is but the first step on the road to disarmament and development. However, Washington and Moscow still seem to have much to do before they can agree on a further treaty that will cut 50 per cent of their strategic weapons. This is the vital next step towards eliminating all the nuclear weapons on earth.

This grand design for world peace may yet elude us. Still, it is a design worth pursuing, and the indications are that the opponents of peace are losing ground – among them, ironically, those Third World client states whose authoritarian governments thrive on a tense international environment. Their survival depends on the support, overt and covert, which they receive from one or other of the major powers.

External support enables these countries to act as phoney frontline states. It is as mini-crusaders in a giant ideological struggle that their leaders divert a major portion of national resources into arms purchases or into their own pockets. They use the weapons to suppress the people, while denying them health, education and employment, and to carry on their border fights and other petty squabbles.

Peace will put all such states on notice. They will be forced not only to think seriously about settling disputes with their neighbours, but also to respond to the wishes of their people.

Soviet leader Mikhail Gorbachov – proponent of new thinking that has electrified his country and the world.

South Syndication

(Altaf Gauhar is Editor-in-Chief of *South Magazine* and *Third World Quarterly* and the Secretary General of the Third World Foundation for Social and Economic Studies, London. He is a former Pakistani diplomat)

Disarmament and Development

By A Kireyev

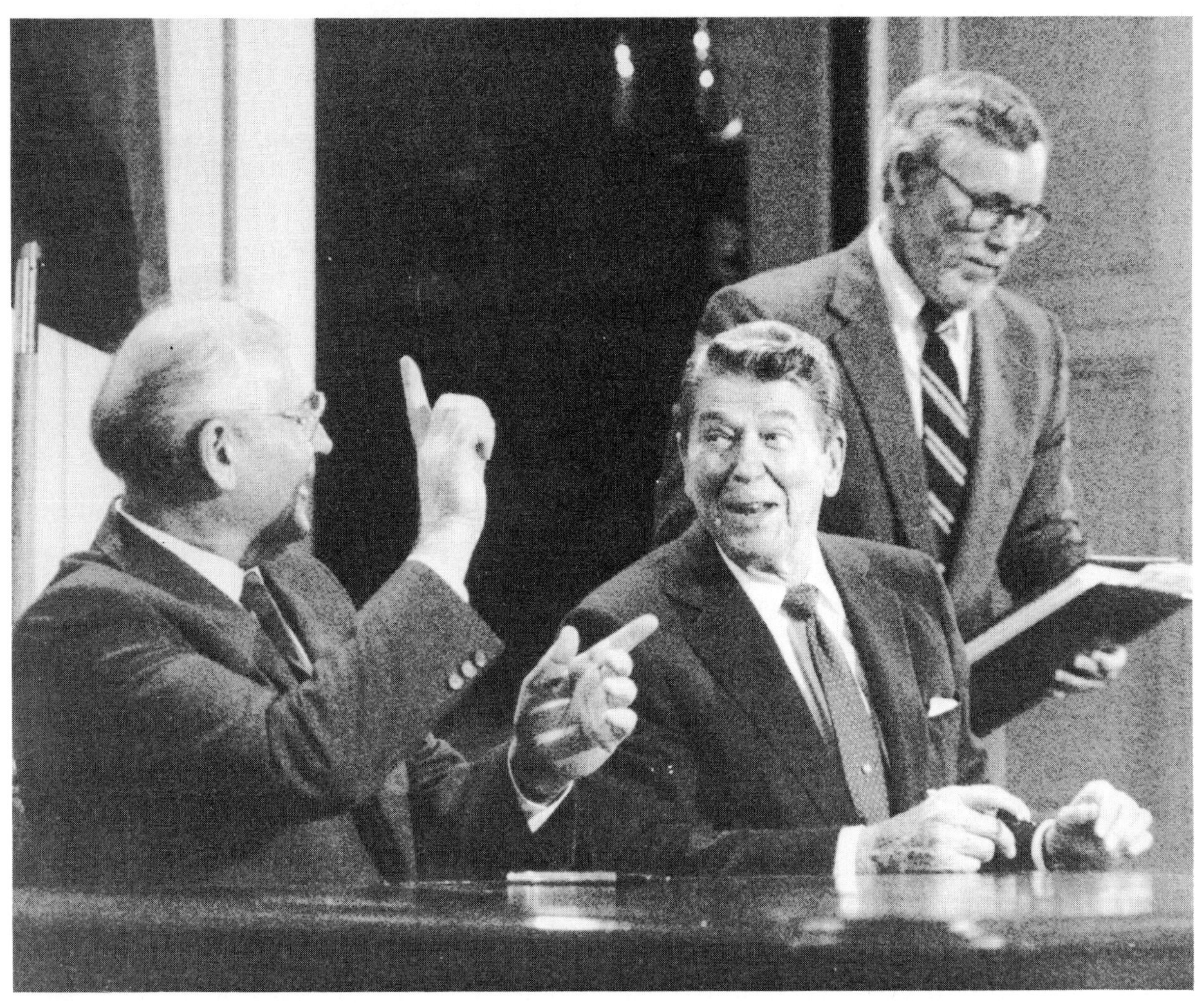

Soviet leader Mikhail Gorbachov and USA President Ronald Reagan together in Washington DC in December 1987. Despite all difficulties their relationship has started to make the world a safer place.

An Israeli soldier threatens defenceless Palestinian women – what has the world learnt since the 1930s?

The annual volume of global military expenditures progresses to the trillion-dollar mark apace: this is a sum already comparable to the developing countries' total foreign debt accrued over the decades. Since 1960, the world has spent 14 trillion dollars on military purposes, as against the 8.6 trillion dollars increase in the global volume of production, according to the International Conference on Inter-relations between Disarmament and Development held at the United Nations headquarters in New York. The priority growth of non-productive military expenditures stifles world economic development.

Three to four years of every human life on Earth are spent on work to feed the monster of war, while 20 per cent of humanity live in appalling poverty. With every new bomber, tank and submarine, the world loses the hope of having several more factories, schools or hospitals. The arms race means measures are never implemented that could fight hunger, disease and natural calamities. It means new millions joining the army of the homeless, illiterate and unemployed.

Imposed on the world by imperialism, the arms race impacts the worst on developing countries. In the recent period their military expenditures have grown twice as fast as those of industrial states to account for more than 20 per cent of the global total. The skyrocketing import of arms is largely to blame here. In the 1960s, the costs of weaponry imported amounted to less than 30 per cent of the total volume of foreign aid. In 1987, developing countries' expenditures on arms imports far exceeded the aid they received. Hence their snowballing foreign debt.

Iranian Prisoners-of-War from the Gulf War – the human price of senseless conflict.

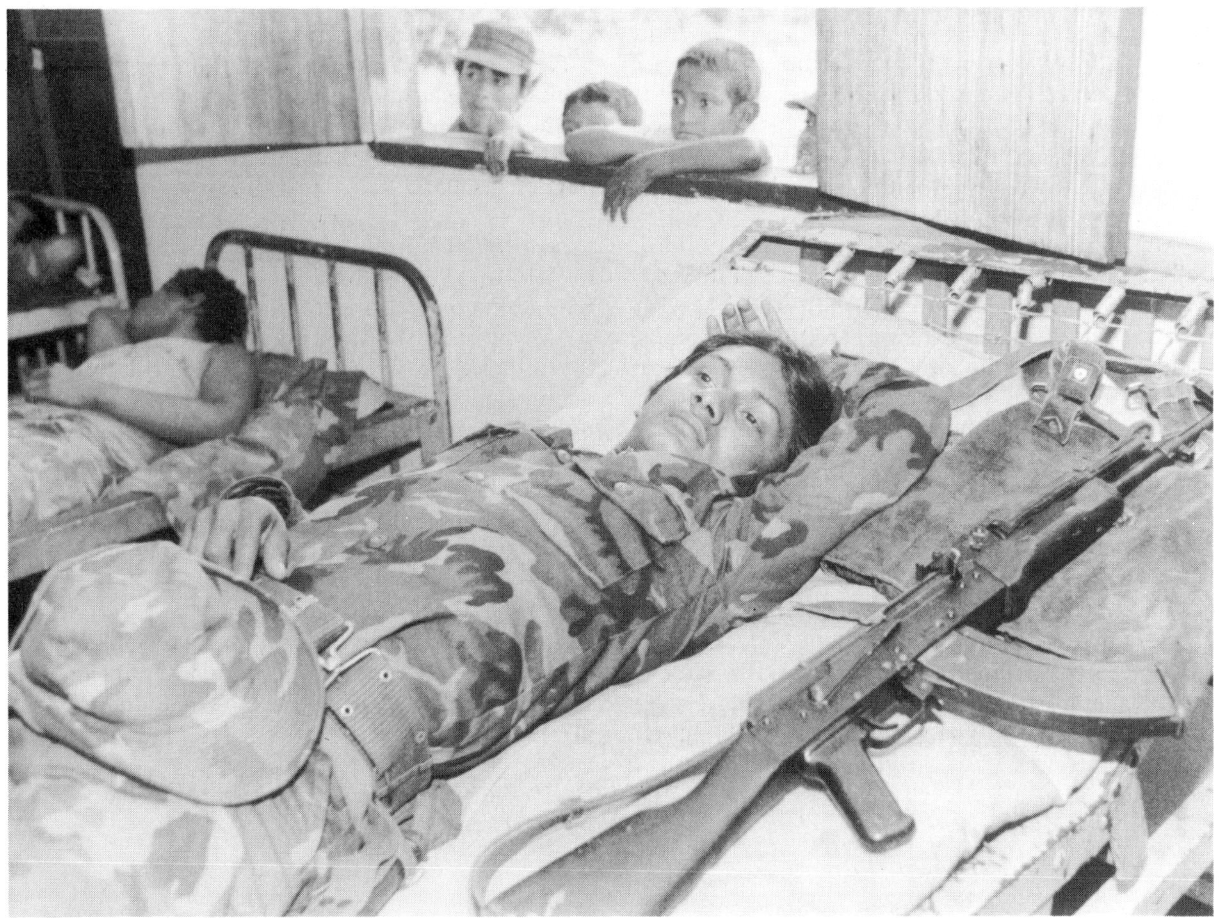

A young Nicaraguan soldier lies wounded in a hospital bed – a victim of Reagan's aggression and terrorism.

Such are just some of the trends of world economic development, with its rapid militarisation. As socialist countries see it, only practical steps to drastically cut armaments can provide the major extra sums needed to solve development issues in the forseeable future. Life poses these issues before all countries without exception.

As the New York City conference, and later statements by Western leaders showed, the West does not formally deny the interdependence between disarmament and development, but seeks to veil it in words, as it ties in both issues with security. It is too early to speak of disarmament before we attain security, says the West.

To be sure, it is vital to attain international security, say both the socialist and developing countries. But such security remains a castle in the air in a hungry world armed to the teeth, they further argue. The world needs practical steps to disarmament, necessarily accompanied by development allocations. With that goal in view, the Soviet Union proposed that an international fund "Disarmament for Development" should be set up, and that NATO and Warsaw Treaty military doctrines should be compared. Such comparison could grow into a realistic one of military budgets with a view to putting an end to their growth by limiting them to a level of reasonable sufficiency. Newly-free countries, in their turn, see development issues as first priorities, with stress laid on non-military threats to social and economic progress, like hunger, disease, illiteracy, the growing foreign debt, and suchlike.

If implemented, the principle of disarmament for development would bring humanity precious gains.

As UN experts estimate, if the arms race

slackens, and global military expenditures are cut by about 30 per cent within this century, the world Gross National Product (GNP) would grow by 3.7 per cent, agricultural produce by 4.6 per cent and, fixed assets by 5.3 per cent, the corresponding figures in developing countries varying from 10 to 14 per cent. So a slower arms race would greatly benefit the Third World.

Cut military expenditures by 100,000 million dollars, and you will have the money to build 300 thermal power stations, each with 120,000 kWt capacity, or a thousand chemical fertiliser plants. It costs 3,000 million dollars to provide 1,200 million Third World townspeople with drinking water. To make developing countries self-sufficient in food in the years ahead, a mere 0.5 per cent of global military expenditures would suffice.

Disarmament would help to fight AIDS. The United States estimates the cost of treatment for 50,000 patients at two million dollars, a sum to be obtained by cutting the federal military budget by a negligible fraction of one per cent.

All that will remain wishful thinking unless arsenals are cut promptly and drastically. The Intermediate Nuclear Forces (INF) Treaty, signed by the Soviet Union and the United States, was the first practical step to such a cut.

Now, the world needs its economic model for a period of disarmament: an especially topical task in the Disarmament for Development effort. That model must include planned shifts of military industries to civilian production in developed countries, an international experts' study of all aspects of such industrial conversion, bilateral and multilateral negotiations to be started on limitations on trade in conventional arms.

New political thinking demands that these topical tasks be solved. Every step to rid humanity of nuclear and other weaponry must not merely build up international security but also improve living standards. Imperialism has long imposed on the world the principle "Armament Instead of Development". It is high time to replace it by the reverse: "Disarmament for Development".

(A Kireyev is a Soviet academic specialising in Economics. This article was originally published in *Trud,* the newspaper of the Soviet trades unions, in March 1988.)

Nelson Mandela – Freedom at Seventy

Nelson Mandela is one of those rare individuals who personify and embody in themselves the aspirations and identity of an entire people. As with such people generally he is also acclaimed as an international leader and a representative of all that is finest and most noble in humanity.

Born on July 18, 1918 Mandela, like millions of his compatriots, grew up in a society where a minority of whites had seized the land and confined the indigenous people to barren and remote areas, where their main function was to supply cheap, slave-like labour to the factories, mines, farms and homes, making South Africa one of the most profitable areas on earth for imperialist interests.

Nelson Mandela was able to obtain further education and became one of the few black South Africans of the period to qualify as a lawyer. But he was a lawyer at the service of his oppressed people. In 1944 he joined the African National Congress (ANC) and soon became one of its leading activists.

In 1956 together with 155 other leading opponents of apartheid, he was arrested and charged with high treason. After five years all the accused were acquitted.

In April 1961 – following the banning of the ANC in the wake of the Sharpeville massacre – Mandela took on additional responsibilities within the liberation movement, including preparation for the stage of armed struggle. Going underground he eluded the apartheid authorities for 15 months and visited a number of countries to build support for the struggle. On August 5, 1962 he was arrested and later sentenced to three years imprisonment on charges of inciting people to strike and illegally leaving the country.

In 1963 Mandela – a founder of the ANC's armed wing, Umkhonto we Sizwe – stood trial again, with nine others, for sabotage. He was sentenced to life imprisonment on June 11, 1964.

Whilst on trial Mandela, the lawyer and freedom fighter, put his accusers on trial and declared passionately that he was prepared to die for his beliefs. At his 1962 trial he made it clear from the outset that "this case is a trial of the aspirations of the African people".

In the more than quarter century that Mandela has been incarcerated his stature has grown and grown nationally and internationally. He remains unbeaten and unbroken – like his people with whom he has constantly reinforced his political, spiritual and emotional bonds. Young people who were not even born before his imprisonment engage in death-defying struggles with his name on their lips. The whole world knows that if South Africa's people could vote, Mandela would be in the Presidential Palace, rather than in Pollsmoor Prison. Internationally, he is more known and more respected than the majority of heads of state and government in the world.

This esteem is reflected in the 'Nelson Mandela – Freedom at 70 Campaign', one of the political and cultural highlights of 1988. The peoples of the world greet the 70th birthday of Nelson Mandela. They do so in full confidence of victory in the struggle to which he has dedicated his life.

Maggie or Three Nations?

A look at the impact of three terms of Thatcherism on Britain's visible minority communities.

Mrs Margaret Thatcher is not only the longest serving British Prime Minister of the century – she has also proved herself to be the most radical, in a bizarre sense one can say revolutionary, Premier of the period. To find a point of comparison one has to look at the record of the 19th century 'Tories' who were considered radical – such as the long-serving Benjamin Disraeli, whose period of leadership coincided with the heyday of jingoistic 'Rule Brittania' chauvinism. Therefore when we talk of the radicalism of the present series of Conservative administrations we are referring to what may be described as a type of "negative radicalism" – one that is innovative, daring and ideologically motivated but in the service not of progress but of turning the clock back and of reinforcing whatever is backward, and ultimately divisive, in society.

Such policies affect every area and section of society – the majority of them adversely. Indeed – although the protagonists of what has become known as 'Thatcherism' are too short-sighted to realise this – there are important ways in which all will suffer from these policies, even though they may benefit, some of them very handsomely, in other areas. This is the case because the general diminution of the standard and quality of life and the opening of chasms between different sectors of society affects the environment of all and, without being alarmist, will lead in the future to a general erosion of the fabric of society, including of standards and facilities that have been built up over centuries.

In this article we concentrate particulary on the question of the visible minorities – but in the most oppressed and most persecuted section of the society, one can see a microcosm of society as a whole and a portent for the future. We can also see the conditions that are being created in one section of society that may, if they are allowed to continue and worsen, light a fuse leading to a conflagration in the whole of society.

Developments in Britain are actually changing the face of the world. In what has hitherto been considered a modern society, and in a country which constantly lectures on so-called 'Western civilisation', the visible minority communities are gradually being forced back decades so that millions of people are condemned to live in conditions that should shame a country that has grown rich by plundering and exploiting half the world for centuries. Britain is now creating within itself the every divisions which it played a pivotal role in fostering on a global scale.

Since the present series of Conservative administrations began in 1979 we have members of our community who, in this period of almost a decade, have never had a job – even though despite every disappointment they have explored whatever avenues have been available. To add to this, we now have the situation where children of 15 and 16 are preparing to leave school having been educated entirely under Tory rule and the constraints of cost cutting and penny pinching,

being consequently ill-educated in both the academic and social senses. Perhaps it is as well that there are so few jobs available to them as many of them would be unable to satisfactorily undergo even a basic job interview. To complement the unemployment situation a nation of unemployables is being produced! It is as though a bizarre master plan was in operation.

The decline in education is matched by the crisis in housing. Because of central government restrictions the building of new homes by local authorities has all but come to a standstill. There is less and less money for repairs and renovations – although the Town Halls are holding millions of pounds from compulsory sales of homes which they are forbidden to use in improving housing. The possibility of buying or even renting a decent home in the south east of England, in particular, becomes more and more of a dream as the value of property starts to lose any semblance of a connection with reality. People and families are therefore forced into ever more overcrowded conditions just as in the immediate post-World War II period – only this time there is no post-war reconstruction being planned.

Beyond the question of overcrowding lurks that of homelessness. A society where thousands of people have no roof over their heads can barely lay claim to the mantle of civilisation; yet the continued crisis in housing, combined with the new housing bill and the general economic crisis and legislative programme, mean that what is already a grave problem will escalate beyond anything that has previously been seen. The 'Poll Tax' in particular, will turn a roof into an unaffordable luxury for many.

Prime Minister Margaret Thatcher once said: "The National Health Service is safe with us." The reality is that there is a two-tier system emerging whereby health must be bought with wealth whilst others die for want of basic treatment and care, adequate facilities and the means to produce a correct diagnosis.

Established after the Second World War, the National Health Service (NHS) was one of Britain's greatest gains for the working people and a lynchpin of the welfare state. But the NHS would never have been a viable project were it not for the many thousands of people from the Caribbean, Asia and Africa who staffed the service – generally in the worst and most low-paid positions doing the most dangerous, dirty and unwanted jobs. When the NHS is under attack these workers have struggled and are struggling not only on questions of their own jobs, pay and conditions but also to safeguard the service itself. However, saintliness does not pay the bills or provide the means for running a home and raising a family. An increasing number of NHS staff feel unable to take the steadily mounting pressures, the low wages and the ingratitude of those on high. Their departure is further exacerbating an already acute situation.

The Prime Minister's stated goal is to "destroy socialism" in Britain (and probably in the world if she could get away with it) and to her "socialism" appears to mean anything that is not run strictly according to market principles and for the benefit of private enterprise. There is therefore a hostility to the public sector, and in general to the people in the inner cities and to anything that cannot instantly make a "fast buck". Lurking behind these tastes and prejudices, there is an ugly dose of racism – at the same time such policies themselves serve to further fuel racism.

Precise definitions vary but public services currently employ in the region of five million workers and cover many areas of people's lives, including health, education, public transport and the road. They used to cover gas, and, for the moment at least, still include water and electricity. In a recent lecture, Rodney Bickerstaffe, General Secretary of the National Union of Public Employees (NUPE), noted that:

"Past generations have been willing and able to extend and improve public provision, frequently where the market failed to meet or even to recognise need.

"This isn't to say that their achievements were flawless or perfect, but that their principal orientation was social and beneficial.

"Against this, the current Conservative administration prefers the market, individuals and dog-eat-dog. Those who can, might, if the price is right, and those who can't, don't even have the chance to exercise their choice."

Thatcherism has come in three waves since 1979. In the first, a governmental priority was to pursue economic policies that drove up unemployment and created a climate whereby new anti-trade union laws could be introduced.

In the second period, which followed the 1983 general election, fought on the Malvinas/Falklands return to jingoistic gunboat diplomacy, there was a campaign to sell off public industries. In the third phase, inaugurated by the 1987 general election, the chief target of the government has become the public services themselves.

A particular target is local government and its services – a sector already suffering as a result of compulsory sales of housing, rate capping and other financial restraints. Added to these are four major pieces of legislation currently being forced through parliament.

Firstly, the Local Government Act. This compels every council in the country to 'invite' private contractors to bid for vital local services like school meals and refuse collection. This means that over half a million of the lowest paid council staff will be told that they must accept lower pay and worse conditions or lose their job to an outside company. The job of private companies is to make profits not to provide services. When services have been privatised it has been to the detriment of both workers and consumers.

Secondly, the Local Government Finance Bill. This is the bill which provides for the introduction of the 'poll tax', something that goes fundamentally against the principles of modern taxation, namely that they should be based on ability to pay. The poll tax is also a racist measure, as it has been clearly shown in a number of studies not only that the overwhelming majority of visible minority households will be worse off than they are at present, but that they will also be worse off than their white neighbours. However, whilst the poll tax has at least become a national issue, hardly any attention has been focussed on another measure whose consequences could be nearly as grave. Under the new plan for business rates, councils will not only lose control over them but also the income from them. All the money raised will go into a national pool and be shared out among authorities simply according to population, without any regard for the relative wealth and prospects of an area or of any special or particular needs. The result of this will be that any council wanting to improve its services beyond the fixed level set by the government will have to raise *all* the extra money from the poll tax. It is estimated that a one per cent increase in spending will mean a poll tax increase of four per cent. The inevitable result is that councils will be under enormous pressure to make cuts. It is a means of punishing the poor for their poverty and executing a major redistribution of wealth away from the already poor to the soon-to-be even richer.

Thirdly, the Education Bill. Under this proposed law schools will have the right to 'opt out' from local authority control. The Inner London Education Authority (ILEA) is to be abolished and a range of financial powers will pass from councils to head teachers. The Education Bill is really a back door means to reintroduce selective schooling, whereby the privileged few receive a first class service whilst an under-funded, under-staffed service is reserved for the rest who, of course, include the visible minorities. The education of unemployables for a future of unemployment is scheduled to become institutionalised. This represents a classic way of keeping the masses of people under control. Uneducated people are easily managed and manipulated. This is either being done consciously or people have not realised the full dangers.

Fourthly, the Housing Bill. The government advertises this as giving council tenants the right to switch to private landlords. What it really does is to give those private landlords the right to buy council properties. The only right that a council tenant will have will be to object to private landlords' bids, and only if at least half the tenants make a formal objection can a sale be stopped. The role of local authorities as providers of homes will be crippled and tenants' rights and the quality of housing will be knocked back decades.

These measures cover different areas but they are not random or isolated attacks but rather a part of a conscious, deliberate and comprehensive strategy. They will make life more difficult, if not impossible, for millions.

For our people life will become almost intolerable. We do not seek to accuse any individual of malign intent or to indulge in conspiracy theories, but the direction of policies can almost lead one to believe that there is some deliberate plan to engineer the removal of visible minorities from British society. Such a thing has happened before, as during the reign of Queen Elizabeth I, when "diverse blackamoors" were ordered to be driven from the kingdom.

Whilst mass physical removal may not be on the agenda it is a fact that a process of economic, social and cultural removal is already underway. Premier Margaret Thatcher elevated herself into office with a demogogic speech justifying people's supposed fears (her own fears perhaps?) of being 'swamped' by those with an 'alien culture'. By marginalising the visible minorities completely the danger of such 'swamping', if we may use this unpleasant word with its inanimate connotations once again, is presumably resolved. But historical lessons show that such processes once unleashed acquire a momentum of their own and are fraught with grave and unpredictable consequences for all concerned – the aggressors as well as the aggressed. In this context we must note that preliminary soundings are starting to be made for the post – Thatcher succession. A clear danger is emerging that people will learn from her bad example and this, in turn, could easily lead to greater extremism.

The totality of the racist package is reinforced when one remembers that as well as making life unbearable for families, the very right to family life is and has been under attack. Racist laws passed by successive governments have kept Asian, African and Westindian families divided for years and imposed terrible humiliations on children who must attempt to prove their parentage. The new Nationality Act will further tighten those screws and will also revoke certain pledges that were given the force of law by previous acts. The stipulation that those who seek family reunion must prove that they will do so "without recourse to public funds" – public funds which in many instances the head of the family has contributed to through taxes levied on wages earned through back-breaking labour or funds disbursed by the very organisation that is employing the person – introduces a racial means test into the provision of services of a kind which the South African regime would truly envy.

Margaret Thatcher talks a great deal about family life and projects a public image of herself as a family person. It is actually something of a trade mark for her as she seeks to keep her wisdom not simply for domestic consumption but lectures the Soviet Union and other countries on the matter as well. But the policies of her government suggest that she is only talking about white family life.

Some of the local authorites – and in particular the former Greater London Council (GLC) and the other disbanded Metropolitan authorities – have provided just about the only layer of protection for the community in the face of this government offensive. That is why they too have been placed in the firing line, why they have been either abolished or completely hamstrung.

To the extent that the government sees any need for ameliorating the worst results of its policies it will grudgingly consent to and arrange only the most superficial and short term measures that serve to paper over the contradictions rather than resolving them. Indeed they continue to pursue the policies that are raising those contradictions to the level of antagonism.

It is fortunate from the point of view of the stability of British society as a whole that the visible minority communities are not highly organised from the point of view of waging a violent struggle. Contrary to the reports that appear in the sensationalised media with increasing frequency, outside forces have not infiltrated into our community with any degree of success, nor are there significant indigenous forces within the community who would want to make those kinds of approaches. But it should be stressed that this is entirely due to the good sense and responsibility of the minority communities, not to any shortage of provocations on the part of the authorities.

Barring any unforeseen eventualities the Conservative Party is set to rule Britain for the whole of the 1980s. One has to go as far back as the earlier part of the nineteenth century to find a similar period in British history of uninterrupted rule by a single party over a calendar decade. But the relationship to the nineteenth century does not end here. As in that era we are witness to – indeed we are victims of – a divided and divisive society marked by the yawning gap between the 'haves' and the 'have nots', where exploitation is rendered acute, being classified an aggravated by special levels and types of oppression.

It is certainly an achievement to be the longest serving British Prime Minister of the twentieth century, but whilst she has been in office Mrs Thatcher has totally disrupted the quality and standard of life of the country. The one thing that must be placed on the credit side for her is that she has been careful to more than help a tiny minority who have benefited handsomely from her rule. This handful of people are precisely those who most ensure – financially and in other ways – that she remains in office.

Much is made of the present divide between 'north' and 'south'. But to that very real division it is now necessary to add that between the visible minorities and others. Increasingly it can be said that Britain is three nations with a one party state. How long will it last?

First they came for the Jews
and I did not speak out –
because I was not a Jew.

Then they came for the communists
and I did not speak out –
because I was not a communist.

Then they came for the trade unionists
and I did not speak out –
because I was not a trade unionist.

Then they came for me –
and there was no one left
to speak out for me.

Pastor Niemoeller
(victim of the Nazis)

NORTH • LONDON • BUSINESS • DEVELOPMENT • AGENCY

The North London Business Development Agency is one of the three Enterprise Agencies established by a unique initiative of the Home Office. This Agency is a partnership between the Home Office, the London Borough of Hackney, the London Borough of Haringey, the Private Sector, local businesses and community groups.

The active participation of such organisations in this VENTURE proves the need of the existence of the North London Business Development Agency in this inner-city area of Finsbury Park to address the needs of the local community and at the same time serve the three neighbouring Boroughs of Islington, Hackney and Haringey.

Various Government Departments joined forces together with the two local authorities to provide premises and financial support for the creation of this Agency.

The problems of the Inner Cities can best be tackled by the local communities with expert advice, training, and financial opportunities and, hence, the creation of these local Enterprise Agencies to provide the encouragement for the development of small businesses, job creation and self-employment especially amongst the unemployed.

It is essential for small business, particularly black business, to produce high standards of presentation and business packages, to the lending institutions, and in today's competitive market in the general business world.

The encouragement which has been shown by the funding bodies to this Agency and the enthusiasm and interest of Board Members has given the Agency the added impetus to realise its objectives.

The Board Agency consists of representatives of our sponsor companies, local businesses, the two local authorities and local community groups.

For further information contact Manny Cotter, Executive Director at 35-37 Blackstock Road, Finsbury Park, London N4 2JF.

Telephone 01-359 7405/7

The Third World and the Western media monopoly

The case for an independent news agency of the non-aligned countries

by Mohammed Arif

This article by Economics lecturer Mohammed Arif is based on a paper that he presented at the International Conference on Non-Alignment and World Peace, held in the Indian capital, New Delhi, in August 1987. He is continuing his research on the subject.

It is not so long ago that Non-Aligned states, particularly in Asia and Africa, emerged from colonial domination. Since then they have been fighting to shake off that colonial past and to build just, humane, egalitarian and prosperous societies, based on industrialisation in a world free from the threat of nuclear and conventional armaments and warfare.

Owing to their strategically vital location and their vast resources, they are today being subjected to neo-colonial plunder and veritably to psychological warfare. They are exposed to systematically planned campaigns of ideological subversion. This distorts their thinking and behaviour and leads to moral degradation. Western propaganda tries to falsify the essence of non-alignment, slanders the aspirations and criticises the course which young states choose for their economic, political and cultural independence.

In recent years the western world has sharply intensified its ideological propaganda against Afro-Asian and Latin American states.

This might be partly explained by the economic failure of western societies to maintain full employment and growth and partly by the emergence of three notable trends: a) Privatisation; b) Technological development; and c) A new aggressive conservatism. Reagan in the USA, Thatcher in Britain and Kohl in West Germany represent this new aggressive conservatism which is based upon the theory of 'new classical economics' and cold war militancy. One result is a greatly increased intensity in the crisis which grips the world economic system. In fact instead of leading national policies towards freedom, they are leading them in the direction of a new reactionary authoritarianism in various forms and guises.

Vast resources have been allocated by western states and multi-national companies for the continuance of psychological warfare. They are trying to brainwash people in developing countries through their domination of the mass media, TV, films, cinema, theatre, advertisements, cultural and scientific exchanges and so on.

Noteworthy is the resourcefulness of western propaganda generally and its ability to change form, choice of means and co-ordination between the state and private sectors. The object is to influence the masses in the political, cultural and economic fields.

In the political field the objective is to enforce bourgeois ideology and to smear socialism; to malign liberation struggles and to describe developing people's defensive actions as an unwarranted resort to violence, to put it mildly.

In the economic field the object is to bring about a kind of nineteenth century laissez-faire attitude in encouraging private enterprise and the dominance of multi-national companies. The continued economic dependence of developing states on the western powers is the obvious objective. The corollary is continuing exploitation of areas which were formerly colonies.

In the cultural field non-aligned countries are subjected to cultural subversion, and, cultural colonisation. Soap operas, such as *'Dallas'*, *'Dynasty'* and *'The Colbys'* are shown in many non-aligned countries without editing. These programmes interrupt and interfere with established indigenous ways of life and values and impose surreptitiously a specific life style, standards and values. The result is that youth in developing societies are torn from old moorings, and have no anchor in any culture. This bewildered and rootless youth are putty in the hands of United States and west European propagandists. The US is known for subsidising these so-called cultural programmes and their screening in poorer countries. Such programmes are subsidised by multinational companies. With technological developments such as cable TV, the danger is that the showing of these soap operas may increase substantially in Third World countries.

The effect of all this is that the people of Africa, Asia and Latin America do not see themselves through their own eyes but the eyes of the West. They are led to believe in the superiority of the western media, bourgeois political beliefs, culture and values.

A study of the western media – in particular the British in relation to Commonwealth countries – is important not only concerning its effect on the western world but even more so for its effect on the Third World.

The western establishments first tried to perfect brainwashing techniques by applying them to their own people; an example is the use of Saatchi and Saatchi in Britain by the Conservative Party in the 1983 and 1987 elections. The success they achieved in moulding public opinion is a case in point. Further, if one looks at Britain, the entire press is virtually controlled by four or five multinational companies, with the exception of a few newspapers, and all are losing money. These losses are made up by profits in industry. One cannot justify publication of these newspapers; purely on commercial criteria. Our profit – maximising criteria only a few should have survived. The fact is, the criterion is not commercial, it is political. The press in Britain is centralised, and pro-Conservative Party.[1] It is right-wing, pro-capitalist; and it expresses the opinions of its proprietors.

So far as radio and TV are concerned, it is known that the BBC is a state-financed institution. Commercial TV companies are owned by multinational companies. Obviously, he who pays the piper calls the tune. Moreover, the appointment of programme makers is subjected to vetting by the security service of the state. "Those who have been politically active on the left can expect to be turned down, as others who have without political commitment been associated with persons known to be active in this way. So far as commercial TV companies are concerned there is evidence of close contact with the security services and the exchange of information with them".[2]

The press in Britain is divided into the 'quality' and the 'popular' papers. The popular papers are mostly tabloid size, smaller than the quality, but they sell five times as many copies. This plays an important part in maintaining divisions in society as well as cultural gaps between classes.

Most of the studies conducted by objective scholars have come to the conclusion that the western media, day after day, pumps out propaganda in favour of class exploitation, imperialism, subtle racism and sexism.[3] The objective of this is to discourage progressive change and cooperation between different peoples and sections of society against the status quo.

In this context I would like to draw attention to the roughly eight million Afro-Asian people who live in western Europe; out of this three and a half million live in the United Kingdom. These people suffer more than the white population. The British media supplies the white population with a series of racist images of black people. Black people themselves are, however, practically absent from the public debate about themselves. They are presented as immigrants, a problem, parts of the barbaric former colonial empire, representative of a backward and disorderly part of the planet. There are very few programmes, certainly not the popular ones, which show the contemporary or historical dignity of Afro-Asian people, their creativity, their resistance to oppression, their cultural and scientific contributions.[4] All this helps to reinforce illusions of racial supremacy among white workers and prevents communication between white and black workers concerning cultural traditions and common interests. Clear evidence of this was found in the statistics of the general election, 1987, which showed that all Afro-Asian candidates did less well than their parties' regional average. In the case of Labour there was a drop of 2.2 per cent, in the case of Tories there was a drop of 2.5 per cent, and in the case of Alliance a drop of 5.2 per cent overall. All this shows that race was still a real issue in the minds of voters, though it did not surface in the words and speeches of politicians during the national campaign to any great extent. Instead law and order became a major political issue and one which the British media has connected in the public mind with Afro-Asian people.[5]

I believe that Afro-Asian people who wish to

communicate with each other, and with others, must do so without, indeed against, the established media. These people obviously require, and are anxious to obtain, information from alternative sources.

The influence of the western media in the Third World in general, and the non-aligned world in particular, is largely the result of the latter's dependence on multinational companies which control newsagencies, and produce printing equipment, radio and TV equipment, paper and advertising. To give examples: 80 per cent of daily newspapers in non-socialist countries are controlled by a handful of multinational companies.[6] The West also controls 90 per cent of radio waves and 95 per cent of TV capacity in the international range outside the Socialist world. About 80 per cent of the information broadcast and printed in non-aligned countries is supplied by four major western news agencies; they are UPI, AP, Reuters and Agence France Presse. Further studies have shown that the USA controls 75 per cent of the world's flow of TV programmes, 50 per cent of film show time, 35 per cent of published books, and 90 per cent of TV news (together with the British Visnews), 60 per cent of records and tapes, 82 per cent of the production of computers used in mass communication, and 89 per cent of computer-fed commercial information. Research also confirmed that the western share of correspondents worldwide is above 70 per cent.[7]

On the other hand, a disappointing picture emerges in the case of news agencies of newly liberated Afro-Asian countries: they own 74 new agencies out of 104 (see Apendix). Most of them lack the technical, financial and human resources to be effective both nationally and internationally. The result is that they are forced to depend on the giant western news agencies for the coverage of international events. Further, with the expansion of information and communication, these giant news agencies are also a major source of information for mass communication media, particularly newspapers and radio. We often see newspapers publishing reports received from such agencies in the same wording and style. It is sad to observe that the 'Tuesday morning American Embassy briefings' on Afghanistan in Delhi, which are full of misinformation, are splashed up by these giant news agencies and are produced by newspapers the following day in Afro-Asian countries, as well as in the West.[8]

A highly respected British journalist, after visiting Afghanistan, attended one of these disinformation sessions and reported that he was astonished to hear that the town of Paghman, just outside the Afghan capital of Kabul, "appears to remain firmly in the hands of rebels." Eight days earlier he had been taken to Paghman by Afghan government officials whom he had challenged to prove that what the western embassies were saying was wrong. From his observation, the Afghan government was right. He also reported the kind of journalists invited to the briefing "included a Pakistani representative of the Associated Press" (who also writes for the *Daily Telegraph)*, and others from Agence France Presse, the West German DPA, and the Saudi news agency. There was a man from the Japanese 'Moonie' paper Seki Nippo, a man who doubles for Radio Free Europe and another "Moonie" paper, *The Washington Times* and a "US freelancer"[9]. This only goes to show that the moment a national liberation struggle starts in any country it at once becomes a target for disinformation and the western propaganda machine begins to work at full capacity.

There is an ideological confrontation between political systems in the world, and we would be dismally failing in our duty to proliferate the truth, if we tried to avoid discussing the fundamental principles underlying this issue.

There is indeed a struggle in progress for the minds and hearts of men and women in Asia and Africa, and our future depends to no small degree on the outcome of the struggle.

The arms race, hunger, poverty, international tension and the retarding of progress in Asia and Africa – all these spring from the fact that those who rule in the western world insist on taking the ideological confrontation into the military arena, and exacerbating the situation further by economic and psychological warfare. This is why they are critical of the United Nations. This is why they are attempting to break up UNESCO and spreading lies about the new international economic order, and this also is why they are spreading lies about the new international information order.

However, in spite of continuous efforts by Third World countries to restructure international relations in the field of information and to establish freedom in culture and communications; and in spite of the 39th U.N. General Assembly resolution, by a vote of 77 in favour, 6 against (USA, Britain, West Germany, the Netherlands, Israel and Japan), when it was decided to decolonise information and assist developing countries to build their own information and communication infrastructure,[10] I feel little headway has been made in this field. The impact of the resolution has not been felt by Afro-Asian people.

I dare suggest that the members of the Non-Aligned Movement should create their own news agency jointly. India, Algeria, Syria and Cuba would be the natural leaders in this. They have the skill, technical resources and are less prone to international pressure. I do not feel that most non-aligned countries have the resources individually to enable them to create an agency which could have an international impact and could compete with multinational news agencies on an equal footing.

I believe that in order to compete with western multinational companies Afro-Asian countries need to create their own multinational news agency. We need this agency desperately because I believe that the peace and progressive movements in Asia and Africa should grow, it is only necessary that these grow en masse and yet remain healthy and strong by continual raising of the level of political education and debate". We need a new international information order to educate people about the massive socio-economic, cultural and political exploitation to which they have been subjected, and are still. To restore their confidence in themselves we need to expose in the international field, who is for peace, who is for military aggression, and who is trying to consign our culture, our language, our political freedom to the dustbin of history. We also need to show who is for sharing the world's resources and scientific development for the good of all mankind and who is using all those things for their own small and sectional ends and who is dividing the world into spheres of influence to serve their own interests.

Above all we have to explore who supports the policy of progress, freedom and national liberation and who follows the policy of backwardness and enslavement. I firmly believe that the non-aligned countries must move forward; otherwise the west will push them backward. The choice is between freedom and barbarism.

I also believe that the eight million Afro-Asian people who live in Europe are equally eager to see the establishment of an independent news agency which will provide them with genuine information about the peoples of African and Asian countries with whose struggles they have historic links of solidarity.

References

1. John Whale, 'The politics of the media', Manchester University Press, 1980.
2. Stuard Hood 'On Television', Pluto Press, London, 1983.
3. Ibid – 2
4. John Downing, 'The Media Machine', Pluto Press, 1980.
5. 'New Statesman', London, August 1987.
6. News Bulletin No. 74, Novosti Press Agency, 1986.
7. Philip Harris, 'BBC Inside the News', 1982.
8. Peter Gill, 'New Statesman', 3rd August 1987.
9. Jonathan Steele, 'Bull about Kabul', The Guardian, London, March 10, 1986.
10. 'World & National Newsagencies', Working Paper, AAPSO, Second International Conference on the New International Information Order, Kabul, 1986.
11. Dennis and Cynthia Roberts, 'How to secure Peace in Europe', London, 1985.

Appendix

The Agencies:

- The European Continent,
  North America, Oceania – 30 Agencies
- The African Continent,
  Asian Continent,
  The Arab World,
  Latin America – 74 Agencies

Problems for small news agencies:

- Little technical information experience
- Little material and technical resources
- Restricted activities, in the larger part, to national key cities
- Contemplating opening an office in the former occupying power before thinking of opening an office in neighbouring states or in major Third World countries
- Few correspondents on the national or world levels

Major western agencies:

- Associated Press A.P.
- United Press International U.P.I.
- Reuter
- Agence France Press A.F.P.

The Third World receives 80% of world news from such agencies and only 20% from other sources, i.e. their own agencies or the agencies of socialist countries.

Hammersmith
& Fulham
Serving our Community

London Borough of
Hammersmith & Fulham
Town Hall
King Street W6 9JU
Telephone 01-748 3020

Ethnic
Minorities

ETHNIC MINORITIES DEPARTMENT

The London Borough of Hammersmith and Fulham has established this new Department to take responsibility for leading the Council's commitment to equal opportunities, particularly in its provision and delivery of services in our multi-racial community. The Department is charged with the task of critically scanning and assessing the relevance, accessibility and accountability of Council services to black and other oppressed minority communities. In this context the Department will be in the forefront of developing the Council's anti-racist strategies, and has a clear commitment to working with and forging a credible alliance with the local black and other oppressed minority groups.

This newly established Department, staffed by a small team of dedicated professionals, led by the Director Jim Baker, and the Chair of the Ethnic Minorities Committee Councillor Ken Martindale, posesses expertise in areas like community work, anti-racist training, management and other disciplines, and all have direct experience of working with black communities and knowledge of their needs, aspirations and demands. The recognition of and commitment to eliminating the structural inequality and racism facing black communities is central to the work of the Department.

Nationally the reality is that Equal Opportunities Policies have not changed the position of black communities. The extent of racial discrimination in Britain remains the same as in the fifties. The Department is under no illusion as to the extent and pace of change in institutional and professional practice, and response towards the reality of a black and white community in the arena of racial equality and justice. The Department has developed the concept of Action Planning as the core element of its corporate anti-rac st strategy. This concept defines realistic targets and implementation dates with clear input from local black and other oppressed communities.

The Ethnic Minorities Department will be critically examining the corporate and departmental policies which have been developed in a black and white community, as well as the practices of caring professionals. The department is under no doubt that it will extend the parameters of current corporate and professional thinking on policy and practice in the arena of anti-racist initiatives.

COUNCILLOR KEN MARTINDALE

DIRECTOR JIM BAKER

The History of Jazz 1619-1960

By Sharon Atkin

Most people find it difficult to define Jazz; equally they have difficulty tracing its origins.

In 1619 an indentured slave named Isabella, the first black woman brought to America, landed at the settlement in Jamestown, Virginia, and with her came sounds and instruments that were previously unknown to that continent.

In those early days black women and men brought a birthright and bloodright of music from Africa, a heritage of improvisation, rhythm, call and response, antiphony and a musical passion that would be retained.

Early Jazz is an amalgamation of several musical developments and a synthesis of march and dance beat, Afro-Caribbean roots, the work songs of the slaves, chants like spirituals and the secular blues.

The development of the music was for long contained in the southern plantations and cities and its retention was largely due to the fact that communication between those in bondage was prohibited for most of their waking hours.

Duke Ellington

Bessie Smith

Unlike most other southern cities New Orleans was a very cosmopolitan area. There were women of colour who had been transported from Haiti. In some cases they lived as free women because they were recognised as having powers. They were known as the 'Queens of New Orleans'. In fact they practised the old art of Voodoo.

Their ceremonies were usually held at night by the river bank and the way that they were able to call the faithful together was by chanting. These 'chants' were often repeated by servants in the households of the white slave owners. Each chant contained a message and, more importantly, gave instructions regarding the venue of the ceremony. Once assembled the rituals always featured music usually played by assistants to the High Priests or Priestesses. The instruments had all come from

Bud Powell

Africa and they produced sounds and beats that were alien to the white inhabitants of the 'New World'. They also varied considerably from the drums and instruments of the indigenous American Indians.

All this added to the fear and wonder that was increasingly prevalent amongst the white community in New Orleans – but for the slaves it was a way of communication and control of their culture.

The working life of slaves on the plantations was even more degrading and hard than that of their city counterparts. The music and chants were considerably different and would be described in western terms as a lament or dirge.

Charles Mingus

The work songs symbolised misery and suffering and also sent coded messages. This music was the forerunner of the secular 'blues'.

The third type of music, which blended to influence the musical form called Jazz was religious tunes of the churches. These were the spirituals and while the messages of the songs talked of God and redemption and hope the structure of the music was very similar to the secular blues and the work songs.

"Negro music is essentially the expression of an attitude, or a collection of attitudes about the world, and only secondarily an attitude about the way music is made."
Le Roi Jones (Amiri Baraka) – 'Jazz and the white critic'

Dizzy Gillespie

The celebrated pianist Mary Lou Williams says in the book 'The History of Jazz' that, "the main origin of American Jazz was the Spiritual. Because of the deeply religious background of the black American, he (she) was able to mix this strong influence with rhythms that reach deep enough into the inner self to give expression to outcries of censored joy which became known as Jazz."

At the turn of the century, Jazz was in its embryonic state. It was largely due to the outbreak of the First World War that the music of black people was heard outside of the southern states of the USA.

Charlie Parker

The newly established record companies recognised that, after the success of the Maimie Smith recording of 'Crazy Blues' on Okeh Phonography, they probably would have a market among black servicemen who were overseas – so the Race Records were therefore produced.

The Jazz of New Orleans was gaining popularity, as was the written Blues of writers like W C Handy and the Piano Rags of Scott Joplin.

The music of the twenties was dominated by King Oliver, Louis Armstrong, Jelly Roll Morton and the great Blues singers like Maimie Smith, who was the first black artist to make a record, and Bessie Smith (no relation to the former).

This was the era of New Orleans Jazz and its white counterpart, Dixieland. The twenties saw the young Edward Kennedy Ellington (Duke), putting together his first band. He was from Washington DC and had been heavily influenced by the pianist Earl 'Fatha' Hines. Ellington was to dominate the music scene for over forty years and became one of the best-known ambassadors for the USA.

In the thirties Duke Ellington wrote a song entitled 'It don't mean a thing if you ain't got that swing', which was sung by Ivy Anderson. The popularity of the song gave rise to the title 'Swing', which heralded the new Big Band music of the times led by Count Basie, Fletcher Henderson, Ellington and Cab Calloway.

The focus of activity had moved from New Orleans and the South to the Northern states. The Cotton Club in Harlem was the best known haunt of gangsters and outstanding jazz musicians. It became a very fasionable haunt for white socialites but black customers were barred from the club as discrimination was still rife in the USA. Singers like Billie Holiday shot to prominence in the thirties thanks to films which were being made in Hollywood, offering opportunities to the up and coming Jazz stars.

As the Second World War approached the big bands were still popular but some soloists also became household names, their music was heard on the radio and bands like that of clarinetist Artie Shaw were making history by employing the talents of Billie Holiday who toured with his all white band.

Max Roach

It was during one of the tours down south that Holiday was to encounter the harrowing work of the Ku Klux Klan when she made a stop to visit the 'bushes', she noticed that the birds were circling overhead. On close inspection she saw bodies of black men swinging from the trees – they were the victims of a lynching party. The vision of those dead bodies stayed in her mind and when she was asked to sing a song called 'Strange Fruit', which was written about lynchings, she brought a quality to the song that would make most listeners burst into tears.

Billie Holiday also developed a musical partnership with Lester Young during the thirties and forties. He was an outstanding soloist in his own right (see 'who's who').

The other major artists of the period were undoubtedly Coleman Hawkins, Ben Webster and Sidney Bechet.

With the onset of World War II, Jazz stayed much the same but in the post war period new musical developments were afoot.

Charlie Parker developed a new faster music which was built on an entirely new chord structure and time sequence. The old style Jazz was largely played in 2/2 time whilst the Parker Be-Bop was played on 4/4 beat. His collaborators were Dizzy Gillespie, Max Roach, Charlie Mingus and the superlative Bud Powell.

Sidney Bechet

Louis Armstrong

Parker, or Bird as he was more usually known, revolutionised Jazz. Most contemporary critics found the new sound and time hard to grasp, but the fantastic quintette made an historic recording at Massey Hall on a rough tape recorder which belonged to the bass Charlie Mingus. Because of contractual problems the record, when finally released, went out in the name of Charlie Chan, but Parker's style was unmistakeable. Today the record is hailed as a masterpiece.

It is undoubtedly true that Be-Bop was the music of the forties. It gave rise to unique soloists and instrumentalists of the calibre of Miles Davis and Dexter Gordon, who in the eighties was the first Jazz musician to be nominated for an Academy Award for his acting role in the Jazz film 'Round Midnight'. Be-Bop was a music that most white musicians could not play, so they sought white Jazz artists like Lennie Tristano and Lee Konitz to rationalise the Be-Bop sound and make it more relevant to the music of the classical schools. It was therefore not surprising that the days of the big bands were past and that the quartettes and trios where to become far more popular.

Billie Holiday

The Birth of the Cool was a fifties phenomenon and gave prominence to classically trained musicians. Miles Davis, the Modern Jazz Quartette and Chico Hamilton, typified the move to concert halls and the geographical shift to the west coast of the USA. The technical abilities of the exponents of the 'Cool Jazz' era were never in doubt but their music lacked the passion and originality of Parker and Hawkins. They introduced Elizabethan Virginal music and Chamber pieces and then dressed it up as Jazz. Fortunately their work was seen by the majority of black listeners, as well as musicians, as desanitising a music that was born out of real hardship and pain.

Count Basie

Every generation has its geniuses. fortunately John Coltrane, Sonny Rollins, Joe Harriott and Ornette Coleman, dominated the music of the middle and late fifties, as well as the sixties, when their music, which spanned both the USA and Europe, proved that the statement of Albert Ayler was true, namely that "Jazz was not soley about the structure and sequence of notes anymore, it was about feelings". The Black Power movement of the sixties had an undoubted influence on the music and its exponents.

John Coltrane

Harriot was the symbol of blackness, revolution and inspiration in Britain. His work stands alongside any of his US-based counterparts. Therefore his contribution to Jazz has to be understood in the context of the wider scene, and the fact that until the arrival of Harriott in Britain, Jazz had seen few innovators and only interpreters.

Jazz is not a static music. It has been played all over the world and at the present time it is enjoying a revival – but it still *remains* a black art form and means of communication that for black people transcends spoken language divides.

Art Blakey – Drums

Art Blakey was born in 1919 and unlike his many musical contemporaries is still going strong. He, along with Max Roach, almost singlehandedly changed the focus of the drums in jazz, from background accompanist to front line instruments.

Blakey has had the drive and commitment to jazz to always develop new sounds. He is constantly finding young innovative musicians, who are collectively known as the Jazz Messengers.

Over the past thirty years the musicians that were nurtured by the Blakey stable have in turn become the foremost Jazz leaders less than a decade later. They include Horace Silver, Wayne Shorter, Freddie Hubbard and Cedar Walton. His style is characterised by drum rolls and the cymbals squashing down. Weak players find the Blakey style overbearing but to most he has a drive and a sense of timing that is rarely equalled. Hear him also on the album, *Free For All*, and then contrast that with an earlier record of the Funk era with the classic 'Moanin' from the pianist Bobby Timmons (on the album of the same name).

Joe King Oliver – Cornet

King Oliver was born in 1885. Many historians and musicians chart the origins of Jazz with the band and recordings of Joe King Oliver and Kid Ory. In 1914 King Oliver joined a group called Brownskin Babies. They became famous for the use of mutes. By 1918 he had left Kid Ory to form his own Creole Jazz Band. Kind Oliver sent for a young Louis Armstrong to augment his band in 1923. It was that band which became the first to record in the New Orleans style. It is said that their standard has never been surpassed.

The great Classics of the period were 'Dippermouth Blues', 'King Porter Stomp' and 'Tom Cat Blues.'

King Oliver found difficulty adapting to the new musical style and climate, particularly in the 1930s. Sadly he died working as a caretaker, a forgotten genius.

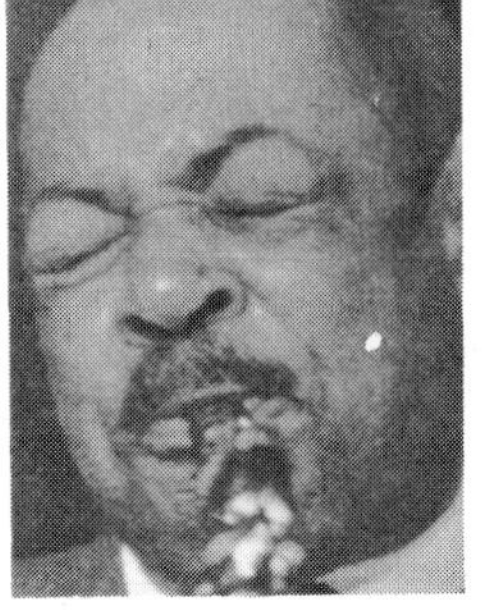

Coleman Hawkins – Tenor Saxophone

Coleman Hawkins was born in Missouri USA in 1904 and was singlehandedly responsible for bringing the saxophone into prominence as a solo instrument of note. Previously it had been viewed as a joke instrument. Coleman Hawkins' career spanned more than forty years. Throughout all the changes and developments in Jazz he remained one of the undisputed masters, ranking alongside Parker, Coltrane, Webster, Bechet, Young.

His recording debut was in 1923 with Mamie Smiths Jazz group and concluded with his old friend Ben Webster in a recording date in 1969 shortly before Hawkins' death.

He is perhaps best known for his rendition of the song 'Body and Soul,' which was recorded in October of 1939, and can be heard on the record *Coleman Hawkins Vol I 1924-1940.*

Body and Soul encapsulates the unique artistry of Hawkins. Many examples exist of the excellence of Coleman Hawkins in many different settings, including recordings with Sonny Rollins and Thelonious Monk and 'sparing' with his rival, Lester Young.

Lester (Prez) Young Tenor Saxophone and Metal Clarinet

Lester Young was born in 1909. His talent came to the attention of the public and critics when he recorded in 1936, as a member of a small group called Smith and Jones Incorporated. He was quickly drafted into the Count Basie Band, and was soon lauded as its finest soloist. Lester Young was an important influence on the musicians of the late 40s and

Art ensemble of Chicago

early fifties, notably Charlie Parker, Stan Getz and Zoot Simms. Young was a member of the original 'Blue Devils' in 1932 and left the following year to work with Bennie Moten. His spell with Basie brought him into contact with Billie Holiday. Theirs was the perfect musical partnership: his tenor playing complemented the vocals and phrasing of Billie Holiday and they had an almost telepathic relationship, which was mutually testing. It was Billie Holiday who nickmamed him 'Prez' and he in turn called her 'Lady Day'. His death in 1959 saw Holiday distraught and many felt she too gave up the will to live, her death coming only a couple of months after his. His finest recordings were made with the Basie Band and also later on the Jazz at the Philharmonic series. He was the 'Bridge Man' between the music of the thirties and the Parker Be-Bop of the forties.

Joe Harriott – Past Master

Historically black Jazz musicians could not expect either commercial rewards or artistic recognition, from a racist music industry or from uneducated critics.

In the case of Joe Harriott this was especially true. Born Arthurlin Joseph Harriott, in Jamaica on July 17 1928, Joe emerged as the greatest alto saxophonist that the Caribbean has ever produced.

Joe's early life was spent in a Catholic institution called Alpha, in Kingston, Jamaica. Alpha was also home to a number of fine musicians, notably Bobby Breem, singer and percussionist and Harold MacNair, the magnificent flautist and tenor saxophonist.

His early life and influences are not well recorded, but it seems that he showed an early aptitude for the orchestra. His first instrument was the clarinet, but as he got older and heard the imported records of the early jazz masters, he decided to switch to saxophone.

As a young man he became a popular guest with some of the dance bands which played around Kingston.

In 1951 the Ossie D'Costa band set sail for England and with them the young Harriott, who by this time played everything from Bass Saxophone to Alto.

Modern Jazz was still in its infancy in early fifties Britain and Joe's unique style was hard for people to initially accept. Underterred he played around London in the jazz clubs with Ronnie Scott and others.

The critics likened his early playing to that of Charlie Parker whose music was still much misunderstood, consequently Harriott did not receive instant recognition. However most could see that Harriott was talented and also lacked the musical contemporaries to keep pace with his innovative style.

Harriott's musical genius was as complex as his personality, he could not easily be contained, since his love of music transcended narrow divides.

Joe was equally at home playing traditional Jazz with bands like those of Chris Barber or Ken Colyer as he was developing 'Freeform' music, a term he used to describe Avant Garde Jazz.

For over two decades he silenced critics by constantly setting the musical agenda.

He equally frightened musicians by developing music without chords, fusing Indian music and Jazz together and writing hit tunes for the Chris Barber band.

The brilliance of Harriott is on many levels: Firstly, he was an outstanding alto saxophonist. His strident approach to the instrument led to amazing speed and control even in the upper register. There was a strange, haunting, lyrical sensitivity when he played ballads, such as 'Lover Man' or 'Polka Dots' and 'Moonbeams', the combined effect leaving others gasping with wonder and awe.

Secondly, his abilities as a composer should not be overlooked. He wrote a tune called 'Revival', which was recorded by the Chris Barber Band and subsequently earned Barber a place in the pop charts and Harriott an Ivor Novello award for popular song. More recently the widow of the actor Trevor Howard, chose this music for his funeral.

In much of the music written by Harriott his Caribbean roots are drawn on, not in the same way as Sonny Rollins uses Calypso, but more to reflect the tempo and warmth of Jamaica.

Thirdly, even though he was a brilliant soloist his intuitive playing behind poets of the calibre of Dannie Abse and Laurie Lee brought him to the attention of a wider artistic audience.

What sets Harriott aside from the rest was that he pushed the barriers of music further than most, so he was often the first to achieve previously undreamt of goals.

He was the first artist in Britain to record with strings, and he scored for the London Philharmonic.

He was also the first British-based musician to be awarded a five star rating for the highly innovative Free Form Album from the United States' Jazz publication *Downbeat*.

It was certainly true that Harriott was not in the least bit interested in mirroring his US counterparts. It was also the case that he was not influenced by the discovery and development in the USA of Avante Garde Jazz by Ornette

Joe Harriott

Coleman. Yet they were both travelling in the same direction musically, and that was a very revolutionary road in the late fifties.

Harriott was uncompromising personally and professionally. He refused to accept the racism which was so prevalent in post-war Britain. He had a deliberate policy of hiring and working whenever possible with black musicians.

In the fifties and sixties this in itself was a fairly revolutionary act of faith. He often worked with the celebrated trumpeters Shake Keane and Dizzy Reece, both of these musicians subsequently left England to work in Europe and more latterly the USA.

Joe Harriott was totally dedicated to his art and culture, when Jamaica gained independence in 1962, Joe who was by then well established in Britain, chose to remain a Jamaican national. The records of the High Commission celebrations of Independence show that Joe Harriott's quintette was the star attraction on the night.

He never played safe and like many true revolutionaries he had a goal but just failed to achieve it.

In the sixties his most commercially successful venture took shape. He was introduced to John Mayer, an Indian classical musician, who put together a double quintette – made up of five Indian musicians playing tabla, sitar etc., with Mayer playing harpsichord and violin.

The Jazz input which was led by Harriott saw flutes added to form the bridge between two very different musical meters. The Indo-Jazz Fusions as they were to be known confounded the view held by Rudyard Kipling, namely that 'East is East and West is West and never the twain shall meet'.

In fact while a pop group, The Beatles, were just discovering India, Harriott and Mayer pre-empted the popularity and subsequent drift to the east which was soon to take place. The double quintette played at the Jazz Expo Concert at Hammersmith, on the same bill as Max Roach and Stanley Cowell, of 'Blues for the Vietcong' fame.

A string of television appearances and concerts followed which were in turn put down on discs. A number of albums were produced in that period and were seen as commercially viable.

Harriott's retrospective view was that to put the two musics together was highly ambitious and did not always work, but he concedes that there was some very pretty music written, played and recorded during that period.

In the seventies Joe Harriott embarked on his last recorded musical colaboration with the Goan guitarist Amancio D 'Silva. They recorded an album Hum Donno and used the vocalist Norma Winston on some of the tracks.

In early 1972, Joe Harriott became disillusioned with the Jazz scene in London. He decided to undertake a tour of England, guesting with local Jazz combos. On one occasion he was sitting in at the Great Harry, Warsash near Southampton when he was taken ill. A few days later he was admitted to the Royal South Hants Hospitalwhere he underwent an operation on his spine. Cancer of the spine was diagnosed and a long battle was then fought to overcome the rapidly encroaching disease.

This was in September 1972. He never left hospital and died on January 2 1973. During his illness he showed great courage and was hopeful of making a recovery. He was a complex man scared of showing his emotions to most people but his playing revealed his soul. There were times when his cynicism was noticable in his playing, but more often than not it was his sensitivity and vulnerability that shone through.

Younger musicians owe much to the pioneering spirit of Joe Harriott – Jazz has claimed a lot of geniuses before their time including Parker, Coltrane, Eric Dolphy and MacNair.

Britain was not blessed with any artist of the calibre of Joe Harriott.

His funeral at the Church in Bitterne near Southampton read like a Who's Who of the Jazz world. Annie Ross, John Mayer, Michael Garrick Dave Green and Coleridge Goode were all there.

He was interred in the same Church yard and the inscription on his grave stone reads 'Parker there's them over here can play a few aces too.'

It would be nice to think that Jamaica would recognise the immense contribution made by Harriott and posthumously make him a National Hero.

(This is an extract from a forthcoming biography by Sharon Atkin)

Gail Thompson – Young, Gifted and Black

Gail Thompson (Courtesy of Ian Thompson)

Gail Thompson is one of the best known Jazz musicians in Britain. She was born in south London and has remained a resident of the area since her childhood.

Gail's parents were born in Trinidad and Tobago and emigrated to Britain in the fifties. She was born into a family of three brothers and concedes that as a young girl she was not too interested in playing music, although all her brothers are accomplished musicians in their own right.

At school she became interested in music and joined the school orchestra. Her first instrument was the clarinet and she showed amazing aptitude for reading and harmony.

At school Gail did not play jazz and had little or no opportunity to hear it at home, but one day whilst shopping she bought a cheap record of Stan Getz which she says changed her life.

When she heard the saxophone in a jazz setting she knew instantly that she had to play it. In the school orchestra she switched to tenor saxophone.

Locally there were musicians from the Caribbean who helped her develop her style and range. Gail studied Steel Drums, African Drums, and Calypso and she was ultimately to incorporate all of these art forms into her music. For her the Grand Masters of Jazz were Parker, Coltrane, Ellington, and Coleman Hawkins. Like many musicians she was not keen on vocalists, but Billie Holiday has remained a firm favourite.

As she advanced with playing Jazz she decided to join the National Youth Jazz Orchestra and remained in the reed section for many years, being one of the party who toured the Soviet Union.

Although Jazz still has a minority appeal in Britain, it has, over the past few years, enjoyed something of a revival and Gail has been at the forefront of this renewed interest. She served her apprenticeship with various rehearsal bands, but at the age of nineteen Gail landed a job in the orchestra of the hit show 'Bubblin' Brown Sugar' which charted the history and development of Jazz and Blues in the USA.

She says that when she first appeared in the Band room of the theatre she was asked whose girl friend she was, so rare was it for young black women to be playing Jazz professionally. Undeterred she went out and played in the orchestra pit for the following two years.

By the age of twenty Gail had learnt to play a variety of instruments from bass guitar to baritone saxophone, which is not only a difficult instrument to play but one that many strong men would find difficulty in lifting. Few people find that they can cope with the Baritone as an instrument and consequently very few musicians undertake to try and play it.

Over the past ten years Gail has made an astonishing contribution to music. She recognised early on that it was not enough to play, but that as a black woman in Jazz she would have to cope with both racism and sexism, therefore she would have to address the political issues around the arts and resources available to her music.

To this end she serves on the Greater London Arts Association as an advisor on Jazz and the minority communities.

Fortunately, Gail has never been satisfied just to confine herself to playing. Her most notable achievements to date include a concert at the Royal Festival Hall, running a successful womens' jazz group called Gailforce, and co-founding the very popular and critically acclaimed 'Jazz Warriors'.

In 1986 the 'Warriors' played with the lengendary Art Blakey and the Jazz Messengers at the Camden Jazz Festival. Gail was featured on baritone saxophone and was given quite a lot of prominence in the ITV documentary on Blakey which followed his performance at the festival. The BBC then decided to programme a Jazz Week and invited Gail to be the guest presenter and linkperson for the week. She thus claimed another first for female Jazz musicians. Since 1984 Gail had developed a keen interest in teaching young black children to play and realised that there were few facilities to teach music, particularly Jazz. She decided to start a saxophone school but was so inundated with applications that she found it impossible to meet the demand. However Gail set about trying to secure funding to open a music school in her locality. She approached Lambeth Council who were enthusiastic but offered little in the way of financial support. In less than two years Gail Thompson opened Music Works in Stockwell Road, Lambeth.

It is now one of the best schools teaching every facet of music, in particular, Jazz, Vocals, Harmony and Composition, together with training on a variety of instruments for all age groups and every level of musical competence. Students from all over the country are queueing up for places at Musicworks.

At the same time Gail was opening the school she still found time to write a Jazz Opera which was performed at Covent Garden, arrange music for the US-based Mel Lewis Big Band and take on the Musician-in-Residence job at the Festival Hall. As a musician she felt that it was necessary to organise a Big Band and so the 'Blue Haze Jazz Orchestra' was formed under her direction. Not only was she still running the highly successful Gailforce but she found time to start a Gospel Group of over fifty female singers.

In 1987, Gail Thompson suffered some problems with her mouth which prevented her from playing. She also felt at the time that Jazz in Britain was not advancing and so she departed for Kenya, on an overland trip. Before she departed she said that she was interested in tracing the origins of Jazz in Africa and perhaps would respond to some requests to establish a Jazz school in that part of the world.

Gail would be the first to admit that she has not yet realised her full potential, but, not unlike Joe Harriott (whom she greatly admires), she has done much to advance Jazz in Britain and has given a new status to black women in this country. Her commitment to music and her positive approach to achieving new heights stand as a complement to Harriott and those early pioneers of Jazz in Britain.

The black contribution to British classical music

by David Roussel-Milner

Jessye Norman

British classical music owes much to the traditions established on the European mainland, and can, therefore, hardly be described as an indigenous art form. Where would music be in England without the Russians, French, Italians and Germans? Historically black people have contributed to European classical music to a greater proportion than might be expected from the numbers resident. A few names of black artists spring immediately to mind: Samuel Coleridge-Taylor, who was famous for his composition of massive choral pieces such as *Hiawatha;* Ulysses Kay, another black composer known particularly for his *Suite from the Ballet Dance Calina;* Dean Dixon, the conductor; and George Polgreen Bridgetower, a son of Poland as well as the son of an African King, who two centuries ago displayed his virtuosity as a violinist at the tender age of ten in cities all over Europe. One of the greatest composers of all time was Johannes Sebastian Bach, who was known as 'The Black Spaniard'.

In the Westindies, in particular, the study of classical music used to be considered essential for middle .and upper class black people, and the standard of musical performance, as well as appreciation, is exceptional amongst many of the older generation of black people in Britain. For example, Britain's first black hairdresser, Carmen England, studied piano and singing at the Royal Academy of Music, qualified as a Licentiate of Trinity College, London, and became Trinidad's leading recital accompanist during the World War II years, before taking up the hairdressing profession for which she is best known.

Black people continue to make a substantial contribution to classical music in Britain in spite of the particularly difficult problems placed in their paths, although United States' singers such as Shirley Verret, Grace Bumbry and Jessye Norman, who have already made their names on the stages of the greatest opera companies around the world, are warmly welcomed in Britain where they often command the highest fees. Black faces in the major orchestras are a rarity, however, although young artists from the Third World have been able to shoot to international fame after winning international competitions.

The hurdles remain for the black British artist, who frequently is forced to turn to jazz or 'pop' in order to pursue a musical profession even when their preference and aptitude would suggest a career in classical music. The prestigious Glyndebourne Opera Company has recently presented Gershwin's operetta *Porgy and Bess* and could hardly have avoided using black singers. Their success should ensure that they are engaged in future to perform in "white" roles, but the Arts Council, if it is to honour the promises it made two years ago in launching its Action Plan, must now make sure that integrated casting policies are followed for all productions presented by their clients. In particular, action must be taken to assure aspiring singers, players, conductors, directors and technicians from the ethnic minorities that the long hard training they must undertake will receive equal recognition from organisations in receipt of subsidy from the Arts Council.

The greatest pressure must be brought to bear on the major orchestras to remove the apparent discrimination against black players, and consideration should be given to changing the system by which orchestra members are able to ensure that their (usually white) friends are used as deputies.

A brief examination of the records of the National Opera Studio would no doubt reveal that a number of Third World singers have received training there but, as is the case with black graduates in every profession, their chances of employment have depended more on the shade of colour of their skins than their relative artistic abilities.

Hyacinth Nicholls

The tenor Willard White is one singer who has had a measure of success, and he was one of the leading performers in Glyndebourne's production of *Porgy and Bess;* other black singers who appeared with him were Curtis Watson, Pauline Forrest, Rhoda Graven, Angelina Phattame-Doswell and Hyacinth Nicholls. As is always the case, white society itself suffers when it discriminates against black people, and the loss of the considerable talent within the minority communities is immeasurable.

The Struggle for Caribbean Music

Get up, Stand up, Stand up for your rights,
Get up, Stand up, Don't give up the fight.
(Robert Nesta Marley)

The success of that particular tune might never have been had it been left to the multi-nationals who control the music industry.

In Britain the trends in and popularity of music are assessed by the only national music polls, which are produced weekly by Gallup and M.R.I.B.

The consumers and purchasers of popular music are 'educated' by the media, newspapers and advertising and are told what type of music we should like and 'better' still what music enjoys mass appeal.

For people of Caribbean origin who live in Britain it is almost impossible to hear the current exponents of Calypso or Reggae.

Few people today remember that Bob Marley and the Wailers had been singing and writing music for a number of years but had little or no opportunity to have their music recorded, thereby insuring that they could not appeal to a wide audience.

It was in fact Chris Blackwell, an independent record producer who had recently established the Island Records label, who trusted Marley with his first advance of £5,000 and on his own admission he never expected to see the young Marley again.

The fact that Marley used Reggae to convey social, political and spiritual messages was seen by the music bosses as having little appeal or commercial viability for the record companies. However, when Eric Clapton recorded the Marley classic, 'I shot the Sherrif', his version was given widespread promotion by the powers that control the industry.

If the music of Marley had little appeal for the majority European music purchasing audience, then why was Clapton's cover version promoted?

Musical Youth

The answer is simple – the music industry has always preferred to find a white alternative to promote, rather than give exposure to black artists. An example of this was during the post World War II period in the USA when Elvis Presley was able to copy the sound of the black rhythm and blues artists who were confined to recording on the 'race record labels'.

In Britain in the post war period the only black

artists to appear in the charts were those who had become acceptable in mainstream USA.

It was to be many years before we were to see Caribbean musicians in the Top Twenty. The origins of the Calypso are in Trinidad and Tobago and the power and appeal of the Calypso has been demonstrated over years, having considerable influence on the politics of the country.

Gypsy is a well known Calypsonian who wrote and recorded a song about the economic decline of the Trinidadian economy under the leadership of the then Prime Minister George Chambers, entitled 'The Sinking Ship'. It was a huge success but the influence of the song and Gypsy's credibility were dented when he accepted an invitation to dine with the Prime Minister who subsequently lost the election, the first time his party had been defeated in twenty years.

The enormous power of some of the Calypsonians is evident, yet they have never had the exposure that they are due.

The critics claim that Calypso is only for a minority audience but the real truth is that the music moguls have very few of the Calypsonians under contract, therefore they are reluctant to promote or distribute their material.

The same is, of course, true of Reggae music, with notable exceptions, such as Marley, McGregor and Grant.

Bands like Misty-in-Roots have a very large following within Britain yet the major distributors have so far been able to ignore their music. This is partly due to the fact that as black people we represent about four per cent of the population and so are not yet considered to have the purchasing ability necessary to be able to influence the market.

It is also because racism is still prevalent within the industry as a whole. In recent years groups like The Police and Boy George and Culture Club have been encouraged to develop Reggae songs for a European market. It is not the style or the tempo of the music that is unpopular, but it is the bosses, working with the promoters of the popular charts, that have the ability to make or break careers.

If you look at the television and radio programmes that are a regular means used to advertise and 'sell' sounds it becomes obvious that few black Caribbean artists or promoters will have access to nationwide coverage.

Minority interest programmes are reserved for the radio and television studios' late night or early morning slots. In the case of some local and commercial radio stations black programmes have been dropped altogether.

Rudy Grant

The real opportunities for the advancement of Caribbean music in Britain lie with the pirate radio stations. It is envisaged that community radio stations will be able to fill some of the gaps left by the establishment. The obvious problem facing both Reggae and Calypso is capitalism – supply and demand tinged with racism.

Profits count more for business people than equality of opportunity. Only as more black people move into broadcasting and start to manage and control the means of production will Caribbean music cease to be marginalised.

The breakthrough for black recording of Soul and Blues artists in the USA came when Berry Gordy developed the Detroit Sound through the birth of Tamla Motown. Would we have seen a

Stevie Wonder, a Diana Ross or even a Michael Jackson had it not been for black people setting up their own labels and controlling the distribution of their products, together with having record stations and black charts to promote black music?

The importance of Marley was that he understood the politics of music and therefore his songs were socio-political commentaries on a society which glorifies the contributions of Europeans and of those black people who aspire to be white and thus denigrates the immensely powerful music of the black population.

A recent report prepared by the Adam Smith Institute for the British government on the planned future of the Arts makes no mention of Reggae, Calypso or Jazz in its section dealing with music. The only musical forms which merit a mention are Opera and Classical music, these two being the only ones which are recommended for future funding.

It is further suggested that music teaching becomes a local council responsibility and be removed from the education budget altogether.

The implications of such actions would be to deny the presence of black music in Britain and to deter young people from having any interest in studying the music of the Caribbean. It also means that in the eyes of the 'experts' the only valid music is that which is European in origin. Experience has shown us that whatever the Adam Smith Institute recommends, the present government is likely to put into practice.

Trevor Walters

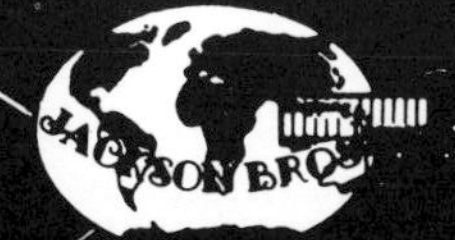
JACKSON BROS

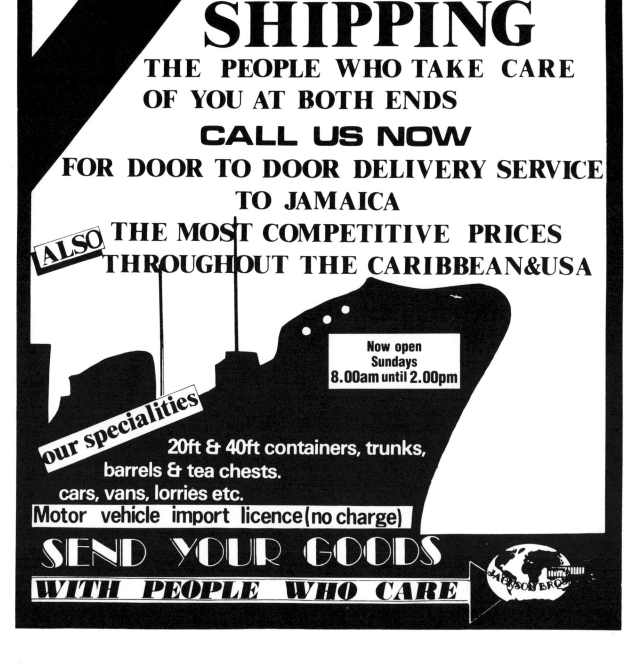

Carnival is we 'ting

by Kwesi Bacchra

For all those in the media, local and national government and elsewhere who try to promote the lies that Westindies cannot organise anything or that they are indolent or lacking in artistic creativity, the musical and colourful extravaganzas which joyfully explode each year all over Britain in a riot of harmonious multi-racial togetherness are proof of our denigrators mendacity.

What other group in Britain, including the native population, has been able to organise in the face of official obstruction a street festival which can attract upwards of two million people, tens of thousands of whom come from abroad, bringing their dollars, marks and yen, with a paid administration staff of four, and an unpaid management committee of half a dozen? That is the scale of the small organisation behind the Notting Hill Carnival in London, which not only co-ordinates every August bank holiday by becoming Europe's largest street festival by far,

but also promotes a number of events throughout the year bringing Caribbean entertainment to many, black and white. No wonder the former Mayor of the Royal Borough of Kensington and Chelsea, Councillor Cox boasted that he was the Mayor of Notting Hill when he was abroad.

Almost every major city in England and Wales can boast its own Caribbean Carnival with imaginative floats and colourful costumes winding, moving and dancing through the streets to the sweet pan music of instruments painstakingly hammered out of oil drums. Men, women and children spend their hard earned money and labour for hours on end painting, sewing, glueing and bending wire to produce a creation to be worn for a few hours in competitive glory before the hard work starts on next year's replacement masterpiece. How dare they suggest, after exploiting our labour from slavery and indentured labour for centuries, that our people, old or young, are lazy!

In some towns Westindians have brought new vitality to an ancient or existing festival, as at the Goose Fair in Nottingham or at Roundwood Park in the London Borough of Brent; while in many cities our Carnivals have served to brighten dreary, run-down areas. At different times of the year, usually around bank holidays, the grooving melodiousness of steelbands combines with the hypnotic rhythms of Africa to entire spectators and participators to jump-up and reel in cities and towns like Oxford, Reading, Leicester and Leeds; Manchester; Preston, Dudley, Coventry and Huddersfield, Rotten Park and Handsworth in Birmingham, St. Paul's in Bristol, Bute Town in Cardiff, not forgetting Liverpool and Merseyside. Where local education authorities have a positive approach to multi-cultural education, schools have been encouraged to develop music and art projects. These projects catch the imagination of children, sometimes spinning off to provide a greater geographical and historical understanding of the Caribbean region, which has been used over the centuries as the cockpit of struggles for pre-

FIRE

eminence between European nations.

As the foreign currency spending tourists flow into England, one might expect that a spark of interest might be generated within the bureaucracy of the English Tourist Board and its local counterparts in London and other English regions, yet, in spite of innumerable approaches by Carnival organisers, they have shown not a whit of interest. Other English events enjoy their patronage and the accompanying financial support but, apart from a modicum of advertising assistance, black people must do their own thing without the backing which, perhaps, those with lesser ability must obtain to survive.

Strangely, greater recognition has been granted to Westindian Carnivals in Britain by authorities on the European mainland than here in this country, which we count as home and in which we pay our just share of taxes. Several years ago black groups in Holland, Belgium and France drew inspiration from the spectacular Caribbean events they came to enjoy on the streets in England, and they started to do their own thing in their home towns. Then three years ago the Foundation of European Carnival Cities, based in Amsterdam, invited the chair of the Notting Hill Carnival and Arts Committee, Alex Pascall, to be a vice-president with responsibility for the arts. The Mayors of cities as far afield as Italy and Greece are proud to host visits by steelbands and masqueraders from Britain. Mainland Europeans find it strange that Carnival in England, which brings pleasure to millions, trading profits to hundreds and money into the country, receives so little support from the authorities.

In 1988, at a time when demands are being placed on the organisers of Notting Hill Carnival to improve their administration, the Arts Council is reducing its grant to £50,000, while the London Borough Grants Scheme and Greater London Arts will not increase their subsidy even to cover inflation. The Royal Borough of Kensington and Chelsea cannot yet make up their conservative mind what money they will graciously donate, while indications from the City of Westminster are that they are unlikely to provide any funds in spite of the pleasure and employment Carnival brings to so many of their ratepayers, not to mention the

profits generated for the businesses within the borough.

It is the widely reported unfortunate events at the 1987 Carnival in Notting Hill, including a tragic killing, which have been used as an excuse by members of government and other MPs, local authorities and certain councillors to force the Metropolitan Police to call for a ban. It is known that there are people who strongly object to Carnival celebration and do not wish to recognise the artistry, beauty and cultural heritage of the Caribbean people. They prefer to live with their prejudices, and believe that we have no culture, or distinctive merit. The Carnival with all its splendour, attracting so many people of all races, threatens these prejudices. They know they cannot physically stop it, so they have attempted to usurp the administration by setting up their own "Steering Committee" which could then be used to suck the life out of Carnival until it would die, they hope, a natural death. They had not reckoned with the long suffering tenacity of Caribbean people, developed during 400 years of brutal oppression, so more recently the authorities have played the age old ploy of patronising pressure of divide-and-rule policies while squeezing the financial support which is our due.

The behaviour of the Arts Council is particularly deplorable as it always boasts to be totally independent of governmental control. Their allocation for Carnival remains the same in 1988 as it was in 1987 but, without any consultation with Carnival organisers, the Arts Council decided to reduce the grant for administration by £15,000 while increasing the money for costume bands by the same amount. While one must acknowledge that the bands need and deserve the extra money, it is galling that once again the white bureaucrats at the Arts Council have had the arrogant presumption to decide what should be our priorities.

At any event attracting hundreds of thousands of people, there will be those who will take advantage to pursue their criminal ends but, it is only when they steam through *our* Carnival crowds that the gutter press splash such behaviour, which decent black people equally deplore, across their front pages. It is a fact that, for the number of people attending the Notting Hill Carnival, the level of crime is less than it would be, say, at a football match. Nevertheless, if potential sponsors, for whom all our Carnivals could be a rewarding opportunity, were not so, shall we say, blinkered, they would not use

criminal activity as an excuse for not supporting our artistic excellence. But then, a glance at the pages of any black newspaper or magazine will reveal their unwillingness to put back even a smidgen of the profits they amass out of the billions of pounds black people spend.

It is a fact that, apart from business use, black people spend far more per head of the population on international telephone calls, but I do not see the name of British Telecom supporting any of our activities. In the insurance world, companies like American Life Insurance earn millions of pounds from us, and they even employ black agents to persuade us that they are the best company for black investors. While small black record companies have done their bit, the large companies like Island and Virgin, whose business is substantially dependent upon the black community, are conspicuous by their absence from the sponsorship field. On the streets at Carnival time, up and down the land, higher than normal profits are made from the sale of Pepsi Cola and Coca Cola, but they put nothing back into our communities. The brewers do well during Carnivals but, with a few notable exceptions including Red Stripe, Carlsberg, Tennants and Pink Lady, the majority fail to honour their responsibilities. It would be possible to fill several pages of this book with the names of companies which, although they are aware of the financial benefit they would derive by sponsoring a steelband, a costume band or a carnival tent, prefer to turn a blind eye to the fact that an adequate, and so more efficient, administration would prevent those occurences which tend to occasionally drag one down towards the level of a football mob.

All over the country black businesses give their support to Carnival events and without them a great deal would just not be possible. Perhaps the banks, who profit out of their financial dealings as well as out of the millions of black peoples' accounts they hold, will one day realise that we can all choose where to put our money.

The message from Carnivals in 1988 must be *"Carnival is we 'ting"*. Caribbean people have developed it to a standard which surpasses all other such events in Europe, even rivalling those other black spectacular carnivals in Trinidad, Rio de Janeiro and New Orleans. Carnival will remain *"we 'ting"* and, all over Britain, we shall continue to excel.

Black pioneers in style

by Seta Niland

Rifat Ozbek – one of the top British Directional Designers

Unlike our international counterparts, fashion has rarely been seriously addressed in Britain – that is until quite recently. Often dismissed as trivial and inconsequential, fashion amounts to more than just images of glamorous models gracing the pages of the 'glossies'. The fashion industry in Britain today has discarded its once eccentric profile to become the fourth largest industry, generating a substantial amount of employment and revenue for the national coffers.

Working today in the fiercely competitive environment of fashion has meant, alongside predominant Thatcherite values, a sharpening of mores and practices throughout the fashion infrastructure. The black community in Britain has contributed greatly in recent years to the diverse and eclectic nature of the fashion industry. British fashion has grown up and with it a new league of black artists who represent the different professions across the fashion spectrum. No longer relegated solely to textile manufacture, the black community has shaken off the mantle of disadvantage and despair to assume a more prominent role in the higher echelons of the fashion world. Designers, journalists, stylists, photographers, and retailers, all have pushed aside the barriers, establishing significant inroads into a once insular fashion industry.

The one name that instantly springs to mind is that of Bruce Oldfield, accredited with the restablishment of Britain on the couture map. Yet Oldfield has proved to be more than a designer; visionary, shrewd businessman and diplomat (he represented Britain at the 'Australian Bicentenary' using designs inspired by Aboriginal art). Oldfield's empire has extended to all corners of the global fashion centres. He attributes his success to sheer hard graft and patience, a testimony confirmed by fellow leading lights of the industry. The competitive nature of fashion demands unswerving devotion, countless working hours, and acceptance of initial low returns with high outlay.

Contemporary fashion must be commercially viable while retaining wit and originality in design. The same precepts are applied right across the fashion spectrum. Oldfield's biography might read like the classic rags-to-riches fairy-tale, but as the great maestro himself acknowledges, nothing is achieved without the accompanying blood, sweat and tears.

Top designers' liaison with art and design colleges has helped towards a restructuring of the traditional curriculum to include work placements and practical experience. The onus is to improve the awareness of students to the prerequisites of the industry, whether as designers, writers, illustrators or models. Work placements and industrial training encourage undergraduates not only to sample the feel of a real working environment, but equally to experience at first hand the machinations and problems that arise daily at the workplace.

A graduate of St. Martin's School of Art, and one of the most respected designers today, Rifat Ozbek knows only too well the problems that students face on graduation. The reality is often different from the dream. Ozbek's reputation lies with the well-cut and wearable clothes that he produces with every collection. As Joan Burstein enthuses, Ozbek is a sophisticated designer, whose clothes are ideal for the busy working woman. Backed by Gulf Shipping, a Pakistani-owned Swiss-based company, Ozbek stands firmly on the success of each collection.

Another young designer, Darlajane Gilroy, has recently worked on a joint venture with the Design Council to produce a video and pamphlet to help other young hopefuls. Entitled 'Fashion Means Business', it traces the development of a new collection of Gilroy's, and covers each stage of the process: from sourcing fabrics, pattern cutting, to marketing, promotion, design protection, and cashflow projections.

Brenda Polan of *The Guardian* features an overview of the industry and British fashion, with guidelines for young aspirants among other topics, in the illustrated booklet that accompanies the video.

This venture emphasises the gravity of setting up in fashion and the practical approaches in climbing the ladder to success. Yet design is merely one facet of a major industry.

Modelling is undoubtedly one of the most visual aspects of fashion and is certainly perceived as the most glamorous. Many a 'teen dream' has been fuelled by the lure of international travel, exorbitant fees, and the other perks that are part and package of a top model's earnings.

Potential models should realise however that internationally renowned models like Imman are few and far between and owe their deserved recognition more to luck and circumstance than to

Darlajane Gilroy – working with the Design Council to help young hopefuls

any concerted effort to help the lot of black models. The pitfalls that await young hopefuls are too numerous to detail, though the most common complaint is the treachery of bogus agents, and 'cowboy' photographers. In addition, the current vogue in European publications to feature black models should not be simply interpreted as long-awaited and deserved recognition. Rather it smells suspiciously of 'ethnicity' as fashion. After all, black represents the all-time fashion classic colour, so why not extend it to models! Features pertaining to the black community rarely accompany or complement the fashion pages, and when they do, belie an ignorance and unwillingness to scratch further than the glossy surface.

Naomi Campbell has earned herself a formidable reputation inspiring other youngsters (she's only 17) to follow in her elegant footsteps. Poise, personality, and professionalism are essential to success in modelling as are striking good looks – and though appearance on the covers of top 'glossies' like *Vogue* has still not warranted an in-depth coverage of the problems that black models constantly face, the exposure she has recently received has proved beyond doubt that black is as beautiful as is necessary. Black models still have a long way to go but as the old adage goes, when the going gets tough, the tough get going.

On the other side of the camera, photographers battle against ingrained racist attitudes from diverse elements of the public relations industry. As Suresh Karaida of *The Independent* succinctly puts it, being a member of the ethnic minority communities in the national media only seems acceptable if an individual is fortunate enough to represent a high-profile publication like *The Guardian* or *The Independent*. He quotes a recent incident at an airshow for the press. An eminent member of the representative PR company indiscreetly queried Suresh's presence at the airshow only to retract his statement on learning that he was in fact from *The Independent*.

Though these attitudes can discourage or dishearten, it is more important to keep up a high profile and a fighting spirit in the face of such adverse reactions. The British fashion industry remains one of the most elitist, its old boy/girl network still the most effective barrier to young black talent. Often a job vacancy will be filled not simply through merit and the principle of the best person for the best job but quite likely through the number of contact names in the ubiquitous filofax.

Thus fashion cannot be strictly measured according to design, fashion pages or other visuals of that ilk. Indeed, fashion gurus and sociologists stress that fashion is the product of factors, a social interaction of the influences in our society, a reflection of the changes that occur daily in our lives, a sign of the times. The new assertive league of black designers, journalists, editors and artists confirm that the black community in Britain in the '80s plays an integral role in the growing maturity and internationalism of British fashion.

Bruce Oldfield – international British couturier

(Seta Niland is Fashion Editor of *Root* magazine)

The Literary World

by Alison Daiches

Dr David Dabydeen

As the decade of the 80s approaches its end, an assessment of literary activities among Britain's black population reveals spectacular successes as well as a degree of failure.

A new generation of poets have been spawned, some achieving national and international prominence. Faustin Charles, a black Trinidadian, published his *Days and Nights in the Magic Forest* to somewhat reserved acclaim: the book went virtually unnoticed among white critics and whilst some of the pieces could be said to have been overwrought and indisciplined, the poems on cricket revealed Charles' formidable lyric gift and penetrating insight into the violence of Caribbean history.

David Dabydeen, an Indo-Guyanese, won the Commonwealth Poetry prize and Cambridge Quiller-Couch Prize for his first book of poems, *Slave Song.* The achievement was all the more remarkable because the poems were written in Creole and because they dealt with the pornography of Empire in a stark and disturbing way. His second collection, *Coolie Odyssey*, received high praise from the older generation of writers like Wilson Harris and Samuel Selvon, although it is regrettable to see Dabydeen's drift towards a Naipaulian despair, possibly provoked by a sense of the alienation and dispossession of people of Indian origin in the Caribbean.

Fred D'Aiguar, of mixed race (a descendant of the most powerful Portuguese merchant family in Guyana) published his *Mama Dot* which contained delightful vignettes of childhood innocence and family warmth but which also completely neglected the vision of wounded passion and violence of the previous two poets. Can Caribbean poetry be a composition of childhood pleasantries recollected in the tranquillity of the metropolis? It is perhaps because the poems were so obviously 'safe' dealing with the 'universal' issues (by turning away from embarrassing particularities like mass malnutrition, class predacity, post-independence corruption, inter-racial massacre, American invasion of territory and mind) that *Mama Dot* was received with such acclaim by white 'establishment' critics. It would seem that acceptance into the body of 'mainstream' English poetry demands acquiescence and mimicry from the 'black' poet: he/she must take a wry, detached view of life. Their work must belong to the camp of Dylan Thomas and Philip Larkin and must strenuously ignore the fact that Thomas Hardy, D.H. Lawrence, T.S. Eliot and Ezra Pound existed. Poetic assimilation therefore has parallels with the social situation in which black people have to be submerged into the white body politic and so make themselves either invisible, harmless or 'universal' – 'universal' in this instance merely meaning the negation of cultural identity.

The present divide between sub-Larkin black poets and those who labour in the vein represented by Linton Kwesi Johnson (which has been described elsewhere as the divide between 'house negroes' and 'field negroes') is reflected in the relationship between 'mainstream' (white) and 'minority' (black) presses. Put bluntly, the mainstream presses view minority presses with a classically liberal mixture of contempt and compassion: contempt arising out of a natural sense of superiority over black 'scribbling', and compassion because of the literary nobility of that emotion. The 'minority' presses are, as expected, down-to-earth in their response: they repudiate the privileged resources of the 'mainstream' presses, their easy access to media hype, and above all their 'club-of-gentlemen' exclusivity. Can it be seriously disputed that contemporary English poetry is controlled by a handful of minority whites: they edit the literary pages of the 'quality' press and hold sway over bodies such as the Poetry Society and the Arts Council. Roger Clarke is right when he declares that "the poetry world is small and clannish, and often members will devote more energy to the pursuit of vested interests and jealous fending than to excellence". *Listener*, 21.1.88). Now and again, to balance the books, they will take up a token black writer. Black publishers cannot yet fully hope to compete with the accumulated privileges and access to power of the 'mainstream' presses. But they may take consolation by remembering Dr Johnson's dictum that great literature is that which survives epochs. We see here, in the literary world, another parallel with the social reality of black people – deprived of justice on earth, the experience of slavery forced them to look for heavenly rewards and the avenging hand of God, an attitude spurred on by missionary Christianity. Perhaps in some other era, a new God-Leavis will appear to assess the poetry of the 1970s and 1980s and proclaim new bearings in English poetry, new pathways beaten out by black writers. Perhaps then the radical linguistic departure that black poetry today signals, its demotic oral energy and ferocity of ideas and feelings, will come to be recognised as a new awakening of great English language poetry.

John Agard in conversation with fellow writer Grace Nichols

The 1980s must be remembered too for the emergence of black women writers. Grace Nichols consolidated the stunning success of the first book of poems, *I is a long memoried woman* with a new publication, *The Fat Black Woman's Poems* which challenged stereotypes about 'femininity'. She also published a poetic novel of childhood, and two books of children's stories, adding further to her reputation as a gifted writer. Amryl Johnson's *Long Road to Nowhere* and Valerie Bloom's *Touch Mi, Tell Mi!* proclaimed new poetic talents, and Joan Riley published a novel *The Unbelonging*, a disturbing account of the impact of race on the psyche, leading to a withdrawal of self into a nightmarish world of schizoid tendencies.

Male writers of fiction also came to prominence: Caryl Phillips, hitherto known solely for his plays, published two well-received novels and a travelogue, the first *The Final Passage*, winning the Malcolm X Prize in the 1985 Greater London Council (GLC) Literature Competition. James Berry, better known as a poet (he won the 1981 National Poetry Prize for his superb poem 'Fantasy of an African Child', and edited *News for Babylon*, an anthology of black British poetry), won the 1988 Cadbury Smarties Prize for *A Thief in the Night*, a collection of short stories for children. John Agard, another distinguished poet, and a superb performer in the calypsonian tradition, published *Letters for Lettie* (1979), short stories complementing his other collection of children's verse (*I din do nuttin* and *Say it again, Granny*).

Eclipsing all these works of fiction in terms of sheer genius and originality of prose were the two novels of Salman Rushdie, the first of which, *Midnight's Children* won the Booker Prize. Its style was a dazzling synthesis of the 'magical realism' of contemporary Latin American writers, the narrative sagas of Indian scripture, and the dishevelled prose of Laurence Sterne. Rushdie has rapidly established an international reputation as weighty as that of older writers in Britain like V.S. Naipaul and Wilson Harris, both of whom continue to publish novels of distinction: in 1987, Naipaul's *Enigma of Arrival* added to his stature as a controversial figure, and Harris' recent *Carnival* and *Infinite Rehearsal* once again confirmed his reputation as one of the most formally innovative novelists in the world. He was awarded the Guyana Prize in 1987.

V.S. Naipaul

In the field of drama, there was a relative and comparative paucity of material. David Simon, a young novelist (*Secrets of the Sapodilla*) started a theatre workshop in Lewisham where his own play, a dramatisation of *Railton Blues*, was performed. Edgar White wrote several pieces, including two dealing with Westindian family life in England (*The Nine Night* and *Ritual by Water*). The most successful play produced in the decade was Hanif Kureshi's *My Beautiful Launderette*, which, in film form, was judged British Film of the Year in 1985 (*Evening Standard* Award).

Asian Film Makers in Britain

by Naqi Ali

The new wave of Asian arts in Britain surged forward in the post-war period with the influx of members of the visible minorities. In the formative years of the 1960s and '70s the arts were kept alive by many small groups, mainly consisting of artistes, dancers and musicians who made this island their new home. Their cultural expression was stifled by racism and a reactionary media and was also hindered by the immigrants' search for a better life. However, with the growth of the new generation of Asians, coupled with the enlightened policies of the Labour councillors who were elected to the last Greater London Council (GLC) in 1981, as well as those in other metropolitan boroughs, an impetus was given to multiracial and multicultural activities.

Therefore, despite racism, a reactionary media and the maintenance of a right Eurocentric approach to the arts, as well as restrictions placed on artistes borne out of societal orthodoxies, Asian arts in Britain have made tremendous strides. This is due mainly to individuals, dedication of the artistes and the unequivocal support given to them by the Asian communities. The progress Asian arts have made in Britain bears testimony to the tenacity of Asian people and their resolve to preserve and promote their cultural traditions.

Britain can now boast many professional Asian theatre groups, dancers, musicians, writers and artists. Whereas the performing and visual arts are thriving, very little progress has been made towards establishing a truly Asian film culture. The reasons are obvious. Film making is a conglomeration of many arts. It costs a lot of money and demands a thorough professional and technical training. And the competition is fierce.

Indian films have been distributed in Britain extensively over the last thirty years. Before video cassette recorder ownership reached its present hysterical pace there were over 1,000 part-time cinemas showing Indian films. In terms of art films the National Film Theatre, and in recent years Channel 4, have adopted a progressive policy of introducing good Asian films into their programming. Many Asian actors – such as Saeed Jaffrey, Zohra Sehgal, Zia Mohiuddin, Roshan Seth, Renu Setna, Tariq Younus, Madhur Jaffrey – have made their mark on British films and television. Yet until 1980 the only Asian film maker to be reckoned with was Waris Hussain. Two more names, although attached to BBC or commercial television, were those of Zia Mohiuddin and Yavar Abbas. Yavar Abbas has produced a number of documentaries on subjects related to the subcontinent of India and Pakistan, which were shown on BBC and Channel 4.

The great Faiz Ahmed Faiz (from the Faiz family archive)

The advent of Channel 4 and the new Labour leadership at the erstwhile GLC opened new vistas for Asian independent film makers and also encouraged any film and video collectives and cooperatives to come forward. Especially since Farrukh Dhondy became the commissioning editor of Channel 4 the company followed a policy of allocating resources to small independent companies and collectives.

Bandung Production

Farrukh Dhondy's first venture was to support Bandung Production. Thus the spectacle of childish petulance, juvenile truculence and amateurish nonsense of the *Eastern Eye* programme was replaced by *Bandung File*. It comprised a series of six programmes on issues of public interest at home and abroad. Bandung is run by Pakistani-born Tariq Ali and Trinidadian-born Darcus Howe. The first series of six programmes was extended for the second year. This was a commendable effort to bring Asian and Third World programmes out of the boxes and inward looking tunnel vision and to appeal to a broader audience. In 1987 Bandung also produced a feature *The Partition*, based on Sadat Hassan Manto's story *Toba Tek Singh*.

Retake Film And Video Collective Ltd

Retake is the first Asian film and video collective to be fully franchised under the ACTT workshop declaration. It is the brainchild of two brothers – Mahmood Jamal and Ahmad Jamal. Mahmood was born in Lucknow, India, in 1948. He came to Britain via Pakistan in 1967. A poet in his own right, with two collections to his credit, he has translated modern Urdu poetry for *The Penguin Book of Modern Urdu Poetry*. Ahmad Jamal is a graduate of the London International Film School.

Retake, based in Camden, have been closely involved with the local community and have produced documentaries in response to the needs of that community, including community consensus for research into actual issues to be included in the programmes.

Living in Danger, which was made as a contribution to the 1985 Anti-Racist Year Programme deals with racial harassment on the housing estates and was their first documentary. This was followed by *An Environment of Dignity* and *It's Our Right*. They deal respectively with

A scene from Retake's An Environment of Dignity

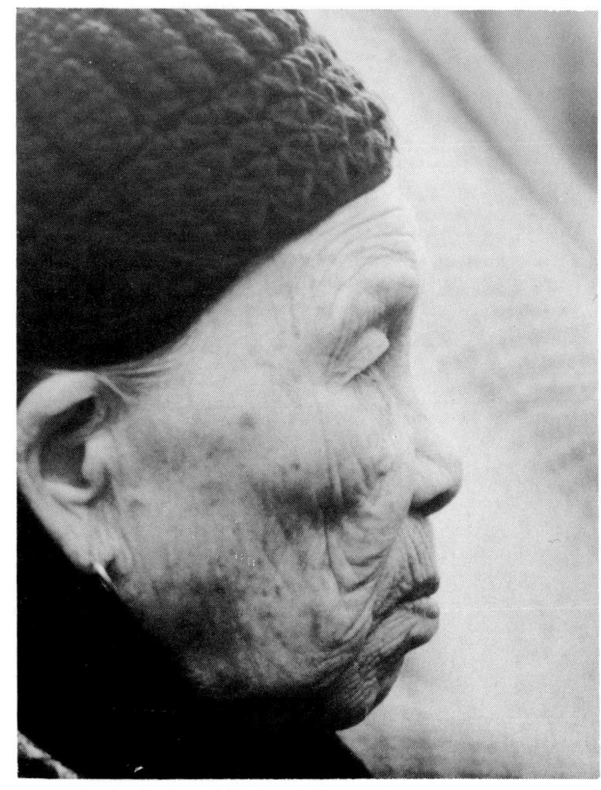

A scene from Retake's An Environment of Dignity

From Retake's documentary Hotel London

issues such as housing, diet and leisure provision for elderly Asians; and the welfare state in the family and cultural context of the lives of Asians in Britain. The latter was dubbed into five Asian languages. Another Retake documentary, shown on Channel 4 in July, 1987, was *Sanctuary Challenge* wich deals with the struggle of two Cypriot refugees fighting a deportation order.

Retake have also made two drama documentaries – *Majdhar,* the first feature, was shown on Channel 4 and was also screened at the 39th London Film Festival. It is the story of a young Asian woman who is abandoned by her husband soon after her arrival in London from Pakistan. Instead of returning to Pakistan she stays in London and fights to establish her own destiny.

The other drama documentary was unspooled at the 31st London Film Festival in November 1987. *Hotel London,* shot in an actual London 'bed and breakfast', examines the housing crisis in London and the effects it has on families and single people.

Penumbra And Azad Productions

Channel 4 also opened its doors to H O Nazareth and Faris Kirmani's Penumbra and Azad Productions. Nazareth has been making films under the banner of Penumbra Productions, which was set up in 1981 to make TV programmes and non-broadcast films and videos about the history, culture and politics of Africa, Asia and the Caribbean. Penumbra's first production was a series of lectures by the Marxist historian C L R James for Channel 4. This was followed by *Music Fusion,* a video of the concert by a renowned Pakistani composer, Imdad Hussain.

H O Nazareth was born in Bombay, India. He came to London in 1965 and became a political activist and a journalist, writing regularly for the radical political magazine *The Leveller.* In 1981 he co-wrote a BBC Play for Today *'The Garland'* with Horace Ové. The Garland deals with the inhumane practices perpetrated at immigration control in British ports and airports.

An East London Mosque featured in The New Eastenders

The eloquence of The Fearful Silence

Encouraged by Channel 4's support a sister company to Penumbra, Azad Productions, was set up in October 1984 with Faris Kirmani and Sulekha Nath, both graduates of the London International Film School. Their first production *State of Limbo*, a look at Pakistani exiles living in Britain and their views of the Zia regime in their homeland, was directed by Sulekha Nath and shown on BBC's *Open Space* slot in August 1986.

A Corner of a Foreign Field, an intimate look at Pakistani settlers in Britain was followed by *A Fearful Silence* – a documentary about domestic violence against women in Britain's Asian communities – and about women organising against it. The documentary was shown on Channel 4 in August 1986 and was followed by a campaign to alleviate the suffering of the victims of such violence.

Azad Productions have come a long way since *A Fearful Silence* and have made *Baluchistan – The Gathering Storm; Faiz – Poet in Troubled Times; Qwali – The Sabri Brothers; Habib Jalib: Poetry of Defiance*, and *Nazrul: The Rebel Poet of Bengal*. They were all shown on Channel 4. *Qwali – The Sabri Brothers* was also screened in the 31st London Film Festival on November 1987.

Nazareth has just produced a documentary on Apartheid for Penumbra Productions, *The War Against Children*. Shot on location, using interviews with black and white children, parents, social workers and lawyers and with the use of archive footage, it describes the reality of Apartheid and its effects on children. *The War Against Children* is awaiting prime-time transmission on BBC.

Other film makers include Suj Ahmad *(East End Story)*, Uday Bhattacharya *(Circle of Gold)* and Rahul Amin – whose finely constructed feature *A Kind of English* was unspooled at the 30th London Film Festival.

Salman Peerzada is another filmmaker with a good future. Salman started his career as an actor 25 years ago in *Emergency Ward 10*. He was also the lead character in Jamil Dehlavi's celebrated film *The Blood of Hussain*. Salman then went back to his native Pakistan and under hazardous circumstances shot his first film, *Mela*, on the turbulent state of politics in Pakistan. *Mela* was shown on Channel 4 and at the Third Eye Festival organised by Parminder Vir. The film became the victim of a strenuous campaign by the Pakistani authorities and earned Salman exile as well as victimisation for his family in Pakistan. Salman now commutes between London and New York and has been working on a number of projects.

The man who gave the world The Blood of Hussain

Jamil Dehlavi is the first and only British-based filmmaker from Asia to rise above the norm and join the celebrated rank of internationally renowned film makers. With his first full-length feature *The Blood of Hussain,* Jamil Dehlavi has created for himself a niche in the world of international films.

Jamil Dehlavi was born in Calcutta, India, in 1944. His family migrated to Pakistan after 1947. He studied at Rugby and Oxford in England graduating in French Literature, Politics and Law. After practising as a lawyer in Lincoln's Inn Jamil moved to the United States to study film and theatre. After graduating in cinematography at the South California Film Institute and in Film Directing at Columbia University, New York, he returned to Europe to attend a drama school in Paris. He then became an assistant director with French Television moving on to New York to work as a freelance cameraman for the United Nations Radio and Video Services.

The artist as filmmaker – Jamil Dehlavi

In 1980 Jamil Dehlavi created a storm in the film world with *The Blood of Hussain,* endearingly beautiful, evocatively simple, yet a forceful visionary political drama. *The Blood of Hussain,* a metaphor for the life and martyrdom of Iman Hussain, forecast the military coup in Pakistan. It is an elegy written on a poor country prostituted over the years by its politicians and raped continually by its army – merely to serve the

Salmaan Peerzada in Jamil Dehlavi's The Blood of Hussain

Salmaan Peerzada in Jamil Dehlavi's The Blood of Hussain

vested interests of its landed gentry and the imperial powers.

The Blood of Hussain was selected by 'The Directors Fortnight' at the 1980 Cannes Film Festival. It was awarded the Grand Prize at the Festival of Nations in Taormina, Italy, the same year, and the Gold Award for the best feature film at the Houston Film Festival as well as many other international accolades.

Five years before *The Blood of Hussain* earned Jamil Dehlavi exile as well as international recognition his earlier medium-length feature *Towers of Silence* has earned him the coveted Grand Prize as the best experimental film at the Festival of Americans in 1975, and was an official entry from Pakistan to the world's leading international festivals. It was also shown on Channel 4.

In 1985 Jamil Dehavi sprung another surprise with a hauntingly beautiful surrealistic documentary, *Qaf,* on the power of volcanic

A scene from Born of Fire *by Jamil Delhavi*

A scene from Born of Fire *by Jamil Delhavi*

eruptions. It won the Gentian Award (Best Mountain Film) at the Terento International Film Festival, Italy; Special Jury Award, at the Houston International Film Festival; Diable D'Or at the International Film Festival, Switzerland; and Special Jury Award at the Telloride Mountain Festival (USA).

Volcanic eruptions also flow in his latest film *Born of Fire* shown recently on Channel 4 and in many cities in the USA. It has also been scheduled for Japan and for French and German television. *Born of Fire* is a mystical fantasy in which Peter Firth plays a flautist who finds his playing taken over by mysterious music, conjuring images from a strange and different world. The trails lead him to seek the master musician in the wild countryside in Turkey where good fights evil and music fights fire. *Born of Fire* has won the Special Jury Award at the Madrid International Film Festival and a Gold Award at the Houston International Film Festival (1987).

Jamil Dehlavi is now working on a live-action adaptation of Rudyard Kipling's *The Jungle Book,* a six-part series for Channel 4 with the participation of various European television channels. He is also in the process of developing a feature film, an adaptation of D H Lawrence's *The Woman Who Rode Away,* to be filmed in Mexico.

Jamil Dehlavi is a stylist whose style is an outgrowth of his thought, vision and expression. He combines an insight into human souls with symbols, realities of life and dreamlike sequences.

Born of Fire has once again proved the versatility and genius of Jamil as a world class film maker.

Problems and prospects

With the exception of a few, a true Asian film culture has not developed in Britain. The film makers, actors, technicians and journalists find themselves in a 'Catch 22' situation. There are not many Asians in positions of power and authority in a society rife with racism. And this is bound to reflect itself in films and film making. Too little progress has been made in the area of integrated casting and using Asian film makers, technicians

Rita Wolfe in Ahmed Jamal's Majdhar

Film maker Horace Ové with novelist James Baldwin

A still in Jamil Dehlavi's Tower of Silence

Mahmood Jamal

and artistes in the mainstream cinema. Too much reliance on funding agencies and Channel 4, or occasionally BBC and other ITV networks, leave most of the Asian film makers to focus on problems and issues confronting the minority communities or subjects connected to the subcontinent of India, Pakistan and Bangladesh. There is a danger of their art being ghettoised.

H O Nazareth of Azad Productions appreciates this. Talking to *The Guardian* recently, Nazareth said: "The programmes we make aren't exactly mainstream. So it's never easy to persuade people to put money into them. And while we do get a certain amount of work from Channel 4, it's almost as if the other three feel they can leave it to Farrukh."

Consequently, they have a narrow base. Retake Collective is in no better position. Although they have made two features as well as documentaries, most of their finance comes from local authorities and other semi-governmental funding agencies. They are not tied to commercial strain like independent film makers, but this complete reliance on funding agencies puts them in a box. Mahmood Jamal agrees that Retake have serious problems of being boxed in but sees no alternative until the power structure in society changes. Perhaps Asian film makers should broaden their horizons and, like Norman Jewison *Moonstruck*) and Sorceress, make films based on minority communities but with a wider appeal. With Asian characters there is also a problem with costumes or accents. But to be honest, most of the output by independent film makers and by the collectives so far has not been of the high quality or standard necessary to lure financiers. No doubt they suffer like artists in other fields, from lack of training and other objective difficulties. But they still have to learn a lot and create a style of their own if they are to impress the wider audiences. The extra little touches, imagination and a crisp script that make a good film great do not cost money. Perhaps here they can take a leaf from Jamil Dehlavi.

Many of these film makers, themselves, are reluctant to be restricted to one source of work or one sort of product.

"Although our experience, our expertise is in the ethnic area we don't want to be limited to that. Second, we don't want to stick to documentaries – we want to do drama. And third, we want to be known basically as a professional production company: we don't want to be patronised. We simply want to produce programmes which will stand up against any other," says Nazareth.

Only time will tell.

HACKNEY'S RESPONSE TO RACISM

OUR MOTTO IS 'RACIAL EQUALITY=JUSTICE'

The Borough's response to racism is a direct and immediate challenge. The Borough's Race Relations Programme attacks racism in all it's manisfestations through firm policies, procedures and practices.

1. THE RACE RELATIONS COMMITTEE

The Committee is comprised of elected Councillors and co-opted representatives from community organisations. Its brief is to develop specific policies and assist with their implementation in order to meet the needs of Hackney's black and Ethnic Minorities.

2. EMPLOYMENT

a) The Council has accorded a very high priority to tackling racism in the recruitment process, and by the end of December of 1987, 38.7% of the Council's total workforce were Black and Ethnic Minority, against a target of 32%.
b) Black people constitute 21% of the Top 70 Posts in the Council, but Black Women are a mere 3%. Not good enough!
c) The Council's goal is to completely redress the imbalance in it's work-force; by 1990 Black and Ethnic Minorities should constitute 48% of the workforce.

3. INDUSTRIAL RELATIONS

With our success in recruitment, attention is increasingly on racism in Industrial Relations, e.g. induction and training, career development and promotion, disciplinaries and grievances, and general support mechanisms for Black and Ethnic employees.

4. SERVICE DELIVERY

Central to everything, the Council's aim is to deliver the services in a manner free from racism, meeting the needs and aspirations of the Borough's Black and Ethnic Minority community.

5. OUTREACH/LIAISON WORK

The Council recognises that it's Race Relations Policies and strategies, and their implementation can **only** be meaningful if they are inspired by the Black and Ethnic Minority communities themselves. Hence, the importance of proper and full consultation, and involvement, liaison, and general outreach work, much more is required.

6. ANTI-APARTHEID AND OTHER ISSUES

Hackney is not an island, and therefore, our anti-racist concerns and work extend not only to the rest of the Country, but also internationally.
Specifically, we do our best towards the elimination of the Apartheid system in South Africa and Namibia.

7. THE RACE RELATIONS UNIT

The Race Relations Unit is vigorously working for the effective implementation of the Council's policies to eradicate racism and to establish effective consultative mechanisms with Black and Ethnic Minorities so they can contribute to the shaping of Council policies.
Councillor Mamesia Margai, Chair of Race Relations Committee, and Dan Thea, Principal Race Relations Adviser, and all of us at the Race Relations Committee salute the eighth edition of Third World Impact.

RACE RELATIONS UNIT, HACKNEY TOWN HALL,
MARE STREET, LONDON E8 1EA.
TEL: 01-986 3123

THE LONDON BOROUGH OF HACKNEY

Inner London Education Authority – victim of the New Right and Racism

by Paul K Coleman

For over a century a consensus has prevailed that every child in London must have access to a decent education. It is still part of this consensus that education is provided despite the ongoing presence of poverty and a widening gap between rich and poor. Since the late 1950s black people have campaigned to ensure that this consensus also embraced a resolve to overcome the additional burden of racial oppression carried by black working class children, in particular.

Yet as the 21st Century approaches, London is a city still unwilling to accept its multi-racial reality that has existed for at least 40 years.

In spite of this, black community pressure secured significant gains as the Inner London Education Authority (ILEA), since the late 1970s, was forced to develop strategies aimed at tackling racial oppression in education.

But these advances will be eradicated by the intention of the third successive Conservative government, elected in June 1987, to abolish the ILEA and dispense with the hitherto existing consensus. Dismantling the ILEA was an oblique inclusion in the Conservative Party's election manifesto, *The Next Moves Forward*. Opponents referred to the abolition of ILEA as part of the Conservative Party's hidden agenda. But the plans for educational change in Britain – change which will not merely ignore the existence or racial oppression but which will virulently aim to destroy any strategy developed to resist that oppression.

Lincoln Crawford

Tacit support for the changes outlined in the manifesto was gained by the constant repetition of folksy catch-phrases: "Parental choice", "Parental Power", "Parental Consultation", "Accountability of schools and teachers to parents". All these political jingles were part of the Conservatives' hard-sell of their plans for a national core curriculum with attainment tests for children at ages 7, 11 and 14. Opposing voices warned that any curriculum sensitive to the needs of children from multi-racial backgrounds would be the first to suffer, being 'swamped' by the requirements of the Core Curriculum of so-called 'basic' subjects.

Attainment tests would brand children as failures as early as seven and would particularly disadvantage black children who, as report after report has shown, are branded as academic failures and as 'educationally sub-normal'.

But the simplistic appeal of the catchphrases drowned the critics. Invoked too for parental consumption was the spectre of the "loony-left, Marxist teacher". The ILEA, if papers like the London *Standard* are to be believed, is full of such devils. The manifesto stated: "In certain cases, education is used for political indoctrination and sexual propaganda. The time has now come for school reform."

Significantly "racial propaganda or indoctrination" was omitted. The New Right ideological thinkers behind the Conservative Party's plan for Britain wish to suppress or control all discussion of race, particularly when Britain's historical legacy of racial oppression rots away at the basic 3Rs core of the Core Curriculum. The New Right – the Adam Smith Institute, Roger Scruton, Ray Honeyford, the United States Heritage Foundation et al – are fully aware of the potential of education authorities like ILEA teaching their pupils that the 'Great' in Great Britain comes from its history of colonial plunder, slavery and racial oppression. Docile, unquestioning consumers and workers do not emerge from a curriculum which reveals the reality behind Britain and notions of Britishness. Nor, of course, do they vote Conservative. The New Right fears any education authority that might increase its democratic responsiveness to the point where a curriculum emerges that guides children *away* from the New Right goals of status and material position but *towards* critical perspectives of society and a sense of personal worth. Race is of crucial importance to the government's own objectives and ILEA is set to follow the Greater London Council (GLC) as one of the victims of this battle for the hearts and minds of London's people.

The racial oppression that ILEA has identified and sought to confront over recent years has its source in the structure of inner London society itself. The ILEA described the area as "one of the most disadvantaged areas in the country with very high proportions of poor families, unemployed parents, children speaking languages other than English, single parent families, homeless families and old school buildings." The authority argued that London has always had special educational needs and justified its higher spending levels on the grounds that "all services cost more in London. Policing London, for example, costs twice the national average."

Herman Ousley – Chief Executive of ILEA

Government spending restrictions have hampered ILEA. Only six per cent of ILEA's net costs are met by specific government grants. The other 94 per cent has to be borne by inner London ratepayers. The government does not pay ILEA any block grant which, on average, accounts for 40 per cent of the net cost of local government services. Expenditure level for the ILEA in 1988-89 was set on July 23, 1987, by the Secretary of State for Education, Kenneth Baker, at £955 million, a reduction of between £138-£163 million. The authority claims to have made strenuous efforts to improve efficiency and save costs but claims equally to have been starved financially on political grounds. The budget restrictions and the impending 'reforms' threaten much of ILEA's multi-racial education provision.

ILEA's provision of language support to those

children for whom English is a second language will be severely missed if, as is the likely prospect, the London boroughs which take over inner London's education service do not wish to or are unable to replace such provision. ILEA said in one of its responses to the government that "the loss or reduction of language teaching support, in particular, would be catastrophic". One in four of inner London's pupils speak or use a language other than English. An ILEA report showed that overall these children speak over 140 different tongues. Some 45,000 pupils in inner London schools need help with English.

ILEA provides six inspectors and 190 language teachers for this purpose, deployed across the ILEA in 35 teams. It provides in-service training for teachers to develop skills, strategies and resources to work effectively in multi-lingual classrooms. It also provides assistance for specialist staff in schools, funded under the Section 11 provision. These staff are involved in home school liaison for black children, establishing school-community links and devising teaching methods and teaching material better equipped for a multi-racial classroom. Material comes from ILEA's Centre for Learning Resources and include packs, books, jigsaws, audio and video cassettes.

In its recent history ILEA has employed 12 Education Liaison Officers (one in each inner London borough) who work with the black communities. ILEA's Equal Opportunities Unit has aimed to develop such policies within the authority, both as an employer and a contractor, the latter involving the development of a Contracts Compliance policy. The Unit's work was backed by an Equal Opportunities Inspectorate. A Multi-Ethnic Education Inspectorate, with an officer assigned to each of ILEA's ten divisions, provided courses for teachers and lecturers in anti-racist education.

The scope of ILEA's provision can be measured by looking at Tower Hamlets where it is spending some £70 million. Unlike the rest of London, school rolls in Tower Hamlets are rising. In January 1987, the authority said there were 12,780 children, aged 5-11, in primary/junior schools in the borough, a rise of nearly 2,000 since 1980. ILEA announced last summer that it is to spend £16 million to build a further 3,000 primary school places by 1990. This was partly in response to fierce criticism from the local Bangladeshi community, owing to the fact that about 1000, mainly Bangladeshi children, are unable to attend local schools because they are full to capacity. An internal ILEA report described the situation as "an unprecedented crisis".

Fierce criticism of ILEA is not new. But one of its Education Liaison Officers said that the Bangladeshi community was expressing concern about what will happen to their children when ILEA is abolished. The Social and Liberal Democrat – controlled council at Tower Hamlets, which would take over from ILEA, is implementing a decentralisation programme which could lead to the creation of under-resourced 'sink' schools for Bangladeshi and Bengali children. The local community has expressed little faith in the council's ability to take over the responsibility from ILEA for the education of their children. This would be the same council which has dragged homeless Bangladeshi families to court on the notoriously 'racist' contention that they made themselves 'intentionally homeless' by leaving their 'accommodation' in Bangladesh.

None of the boroughs planning to take over from ILEA have shown any commitment to responding to the needs of their black school population. Others more sympathetic will be unable to do so because of their own spending limits imposed by the Conservative government. The government's Education Reform Bill, published on November 20, 1987, proposes that individual boroughs should be allowed to 'opt out' of ILEA on April 1, 1990 or on April 1 in any following year. A simple majority vote of the borough council without any requirement to consult voters or parents is all that it would take. The Bill also proposes to allow individual schools the right to 'opt out' from borough control. A simple majority of parents would be needed. In schools where black parents are not a 'simple majority', their views could be totally ignored. In April 1988 the government dismissed the result of a poll conducted among inner London parents, supervised by the Electoral Reform Society, that showed that a clear majority opposed the government's plans for ILEA. The abolition plan led the Black Governors Collective to ask whether Conservative councils like Westminster would agree to co-opt black people onto school governing boards. This was an ILEA policy and has led to 1,000 black school governors being installed in inner London schools. So much then for the government increasing parental power.

ILEA was formed in 1965 to take over responsibility for London's education service from the London County Council. Its overall loss to London can be measured by recapping the services it provides. ILEA, the only directly elected single purpose education authority in Britain, is responsible for education in 12 inner London boroughs and the City of London. It has over 289,000 children attending its 1,057 schools (758 primary, 140 secondary, 49 nursery, 104 special schools and six hospital schools). Another 31 nursery schools are about to open or are in the planning stage. However, because of the Department of Education and Science's building allocations there is a shortfall in nursery provision, aggravated by the national shortage of nursery teachers and nursery nurses.

ILEA has over 500,000 students attending its 18

Irma Crichlow – ILEA member

Further and Higher Education Colleges, five Polytechnics, and 20 Adult Education Institutes. It also funds or maintains 80 youth centres and hundreds of youth projects and clubs. The British reggae band, Aswad, recently highlighted an alarming trend, where, following the closure of youth clubs in south London, youngsters began flooding into amusement arcades, fuelling a gambling craze with money stolen from their own parents. This shows how high the social stakes are set if ILEA's Youth Services are swept away. Again, would Conservative councils realise the need to fund black youth projects? Attempts by Kensington and Chelsea to repossess premises used for rehearsals by the Mangrove Steel Band is an example that gives rise to such concern.

The representative structure of ILEA allows its black members and officers to impress a black perspective onto education policy. Few of the black members, like Bernard Wiltshire, Anstey Rice, Irma Crichlow, Lorna Boreland-Kelly, Jean Barnard or Lincoln Crawford would dispute that struggles have had to be fought and won. Herman Ouseley, now ILEA's Chief Executive would not claim that ILEA is perfect. But abolition and devolution to the boroughs would set this black perspective back many years. The input from the Department of Education and Science would predominate. The race dimension would likely be substituted by the facile harmony language of 'let's all live together'. Even this pithy measure of acceptance that racial inequality in education needs tackling would not be guaranteed a hearing.

Neither is it morbid scaremongering to consider the prospect of ghetto, under-resourced 'sink schools' enforced by unofficial, but nonetheless effective, colour-bars. Black pupils presenting potential employers with a background of 'sink' schooling will do nothing but worsen their job prospects. Black people will still be confronted with their post-1945 legacy of low-grade, unskilled employment. When prospects die so does hope, and when that goes the social cocktail becomes explosive.

Prophetic accounts of what may be the effects of the abolition of ILEA are more than just idle speculation. As with the 'Poll Tax' it takes little foresight to see that black people will be among the hardest hit. Black community self-help and organisation may absorb some of the blows and will work to actively resist the potentially larger and more lasting effects of abolition. But the end of ILEA will signal the start of an education free-for-all. But free it will not be, and political power and money will buy educational achievement. Black parents have relatively little of either right now.

Without an ILEA cushion black children will be vulnerable to the Core Curriculum aim of furthering the division of all children, along lines of class, sex and race, into two groups; those who can service the economy through their mental labour, and those who are streamed into the economy's manual labour areas. ILEA represents a

Jean Bernard – ILEA member

danger as it has tried to break away from imposing these convenient definitions on its children. Under ILEA many black and female pupils have received a technologically-based education. But this escape route from being penned in on the manuel labour side of this mental manual divide will be shut off if ILEA is lost. The New Right dislikes the self-empowering quality of knowledge and of access to technology. The attack on ILEA represents an attack on an attempt to equalise the distribution of technological capital.

It was a mixture of Victorian paternalism and philanthropy that in 1870 established ILEA's original forerunner, the London School Board. Historians also documented the Victorian ruling class' fear of a revolutionary reaction to poverty and enforced ignorance. The Conservative government, entering the 1990s, is not fearful of the consequences of spreading poverty or ignorance. For example, as a result of the Social Security Act 1988, up to 22,500 ILEA pupils lost their right to free school meals on April 18 1988. This has increased the burden endured by many black families on low incomes.

Chancellor of the Exchequer Nigel Lawson's March 1988 budget effectively liberalised the law on charities to encourage them to plug the gap that the state sector is no longer allowed to fill and that the private sector is not interested filling. In one sense, both black and white children in inner London are victms of a return to Victorian notions of philanthropy. But the New Right do not fear that they will reap what they have sown. They have rejected the consensus and Victorian qualms about ignoring some degree of social responsibility. The education of children in inner London is less the victim of a return to Victorian values but more the victim of the New Right. It is a new, callous and ruthless direction.

Education

Education synthesises the achievements, discoveries and consensus of the past and prepares and researches for the future. It is therefore both a product of history and an architect of the future. The importance of education cannot be underestimated and, furthermore, whilst it can influence the future direction of society it is also inevitably moulded by what has gone before.

Therefore, because Britain is a society that essentially took shape in the context of the era of imperialism and is consequently characterised by racism, this has conditioned the nature of the British educational system which has in turn then served to perpetuate that form of society and that world outlook. The struggle that has been waged by the visible minority communities and their allies in the sphere of education has therefore essentially centred on whether to reject that heritage and to substitute a progressive alternative or to reinforce an education system that would instil in children – both black and white – the view held by Prime Minister Margaret Thatcher that Britain is still "the nation that built an empire that had ruled a quarter of the world."

Such a belief is, of course, the very antithesis of a genuinely educated and educational outlook and it is therefore hardly surprising that the educational field is one of intense ideological and political struggle. Before she toppled Edward Heath from the leadership of the Conservative Party, Mrs Thatcher served as the Secretary of State for Education. She achieved political notoriety by ending the practice of providing children with free school milk – earning her the epithet 'milk snatcher' – and by attempting to hamstring the independence of student unions, the National Union of Students in particular. In 1988 the attempts to find a legal way to destroy student unions continue – and this is hardly a coincidence because education has been, in a sense, a priority area for the reactionary onslaughts of the last three Conservative administrations.

The Education Bill of Secretary of State Kenneth Baker is one of the most important of current pieces of legislation, coming as it does in the period when attempts are being made to make the 'Thatcher revolution' irreversible, which inevitably means fashioning the next generation according to the required image.

An entire legacy and system of imperial racism was the reality that confronted minority children when they entered the British school system – the ancient civilisations built by non-white peoples in Africa, Latin America, the Middle East, India, China and elsewhere at a time when Europe was in the 'Dark Ages' or before were ignored, denied or ridiculed. On the basis of curricula that were at best inadequate, IQ tests were devised that tested not intelligence but the degree of immersion in European cultural values.

Alongside such institutionalised racism and discrimination, children and their parents also had to cope with the racial prejudices of many teachers, the racist abuse and attacks from fellow pupils and, particularly in the case of Asian pupils, the dilemma of having a first language other than English and the lack of facilities and, worse, understanding to deal with this matter.

All of these questions meant that problems were being stoked up for the future, and in the late 1960's it became clear that there was an insidious campaign being waged by the educational authorities and their collaborators elsewhere in the establishment to shift the blame for their failings onto their victims and to simultaneously shuffle the problem out of public view. Using the flawed IQ tests in particular black children were disproportionately and callously labelled as 'Educationally Sub-Normal' (ESN) and shunted off into special schools – out of sight and conceivably stigmatised for life. As black activists were to make clear in their researches and campaigning it was the British education system that made the Westindian child 'sub-normal'.

Black people who had migrated to Britain in the '50s and '60s came with high hopes not so much for themselves as for their children. It was felt that their sacrifices and hard work would make a better life for the generation that followed. Naturally they expected teachers and education authorities to be their allies in this struggle and aspiration.

Therefore when black parents realised what was being done to their children the response was one of bewilderment and rage. From this the view arose that if the education authorities were not educating the children then the community would have to take on the job itself. This was the starting point for the 'Supplementary Schools' movement, which went on to become one of the most enduring and positive examples of black self-organisation in Britain. Some of them, naturally, were transient but others are still going strong after more than a decade. They have taken many forms – some helping children to 'catch up' and improve their general academic standing, whilst others have had a conscious cultural and essentially political orientation of seeking to educate the children of the community to be aware of and take pride in the history and achievements of Third World peoples – to literally reclaim what had been 'hidden from history'.

Although the precise circumstances of different national communities vary, in many respects a common factor has been an appreciation that the British school system is not fully equipped to cater for the needs of ethnic minorities. A variety of forms have therefore emerged such as the network of language schools that exist throughout the Chinese community. They are seen as essential if the rising generation is not to forget its roots and lose its identity. Furthermore, an ability to speak Chinese is often an important factor in ensuring proper communication between parents and children.

Likewise the Tamil community, first and foremost the West London Tamil School, have moved to promote their language and culture, a move given added poignancy by the wave of tragedies that have overtaken the Tamil people in Sri Lanka in recent years and the resultant refugee crisis.

The various forms of supplementary schools acted as an inspiration and example to many in the mainstream of the education world to re-examine their perspectives and to reformulate curricula to reflect Britain's multi-racial, multi-ethnic composition. Others opportunistically saw the possibility to co-opt another area of the black community's struggles into the grip of the establishment, and felt that with certain adjustments and concessions the educational system could be further refined as a means to control the rising and angry generation.

From this unlikely combination was born the concept of 'multi-cultural education', which came to be particularly championed and promoted by progressive Labour-controlled bodies, such as the Inner London Education Authority (ILEA) which is now facing dissolution at the hands of Tory central government. Many schools have sought to overcome a 'Eurocentric' bias, including in the realms of literature, history, geography and religious education.

A governmental response on these questions – with particular reference to the provision for language teaching – came with the 1985 report (produced after six years of deliberations) entitled 'Education for all', or more commonly known as the 'Swann Report' after the committee's chair, Lord Swann. Acknowledging that prejudice is a fact of life in British society, Swann debunked the by then discredited link between 'IQ' and achievement, but on provision for mother tongue teaching the report was disappointing. It noted the argument that mother tongue teaching is of value and "that all languages should be valued and maintained as part of our national linguistic resource". But it undermined this observation by claiming that no evidence existed to suggest that mother tongue teaching enhanced a child's academic performance. There are many retorts to this but the most fundamental one is clearly that the report's authors saw academic attainment in an abstract and one-sided fashion, or more crudely through white-tinted spectacles.

In a classically muted response, the Commission for Racial Equality (CRE) stated: "We are concerned at the apparent contradiction between the Committee's positive advocacy of multilingualism on the one hand and their limited conception of the role of the school in promoting that multilingualism on the other." But the contradication was not simply apparent – it was real.

However, whilst the main criticism of the Swann report was that it was ineffectual, more direct attacks were in the making. These came to prominence in the now notorious 'Honeyford Affair'. This hitherto obscure Bradford headteacher was forced into 'early retirement' in 1985 after a long and bitter campaign spearheaded by the Drummond Parents Action Committee and supported from the mosques and by numerous anti-racist groups.

Honeyford's mistake was to go into print with what many privately thought. In a 1982 article in the *Times Educational Supplement* Honeyford said that some teachers – clearly implying that he was among their number – regarded "the whole notion of multi-racial education with scepticism and even resentment." He went on to talk of "the tendency we all have, whatever our colour, to adopt a narrow and rejecting view of others". Sadly Honeyford's trade union, the National Association of Head Teachers, backed him all the way. And his admirers included the Prime Minister. At the height of the controversy he was invited to 10 Downing Street in order that Mrs Thatcher could listen to his educational 'theories'.

But the harsh reality has always been that whilst ire has been focussed on any move, no matter how tenuous, towards an anti-racist perspective minority children throughout the country, in deprived inner cities and prosperous villages, are subjected to racist taunts, bullying and attack.

Early in 1988 the CRE issued a report, "Learning in Terror", which affirmed that racial harassment and violence in schools and colleges is a serious, widespread and persistent problem throughout the country – and that in most areas very little is done about it. The attacks and harassment, noted the report, are not just concentrated in deprived inner city areas with a high proportion of visible minorities. They are just as likely to occur in nearly all-white middle class suburban areas. In launching the report, Dr Aaron Haynes, Chief Executive of the CRE, said:

"Young people in schools and colleges suffer no less than men and women on the streets and in their own homes on housing estates. As in the wider environment, their walls may be daubed with the same threatening symbols of hatred and oppression. Acts of aggression and outbreaks of violence are not uncommon.

"The perpetrators span the age range from infant to adult, and they include pupils, students, teachers, lecturers and parents, all of whom may be described as ordinary, everyday members of the learning community. We need to disabuse our minds of the idea that racial harassment is solely or even mainly the work of the lunatic fringe or outside extremists. Incidents occur in the classroom as well as in the corridor and playground. They range from racial abuse to racial violence, leading to injury and even death. They are a feature of largely white schools in rural and suburban Britain, as well as of schools in the cities."

Dr Aaron Haynes, Chief Executive of the Commission for Racial Equality (CRE)

Amongst the CRE recommendations were a number directed to the Department of Education and Science. One was that school inspection reports should feature racial harassment as an item for enquiry and observation. Their "publications on discipline and behaviour should include a special section on racial harassment because of its unique effect on individuals and the community."

Another 1988 report from the CRE showed that as a result of discrimination black school teachers have lower job prospects in their chosen profession, whilst the previous week a report on the west London borough of Ealing also revealed extensive discrimination against black teachers. The CRE survey showed that some 80 per cent of their number were to be found on the two lowest pay scales, compared with 57 per cent of white staff. A mere five per cent of non-white teachers available were to be found in the more senior posts whilst the figure for white teachers stands at 13 per cent. Teachers from the visible minorities made up just two per cent of the total in the areas surveyed, even though they included Newham and Brent, where the respective proportions stood at 26.6 per cent and 33.5 per cent. The survey was conducted among 1,189 primary and secondary schools within eight boroughs having a larger than average visible minority community. The report recommended that measures be taken by the Department of Education and other bodies concerned with the training, appointment and career progression of teachers to ensure that a non-racial policy is actively pursued.

But whilst the CRE was putting forward reasoned and considered ideas, the juggernaut of the third and most radical phase of the Thatcherite counter-revolution had other ideas. The largest teachers' union in the country, the National Union of Teachers (NUT), commented:

"The government claims its bill, misleadingly called the 'Education Reform Bill', will give parents greater choice by allowing open enrolment, raise standards through a National Curriculum and Testing, and increase diversity of provision by allowing schools to 'opt out' of local authority control. The NUT and many other educational organisations strongly contest these claims and argue that, in fact, the bill's proposals would be divisive and lessen opportunities for the majority of children. We also deplore the fact that the government's proposals do not take account of the needs of our multicultural society." The NUT and other concerned organisations have also noted that no mention is made in the section of the bill dealing with the establishment of a national curriculum of 'core' and 'foundation' subjects of the requirement that such a curriculum should reflect the diversity of modern British society, and should prepare all pupils for life in that society. The proposed curriculum in fact has a narrow list of subjects which do not deal with what is required to become a responsible citizen of a modern country.

"No mention is made of the need to include a multi-cultural and anti-racist perspective in all subjects, nor does the list allow for the developments across subjects such as in humanities teaching which can include teaching about race relations, racism and anti-racism, information about other cultures and preparation for citizenship."

It is noted that the list of subjects includes a modern 'foreign' language – but this will surely mean a European language and not a community language – Thus the position of these languages will receive even less support from the schools, and students who would benefit from being able to study, say, Urdu or Chinese, will be forced to study French or German instead.

Another specific objection raised regarding the bill is that the proposal to test at the ages of 7, 11, 14 and 16 will disadvantage those children for whom English is a second language, especially at the earlier stages. "The tests themselves may be culturally biased, unless the people setting them are advised by experts in culturally unbiased testing."

The government's proposal that schools should have the option of 'opting out' of local education authority control raises the danger that some schools may be forced to close owing to falling rolls as parents chose to send their children to the more 'popular' schools. This could have the effect of depriving some areas of their local community school, particularly in inner city areas. This in turn will put areas with a strong visible minority presence at a disadvantage and so actually decrease choice. The NUT state: "It could even lead to racial segregation if white parents follow the example of Dewsbury and wish to send their children to 'all-white' schools."

The reference to the West Yorkshire town of Dewsbury recalls the actions of a group of white parents who, in the autumn of 1987, refused to send their children to the local designated school on the grounds that the majority of pupils were of Asian origin. A number of lurid and untrue tales were spread about academic standards at the school and the nature of the curriculum. It was said that the Christian religion was not taught at the school, even though it was a Church of England one! Although the parents' actions were provocative, morally offensive and of dubious legality, no measures were taken to prevent them. They were backed by wide sections of the press, and the attitude of much of officialdom was ambiguous to say the least. It was pointed out that the chaotic scenes at Dewsbury, which became a cause celèbre for every right wing extremist in the country, could be repeated up and down the country in perfect legality following the passage of the Education Bill. This logical opinion has never been refuted and the bill continues its legislative passage.

It is in this difficult situation that minority teachers, parents, students and pupils, supported by anti-racists in the indigenous community, are having both to defend existing gains, however modest, whilst promoting constructive alternatives.

Important debates were held at the March 1988 conference of the Labour Party Black Section in Manchester. The conference noted that, "Black Section supporters have played a leading role in the Black Governors Collective Movement which demands the greater involvement of black people, including parent, student, teacher and governor, in the running of the schools." Even in the present difficult situation there is great scope for members of the community to avail of the opportunity to become school governors and thus have a real say in the future of our children. If it is seriously understood that reliance cannot be placed on external institutions then it is necessary to be serious about self-reliance.

The conference – and this is indicative of wider trends within the movement – took up the question of what have become known as "black schools". One proposal advanced was for local education authorities "to provide for black schools with the same level of support and resources available to similar establishments in the independent and church sectors".

A discussion paper commented: "This is not the big problem for socialists that it may seem. There are *de facto* black schools already. It is just that, though they may have a black majority or near majority among the student population, this is not reflected among the teachers, curricula, governing body or general ethos of the school. Black Church schools exist in the independent sector and turn out excellent results – sometimes better than the local education authority. ...At least one of these is investigating how the proposed opt out system might be of benefit."

However, a supplementary paper stated: "We need to look at what independent black schools will mean in practice. First they mean Afro-Caribbean, Muslim, Hindu, or Sikh schools and not black in the political sense. The idea is therefore divisive to the black community. In practice, they will either be privately funded or opted-out schools, and usually religious schools. They will therefore only cater for an élite (and the lucky few working class children who can get scholarships)... In addition, religious schools often have a narrow curriculum which stunts the development of children."

However, this statement did correctly note (and it is a point that is often overlooked by people who should know better) that "within the context of current legislation which allows grant-aided religious schools, black religious schools should have the same rights as Church of England, Catholic, Jewish, etc. schools." (An essentially similar point was made in an April 1988 document from the Labour Party itself.)

Whatever final judgement is made on this complex problem it is surely right that such an aggressive but constructive approach be adopted as is to be found in both these positions; for it is a fact that whilst press hysteria has been engendered around subjects such as the 'positive images' campaign, a survey published in April 1988, for example, showed that, according to the newspaper *The Independent*: "An examination of reading schemes used in 196 primary schools in Sheffield shows that Chinese and Japanese are massively underportrayed... and that when they are represented they are characterised in terms of racially-offensive stereotypes."

Sheffield school teacher Ian Rice, who undertook the research, said: "One can only guess at the bewilderment and indignation of an ethnic Chinese/Japanese child in a British school faced with such a patronising and ignorant portrayal of his ethnic culture."

If government plans for a core curriculum taking up some 90 per cent of school time, for stringent controls on finance and the disbandment of progressive local education authorities, and for 'opted out' schools not having to comply with equal opportunities policies and practices come into effect, the prospects for rectifying such areas, short of a massive struggle, are slim indeed.

For the future of a multi-racial Britain it would not be the best outcome were the minorities to conclude that they no longer have a suitable place in the mainstream of the British educational system and that they must avail themselves of the new facility of 'opting out'. The idea of special schools for particular groups – whatever the outrage generated when those groups happen to be from the visible minorities – are not a new idea as the multitude of Church of England, Roman Catholic, Jewish and other schools bear witness to.

The proposed new system could well mean that unless the basic standard of education improves greatly the Asian and Westindian communities will set up their own schools and go to the state for the necessary finances. But Britain is a multi-racial society and will be even more so in the approaching 21st century. It is doubtful, to say the least, that the best way to prepare for that next century would be to divide the younger generation as they go through the educational process. It is surely necessary to educate all children in respect for the cultures and traditions of all. Nothing short of a complete change of educational strategy by the government can prevent major troubles in the future, which will damage the interests of all in society.

Black children in school

by Elaine Sihera

Elaine Sihera is a Jamaican born educationalist and broadcaster who has been teaching English to Secondary School children in Britain for the past 12 years.

Education is not just the acquisition of knowledge for its own sake but the preparation for taking one's place in the community. In that respect many black children are stateless, having been educated in the norms and values of a country which does not regard them as *bona fide* contributing members. Invisible in the classroom, they remain reluctant spectators for most of their lives, trapped on the periphery of British society.

It was Lord Swann, in his Committee's report of 1985, who finally laid to rest the notion that black children were failing in the British system because of the structure of their family or low average IQ. Instead he emphasised the major problem as discrimination in the schools themselves, and society at large, which directly – and indirectly through deprivation – affected a child's life chances. The most important finding was that Westindians were definitely underachieving. The key question is: why has there been little change in the status quo since the report? For the reason we must go back into the past.

Eager Westindians arriving in Britain in the fifties, or earlier, regarded things from a colonialist perspective. They were coming to the 'mother' country to seek a better life. While they had differing aspirations, the idea of the white person being somehow 'better' was still etched on their subconscious as a legacy from the past. Into this society their children came, also full of expectations. However, despite the fact that the black child had been exposed to a system of education in the Westindies which reflected the English structure of education, he/she had difficulty adjusting, reinforced in no small way by the white Briton's stereotyped view of the black person as being 'inferior'.

Caught in a system where their language was not reinforced in any way, their culture was not promoted or recognised, their very presence was tolerated rather than positively encouraged, and where their parents might repeatedly speak of returning 'home' at a future date, many black children became confused, introspective and apathetic. Soon enough, they were then regarded as educationally sub-normal (ESN) by teachers who saw that label as a good way of isolating them even further. This derogatory label also served a second purpose: that of legitimising and reinforcing the teachers' own prejudices. It was left to black parents, academics and campaigners to alter the way these early first generation children were assessed.

Today, walk into any British school, even in areas of high ethnic minority population, and the structure is depressingly homogenised. There is invariably a white headteacher (even in schools where there are 80 per cent black children), the senior staff will all be white and any black teachers will be stuck firmly to the lowest teaching grades. On top of that black children will be in the lowest streams, and ESN has now adopted a fashionable name – Special Needs. The idea of a 'multicultural' awareness in schools, accepting that people are different but equal, is only restricted to certain schools: i.e. those which boast a large black community. It is taken as axiomatic that predominantly white schools will not need such 'multicultural' education as they are unlikely to find it of any use. The irony is that it is precisely in these establishments where multiculturalism should flourish because, armed only with heresy and one side of the argument, many of these pupils lack the exposure of face-to-face contact with their black peers. Result: personal prejudices are solidified into irrefutable 'truths'.

The black child in the British education system suffers from a chronic lack of identity and of positive self-image. His/her culture is not regarded as valid, yet any identification with mainstream culture is resisted because of the colour of his/her skin. Even more important, the success of black children is hampered by the following: few existing role models to reinforce their worth and capacity to excel; low expectations by teachers; no reflection of their presence in the media or society; talent primarily channelled into sports or other low-status activities; lack of positive career guidance; racist environment of both school and community where bullying is ignored; lack of any positive contribution to the curriculum; any difficulties mean pupils seen as a 'problem' by teachers; too many punitive sanctions, insufficient praise and a curriculum which is geared to the needs of the majority.

Back in the Westindies, parents also regarded the education of their child to be the prerogative of the professionals; the people who knew best were the teachers. They did not interfere and gave school staff a free hand in the discipline of their children. There was nothing irregular or untoward about this parental approach. On the other hand this non-interventionist style of some black parents is often seen by British staff as negative influence. It is interpreted that parents 'do not care' about how their children are doing because their actions do not reflect the school-home partnership. Yet there is no direct evidence to date to show that reluctant visitors to the school care any less for their offspring. As a matter of fact this might be a pointer to their own feelings of impotence in helping their child positively, particularly in the face of so many educational changes, and of ultimately bowing to professional expertise to improve their child's performance and progress.

The biggest obstacles to our children's future success are still low achievement and a very poor self-image. The road to the future is paved with good intentions from successive governments who have refused to grasp the nettle of true education for all. Children cannot strive for equality in an unequal society where differences are treated as inferior attributes and other cultures or perspectives are regarded as irrelevant to the mainstream culture. We are still a long way off from Swann's recommendations that **'all** schools should adopt clear policies to combat racism' and, as the under-representation of ethnic minorities in teaching was a 'great concern' (being the subjects of racial prejudice and discrimination), far greater efforts should be made to "attract more black teachers through equal opportunities policies and ethnic monitoring". If anything, the situation is getting worse. There were only 2.5 per cent black teachers in training colleges during 1986, a fall of 2 per cent on the previous year.

To make matters worse teachers who have been employed under the government's Section 11 funding for ethnic minorities find themselves marginalised to obscurity within the profession, not eligible for promotion within mainstream teaching and not seen as having much to offer their respective schools in curricular development. Indeed the London Borough of Newham was actually taken to court recently for actively thwarting the promotion of Section 11 teachers. They had sent circulars to Heads with the instruction that teachers employed with Section 11 funding were **not** eligible to be considered for internal promotion. This was only revealed because a teacher was prepared to take his case further. He was awarded damages but the implications for hundreds of black teachers in similar positions are alarming.

Throughout their lives in Britain black children have been expected to assimilate the society's culture instead of accommodating it along with their own. This is the chief cause of a negative self-image, the absence of a reflection of their very presence in society. There is much we can do to offset this negative impact on our children. Parents can, and should, try to take a much greater interest in their children's school careers and to contribute where necessary. For example, being a governor in a school is an excellent starting point. Black teachers can also do much by seeking positions of influence within the system to provide essential role models. However, the onus is on the society which the government represents, and until the neo-colonialist image of the black person is swept away our children will be swimming against a most horrendous tide of prejudice, discrimination and inequality.

Opening an academic window

by Alfred Ford

With reference to a few examples, Alfred Ford shows that 'underachievement' is only part of the story.

For twenty years or so, public discussion on the education of British children of Westindian origin has focused overwhelmingly on the issue of 'underachievement'. It is a word that has become synonymous with young black people. A dozen Ph. D theses, and major public documents (the Eggleston Report; the Swann Report, etc.) have piled up statistics, have provided diagrams, charts, paradigms and theories to prove the existence of 'underachievement'. Local Education Authorities up and down the country have set up research teams to enquire into the nature of this 'underachievement', have issued 'multi-cultural policy statements' and have appointed specialist staff to cope with the problem.

All of this is welcome, especially the supplementary schools set up by concerned black teachers. The community welcomes the provision of resources and the sensitivity to its educational plight. Yet I cannot but regret the fact that 'underachievement' is such a dominant concept, conditioning perception of our young black people. These young people are burdened with other automiatic associative terms – 'muggers', 'lazy', 'criminal', 'rapists'. 'Underachievement' is an addition to their burden of stereotypes.

I fear too that talk of 'underachievement' is a self-fulfilling prophesy. Young people will merely become what is expected of them. If all the academic research is on 'underachievement', if it is the term that determined official reaction to young black people, and the term that shapes 'remedial' structures and programmes, then young black people *will* continue to 'underachieve'. Surely the time has come to correct our knowledge of the educational potential of our Caribbean people by focusing on the quality of scholarship that, historically, has emerged from the Caribbean region; by a focus on Caribbean academics in Britain; and finally on the young black people who are presently attending universities and who will be the future's scholars and leaders.

In the first aspect, let me begin with the indisputable assertion that scholarship has always been our major priority in the Caribbean. Those of us born and brought up in the region will remember the discipline of schools, the great respect (indeed terror!) for teachers, the burning desire to learn, but specifically the pressure, sometimes beatings, our parents applied on us to study. We will remember our pride at coming first, and our deep shame when we ended up at the bottom of the class. Children and families, were identified according to their academic ability: so-and-so was a bright child, and his/her whole family were known to be equally bright. Our concept of aristocracy was based not on money or breeding but on intellectual ability. The children with shining 'O' or 'A' level results were regarded with awe by the younger ones, figures to be emulated. And there were dozens of children with such high passes: *academic achievement was a day to day reality,* it was taken for granted, it was never questioned.

We produced scholars with an international reputation – historians like Walter Rodney and Eric Williams, economists like Sir Arthur Lewis (winner of the Nobel prize), writers like V.S. Naipaul and Wilson Harris (who between them have won a handful of the world's major literary prizes). Our Caribbean tradition is one of eductional *achievement*.

In the second respect, let us never forget that Western Universities, from Harvard to McGill to Cambridge, are staffed, inter alia, by Professors and Lecturers and Fellows of Caribbean origin. They may not number in vast quantities, but what matters is not the quantity but the quality of intellectual contribution. In any case, the Anglophone Caribbean have relatively tiny populations, so it would be unrealistic to expect that we would produce intellectuals in the thousands. These Caribbean academics not only contribute their knowledge and skills to the world community of academic scholarship, but they can be crucial models for young black people in Britain who are grappling with racism in schools and the wider community which supresses their talents.

The following selective potted biographies show some of our achievers and a couple of young hopefuls:

Elizabeth Thomas-Hope

Elizabeth Thomas-Hope was born and educated in Jamaica where she took her 'O' levels and 'A' levels. She went to the University of Aberdeen, in Scotland in 1963 where she read for a degree in Geography. Between 1967-69 she studied at Pennsylvania State University, obtaining her Masters degree in Geography and Computer Studies. She then returned to Britain, to Oxford University, where she was awarded her doctorate. She is presently Lecturer in Geography at the University of Liverpool. She has held Lectureships and Research Fellowships at City University, New York, the University of London and the University of the Westindies. Her main fields of academic interest are Caribbean migration, contemporary Caribbean society and culture, and Caribbean minorities in Europe and North America. She has published widely in a variety of academic journals, including *Social and Economic Studies, Oral History* and *New Community*. Her book publications include *A Geography of the Third World*, published by Methuen in 1983.

David Dabydeen

David Dabydeen was born and educated in Guyana. He moved to London in 1969, doing his 'O' and 'A' levels there before going to Cambridge University where he read English Literature, graduating with the University's Quiller-Couch Prize. He obtained his doctorate in English Literature in 1982, went to the USA as a Fellow at Yale University, then took up a post-graduate Junior Research Fellowship at Oxford University. Between 1982-1983 he served as a Community Education Officer in Wolverhampton. In 1984 he was appointed Lecturer in Caribbean Studies at the University of Warwick. Dr Dabydeen has published eight books so far (his first book of poems winning the Commonwealth Poetry Prize in 1984), including two studies of British Art. His numerous awards include those from the British Academy and a Greater London Council (GLC) Literary Award in 1985. He has given guest lectures and readings at some of the world's most prestigious institutions, including Yale University, Oxford University, Cambridge University, Aarhus University (Denmark), the University of Singapore, the Swedish Royal Academy, the University of the Westindies, the University of Rome and the Sorbonne (Paris). Much of his work has been featured by British television, including his one-hour documentary for ITV on art and slavery, entitled *Art of Darkness*.

Clive Harris

Clive Harris was born in St. Kitts, studied Sociology at Birmingham, obtaining his Masters degree from the University in 1976, and his doctorate in 1981, which was supervised by Professor Stuart Hall. He taught at the University of Birmingham and at Wolverhampton Polytechnic before taking up a Research fellowship at the University of Warwick in the School of Race and Ethnic Studies. He was appointed to a Lectureship at Birmingham Polytechnic in 1987. His research interests are in Migrant Labour in Capitalist Social Formations, and in Monopoly Capitalism in 'Underdeveloped' Social Formations. His community experience includes a three-month placement with Wolverhampton Council for Community Relations, a six-months placement with Birmingham's Social Services Department and some remedial teaching at the Harambee Self-Help Project in the West Midlands. His forthcoming publications include *Formal Capitalism in Jamaica 1834-1900*, to be published by Zed Press.

Philip Nanton

Philip Nanton was born in St. Vincent, did his 'O' and 'A' levels in Sussex, took a Higher National Diplomae in Business Studies at Hendon College of Technology, a post-graduate Diploma in Economic Development (with distinction) at London before going to the University of Birmingham in 1971 to do a Masters in Economics and African Studies. He obtained his doctorate at the University of Sussex in 1986/7 and is presently Lecturer in Social Policy at the University of Birmingham. He has published widely on Caribbean history, and his interest in Caribbean literature was expressed in his editing of an anthology of Pan-Caribbean Writing, *Melanthika.* He has also recently published two plays, *Anancy's Magic,* with Longman's, Dr Nanton's involvement in community work is a long one. In 1982 he was appointed to Northampton's Race Relations Service and played a major role in the Borough's establishment of an Equal Opportunities Policy.

Harry Goulbourne

Harry Goulbourne was born in Jamaica, and grew up in London, attending Peckham Manor Comprehensive School. He read History and Political Theory at the University of Lancaster, and obtained his doctorate at the University of Sussex with a dissertation on Education and Politics in Jamaica between 1880 and 1968. He took up a Lectureship at the University of Dar-es-Salaam in Tanzania between 1975-1978 before moving to the University of the Westindies where he became Vice-Dean of the faculty of Social Sciences, at Mona. He has published several articles on African and Caribbean political issues and was awarded a Leverhulme Fellowship at the University of Warwick's Centre for Caribbean Studies in 1984. He is presently a Senior Research Fellow at the University of Warwick. His books include *Politics and State in the Third World* (Macmillan, 1979). Dr Goulbourne is a member of various academic bodies including the Caribbean Studies Association, the Association of African Political Scientists and Gray's Inn, London.

Sheila Nasta

Sheila Nasta, of Indian and English parentage, is currently lecturer in Literary Studies at Portsmouth Polytechnic. She read English at Kent Univesity, doing an M.A. thesis on the work of Samuel Selvon and V.S. Naipaul. She has taught in schools in Kent, Buckinghamshire and London for several years and acted as an Assistant Examiner for the Oxford and Cambridge Examination Board. In 1984 she founded and edited an educational journal concerned with the teaching of African, Caribbean and Asian Literatures, *Wasafiri.* Her current research interests are the Literatures of the Indian diaspora and Women's Literature from the Commonwealth. Her publications include 'A Select Bibliography of Samuel Selvon' (*Journal of Commonwealth Literature,* 1983) and two forthcoming books, *Critical Perspectives on Sam Selvon* (Three Continents Press) and *Mothers and Minors: Black Women's Writing* (Women's Press).

Diane George

Diane George, born in Islington of Trinidadian parents, was brought up in south London. She attended St. Veronica's School, then Southwark College, where she obtained nine 'O' levels (with distinctions in sociology, religious education and integrated humanities) and three 'A' levels in English, History and Music. She is presently a first-year History undergraduate at the University of Warwick. She plays the clarinet, guitar and piano for recreation and has a strong interest in drama. She has ambitions of becoming a lawyer.

Natalie Glitzenhirn

Natalie Glitzenhirn was born in Islington and grew up in England, Germany and Montserrat. She studied for her 'O' levels at Slough (St. Bernard's Court), passing eight subjects, with a distinction in German. She went on to achieve 'A' level passes in German, Spanish and Business Studies. Natalie is presently a first year undergraduate at the University of Warwick, reading German and International Studies. She enjoys sport, playing basketball for the University. She wants to become an accountant.

Housing

The attempts by the present Conservative government to return the country to the Victorian era have certainly not overlooked the housing sector. The state and quality of housing available to the working people of Britain has long been a disgrace in many parts of the country and the visible minority communities have tended to suffer worst of all.

The Housing Bill, which is currently making its way through parliament, will strip tenants and others of practically all rights – under the by now familiar deceptive signboard of 'freedom of choice' – and in so doing complete the change from housing being a basic right to being a luxury, rendering many thousands more homeless in the process. As with practically all such attacks on living standards and democratic rights it is invariably the visible minorities who are affected first, hardest and longest.

The right to a home is one of the basic human rights, but it is one of those rights that a system based on private enterprise and private profit finds most difficult to satisfy. This is the reality that underlies a shifting pattern of forms.

In the 1950s and early 1960s a typical sign to be found in landladies' windows throughout the cities of England would read: "Rooms to let. No coloureds. No Irish. No Children. No Dogs."

Such was the welcome extended to those who were invited and enticed to Britain to help in the post-war recovery and to labour to create the boom.

It was the national disgrace of signs such as these that helped to prepare the ground for the passage of legislation aimed at eliminating racial discrimination. But whilst legislation can certainly help, the ideology and practice of racism is so pervasive and tied to various other social and economic factors that it cannot simply be banished by virtue of an act of parliament.

All surveys and studies consistently show the disadvantaged status of minorities in the housing sector. A Political and Economic Planning (PEP) report published in 1974 showed that for every white household living at a density of two or more persons per bedroom, there were three times as many Westindian and four times as many Asian households in the same position.

In the 1979 National Dwelling and Housing Survey, figures for London showed 27 per cent of Asian households and 18 per cent of Westindian households living in over-crowded accommodation, compared to six per cent of white households. Subsequent research shows that the situation since then has worsened.

In terms of amenities, too, Asian and Afro-Caribbean households fare worse than white households. According to the same National Dwelling and Housing Survey, some 30 per cent of Asian and 14 per cent of Westindian households in London lacked the use of one important amenity, compared with 12 per cent of white households.

According to PEP reports over half of Pakistani households in Britain, compared with 11 per cent of white households, lacked their own bath, hot water and inside lavatory.

Repeated studies by a series of bodies, including the Policy Studies Institute, the Runnymede Trust and the Commission for Racial Equality, have yielded firm statistical evidence to show that, compared to white households, minorities are systematically allocated to undesirable accommodation, such as 'hard to let' flats on the older and more dilapidated estates, by local authority housing departments.

Many of the inner city areas where major communities of visible minorities live suffer from some of the most deplorable housing conditions in Britain. A 1981 survey carried out in the Handsworth area of Birmingham by a market analysis firm established that in a circle half a mile in radius from the centre of Lozells Road one would find an area in which one house in ten either shares or has no inside lavatory or bathroom. Just a quarter of houses were owner-occupied, compared with 56 per cent nationally. 60

per cent were owned by the local authority, compared with 33 per cent nationally. 12 per cent consisted of just one or two rooms and 14 per cent accommodated more than one person to every room. Nearly 53 per cent of houses in Britain were centrally-heated, but in Handsworth the figure was just 36 per cent.

An analysis of the housing policy of Hackney Council in east London by the Commission for Racial Equality (CRE) some years ago was in many respects a landmark in its field. It found that amongst white applicants 16 per cent received houses, 19 per cent maisonettes and 65 per cent flats. However, among black applicants four per cent received houses, 11 per cent maisonettes and 85 per cent flats. Of all houses, maisonettes and flats allocated to black and white applicants, 79 per cent of houses were allocated to white people compared with 21 per cent of black people; 64 per cent of maisonettes were allocated to white people compared with 36 per cent to black people; and 46 per cent of flats were allocated to white people compared with 54 per cent to black people.

A larger proportion of white applicants received new properties, whilst black applicants tended to be allocated to inter-war properties that had been modernised but to a relatively low standard. Of white applicants, 25 per cent were allocated new properties, compared with three per cent of black applicants, while by comparison, 24 per cent of black applicants were allocated to inter-war properties, compared with seven per cent of white applicants. 88 per cent of all new properties allocated to the waiting list subsequently went to white applicants, and 75 per cent of the inter-war properties went to black people.

However, institutionalised discrimination – intentional or unintentional – is clearly not the only aspect of the problem. Also compounding the housing problems of the community are the prevalence of racial harassment and racial attacks on peoples' way to and from their homes. White racist neighbours are amongst the major perpetrators of these attacks which, as well as resulting in a great deal of individual suffering and misery, can contribute to the emergence of a housing situation which can be likened to that of *de facto* apartheid. As well as straight-forward thuggery it is known that so-called 'Residents' Associations' have long been a favoured method of organisation for white racists. On numerous occasions, such supposedly 'independent' groups have been exposed as fronts for the National Front and similar extremist parties.

The levels of harassment and attack suffered by minority residents and tenants range from seemingly trivial verbal abuse all the way to arson attacks that have repeatedly resulted in death, sometimes of whole families, and have in turn provided the focus for some of the major anti-racist campaigns.

Yet despite the seriousness of the problem –, attempts by local authorities to evict tenants responsible for the racial harassment of their neighbours have been tried only rarely and even then it has generally been the case that the political will to see the process through to a conclusion has been lacking. This is in spite of the fact – all other considerations notwithstanding – that it is perfectly normal for a tenancy agreement to include a clause to the effect that tenants must not harass or be an unreasonable nuisance to their neighbours.

Amongst the litany of grievances of the minority communities on the housing front, probably the most deplorable is the long-running case of the Bangladeshi community in east London, particularly in the borough of Tower Hamlets. Their plight has caught national attention and created national precedents. It has involved different parties in the leadership of the council at various times as well as the former Greater London Council (GLC). A report published in March 1986 said that local GLC officers responsible for allocating homes to Bengalis believed that they should be housed together on the worst estates because they were "dirty, noisy and potential sources of social conflict". The study was conducted by Deborah Philipps, an academic from Leeds University, and was focussed over five months in 1984. Many housing officers, the report revealed, gave the worst housing to Bengalis on the grounds that "they would turn them into slums anyway".

The report said that very few Asians were given the opportunity to view property on traditionally white estates and on nine modern estates their proportion varied between three and eight per cent. But on many of the older estates, more than half of the offers were made to Asian people – on the rundown Berners estate the proportion was 90 per cent.

It was above all Tower Hamlets that became notorious for the practice of placing families in so-called 'bed and breakfast' accommodation – an action that was as unsuitable as it was unpleasant as it was uneconomical. But in 1987 the council – controlled by the Liberals, soon to become the

Social and Liberal Democrats – went a step further by seeking to absolve itself of all responsibilities towards the unfortunate families. In a July 1987 High Court ruling – a verdict which was challenged on an appeal whose result is currently awaited – it was considered reasonable for Tower Hamlets to regard as "intentionally homeless" families who had exercised – frequently after an inordinate delay – their legal right to come to live in Britain.

By categorising the families as "intentionally homeless" the council is freed of its legal obligation to provide them with accommodation. The ostensible reason was that people had voluntarily left accommodation in Bangladesh, even if that accommodation was totally inadequate and even if it was necessary to leave it behind in order to realise a long cherised ideal of living together as a family. Concretely this means that men who have lived and worked in Britain for up to 20 or even 30 years are said to be ineligible for housing under the Homeless Persons Act. The High Court ruling also said that the council had no duty under the child care laws to ensure children's welfare by housing their family when it has been deemed to be "intentionally homeless".

This legal wrangle places an important housing safety net under threat. The National Assitance Act of 1948 set out to abolish the shadow of the work house by placing a duty on social service departments of local authorities of providing temporary accommodation for those in urgent need. This generally meant homeless families. However, the laws was not flawless and did not resolve the problem of homelessness.

Further progress came with the 1977 Housing (Homeless Persons) Act, introduced as a private member's bill by a then Liberal MP. It placed a duty on local housing departments to provide temporary accommodation for homeless families and other priority groups. The only way in which a family could find itself excluded from help was if they had deliberately left accommodation which it was considered reasonable to continue to occupy. But this "intentional homelessness" clause was not part of the original bill and it was never envisaged that it would apply to more than a handful of cases. But today it is probably the major reason given for the denial of housing to the homeless.

Furthermore, Tower Hamlets' refusal to house families on the grounds that they voluntarily left accommodation in Bangladesh and are not settled in Britain (a policy that has also been taken up by Labour-controlled Camden council with regard to Irish families) foreshadows an important forthcoming change in immigration law. This will remove the right given by the 1971 Immigration Act to men who settled in Britain before 1973 to bring their wives and children to join them. In the near future such people will have to show that they can support their families without "recourse to public funds" – funds to which they have generally been contributing through taxation. One of the consequences of this is that such families forfeit the right to be housed by a local authority.

Home Office ministers have stated that the Tower Hamlets situation is one of the factors that induced them to initiate the rule change. But campaigners, in particular the Tower Hamlets Homeless Families Campaign, point out that the council's policies have significantly worsened the situation. They cite the following factors:

– Racial discrimination in housing allocation which keeps Bengali families in hotels far longer than dictated by the shortage of housing;

– Planning and investment policies which fail to make use of the opportunities for building large houses for rent;

– The sale of entire council estates to private developers for resale to the rich who want to live near the city.

The Homeless Families campaign state: "The council has followed policies which have resulted in large numbers of Bengali families in hotels, has then said it cannot cope with the demand, and pressed for changes in immigration policies, to stop families coming to a place where they have a right to live."

Tower Hamlets council has essentially given three reasons for their decision to try and evict the families. They cite a shortage of money to pay hotel bills; a shortage of homes for homeless families; and that certain Bangladeshi families should not be given council flats anyway.

Against this, campaigners question both Tower Hamlets' policies and record. They note that since 1983 the council has sold off more thn 500 homes and a further 1700 are presently under threat. They also state that although Tower Hamlets council built 8,556 new homes between 1964-84, only seven per cent were in the E.1 postal district, the heart of the Bangladeshi community. Not one has been built in Spitalfields, the ward with the worst housing conditions and the most Bangladeshi residents. The council allocates only 30 per cent of its housing to homeless families whilst some other London boroughs provide twice as much. Two major independent reports, as well as an investigation by the Commission for Racial Equality, have declared that the council's allocation of housing is discriminating against Bangladeshis.

The High Court ruling accentuates the discriminatory aspect by stating that "intentionality" should be assessed taking into account "the general circumstances prevailing in the area" (ie Bangladesh in this case) as well as the customs and lifestyle of the applicants' own community. It was also "relevant" that an applicant had never had a continuous place of residence in Britain and that "his ties were never very close".

This judgement, tinged with racism, nevertheless, also has serious implications for any family that finds itself in the trap of homelessness, as "intentionality" would now be interpreted much more widely than before.

The Bangladeshi families in Tower Hamlets have suffered for many years and there is every chance that their suffering will be reinforced and generalised with the force of law. What is particularly dangerous is its coincidence with the government's new Housing Bill. Since 1976 successive governments have cut the amount of money available to house the homeless but the new bill will worsen the situation by far. By reducing the amount of money to councils and housing associations it will force rents up, thus making many more people homeless. It will also cut even further the number of homes that a council has to offer the homeless by allowing private businessmen to come in and take over whole estates. Such changes are also inter-related to the forthcoming introduction of the 'poll tax', and the Social Security Act which came into force in April 1988. Together they mean that people face an effective end to rent controls and building standards and more generally the prospect of an end to council housing in any form that has hitherto been considered recognisable. Whatever the shortcomings of municipal housing, and whatever the criticisms that have been levelled – and there are many on both counts – this can only be seen as a major assault on both the visible minorities and working people generally. These are vicious attacks which are fraught with explosive social consequences. From a legacy of neglect and discrimination we appear, sadly, to be moving into a period of immense suffering – suffering which the younger generation, in particular, will certainly not endure in silence.

Cable Street to Brick Lane

by Ivan Corea

Sri Lanka-born Ivan Corea has worked for several years with the Bangladeshi community. He takes a look at the 'real' East End, through the cracked windows of a deprived community.

The commercials tell a different story. The Docklands is depicted as the "in" place to be: luxury flats – anything from a mere £450,000 upwards, smart housing; clean streets; City whizz-kids with the symbols of the new rich – the Porsche, yellow tie and filofax. It resembles a view and a total policy statement for Britain's inner cities put forward by Prime Minister Margaret Thatcher and the present Conservative government.

However, you only need to scratch the surface to see life beyond the filofax – the stark reality is Brick Lane and the surrounding area of Stepney with its racist slogans, bad housing, suffering and official indifference. This is the real East End – away from the 'yuppies' and the 'Eastenders' television soap opera.

The East End of London has always been a first stop settlement area for immigrants. For over 300 years people of different races, religions and backgrounds have come and gone. The Romans established a settlement just outside the city gate 'Eald Gate' (now known as Aldgate) during the reign of Claudius (who invaded Britain in 43 A.D.). The area was famous for spittal sermons preached in the pulpit near the hospital church (founded in 1197 by London merchant Walter Brune and his wife Rosia). The non-conformist preacher John Wesley and the Dean of St. Paul's Cathedral, Dr Donne, preached here.

The Huguenots were the next settlers – they were French Protestants who fled persecution in France, particularly after the St. Bartholomew's Day Massacre in 1572. In 1687 there were 13,000 Huguenot immigrants living in Spitalfields. They were silk weavers who lived in Fournier Street, Leman Street, Duval Street and they became extremely successful. The rich and famous travelled to the East End to buy their silks. Resentment grew and so did racist attitudes – sadly it is very much a part of the East End legacy.

The Jewish community, who followed the Huguenots, were to suffer the same fate. Many Jewish immigrants lived in terrible conditions as did the Irish settlers who tended to live in the

Brick Lane in east London

Bangladeshi families live in appalling conditions in the East End

Spitalfields area. There were around 130,000 Jews who lived in the "Jewish Quarter" in the East End by the end of the First World War. Some of them became successful as clothing manufacturers and their very presence led to the Battle of Cable Street (now depicted on a large mural on the side of St. George's Town Hall, 236 Cable Street, E1) which by street resistance sealed the fate of Britain's fascists as a viable political force. Sir Oswald Moseley and his black-shirted British Union of Fascists attempted to march down Cable Street aiming to provoke and no doubt attack the Jewish Community. On Sunday 4th October 1936, 100,000 people massed on the streets and made their stand against racism.

Other significant communities of 'Eastenders' have included the Chinese and the Somalis.

In 1978 the latest wave of immigrants to the East End, the Bangladeshi community, faced something depressingly similar to the challenge of the 1930s. Spitalfields has been described as Britain's "largest Bangladeshi village". Nearly a third of the population of Tower Hamlets are Bengalis. The early settlers were mainly seamen who decided to live in England, they 'jumped ship' and lived in Stepney. Many more people arrived mainly from the Sylhet district in Bangladesh (then east Pakistan) in the late 1950s and the 1960s. They were largely single men who were 'sponsored' by the seamen who were their family members. They settled in Spitalfields and outside London in Bradford, Birmingham, Luton, Leicester and other inner city areas.

The Bangladeshis of the East End have had to face intense racism. They are hard-working people –many work in the factories dotted around Brick Lane. They are also devout Muslims. They believe in the values of family life and follow what is very much the extended family system. Yet the harsh implementation of Britain's immigration and nationality laws makes family reunion one of the main concerns in the community. The Bangladeshis have had to live in terrible conditions and many still do. They face institutionalised racism in housing, education, employment and even in the realm of religion. Extremist organisations like the National Front still sell their publications on Sundays calling for forcible repatriation.

However, it is to the credit of the local community that the National Front are no longer able to maintain a high profile. People have not forgotten the events of 1978. They started with the murder of a young Bengali factory worker, Altab Ali, who was stabbed by white racists in Adler Street, E1. His murder sparked off massive demonstrations by the Bangladeshi community and anti-racist organisations who felt that "enough was enough". The police were not protecting the Bangladeshi community; the Nazi bully boys were able to freely embark upon a rampage of Brick Lane, to organise meetings and provoke violence. Bangladeshi families were living in fear. Their children were assaulted and spat upon, racist abuse was hurled at Asian people and burning rags pushed through letter boxes.

On July 16th 1978, a massive protest march was organised and the Asian community joined by many other anti-racists occupied the top of Brick Lane and prevented the National Front from selling their papers for the first time. A sit-down protest was also organised outside Bethnal Green Police Station to protest police racism. It resulted in a victory in the fact that racism was challenged; the Bangladeshis shook off apathy and a new era dawned where a hidden minority became a visible minority. They were not going to be trampled

Brick Lane drawn by Bulbul Bibi Ali of Mulberry School, London E1

over. They stood up for their rights and won.

Ten years on and the Bangladeshi community are still suffering. Much has been said about the 'ghetto' policy of the former Greater London Council (GLC) under which Bengalis were allocated council flats in the same area and white families were given the cream of the available housing in Bethnal Green. Although the ideal situation is multi-racial housing, the reality is that the races are separated.

The housing situation is now worse. There are over 1,000 Bengali families living in bed and breakfast accommodation. The ruling Liberals in Tower Hamlets Council have caused an uproar by attempting to evict nearly 100 families living in bed and breakfast accommodation, stating that they have made themselves "intentionally homeless" having left their homes in Sylhet, Bangladesh. This can only be described as a blatant case of racism.

Abdus Shukur, Chair of the Federation of Bangladeshi Youth Organisations (FBYO) has stated that the "situation is appalling. The hard-hearted act of Tower Hamlets Council is racist in the sense that you don't deprive a human being of the basic right of shelter because they have left one country to live in Britain. For most of the Bengali people, their main home is in Britain. In any case the property they have left behind in Bangladesh is shared property because of the extended family system."

According to Abdus Shukur the concrete solution is for Tower Hamlets Council to build more homes and to put pressure on central government to give more funds for tackling the homeless situation in the borough. The Bangladeshi organisations have joined forces and have embarked upon a campaign to fight for the rights of these Bengali families. The Homeless Families Campaign based at the local Brady centre has steadily gathered momentum.

A recent All-Party Home Affairs (House of Commons) Report, "Bangladeshis in Britain", highlighted the fact that the Bengalis are a deprived community. Their children are under-achieving in schools, unemployment is high, the housing situation is far from adequate, the

The East London Mosque in Whitechapel Road

Bangladeshis face racism from all sides. The need is urgent, east London will explode if the government does not give support to the community.

The inner cities are crumbling. When Prince Charles visited the East End he was visibly moved by the plight of the Bangladeshi community. One glimmer of hope for the generation of tomorrow was provided by the Prince of Wales' visit when he launched the Inner London Education Authority (ILEA) Compact at Mulberry School for Girls in Stepney. This unique partnership between schools and business aims to guarantee jobs for young Bengali teenagers in the area. But there will need to be far more glimmers before there is light at the end of the tunnel.

Indian Indenture – Another Slavery

by Ron Sanders

May 5, 1988 will mark the 150th anniversary of the first arrival of Indians in the Westindies. Three hundred and ninety six of them were landed in Guyana on board the vessels "Whitby" and "Hesperus" which had set sail from India on January 5 and 29 respectively. For the next 79 years, until 1917 when Indian indentured labour was abolished, Indians suffered the same brutal and dehumanising processes which had characterised African slavery. Yet, in Guyana and Trinidad, after 150 years of living side by side, the descendants of African slaves and Indian indentured labourers exist in an uneasy relationship characterised by racial suspicion and a refusal to share power as equals.

This article will examine the current relationship between the two major races in Guyana and Trinidad and Tobago. But integral to understanding how that relationship was fostered by a white plantocracy, concerned about the possibility of a united revolt, and developed by politicians who found racial sentiment a natural convenience for maintaining political office, is a background to how Indian indenture to the Westindies began.

It was Sir John Gladstone, the father of two British parliamentarians, one of whom, William, was later to become Prime Minister, that introduced Indian indentured labour to the Westindies. He owned several sugar estates in Guyana and his sole purpose in importing Indians was to make the plantations 'independent of our negro population'. He was assured by the Calcutta firm of Gillanders, Arbuthnot & Co., which had already supplied Indians as labourers to Mauritius, that the Indians 'would cost less than half of slaves'.

African Slavery Abolished

Slavery was abolished in the English-speaking Caribbean in 1834 by the passage of an Act in the British Parliament the year before. The Act of Abolition created what has been described as 'a unique and unprecedented status for former slaves – it made them half-slave and half-free'. For the Act provided for a seven-year period of apprenticeship during which the former slave would work a compulsory 40½ hour week for his old master *unpaid*. In the words of Viscount Howick, Parliamentary Under Secretary for the Colonies, the Act 'gave with one hand and took back with the other'.

The legislatures of all the colonies were controlled by the sugar plantation owners who had already received some £20 million as compensation for their slaves; yet, they decided to enforce the apprenticeship provision of the Act. The only exceptions were Antigua, The Bahamas and Bermuda.

Apprenticeship Opposed: Brutally Enforced

In the first few days following the abolition of slavery, the response of the former slaves to the enforced period of apprenticeship was predictably unhappy. In St. Kitts, Montserrat, Trinidad and the Essequibo region of Guyana, the 'apprentices' refused to accept the new system and they demonstrated in the streets. In St. Kitts and Trinidad, the militia had to be called out and the protests were brutally put down.

Historian Hugh Tinker records that 'according to some writers, the apprenticeship system was distinctly worse than the previous slavery: the employers knew that the time when they could exploit their former slaves without reply was strictly limited, so they vowed to extract the last drop of sweat from them'. The planters took advantage of their control of local legislatures, to revive oppressive laws which had become obsolete and to devise new ones to govern, *inter alia,* the confining of apprentices to one area, the setting of low wages and compulsory apprenticeship for children. Under these laws, workers sentenced to penal labour were sent out in chain-gangs to work for their own employer.

The disquiet of the former slaves over the apprenticeship system continued; their old masters matched the increasing level of dissent with a rising scale of brutality. During the short space of two years in Jamaica, 60,000 apprentices received an aggregate of 250,000 lashes and 50,000 other punishments. And Jamaica was by no means the worst example; the apprenticeship code in British Guiana appeared 'to have been the harshest in the Caribbean, and their experience of it hardly disposed the ex-slaves to a life of wage labour on the plantations'.

In the face of bitter apprenticeship strikes and unrest, the scheme of forced labour had to be terminated in 1838, three years earlier than scheduled. With its end came a crisis of labour for the owners, particularly in Guyana and Trinidad where the land available to the former slaves for purchase or squatting was plentiful. The freed slaves had no intention of staying on the estates unless they received better compensation and when the planters refused to meet their demands they left in droves.

The planters scrambled around in every direction looking for new labour. Immigration agents were sent to other parts of the Westindies to entice freed slaves but they attracted only 2,900, mainly from Barbados. They also recruited some from Antigua where there was no apprenticeship system and all the slaves had been set free. But these freed workers quickly left the plantations to join the villages being rapidly established by the former Guyana slaves. In the meantime, the other Westindian colonies took steps to keep their workers at home; in Antigua, for instance, the planters passed an Act to restrict emigration to British Guiana and Trinidad in an effort to hold on to their 'artificers and handicraftsmen'.

Portuguese were imported in large numbers from Madeira, 599 of them landing in Guyana in 1835. But they preferred the retail trade to plantation labour and while, by 1856, they controlled nearly all the retailing businesses in the country, the plantations still needed new labour or the owners would have to meet the wage demands of their former slaves.

Indian Indenture Begins

Thus it was that Indians were brought to the Westindies by planters who wanted to make the sugar estates 'independent of our negro population'. The Guyana plantations got 89 per cent of the Indians brought to the Westindies; approximately 238,216 landed between 1838 and 1917. Trinidad got 143,900 (33 per cent) and Jamaica 36,400 (8.4 per cent). The Leeward and Windward Islands had less land space and, therefore, their former slaves had little option but to continue working for their former masters for whatever they were paid. Hence, fewer Indians were imported to those islands: 5,900 (1.4 per cent) went to Grenada, 4,400 (1.0 per cent) to St. Lucia, 2,500 (0.6 per cent) to St. Vincent and 300 (0.1 per cent) to St. Kitts. Barbados, Dominica and Antigua had more than enough workers for their land size and no Indians were imported into those territories.

There was a lull in the importation of Indian labour to the Westindies after the first shipment in 1938. John Scoble, the Secretary of the British Anti-Slavery Society was in Guyana at the time and he was appalled by the atrocious conditions set for the Indian labourers. He publicised these conditions in England and Indian emigration to the Westindies was stopped. But not for long.

In 1846 a Sugar Duties Act was passed in Britain equalising import duties on all sugars after 1851 (later postponed to 1854). The heavy competition brought about by the expansion in sugar supplies to Britain led to falling prices for Guyana's sugar. This crisis for the planters was made worse by the demands of the former slaves for higher wages. Thus, as Guyanese economist Clive Thomas points out, 'the planters developed, with British government support, a policy of indentured immigration in a major effort to maintain their supply of servile labour'. From 1851 to 1871, there was a large influx of Indian labourers to Guyana and Trinidad.

The rigours of African slaves crossing the notorious 'Middle Passage', overcrowded, ill-fed and open to disease, have been well documented and are well known. Guyanese historian, the late Walter Rodney, has recorded that the number of deaths averaged in the vicinity of 15 to 20 per cent.

Less well known are the hardships suffered by the Indians in their journey from Calcutta to the Westindies. The slaves making the passage from West Africa to the Caribbean were compelled to endure from four to six weeks at sea; the Indians shipped to the Caribbean had to face three or four months at sea. Many died; victims of cholera, typhoid, dysentery and a dozen other diseases which were a common feature of shipboard existence.

The mortality rates of the Calcutta-Caribbean ships tell their own story. In 1865, the Golden South had a mortality rate of 29 per cent; in 1869, the Shand's death rate was 21 per cent and these were lower than the rate of death in the 1850s. In this, as on the plantations, Indian indentured labourers shared a brutal experience with African slaves.

The Indian indentured labourer was owned only for five years with the promise of a free return passage to India at the end of this time, therefore the estate owners were determined to extract every ounce of labour. The planters, ignoring any need to acclimatise them, ruthlessly worked the Indians from the moment of their arrival. They died in large numbers.

According to one chronicle, large numbers of Indians attempted to escape from the plantations, some even striking out for India through the bush, and their bones were now commonly seen whitening under the tropical sun, while their compatriots lay sick and dying in the public roads. Between 1841 and 1851 over 42,300 entered British Guiana but the population increase recorded was only 29,500.

Indenture Indistinguishable From Slavery

The contracts for Indian labourers under the indenture system were vastly inferior to the terms given to 'free' labour in Guyana. The indenture conditions included nine to ten hours of work per day compared with the prevailing 7½ hours; pay was fixed at 16 cents per day, plus food allowance, compared with 32 cents per day for other labourers.

Barbadian novelist George Lamming states: 'There can be no question that Indian workers were now condemned to a history of humiliation almost indistinguishable from the memories of African slavery'. In the Westindies beating and flogging of indentured Indians was a routine element in plantation discipline right into the twentieth century. In Guyana, up until the 1870s, indentured Indians who reported sick were placed in stocks.

It is an interesting footnote to the history of the barbarities suffered by indentured Indians that when their ill treatment on John Gladstone's plantation in Guyana was disclosed he 'sold his interests and severed all connections with the colony'.

There were other cruelties meted out to the indentured Indian, including imprisonment for petty crimes for which he bore no guilt but could make no appeal. An unexplained absence from work was classified as 'desertion under the labour laws and constituted a criminal offence punishable by a fine or imprisonment. Thus, in 1901, out of an indentured population of 14,609 more than 23 per cent (3,423) were prosecuted and 1,922 were convicted. In exceptional cases when court officials felt obliged to disassociate themselves from the established practice of prosecuting the Indians, they incurred the wrath of the planters "for revealing what the reality was like".

The measure of the brutal treatment of the indentured Indians is the fact that several riots and strikes occurred on the estates between 1869 and 1917, when indenture was abolished. The first riot occurred in 1869 followed by two more in 1873. In 1886 there were 31 strikes and disturbances, 15 in 1887 and 42 in 1888. From 1884 to 1905, there were 10 or more disturbances each year. The Indians were obviously not a people content with their lot.

They were quartered in squalid accommodation which remained unchanged throughout the 79 years of indenture. No provision was made even for a modicum of sanitation and every tenement 'logie' was shockingly overcrowded. Tinker records that a Royal Commission which visited Guyana in 1871 reported finding 'twenty or thirty' Indians packed into one barrack room. He said the same commission dismissed such plantation hospitals as existed as 'filthy holes'. In 1882, only 18 per cent were classified 'reasonably healthy'.

In the 18th Century, the planters in Guyana received strong backing from the British government in their determination to maintain slave labour as a means of reaping high profits for sugar. The arguments then are not dissimilar to the arguments heard now in support of the British government's refusal to apply sanctions against South Africa which uses apartheid, to provide a permanent subject labour force kept rigidly separate from the ruling class.

Today, the British government justifies its actions by saying that British jobs would be lost and British industry hurt by the imposition of economic sanctions against South Africa; a century and half ago, the British government excused its decision not to end African slavery in the Westindies by pointing to 120 refineries in Britain providing thousands of jobs and a lucrative re-export trade in sugar to the European continent. There was no need to mention that Parliament was dominated by families with Westindian sugar interests.

As the British government refused to end African slavery while it suited them, so they rejected terminating Indian indentured labour which the Secretary for the Colonies, Lord John Russel, opposed in 1840 describing it as 'a new system of slavery'.

African and Indian Civilisation Maligned

But if British government support for the inhumanity of African slavery and Indian indentured labour was inexcusable, the participation of the British intellectual community in the justification of these wicked systems was unforgiveable.

Dr Eric Williams drew attention to the fact that African civilisation had to be distorted and maligned by the European establishment to 'find an alibi for negro slavery' and in the same way 'they distorted and maligned Indian civilisation in the 19th Century to justify Indian indenture'.

Williams identifies the great names in British intellectual history such as Hume, Trollope and Froude with 'the distortion of African civilisation and the defamation of the African character' and, in particular, Lord Macaulay, the historian, and Lord Acton, the Professor of History at Cambridge College with 'the distortion of Indian civilisation and the defamation of the Indian character'.

He cites Lord Macualay's work of 1834, 'Minute on Indian Education', as saying:

> I have no knowledge of either Sanskrit or Arabic. But I have done what I could do to form a correct estimate of their value... It is, I believe, no exaggeration to say that all the historical information which has been collected from all the books written in the Sanskrit language is less valuable than what may be found in the most paltry abridgements used at preparatory schools in England.

Fifty-four years after Lord Macaulay's arrogant and chauvinistic dismissal of Sanskrit's contribution to knowledge, James Anthony Froude, Regius Professor at Oxford University, displayed the same narrow chauvinism and racial arrogance when he wrote of Westindians of African origin:

> We have a population to deal with, the enormous majority of whom are of an inferior race. Inferior, I am obliged to call them because as yet, and as a body, they have shown no capacity to rise above the condition of their ancestors except under European laws, European education and European authority... their notions of right and wrong are scarcely even elementary; their education, such as it may be, is but skin deep and the old African susperstitions lie undisturbed at the bottom of their souls.

The experience of African slavery and Indian indentured labour in the Westindies and its unjustifiable defence have, understandably, left a residue of bitterness in the minds of successive generation of Westindians. The Westindian struggle for political rights and economic justice, the movement to be rid of British colonialism and to establish independent states were natural outgrowths from the anger aroused by these two brutal systems.

The Legacy in Guyana and Trinidad

The challenge to accept their shared background and common citizenship applies today in a particularly poignant way to the descendants of African slaves and Indian indentured labourers in Trinidad and Guyana whose populations are largely made up of the two groups. In both countries there has been an uneasy relationship between the races since the importation of Indians.

Writing of the Independence of Trinidad and Tobago in 1962. Eric Williams said, 'Two races have been freed, but a society has not been formed'. Similar sentiments could have been expressed about Guyana.

From the outset, the African regarded the Indian's arrival as a fatal blow to their power to bargain for higher wages on the sugar estates. Their feeling was that the Indian 'takes bread from the negro labourer and lowers the price of labour' and they blamed the Indians and not the planters for this perceived injury.

The plantation owners quickly recognised the strategic importance of this. Clive Thomas records that in Guyana the planters,

> 'manipulated the ethnic groups to their own advantage. This process was made easy by the tendency of the Africans, after the abolition of slavery, to move off the estates. Those who remained opted primarily for work in the factory and left more arduous, low wage fieldwork to the newly arrived immigrants.... this pattern created a functional basis in the division of labour among the two ethnic groups of sugar workers and later generated two distinct areas of settlement near to each estate: the so-called African and Indian villages'.

Before the establishment of 'free' Indian villages, the planters intensified the animosity between the two groups by cocooning the indentured Indians on the sugar estates and prohibiting them from journeying outside without a pass. Consequently there was little or no contact with the African community who had left the estates and established their own villages. Moreover, the Indians were allowed to maintain their religion and customs which were strengthened by the arrival of every new batch of indentured labourers and which were very strange to the African community who had been forced to adopt the religion and practices of their former masters. Both in physical and cultural terms, the Indian indentured labourers became an enclave society – separate and distinct from the Africans.

It is noteworthy that in the Windward Islands and Jamaica, where fewer Indians were imported, they have become completely absorbed into the creole societies, by inter marriage. In St. Lucia, many of them speak French Patois, the language of the rural workers, even though the French occupied St. Lucia long before the arrival of labourers from India. The reasons appear obvious: the Indians were not separated from the African community and when their religious instructors died, there were none to replace them. The Indians became Christians adopting the dress and culture of the St. Lucian of African descent.

But in Guyana and Trinidad, where the numbers were greater, neither the planters not the colonial governments wanted an alliance between the Africans and Indians, for such a partnership could end not only their stranglehold on cheap labour for the estates, but their control of the country. Indeed, in one brief period in Guyana between 1950 and 1953, a nationalist political party, the People's Progressive Party (PPP), led by an Indian, Cheddi Jagan, with an African, Forbes Burnham, as its Chair, 'united rural Indians and working-class Creoles (Africans) in opposition to British colonialism and the local elite'. Commenting on the period, the late Guyanese newspaper editor, Carl Blackman, recalled his months of 'elation, euphoria and nationalistic pride as that juggernaut headed by the nation's favourite sons, Cheddi Jagan and Forbes Burnham threatened the power of King Sugar, sent the Water Street shipping and shopping barons cowering in their panelled boardrooms and temporarily toppled the old order under a mountain of votes'.

The elation did not last long. For far from 'cowering' the planters and the British government, decided action had to be taken against the PPP which, in the words of Professor Gordon Lewis, 'was interested primarily in the total transfer of power'. Thus, the Guyana government's legislative programme was provocative and included removal of legislation which banned radical literature and measures aimed at weakening the sugar plantation owners. The British Parliament was told that 'Britain had taken the first steps to forestall a communist threat to sieze power in the colony' and British troops 'were hurried across the Atlantic in warships and aircraft to put down a communist coup'. Guyana's Constitution was suspended on October 9, 1953 and its first national Government brought to an end after 133 days.

Writing on the suspension of the constitution and the overthrow of the government, elected democratically in the first-ever election to be held under a system of universal adult suffrage, Lewis concluded that 'much of 1953 and after was caused by the imperialist need to smash the remarkable unity of the Guyanese African-Indian majority'.

In the event, there was not to be another such massive demonstration of unity by Africans and Indians in Guyana for, in the wake of the government's overthrow, the PPP effectively divided along racial lines in 1955 – the majority of Africans backed Forbes Burnham and the overwhelming number of Indians stood behind Cheddi Jagan. The two groups returned to their old relationship which had never changed in Trinidad and which Lewis has summed up as:

> '....the Africans, in the main, were an urban mass hating the land and its slave memory and identifying itself with its middle class brethren who had become the white collar proconsuls of the colonial structure, while the Indians were a rural mass trapped in the sugar estate prison. But the differences came to express themselves in racial terms'.

These differences have had a profound effect in both Guyana and Trinidad. To a great degree, despite the 'creolisation' today of an increasing number of younger Indians, the differences still plague the politics, and therefore the economic and social development, of both countries.

A report compiled in 1964 indicated that, in relation to co-operation between Guyanese of Indian and African extraction, while government officials of African descent,

> 'stressed that there was a growing racial co-operation in politics, they did not notice a complementary cultural integration. Indeed, they did not welcome such a move and their arguments against racial integration betrayed an appalling ignorance of the customs and attitudes of fellow Guyanese'.

A similar study of the Trinidad and Tobago society in 1960 revealed that to the majority of Indians 'the idea of the East Indian group losing its ethnic identity and disappearing into the Westindian population is not acceptable'. The same study concluded that 'the East Indian might like his circumstances to be bettered, but he has no desire to be anything else and least of all a Westindian'.

Yet, when every Indian in Guyana and Trinidad and Tobago was offered Indian citizenship 'by descent' under India's Citizenship Act of 1955, very few accepted it. According to Trinidadian novelist, Sam Selvon, the number in Trinidad 'that showed interest in the venture came mostly from the country districts where the majority were still adhering, or trying to adhere, to the traditions and customs brought from India'.

Controversial Calypso

In 1979, controversy over a calypso in Trinidad and Tobago caused the relationship between Africans and Indians to be scrutinised once again. The results of that examination indicate that Indians are not fully accepted as Westindians by the African community. This may have as much to do with the way in which Indians have presented themselves to the rest of the Westindian society as with a continuing belief by the African section of the population that they are the authentic Westindians and Indians are immigrants who 'took bread from their mouths'. In any event, the calypso suggested that 'the Caribbean man' is of African descent and, therefore, by implication the Indian is not a Caribbean man:

> 'Dem is one race – De Caribbean Man
> From de same place – De Caribbean man
> That make the same trip – De Caribbean man
> On the same ship – De Caribbean man'.

When the Federation of the Westindies was being debated in the 1950s, leaders of the Indian community in Guyana and Trinidad were not in favour of the idea. They feared that in such a Federation they would become a permanent minority. In December 1954, when the Trinidad Legislature voted on a constitutional plan drafted in London, of the six people who voted against it, four were Indians. Two other Indians, including Ashford Sinanan, did not vote at all and Adjodha Singh, who was a Minister, left the chamber before the vote was taken.

Guyana had opted to stay out of the Federation and while many other groups also opposed Guyana's participation, the leaders of the Indian community were definitely hostile to the idea.

An observer of the debate on the question of Federation in Guyana's Legislative Assembly concluded that,

> 'the East Indian community in general is against Federation.... if British Guiana remains outside the Federation the Indian community, it is thought, can continue its gradual increase of power by reason of its numerical superiority and its mercantile interest.... But in any Federation of the Westindies the Africans would form a vast majority and the East Indians would suffer a consequent decline in power and influence'.

Some Indians in Guyana were strongly supportive of Guyana's participation in the Federation. Among them was J I 'Jimmy' Ramphal and Rahman Gajraj. In the debate in the Legislature, Ramphal even advanced the opinion that Guyana 'shall have lost paradise if we do not enter into Federation'.

In the event, Guyana stayed out of the Federation and its racial division, excited by politics, flared up in communal riots between 1962 and 1964 leaving many people dead and many others permanently maimed. The tactics of divide and rule, implemented by the planters when the Indians were first introduced to the country, had reached out across a century and exacted a terrible toll in blood.

The descendants of Indians and Africans in Guyana and Trinidad are yet to resolve the issue raised by Eric Williams of whether they are 'two races' or 'a society'. Some will argue, with justification, that while Williams the academic and historian, was capable of analysing the problems of racism, Williams the politican helped to perpetrate it in Trinidad by indulging in the politics of race to keep his People's National Movement (PNM) in power. Whether or not this is so, his challenge to form 'a society' from the liberation of two races remains valid.

Indeed the challenge has become urgent today and rests squarely at the door of the leaders of the two races in both countries. Those leaders include not only the politicians but academics, religious leaders, trades unionists and media operators. And it is not sufficient for the descendants of Indians merely to acknowledge their Westindian identity (though they must do so); they must also join meaningfully in the work of proclaiming it which, so far, only some, such as Guyana's Sonny Ramphal and Trinidad's Kamalludin Mohamed have been prepared to do.

In this connection, every Indian descendant would do well to recall the words of India's independence Prime Minister, Jawaharlal Nehru who said in the Indian Parliament in December 1957, if Indians 'adopted the nationality of the country (in which they settled) they cease to be Indian nationals'. He went on to make it clear that 'Indian settlers should associate themselves as closely as possible with the interests of the country they have adopted'. How much more valid is this exhortation for those who were born and grew up in Guyana and Trinidad, the children of Indians who were also born and grew up there.

But, by the same token, the Westindian descendants of Africans also have to accept and acknowledge that a common history of transplantation and exploitation, together with 150 shared years of contribution to the development of

Guyana and Trinidad, bind them inseparably to the descendants of Indians and there must, therefore, be room for both in national life.

In this context, the two groups have to learn to share power and positions not as adversaries but as equals; not out of political accommodation but out of shared citizenship. Many had great hope that the formation of the National Alliance for Reconstruction (NAR) under A N R Robinson and Basdeo Panday would have been the catalyst for such an understanding in Trinidad; one which would have spilled over into Guyana.

But the fracture of the NAR Government has not relieved either Robinson or Panday of their obligation to maintain the racial unity of Trinidad and Tobago which their brief association demonstrated was possible. Indeed, a greater obligation now devolves upon both of them to ensure that their personal differences are not made the fuel for igniting racist fires such as those that followed the separation of Jagan and Burnham in Guyana.

In this year which marks the 150th anniversary of the end of the 'apprenticeship' system for Africans and the start of 'indenture' for Indians, the leaderships of Guyana and Trinidad and Tobago, regardless of political party or ideology, should make a major effort to ensure that their people respond to the challenge to form 'a society'.

The alternative is continued racial division which will always impede the economic growth and social development of both Guyana and Trinidad and Tobago.

Features of Indo-Caribbean History

by David Dabydeen

1838 was a year of profound significance to Caribbean peoples. It was the year of the Emancipation of African slaves. For two centuries, Africans had been shipped to the region to work on the sugar plantations. Their labour underpinned Western economic development, creating vast wealth for European nations. According to seventeenth and eighteenth century opinion, black people were "the strength and sinews of this western world" and the slave trade "the Hinge on which all the Trade of this Globe moves on."

The late Eric Williams, in his seminal study *Capitalism and Slavery,* asserted that slave trade profits "provided one of the main streams of that accumulation of capital in England which financed the Industrial revolution", and though his thesis has been subject to varied degrees of interpretation since its publication, his work on the impact of slave revenue on the development of British cities (Liverpool, for instance, evolving from a mere fishing village in the seventeenth century to a major world seaport in the next century) remains beyond dispute.

Sir Shridath 'Sonny' Ramphal

One of the consequences of Emancipation was the importation of hundreds of thousands of Indian people to the region, indentured labourers whose descendants today form the majority ethnic group in Guyana, Trinidad and Surinam. The reasons for Indian emigration were varied. Lower caste Indians, sometimes existing in a state of virtual slavery in India (their labour, and sometimes that of their children pledged to creditors for a lifetime), were glad to flee their landlords and money-lenders for the prospect of a new beginning in new lands. Others were enticed by the fanciful tales of recruiters employed by the British, and deceived by false promises of plenty. Famine and civil war further swelled the numbers of emigrants. Some were simply kidnapped in time-honoured fashion and dumped on board departing ships. The British, short of labour in one part of the Empire, were only too happy to find supplies in another.

The Indians occupied the old slave quarters and worked in the sugar plantations, inheriting many of the conditions of servitude of the previously enslaved Africans. In Professor Hugh Tinker's phrase (quoting Lord John Russell, the British Secretary of State in 1840), indentureship represented "a new system of slavery". Many plantation laws reeked of slavery in their severity: for arson, an Indian could be sentenced to fifteen years imprisonment, and for burglary, eight years' hard labour in chains. Dr Brinsley Samaroo, writing of the self-destruction that resulted from such oppression, cites a group of nineteenth century Surinam immigrants who testified that "if any coolie fails to work for a single day of the week, he is sent to jail for two or four days, where he is forced to work while day and night kept under chains. We are tortured very much. For this reason, two or three people died by swallowing opium and drowning themselves."

Such conditions of human and economic squalor were not endured passively. Like the African slaves, Indians rebelled through strikes, riots, acts of arson and other forms of violence, laziness, theft and sabotage. Dr Kusha Haraksingh has written that "even on board ship, as during the voyage of the *Hesperides* in 1882, violence could break out. In the fields, violence was never far below the surface... The vulnerability of the drivers to a sudden assault in a deserted cane piece by an aggrieved worker wielding the tool of his trade – a cutlass – did force many of them to moderate their demands on the workers." Tyran Ramnaraine shows how, from 1869, the militancy of indentured labourers became a feature of Guyanese plantation life (Indians were recruited first to British Guiana in 1838, to work on the plantations of John Gladstone, father of the British Prime Minister). In July of that year Indian labourers at Plantation La Jalousie rioted over wages; in August, they struck at Mahaicony, and in December at Plantation Enterprise, beating up some African constables who had attempted to arrest one of their gang. The unpleasantness of immigrant life was described by John Jenkins, a representative from the Anti-Slavery Society, in evidence given to the 1870 Commission of Inquiry into the Treatment of Indian Immigrants:

> Take a large factory in Birmingham or Belfast, build a wall around it, shut in it work people from all intercourse, save at rare intervals, with the outside world, keep them in absolute heathen ignorance and get all the work you can out of them, treat them not unkindly, leave their social habits and relations to themselves, as matters not concerning you who make money from their labour, and you would have constituted a little community resembling, in no small degree, a sugar estate in British Guiana.

Women immigrants were not exempt from the world of violence. Basdeo Mangru's researches highlight the difficulty that recruiting agents faced in enticing women to emigrate. "There were few unattached women because of the Indian custom of child betrothal and marriage at puberty". The male emigrants were also reluctant to submit their wives and daughters to the perils of a sea voyage, planning instead to "brave themselves for the sake of gain, hoping to return to share it with their families". According to Mangru, the women who boarded emigrant ships tended to be mostly widows, prostitutes or those who had for whatever reason severed all ties with family. Recruiters took to kidnapping women in order to fulfil sexual quotas (in 1857, the law stipulated that

Basdeo Panday

there should be a ratio of 35 women to every 100 men shipped to the Caribbean). In the 1860s, an Indian newspaper, the *Pioneer of India,* denounced the forcible emigration of women by kidnapping: "here in India, as formerly in Africa, the slaves are seized by force and detained against their will, despite their tears and entreaties."

Violence was one consequence of the sex ratio imbalance on the Caribbean plantations. As Mangru explains, "the paucity of women created a grave social problem and seemed the principal cause for the alarming number of murders of unfaithful wives. It promoted unsettled habits, tended to lower the standard of morality, produced unhealthy competition for the available women and made seduction more likely." Immigrant riots were sparked off when white overseers formed connections with Indian women since this further depleted the choice available to Indian males. Caste prejudices prevented cohabitation with Afro-Caribbean people. Male Indian possessiveness of womenfolk was therefore surcharged in the plantation system. Women, more than ever, were guarded as precious commodities, and sexuality was a matter of trade. There is evidence however that some women were able to exploit their power deriving from their scarcity, and were able to control their menfolk by the threat of desertion and infidelity. In so doing they were able to exert a freedom, however minimal, and challenge traditional male domination and oppression. It was a challenge fraught with extreme danger: between 1884-1888 there were 33 recorded incidents of wife-murder. Today in the Caribbean the abuse of women is one of our major disgraces: the multiple wife-beatings in Naipaul's *Miguel Street* and *A House for Mr Biswas* reveal how ready the violent male hand is. The modern tradition of wife-beating is one rooted in a shameful ancestral past of sexual competition in the plantation.

Men and women however endured and survived plantation existence, and some triumphed over the experience of brutality. The descendants of the indentured Indians count among them politicians of international eminence, like Cheddi Jagan (who spearheaded the Caribbean movement to independence), Commonwealth Secretary General Sir Shridath Ramphal and Rupert Roopnaraine, a leader of the Working People's Alliance of Guyana.

In the arts, Indian writers like the Naipaul brothers and Samuel Selvon have made permanent contributions to world literature.

In the field of sport, cricketers like Rohan Kanhai and Sonny Ramadhin dazzled millions through the sheer genius of their stroke-play or bowling. Kanhai actually created a new batting stroke, the famous sweep that so excited commentators like C.L.R. James and which has been brilliantly analysed by scholars like Frank Birbalsingh and Clem Shiwcharan.

But the true Indian contribution to Caribbean history lies not in the singular deeds of a handful but in the mass action of the unnamed. I refer to the canecutters, ricefarmers and peasant workers whose names have been unrecorded but whose labour fed and still feeds the region. Their labour is the true spirit of our ancestors, and that spirit still resides in the Caribbean countryside, in the architecture of wooden houses propped on stilts, in the cleanliness of daubed bottomhouses, in the mud firesides stoked by coconut-shells and in the spires of Temples and Mosques erected by communities in their resolve to keep alive religious traditions that go back hundreds or thousands of years.

Cheddi Jagan

The spirit of ancestry resides too in the habits of people, in the self-sacrificial attitude of parents to children, in the lifestyle of diligence and frugality, and finally in the instinct for a principled survival.

Bibliography of Hansib Publications on Indo-Caribbean History and Culture

Frank Birbalsingh and Clem Shiwcharan, *Indo-Westindian Cricket*

Willi Chen, *The King of the Carnival and other stories*

David Dabydeen, *Coolie Odyssey* (poems)

David Dabydeen and Brinsley Samaroo, *India in the Caribbean* (essays and poems)

Basdeo Mangru, *Benevolent Neutrality: Indian Government Policy and Labour Migration to British Guiana 1854-1884*

Jeremy Poynting, *The Second Shipwreck: A Study of Indo-Caribbean Literature*

Angus Richmond, *The Open Prison* (novel)

John Thieme, *The Web of Tradition: Uses of Allusion in V.S. Naipaul's Fiction*

Ron Sanders, *Inseparable Humanity: An Anthology of Reflections by Shridath Ramphal*

World Minorities and Justice

A society's claims to be civilised and democratic must be judged not least by the attitude it takes towards its minorities. In this light it must be said that, in the main, the world remains an uncivilised and undemocratic place.

The struggle of the black majority in South Africa is at root a struggle for the return of the land seized by outside settler colonial forces and herein lies its essential identity with the struggles of indigenous peoples in the United States of America, Canada, Australia and New Zealand. These peoples have truly been victims of genocide. A recent study shows that about 70 per cent of North America's 16th century Native American population was wiped out by smallpox and other diseases introduced to the continent by European settlers. Between 1492 and 1600 their population is estimated to have been reduced from 14 million to around four million.

This genocide is not simply a matter of history – it continues today. In 1988 white Australians have celebrated 200 years of 'nationhood'. 200 years of criminal invasion and usurpation would be more appropriate – the real Australians have a history of nationhood going back at least 20,000 years. Whilst white Australians have one of the highest standards of living in the world the Aboriginal standard is one of the lowest. Trachoma – an inflammation leading to partial or total blindness is endemic. In Western Australia some 75 per cent of Aborigines under the age of 21 display symptoms of the disease. The Aboriginal population in the Kimberely region have the highest incidence of leprosy in the world with an attack rate of 107 per 100,000. In Victoria state an Aborigine is 45 times more likely to go to prison than a white and the deaths of Aborigines in police custody are now arousing global concern.

The question of national minorities lies at the root of many of the conflicts in the world. Few, if any, states have a blameless record. Yet a basis for justice is already enshrined in international law. On December 10 1948 the General Assembly of the United Nations adopted the Universal Declaration of Human Rights. It states:

"Article 1

"All human beings are born free and equal in dignity and rights. They are endowed with reason and conscience and should act towards one another in a spirit of brotherhood.

"Article 2

"Everyone is entitled to all the rights and freedom set forth in this Declaration, without distinction of any kind, such as race, colour, sex, language, religion, political or other opinion, national or social origin, property, birth or other status."

Forty years on its implementation is long overdue.

THE RELIABLE SHIPPERS

- SHIPMENTS TO ANY DESTINATION GUYANA, BARBADOS, ST. LUCIA:
- FREE QUOTATIONS, FREE COLLECTION, FREE STORAGE
- TRUNKS, BARRELS AND T-CHESTS SUPPLIED & SHIPPED
- 20ft & 40ft CONTAINERS LOADED AT YOUR DOOR WITH CARS AND FURNITURE
- DOOR TO DOOR SERVICE
- AIRLINE BOOKINGS TAKEN

VISIT OUR SHOWROOM OPEN MON-SAT

AGENTS:
HUDDERSFIELD
MR PROUTE
0484 549978
READING
MR EVANS
0734-867451

10 KINGSLAND HIGH STREET
DALSTON, LONDON E8 2JP
PHONE 01-241 5111, ASK FOR EXT 4

ARE YOU MOVING ABROAD OR SHIPPING ONE TEACHEST, BARREL, MOTOR VEHICLE ETC?

WE TAKE THE GREATEST CARE OF EVERYTHING

- WE SUPPLY STEEL/PLASTIC BARRELS, TEACHESTS, CARTONS, PACKING CASES
- DELIVERY AND COLLECTION NATIONWIDE
- FREE SECURITY STRAPPING/SEALING/ LABELLING AND STORAGE

OFFICES IN GUYANA AND JAMAICA
RING NOW FOR A FREE QUOTATION AND BROCHURE

01-681 5631 (6 LINES)

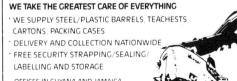

Health and Nutrition

by Devinia Sookia

Cervical Cancer

Janet Adegoke will go down in history as the first black woman mayor in London. She rose to the most prestigious position in the London Borough of Hammersmith and Fulham only two years after her election. Sadly, Janet Adegoke died from cervical cancer on October 1, 1987 at the age of 45. This tragic death reminds us once again of how the disease is no respecter of distinction or achievement. It places all women at risk.

Cervical cancer can be treated if it is discovered early enough and no woman should contract cervical cancer today if she has regular smear tests. The death rate among women under 35 has doubled over the last 20 years. According to the Women's National Cancer Control Campaign, about 550 cases of the disease are registered in this age group in a year, twice as many as in the mid '60s. More than 2,000 women die every year from cervical cancer, and although the majority are over 45, there has been a marked decrease in the past two decades in the death rate of middle-aged and elderly women.

Cervical cancer is one of the easiest diseases to cure and, if a woman has regular smear tests, it is very likely that if she has acquired the disease it will be diagnosed at an early stage and treated satisfactorily.

At an early stage the abnormal cells are easily treated but the progression from abnormality to cancerous is very fast in some women, particularly younger women. So a screen test at least once every three years is very important.

Most experts think that the major cause of cervical cancer in younger women is the sexually transmitted human "papilloma virus" (HPV). Cervical cancer contracted in this way seems to progress faster than those suffered by older mature women. Women with more than one sexual partner are most at risk of coming into contact with HPV – the virus which causes genital warts. However, these warts are small and hardly noticeable. Therefore a woman might not even know that she is infected.

Janet Adegoke

Scientists are trying to find a vaccine against HPV, but the only prevention against cervical cancer for the time being is regular screening. Health authorities are under pressure to call all sexually active women for screening at least every three years. The smear test is very simple. The doctor inserts a speculum to open the walls of the vagina, then rotates a wooden spatulum to collect cells from the surface of the cervix. The sample is then sent to a laboratory to see whether it is negative, meaning everything is normal, or positive, meaning that some abnormal cells are there. There are three types of positive smears, technically known as CIN (certival intra-epithelial neoplasia), 1, 2 and 3 which mean mild, moderate or severe pre-cancerous cells.

CIN 1 is slight and usually the cells revert to normal within six months. Repeat smear tests should be carried out every three months. If after the smear, the cells are still the same, a gynaecologist should be seen.

CIN 2 is more likely to progress to cancer. If after repeat smear tests every two months, the cells are still abnormal, the abnormal cells should be located and destroyed. The cells are removed by one of two methods: laser treatment which removes the area of abnormal surface tissue on the cervix by vapourising it with an intense beam of light or by cryocautery which destroys the abnormal cells by freezing. Both are done under local anaesthetic.

CIN 3 is the most severe form of pre-cancer which can be lethal if it is not taken care of. If the abnormal cells have spread from the surface of the cervix into the cervical canal it is usual to remove part of the cervix in a cone biopsy operation. The stage after CIN 3 is cancer which is treated either by a six-week course of radiotherapy or by an extended hysterectomy, involving the removal of the top half of the vagina and the womb.

The means to diagnose and treat cervical cancer do exist. In tribute to Jane Adegoke, and all the victims of this disease, we need to fight to make sure that they are available. The *Janet Adegoke Memorial Fund* as been formed so that donations can be made towards a new microscope at Charing Cross Hospital to support local screening services for women in Hammersmith and Fulham.

Donations should be sent to:
Women's National Cancer Control Campaign,
1 South Audley Street,
London W1Y 5DQ.
Tel: 01-499-7532

Premenstrual Syndrome

Premenstrual syndrome (PMS) is now accepted by experts as a medical condition, though it cannot be classified as a disease.

PMS is a state of discomfort, both emotional and physical, which happens every month just before a woman menstruates. The symptoms are depression, anxiety, tension, tiredness and irritability. Many women also feel bloated and their breasts become tender. These feelings may start as long as 14 days before the next period. The severity of the symptoms vary and they can be very severe in some cases. However, as soon as the period starts, the woman feels relief.

It is impossible to say how many women suffer from PMS but a large number notice breast swelling, mood changes and a feeling of irritability in the few days leading to a period. One in 10 women suffers so badly from PMS that she has to seek medical help. Symptoms are more severe in women aged between 30 to 40.

Some women find it extremely difficult to go on with their daily work as a result of PMS. But research has proved that a woman's work performance never gets worse when she is in that state as she puts more effort and concentration than she normally would. However, PMS seems to affect women in their domestic life, sometimes leading to divorce. PMS women may also be involved in crimes, accidents and suicides.

In France a woman who commits a crime while she is suffering from PMS can use this in her defence. In Britain there has been one case where PMS was used as a mitigating factor for a woman accused of murder.

Though the cause of PMS is not yet known, a diet with less sugar, more fibre and an intake of vitamin B6 helps in lessening the feelings of tiredness, irritability and tension. Oil of primrose also relieves PMS.

Is a Vasectomy Final?

Vasectomy is the most effective form of birth control and about 75,000 men have vasectomies performed every year according to medical research. But more and more men are regretting their action and are seeking to have the operation reversed.

Many men decide to have a vasectomy reversed because when they divorce and get married again they want to start a new family. Others want it because one of their children may die or they just feel like having children again. The success of fathering children again after a vasectomy reversal is not certain. Between 70 and 80 per cent of men operated on regain sperm production, and of those 40 per cent make their partners pregnant within two years, according to surgeons at the King's College Hospital in south London.

A vasectomy reversal, also known as a vasoplasty, can be performed on the National Health Service or privately. Surgeons use a fine needle and thread to reconnect a tube of one hundredth of an inch in diameter. This acts as a channel for the sperm that a man produces.

A vasectomy cannot generally be reversed 10 years after the operation. Many surgeons do not want to perform a vasectomy in cases where a couple has only one child or are very young. They also refuse to carry one out unless they have a written consent from the man's wife. Most operations are discussed with both husband and wife, as it is often the wife who encourages her husband. This ends the anxiety over conception and the wife is relieved from taking the pill or using any other method of contraception.

Some men are so eager to have children again after a vasectomy that they are prepared to go through more than one vasoplasty. There are cases where even three reversal operations have failed.

The Cures of Natural Medicine

Much of modern medical science dismisses Natural Medicine as unfounded and states that some natural remedies are more harmful than helpful. However, many of us have heard from our grandmothers of cures such as peach tree leaves which keep a headache away, mint tea which is good for indigestion and many others.

Our ancestors, be they of African or Asian descent, grew up in an era when barks, roots and herbs were said to have amazing healing powers. They were also familiar with some household products which when rubbed on the body were supposed to heal sores, cuts, burns and rashes and even cure the common cold. Vinegar can heal rashes, insect bites and sores. Rolling peach tree leaves in a wet light cloth and wrapping it round the head can cure headaches. Boiled peach tree leaves can also be used to sponge down the body and lower fever. Boiling the bark of a red oak tree and using it to gargle can cure a sore throat. Rubbing down the fat from a sheep on the body can be an overnight cure for a common cold. Plain flour is a good remedy for burns and baking powder mixed with water can be used to clear up rashes. A child's nose bleeds can be stopped by placing keys on his back.

In Jamaica, cuts and bruises are healed with banana roots. Lemon peels can be placed on the head to stop headaches. Aloe vera juice has been known to normalise body functions, help circulation, ease ulcers, kidney and bladder disorders, high blood pressure and asthma. Aloe vera also helps headaches and toothaches, stimulates hair growth and relieves allergies. Aloe Vera loses its healing ability as it becomes oxidised by the atmosphere. In the 1970s, a Texas pharmacist, Bill Coats developed a stabilisation process by which portions of the plant could be used allowing only the least possible amount of oxidation to take place and producing fresh Aloe vera juice. Aloe vera juice is reported to have done

Convenience foods are becoming increasingly popular – but are they a mixed blessing?

wonders for diabetics. It can help diabetics to control the disease without the use of insulin after six months of daily intake of 4 oz. doses per day according to "Forever Living Products", distributors of Aloe vera juice in the United States.

A few years ago many people would not have considered using herbs and roots. But nowadays more and more people are turning to natural remedies. Even members of the Royal Family, such as Prince Charles, trust the healing powers of medicinal plants. Drugs prescribed by doctors have so many harmful side effects that some people prefer to have roots and herbs instead. They need relief without the fear of harmful side effects. There are many cases where car accidents happened because the drivers fell asleep whilst driving, as they were unaware that the non-prescribed drugs they had taken for either hay fever or a common cold could cause drowsiness.

Try Not Eating Your Heart Out

The human heart is a very important organ. It works day and night. When we are asleep, it pumps nearly five to six litres of blood per minute and when we are active the volume nearly doubles. Heart disease is however very common among both men and women nowadays. In 1987, 104,467 men died of heart disease compared with 82,131 women throughout the United Kingdom according to Anne Dillon, Director of the Coronary Prevention Group.

One of the major causes of heart attacks is "atherosclerosis", which is characterised by thickening of the walls of the blood vessels. When the coronary arteries, which supply blood to the heart muscle, are affected, they become narrow due to the deposit of plaques containing a fat-like substance known as cholesterol. Sometimes this plaque becomes so thick that the inner lining of the blood vessels bursts leading to clot formation or thrombosis which blocks the blood supply to the heart completely. The heart muscle then suffers from a lack of oxygen. If the damage is severe, death may occur immediately. "Atherosclerosis" of the cerebral arteries causes paralysis or a stroke, and that of renal arteries leads to high blood pressure. The thickening of the arteries starts at a young age but may not become apparent until middle age.

A coronary "occlusion" occurs when one or more of the coronary arteries become blocked, stopping blood flow to the heart. It is characterised by a squeezing pain in the centre of the chest behind the breastbone. This pain may spread to the shoulder, arm or neck. The patient has sweating, nausea and vomitting. If unattended death may occur.

Excess weight puts an extra burden on the heart. Therefore, controlling your total calorie intake is necessary to avoid the formation of cholesterol or fat deposits and diet plays a major role in the development of "atherosclerosis". Other factors responsible are high blood pressure, cigarette smoking, diabetes, lack of exercise, worries, pressure, heredity and age.

A healthy diet with less fat, less sugar, less salt and more fibre, is very important for a healthy heart. The amount and type of dietary fat can give rise to "atherosclerosis". Saturated fats such as butter, ghee (Indian clarified butter) and coconut oil and soya oil are rich in poly-unsaturated fatty acids and lower blood cholesterol. Fish and shellfish contain unsaturated fats. Poly-unsaturated fatty acids prevents thrombosis formation whereas saturated fats promote coagulation. People with high levels of cholesterol in their blood have a greater risk of suffering a heart attack. Asian people tend to consume a lot of ghee as most of their food is prepared in it, which partially accounts for the high percentage of heart conditions among the community.

Extra calories over a period of time increases weight, and being overweight puts extra work on the heart and lungs. A heart surrounded by fatty tissue has to work harder to pump blood to the body.

Dietary fat is of two types: visible and invisible. Invisible fat exists in natural foods such as pulses and milk. Fresh vegetables and fruits have very little fat. Visible fat is the fat added to food during cooking. For a person the average intake of visible fat is 20-30 grams a day. Animal foods such as meat, eggs and by-products are high in cholesterol and should be restricted to the minimum. Consumption of whole milk is to be discouraged. The use of whole cereals and pulses is recommended in the place of refined products. The dietary fibre in cereals, pulses and vegetables reduces fat intake. The pectins that exist in fruits reduce blood cholesterol. There is no doubt that a vegetarian diet with skim milk is beneficial to those who are susceptible to atherosclerosis.

The Natural Goodness Of Health Food

Health food is being taken more and more seriously by those of us who want to live a cleaner and healthier life. "Health food" is a term which is used for different organically grown fruits and vegetables. It also covers herbal remedies and beauty treatments.

More than a million and a half people in Britain are now vegetarians, some of them "vegans", who avoid not only meat but also animal products like milk, cheese, butter and eggs. A recent Gallup poll shows that one in three Britons has reduced his or her consumption of red meat. Public concern about excessive sugar, salt in food and the use of

A healthy packed lunch

chemical additives to preserve fruits, vegetables, meat and drinks has increased. The health food shop is no longer a back street oddity frequented only by eccentrics. In London and the south east alone there are more than 1,000 health shops and supermarkets with health food departments. Professor John Dickerson, a University of Surrey nutritionist, says: "Health food is one of the fastest growing businesses in Britain, and this reflects the public's intense interest in preserving their health". The pharmaceutical and supermarket chains are promoting health foods. Even the doughnuts you buy in those supermarkets are wholemeal and the jam filling is free of refined sugar.

Many supermarket chains sell organic fruits and vegetables such as red cabbage, apples and others which are grown without chemical fertilisers. Health food stores offer a range of low-salt, low-sugar foods and make fibre-eating easy with dried apricots and figs, exotic beans and whole-grain breads. Health foods replace saturated-fat red meat and dairy products with nutrient-rich beans. There is even cow's milk in which poly-unsaturated sunflower oil is substituted for dairy fat, reducing saturated-fat content from 14 grams per pint to a mere 0.3.

Many health-food offerings are directly in line with the key recommendations of NACNE (National Advisory Committee on Nutrition Education). Not only do they have additive free yoghurt and wheatgerm which is good for the nerves, they even have natural body and hair care treatments made with the finest quality of oils such as jojoba, almond, sunflower seed, wheatgerm, carrot, avocado and peach kernels.

While doctors think highly of the food and beauty products available at health-food stores, they do not trust health-food "cures". Many of them are classified under "old wives' tales". They might be harmless but they can lure the sick away from proper medical treatment. A herbal tablet found in most of the health food shops is promoted for complaints from constipation to appendicitis.

According to the Ministry of Agriculture, Fisheries and Food, which regularly analyses food samples, goods grown with animal manure are not different from those fertilised with chemicals. Dr John Brown, a nutritionist with the Health Education Council, says that nobody knows the health risks of very small traces of pesticides found on fruits and vegetables. When a California laboratory analysed 28 samples of "organic" vegetables and fruits from health-food stores in the United States and 14 similar non-organic ones from supermarkets, only two of all of them were free of pesticide residues and one of them was from a non-organic supermarket. In Britain guidelines for growing food organically are produced by the Soil Association, but grower compliance is voluntary.

Carib.

Gravylles
272 BRIXTON ROAD, LONDON SW9 6AQ

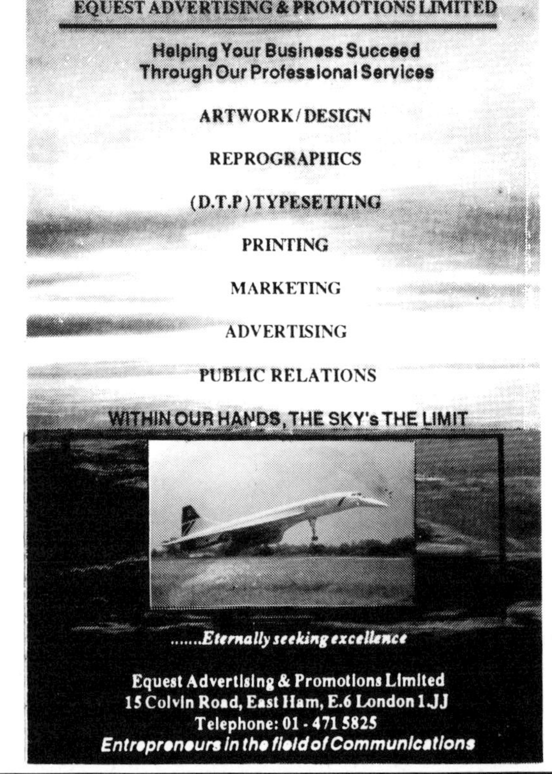
EQUEST ADVERTISING & PROMOTIONS LIMITED
Helping Your Business Succeed
Through Our Professional Services
ARTWORK/DESIGN
REPROGRAPHICS
(D.T.P) TYPESETTING
PRINTING
MARKETING
ADVERTISING
PUBLIC RELATIONS
WITHIN OUR HANDS, THE SKY's THE LIMIT
.......Eternally seeking excellence
Equest Advertising & Promotions Limited
15 Colvin Road, East Ham, E.6 London 1JJ
Telephone: 01 - 471 5825
Entrepreneurs in the field of Communications

Visible minorities get 2nd class treatment in the NHS

by Ashok Varma

Overseas doctors in Britain are becoming increasingly concerned that the racial discrimination, which has resulted in non-white doctors doing the most unattractive and dead-end jobs in the hospitals, is now spilling over into patient care.

Though it is difficult to prove that an inferior standard of care is being provided, this opinion is widely shared by overseas doctors who have worked in the NHS.

The Overseas Doctors' Association (ODA), which was originally formed to look after interests of overseas doctors, is now taking up this matter as no other organisation seems interested. Moreover, the ODA is in a unique situation of looking at the problem from ethnic minority patients' point of view as well as that of a doctor.

At a recent ODA seminar at Birmingham on Primary Health Care in the Inner Cities and Deprived Areas, the association expressed the view that health care provision to the urban ethnic minority population is crippled by a lack of cultural understanding.

Wrong diagnosis

Mental health delivery is particularly badly hit because in several cases diagnosis is made on how a patient expresses his or her thoughts and perceptions. For example it is common for people in Asia and Africa to believe in spirits both good and evil. This belief to a European mind may be strange and tantamount to schizophrenia.

Up to 50 per cent of diseases are wrongly diagnosed amongst ethnic minority patients in some psychiatric hospitals due to a lack of in-depth cultural understanding.

Zombies

Dr Srirama Venugopal, chair of the ODA, says, "People are being inappropriately committed to institutions and some are being turned into zombies by ECT (electro-convulsive therapy) and long-term medication".

Electro-convulsive therapy is the passing of a strong electric current through the brain to induce convulsions. Its use is controversial and its mode of action not fully understood. Its effects were dramatised well in the film *One flew over the cuckoo's nest,* starring actor Jack Nicholson.

Prejudice

Lack of cultural appreciation also affects the attitudes of nurses and other staff towards minority patients. For example, people from the Indian sub-continent are considered 'sissies' and more likely to complain about pain. This view is prevalent despite reports in the *British Medical Journal* which showed that Asian patients demanded fewer pain killers after similar operations than white patients.

Several social scientists have studied expression of pain as a social phenomenon. Amongst Mediterranean and Asian, as well as African society, an ill person is expected and indeed encouraged to express pain. This forms a normal and vital part of the social behaviour of a sick person in these cultures. But despite the weight of scientific evidence, a majority of white nurses and doctors continue to preach what suits their prejudice.

Afro-Caribbean people are considered as 'trouble-makers' and many staff consequently adopt an aggressive and un-co-operative attitude as a defence even before they interact with the patient. Several white members of staff take pride in telling off patients from ethnic minorities and are then 'protected' by other white colleagues. Non-white staff may also turn a blind eye for fear of personal victimisation and even the loss of one's job.

Assaulted

Several of us have felt unable to adequately express ourselves in English at one time or another. Our elderly relations from Asian and African countries sometimes know very little English. But most hospitals in the NHS have no organised provision of interpreters to improve communication with patients. All health care workers are told is that to touch a patient without adequate explanation constitutes assault on that person. Elderly ethnic minority patients are subjected to such assault everyday in NHS hospitals.

Some in the health service admit this lack of understanding and as Mr Clive Firmin, manager of a Birmingham psychiatric unit, says about mis-diagnosis of psychiatric patients, "there are two theories to explain the relatively high rate of institutionalisation among ethnic minorities – the conspiracy theory and the cock-up theory. The second of these is by far the most common explanation – *We just don't understand as much about these people as we could."*

But there are others in the health service who have adapted to looking at an ethnic minority patient as a person with lower intelligence. I once heard a junior plastic surgeon at the West Middlesex Hospital, Isleworth, talking about "those ignorant Punjabis". The man is now a consultant plastic surgeon in the NHS. I wonder if such a doctor can ever provide equivalent care to an ethnic minority patient as he would to a white patient.

Black Politics in Britain

The determined and protracted struggle of Britain's visible minorities to win a degree of representation within the political structures of Britain took an important step forward on June 11 1987 when Diane Abbott (Labour – Hackney North and Stoke Newington), Paul Boateng (Labour – Brent South), Bernie Grant (Labour – Tottenham) and Keith Vaz (Labour – Leicester East) were elected to the House of Commons. They were the first avowed members of the visible minority communities to secure seats since Shapurji Saklatvala held the south London seat of Battersea North firstly for the Labour Party and then for the Communist Party in the early 1920s. It was significant, therefore, that in his own maiden speech to the House of Commons, Keith Vaz should remind his fellow members of Saklatvala's words in the House, where he called for it to "break out of prejudice and find a new place" in the world.

Some six decades separate Saklatvala from today's four MPs but these are not decades of apathy and indifference but of struggle often of a difficult, frustrating and even bitter kind. One person who exemplifies that period is Lord Pitt of Hampstead, formerly David Pitt. A one-time Chair of the Greater London Council (GLC), Lord Pitt failed to take the north London seat of Hampstead (a Conservative marginal) in 1959 and lost the safe south London Labour seat of Clapham in 1970 to the Conservative Party. This latter defeat was a sobering example of the strength of the white racist lobby. A bleak period followed with party bosses concluding that they were not prepared to risk allowing black candidates to contest safe or winnable Labour seats. In that time Labour selected minority candidates for 'no hope' seats only. To turn this situation around required a major political struggle, with the Black Section movement making the decisive contribution. It was therefore a moment of some emotion when Lord Pitt told a gathering one month after the 1987 general election that June 11 (election night) had been the "greatest day of my life". As with all the achievements of the black community, that great day was not achieved without history and struggle. Speaking at the same function as Lord Pitt – a reception organised by Hansib Publishing to honour the four MPs – Diane Abbott identified three factors that had contributed to her victory and those of her comrades:

- The liberation struggles that had led to the fall of the colonial empires and the rise of the Third World;
- The struggles of an earlier generation of activists exemplified by Lord Pitt;
- The struggle of the youth and dispossessed on the streets.

Writing on the significance of the election results in *Campaign Group News*, Bernie Grant noted: "For the black communities it will mean the possibility of a direct input into parliament that simply wasn't there before."

The election of the four was one of the consolations of the last election, which saw the Conservative Party led by Margaret Thatcher sweep back to power in her third consecutive election win. The Conservative Party was returned with an absolute majority of 101. But this does not mean that the Tories received a mandate commensurate with such a large majority. It is the vagaries of the British electoral system that produce such a result with 42.30 per cent of the vote on a turnout of 75.35 per cent of the eligible electorate. The parts of Britain that are particularly adversely affected by the Prime Minister's policies are precisely those which gave her no mandate. In the north of England, Wales and Scotland, Labour scored major gains at the expense of the Tories.

Labour frontbencher Gerald Kaufman noted when analysing the results: "Large parts of the country have revolted and rejected Conservatism. They have created two nations, one of which has elected them and one of which has rejected them."

Together at a reception in their honour organised by Hansib Publishing on their historic victory – from left: Paul Boateng, Keith Vaz, Bernie Grant and Diane Abbott.

With the exception of London there was a decline in the Tory urban vote. It decreased as follows:
Liverpool – 12%
Plymouth – 7.6%
Glasgow – 6.2%
Sheffield – 4.5%
Hull – 2.5%
Edinburgh – 1.4%

No Conservative MPs were returned in Manchester, Leicester, Bradford, Liverpool, Glasgow or Newscastle. In Scotland the Conservatives have been reduced to holding a mere ten seats – essentially in rich rural constituencies.

But as *The Independent* remarked:
"The parts of Britain where Labour has tended to do relatively well...have fewer seats than the parts where the Tories have progressively increased their strength. As long as the Tories can consolidate their support in the more prosperous areas at the same rate as their votes slip in the poorer regions, the laws of arithmetic will continue to produce Conservative governments."

However, despite all this, it is important to note that the 'race factor' has by no means disappeared from the electoral prospects of black candidates. As Ken Livingstone MP has noted there would be at least 26 black members in the House of Commons if the community had parliamentary representation proportionate to its numbers.

With the exception of Keith Vaz, who overturned a Conservative majority of 933, the black MPs all sustained a loss in the Labour vote in their constituency, despite the fact that the party increased its vote nationally.

Whilst Keith Vaz had a swing in his favour of 2.8 per cent, Diane Abbott sustained a swing to the Tories of 1.8 per cent, Paul Boateng a swing of 3.4 per cent, and Bernie Grant a swing of 6.8 per cent. In an election notable for the fact that all the major parties fielded visible minority candidates, a *New Statesman* study showed that for Labour minority candidates the average vote loss was 2.2 per cent, in the case of the Conservatives it was 2.5 per cent and in the case of the former Alliance the loss averaged at 5.2 per cent.

But despite this evidence of prejudiced voting, the most important point that must be registered is that it has been irrevocably and irrefutably demonstrated that visible minority candidates can win elections, can represent their constituencies – above all that they can exercise power.

It should also be noted that the white racist lobby is not an absolute factor, as none of the MPs could have secured election without drawing substantial numbers of white voters to their side. It is also true, of course, that the election of the four arose from the struggles of the community and was supported by the community. All four were elected in areas with large minority communities (including Irish, Cypriot, Jewish, etc. as well as African, Asian and Westindian) and all had a long record of political activity and struggle in and with the community.

It is significant to note that all four black MPs may be described – to varying degrees – as being on the left of the Parliamentary Labour Party. This is a fact that bears on the political maturity of the minority communities, showing, that whilst they will support and promote their representatives, they do so on the basis of their record and standpoint and not by parodying the white racist lobby in reverse. A special opinion poll commissioned for Hansib's newspapers by the Harris Research Centre during the general election showed that 72 per cent of the visible minority electorate intended to cast their votes for the Labour Party. Moreover, when asked to identify the issues that most concerned them when deciding how to cast their votes, unemployment was cited as the biggest single factor by a majority of respondents – 67 per cent in all. Other responses included – Law and Order – 38%; Housing – 37%; Racial Discrimination – 32%; Economic Policy – 28%; Immigration and Nationality – 23%; Poverty – 17%; Defence – 14%.

When asked whether they would be more likely to vote for a minority candidate, 32% said they would be more likely, whilst 51% said that it would make no difference to their attitudes. 10% said that they did not know, whilst 7% even said that it would make them less likely to vote for the candidate.

This is a statistical justification for Paul Boateng's statement on the night of his election: "We go now as Socialist Tribunes of all the people, black and white, in Brent South. Socialist Tribunes who are defenders of their rights, defenders of their health service, defenders of their education service and of their jobs, and we go forward together."

The same point is proved conversely by the experience of the Social Democratic Party's Manzoor Moghal, who stood against Labour's Max Madden in Bradford West. He experienced the biggest negative swing of any of the minority candidates with the Alliance vote in the constituency dropping from 13,301 to 5,675. This represented an Alliance swing to Labour of 13.9%. Bradford West has a strong Asian community but Max Madden, for his part, has a strong record as an anti-racist. It seems, therefore, that the unfortunate Moghal's vote could have been squeezed from two directions.

Whatever the precise relationship of the black MPs to the Black Section movement at any particular time it should be placed on the historical record that the movement was essential in propelling the Labour Party into selecting minority candidates for winnable seats. The three strategic steps that contributed to this were summarised by Labour activist Sharon Atkin (herself the candidate for Nottingham East until she was summarily removed by the party's national leadership two weeks before the general election was formally called) in an article carried in *Interlink*, journal of the Socialist Society:

"The campaign was important on several levels:

"1) To recruit black voters to the party and to encourage registration campaigns.

"2) To increase representation of black people at every level, i.e. Health Authorities, Local Councils, School Governors and Parliament.

"3) To fight for anti-racist policies within the party, to encourage greater international links and support workers in struggle, particularly in Third World countries."

Almost certainly, the election of the four MPs would not only have been rendered difficulty, if not impossible, without the Black Section movement – and the same applies to the experience and achievements that accrued first from involvement in electoral politics at a local level. The considerably more than 100 councillors, the mayors and mayoresses and the council leaders (including Bernie Grant himself) all showed to electors and elected alike what was possible and how to work, and conditioned society as a whole to the historical inevitability of black representatives at Westminster. But the council experience contains a warning too as a number of experiences, most recently the stepping down from the leadership of south London's Lambeth Council by Linda Bellos, illustrate.

Winning power is not the end – it is the beginning of the work of exercising it. This is all the more the case, when national reality dictates that we are talking at this stage more about the form of office rather than the essence of power. Elected represenatives should never forget from where they came and by whom they were elected.

Despite our electoral gains and our other achievements the situation facing our people is still bleak. The average worker from the visible minorities earns only 85 per cent of the wage earned by workers as a whole. Visible minority unemployment is twice the national average – a basic figure that does not fully reflect the areas of real deprivation. Less than 50 per cent of black graduates have found full-time employment one year after obtaining their degrees, compared with 70 per cent of white graduates. It is a matter of having a platform and of using it to build for the struggles ahead.

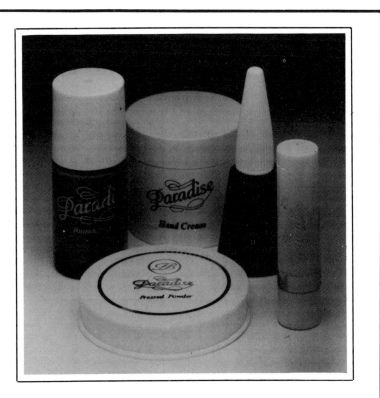

Black People and the Labour Movement

by Bill Morris

Ending racism is a moral and political imperative, because racism is a cause of bitterness and misery for millions of people; it divides and pollutes our society, and it degrades both the oppressor and the oppressed.

As the Deputy General Secretary of the Transport and General Workers' Union (T&GWU), Bill Morris is Britain's leading black trades unionist. In this article he outlines how his general perceptions of the anti-racist struggle relate to the situation in the British labour movement (both the Labour Party and the trades unions) at the beginning of 1988. As an active participant in the struggles on which he writes, Bill Morris displays commitment to the immediate issues combined with a strategic and long-term approach.

I wish to begin from first principles:

Britain is a country which is very deeply divided, a country in which injustice and inequality is everywhere apparent; and in particular it is a country in which racism is a profound and pervasive fact. Indeed, racism is such a fundamental fact of our society that it makes little sense to talk of it as in some way a secondary phenomenon, a product of other divisions – for example of class – although of course the way in which it is experienced by black people is very much influenced by the particular structure and history of the British economy.

From that I draw three conclusions, which I consider to be of great importance when considering the relationship between black people and the British labour movement.

Firstly, since racism is a social fact it is not simply a matter of personal prejudice, however common that may be. Rather it is produced and reinforced through the institutions of white society, and, because those institutions have rules and structures which are themselves the products of racism, there is a sense in which the institutional force of racism has a life of its own, regardless of the attitudes of any individual. The seeming paradox of institutions whose leading figures protest their anti-racism but which can plainly be seen to discriminate is more apparent than real. If it were not so we could solve many of the problems of racism by subjecting the perpetrators to psychoanalysis, an idea that, as might be expected, found some popularity in California but transferred to Britain seems to many of us largely to have missed the point.

Secondly, the institutions of the British labour movement cannot escape the scrutiny of anti-racists. Indeed it would be astonishing, given the history of Britain and its colonies, if organisations based on the British working class were not to some extent polluted by racial discrimination. Therefore any group inside the movement which insists on the primacy, and fundamental explanatory power of class divisions, will soon find the contradictions between neat theory and messy practice too sharp to contain.

Finally, anti-racist strategies must start from a commitment to social and institutional change, to the elimination of injustice and inequality through profound changes in the social order. Any "equal opportunities" policy which does not begin from that premise is likely to fail. Naturally, given that anti-racism involves such change, it is the responsibility of anti-racists to look to those forces in society which, at least ostensibly, exist to promote it.

Hence the great dilemma of black people in the labour movement. On the one hand it exists to promote social change, to eradicate class divisions and to empower the powerless. On the other hand it is itself distorted by the racism of the social order it is challenging. It would seem that black people should be looking to direct and lead the movement, and notwithstanding they should be protesting at its own discrimination and injustices.

This is the kind of dilemma that can last an eternity. It seems to me – as a labour movement activist – to be profoundly important that we do not allow it to do so. In the remainder of this article, I seek to look at some of the areas in which the debate around the role of black people in the labour movement – and the movement's own record of discrimination – is sharpest, and suggest some ways in which contentious issues might be resolved to the general good.

Chair of Black Sections – Cllr Narendra Makanji

The first issue is that of black representation in the Labour Party, and the role of the Black Section movement.

Of course, the debate around the demands of the Black Section has had a number of benefits. Above all, it has helped to ensure the election of four black MPs to the House of Commons, and it has challenged the complacent assumption on the part of some prominent white Labour Party members that the Party can rely on what is referred to as the "black vote", a docile mass that will turn out regardless of how it is treated because is has no other political home to which to go.

In that respect, the role of the Black Section debate as "establishment tree shaking" has had a value. But that may be subject to the law of diminishing returns. The motion to agree to the establishment of Black Sections has been defeated at successive Party conferences, and the majority against is growing. Meanwhile, the Party is at last turning its attention to the sharp decline in its support amongst black people. There has always been a danger that the debate will degenerate into divisive conflict between individual supporters of Black Sections and the Party leadership, a conflict characterised by an ultra-left relish for confrontation and denunciation on the one hand and insensitive repression on the other.

In a sense, the debate has actually begun to assist in a fundamental aim of racist politics – one which has been enthusiastically pursued by the current Conservative government. That is to portray black people as marginal, as at best politically irrelevant and at worst as an alien force, a "threat" to the social order after the inner-city civil disorders of 1981 onwards, and as "outside infiltrators" when they make demands on the labour movement.

The image of an "alien threat" is so basic to Thatcherism, and so profoundly authoritarian and racist in its implications, that there is an urgent need for anti-racists and democratic socialists to stand, clearly and unequivocally, for the right of black people to be at the centre of British political life. On that there can never be any compromise.

It needs to be remembered that black people can and do offer the Party priceless reserves of political energy, enthusiasm and commitment. The black community could help to revitalise a Party that in too many areas has grown stale and weary. All it takes is a Party – leadership and members alike – that really is willing to listen.

That is why it is so pleasing to see that, at the time of writing, both sides of the Black Sections debate are inching towards a satisfactory resolution. The leadership now appears to accept that the case for independent black representation within the Party has been convincingly made, whilst many of the supporters of Black Sections do not want to see their cause doomed to another fractious and sterile defeat at the next Party Conference. That is why the "socialist society" option is now gaining support.

There is a strong case for allowing a national black socialist society to affiliate to the Party on the same basis as the Fabian Society, for example, with the rights of nomination and representation that other affiliated societies enjoy. Such a proposal could deal with many of the technical problems identified by the opponents of Black Sections. And a black socialist society could offer black people the chance of systematic involvement in the Party's current comprehensive review of its policies. But above all, a black socialist society could have an autonomy that a black section never could. It could become the point of contact between the Party and the black communities – and playing a role in the community will be every bit as important as participation in the internal affairs of the Party. Of course, any affiliated society must accept certain basic rules. But those leave wide scope for freedom of action – a degree of independence which any serious black-led movement must have. In this respect at least, the future seems hopeful.

But clearly there remain other problems for the movement to tackle. Internally, there is the whole issue of black representation in the trades unions. And because the structure and membership of the unions is so diverse this is not a problem that can be so easily resolved. There is no simple structural change, for example, that will ensure the election of more black shop stewards and the appointment of more black officers in unions as diverse as, say, the National Union of Mineworkers and the Banking, Insurance and Finance Union.

However, there can be no doubt that black people are grossly under-represented at all levels of the trades unions and the evidence is already strong that that is proving to be a major obstacle in any attempt to recruit new groups of black workers. Stated boldly, too many are looking at the trades unions, seeing only white faces, and writing them off as irrelevant to their needs. It is a notable fact that many groups of black workers continue to rely on informal organisation at the workplace and their communities, and on voluntary networks and advice services to secure their rights at work. That is so despite the well publicised cases – from Grunwick onwards – in which trades unions have fought hard in disputes which predominantly involved black workers. (The cases where this has not happened are, it must be said, just as important – but less well-known.)

There are, however, signs of change – partly prompted by self-interest. Unions like the Transport and General Workers' Union (T&GWU) have identified a major change now taking place in the British economy – the creation of what has come to be known as the two-tier labour market.

In the first tier are permanent workers, tied to established firms, with good pay, good conditions and job security. In the second tier, are the growing army of temporary, casual, part-time and deskilled workers. They are the victims of the employers' drive to "flexibility", which recent disputes have shown to be one of the most hotly-contested issues in British industrial relations. And the growth of the secondary tier has been further encouraged by the removal of wages council protection from young people, the setting up of the Youth Opportunities Programme (YOP) and then the Youth Training Scheme (YTS) at a third of adult unskilled wages, and cuts in the 'social wage' – through benefits, welfare services and so on.

Marc Wadsworth – Campaigns Organiser of the Labour Party Black Section

It is important to note that the position of secondary workers in the labour market is not a function of their abilities and skills. Many are highly skilled, and many others have great, if often unrealised, potential. Rather it is a matter of equal opportunities, because the majority of marginal workers are women, and many are young and from the ethnic minorities.

Since many unions are now extremely keen to recruit and represent secondary workers – the T&GWU is aiming its 'Link-Up' campaign specifically at them – they are obliged to consider the structural changes that are required to integrate them into union structures. Such changes will vary substantially from union to union. The problem, in any event, is not ideas for change – the TUC "Black Workers Charter", for example, was very useful in this respect – but the will to implement them.

Inescapably if unions set up advisory committees, improve the proportion of ethnic minority officers, and promote black people through lay representative structures, that will raise questions of power within the union. To demand that this is done is to say to those now in control of unions, the time has come to cede some of your power to us. Of course that is just. But we cannot be surprised if we encounter resistance.

Unions also need to be constantly reminded of the scale of the task that faces them if they are serious about fighting racism in employment. As the 1985 Policy Studies Institute (PSI) Report, "Racial Discrimination – 17 Years After the Act", showed, in almost every job category, both private and public sector employers were far more likely to offer jobs to white applicants. Moreover many used selection methods that discriminated indirectly, such as 'word of mouth' recruitment, and demanding qualifications in excess of those required. The PSI did not provide direct evidence, but I doubt whether in many cases these practices were the subject of serious challenge by the relevant trades unions, and in some cases there was no doubt active support for them.

This suggests an urgent need for work to reform trades unions' collective bargaining procedures. The TUC booklet "Trade Unions and Black Workers" details the equal opportunities clause that should be included in every collective agreement. Further progress on this is a top priority, as is trades union support for effective monitoring. Of course, this kind of action is not going to eliminate racism at work altogether. It will still be there, and sometimes it will be open and ugly. Racial abuse and harassment is still a fact of life for many black workers – and overt racism exists amongst trades unionists as well as employers.

So there can be no substitute for trades unions taking these problems seriously, and when black workers complain to stewards or officials about such behaviour, action has got to be taken. Rhetoric and pious expressions of concern are not enough. Indeed they are a certain recipe for black peoples' alienation from the labour movement.

I have concentrated on structural action quite deliberately. I believe, both in theory and in practice, that the most effective anti-racist work comes from campaigns for social and institutional change – challenging racism in the labour movement means drawing all sections of the movement into such work. There are inspiring examples to be found, for example of trade union involvement in struggles against deportations. But they are still too few.

There is so much that could be done. The government is challenging the principle of contract compliance, one of the most effective weapons available to local authorities in challenging discrimination. It is pushing the poll tax through parliament. This will hit the inner cities – and hence the ethnic minorities – hardest of all. It is relaxing controls on the private rented sector, and that too will disproportionately affect black people. Everywhere there are battles for the labour movement to fight, in which black people should be taking a central role.

Ending racism is a moral and political imperative, because racism is a cause of bitterness and misery for millions of people; it divides and pollutes our society, and it degrades both the oppressor and the oppressed.

But, of course, black people will continue to find their own ways of fighting it. The question for the labour movement is, do we have a role in that fight or do we not? I passionately believe that we do. As I have tried to show, that's not just right in principle, it's a basic matter of survival.

Bill Morris
Deputy General Secretary
Transport and General Workers' Union
February, 1988

The fight for black political recognition

by Marc Wadsworth

In this article Marc Wadsworth, Journalist and former National Chair of the Labour Party Black Section, surveys the contribution and role of that movement, the responses it has evoked and hints at a future direction.

Explosions of black anger at our continued exclusion from the power structures of British society found a voice in the party to which we have traditionally turned in huge numbers when Black Sections were born five years ago. Previously, there had been countless struggles against racism by black workers. These had included "single-issue" protests over police brutality, racial harassment at work and home, anti-deportation campaigns and the fight for an end to racist education. Industrial battles against employers and trade unions alike had also taken place.

In 1980, St Pauls, Bristol, was the scene of the first contemporary inner city uprising on a large scale. A black and white protest against a fascist march in Southall the previous year saw Blair Peach killed by the Metropolitan Police's notorious Special Patrol Group. St Pauls was followed by uprisings in Brixton, Toxteth and Moss Side as well as in many other cities in 1981. The Broadwater Farm uprising of 1985, following the police killng of Cynthia Jarrett and maiming of Cherry Groce, led to the show trials and subsequent framing up of three people for the murder of PC Keith Blakelock.

Labour Party leader Neil Kinnock – consistently opposed to Black Sections

Prominent Black Section supporter Bernie Grant, then leader of Haringey Council, was vilified by the right-wing press as well as the Labour leadership for saying the police got a "bloody good hiding". He was echoing the view of black youth in Tottenham who had suffered the fate of thousands of others like themselves around the country, namely years of police racism.

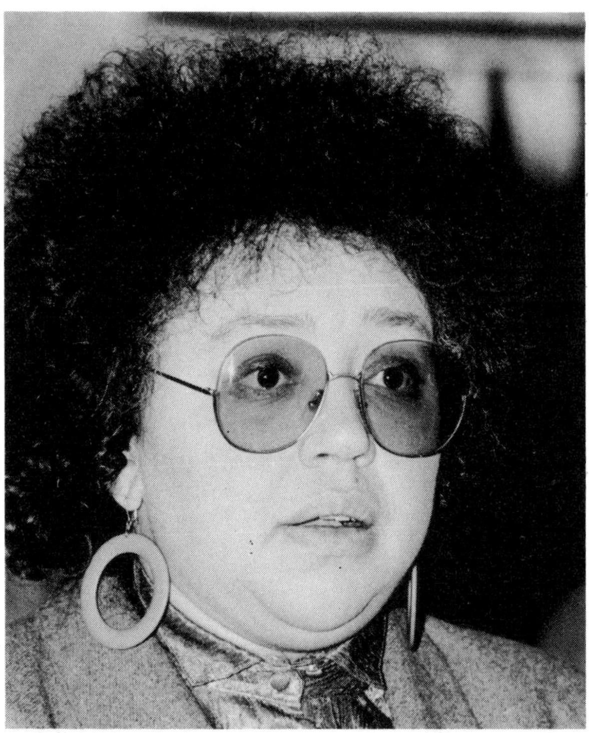

Sharon Atkin – surcharged as a councillor; removed as a candidate

Black self-organisation in the Labour Party could not have taken root had it not been for this long tradition of struggle, based on the same principle of black people themselves leading the fight against racism.

The Black Section had a modest start in London. A handful of black Labour Party members, sick of the party's patronising approach to race, often relying on 'godfather' politics for votes in black areas, joined forces.

Now around 40 groups exist, including in Birmingham, Nottingham, Manchester and Bristol. We argued that for 50 years Labour had permitted separate women's and youth sections. These have their own organisation and specific representation both on constituency management committees and on the party's ruling National Executive Committee (NEC).

Black Sections are needed to make Labour more accessible to black people, to get members of our communities elected to party posts and adopted as local government and parliamentary candidates, as well as ensuring the adoption of anti-racist policies especially in employment, housing, education and immigration.

There was an initial flirtation with the idea of having loosely-organised "caucuses" or "ethnic minority" groups. But Black Sections, open to members of the Labour Party of African and Asian descent, were eventually established. They represent the views and interests of black people and fight against racism within the Labour movement. Originally, the major role of Black Sections was to promote black representation at all levels of the party. Successes have included a three-fold increase in the number of black councillors, three black leaders of councils and the election of four black Labour MPs – all supporters of Black Sections – at the 1987 General Election.

Following the 1984 Black Section conference in Birmingham, attended by 300 black people, our campaign began to attract increasing support among Labour activists in constituency parties around the country. An attempt to alter the party constitution to allow Black Sections was defeated 10-1 by the trade union block votes at that year's party conference. But the following year an NEC working party, specially set up to deal with the issue, recommended in favour, following wide-reaching consultation in the movement.

This was completely junked by the party leadership who had, by that time, dug themselves a trench which they refused to get out of. In 1985, with the help of the public service union, NUPE, and the mineworkers, we reduced the party conference vote against us to 5-1.

The party leadership's answer was to revert to the old trick of paternalism by appointing trusted black party members to a neo-colonialist "Black and Asian Advisory Committee". This was controlled by its powerful white members. The Black Section boycott of the committee was extremely effective. Labour's left-wing joined all self-respecting black members of the party in refusing to have anything to do with it.

In 1985 and 1986 we stepped up our fight for recognition (not permission because we were already established). This we did in the constituency parties where our campaign was strongest. The party leadership's response was to halt the selection of parliamentary candidates in several seats, including Lewisham East where Russell Profitt was standing, because of the involvement of Black Section delegates.

The party leadership, notably Neil Kinnock and his deputy Roy Hattersley, has consistently opposed Black Sections. Cynics note that Hattersley referred to the black people who make up 30 per cent of the electorate in his Birmingham seat as "my Asians". He was deeply nervous about them flexing their political muscle. So much so that when Sparkbrook Black Section was formed he orchestrated the expulsion from the party of two of its supporters, Kevin Scaly and Amir Khan. It was only after a bitterly fought 14-month campaign that they were eventually reinstated.

The leadership's opposition to Black Sections is based on their view that they do not need to concede power to the black people on whose behalf they claim to speak and because of their traditional 'caving in' to white racist voters. Labour did the latter most obviously in government when they introduced racist immigration laws. The leadership's opposition is also based on the labour movement's basic conservatism – its fear of change, especially change not controlled by the white barons already in charge. Furthermore, the Labour leadership's politics are based on British nationalism. And British nationalism depicts the nation as homogenous. It absorbs racial differences into a single 'British identity': an identity based on Britain's imperial past. Hattersley told Labour Conference in 1985 there were no groups of people in Britain who could be "lumped together" and called "the blacks".

Hilary Wainwright, in her book 'Labour – A Tale of Two Parties'. noted: "The gap between the vitriol with which members of the parliamentary leadership respond to Black Sections and the reasonable nature of their case is remarkable."

Neil Kinnock told lobby journalists at Westminster in 1985: "I would not give a damn if the whole Labour Party was against me on this."

And an unnamed member of his shadow cabinet told the *Sunday Times*: "I want these characters out and I don't mind if we lose a few seats to the SDP in the process. It is an insidious disease that has been allowed to spread. It is political AIDS."

This hysteria reached a peak when Sharon Atkin was undemocratically sacked as Labour's parliamentary candidate for the marginal seat of Nottingham East. The pretext for this was an unexceptional speech she gave to a Black Section public meeting in Birmingham. Among the things she said was: "What I will always do is fight for black people, with black people." In response to heckling from a separatist black nationalist complaining about the party and its leaders' record on race, she added: "I don't give a damn about Neil Kinnock and a racist Labour Party."

Former Greater London Council (GLC) leader Ken Livingstone MP commented: "When I say the Labour Party is racist from top to bottom, no action is taken against me, but when a black woman says it, it sends the Labour Party into a great lather."

A panic statement from four other black candidates in winnable seats, Paul Boateng, Diane Abbott, Bernie Grant and Russell Profitt, which pledged allegiance to the party during the row, was construed as them distancing themselves from Sharon Atkin in her hour of need. This put great strain on Black Section unity at a time when it was most crucial.

Prior to this the Black Section held a hugely successful annual conference in Nottingham titled, "Going on the Offensive with the Black Agenda".

Ken Livingstone MP – has supported principles of self-organisation

It passed policy opposing the racist immigration laws, supporting anti-racist education, a package of measures to put unemployed black people back to work and to make the police a democratic and accountable force. Our movement stepped into a new phase when a parliamentary black caucus, with Bernie Grant, now MP for Tottenham, as its first secretary, was set up at the conference.

Bernie Grant said: "The issue of whether or not the black MPs are going to work together is decisive. If we can achieve that we can go on to consider how best to relate to the black communities."

Diane Abbott, MP for Hackney North and Stoke Newington, said: "The danger is that unless we work together and work around agreed aims and objectives, the rest of parliament will divide and rule and we will become, as individuals, isolated and marginalised."

And Leicester East's new MP, Keith Vaz, commented: "It is inevitable that, one day in the not-too-distant future, we will all sit together. It is unthinkable that there will not be differences and also agreements about policy objectives."

Paul Boateng, of Brent South, said he was against a Parliamentary Black Caucus. He told the US magazine *Newsweek* (January 11 1988): "My agenda is the agenda of the party."

The Black Section will now step up their activity in an attempt to get greater political results for the black communities. This cannot be achieved by, as a columnist in a black newspaper proposed, contributing a £100 cheque towards a "secretariat" for black MPs; it will only come through struggle directed by the grassroots, to which our representatives must be responsive and accountable. This is the newest and most challenging phase of the struggle for black self-representation in the Labour Party.

There have been changes in the trade unions which are positive developments for our struggle. Britain's largest, the Transport and General Workers which appointed a black deputy general secretary, Bill Morris, in 1986, now has conference policy in favour of black self-organisation in their own ranks. This must now be translated into support for Black Sections in the Labour Party.

The advance in the T&GWU, fought for by Black Section supporters in the union, liberated Bill Morris enough for him to propose a compromise in the Labour Party. He says there should be a Black Socialist Society. But even this concession to the Black Section campaign faces an uphill battle with Labour's establishment.

Bill Morris said: "The case for some kind of independent black representation in the party has surely been made." And: "Black self-organisation, formally recognised or not, will play a central part" in the anti-racist struggle.

The Black Section reaction was to welcome this contribution to an important debate we had begun five years earlier. But we stressed that the Black Section remained fully committed to a change in Labour's constitution which would guarantee black representation at all levels. Eric Heffer, then chair of the Labour Party, had made a similar proposal in 1985 but it never got off the ground. The NEC defeated his plan for black groups to affiliate to the party by 16 votes to 8 – those against including Neil Kinnock and Roy Hattersley.

Kuomba Balogun – Bristol activist and target of criminalisation

The Black Section, determined not to get tied down by internal party trench warfare, has increasingly been leading the left in turning outwards. For example, our supporters like Martha Osamor, former deputy leader of Haringey Council, played a leading role in the Broadwater Farm Defence Campaign.

The aim has always been to play a positive supportive role as black activists, rather than a cynical one like certain members of White Left tendencies.

We have been represented on the support committees of three important industrial/ workplace campaigns, Kenure Plastics, Wheelers Restaurant and the Diamond Four. Our activists also swelled the ranks of protests at the police killing of Clinton McCurbin in Wolverhampton, the threatened deportation of Som Raj in the same city and over the Harwich Ferry refugees.

Leading members of the Black Section, including the national youth organiser, lent support to the Family and Friends of Trevor Monerville campaign in Hackney, east London. Trevor twice received unexplained injuries following periods in police custody – the most serious led to him needing an emergency operation for a blood clot on his brain.

Youth members, particularly in Birmingham, took an important lead organising against racist South Africa's apartheid regime. Several meetings on the issue of Azania have been held by Black Sections up and down the country including one to mark the anniversary of the murder of Steve Biko and another to promote a tour of black groups by the editor of *The Sowetan,* Thami Mazwai. We continue to play an active part in the affairs of a new umbrella organisation we helped to found, Black Action for the Liberation of Southern Africa (BALSA).

A Black Section trip to Belfast as guests of Sinn Fein firmed up links with the Irish liberation movement. One of the delegation members, Kuomba Balogun, chair of Bristol West Black Section, was sacked from his job with St Pauls Local Development Agency following a viciously orchestrated campaign against him by Home Secretary Douglas Hurd and the gutter press.

Priorities for the future include a major policy initiative on the inner cities, drawing attention to issues like those raised by the Kuomba Balogun case, and campaigns against the government's education, poll tax and local government bills.

Black unemployment now stands at 20 per cent – twice that of the white community. A top report has stated that race attacks are running at the equivalent of one an hour. Our communities – particularly the young among us – are still being criminalised by the police and the courts. The picture is bleak.

Black political unity can change all that and Black Sections are ideally situated to play a major role in the process. But they will not deliver the big prize of a mass national black movement in Britian unless they draw their strength and legitimacy from the many grassroot campaigns in our communities which have sustained us thus far.

Trades Unions

With Mrs Margaret Thatcher now the longest serving British Prime Minister of the twentieth century, a strategic reversal appears to have taken place in the fortunes of the nation's trades union movement. The voices of a decade ago alleging that the trades unions were "holding the country to ransom" are seldom heard at the end of the 1980s – indeed they would seem cruelly out of place.

Yet, if one were to conclude from the reverses suffered by the movement that it has ceased to be one with both power and influence, one would be making a profound mistake. Millions of people – many of them at the point of production – remain organised within the unions and, as the experience of the mineworkers shows, not a few of them are intensely loyal to the movement and its ideals. We are dealing not only with a movement with a history but with one that retains a great deal of its standing at both home and abroad. In the international context this can be seen not only in the Trades Union Congress' (TUC)'s prominent role in the Commonwealth Trades Union Council (CTUC) – not infrequently alongside unions it helped to found – but also on major questions of contemporary international life. For example when the International Confederation of Free Trades Unions (ICFTU) decided to send a delegation to Moscow to discuss nuclear disarmament with Soviet leader Mikhail Gorbachov one of its prominent members was Norman Willis, TUC General Secretary.

That the British trades union movement enjoys such standing, even after having suffered a series of reversals, is a tribute to its history – a history that has changed Britain and the world. The words of the movement's anthem that describe its red flag as having been "shrouded oft our martyred dead" accord with the historical facts. Before the unions emerged, the working people of Britain floundered in the depths of oppression, unalleviated poverty and brutal exploitation – this was the era that framed the 'Victorian values' so beloved of the present Prime Minister. In that era

Bill Morris – Britain's leading black trades unionist

ordinary men and women suffered and died, were hounded, imprisoned and transported to Australia as convicts as they sought to assert basic human rights, something accorded hitherto solely to the holders of titles and the owners of property. Without their sacrificies many of the rights and social benefits that nearly everyone in Britain takes for granted – or did until very recently – would have remained unthinkable.

In certain areas the British trades union movement has few parallels. For example it is united in one federal body which is independent of state control and transcends craft, political, ideological and religious differences – a rare achievement.

Whilst there are a growing number of trades unions that recognise the importance of their black membership, the fact that the history of the black community in Britain is intimately bound up with the development of the trades unions from the earliest days is still only dimly perceived. It is to the credit of progressive writers such as Ron Ramdin and Peter Fryer that this area of people's history is being progressively demystified.

Robert Wedderburn, who was born in Jamaica, most probably in 1762, came to England in his late teens in 1778 having already witnessed many atrocities. Having worked at sea he became a jobbing tailor. His experiences in life led him to espouse anti-establishment views and in 1817 he launched the broadsheet *The Forlorn Hope* which was committed to campaigning for a free press. Soon imprisoned on charges of 'sedition and blasphemy', he maintained an abiding faith in the principles of revolution, writing that "the poor would be victorious should a civil war commence". With an amazing degree of foresight he insisted that the battle had to be fought on two fronts: "a simultaneous revolution of the white poor in Europe and the black slaves in the Westindies."

William Davidson, who, having been born in Jamaica, came to England in 1786, was one of a number of people drawn into an attempt at insurrection from the ranks of radical movements by the activities of an *agent provocateur*. A plan was hatched to kill the entire cabinet whilst they were dining at the home of Lord Harrowby in Grosvenor Square. William Davidson had once worked for Lord Harrowby, who had described him as a "damned seditious fellow". It was hoped that the mass assassination would spark an insurrection culminating in the formation of a provisional government. Davidson was given the task of raising money and buying weapons and he took the responsibility of hiding weapons, in a loft in Cato Street.

Arrested on the eve of their planned action Davidson was amongst five people charged with high treason, in what became known as the 'Cato Street conspiracy', who were sentenced to be hanged early on the morning of May 1 1820. Davidson had pointed out to the court that, although his home had been ransacked, no incriminating evidence had been found. One of the items which Davidson guarded from capture was a banner which read: "Let us die like men and not be sold like slaves."

The insurrection on which the conspirators of Cato Street had placed their hopes did not materialise, but they were none the less active in a period of revolutionary ferment. In Scotland the towns of Glasgow and Paisley saw 60,000 weavers on strike in the same year. The rise of the working class was leading to the rise of the working class movement.

The Chartists were Britain's first mass organised working class movement, arising in the later 1830s. One of their central leaders was a black worker, William Cuffay. Cuffay (alternately called Cuffey, Cuffy and Coffey) stood out amongst his contemporaries as an indomitable working class leader. Before joining the Chartist movement in 1839 he had already lost a job of many years for having joined in strike action. In October 1839 he helped to form the Metropolitan Tailors' Charter Association, which recruited 80 members on its first night. He was a strong supporter of the 'People's Charter' which was drawn up by William Lovett and Francis Place. Its demands included universal male suffrage, annual parliaments, vote by secret ballot, payment for MPs (then an essential demand if working people were to stand any chance of getting into Westminster), abolition of property qualifications for MPs and equal electoral districts.

Cuffay soon emerged as among the dozen most prominent members of the Chartist movement in London. In 1841 he was elected delegate for Westminster to the Metropolitan Delegate Council. A few months later, in 1842, when George Harney and other national leaders were arrested, Cuffay was amongst the four leaders appointed as an 'interim executive'. Cuffay's influence among London Chartists was high. *The Times* referred to them as "the black man and his party". This type of publicity lost Cuffay's wife her job as a charwoman. It seems as if some things don't change!

In 1844 he was a member of the Masters' and Servants' Bill Demonstration committee in which capacity he was opposed to the power vested in magistrates to imprison a 'neglectful worker' for two months on the strength of an employer's oath. He was also one of the ten directors of the National Anti-Militia Association and, in keeping with the internationalist standpoint of the Chartists, was a member of the Democratic Committee for Poland's Regeneration.

During the National Convention of the Chartists in 1848 Cuffay was a London delegate and he took a hard line. The main business of the Convention was to call a mass meeting on Kennington Common in south London and a procession to take a petition containing around two million

Striking nurses on a south London picket line

signatures to the House of Commons. Cuffay seconded an amendment that "in the event of the rejection of the Petition, the Convention should declare its sitting permanent and should declare the Charter the law of the land". Eventually the idea of a National Assembly was accepted. When the Committee for managing the procession was established, Cuffay was elected to its Chair. The abandonment of the march on parliament after assembly at Kennington Common was a severe blow to Cuffay. He then joined a smaller group who saw insurrection as the only way forward. He was arrested in August 1848, the day after a meeting had been held at a public house in Bloomsbury, allegedly to plot a series of acts of arson to act as a signal for a rising. Cuffay had refused to go underground after his comrades had been arrested "lest it should be said that he abandoned his associates in the hour of peril." Evidence against Cuffay was given by two police spies and despite a powerful speech in his own defence he was found guilty, and with some fellow Chartists was sentenced to transportation "for the term of their natural lives". "A severe sentence but a most just one," *The Times* opined. Again, some things don't change!

Cuffay's voyage lasted 103 days and he landed in Tasmania in November 1849. Allowed to work as a tailor, his activities in the working class movement made him a public figure in his new home. As with his pioneering role at the dawn of the modern movement of the British working class, Cuffay's life in Australia demonstrated the internationalism displayed so readily by black workers.

In dwelling on the significance of Cuffay's life and work at the beginning of the organised working class movement in Britain, one is drawing attention not merely to something of positive significance, but also to a significant lack of reciprocity. The racial riots directed against the black communities of Liverpool and Cardiff – and to an extent Glasgow – in 1919 were connected not least to problems of chauvinism within the seafarers' trades union. In the years that followed, the working class movement laboured not least to keep black workers off the ships and away from the docks. In a June 1936 report of the Cardiff Docks register it was shown that, of a total of 690 unemployed firefighters, 599 were black. In the face of such discrimination Africans, Westindians, Arabs, Somalis and Malays united into the Coloured Seamen's Union. Since the early years of the century, Chinese seafarers had also faced the sustained hostility of the trades unions.

In 1930 the Trades Union Congress passed the following resolution proposed by a delegate from Cardiff:

"That this Congress views with alarm the continued employment of alien and undesirable coloured labour on British ships to the detriment of British seamen and calls upon the government to use all their powers to provide remedial action."

There is, of course, an inter-relationship in the fact that the earliest cities in Britain to host a stable black community should also be those who derived particular profits from the slave trade and the related 'sugar triangle'. The resources generated from what Marx and Lenin respectively dubbed 'primitive accumulation' and 'colonial super-profits' were naturally diffused throughout British society, albeit highly unevenly. British workers therefore lost the revolutionary impulse that they had had during the period of the Chartists. Early in the twentieth century the Russian revolutionary leader, V.I. Lenin, noted:

"In Great Britain the tendency of imperialism to divide the toilers... to encourage opportunism amongst them and to give rise to a temporary organic decay in the working class movement, revealed itself much earlier than the end of the nineteenth and the beginning of the twentieth centuries. For two big distinctive features of imperialism applied to Britain from midway through the nineteenth century: vast colonial possessions and a monopolist position in the world markets. Marx and Engels systematically followed, over some decades, this relation between working class opportunism and the imperialistic peculiarities of English capitalism."

There were many in the working class movement who understood this well, although from a thoroughly reprehensible standpoint. In 1946 the Labour trade union leader Ernest Bevin told the House of Commons that he was not prepared to sacrifice the British Empire because its demise would, he alleged, lead to a considerable fall in the standard of living of his constituents.

The historical legacy of the internationalism of black workers and the chauvinism – indeed racism – of the established labour movement and white workers themselves is a part of the background that shapes the contemporary history of the visible minority communities. It was the economic conditions created by the 'post-war boom', characterised, inter alia, by relatively full employment and Keynsian economics which propogated the amelioration of class contradictions, that led to the migrations which in turn moulded today's visible minority communities in Britain in their essential outlines.

At Britain's request thousands came, principally from the Caribbean and the South Asian sub-continent, to staff the hospitals and run the public transport in the cities of what they were cynically told, by Enoch Powell among others, was their 'mother country', as well as to generally fill all the jobs that the relatively prosperous white workers of the day were not prepared to take on. Such jobs, not surprisingly, included those that were dirty and dangerous and those with a high rate of anti-social shift work.

The people who came in the 1950s may have had certain illusions regarding British people and society but they also, generally, had a high degree of class and trades union consciousness. The main political parties in India had organised their trades unions from early on, whilst in the Caribbean many of the political parties, of both left and right, had actually been established by the trades unions in the wake of the epic labour revolts of the late 1930s. Such people joined the trades unions without hesitation, but the response from the movement was ambiguous, as can be seen from this resolution proposed at the 1958 Trades Union Congress:

"The coloured people coming to England are British subjects only seeking a means of existence which is denied them in their place of birth. We implore all trades unionists to do all in their power to help them obtain employment and join their respective trade unions, thus enabling them to work and live as decent human beings.

"It is time a stop was put to all foreign labour

entering this country: they constitute a danger to the workers of this country. In the event of a slump occurring, the market would be flooded with cheap foreign labour and a serious deterrent to trade union bargaining power."

On the one hand a sympathetic – if somewhat patronising – call is made to visible minority workers to join the trades unions but on the other hand a call is made to keep these same people out of Britain. This contradiction represents the expression of the division of the world into oppressed and oppressor nations and the resultant split in the working class.

To this day a view persists that the failure of the trades unions to properly represent black workers and to effectively tackle racism within and without arises from the minorities not being adequately unionised. This is a false and ignorant misconception.

According to a survey, *Black and White Britain,* published by the Policy Studies Institute (PSI) in the mid-1980s, 56 per cent of all Asian and Afro-Caribbean workers were in unions compared with 47 per cent of white workers. For male workers the figures were 64 per cent for Westindians and 59 per cent for Asians, against 57 per cent for white males.

Looking at women workers the figures become even more pronounced. The unionisation figure for all women workers was 34 per cent, but for Westindian workers it was 57 per cent – this large gap being partially explained by the industries they work in and the fact that more of them have full-time jobs. Visible minority and white workers attend their union meetings in about the same proportions – some 40 per cent.

But this willingness to join unions is not reflected in terms of involvement in the structures of the movement. Only four per cent of visible minority members were found to hold union posts compared with 11 per cent of white members.

It is not surprising, therefore, that the struggles of minority workers in Britain have been moulded by considerations of both race and class – and have even included the unions themselves amongst the adversaries. From early days ambiguous attitudes and racist presumptions coexisted with a 'workerist' attitude that affirmed that race was "not an issue" on the part of union leaderships and bureaucracies. On the shop floor it was more common to find straightforward racist attitudes and behaviour. Invoked 'tradition' and, ironically, the very power and authority of certain unions kept – and occasionally still keeps – minority workers out of certain industries and trades. In particular some of the older, more craft-oriented unions acquiesced in or promoted racist codes and practices, with many of the union officials being racially prejudiced themselves.

What is generally considered the first strike of visible minority workers in Britain took place at the Courtaulds Red Scar textile mill in Preston, Lancs in 1965. The workers' action was directed at management efforts to enforce an effective pay cut on the grounds of the introduction of new technology which would involve workers manning a greater number of machines. But the deal which the mainly Asian workers were to reject had been negoitated above their heads and behind their backs by white union officials. With the union officials standing with management and the white workers allowing prejudice to prevail over class solidarity, the strikers were eventually defeated. But like many other defeats in history the struggle was not without its positive lessons. It established that workers in Britain of Third World origin would fight for their rights and those of all workers. The fear – genuine or mischievous – that these new sections of the working class in Britain would prove to be "scabs" legitimising cheap labour and other exploitative practices was proved to be without foundation. Indeed, if anything the reverse was the case.

Secondly a link was made that was to recur in future struggles – that between work place and community, which in turn represents in itself the inter-connection between race and class both in consciousness and struggle. Abandoned by the trades union the workers received support from the community organisations – in this case from the Indian Workers' Association and the Racial Adjustment Action Society. Two decades later the miners' strike was to see literally hundreds of community organisations throw their collective weight behind one of Britain's most heroic and significant industrial struggles.

The factors that were seen in operation at the Red Scar dispute revealed themselves even more directly in the 1974 Imperial Typewriters strike in Leicester. It is worth quoting the views of a would-be 'leader' of the working class at some length. George Bromley, a Justice of the Peace, negotiator for the Transport and General Workers' Union and a 'stalwart' of the Leicester Labour Party, had this to say:

"The workers have not followed the proper

disputes procedure. They have no legitimate grievances and it's difficult to know what they want. I think there are racial tensions, but they are not between the whites and coloureds. The tensions are between those Asians from the sub-continent and those from Africa. This is not an isolated incident, these things will continue for many years to come. But in a civilised society, the majority view will prevail. Some people must learn how things are done."

Bromley may have insisted that the tensions were not between "whites" and "coloureds". He did not mention that at the previous election the National Front had polled 9,000 votes in the city. He was, however, prepared to indulge the lurid tales that alleged that the strikers were in receipt of "Chinese communist money". "I've had reports", he said, "of £5 notes changing hands on the picket line."

The workers in fact had a litany of grievances starting with bonus rates, but ranging over a number of issues, including the difference in treatment accorded to white workers and the "dignity of human beings, the right to go to the doctor when they are ill or take time off to look after their children."

Deprived of union backing and with stories of "Peking gold" being rightly treated as a sick joke, the strikers incurred real financial hardship. What support they did receive came from community organisations such as the Indian Workers' Association and local Sikh *Gurdwaras*.

As the strike continued the Asian workers brought to it, in the words of one commentator, "a vivacity and style... that makes it unique". Women played a major role in the strike – their status meant that they felt the effects of the economic crisis both in terms of their wage packets and in terms of inflation when they shopped for their families. Asian youth came forward to support the strikers. In the words of historian Ron Ramdin:

"The emergence of Asian youths in the struggle worried state officials who were already faced with controlling Westindian youth. Later this would have implications on social policy. Together, these youths, with no background of employment experience and no real work prospects in the foreseeable future had little to lose by demonstrating the plight of the black working class."

By the end of July 1974, after nearly three months on strike, the attention of the workers, who had undergone innumerable hardships, shifted to London where 200 people lobbied Transport House (then the headquarters of the Labour Party) calling for the strike to be made official. But all they received was a promise of an inquiry by transport union leaders, Jack Jones and Moss Evans. The role of the trades unions in the Imperial Typewriters dispute was truly one of

Norman Willis – General Secretary of the Trades Union Congress (TUC)

acting as the "labour lieutenants of capital".

Strikes have been described as a "school of war but not the war itself". Extending this analogy a little it can be said that disputes such as that at Imperial Typewriters were the school for the real war that took place in north London – at the Grunwick photo processing plant of George Ward. This dispute, lasting nearly two years, was to become a legend in trades union history and a landmark in the history of the community etched with pride and bitterness. With a workforce making heavy use of student part-timers and otherwise largely made up of Gujarati-speaking East African Asians, many of them women, the regime at Grunwicks was characterised by compulsory overtime and arbitrary dismissals. Furthermore the workers, many from conservative backgrounds, had to put up with enormous indignities from white managerial staff, such as not being allowed to go to the toilet without first putting up their hand to get permission.

The strikers were led by a Gujarati-speaking Indian woman, who had previously lived in East Africa, Mrs Jayaben Desai. The oppressive and humiliating working conditions, the arbitrary and excessive use of compulsory overtime and the general "atmosphere of fear" were the immediate causes of the strike. Having walked out the workers joined the 'white collar' union, APEX, and received support from the local Brent Trades Council. When the strikers were dismissed and the company refused to recognise the union – which soon recruited 137 striking workers to its ranks – the wider trades union movement saw the dispute as one of 'recognition' and rallied to its support. It was fortuitous that the Trade Union Congress met some two weeks after the beginning of the dispute and therefore proclaimed their support.

In a strike that lasted very nearly two years the class forces in British society were sharply and clearly polarised – weekly mass pickets were held, frequently drawing thousands of supporters, including miners brought down from South Yorkshire by their then area president Arthur Scargill (himself one of the hundreds arrested on the picket line) in an act of solidarity that was to be more than repaid by visible minority workers during the historic miners' strike of 1984-85. More token appearances on the picket line were made by members of the then Labour cabinet. But the class forces were being equally firmly ranged on the other side – at one time a quarter of the entire Metropolitan Police were involved in the attempts to suppress the strike and pickets; and government minister Merlyn Rees defended the actions of the police stating: "I learnt this in Northern Ireland: operational control must be in the hands of the police." On one day alone 243 pickets sustained police-inflicted injuries.

But, although there was no shortage of statements and affirmations of solidarity, the familiar problem of the chasm between words and deeds in the stance of the trades union leaders was once again the achilles heel of working class solidarity. Defying TUC resolutions, and their own bombastic promises, trades union leaders not only refused to cut off essential services but actually disciplined rank-and-file postal workers who moved to put this strategy into effect. With the oppressive forces of the state determined to bus the scabs in each morning come what may, the refusal to halt essential services to this mail order photo processing company meant that there was ultimately no way in which the strikers could win their immediate demands, irrespective of their level of courage and sacrifice. In November 1977 in an act of bitter defiance and disappointment, Mrs Desai was joined by fellow strikers Vipin Magdani, Johnny Patel and Yasu Patel on a hunger strike on the steps of the TUC headquarters, Congress House. When two other strikers joined them, these two had their strike pay withdrawn and their union membership revoked – a most bitter twist to a struggle for union recognition!

Ten years and more later the lessons of the Grunwick dispute remain a cause for study and struggle with many people holding the view that it was a tactical error to closely follow the left wing of the trades union movement in focussing on the struggle for union recognition rather than on the wider question of the rights and dignity of Asian workers. Following from this, debate still continues as to whether the balance of efforts in raising support should have been directed to the unions or to the community.

But there are certain factors about the Grunwick dispute that are timeless and indisputable – and not least amongst them is that a new page was turned in the annals of the community's workplace struggles. During the Grunwick strike workers at the nearby engineering factory, Desoutters, where Mrs Desai's husband was employed, went on strike and shortly afterwards the Grunwick example was taken up by the Asian women workers at the Chix bubble gum factory in Slough. Nor should it be forgotten that the 1978/79 'Winter of Discontent', essentially waged by low paid workers in the public sector which broke the back of James (now Lord) Callaghan's Labour government, was waged in no small measure by black women organised particularly in the National Union of Public Employees (NUPE) and the Confederation of Health Service Employees (COHSE). It was these militant struggles of oppressed workers, alongside the growing involvement of black people at various levels of the trades union movement and the development of the anti-racist movement generally, that contributed to a change in the formal attitudes of the movement. At its 1976 congress the TUC put forward a clear denunciation of the National Front and its policies which was passed unanimously, with Bill Keys of the print union, SOGAT, declaring: "These people who peddle race hatred are no different from the people who peddled the hatred in Germany in the 1920s and 1930s."

In June 1981 the TUC published its 'Black Workers Charter' which stressed the need for unions to be closely involved in the development of policies for equal opportunities at work. It recommended that trades unions and management should regularly review employment practices and the structure of the workforce to see that there was no discrimination – direct or indirect – in the areas of recruitment, promotion and training opportunities.

Following the publication of the TUC's charter, the Commission for Racial Equality (CRE) undertook a series of investigations which highlighted how certain employment practices can put minority workers at a serious disadvantage.

Amongst the practices uncovered by the CRE were:

* That the use of word-of-mouth and employee recommendation as a major recruitment method may have caused unintentional indirect discrimination against black people at a number of branches of Unigate Dairies;

* That reliance on internal advertisement of job vacancies by Kirklees Council tended to exclude black applicants and give an advantage to the existing, predominantly white workforce;

* That the promotion procedures used by Dunlop's Polymer Engineering Division, in particular the spoken and written communication skills required, were not closely enough related to the actual needs of the job and indirectly discriminated against Asian applicants;

* That procedures which left recruitment practices and decisions to individual supervisors at St. Chad's Hospital allowed discrimination to occur.

These are individual examples – but representative of long-established national trends.

In the wake of the CRE's findings, the TUC, in 1984, urged its affiliates to ensure that discriminatory practices were stamped out in the country's workplaces. But the gap between rhetoric and reality remained, so that a report published in the same year and prepared for the West Midlands TUC could state:

"Black members see unions as white organisations which are either indifferent or hostile to the concerns of black people. There is a lack of confidence in the ways in which unions represent their black members. Grievances are not taken seriously, officials will not challenge management over issues of race."

Lionel Morrison – Former President of the National Union of Journalists

According to the TUC's 1986 publication, *Trades Unions and Black Workers:*

"The challenge facing the trade union movement is to translate its commitment to equal opportunities into a reality in terms of its structures and procedures and its collective bargaining objectives... The fact is that despite the movement's policies of opposition to racism, instances of discrimination by union representatives, discrimination by employers and discriminatory employment practices still persist... The gaps between union policy and what happens in practice need tackling urgently."

There has in recent years been a greater awareness among the more progressive union leaders both of the need to expurgate racism from the union movement and of the potential role of the unions themselves in the fight against racism.

Ray Buckton, the veteran leader of the train drivers' union, ASLEF, wrote: "Racism is a disease which poisons the heart and warps the mind, a corrupter of souls, an evil which undermines the ordinary human sympathies which are at the core of trades unionism."

With regard to union participation in the wider anti-racist struggle, particular mention should be made of the defence of members facing deportation under Britain's racist immigration and nationality laws. The National Association of Local Government Officers (NALGO) has been particularly prominent in this regard, as in the cases of Mohammed Idrish, Shahid Syed, Rose Aloso and Marion Gaima. NUPE has struggled against the threatened mass deportation of nurses from the Philippines. On a broader level, a greater number of unions are affiliating themselves to the Campaign Against Racist Laws (CARL) and – in what was something of a first – TUC leader Ken Gill spoke at the CARL demonstration against the new nationality law in March 1988 on behalf of the movement. Also worthy of mention in this context is the greater interest being shown by the TUC in the struggle in South Africa – a central concern of black people throughout the world – as illustrated in the 1988 document, "Beating apartheid: The current crisis in South Africa – and the TUC's programme of action."

But a 1983 survey by the TUC of its affiliated organisations found that only eight unions had black officers. Two years later a survey of the 33 biggest unions carried out by the independent Labour Research Department (LRD) found that 13 of them had appointed officers from the minorities. However many barriers still remain to the full participation of workers from the visible minorities in the trades unions. One is that far more black people work shifts as compared to whites, and this tendency is increasing. It is estimated that just under a third of black men work shifts as compared with one in five among white men. Naturally, shift workers find it harder to attend union meetings and generally to participate in its affairs. Furthermore many Asian workers are prevented from entering public houses by religion or custom yet rooms above bars remain a favourite location for trades union meetings. This practice particularly works to exclude Asian women. Fear of racial attack can also prevent many black workers from travelling long distances at night to attend meetings. The 1987 TUC leaflet, *Black workers – a TUC charter for equality of opportunity* states: "Particular attention should be given to encouraging black members to become shop stewards, branch officials, regional and national officials. This may require specific thought being given to when meetings are held, removing potential barriers or hurdles; for example account might need to be taken of Muslim religious holidays." There has also been some progress in issuing union material in Asian and other minority languages.

Some of these efforts are now starting to pay off not only at the middle level, but actually at the top rank. Lionel Morrison, originally from South Africa, recently completed a one-year term as President of the National Union of Journalists (NUJ) whilst Bill Morris, the Deputy Secretary General of the Transport and General Workers' Union – still the largest in the country – is, after long years of patient activity, about to join the General Council of the TUC, the movement's highest executive body. Morris thus becomes the first black person elected as a central leader of the British working class movement since the days of William Cuffay.

This essential step towards creating the conditions for the unity of the ever more multi-national working class in Britain could not be more timely. Under the recent succession of Conservative governments, unemployment, the fear of it and the ravaging of social security provisions and entitlements has been used to keep down the working people.

The government chose to finance a level of four million unemployed in an attempt to break the power of the unions. It was on this, rather than on any of the country's innumerable needs, that the finite revenue from North Sea Oil was expended. In a vindictive action that left the nation as a whole poorer, spending on health, education, science, research etc. was restricted and slashed, new anti-union laws were brought in and inevitably a green light was given to ruthless employers of the Rupert Murdoch type who drew understandable inspiration for their own anti-union crusades. These attacks were, in turn, facilitated by the shortcomings of the unions themselves – their bureaucracy and their indifference to the needs and concerns of the ordinary members. Margaret Thatcher was able to attack a trades union movement that had been weakened from within. These considerations apply with particular force to black unionists. A 1988 report from the Runnymede Trust showed that black workers are

Mrs Desai, leader of the Grunwick strike

Asian women have been to the fore in industrial struggles

no better off than they were before the Race Relations Act became law 20 years ago and in some cases are in a worse position. The fact is that, if the trades union movement had held out for equal opportunity policies in the 1950s and 1960s, they could have been implemented at a stroke – as we have seen they did not.

In 1987 Chinese workers at the exclusive Wheelers fish restaurant in Brighton went on strike and looked to the powerful Transport and General Workers' Union for support. Decades after the union movement revelled in its discrimination against Chinese seafarers, the union proceeded to prevaricate on the translation of leaflets and recruiting material, withdrew recognition from the dispute and revoked the position of shop steward held by one of the strikers. This in turn facilitated the development towards the formation of a Chinese Workers' Association – a sign of the continuing times in that the Indian Workers' Association celebrates its 50th founding anniversary in 1988. Such independent organisations of minority workers continue to play an essential role.

The task now is surely to build on the gains already achieved within the movement, to be realistic about them, to extend them at every level and in every area and to do so in a way that strengthens the movement and its ability to pursue the objectives championed from William Cuffay to Bill Morris.

50 years of the Indian Workers' Association (GB)

by Prem Singh

The Indian Workers Association (IWA) (Great Britain) is one of the oldest organisations of black people in Britain. Its foundation stone was laid at Coventry in 1938.

More particularly, it is the first as well as the oldest association of Indian emigres in this country, which was given its working class character both by naming it as such and by adopting a programme designed to serve the interests of this class in a broader context as a mass organisation.

From this it becomes clear that its initiators belonged to a revolutionary school of thought. And they represented a new way of thinking which was emerging in India of those days. The Indian National Congress, which was heading the independence movement, was becoming isolated from the younger generation and intelligentsia because of its compromising and collaborationist policies towards the foreign rulers. The resultant consequence of this changing political climate was that a considerable section of activists wielding considerable influence on the masses became disillusioned. They began to look for new ways.

In the meantime, the Communist Party of India became a force to be reckoned with in this movement. They realised that without resorting to revolutionary techniques of struggle, as the communists say, no new impetus could be enthused in the fight to liberate India. Guided by this new thinking many joined forces with the communists and began to organise the working class and poor peasantry, the real revolutionary classes, along these lines.

In Britain, too, such a conflict between the two diametrically opposed political view points had emerged. The IWA stood for the revolutionary overthrow of imperialist rule and its replacement by a type of government which would pave the way for the establishment of a socialist mode of production. On the other side were various combinations including the India League which followed the footsteps of the Congress leadership of India and kept advocating the struggle for limited gains, far short of total independence. However, these differences remained dwarfed in the face of a very hard and long struggle.

Prem Singh – National President of the Indian Workers' Association (GB)

Whatever the circumstances, historical facts reveal that the IWA played a major role in the fight for India's freedom. It raised funds for the movement, carried a propaganda campaign with a view to mobilising public opinion and, above all, the working class of this country was called upon to play its historic role in solidarity with their fighting fellow workers of India.

After the attainment of national independence, many organisations, leagues and groups of Indian migrants in Britain which were working towards this aim wound themselves up. The IWA continued its activities, because its mission did not end there. However, it had a very low profile at this time.

The city of Coventry has earned a unique place in the history of IWA. This uniqueness lies in the fact that it was this city which hosted the inception of IWA to begin with; it was Coventry where the Association was revived later on in 1953, and where it was subsequently centralised in 1958. Further, it is a matter of great pride for us that Coventry still has a very much alive branch, which is part and parcel of the centre.

The IWA's reactivation was effected in totally changed circumstances as compared to those in the early period. This time the composition of Indian immigrants was basically of a different character. The bulk was composed of members of the proletariat and semi-proletariat as well as people from rural backgrounds who had minimal industrial experience and therefore faced trials and tribulations in a metropolitan environment.

The IWA has always identified itself with the cause of the working class because it regards itself as part and parcel of this class. It has been participating and expressing solidarity with the struggles of the workers whenever they were waged. Its whole record bears out this testimony. For this it deserves its share of credence.

In addition to the problems being confronted as workers, racism, with which British society is riddled, has been one of the major problems that the IWA has had to fight against. After its reactivation this struggle has acquired new dimensions. In fighting racism the IWA is guided by its tactical line enshrined in its constitution. Article 3s(v) directs the Association "to organise Indians to fight against all forms of discrimination based on race, colour, creed or sex, for equal social and economic opportunities and to co-operate with other organisations to this end." For the IWA racism is a class issue. It operates as an instrument of exploitation and therefore the fight against it is closely related to the struggle against class exploitation. The Association is of the view that this analysis of racism is in no way contradictory to the conception of broad front. In fact, such a broad front does not become a reality without the overwhelming participation of the working class within it. The IWA will keep on working towards this end until the required success is achieved.

Finally, I must lay the necessary emphasis on the fact that the 50th anniversary of the inception of IWA falls in this year. The main body, which I represent, has planned to organise functions, rallies and other related festivities, marking the anniversary of its golden jubilee, in various towns. A request is therefore being made to a cross-section of people, the media included, to physically participate in these celebrations, and to donate generously in financial terms.

Donations can be sent to Prem Singh, National President, 34 Shamrock Street, Derby DE3 6PT.

Immigration, Nationality and Deportation

Frightened for their lives – Tamil refugees strip on the runway at Heathrow Airport to prevent their forcible removal to Sri Lanka

"You might be forgiven for thinking that even Mrs Thatcher's government would have difficulty in finding yet more laws to introduce to restrict black immigration."

These words, which reflect the thinking of many people in all parts of the community, appeared in a March 1988 article published in the *Morning Star* newspaper and written by trades union leader, John Daly. The General Secretary of the National Association of Local Government Officers

(NALGO) continued: "But you would be wrong: a new Immigration Bill is going through parliament and its sole purpose seems to be to harass black people in this country and keep immigration alive as a divisive 'issue'."

With the third Conservative administration of Mrs Margaret Thatcher unveiling a comprehensive package of legislation – one of the tightest that has ever been hoisted on a House of Commons year as a result of a Queen's Speech – aimed at making the Thatcherite counter-revolution irreversible it would, perhaps, have been too optimistic to hope that we would be spared the burden of yet another racist law.

We were not. The Queen's Speech duly contained provision for a new immigration law. Considering that primary immigration into Britain all but ceased quite some time ago, any fresh legislation can only have the object of further undermining the unity of families and destroying other basic democratic rights.

One of the most disturbing features of the new bill is that it gives summary powers to the police to deport anyone they think has overstayed their temporary leave to remain in Britain. By definition, the act of summary deportation deprives those affected of any right to attempt to prove that they have, or ought to have, a right to remain. The present legal safeguards – inadequate and flawed as they are – would be removed. This includes appeals to the Immigration Appeals adjudicator. In place of at least a semblance of a judicial process alleged 'overstayers' would be simply hustled away to the airport.

A related provision in the new law gives the police the right to deport anyone who claims to be a British citizen but who cannot immediately produce a passport to prove it.

This is more than just a "deport first, ask questions afterwards" policy. It also openly invites the police to engage in "fishing expeditions" – staging raids on members of the black community where they live, work and socialise and threatening those who cannot produce a British passport. Theoretically, a person who lost their passport whilst on holiday could be refused re-admission to Britain despite being a British citizen, although it is doubtful that this sanction would be invoked against white people.

A third provision of the bill makes overstaying a criminal offence for the first time in Britain. This means that overstayers can be convicted and sent to prison for lengthy periods prior to being deported. Each day overstayed will constitute a separate offence.

As stated above, an attack on the right to family reunion is a central feature of the new law. The right of British citizens and others settled in the country to be joined by their spouses and children, a right already compromised, is now to be thoroughly undermined.

It will become necessary for the British residents to prove that they can "support and accommodate" their family member/s before they are allowed residence in the country. As the government clings to the fiction that its immigration and nationality laws are not racist in motivation or content it claims this as a general provision. But it will undoubtedly be used in a racist fashion. A white British person is unlikely to find any difficulty in bringing in his Austrian wife, but a Bangladeshi worker in Tower Hamlets will have a lot less chance of bringing his wife from Sylhet. This reference to "support and accommodate" is sexist as well as racist because these matters must be ascertained without any consideration of a partner finding employment.

Probably the most transparent way in which the bill attempts to stir up racism lies in its provision on polygamous marriages. "Second and subsequent" wives in such cases are to be prevented from coming to Britain under any circumstances. Aside from cultural and religious considerations – and the possible consequences for those women who find themselves in this position – it is important to note that in terms of immigration statistics this is a non-issue.

Less than 30 people in this category a year apply to come to Britain. But the possibilities for whipping up a climate of racism and bigotry through the manipulation of this handful of cases are almost limitless.

Therefore, the new bill is designed both to restrict family reunions and to minimise the potential for organising and building anti-deportation campaigns. On April 21 1988 the bill was read for the third time in the House of Lords and passed. It now awaits the Royal Assent.

The ability of Members of Parliament to intercede to prevent deportations and removals has been successively eroded by government decrees over recent years. The provisions in the new law amount, as explained, to the institution of summary removals. One reason for this is that since the beginning of the 1980s – and to an ever increasing extent – a growing number of anti-

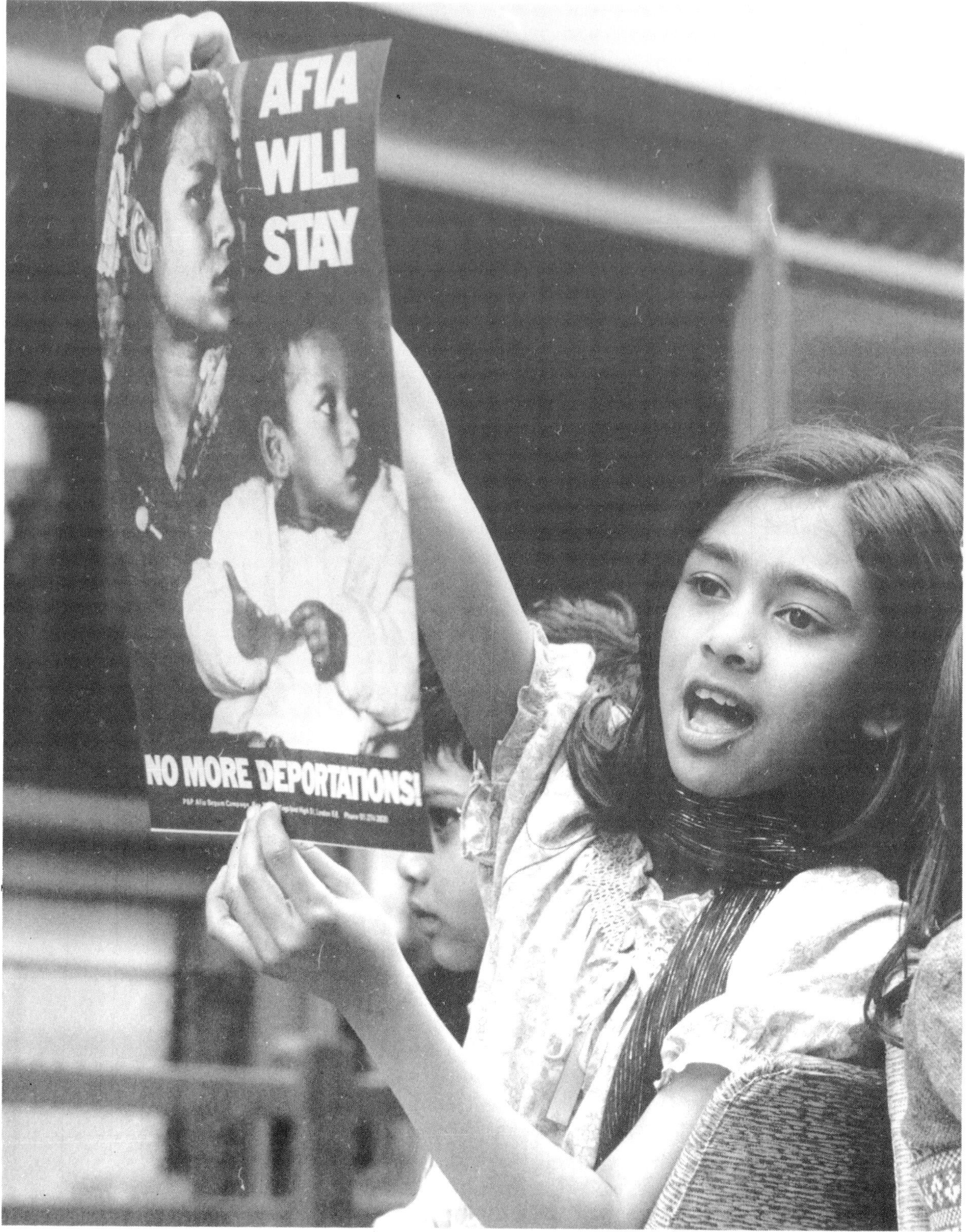

A Brick Lane Protest supports Afia Begum. Despite a massive campaign this young widow was deported to Bangladesh. She had been in hiding in Britain for a number of months before her arrest

Delegates and visitors to the 1988 Labour Party Black Section conference in Manchester visit the Church of Ascension to express solidarity with Viraj.

deportation campaigns have been organised – indeed they have become a vital part of Britain's anti-racist and progressive movements.

These campaigns – employing a variety of tactics – have sprung up with increasing frequency and in nearly all parts of the country. They have enjoyed support from members of political parties, organisations within the visible minority communities as well as those communities themselves, trade unions, students and from all the major religions. By focussing on humanitarian issues they have severely embarrassed the government and damaged its international standing in terms of human rights. For all these reasons and others, anti-deportation campaigns have a good record of success – indeed they constitute one of the few areas where the Iron Lady and her government have "been for turning". But examples of how it is possible to score victories over the government and the state are not something that they would wish to see encouraged.

It follows, therefore, that a major aspect of the bill is a political attack on anti-deportation campaigns. There is, of course, an antidote to each measure – and herein lies the potential significance of the 'sanctuary' movement that is already developing. In the past a number of legal procedures could be gone through before a deportation was executed. An anti-deportation campaign could develop in parallel during this period. With summary exclusion this degree of cushioning is removed and a number of activists are already arguing that only by going into sanctuary in a place of worship, can the necessary time be secured to build a movement. A number of people have already availed themselves of sanctuary which has been extended by various Christian denominations, Hindu temples, Sikh Gurdwaras and mosques. Although the concept of sanctuary is no longer enshrined under English law the authorities have so far shied away from incurring the odium that would certainly follow a forced entry into, and the forcible removal of a person or persons, from a place of worship.

Above all, the sanctuary movement is symbolised by the case of Viraj Mendis who has been in Manchester's Church of Ascension since December 20 1986, after all legal efforts to prevent his deportation to Sri Lanka failed. Viraj is supported by a nationally organised defence campaign and has also inspired a number of other sanctuary cases which rapidly won victory. It is also believed that Viraj Mendis was originally singled out for deportation largely because he had himself been a central figure in a whole series of successful anti-deportation campaigns in the Manchester area.

The case of Viraj Mendis – which has long since become a *cause celebre* for anti-racists – is also connected with the growing attack on the internationally enshrined right to political asylum for refugees – a right that is under growing attack throughout Western Europe. Although he is of the dominant Sinhalese nationality himself, Viraj is known as a strong supporter of the Tamil minority and it is therefore argued that his liberty and perhaps even his life could be in danger were he to be forced to return, either from the authorities or from extreme right wing and chauvinist forces. Amongst the organisations supporting Viraj is Amnesty International.

The power of summary removal is fraught with particularly dangerous consequences for political refugees – and a number of desperate and dramatic airport protests have already been staged by Tamils, Kurds and others. Particularly with the Sri Lankan crisis of recent years, the right wing press and the government have concentrated much of their venom on refugees, particularly on trying to undermine their claims of danger and persecution whilst ignoring the fact that most conflicts in the Third World have their roots in Western interference and oppression, whilst the majority of repressive regimes in the Third World are created and sustained by the metropolitan powers.

The Aircraft Carriers Liability Act is a particularly dangerous piece of legislation. It makes the airline of any country financially liable for carrying people to Britain without the correct papers and also strips such people of the few rights they were previously entitled to claim. This law makes a nonsense of the very notion of being a 'refugee'. By definition a refugee is unlikely to possess all the normal papers. A Jew fleeing from the Nazis in 1930s Germany was unlikely to have first sent a letter to the British Embassy in Berlin requesting an entry visa and an identical letter to the German Ministry of Home Affairs for an exit permit – and there is no reason why today's refugees should be facing a different situation other than in the details.

The fact that airlines are forced into policing the laws of Britain – frequently in countries thousands of miles away – is another matter with serious implications. Firstly, airlines are civilian commercial enterprises not law enforcement agencies. Nearly all of them are surely reluctant to take on this extra role and one can envisage the situation arising where a number of airlines might feel that they have no alternative but to curtail their flights to and from Britain.

The second reason is more particular. This law enforcement role can actually be placed in the hands of the national carrier of the country from which the refugee is trying to escape – what attitude, for example, may we expect South African Airways to adopt towards a would-be black political refugee?

Britain's reluctance to accept Tamil refugees from the conflict in Sri Lanka – a conflict which has its origins in British imperialism's 'divide and rule' and in which Britain has continued to meddle – also contributed to the reinforcement of discriminatory visa requirements, which in turn helped prepare the way for the latest law. After a scurrilous campaign in press and parliament, visitors from Sri Lanka became the first Commonwealth citizens to need visas to enter Britain. This requirement was then extended to visitors from India, Bangladesh, Ghana and Nigeria, as well as ex-Commonwealth Pakistan, helping in the process to prepare public opinion for new laws, and furthermore providing acres of inflammatory reporting for the tabloid press.

Individual and local events also played a role in formulating parts of the new law. It was the campaign waged against the homeless Bangladeshis of Tower Hamlets that inspired the

Britain's boat people – Tamil refugees were detained on a ship at Harwich amidst a climate of racist hysteria

clause on "supporting and accommodating", whilst another clause was also framed in response to a 1985 ruling against Britain by the European Court of Human Rights in Strasbourg.

These women alleged sex discrimination and the infringement of their family life because, although they were settled in Britain, they were not British citizens and, unlike men, were therefore precluded from being joined by their spouses. The court found this to be a case of manifest discrimination and in August 1985 the government changed the immigration rules to put men in the same position as women. Obeying letter but not the spirit of the court ruling they reduced the rights of all, rather than extending the rights of those aggrieved.

But under existing legislation the government was still compelled to give preferential treatment to the wives and children of Commonwealth citizens settled here on January 1, 1971. The rights of these people, based on traditional common law, had been specifically exempted from control by section 1(5) c of the Immigration Act, 1971. Therefore the 1988 law confers no absolute rights but makes all entry dependent on the aforementioned ability to "maintain" and "support".

Most family reunions have in fact now taken place and the remaining number is mainly made up of some 8,000 Bangladeshi families. It is hard to escape the conclusion, therefore, that the main issue is not one of individual numbers but of ideology – the ideology of racism.

The same consideration applies to the British Nationality Act under which many Commonwealth citizens (and those of the Republic of Ireland) lost their right to automatically claim British citizenship unless their application had been received by the end of December 1987. This move – as well as unilaterally revoking a solemn promise given by a previous British government – has also caused widespread fears and chaos at the Home Office department at Lunar House, Croydon – a chaos one of whose effects has, ironically, been to prevent a number of people who wished to leave Britain from doing so as their passports had sunk without trace in the bureaucratic logjam.

It is clear, therefore, that events of the last few years have largely framed the recent legislation. But what is equally true is that we are dealing with the latest in a long line of measures which can only be understood in terms of the relationship between imperialism and the national composition of Britain. The saying promoted by a number of Asian youth organisations in recent years – "We are here because you were there" – illustrates the relationship almost to the point of perfection.

The post-war black presence in Britain arose inexorably from the imperial legacy and it is above all for this reason that black people stake a *right* to make a home for themselves in Britain and why the struggles against deportation and for family reunion are, in essence, anti-imperialist struggles and a continuation of the struggles that brought almost one hundred nations into the era of independence.

Racism and xenophobia have always had a place in the life and make-up of the British (and before it the English) state. In previous centuries the Jewish community was expelled from the country on two occasions. In the sixteenth century Queen Elizabeth I ordered the deportation of all black people living in England and in the next century Oliver Cromwell deported thousands of Irish people to the Caribbean, many of them as slaves. It almost goes without saying that colonialism, the slave trade and imperialism were all justified by racism and in turn served to further fuel racism.

Down the centuries, although the black community in Britain was relatively small, there were periodic calls for the removal of the black presence in British life. At the start of the twentieth century the Aliens Act was passed aimed at excluding Jewish people fleeing from anti-semitic pogroms in the then Tsarist Russia and the countries of Eastern Europe – many of them were considered to be carriers of dangerous socialist ideas. Many of the terms of this act are strikingly similar to those passed in the latter part of the century.

However, despite its relative autonomy, racism is not unrelated to other areas of society's life and, moreover, can be expressed in varying forms. Accordingly, there have been times when black people and other minorities have been invited and 'welcomed' to Britain, when their presence has been considered necessary for military or economic reasons.

People from the then colonies fought for Britain in large numbers during the two world wars and other conflicts. In the years following World War II Britain experienced the 'post war boom' with an unprecedented rise in living standards. The resulting situation of nearly full employment

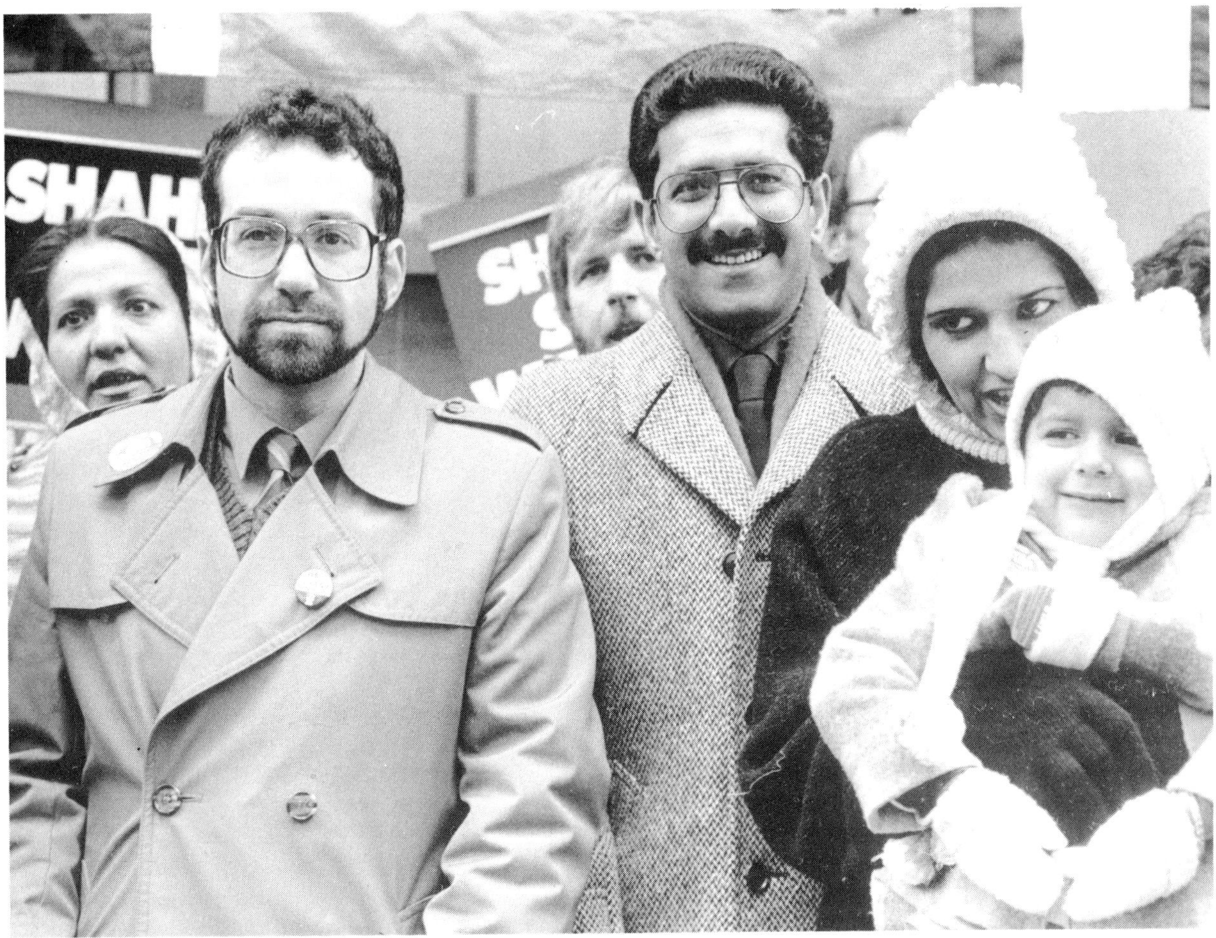

Shahid Syed, an accountant employed by British Gas, was threatened with deportation to Pakistan. His wife suffers from a serious heart condition and it was feared that if she were forced to leave the country she might die. Shahid's campaign was one of a number that has been supported by the trades union NALGO. He is seen here being supported by local MP, Harry Cohen, a consistent anti-racist

meant that people were needed to do the dirty, dangerous, arduous, low-paid, low status jobs that were now being spurned by native workers from England, Wales and Scotland. Thousands came from India and Pakistan to the textile mills of Yorkshire and the foundries of the West Midlands; crews for public transport and nurses for the newly created National Health Service (NHS) came in large numbers from the Caribbean; whilst the new homes and the network of motorways were built by workers from Ireland.

It was during this period that a then government minister – later to become a notorious figure in British politics – went to the Caribbean to recruit workers with all sorts of promises. His name was Enoch Powell.

But the needs of the labour market do not dictate popular prejudice, and the first Race Relations Act was not passed until 1965, before which there were no legal constraints on prejudice and discrimination which were manifested on signs in landladies' windows boasting of a refusal to accept black tenants and the refusal of service in pubs. The contrast with what people had been promised and what they encountered was bitter and ironic. Nor were such attitudes confined to the less educated members of society. The Cabinet papers for 1955, released under the '30 year rule', showed that whilst they accepted the need for black labour, the Conservative ministers had grave fears regarding their permanent presence. Prime Minister Winston Churchill and some of his colleagues were said to have an "almost pathological obsession with questions of the purity of the race".

The Labour Party was scarcely better. In June 1948 – exactly 40 years ago – the SS Empire Windrush docked at Tilbury bringing the first 500 post-war Jamaican immigrants to Britain. Labour's Colonial Secretary (sic), Creech Jones, assured people that they would not survive a single British winter. Their reunion is planned for later in the year!

There was, therefore, a consensus in white British society that lent itself to the introduction of racist immigration and nationality laws whenever the economic climate altered the pattern of labour needs.

The Commonwealth Immigration Act of 1962 was the first major step in halting the movement of black people to Britain and as it approached the statute book there was a desperate rush on the part of many people to come to Britain. In 1965 Harold Wilson's Labour government tightened the controls with a second act of the same name.

These two acts were steps on the way to basing immigration law more and more openly on racist concepts. At the time of the 'Kenyan Asian crisis' of 1968, when people who had been encouraged to retain their British citizenship as part of Britain's continued 'divide and rule' strategy, felt the need to come to Britain, the then Labour Home Secretary James Callaghan laid an act before parliament to restrict their entry.

It was passed without debate, the first of a number of signs that for non-white peoples British passports can be instantly rendered into worthless scraps of paper. Thousands of people became stateless overnight and many endured an agonising wait of years before gaining admission. In history few nations had ever treated their citizens in such a shameful manner. In 1973 the European Court of Human Rights delivered one of its many judgements against Britain – ruling that the terms of the 1968 Act were racially discriminatory.

The Immigration Act of 1971 generalised the provisions of the 1968 Act and introduced the racist concept of 'patriality' whereby those people whose entry to Britain was guaranteed were those who had a parent or grandparent born in Britain – in general terms, white people.

This was again codified by the Nationality Act of 1981 which categorised British passports into various types and considerably lengthened the times spent waiting for family reunion. Historic responsibilities were also ignored, such as those to the people of Hong Kong. The third class citizenship they were accorded left them with absolutely no right to enter Britain. This is a source of concern to many people who fear the consequences of the 1997 resumption of sovereignty over Hong Kong by the People's Republic of China. Whether groundless or not, these fears were real and apply particularly to Hong Kong's minority communities, mainly Indians, who fear a stateless future.

Britain's attitude is in stark contrast to that displayed by Portugal which guarantees full rights to the people of Macau (which returns to Chinese rule in 1999). Mrs Thatcher is even believed to have put diplomatic pressure on the government of Portugal to follow her disgraceful stand.

The racism at the core of Britain's treatment of the Hong Kong people can be seen by contrasting it with the exceptions made for the inhabitants of the analagous colonial enclaves of Gibraltar and the 'Falkland' (Malvinas) Islands. In 'blood and honour' terms it was explained that (presumably in contrast to the 'yellow peril' and the unfortunate refugees from Vietnam who are rotting in concentration camp-like conditions in Hong Kong year after year) these people were of "British stock", had "racial ties" with the country and that "they were British and wanted to remain British".

One expert on immigration law has commented regarding the 1981 Act: "Had it been enacted 25 years earlier, hardly any black man or woman would have qualified for British citizenship".

It is necessary to place on record that almost every year since the Second World War more residents of the UK have left the country than have become resident in it from overseas – over 450,000 more between 1971 and 1983. Meanwhile the wait for divided families in the South Asian sub-continent frequently stretches over four years. Entry Clearance Officers (ECOs) and other British officials have tried by every means to prevent people from exercising their right to come to Britain – imposing long delays, demanding impossibly high levels of proof of familial relationships, seizing on any real or imaginary discrepancy and not infrequently stretching the delay until children reach the age of 18 or marry and therefore become ineligible. And all of this before the latest rules on "supporting and accommodating".

Between 1977 and 1983, 50,750 women applied to join their husbands in Britain. 10,720 were refused, that is more than one in five. The percentage of refusals has constantly increased.

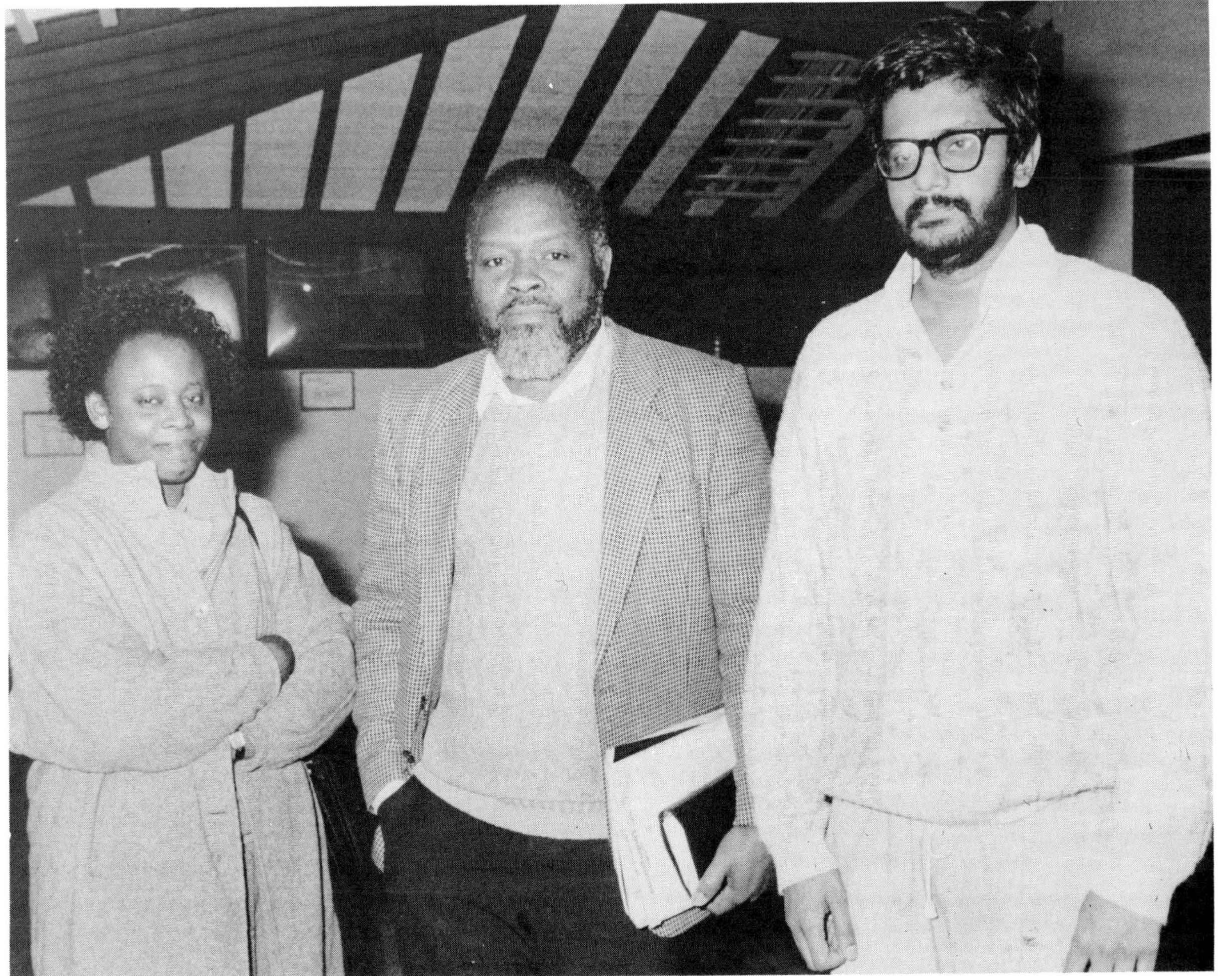

Tottenham Labour MP Bernie Grant in the sanctuary with Viraj Mendis and Tina Olowokanga, a Nigerian mother of six, who is also facing deportation.

Previously, the refusal rate had been around 19 per cent. In 1982 the rate rose to more than 25 per cent and in 1983 to over 30 per cent.

Between 1977 and 1981, 99,510 children applied to join their parents in Britain. 38,300 were refused, that is more than one in three. By 1983 the figures for refusals had reached almost 50 per cent. In Pakistan and Bangladesh the waiting period is up to two years from putting in an application to being given the first interview, and it is only after that interview has taken place that the whole humiliating and bureaucratic procedure begins.

It is a sad fact that Entry Clearance Officers do not have a brief to help applicants but rather to try by every means to keep black people out of the country. Not only are the laws racist but a "climate of racism" is fostered amongst those who administer them. There are, of course, hardly any black people employed in the immigration service.

In 1985 the Commission for Racial Equality (CRE) published a report on a formal investigation into immigration control procedures. On the basis of meticulous research it concluded that the service was indeed operating within a "climate of racism" that bred intolerable behaviour from individual officers.

It said that in Britain Asian families were living in fear of police harassment and immigration "fishing raids" whilst being under the "sword of deportation".

One of the investigators, Ms Juliet Cheetham, said that the rationale behind immigration practice was that all people from poor countries were likely to "cheat and lie" to get into Britain. The report

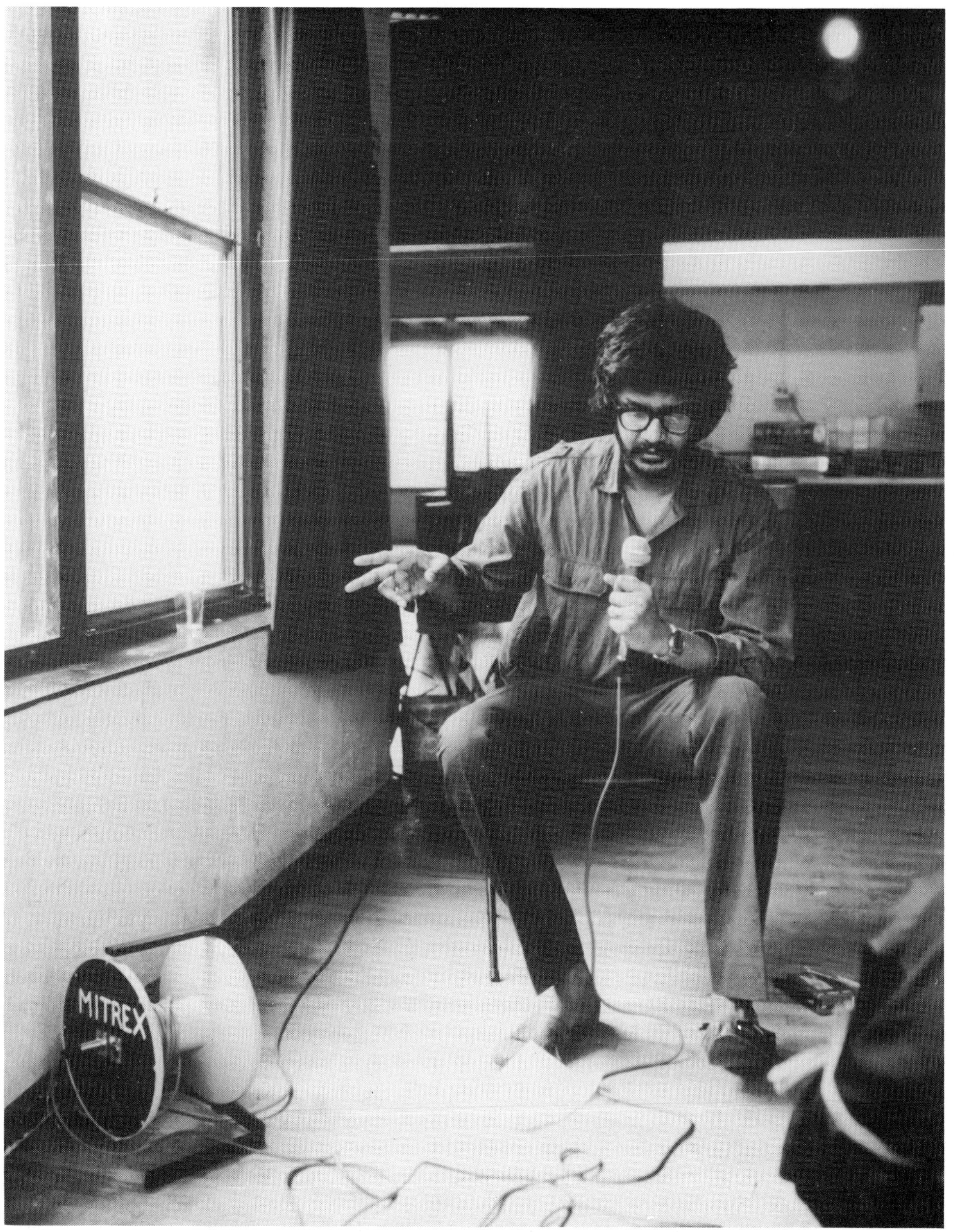

Viraj Mendis, speaking from sanctuary, addresses supporters.

found that Bangladeshi visitors were 30 times more likely to get restricted entry conditions, known as Code 3, than were white Americans.

The report finally proved, if further proof were needed, that the immigration service itself is racist: "Moroccans from the 'immigrant' areas seem, like Mirpuris, to be both simple and cunning." (P 85) "Ghanaians... many are like lost and confused children... like Ghanaians, Nigerians tend to have ambitions and plans out of all proportion to their capabilities and circumstances." (P 86)

CRE staff who observed interviews in Dhaka (Bangladesh) and Islamabad (Pakistan) noted that the ECOs only rarely spoke directly to those they were interviewing and often gave the impression of being bored or irritated. In individual case files words such as "drivel" and "arrant nonsense" were used and in one case the applicant was described as a "bloody liar". A sponsor who attended for interview dressed in a green suit was described as looking "like an Asian Robin Hood".

A note by an ECO on one file warned other officers not to handle it: "I want to do this interview myself. Hands off. This must be this year's strongest refusal."

Whether it is expressed in the views of an individual employee or in the laws framed and passed by parliament, this represents the authentic voice of British racism. It is the voice of those who have raped and pillaged throughout the world, who have treated human beings as chattels and continue to do so to this day. Fundamentally, the control of the labour market by racist laws and the slave trade differ in degree and form not in essence. It is against this that the black community is struggling. It is that struggle that shames Britain before the eyes of the civilised world.

Viraj Mendis

32-year-old Viraj Mendis was born in Sri Lanka on April 1, 1956 and came to Britain in October 1973 to study Engineering at the University of Manchester Institute of Science and Technology (UMIST). By 1975 shortage of money forced him to give up his studies and he took a labouring job in a bakery. It was his experiences there that led him to become a communist. Recalling the period Viraj said: "I worked for 72 hours a week – 12 hours a night, six nights a week... Most of the foremen were white. Most of the workers were Asian."

After losing his job for standing up to racial harassment Viraj took up political activity in the community in Manchester and in 1980 became a member of the Revolutionary Communist Group (RCG). He played a leading role in all the anti-deportation campaigns in Manchester, a large number of which were successful. His own struggle against deportation began in May 1984 when he received a visit from the police informing him that he was an "overstayer". The following month the Viraj Mendis Defence Campaign (VMDC) was formed and since then it has become the highest profile anti-deportation campaign in the country. As a committed supporter of the Tamil people's struggle, Viraj Mendis' life would be in danger were he to be deported to Sri Lanka. Since December 20 1986, he has been in sanctuary at Manchester's Church of the Ascension and his courage has become a source of inspiration to thousands.

Police

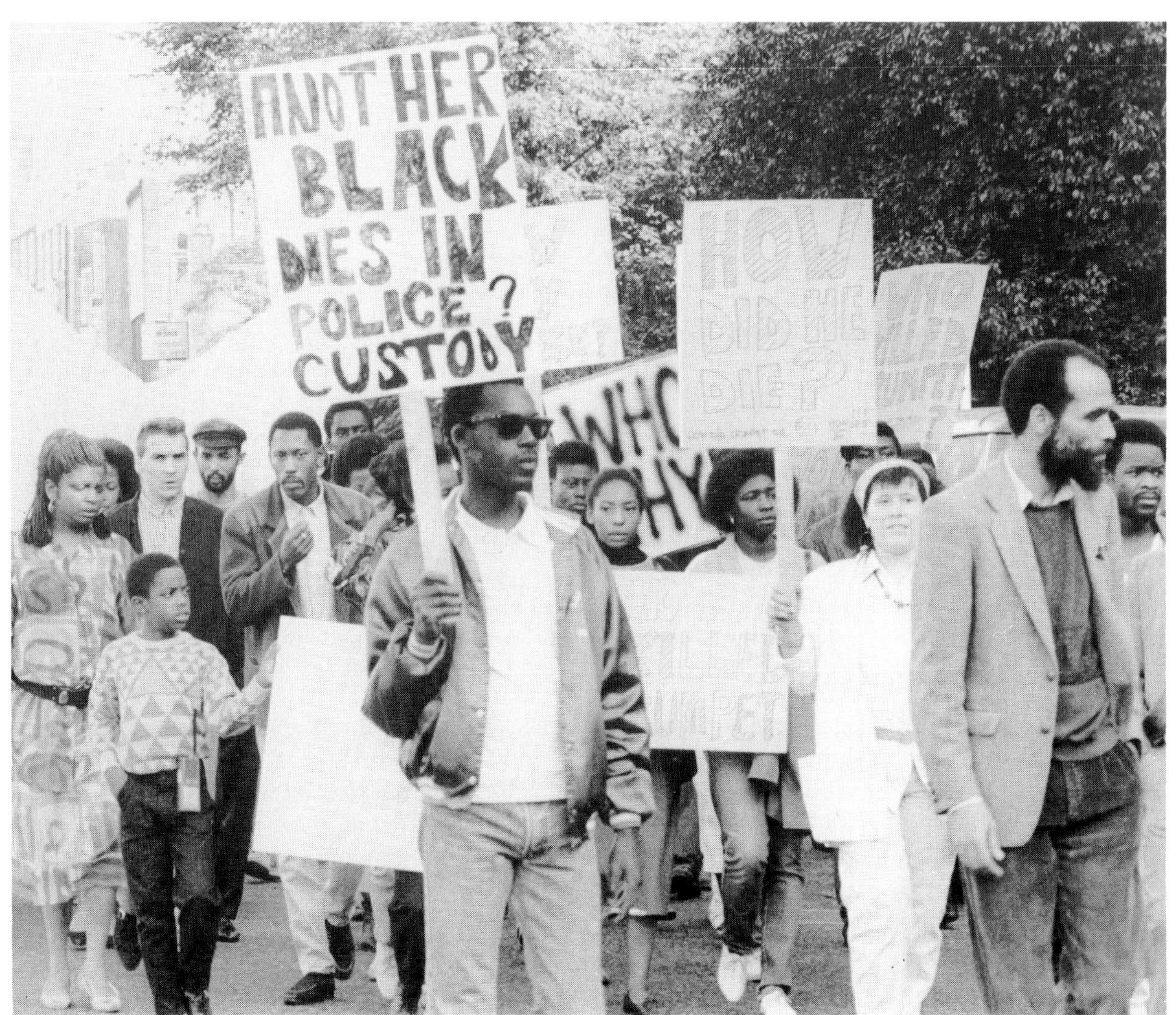

Anthony 'Crumpet' Lemard, a popular local man, died in police custody in the Notting Hill area of west London.

Britain is faced with a crisis of policing that is affecting ever broader sections of society. The police are, in general terms, the frontline force of the British state, with which people, and black people in particular, come into frequent contact. It is the police who enforce the laws and play a major part in defining the attitude of the public to those laws. Considering the economic climate, and considering the types of laws that have been passed and others that are in the pipeline, it is hardly surprising that the attitude of the public towards the police should tend towards the negative. But this stems not simply from the law and the economy, but from the attitudes of the police themselves.

The police frequently complain that they are misunderstood and that they are shouldered with an invidious burden. But against this must be set the overt politicisation of the police – neither should it be forgotten that the formation of the police was a political act arising from the conditions of the time, and that every step in their development has been political.

This overt politicisation manifests itself at the highest and lowest levels. The Policy Studies Institute (PSI) reported that in the Metropolitan Police, "racist language and racial prejudice were prominent and pervasive amongst officers – racist talk on the whole is expected, accepted and even fashionable".

In the higher echelons it is only the form that differs. The outbursts of Manchester Chief Constable James Anderton are notorious, but his is just the most extreme example. Political statements by top police officers are becoming increasingly commonplace – and because they invariably represent the right wing of the political spectrum this trend goes unchallenged; rather it is encouraged by other sections of the establishment.

In 1987 former Commissioner of the Metropolitan Police, Sir Kenneth Newman, made a speech to the Society of Conservative Lawyers in which he identified inner-city areas with their "highest crime rates, the most widespread and most established drug abuse, and the greatest potential for public disorder" as those which presented "a challenge to the style of British policing upon which we have relied since the foundation of the Metropolitan Police in 1829". He went on to state that the police "have to take positive and specific action in such places, carefully managed and persistent action, to prevent the sort of divided society developing of which Lord Scarman speaks, and of which we have seen the nadir in Northern Ireland".

The Director of the Institute of Race Relations, A. Sivanandan, has noted in this context: "But the prevention of 'a divided society' is the business of the government and the political parties, not the police. Conversely, the more a government rules without reference to whole swathes of people – poor blacks, working class, workless – using the consent it gains from some to coerce the obedience of others – and, in that exercise, sets the police against sections of the public – the more it devolves its authority on to the police. Worse, such political use of the police force makes the police themselves more political – to the point where Police Chief Newman could declare, in reference to the possible use of CS gas and plastic bullets, that he was now putting 'all people of London on notice' or the Police Federation imply that a Labour government may not have the co-operation it desires from the police unless it co-operates with the police."

Peter Imbert – new Commissioner of the Metropolitan Police. Change on the way?

The corrosion of the black community's attitude to the police has taken place over a period of time and has reached the extent that possibly the majority of black victims of crime will not call the police for help because they have too many bitter experiences of black victims being treated as suspects and being labelled as criminals.

The riots that have occurred in the 1980s are therefore a product of historical experience, which includes the police standing by when racist mobs went on the rampage in Liverpool, Cardiff and Glasgow in 1919, the identical police behaviour in the west London area of Notting Hill and elsewhere in the summer of 1958 and the years of

Martha Osamor

frame-ups, stop and search, 'sus' laws and deaths in custody.

The report "A different reality", commissioned by the West Midlands County Council in order to probe the wider background to the 1985 riot in the Handsworth area of Birmingham, noted: "The police are viewed by a substantial proportion of Handsworth residents as an ill-disciplined and brutal force which has manipulated and abused its powers in dealings with the black community over a long period of time."

But there had been no shortage of warnings. In 1969 Gus John prepared a report on the area for the Runnymede Trust. The sad fact is that it could have been produced at almost any time. He described the Thornhill Road Police Station as "one of the buildings most dreaded and hated by black Handsworth". He said that it was impossible "to set foot in Handsworth without sensing the tension between police and black people". He found that it took no time "to hear complaints of police harrassment, police brutality, of men reluctant to go and complain at the police station for fear of being beaten up, of youngsters who are stopped and searched apparently indiscriminately".

After the Handsworth riot of 1981 a Home Office research report was commissioned and its findings were published in 1982. The report stated that "so long as unemployment levels remain high in the Handsworth area of Birmingham the danger of riots may remain".

This factual assessment rests uneasily against the public protestants of establishment figures, from Margaret Thatcher downwards, that the riots represent an outbreak of criminality and wickedness, as typified in the Prime Minister's banal statement that "a crime is a crime is a crime".

Therefore when Tottenham police stopped Floyd Jarrett whilst he was driving his own car, charged him with a trivial motoring offence and, whilst holding him at the police station took the keys to his mother's home, let themselves in and began conducting a search for "stolen property", displaying an attitude that led Mrs Cynthia Jarrett to collapse and die of a heart attack, the youth of the nearby Broadwater Farm estate felt that they had numerous historical scores to settle, as well as an immediate one, when they embarked on their uprising. The most serious riot in Britain in a generation, which involved the use of at least one firearm and saw the unfortunate death of Police Constable Keith Blakelock, had been prepared and nurtured by history.

Such being the case, it is hardly surprising that the repression and trials that followed were based closely on another pattern – that of British actions in its colonies, most recently in the north east of Ireland which has served, not least, as a laboratory for British policing techniques.

As Conservative MP, John Biggs-Davison, wrote in 1973, a full seven years before the first major riot, which took place in St. Paul's, Bristol: "If we lose in Belfast we may have to fight in Brixton or Birmingham".

Speaking about the aftermath of the Broadwater Farm riot the local Defence Committee said that the police were engaged in a "massive fishing expedition designed to get anyone, no matter who, in retaliation for the loss of an officer".

In the ensuing weeks 359 people were arrested, some had their doors smashed down at five in the morning and others, frequently children, were held in custody for days without access to either family or a solicitor.

Local councillor Martha Osamor observed: "In their quest for vengeance, they went on to intimidate the community by conducting widespread raids, breaking down doors, threatening people with firearms and arresting hundreds of innocent youths, in a quest to frame some with the murder of PC Blakelock."

With such methods, alongside the use of bought and paid for informers, illegal interrogations and the use of unsubstantiated confessions as sole evidence, it is hardly surprising that three youths were found guilty of PC Blakelock's murder and numerous others were sentenced to savage terms of imprisonment or youth custody. In this case, in particular, the inescapable impression is that the police force had overstepped the bounds of reasonable behaviour and were using indiscriminate force to inflict an act of collective punishment and victimisation – precisely the kind of behaviour that the police are supposed to be combatting.

The determination to see people doing time for the murder of PC Blakelock is a stark example of Britain's sliding scale of justice which has police officers at the top, and black and Irish people at the bottom. The detective who led the illegal raid on Mrs Jarrett's home was neither suspended nor put on trial. He was promoted instead! The police officer who a few weeks previously had shot Mrs Cherry Groce in Brixton, maiming her for life, walked free from court. There is hardly a single case where a British police officer has been judicially punished for an injustice against black people.

Moreover the way that John Stalker, former Deputy Chief Constable of Manchester, was removed from his inquiry, discredited, slurred and ultimately forced from the police force because he took the idea of investigating the policy of 'shoot to kill' in the north of Ireland seriously, can encourage no confidence that miscarriages of justice and abuses of the law by Britain's police and courts may have a legal redress.

The lessons that have been learnt are all negative ones. Thirteen people have been killed by plastic bullets in Ireland and it has been stated that they will be used in the event of future riots in Britain. Over 20,000 of these lethal weapons are held by British police forces – at least half of that number being held by the Metropolitan Police.

Here are some examples of British police terrorism in the 1980s:

* Winston Rose – died in the custody of 11 east London police officers, 1981. No action taken.
* Colin Roach – died from shotgun wounds in Stoke Newington Police Station, 1983. No action taken.
* Cherry Groce – shot and paralysed for life by police officer, 1985. Officer walks free from dock.
* Cynthia Jarrett – harassed to death by Tottenham police, 1985. No action taken.
* Anthony 'Crumpet' Lemard – died in Notting Hill police van, 1986. No action taken.
* Clinton McCurbin – choked to death by Wolverhampton police, 1987. No action taken.

With this being just a part of the record of the police themselves it is hardly surprising that they are notoriously unsympathetic to the victims of racist attacks – an attitude that ranges from low prioritisation and disputing the racial motive to demanding to see the victim's passports and charging them with offences.

Commenting on the death of Clinton McCurbin in February 1987 *Caribbean Times* said: "We are told that the police are trained and instructed to always employ the minimum use of force. But what sort of 'minimum use of force' is it when fit and strong young men in the prime of their lives regularly end up dying?"

The criminalisation policy pursued against the black community means that a disproportionate number of black youths in particular end up in prison. Although the visible minority population in Britain is some four per cent of the total, one study showed that some 25 per cent of the people serving life sentences in British prisons are black, 40 per cent of the inmates of borstals are black and 23 per cent of all prisoners in British prisons are black.

Particularly scandalous is the plight of black women prisoners. In Holloway prison in north London it is reported that over 50 per cent of the inmates are black – the vast majority of them incarcerated for trivial offences not unusually connected to the struggle to feed a family. Naturally no particular community is entirely free of criminal elements but the disproportionate contact that our people have with the state's forces of law and order is dictated by political considerations. The majority of black people in prison have not received justice and simply should not be there. It should also be said that the level of serious crime on the part of the black community is negligible.

Therefore, there is a need for a change of attitudes and for new thinking, not only on the part of the police force but also on the part of magistrates, judges, etc.

Those who hold our liberties in their hands

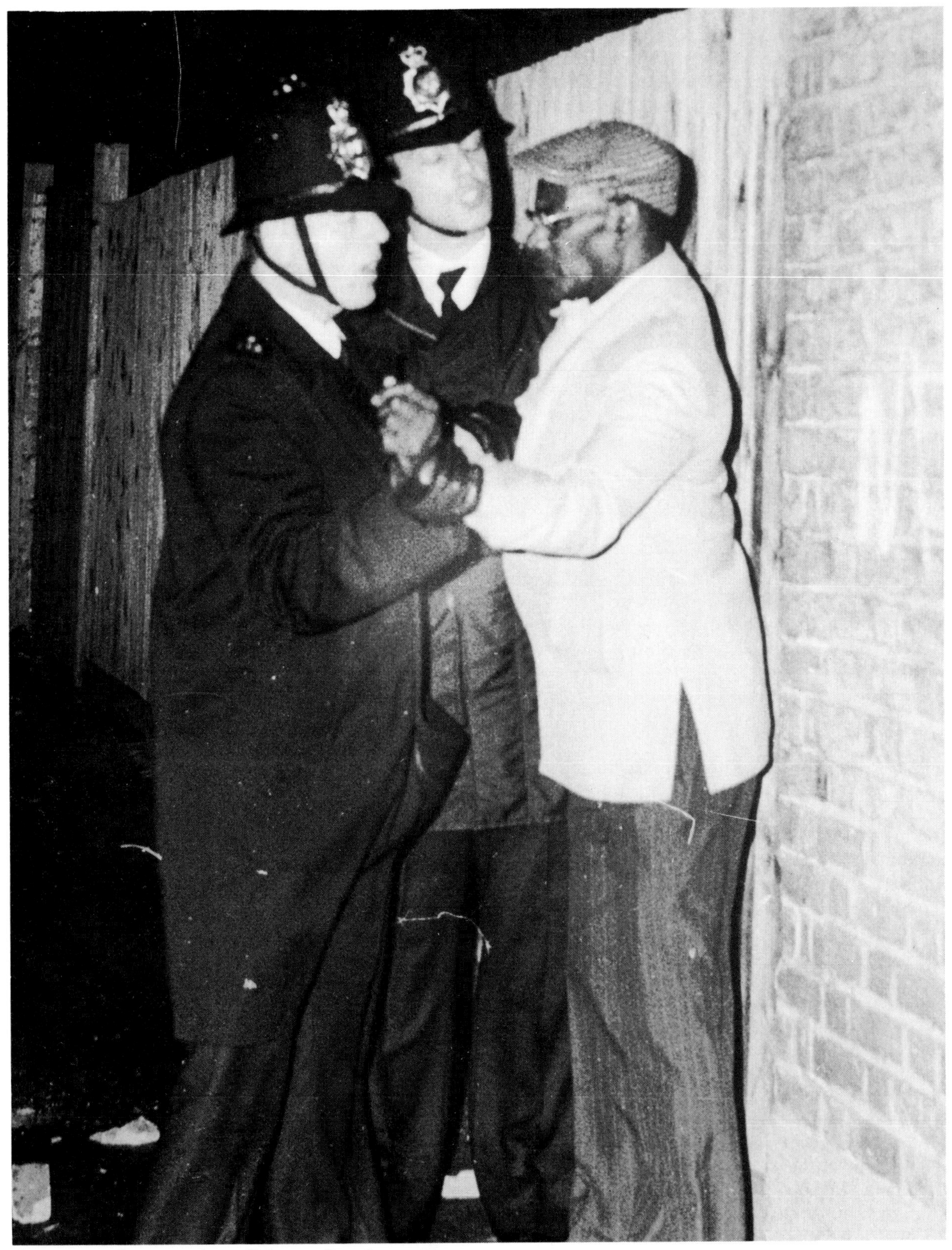

Arrogant and provocative policing on Broadwater Farm

should be in a genuine position to judge when they are being told lies about their fellow citizens and particularly when – as is still too often the case – those citizens are without legal representation or are represented by ill-prepared, half-committed and inefficient lawyers.

The black community's confidence in the police can be said to be at rock bottom. The new commissioner of the Metropolitan Police, Peter Imbert, has said that he wants to change that situation and he has made some tentative moves towards opening a dialogue with the black community. The community will certainly not rebuff any moves in that direction but there must be some caution as regards motivation. It is not to rush to prejudgement to recall Imbert's long period as head of the Special Branch, nor his involvement in the controversial 'Guildford Four' case, nor his 1988 speech criticising the system whereby a person under questioning has the right to remain silent.

If a genuine effort is made, however, it is possible that over time a degree of mutual confidence may return. We may eventually start to move towards a long overdue development – a genuinely multi-racial police force, reflecting latter twentieth century Britain in both numbers and attitudes. At present, it is hardly surprising that so few young black people should seek to join the police force. Many problems could be solved with a change of attitudes and ideas but for that to happen needs more than the efforts and goodwill of one man – even should that man be at the top. It needs co-operation at all levels and here the precedents are not good.

But urgent action is definitely needed. We should not be surprised if the bakeries burn if a whole section of the people are systematically denied even a piece of bread. If such turns out to be the case there will be little sympathy on offer from those who have suffered for so long.

Black Rights (UK)

by Sam Springer MBE DL

Established in January 1982, Black Rights (UK) is one of the leading civil rights organisations in Britain. Following the Scarman Inquiry into the Brixton Uprising of 1981, Barrister Rudy Narayan, supported by *Caribbean Times* **and 16 members of the black community, conceived the idea of an organisation which would continue the work of the** *Caribbean Times* **Free Legal Advice Service and campaign for a Bill of Rights. From this idea Black Rights (UK) was born, with its first Co-Chairmen Rudy Narayan and Sam Springer MBE DL and its first Director Roy Sawh. The present Co-Chairmen are Joe Harte and Sam Springer, with Harold Mangar seconded from the Commission for Racial Equality (CRE) as the current Director. The organisation has always enjoyed the full support of Hansib Publishing and most of Britain's prominent black barristers and solicitors have been known to give of their assistance.**

Black Rights (UK) has scored a number of great successes for individual and collective human rights and has built close ties with the civil rights movement in the United States of America and the countries of the European Community.

Roy Sawh

Black Rights (UK) is an international organisation in the United Kingdom. Its prime objective is the development of a climate within which human rights for all the people can be assured. To achieve this we have taken the leading role in the movement for the entrenchment within the British legal system of an unassailable Bill of Rights which will ensure the protection of the rights of every citizen. The political and legal systems in the United Kingdom are seriously flawed as far as human rights are concerned and Black Rights (UK) is continuing its efforts to remedy this situation. Apart from Australia, New Zealand and South Africa, the United Kingdom remains the only major industrialised nation in the world not having either a Bill of Rights, or the civil rights of the citizen, enshrined within a written constitution. As a result of this, ordinary people frequently find themselves at the mercy of those whose maladministration of the judicial system shows scant regard for the rights enjoyed by the citizens of most other developed countries – *and yet it continues to be the vain boast of the English to be the masters of fair play.*

It is ironic that Britain imposed on its former colonies, written constitutions containing civil rights protective clauses – especially for the benefit of Anglo-Saxon kith and kin where they represented a significant minority. Southern Rhodesia, now the Republic of Zimbabwe, is a classic example.

Britain's appearances before the European Court

of Human Rights are almost equal in number to the total of all other member countries. This demonstrates the need for a Bill of Rights. The necessity to curb the excesses of successive British governments is clearly demonstrated by an examination of legislation enacted and proposed by the current government. Apart from the further curtailment of civil rights which was inherent in the 1987 Nationality Act, sanctions against local authorities, restricting their ability to respond to the needs of their electors, represent a diminution of the right of the people to express their will, at a local level, through the ballot box. Never before has a Bill of Rights been so imperative. The dictatorship of Parliament must give way to the democratic will of the people.

Black Rights (UK) will continue to strive for the removal of impediments to human rights in the administration of the criminal justice system: the restriction on the right to challenge potential juries; the existence of the Diplock Courts in Northern Ireland; the lack of photographic records of identification parades; the absence of a prisoner's right to insist on the presence of his/her chosen legal adviser during questioning; as well as the admissibility of confessions extracted in the absence of the accused's solicitor; the system by which complaints against judges are heard *in secret*. All these militate against the right of an accused person to a fair trial. Their removal is essential and urgent, particularly in a society where racism is endemic.

Another area of reform being sought by Black Rights (UK) is the ending of the anachronistic division of the legal profession into Solicitors and Barristers. We will strive for the fusion of the two professions. It is clear that their division is one of the root causes of the high costs of legal representation. This freqently prevents people from seeking legal redress to which they are entitled, as well as adequate advocacy in criminal and civil matters. There should be an absolute right for anyone accused of a crime to speak directly to a lawyer of his or her choice.

The constitutional changes enumerated above are the reason why Black Rights (UK) was established in January 1982. It has become the nucleus of a civil rights movement in this country, as well as a centre for the coalitioning of those organisations active in the protection of human rights. Conferences and seminars have been held and in November 1988 a conference is planned to involve all organisations interested in civil rights,

Joe Hart, Co-Chairman

Sam Springer, Co-Chairman

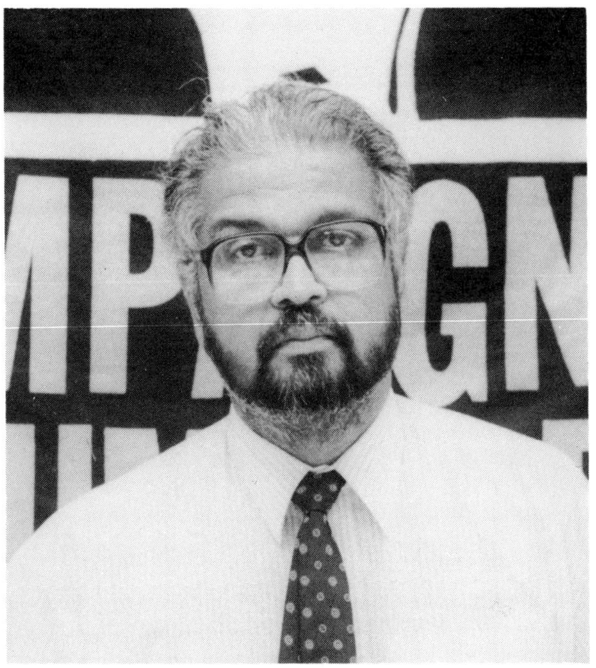

Harold Mangar, present Director

eg. the National Council for Civil Liberties, the Trades Union Movement, etc.

Black Rights (UK) has an international perspective having assisted in the formation of a similar organisation in Holland. As laws within the European Community become progressively standardised it is essential that we work together with civil rights organisations throughout Europe to ensure that the demands for the just treatment of our peoples are articulated. Our concerns are housing, the right to permanent settlement, the right of family reunion, freedom of travel within Europe, freedom from racial harassment, discrimination and the right to vote.

Black Rights (UK) found it necessary to establish an advice centre. Indeed, we inherited the free legal advice service which had been run by the *Caribbean Times*. This work was mainly undertaken by a group of black barristers and solicitors, particularly Rudy Narayan, Tom Kharran, Ashraf Karim, Gulam Meeran, Kuttan Menon and Sibghat Kadri. We continue to host surgeries at our offices (at 221 Seven Sisters Road, London N4 2DA) three times a week, using the services of a team of solicitors and barristers who make themselves available without charge to client or the organisation. Enquiries continue to be received from all over the country covering a wide variety of problems raised by people of all races. Indeed a recent case, which resulted in one of the largest financial settlements achieved by Black Rights (UK), following the resolution of an employment problem, was on behalf of a white person. This ought to finally discredit the views of our critics inside and outside Parliament who allege that Black Rights (UK) discriminates against white people and that the CRE financial support is not used for the benefit of the whole community.

The Nationality Act which came into force on January 1 1988 has the effect of removing the automatic right to register for citizenship. This has affected many black people from Commonwealth countries who did not manage in time to become citizens – effectively for the second time – of this green and pleasant land. It brought a considerable increase in enquiries to Black Rights (UK). During 1987 some 3,000 applications were dealt with by our small staff and volunteers. While we enjoy the support of firms of solicitors who are sympathetic to our aims, particularly where criminal charges have been laid or when a legal opinion is required, the point remains that these cases would be more expeditiously dealt with by our own in-house

Rudy Narayan, Vice-Chairman, creator of Black Rights (UK)

solicitor. This is a very important consideration. We intend, therefore, to recruit a full-time qualified solicitor to our staff as soon as resources are available.

Small cases are as important as those which have hit the headlines – the woman who suffers violence at the hands of her partner, the person who has been sacked for attempting to stop an employer operating discriminatory policies against minority members of staff or job applicants, a child who is being treated as an educational non-achiever because of a teacher's perception that negritude equates with low intelligence, the woman from Bombay who is being refused entry to Britain, by an immigration adjudicator – who could be an ex-South African police officer – to marry her fiancé. All such cases require careful advocacy.

In the important task of providing legal advice we pay tribute to the unselfish support of our legal team – Andrew Gumbiti-Zimuto, Cedric Thomson, John Femi-Ola and Wayne Thompson.

Last year Roy Sawh resigned as Director of Black Rights (UK) to take up the post of Finance Director of Hansib Publishing Ltd. He nurtured the organisation through its embryonic stage and laid the groundwork for the work detailed above. His expertise and commitment have not been totally lost, however, as he remains the Honorary Secretary. Finding a suitable replacement was difficult, but, following an appeal to the Commission for Racial Equality, they were persuaded to second one of their senior officers, Harold Mangar, to fill the post. Harold has worked on the development of race relations legislation over the years. He has also been instrumental in establishing training packages for community relations officers. Harold continues to enjoy the support of Harold Alleyne as Administrative Secretary.

Under the distinguished patronage of the Rt. Hon. Lord Scarman and Rev. Sebastian Charles, the Canon of Westminster, Black Rights (UK) is jointly chaired by Joe Harte B.A. (Hons.) and Sam Springer M.B.E. D.L., while Lionel Morrison, immediate past President of the National Union of Journalists (NUJ), continues to be our able Treasurer.

The case load of the organisation is extremely varied, ranging from wills and probate to matrimonial disputes, child care problems, educational matters, racial and sexual harassment, housing and property, immigration,

Harold Alleyne, Administrative Assistant

discrimination, a range of civil actions and the whole gamut of criminal charges. Our future is precarious as demands on our resources inevitably increase. We are grateful for the support we receive from the Commission for Racial Equality but, if we are to remain the centre of the movement for civil rights, the struggle for a Bill of Rights, and improvements to the status of our people under the law, as well as continuing to provide a high quality of service, we have to increase the financial resources available. We need your support. We appreciate the donations that we receive, often from satisfied clients, one of whom recently provided the funds necessary to purchase a computer and printer. We also appreciate the continuing support of Hansib Publishing. Not only do they publicise the service, but their co-sponsorship of our organisation helps to provide valuable services and facilities.

More, however, is needed. We must be able to employ a solicitor soon if we are to be more efficient in our service delivery. Those interested in helping are invited to contact the Director of Black Rights (UK) at 221 Seven Sisters Road, Finsbury Park, London N4 2DA. Tel: 01 281 2340.

The Urban Trust

Creativity and innovation in the inner city

by Bob Ramdhanie

Given the opportunity, most people would respond to the needs of their fellowmen and women in a very positive and constructive manner. This has been evident on several occasions recently – as Band Aid and Comic Relief, to name but two, have shown.

Within Britain the desire to do something to counter the deprivation found in many of our inner cities is similarly pronounced. The presence not only of government agencies, but the private sector and a variety of voluntary and charitable organisations is testimony to this. The Urban Trust is part of the growing jig-saw of support agencies emerging within the inner city. But what really are we all doing in these areas and who, to use an appropriate phrase 'are sowing the seeds and reaping the benefits'?

Recent experience has shown that money on its own has only a short term impact and many of the projects funded, or in many cases under-funded, struggle from one grant application to another. All too often the commitment and vision of people working within their community becomes reduced to scratching around for financial support. In one sense it would seem that the proliferation of agencies within these areas have done little to have any tangible effect.

As one of the recently constituted charitable trusts, the Urban Trust was born in the wake of the street disturbances of 1985. The pilots of the schemes were greatly concerned about the quality of life within the inner cities and were sufficiently moved to try and do something constructive about it. Thus the last two years have seen a determination to develop a strategy of work within some of our inner cities and this has recently culminated in the appointment of a small team to conduct the work of the Trust.

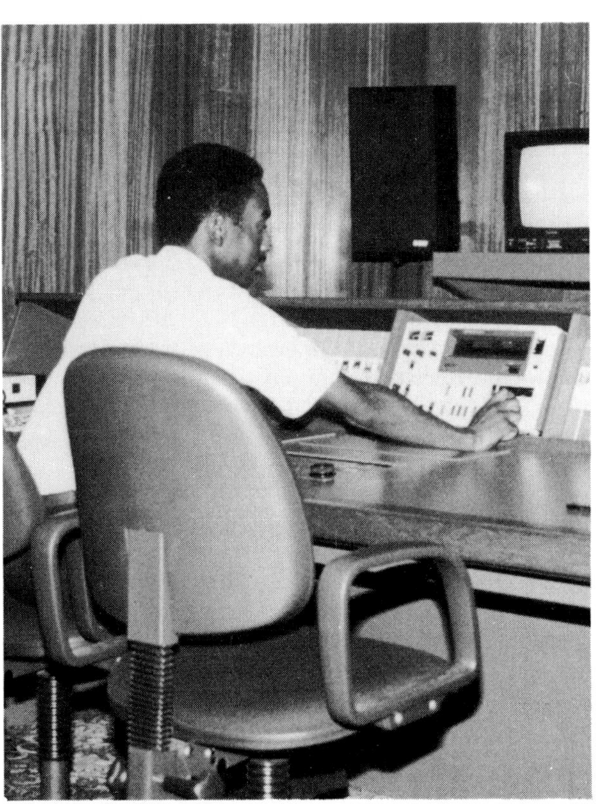

One of the projects funded, in association with others, by the Urban Trust

In many senses, the Trust is seriously handicapped by virtue of its small budget, its national brief and its limited resources, but within this framework also lies its strength. With its limitations, the Trust has to be both creative and innovative in a really tangible way. It does this by working in a manner that complements existing government agencies, other charitable trusts, the private sector and, most importantly, makes sense

Macro Films – Birmingham (video/film training workshop)

to the people and projects within the inner cities themselves.

Primarily, the focus of the trust is geared towards the needs of the black communities within the inner cities and with 75 per cent of both staff and trustees from these communities, it is building on solid, first-hand experiences. The Trust adopts a 'hands on' approach in consultation with projects and provides both cash and 'kind' support in seeing projects through their various stages. Obviously, with its limited resources, the Trust itself will not achieve everything on its own and hence, in creating meaningful partnerships with others, it will bring some degree of economic and social regeneration to some areas across the country. Paramount to its strategy, the Trust is determined to ensure that the necessary skills for long term survival, in whatever context, are grasped, nurtured, developed and implemented by the community groups themselves. In this respect, the success of this new trust will not be gauged by the comments of its trustees or its staff but of the communities with whom it works.

The Urban Trust is based in Birmingham, England, and further information is available from Bob Ramdhanie (Director), or Ian Pearson (Deputy), at 9th Floor, The Rotunda, 150 New Street, Birmingham B2 4PA. Its trustees are:

The First Partnership Bank Project

by Sam Springer M.B.E., D.L.

The background

The problems of black and other ethnic minority communities in attempting to establish businesses have been identified in many inter-city areas. The most common constraints on these entrepreneurs in the development of their business are:-

1. Access to finance, capital and credit facilities;

2. Access to professional business advice and support.

The First Partnership Bank Project, initially researched as the Afro-Caribbean Bank Project, was officially launched by Sir George Young, MP.

The aim of the project was to examine the problems faced by black and ethnic minority entrepreneurs in establishing businesses, and to address these problems through the establishment of a financial institution specifically designed to serve their needs.

Manny Cotter

The concept

The concept of the First Partnership Bank Project has been developed in the London Boroughs of Hackney, Haringey, and Lambeth, and in the cities of Bristol and Birmingham under the auspices of a steering committee. Feasibility Studies have been undertaken to assess demand and market reaction, and to develop the concept within the existing financial system, including approaches to the Bank of England. The objectives of the proposed financial institution are:

1. To establish a financial institution to serve the needs and requirements of the Afro-Caribbean and other minority communities in Britain, through the provision of high-street banking facilities, including the taking of deposits and the encouragement of savings amongst members of those communities.

2. Through such an institution to develop understanding of, and positive assistance to, the business development needs of members of minority communities who wish to establish or expand business enterprises in Britain.

3. To enhance the expectations of the black and

other minority communities by establishing a financial institution, staffed progressively by members of these communities.

4. To ensure, as far as possible, through its financial structure, that such an institution is primarily owned and controlled by the black and ethnic minority communities themselves.
5. To increase wider awareness of the status and economic importance of the communities themselves.
6. To seek to influence the criteria and lending activities of existing banks, by evidence of the success of such an institution.

The early results of the work completed, recommended that a licensed deposit taking institution; ie a Bank, offered the greatest potential out of a range of possible financial institutions examined.

It was also recommended that the proposed bank should have the following targets:-

1. A capital base of a minimum of five million pounds.
2. Deposits of 50 million pounds within three years. On the basis of this level of deposits, the development of a loan portfolio to businesses and individuals, building up to about 1.5 million pounds.

The Committee is chaired by Sam Springer M.B.E., D.L. and has been supported by a group of bankers whose role has been to guide the project along lines which are acceptable to the Bank of England. Their involvement has given credibility to the project and has ensured access to experience and knowledge within the banking community; they will act as a sounding board during the formation of the proposals. This has maintained a balance between what is acceptable in the City and the requirements expressed by the Objectives.

Studies conducted to date consist of a demand assessment and a feasibility study. This demand survey was undertaken by Equinox Consultants and Cooper and Lybrand Associates. It reported these findings and conclusions:

1. There is a very high interest in the idea of a minority financial institution, both amongst businesses and individuals.
2. The majority of respondents have at least one money account and the business repondents were willing to switch accounts to support the institution. The majority of individual respondents would open a new account with the bank.

   Facilities of interest to individuals were the normal bank facilities plus auto-banking, extended hours and foreign exchange transfers; businesses were particularly keen on easier credit access.

3. Experience of racial discrimination was reported by a number of respondents. Nonetheless there was a universal wish for the institution to avoid *any* form of discrimination.

4. The Location was not considered a critical factor providing inter-bank facilities were available.

5. Bank deposit accounts and building society accounts were held by approximately 20 per cent of the respondents.
   The feasibility study was undertaken by Harold Russell, a Banker and Financial Consultant based in Barbados. The Feasibility Study addressed the development concept including discussions with the Bank of England and major clearing and merchant banks.

The findings and conclusions of the study were:

That the most appropriate institution would be a licensed deposit taking institution.

That a draft application for a licence be made to the Bank of England, following further work on the financial structure, management arrangements, and business plan development.

As part of the study, the initial views of African and Caribbean Banks were sought and support was received in principle for both equity participation and reciprocal banking arrangements.

At this point it is worth stressing that the Steering Committee takes the view that there would be no difficulty in obtaining initial equity funding from financial institutions once the bank is formally constituted. However, as stated in the objectives, it is the firm intention to ensure that effective ownership and control is retained by the black and other ethnic minority communities themselves. There will be a campaign to attract financial support from individuals and businesses, at the appropriate time to accumulate the necessary capital.

Benefits

The work conducted to date has identified the following points regarding establishing the First Partnership Bank:

Mobilisation of the personal savings of the minority communities to promote growth.

The attraction of savings from those people currently without bank accounts.

The operation of a non-discriminatory policy.

The introduction of business practices, skills and opportunities to members of black and other ethnic minority communities.

The training of members of minority communities for employment in the banking sector.

Increasing the employment of black and other ethnic minorities in the wider banking industry.

Lowering of available interest rates by providing an alternative to existing lending organisations.

Increasing the available finance for minority business.

The First Partnership Bank Project believes that a bank owes its customers more than just an account. It would like them to take a stake in this new venture so that it becomes their bank, administered and owned by them.

The First Partnership Bank will consider more than just the banking business alone, it will help customers to get a better idea of how to handle their everyday finances, how to set up long range plans, how to get business projects off the ground, and how to put the bank's services to work, helping them to help themselves. The staff will be trained to do more than just open accounts and take deposits. They will be trained to help customers take advantage when they are ahead and advise on how to get out of trouble when behind. In short, it will help solve financial worries and look for the most profitable approach to personal money management.

These studies also produced an assessment of whether branches of the First Partnership Bank in these areas are potentially viable; whether they would have an impact on local problems; would be supported by local businesses and individuals; or whether they should be implemented in a particular way to reflect local conditions and requirements; whether they would open up longer term benefits and opportunities.

Further interest

The areas where all the studies were completed have indicated there is a general wish to see a national institution developed. Demand for this has been identified in a number of quarters over and above the Boroughs and Metropolitan areas. Principally, this has arisen as follows:

Through the medium of the Forbes Trust, interest has been shown in assisting the creation of a business plan to carry the concept forward.

The main banks and government agencies of the Westindies have shown an interest in the establishment of a minority banking institution through which they could develop their services to the Afro-Caribbean population and to trade between the UK and the countries in question.

The way forward

It is proposed that the next stage of development should consist principally of the formation of a Main Board designate comprised of individuals with banking and financial expertise and with standing in the eyes of the Bank of England and the City. This Board designate would be the main vehicle for seeking a banking licence from the Bank of England.

Sam Springer

In addition to the Board there will be a Group to ensure that the Policy, and special interests to be served by the new banking institution will be represented in full without detracting from the business orientation of the Main Board designate.

First Partnership has a new line of thought. This centres particularly on the acquisition by First Partnership Limited of an existing banking institution with a licence to take deposits. Financing this acquisition would be by means of attracting funds by subscription from the black community, and Afro-Caribbean, African and Asian government-owned banks. A Trust vehicle, First Partnership Limited, will be suitably constituted to attract and retain those funds until acquisition was completed. No indication of acquisition and associated costs has yet been ascertained.

First Partnership Limited has made enquiries and has identified two or three suitable candidates which might be acquired.

It remains essential that Board Members of the new institutions be identified, as acquisition of a licensed bank would not be permitted by the government and the Bank of England unless there was full compliance with banking protocol and regulations as laid down by the 1979 Banking Act.

Business plan

In addition to the identification of a Board designate, it will be necessary to present the Bank of England with a fully developed business plan. This will be a substantial document in order to comply with the required standards of the banking industry. Preparation of it will also involve significant funding in order to attract the appropriate skills in financial, legal and corporate areas but First Partnership believe that this support will be achieved from Minorities' National Banks.

The costs associated with the preparation of a business plan will be substantial. These will be in addition to acquisition and setting-up costs.

Pre-business plan

First Partnership, the corporate entity, requires documentation to represent its interests to other agencies. It is therefore proposed that a pre-business plan be drafted which, together with a prospectus, can be used to raise interest and funding. This funding may come from City institutions and/or from national governments, as well as subscriptions from the ethnic minority communities to be served by the new banking institution.

The pre-business plan will need to articulate the following questions:

- ★ what is the concept?
- ★ what are the objectives of the banking institution?
- ★ what role will the community have in its formation and management?
- ★ what are the criteria to be met to acquire a licence to take deposits?
- ★ what size of equity base is required as a minimum?
- ★ what range of services will be offered?
- ★ what geographical locations will be served?
- ★ what social objectives will be established?
- ★ who will be the Main Board members?
- ★ who will be the key managers?
- ★ what staff recruitment policies will apply?
- ★ what relationships with other funding institutions will be established?

The answers to these questions would create the distinct profile for the intended bank which could be marketed both to financial institutions and to the community to attract their interest in principle. It will also be used to underpin a prospectus which would address some of the same issues, but which would be the marketing tool.

Together, the prospectus and the pre-business plan would provide the documentation required to interest sources of funding, necessary both to finance the development of a proper business plan and the eventual acquisition of an existing bank.

Conclusion

The concept of the First Partnership Bank, formed principally to serve black and other ethnic minority communities at retail banking and small business level, is now of a long-standing nature. It has taken a substantial period to bring it forward to its present status because it has depended on the energy and commitment of a small group of individuals with limited access to funds. It is clear that demand has remained considerable and that the concept has a place in the financial establishment of Britain. Research into existing clearing bank services does suggest that they fall far short of the expectations of the black and other ethnic minority communities. There is no evidence that they intend to take any initiatives of a radical or fundamental nature to redress this situation. The opportunity for a new institution is therefore significant and substantial.

The pre-business plan, which will act as an invitation to finance the preparation of a full business plan, will itself answer critical questions. It must demonstrate that there is a practical and realistic prospect of a new institution surviving. It will convey a truly commercial attitude and an awareness of banking requirements. Considerable care will be given to the presentation and content of the prospectus and the pre-business plan so that both can be circulated with confidence.

There is no doubt whatsoever that the First Partnership Bank can tap a body of demand in the community. Its success in doing so hinges on the image it establishes from day one. We believe the sensitive nature of this image will sit comfortably with commercial objectives; the latter will constantly tend to dominate the former. The Group would stand behind the Main Board of the bank and play a key role.

We should not underestimate the complexity of the task of establishing a new financial institution in Britain. The regulations are exacting, and the transition from a Project to a Bank needs careful handling. Nonetheless we do not at this stage see any fundamental problems, providing the necessary level of support both financially and morally is available.

There is a firm intention to establish a financial institution to serve the needs and requirements of the black and other ethnic minority communities.

We have to build a bridge between the Community and the Institution. We must be seen to be the only bank that works hand-in-hand with the Community, in order to establish a mutually beneficial partnership, thereby creating Unity with the Community.

The First Partnership Bank welcomes Third World participation.

The UK Caribbean Chamber of Commerce

The UK Caribbean Chamber of Commerce (UKCCC) is a members organisation which was set up in 1976, by men and women from all walks of business and professional life, to deal with the time-consuming tasks of undertaking market research and providing information and support in various aspects of business.

During its dynamic history, the Chamber has been unstinting in its efforts to "lobby for progress" – making representations to governments at the highest level, both central and local; and initiating practical solutions to problems hampering the development of members and other interest groups.

Such efforts on the Chamber's part brought about the British government's recognition of the need to establish Enterprise Agencies in the blighted Inner City areas, with the specific intention of assisting actual and potential entrepreneurs.

As a direct result of the Chamber's involvement in promoting its members and other business groups, there has been a marked increase in the number of small businesses throughout the country, and the Chamber is now on the threshold of increasing the growth and success of such businesses at a greater level; as we embark on another decade of highlighting the positive contribution made by our members and other small business groups to the nation's economy. It is undoubtedly a credit to the UKCCC when we consider that "out of one organisation comes forth many businesses".

Having reached a first milestone by celebrating our 10th Anniversary (in 1986) it was obvious that the vision of the Chamber had not changed significantly. However, in addition to its original objectives, the Chamber now offers information of relevance to its members and the wider business community, pertaining to their business, trade and profession, and from time to time, updates them with pending government legislation and legislative changes which may affect them, directly or indirectly.

Role

The role of the UKCCC may be defined as:–
"To preserve, protect and defend the rights of its members in the development and prosperity of their businesses and, however controversial, strive to achieve a better deal for members and the community they serve, from governments (both local and central) and financial institutions".

Sponsorship

Through its members, the UKCCC has, from time to time, given sponsorship to students specialising in certain faculties. It is a policy which, it is hoped, will continue in the foreseeable future.

Social Activities

Future social functions and open day meetings will be geared to the specific needs of our members.

Membership

Membership of the UKCCC is granted to companies and individuals engaged in trade, commerce or industry, and certain professional bodies. Membership subscriptions are approved by the Chamber's Executive Council and are payable by categories. The definitions of such categories are determined from time to time by the Chamber at General Meetings.
The present annual subscription is £40 for small firms, extending to £120 for multi-national companies.

Why join the chamber?

Let Members do the talking:

"...because I am a small businessman, I find it cost effective to utilise the Chamber's secretarial, telex and other professional services..." *Mr R.G. Gooden, Tottenham.*

"...to take up the opportunity of improving our business skills by attending professionally-organised seminars such as Marketing, Finance, Commercial Law and other aspects pertaining to business matters..." *Mrs J.E. London, Waltham Forest.*

"... by meeting with other members in other areas of business, we can exchange ideas and gather information to enhance our business and our projects..." *Mr S. Dekker, World Promotions Limited, Liverpool.*

"...my import/export business utilises the information which the UKCCC receives from Caribbean countries..." *Ms P.L. Sinclair, Hackney.*

"...I introduced my colleague, who wanted to start a fashion business, to the Chamber. She found the staff most helpful and, as a result of the information and other assistance received, she is now running a business in Wandsworth..." *Ms Y.J. Odero, Battersea.*

"...my company makes regular daily transactions in the UK and Europe. Because of certain difficulties in Guyana, we now rely considerably on the effective services provided by the UKCCC..." *Mr L. Williams, The Crucible Group, Georgetown, Guyana.*

After attending *BUSINESS FOCUS '86* (the Chamber's annual Exhibition, and Europe's largest event of its kind) *Mr Gidden of Birmingham* wrote:

"...we attended the successful event last year and every praise should be given to the UKCCC for all of its terrific hard work... The Exhibition provided a great Marketing forum, with endless business ideas and contacts nationally and internationally for exhibitors and the public. It proved to be a most apt focal point of the year for small businesses in the UK..."

Exhibitions

Since 1986 the UKCCC has co-sponsored the now annual *Business Focus Exhibition* (together with the London Borough of Haringey and the Department of the Environment through its Urban Programme). This event, which is organised and managed by UKCCC and Trade Limited, has since provided the logical and now proven venue for multifarious entrepreneurs from Britain and overseas to meet, plan and promote their products and services to a captive audience.

UKCCC Business Services Unit

Information

It is true that many heads of companies are unaware of the vital role that information can play in the success of their business. The UKCCC believes that information is a most valuable resource in the armoury of the modern business person. Armed with the correct information, businesses become more competitive, thus aiding their development and growth, saving time, encouraging effective and accurate decisions which increase sales and create greater profitability.

Therefore, the *UKCCC Business Services Unit* is set up with the small business person in mind, functioning as follows:

(a) Trade information through a monthly Newsletter; dealing with business inquiries; import and export trade inquiries; trade regulation files and economic data.

(b) Trade promotions – assisting in the organisation of bilateral trade missions; conferences; seminars and product promotions; distribution of promotional materials and trade directory through the Newsletter.

(c) Negotiating reciprocal agency agreements between members and companies in the UK, EC, Caribbean and other prominent trading areas.

(d) Negotiating preferential rates for cricket matches, travel, car rental, self-drive and chauffeur-driven cars and the theatre.

(e) Providing in-depth management training and specially planned educational seminars.

(f) Conducting market research in the UK and the Caribbean.

Because the majority of the Chamber's UK-based members are small businesses, it is generally assumed that many may suffer from a lack of modern administrative facilities and trained personnel to carry out the time-consuming tasks of office administration. And, since many of our overseas members frequently require administrative and secretarial support, the Business Support Unit will provide the following:

Telephone Service: Messages taken and forwarded by trained personnel.

Secretarial Services: Letter-writing, phone-in dictation, typing and word processing.

Mail, Telephone, Telex and Facsimile Services: Incoming communications are dealt with in accordance with members' instructions.

Confidentiality assured at all times.

Documents and File Storage: Secured file storage for correspondence.

Boardroom: Available for up to 15 persons, on an hourly basis, for small seminars and meetings. Secretarial services optional.

(Contact the UK Caribbean Chamber of Commerce, 99 Stoke Newington Church St., London, N16 OUD.)

Black, British women

By Jenny Rontganger

There is a new woman emerging. Standing tall and proud among the ruins of a 'lost homeland' and a much abused identity. She is the woman of the 90s, a vessel which will carry many to better, greater things; a constant in an era of change. By her name, and despite her name, she has become for all of us, our future. Her name is woman, black woman.

Yet seven years ago the British black woman would have been unable to secure her independence. Aside from prejudice, a married woman was not regarded as an employee within her own right. According to British law she was quite simply an extension of her husband and it was *he* who received the total sum of marriage allowance and tax relief. In fact, this rule applied to almost everything a woman attempted to achieve.

If she wanted to buy her own home, or even a car, unless she was a middle class white woman, she needed a male guarantor, be he her husband, father or lover. Quite simply a woman was regarded by the banks and such-like with the same liability as an unemployed person, the question being – 'how will she afford to pay it back?'

Society prevailed upon keeping the woman at home where they believed her to be more useful, and she in turn depended totally on her husband to live day by day. Thoughts of escaping from sometimes bad marriages were quickly dismissed. Thee was no option for a woman to be independent, especially a woman with children.

Employers invariably refused children into the workplace, deeming them as a distraction, and an unnecessary insurance liability. Anyhow, a woman with children should stay at home or get herself married – men's words that fell on stubborn, determined ears.

This was a time when the future looked none too bright for the black woman in Britain. Knowing herself to have been born at the bottom of the socio-economic pile, she admitted that to survive and to progress things had to change. Through her children she sought that change.

We are the completion of a web spun by our parents and our homeland. We are our oppressors' nightmare – educated, independent, successful. We are a new generation of black, British women who have transcended the limitations and barriers of colour. We are more than even our parents dared to hope we would be...much more.

The fight for self progression

If we had been born in our original countries as our parents before us, then the outcome of our progression would have been very different. However, our development has in part been instigated by this new social and political environment, Britain.

The first major hurdle to overcome was the automatic stifling of our natural mental capabilities. Sitting in racially mixed classrooms with friends we considered as 'equals' the first trip to the careers officer was enough to disabuse any such childish convictions. I wanted to be an architect, a lawyer, a pilot or even a great writer. They suggested nursing. On the other hand, white friends wished to be secretaries, typists and even nurses. They were told to push to the limit of their capabilities and become doctors, lawyers, architects and writers. That is an unforgivable, yet common, mistake. My blood ran thick with stubbornness and, more so, with an anger that was to prove to be my ally in my fight to succeed.

The similarities between our situation and the incidents that had plagued black Americans did not go unnoticed by our parents. When we returned from school feeling disillusioned with the whole educational system, it was they who taught us the words of Martin Luther King and Marcus Garvey. It was they who gave up all so that we could succeed, who suffered so that we could achieve, who gave us the inheritance of a culture that was blatantly ignored in our classrooms.

Statistics have often proved that children of Afro-Caribbean descent succeed in school where their white counterparts fail. We didn't need statistics to prove that – our needs were greater, our urge to succeed surpassed any mental and physical barriers held daily before us. We had no choice, to do well we had to be four times as good as any man and five times better than any white man. We knew the odds and the fight was on to balance those odds in our favour.

This was an age where we were given no chances. We *took* every opportunity and made them work for us. No longer were we to be pushed into lesser positions of subservience, in or out of the home. We were determined to be met as equals, to make our mark on society and succeed. Possibly for the first time in our history as black, British women, we felt perfectly capable of becoming our own breadwinners, despite the heavy costs.

The career woman

It's never been easy to succeed in any one chosen career be you black, white, male or female. But for us, being black *and* female made the task an almost impossible goal. Labour activist, Sharon Atkin, who is the women's officer for the Labour Party Black Sections and an executive member of a new group called Women for Socialism, states: "In this society as a black woman you're definitely bottom of the socio-economic pile. In the Caribbean while there are a number of women who would be classified as 'disadvantaged' I think there are equally numbers of women who are holding positions of authority, active within politics as well as within business. In Britain that is not the case."

However, Yvonne Richards, a highly successful advertising executive currently working for *Reader's Digest*, holds the viewpoint that success is relative to your own perception of yourself and your worth. She attributes her escalating success to confidence in her abilities and maintains, "the prejudices I faced as a black woman are no different from the prejudices faced by being a woman. We've always been the passive, subservient element...not a total person. However, inherent prejudice will always face the minority and I believe that people preoccupied with the negative can never discover the positive."

Though black women are as yet not represented proportionally within society's main professional bodies, we have begun to make a considerable dent in a variety of businesses.

Black women have turned their hand to professions, both diverse and commonplace. Artists, poets, architects, doctors, lawyers, politicians, writers, singers, actresses, sportswomen, newsreaders, teachers, retail manufacturers, fashion designers, models and even grocers – we have bombarded the market with saleable products. The barriers have been stretched, the limitations breached. We have come into our own. Finally.

Yet there is still one major problem for women that some companies see fit to ignore, and that is the difficulties faced by working mothers. Some firms such as BP, ICL, Marconi and Rank Xerox are pioneers of extensive maternity leave given mainly because they cannot afford to let expensively trained employees disappear from their workforce. However, this is a scheme that is usually angled at high-fliers and leading female executives. Support staff who are easier to recruit and cheaper to train may well be left to fend for themselves.

The law states that if a female employee is not covered by a company scheme then, having worked for a company for 26 weeks to two years, you may get a maternity payment of £34.25 per week for up to 18 weeks. If you have worked for two years at 16 or more hours a week, or five years at eight-16 hours a week, you receive nine-tenths of your average earnings for the first six weeks' absence, and £34.25 a week for the remaining period of up to 12 weeks. You have the right to return to your job (or a suitable alternative) up to 29 weeks after your baby is born – that is unless your employer has fewer than six employees. Either side may delay up to a further four weeks if there is good reason.

Many women after having their baby may show a preference for returning to work on a part-time basis. However, there are certain companies that will fight this decision into the courts. The legal profession is one that is reluctant to accept that partners should be allowed to work on a part-time basis, but the Law Society's Working Party on Women's Careers is trying to change this attitude.

Paternity leave is another controversial issue, and Britain alone in the European Community drags its feet over legislating for fathers.

Some employers are making headway on the issue, such as Channel 4, which offers three weeks, Camden Council which offers 10 days leave, and Edinburgh University which allows seven days' leave.

Women who choose to bring their children along to work with them are still facing the problem of finding a suitable creche. But again some companies, which are sympathetic to the needs of their female employees have gone to great lengths to provide fair employment.

Penguin Books, for example, as of April 1988 pays between £17-52 a month to female, or indeed male, parents earning under £14,500 a year who have pre-school children. To finance this, Penguin pays £10 per employee per year into a special fund. Other establishments such as the civil service argue that the cost of premises makes daytime nursery care prohibitive. Yet the BBC has scorned such finer detail and is in the process of building a creche for employees at its new White City headquarters, due to open in 1990.

Within London there is a charity that cares for the needs of working mothers called City Child. They are currently trying to find premises for much needed child-care facilities. The first City Child creche opened at the beginning of 1988. Yet in spite of all these enterprises, company child-care schemes will be a rarity so long as the tax man refuses to link them to tax incentives for employers. For employees, child care is assessed as a perk, not an essential, so you have to pay tax on a place in a creche. Obviously, this is not an encouragement, particularly for those on low salaries.

Changing attitudes

As stated earlier, our development has been, to a great extent, instigated by Britain's social and political environment. There is a larger incidence of women who despite having been born two rungs down the ladder of achievement, now have the opportunity to assert themselves, to assess themselves, and to burn their ambitions full flame. This change has not only provoked a shift in attitude by women themselves, it has also affected the male/female relationship.

By heritage the male has always been the most prominent base of an Afro-Caribbean family, with the female playing a supporting role. Women were expected to work alongside their menfolk during the day and yet still have the supper ready at the table on time, the house clean, and the children well clothed. Arguably this is a role that women throughout the ages have played host and homage to. Change is pre-eminent.

The male ego stated that he should be the sole breadwinner and naturally his wife should bear his children and keep house. Since previously there

Yvonne Richards – Sales Manager for Reader's Digest

were no facilities to accommodate a working mother, this household rule went unspoken thus unchallenged. Additionally the jobs on offer to women meant that it was not worth their while to work unless the domestic financial situation was particularly unstable.

Nowadays, while many women have chosen to follow a career, domestic inequality still exists. Younger couples with a 'nouveau' relationship have split household chores and payments down the middle with each contributing an equal share. However, older couples are still facing the old problem.

Traditional Asian families have been particularly hard hit by these changes. Arranged marriages are being scorned by many men and women alike while the business world has seen a considerable influx of Asian entrepreneurs. Women are altering their subservient role as housekeepers and have broken the rule of not speaking until spoken to.

Ours is a path that has been well trod by women and black people internationally. A path strewn with dilemmas and choices almost too painful to make. Ours is a struggle that is still continuing but will flourish within our children, thus reaching a successful maturity.

(Jenny Rontganger is the Managing Editor of *Root* Magazine)

Olaudah Equiano and the Black British Experience

by David Dabydeen

In 1789 an African, Olaudah Equiano, published his autobiography in Britain entitled *The Interesting Narrative of The Life of Olaudah Equiano.* The book was an instant success. Between 1789 and 1827 it ran into seventeen editions, and it was translated into Dutch and German.

As the two hundredth anniversary of its publication approaches, it is time to take stock of the significance of the work for Equiano's contemporaries as well as for us in present-day Britain. (The book is being reprinted by Longman in 1989 but is still available in a Heinemann paperback edition, edited by Paul Edwards, the African literature critic at the University of Edinburgh).

In 1788, John Newton, an ex-slave captain, describing the interior of a slaveship, wrote: "The slaves lie in two rows, one above the other, like books upon a shelf. I have known them so close that the shelf could not easily contain one more."

A year later, Equiano published his book: black people had moved from being packed in slaveships "like books upon a shelf" to being authors of books. (Apart from Equiano, other British black people in the eighteenth century published books. They included Ignatius Sancho, Ottobah Cugoano and Ukawsaw Gronniosaw.) It was an extraordinary achievement, a triumph over odds that was genuinely heroic, certainly more so than many of the 'heroic' deeds of British history, which mostly relate to warfare in the colonies, celebrated in traditional history books.

Nor was the achievement merely one of slapping down words upon a page. Equiano's narrative is carefully crafted, it consciously attempts to insert itself into the body of British eighteenth century fiction, this being evident from Equiano's 'quotation' of key texts like *Robinson Crusoe* and other works in the travel-book genre. Equiano's range of scholarship, the breadth of his reading and his extraordinary command of the registers of the English language (from the use of grandiloquent apostrophes and other classic rhetorical devices of the period, to prose stunningly beautiful in its measured simplicity) reveal a talent rarely surpassed by his fellow white writers.

Apart from being a master storyteller, Equiano brings to eighteenth century English literature a philosophical depth rarely encountered in the period's fiction. His stories are enjoyable at a surface level but they are also philosophical parables. His story of the theft of oranges (Heinemann edition, pp. 78-80), apart from being a moving statement on the uncertainties of human life, also possibly amounts to the first exploration in English literature of the 'nothingness of being', in some ways foreshadowing the modern philosophy of existentialism. Equiano shows a human being stripped of everything (the condition of slavery), stripped of the power to own, to possess, *things,* and stripped of self-hood. This state of primal nakedness is an intense religious experience, forcing an awareness of the existence of 'God' who is No-thing, beyond all things. These complex philosophical insights are clothed in a simple story, such is the literary giftedness of Equiano. One has to compare Robinson Crusoe's ruminations on God (stranded on a desert island belonging to black people) to Equiano's (stranded on a desert island belonging to white people) to see how banal and conventional the former's are, and how startlingly original and modern Equiano is.

Equiano, however, was not writing for literary critics or philosophers. He was writing, literally, for the liberation of his people, in two ways. Firstly, he was giving voice to the hitherto voiceless. Black people were no longer 'bookless', like Caliban. "Remember first to possess his books... Burn but his books", Caliban had warned, seeing the power of Prospero in the latter's access to 'knowledge'. Now, the situation had changed.

Secondly, Equiano used his book to campaign for the abolition of slavery. He travelled up and down the country to give talks, with readings from his book. He led delegations to the House of Commons to attend the slavery debates. He joined up with leading abolitionists like Granville Sharp to press for a judicial end to slavery. He became known as the leader of the black British community and was described by an eighteenth century contemporary as "a principal instrument in bringing about the motion for a repeal of the Slave Act". For these reasons he was of considerable significance to the eighteenth century, to its literature and its great social movements.

Today, Equiano's autobiography is of relevance to Britain for several equally weighty reasons. At the very least his existence provokes us to revise our knowledge of British social history by recognising a black presence in Britain that is at the very least two centuries old. Black people, in other words, are not recent immigrants to Britain. Nor, therefore, are the problems they encounter in present-day Britain necessarily of recent creation. By recognising the early history of black people in Britain it is possible to discern patterns of racist thought surviving through the centuries and into the present era. We begin to appreciate the hardiness and stubborness of racism, and the way British society has been permeated by anti-black ideology over the centuries.

The solutions for the eradication of racism therefore demand equally persistent and pervasive action. It is not enough to create a Commission for Racial Equality or a network of Race Relations Councils, however welcome these bodies are. Action must involve at least a massive revision of the educational processes whereby the white British arrive at knowledge of non-white British people. In a school context, any effort at combatting racism will necessitate a thorough, scholarly revision of the curriculum to bring to light the hitherto invisible black experience. British history and culture have been so intimately entwined with the history and culture of Africans, Asians and Westindians (through the British Empire, which, for some black people, lasted until the 1980s) that it would be nonsense to teach British history and culture without serious reference to, and consideration of, those of black people. And yet, such 'nonsense' is indeed what characterises much of the present ethnocentric curriculum. The uncomfortable truth is that schools, universities and teacher-training institutions are turning out many people whose knowledge or scholarship, because of its ethnocentrism, is profoundly limited, second-rate and ultimately worthless. Such massive economic investment in ignorance should not continue unchecked; the country cannot afford such a waste of scarce resources, especially now that there is little or no Empire to pay for extravagances.

Equiano's book, then, is a potential lesson in white British self-education, inciting the white British to relearn their history and heritage. For young black people in British schools, Equiano teaches some crucial ancestral truths: firstly, that there *must* be involvement in the wider society for reasons of survival. Separatism and scepticism are ultimately a futile philosophy. Equiano survives and triumphs over racism by mastery of the English language and deep knowledge of English customs. Such education equips him to negotiate with the society for human rights. This mastery of English does not involve a loss of African values: what transpires is in fact an extraordinary co-existence and mutual enrichment of England and Africa. His African consciousness is inevitably extended by the new experience of England, such extension leading to growth in new directions. Equiano becomes multi-layered and multi-cultured, such complexity deepening his imagination. Today's black British youth of African origin should see in Equiano's diversity the potential benefits of their own plural, complex situation, and be encouraged to seize those benefits. The alternative is a ghettoisation of self, an entrapment in 'the castle of one's skin'.

Another powerful lesson is that of self-help, the refusal to lapse into permanent despair and inaction. Equiano is a survivor. He takes whatever limited opportunities for self-betterment are offered and exploits them to maximum effect, this process of conversion from near-nothingness to a form of something being achieved by an act of indomitable will that is never selfish but always principled. He is a person of immense moral principles and he is a person of ceaseless action. He does not wait for state handouts or acts of social pity and charity, nor does he hide behind a barricade of sociological excuses for failure. He takes, but also self-creates, and is not afraid of confessing failure, but then moves forward towards new goals.

Finally, the teacher of literature in British schools should be impressed by the sheer literary talent of Equiano's writing. A close study of the text should reveal the author's superb manipulation of fictional forms and techniques, child-narrative, declamatory rhetoric, understatement, irony, humour, adventure, self-parody, travelbook exotica. Equiano is a *writer*. He can be judged by the same literary criteria that would be applied to any piece of eighteenth century prose narrative. It is important that the teacher judges Equiano as a writer whose place in the educational curriculum is demanded on the basis of literary merit, since all too often black writers are introduced into the classroom for any of the following inadequate reasons:

- the classroom has disgruntled black children, so teaching black literature might keep the children calm and happy;
- black people are a disadvantaged group, so black literature should be taught as a measure of positive discrimination;
- it is good for race relations to teach black authors: the black literature creates positive images of black people in the minds of white and black children, thus reversing a history of negative stereotypes.

In the final analysis black literature should be taught and read in schools not solely for sociological reasons, and certainly not as an instrument of social control, but because the black authors are black people who are *authors:* their works, through the form of prose or poetry, have deepened our insights into humanity.

Amazonian Indians – A dying community?

The Yanomani Indians: the largest tribal group in Amzonia (21,000) whose traditional territory is the remote and forrested border area of Venezuela and Brazil. Now a highway dissects their homelands and the mining companies are moving in. Death and disease are beginning to take their toll. The campaign to secure Yanomani lands has acquired a new urgency.

Working Women of the Third World

The practice of working women in the Third World is so far removed from western understanding. Whereas in Britain, few women have to search for clean water to survive or learn irrigation practices to provide food for their communities, in most Third World countries, heavy work is still shared equally between women and men.

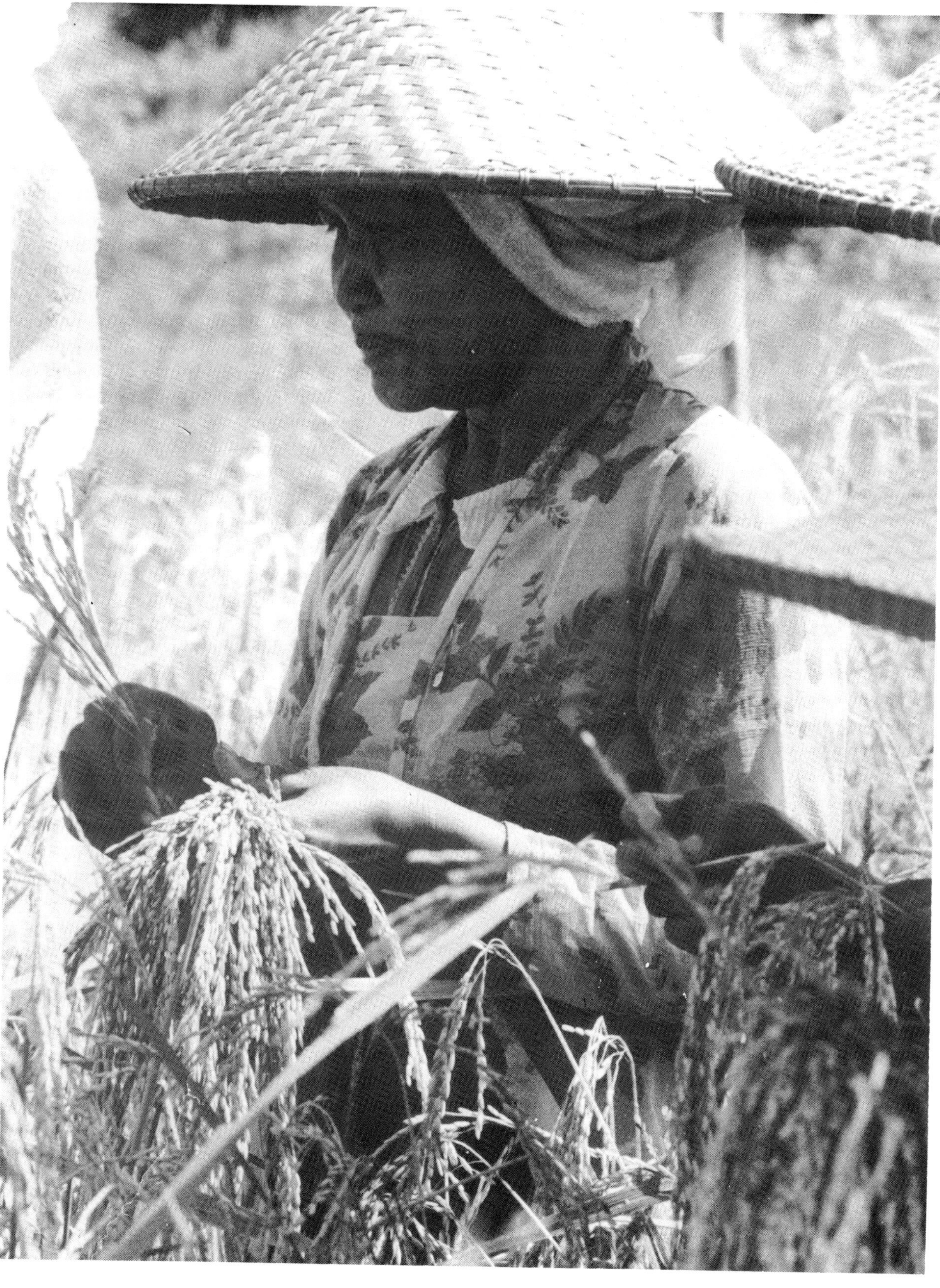

The Children and Year of the Dragon

As seen through the eyes of children from the Chinese Community who keep their culture and heritage alive at the celebrations for Chinese New Year in London.

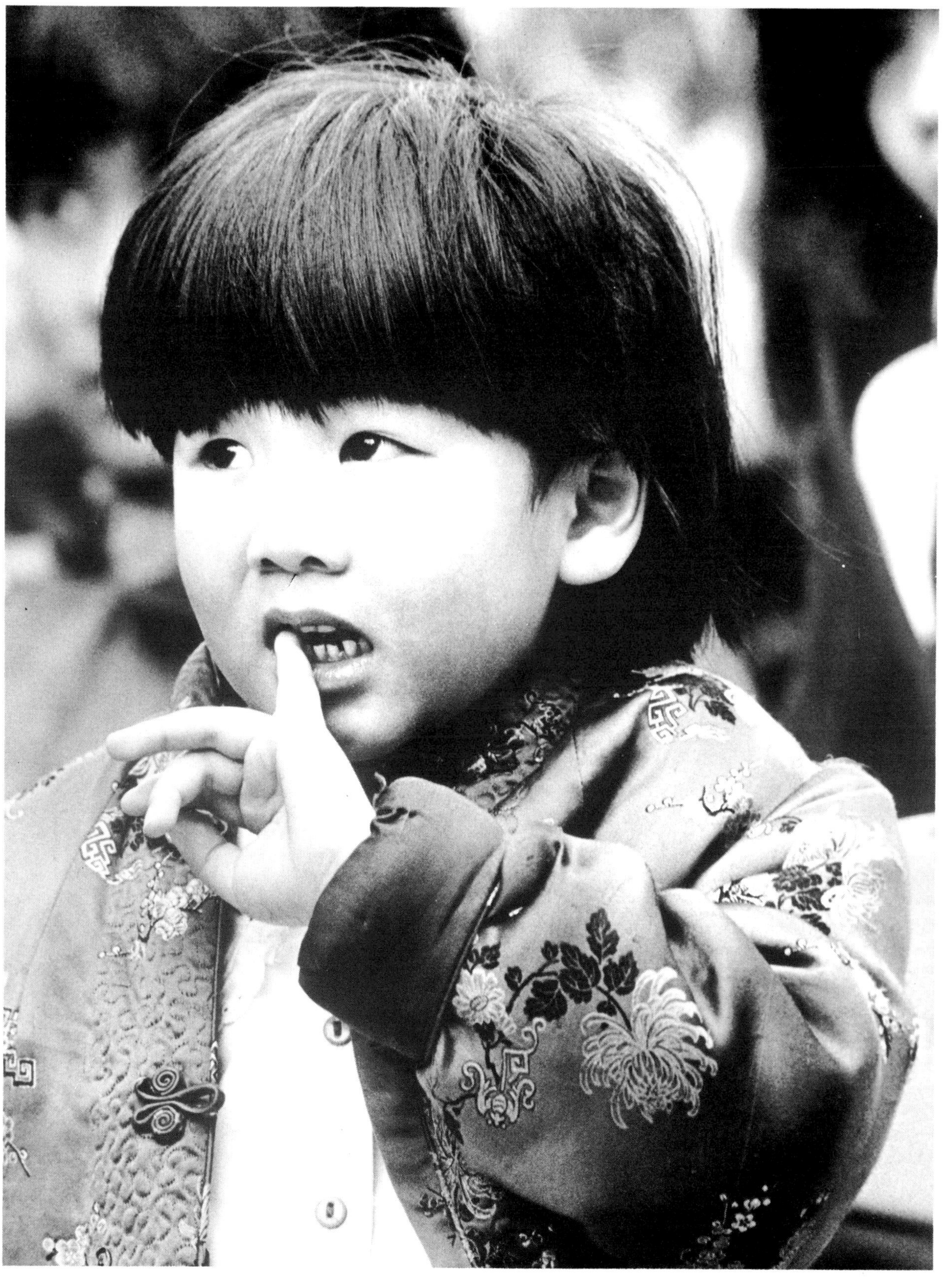

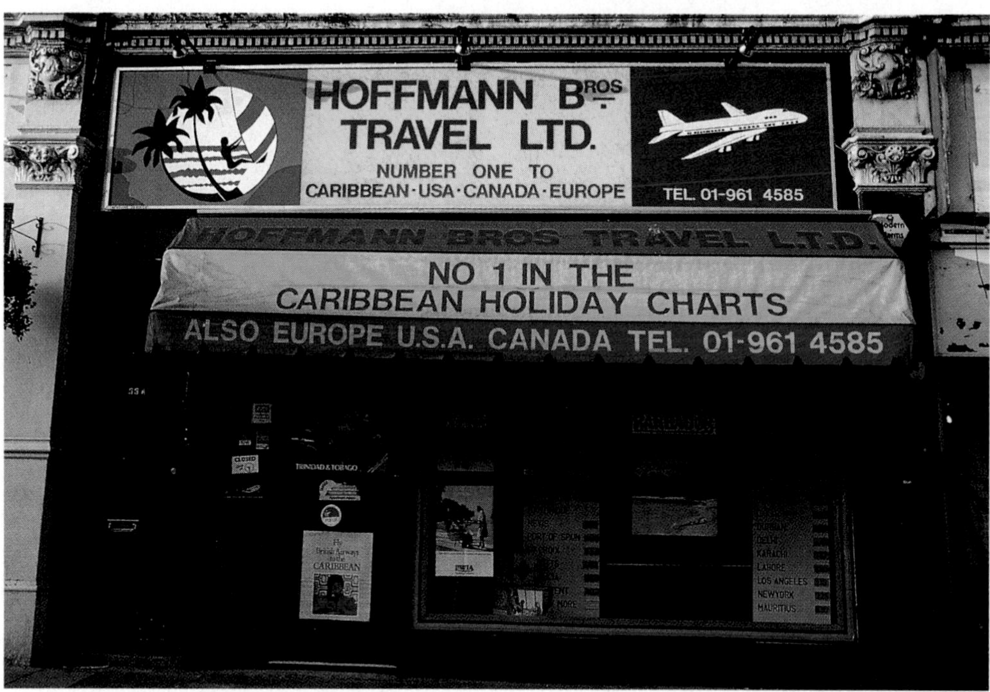

HOFFMAN TRAVEL AGENCY

FLY A GOOD NAME, No.1 to the Caribbean, USA, Canada
Special fares for Group Booking,
Emergency Flights no extra cost – phone your nearest Branch for Details

Kilburn Branch
1a Cambridge Avenue
Kilburn High Road
London NW6 5AA
Tel: (01) 328 2123 (13 lines)

Harlesden Branch
101 High Street
Harlesden
London NW10
Tel: 01-961 4585 (4 lines)

Tottenham Branch
438 High Road
Tottenham N17 9JR
Tel: 01-808 7536 (6 lines)

Streatham Branch
378 Streatham High Road
Streatham
London SW16
Tel: 01-677 0007

New Branch
60 West Green Road
London N16
Tel: 01-809 7700

Pentel Travel
20 Crouch End Hill
Hornsey
London N8 8AA
Tel: 01-348 2448 (IATA and ABTA)

Stoke Newington Branch
20 Stoke Newington High Street
London N16

ACCESS
BARCLAYCARD
& AMERICAN EXPRESS
ACCEPTED

ROOT MAGAZINE

UK 75p
Can $1.50

May 1988

WHITNEY
back in town

FREE!
Michael Jackson tickets

FASHION
Denim & Lace

The Afro Hair & Beauty Exhibition

NEW

ROOT Man

PROFILE
Tony Wade MBE

No Soft Touch:
The bachelor pad

FASHION
Sharp style for the 80's man who works hard & plays for keeps

supplement separating the men

A Hansib Publication

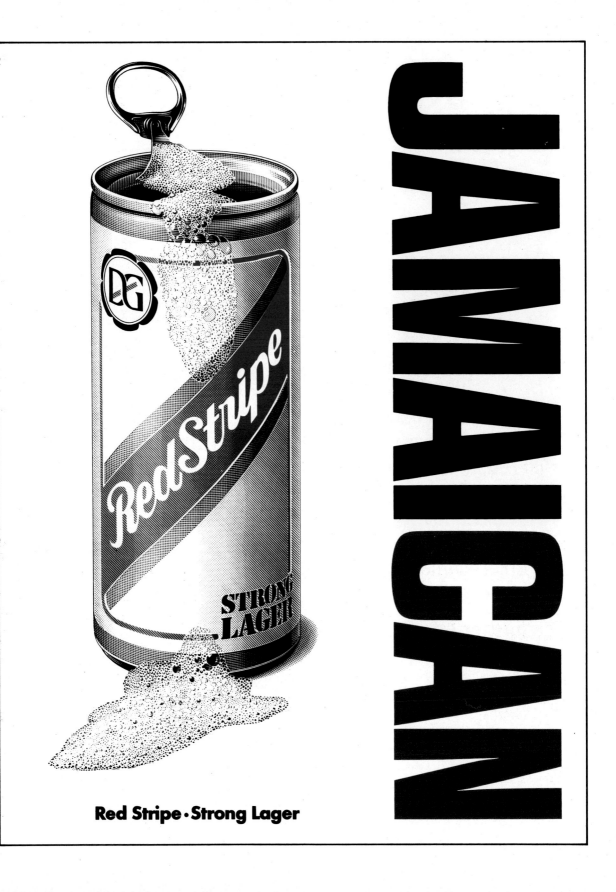

Share My Secret
The secret to my beauty begins with my hair.
With Soft & Beautiful™ No-Lye Relaxer I get
more body, more conditioning, and more style.
Soft & Beautiful, the right choice
for today's woman.
Soft & Beautiful™
BLOW DRY CONDITIONER
NO LYE
CREME RELAXER
OIL SHEEN
JENNIFER WISDOM
PRO-LINE'S SOFT & BEAUTIFUL WOMAN 1985/86
© 1986 PRO-LINE (U.K.) LTD.

The authentic drink of the Caribbean

Caribbean Cool is available throughout the UK, the Caribbean and the USA.

Distributed throughout the UK by A G Barr 0942-882691

People Who Know Demand The Best.

Oil Sheen and Comb Out Conditioner, Extra Dry and Regular

- long lasting sheen
- improves manageability
- helps to prevent breakage
- no itching, no build up, no drip
- moisturizes and conditions

Curl Moisturizing Spray

- restores moisture balance
- penetrates fast to prevent breakage
- conditions with jojoba oil
- gives natural look and lasting sheen

Curl Activator Cream

- restores curl and wave pattern
- contains squalene for added conditioning
- non-whitening formula
- non-greasy

M&M PRODUCTS COMPANY
® THE PEOPLE WHO KNOW YOUR HAIR...AND CARE

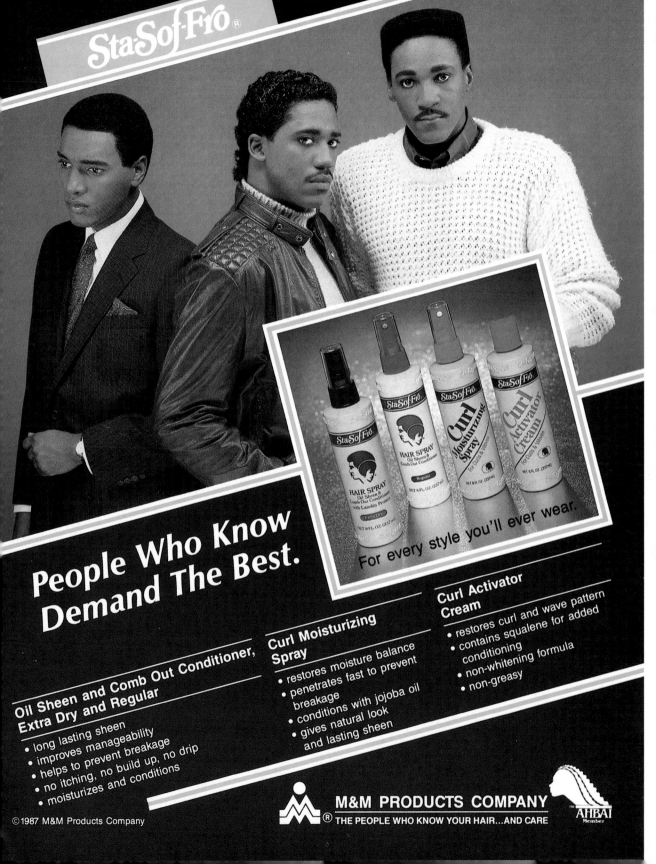

WEST INDIAN DIGEST

No. 152 April 1988 CAN.$1 UK 50p

Commonwealth and Caribbean vista where Africa, Asia and Europe meet the Americas.
Readers in over one hundred and fifteen countries

A Hansib Publication

Contributions of Caribbean people to British society

by Dr Harry Goulbourne, Senior Research Fellow, University of Warwick

It is both relevant and timely to raise the question of the contributions people from the Caribbean have made, and continue to make, to British society. This is so principally because the question cuts right across the usual concern of the media (newspapers, television and radio news as well as drama which claims to be 'realistic') to portray the Afro-Caribbean population in this country almost entirely in negative terms. Sadly, too often the well-intentioned response on the part of decision-makers to this form of social injustice is of the kind which involves the beating of the breast followed by pusilanimous action which may comfort here and console there but does precious little to undermine a profoundly negative perspective on the presence and contributions of citizens of Caribbean background.

To speak of 'contribution' behoves us to speak not just about achievements, but about achievements towards something; and the better something in this context is the construction of a better society in Britain for all. It is important, however, to mark-off or define more clearly, what we mean by the apparently straightforward term 'Caribbean people'. Of course, properly speaking the Caribbean people in Britain should refer to those of us from the English-speaking islands in the Greater and Lesser Antilles which border the Caribbean Sea as well as people from Belize along the Central American Isthmus and Guyana on the northern tip of the South American continent. In other words, the term 'Caribbean people' in Britain has a socio-cultural as well as a geographical definition because they are essentially from the former colonies of Britain in the New World, minus the North American continent and the Malvinas ('Falkland') islands.

The Caribbean region encompasses a strategic stretch looking into the much vaster world of the Americas and an outpost on the strategic trade and former military routes of the Atlantic. It is the region of the world in which many of the battles of Europe were actually fought and which, from the middle of the last century, but especially from the Spanish-American War of the 1890s and again from the invasion of Grenada in 1983, has become what the Reagan administration openly admits to be 'Uncle Sam's backyard'. Perhaps more than any other part of the world, the Caribbean region as a whole is the place where Europe in all its diversity

Linton Kwesi Johnson – frontline poet

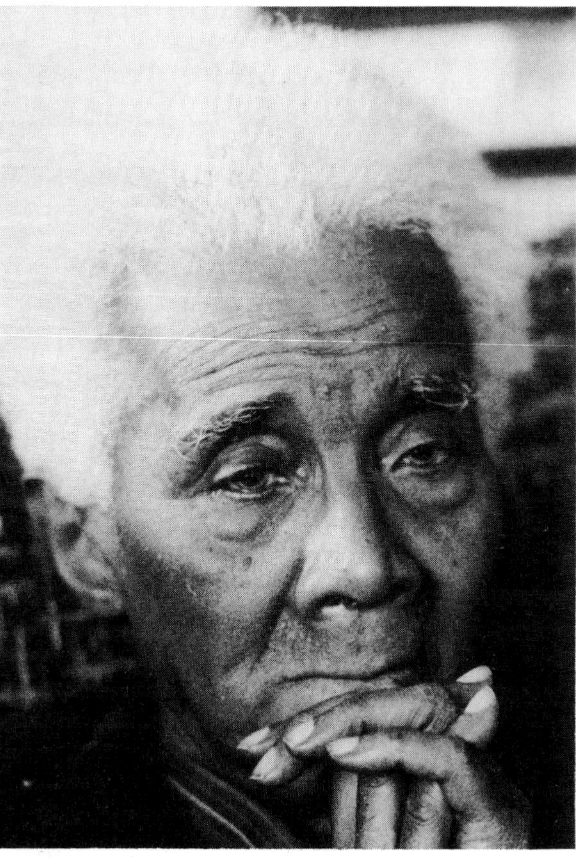

CLR James – veteran writer and activist

has been most directly replicated – in social and political institutions, languages, mix of peoples and so forth. It is also the region of the world in which other parts of the Old World – Africa, Asia and the Middle East – meet Europe.

The region's social kaleidoscope and strategic importance are too little appreciated in Britain, partly because its relative peace tends to keep the affairs of the region out of the news. Of particular importance, when looking at the region through British lenses, is the 'racial' composition of Caribbean societies. Just one example will suffice here.

In Britain there is a distinct feeling that when Fred Bloggs speaks of the Westindies, meaning the English-speaking Caribbean, he has a notion that the area is peopled by 'natives' who are all or nearly all Africans. Of course, there are very few 'natives' – native in the sense of there being pre-Columbian peoples – left in these parts of the New World. And although the majority of people in most of the islands are of African descent (for example, Jamaica, Barbados, St. Lucia, Grenada) there are very sizeable communities of people from the Middle East (for example 'Syrians', a category embracing all people from the region, apart from the Jews some of whom arrived soon after Cromwell's Roundheads came in 1659/60 to conquer Jamaica from the Spaniards). There is also a sizeable population of mixed people, descendants of slaves and overseers, whose presence no doubt occasioned the distasteful and racist term 'coloured people'.

The people who are most often conveniently left out of the picture of the Westindies, however, are the Indian population of the region. For example, few seem to take account of the fact that the single largest ethnic or racial group in Guyana and in Trinidad are people from the Indian subcontinent, 'Asians' as people in Britain would say.

Is this omission as innocent as it appears? I rather doubt it. It too neatly complements what it is difficult not to believe sometimes is a deliberate effort to portray the two major visible minorities, stereotyped as Afro-Caribbean and Asian peoples, in this country in very sharply contrasting terms: Asians are 'high-flyers', law-abiding, industrious – embodying all the virtues necessary for the well ordered, productive society. The Afro-Caribbean people are generally portrayed by the media and some politicians as "bone-idle and lazy" in the words of Terry Dicks, M.P. for Hayes and Harlington, who, according to the *Guardian* (2 September, 1986), 'informed' us that Westindians are "lazy, good-for-nothings who had come across here to sponge and to bring their way of life in the Caribbean to this country". This attitude is part of a long but unworthy tradition, embracing such well-known nineteenth century 'gentlemen' as Froude and Carlyle who saw the Jamaican freedman as indolent, work-shy and inclined to sit under a mango tree until the fruit fell on his head, requiring him only to muster enough energy to eat. It is difficult to believe that this freedman, the small farmer of the Jamaican mountains, was the same social being whom Lord Olivier was later to praise so much for his frugality; that it is the same social type who had been transforming the Jamaican economy from the 1840s after the demise of 'king sugar', by laying the new foundations upon which Jamaica was to survive for the next several generations.

I am trying to make two points here: first, that 'Caribbean people' does not mean solely people of African descent; second, I would like to suggest that the distinction, wittingly or unwittingly, supports an alternative image of the 'well ordered society' from the one I mentioned earlier, namely a society based on racial distinctions, and this is also anathema to the broad egalitarian tradition of the people of the Anglophone Caribbean. This is an important aspect of Caribbean consciousness which has guided the lives of people from the region in this country. And it is important to maintain this tradition so that discussion in Britain on the subject of minorities does not get stuck in the quagmire of racist assumptions and presumptions.

When we speak of the impact and contributions of the Caribbean people we can either take a wide historical sweep or concentrate on the contemporary scene, roughly speaking, the post-World War II period. For quite obvious reasons there must be a preference for the latter, but in order not to lose the perspective it offers, a word about the broader historical view is in order.

Merle Amory – former leader of Brent Council in north London

We could speak of the tremendous contribution of the Caribbean to early modern Britain during the period of the slave trade and of slavery and when sugar was king; when slaves, then sugar, were the premier commodities on a world market dominated by Britannia, who also ruled the waves. These forms of exploitation were to provide writers and film makers later with the backcloth against which to set their adventures on the high seas and on exotic islands of swash-buckling Norse-like buccaneers. More importantly, slaves and sugar provided Britain with the money-capital that many historians, following the pioneering work of C.L.R. James in his seminal work, *The Black Jacobins*, and Eric Williams in his equally celebrated thesis, *Capitalism and Slavery*, see as the necessary spurt for the first industrial revolution. The wealth from slaves and sugar plantations, therefore, did much more than to launch the great nineteenth century liberal politician William Ewert Gladstone on his monumental parliamentary career. And that wealth, created out of this particularly barbaric form of exploitation, is deeply embedded in the very web and fabric of British society.

I do not wish, however, to dwell on this early contribution of the Caribbean people to the development of Britain. Nor do I wish to dwell on the contributions made to defend Britain – nay the Mother Country – during the two World Wars or the contribution to the workforce in the reconstruction of a Britain devastated by the heroic struggle against fascism in Europe. I want to turn instead to some aspects of the contributions Westindians have made in the specific areas of politics and culture to post-World War II Britain.

There is an old spirit alive in Britain today which takes for granted that a multi-cultural, multi-racial (multi-colour is perhaps the best term) society is acceptable if, and only if, we all respect the exclusive, inward-looking, multiplicity of races, cultures, colours as immutable and therefore unchanging from time immemorial and into time and space untold to come. This view is unacceptable to the Westindian or Anglophone Caribbean person because it runs counter to the very grain of the type of social experience which has shaped societies in large parts of the Caribbean. It has been our openness which has sustained us in hostile environments. The Anglophone Caribbean person embraces in his or her social as well as very biological being aspects of those elements which go towards the fashioning of a tolerant society. This in turn entails acceptance of the notions of a fairly open, acquisitive social order based on and defined by social class differentiation which is common in all bourgeois social systems.

Culture and Sports

The general approach to life which is informed by these values has in turn greatly influenced all aspects of Anglophone Caribbean culture and sports. Let us take sports first, and then, let us take cricket as perhaps the best example which brings people of all backgrounds together. This is also perhaps the sport which is quintessentially English; as English as tea in the afternoon.

The origins of the Westindian's love and aptitude for cricket remains vague, but one researcher at the University of the Westindies found that identured Indian labourers arrived in Guyana already with a love of the sport. Another, but not contradictory view is provided by the Grand Old Man of Caribbean commentary on cricket and society, C.L.R. James, in his semi-autobiographical book, *Beyond a Boundary*, and conversations with some of the old boys of and around the sport: what emerges is that a generation of Westindians at the turn of the century, believed that they should be able to defeat the imperialists at their own best game. This is not the Leninist principle of hitting at the imperialist at the weakest link in the chain of control. If this view of struggle has any Marxist antecedents, it must be the notion which is associated with the work of the Italian Antonio Gramsci; namely, that there is a necessity for building an ideology which should be counter to the prevailing ideology of the dominant class in bourgeois society. It was and is a view which holds that whilst developing something out of what has been received, it is possible to compete, if competition is fair, and do as well as the next man or woman. This has also been an important part of the philosophy which has anchored the efforts of Afro-Americans in the USA from before the days of national freedom in the industrial North, through W.E.B. Du Bois, the Rev. Martin Luther King, the Black Panthers, Jesse Jackson and a number of others today.

One leading expert on the study of sports in the USA once informed me that historically Afro-Americans have found it more difficult to enter sports than any of the main professions – of law, medicine, the church and academic life. Of course, this is surprising because it is usually assumed that black Americans are natural sportsmen, arising from what Eldridge Cleaver, in his Black Panther days, used to call the 'myth of the superhuman menial'. The men and women who have excelled in sports in the USA have had to fight against great odds but those who have succeeded have had to contend with more than horses and the swelling of the River Jordan!

John Barnes – Footballer of the Year, 1988

Should it surprise us if we were to discover that the situation in Britain is much the same? Nonetheless, it must be evident that, although many a parent will say that their young Benjamin or Delroy, Clementine or Edwina was never encouraged at school or at the sports centre to develop his or her athletic skills, there are many successful black sportsmen and women in the country. And there are likely to be many more footballers, cricketers, athletes, etc., men and women who enjoy the competition of sheer skill which, once released on the field, cannot easily be ruled against on the grounds of colour.

It is true that, if you listen to a boxing commentator, sometimes you will hear the crude racist or nationalist praising the fallen white competitor for taking his licks well and not a word for the victorious competitor. But once a man is out of the fight – whether it be running, cricket, or whatever – only a Hitler can walk away and pretend that there has not been a demonstration of superior skills. Once the competitors are fairly placed on the field the rules cannot be suddenly and arbitrarily changed by those who control the levers of social and political power. In my view, it is this characteristic of sports which has enabled the black competitor to do so well once on the field. In this respect do I need to say more than that very many major and minor football teams in England have one or more black players and that many of the medals currently won by Britain are being taken by black sportsmen and women. John Barnes, Cyrille Regis, brothers Brian and Mark Stein, Dave Bennett and Lloyd McGraff are a few of the well known black players amongst football enthusiasts, whilst Philip De Freitas and Malcolm Marshall as well as generations of Westindian players are household names in English cricket.

It is, however, both a negative and a positive statement to say that sport is likely to continue to be a major arena of success for Westindians, particularly Afro-Caribbeans, in Britain. Negative because men and women of talent may be pulled exclusively to sport because they know the rules are fairly universal. Positive because, despite the racist chants at football matches, I do not believe that the vast majority of British spectators are necessarily racists in the sense that they have a developed philosophy of ill-intent.

It is not, therefore, because Afro-Americans or Afro-Caribbean Britishers have any innate, primordial edge over other peoples that we excel at sport; rather, it is because the liberal notion of fair competition – once the competitors have managed to pass the entry post – most strongly applies to this province of human endeavour. But it is possible to go on a little too much about sport, because it is an area of life which evokes strong feelings and therefore enjoys a particular salience; achievements and failures are highly visible.

Turning now to culture in a broader sense – the arts, media, religion – it would appear that in them the presence of Westindians has increased. Let us take the media. The active participation of people from the Caribbean in this area of British life has certainly improved over the last several years, but it has to be borne in mind that such a growth is bound to be impressive since its starting point was from zero. Moreover, this participation is still largely limited to television. There is as yet little or no participation in the mainstream press nor on radio. When I say that there is little participation in the news media I do not mean to belittle the contribution black newspapers make to specific black communities as well as the larger community by providing news which would not ordinarily reach the attentive public. Nor do I mean to belittle the efforts of those who have to struggle either to create or make available slots on the box for black faces and drama. But I do wish to criticise the exclusion practices which seem inherent in mainstream British institutions concerned with mass communication.

In terms of religion there can be little doubt that the black churches have done a tremendous amount to bring people of a different colour, class and sometimes even denominations together. The churches, which should have been the main institutions to welcome the traveller, were nearly as exclusive and unwelcoming as other bodies. But it was the church – during the days of slavery and the period of settlement on the land as freedmen – which proved to be perhaps the most general, dependable and tenacious social institution for black people in the diaspora. It may be because the black-led churches in turn have failed to give answers to pressing questions that they too have become less relevant to the needs of the second generation. This has provided the opening for a new faith to enter the lives of many young people. I am speaking here of the attraction of Rastafarianism. Rastafarianism as a religion cannot, however, hope significantly to rival the firm position of the Christian denominations built up over considerable time, even if, like all institutions, they respond late to new demands. Rastafarianism, like Judaism, is essentially restricted in its appeal to certain elements of a 'racial' group. As one response to the types of spiritual/emotional and social deprivation the majority of black people in the Caribbean and Britain have had to struggle against, Rastafarianism may be able to create for itself a social base amongst the poor, the permanently unemployed, and here and there a few sons and daughters of the middle classes suffering from the alienation that society's injustice gives rise to. The contribution of Rastafarianism, however, both to British society as a whole and to societies in the Caribbean, does not lie so much in its contemplation of the religious life but more in the spontaneous release of artistic talents it has effected. This leads naturally to a consideration of

Aswad in action

the contribution of popular music and entertainment.

In a sense this is one area of culture where it should hardly be necessary to say anything at all about the contribution of Caribbean people to contemporary British society. Nonetheless, it is sometimes necessary to state the apparently obvious. It must be difficult to think of general popular music in this country without thinking also of the influence and presence of musical forms which have their roots in the Caribbean. The presence of Carnival both as a street show and a musical event in Notting Hill is a clear testimony of the entertainment and musical contribution from Trinidad, but one which has become 'Westindian' through a wider Caribbean – some would say British – participation because it is surely being moulded into an event which is quite distinct from its Caribbean model. The Notting Hill Carnival is a national event which has the potential to contribute much.

Reggae, arising out of the travails of the Rastafarians of Kingston, and with its principal messengers in the late Bob Marley and Peter Tosh, is a distinct Caribbean form of popular music the presence of which is absent only to the tone deaf. Reggae has also transcended the religious constraints of Rastafarianism to which it owes so much, and it is very interesting to see how Kingston reggae and British reggae have started their different trends, with the latter, in the eyes of many, outstripping the former in both quality and quantity. In Britain Aswad and Black Slate are of course well known groups and earlier, as reggae developed away from the *bluebeat* sound, entertainers such as Desmond Dekker made their appearance. There have also been those singers, such as Jimmy Cliff, who have contributed both to the popular music in the Caribbean as well as in Britain. This, of course, is a tradition established earlier by calypsonians such as Lord Kitchener. And quite apart from the contributions of individual groups and persons, there has been the influence Caribbean music has had on popular music in general, for example, on UB40, The Police and others.

Anglophone Caribbean literature may have been late in maturing but, particularly in the period since the last World War, it has taken off with a 'bang'. One very interesting point about this literary growth is that much of it has blossomed in Britain: George Lamming and Andrew Salkey before they left for the USA did much of their work here; Samuel Selvon and Wilson Harris have long lived and worked in Britain. It is inconceivable that these men had no influence on the present generation of poets such as Linton Kwesi Johnson, Grace Nichols and their contemporaries. Curiously enough, it is still rare to find the British black novelist (Caryl Phillips from Trinidad and Joan Riley from Jamaica are amongst the exceptions) but I sense that it is only a matter of time before we shall see a significant contribution in this area of creative work because the basic ground work is in place and the material, the 'potters' clay', is available in abundance.

But the Caribbean contribution to literature is not to be restricted to the arts: the appearance of a variety of black community newspapers, leaflets and other publications, directed by a self-conscious quasi-political élite, amounts to an important contribution. Historians of the future will be most grateful for these alternative sources of information about late twentieth century Britain – that is, alternatives to the sheer quantity of dead official reports on the conditions of black people in this country. But historians will also be grateful for what may be reflected in these alternative sources about the poor generally in an officially uncaring Britain; a Britain in which many of the victories of the working people, symbolised by the achievements of the immediate post-World War II Labour government under Attlee, were rolled back.

The Political Contribution

These considerations lead me to the comments I wish to make about some of the political contributions people of Caribbean background have made and are making to British society. I intimated earlier that contributions must be understood in terms of putting something towards a greater whole, a recognition of co-operative endeavour. With the essential end of empire, not only is Britain having to face open competition unsupported by fearsome military might (or, to use that very expressive Jamaican word, she lacks the necessary 'backative'), but she is also having to address internal problems which were conveniently set aside during the days of the empire. One of these problems was, of course, the question of the 'nations' which make up the United Kingdom of Great Britain and Northern Ireland.

In the post World War II period, therefore, perhaps the central question for the metropole of a vast empire upon which it used to be said that 'the sun never set', has been what sort of society would emerge in these new circumstances. In the midst of such ponderings, non-white peoples, who have been effectively kept out of the centre of the empire, were beckoned in sizeable numbers to come across, live and work as citizens of an international body – first as members of an empire, then as members of a Commonwealth of Nations. Then, suddenly, problems piled on top of problems; the rapid process of decolonisation in Africa, Asia and the Caribbean called into question, in the most dramatic way, the legal status of the sizeable shifting populations almost everywhere within the decaying imperial boundaries. Whereas Britain could side-step most of the economic and political problems she had helped to create all over the globe, the contraction from being an empire to being simply the island of Britain took place within an overall shift in world economic power and the enlightened, progressive liberalism, which had been an important aspect of the ethos of the imperial order, was caught on the horns of a classic dilemma; it could not say openly that non-whites were not citizens by virtue of their colour but at the same time the managers of the state did not want to see non-whites becoming British islanders. By the 1980s, however, what do we have? Black Britishers, Britishers in a sense quite different from the way that their parents felt that they were British, and so the nationality laws are repeatedly changed. Moreover, a population which used to be regarded as extremely law abiding, and as being from a background where people believed that the safest thing to do is to pay unto Caesar what is due unto him, but to keep a respectful distance from authority, has – within a matter of a generation – been stigmatised by the social accusation of criminality until proved otherwise. With massive economic decline in the seventies and the eighties, the Afro-Caribbean population is further stigmatised as 'unemployable'.

In such circumstances either the people of Afro-Caribbean background in this country can give way to total despair – and indeed a number have! – or, we can look to some of the ways in which we as a people have survived in the past. In my view this latter course of action has been adopted by

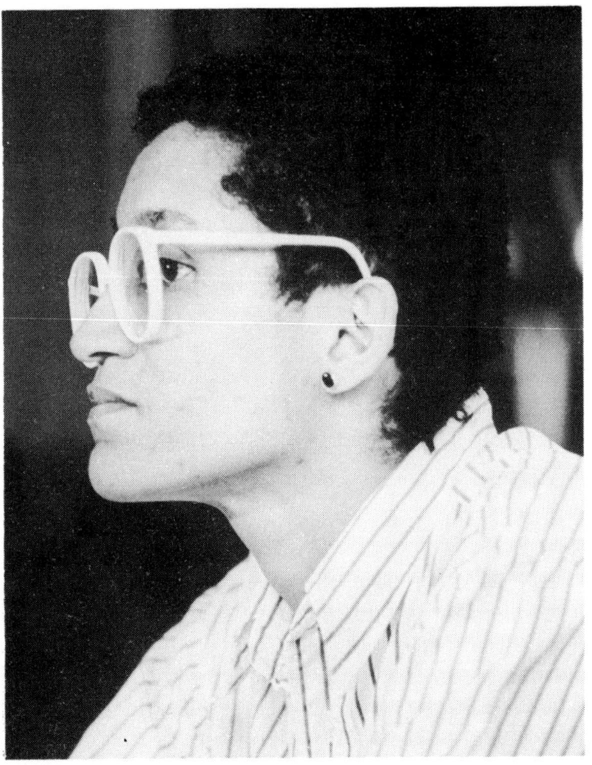

Linda Bellos

Afro-Caribbean people in this country and in so choosing they have made what future historians may come to see as perhaps the single most important contribution to the search for a new, healthier Britain.

The Caribbean people have raised a number of fundamental questions for British society in ways which have forced all elements to stir from any complacency there might have been, particularly with regard to the structures of authority and decision-making. When the black youth speaks and takes action over unemployment this brings into focus not only his or her plight, but that of others of their generation as a whole. When the black activist raises questions about the exclusion of black people from the institutions of power he or she voices the feelings of all the downtrodden as well. When the excessive use of police power is challenged on the streets by black youths, this triggers off a debate of relevance to the whole community about the relationship between the police and the community they are ostensibly employed to protect. The questions raised are not to do with securing any exclusive, particularistic rights; they are questions which apply to society as a whole.

These engagements have made it possible for the professional black politician to make his and her appearance in Britain over the past decade or so. And they have done so as mayors, councillors and, following the general elections of June 1987, as members of the House of Commons. Apart from helping to place radical issues on the agenda for both political discourse and public action, the presence of the politician of Caribbean background, such as M.P.s Bernie Grant and Diane Abbott, as well as Paul Boateng, who is generally regarded as Westindian, contributes to the creation of a significant symbol for younger people, and this can only be to the good of Britain as a whole. The forceful presence of black women such as M.P. Diane Abbott, Merle Amory and Linda Bellos, as well as a number of others in the Labour Party, carries forward the tradition of Westindian women, that is, a tradition of active participation in public life. Perhaps, however, the single most important contribution that politicians of Westindian background could make to contemporary British society is an understanding of the open and egalitarian aspects of Caribbean traditions.

The fundamental reason for this universality of the cause of the overwhelming majority of Anglophone Caribbean folks in this country goes back to some of what I have been saying. Profoundly imbedded in our culture is a rejection of exclusivity, a rejection of a sense of superiority to others and their cultures, the willingness to learn from others, to enter into their folkways, their lanes, their byways, and to see other people's perspectives; and to measure ourselves as partakers of, as well as contributors to, the broad stream of humanity.

Caribbean culture is, of course, fortunate to have benefitted from the great cultures of the modern world – we can lay claim to aspects of Asia, Europe, Africa; we are inheritors of some of the best in the great universalistic religions of humanity. The desire to participate in all aspects of life around us has meant that, whatever we have initiated, developed and refined, has also been equally open for others to enter and partake.

Now, this openness, this willingness to accept others and to expect to be accepted, is nearly always condemned as a sign that Afro-Caribbean people do not have a distinct culture of their own. But I have always found it strange to conceive of culture as being a set of unchanging variables making us as different from each other as possible.

In a talk entitled "Striving to be West Indian" (*West Indian Law Journal,* vol. 6, no. 1, 1982) given at the University of the West Indies in Barbados, the St. Lucian Nobel prize winner for economics, Sir Arthur Lewis, posed the following problem for his audience:

> "Obviously Westindians cannot be different from other men in everything, since we all belong to *homo sapiens,* so one has to ask where we should draw the line; in what respects should we be the same as other peoples, and in what respects should we strive to be different?"

The great man's answer to this problem was that, whilst Westindians do need to be different – and I think it is obvious that we are – in our aesthetics (music, literature, art), if we are not to be boorish, we must also know and appreciate the arts of other peoples. "Difference must be grounded in wide knowledge and not in ignorance of all except the local effort", he argued. Only an ignoramus can say with conviction that Caribbean artistic forms do not exist in abundance and our tremendous contribution here is that we have tried to share this abundance.

The Caribbean people's contribution to British society cannot be assessed solely by statistics nor is it to be measured in terms of any exoticism, strangeness or quaintness. It is quite straightforward. It stresses some values which are not so popular today in the wake of the glorification of ethnic differentiation and exclusivity. Thus, when people of Caribbean background in this country are encouraged to see themselves as utterly different from the 'norm', we are not being asked to contribute to a greater whole, to participate in the broad stream of British society but, rather to actively participate in our own further marginalisation. Fortunately for us, it is an essential part of our culture and history to seek to actively participate in whatever is going on around us, and all we ask is for the ground rules to be clear and for them to be kept so that we may be better able to continue to make the contribution that we are capable of.

NOTE: This is a revised version of a Public Lecture given to the annual meeting of the Hammersmith and Fulham Commission for Racial Equality at the Polish Centre, 6th September, 1986.

Early Westindian Doctors in London

by Jeffrey Green

John Alcindor (left) with unidentified friends (Courtesy of Frank Alcindor)

Despite the numerical weakness of the population of African descent in Britain at the beginning of the twentieth century, and the general colour prejudice including institutional racism, a number of black individuals triumphed in the professions of law and medicine. These black professionals attained a level of social success as well as that within their calling, working in a country that required them to have white clients as Britain's black community was too small to support such black professionals.

Having overcome the obstacles placed in their way by the absence of facilities in the Caribbean and Africa, these black professionals trained in universities and medical schools where they were in competition with the finest minds of the age. They had to obtain experience, gain financial status in order to buy or establish a practice, and then attract a regular income by being of service to the community at large. They were exceptional individuals and their story is part of British social history as well as that of the Caribbean where their absence raises important questions on the 'brain drain' and its effect on the islands. Their work in Britain is also part of the history of the struggle for black rights, for these professionals in Britain seldom distanced themselves from others of African descent.

Theophilus Edward Samuel Scholes, for example, was born in Jamaica in the middle of the nineteenth century and studied medicine in Edinburgh in the 1880s. Under a missionary scheme supported by black people in the United States and headed by Thomas Lewis Johnson, an ex-slave from Virginia, Dr Scholes went to Africa where he laboured in Zaire and then eastern Nigeria. He settled in London by the 1900s and worked on four large books critical of the imperialism and racism of the British. He was known to others of African descent interested in the history and development of their people including the New York-educated Pixley Ka Isake Seme from Swaziland who was studying at Jesus College, Oxford, in 1907.

Seme was to be one of the originators in the establishment of the African National Congress in South Africa in 1911. During his years in Oxford he made contact with Alain Leroy Locke, the first Afro-American to be awarded a Rhodes Scholarship. Before he left Harvard to take up his studies at Oxford, Locke received a letter from Seme who told him that 'others of your race' will be at Oxford. At the end of August 1907 Seme wrote to Locke in the USA recommending that Locke should contact Scholes when he arrived in London: 'Go to 11 Mornington Crescent and there enquire of one Dr Theophilus E. Scholes, the great Negro author. I have told him about you and you are sure of immediate help.'

Locke took his Swazi friend's advice and a letter from Scholes dated 28 October 1907, expressing gratitude to Seme for making the suggestion that the two men meet, is in the Locke papers. In 1925 Locke authored *The New Negro*, a collection of essays that expressed the firm belief in the upward movement of Black America and which reflected the so-called 'Harlem Renaissance' in which Afro-Americans took pride in the achievements and ambitions of their people. In talking to Dr Scholes in London Alain Locke would have received solid advice and gained inspiration for his efforts. Likewise, in 1915, the South African nationalist, Solomon Tshekisho Plaatje, obtained Scholes's advice when preparing his searing indictment of South African land segregation, *Native Life in South Africa*, published in London in 1916. Scholes was also contacted by the Jamaica-born US historian Joel Rogers, who wrote in the *Norfolk Journal and Guide* on 29 August 1925 that Scholes believed that 'England was a bad place for a Negro'; this black newspaper article was headed 'England offers opportunity to Negroes of wealth and artists: no place for masses'.

Scholes was often seen in the British Museum library, and in the 1930s he was visited by Jomo Kenyatta (the future leader of independent Kenya) and Ras Makonnen (a Guyanese whose Manchester restaurants helped finance Pan-African publications into the 1950s.) Scholes's role as a medical missionary in Africa influenced his understanding of colonialism, and whilst it may be regretted that he did not practice medicine in Britain after the 1880s (for his name is absent from the medical registers)* his two volume *Glimpses of the Ages* which predicted that war and revolution would force social changes in the future and detailed how great civilisations had grown and collapsed, suggesting that the British would decline in due course. Scholes also suggested that colonial exploitation would cause the subject peoples to rebel. His writings and conversations were a profound influence on younger black folk in Britain.

Theophilus Scholes was not the only professional black person in Edwardian England, for a Guyanese lawyer named Edward Theophilus Nelson had graduated from St John's Oxford in 1902 having been secretary and treasurer of the Oxford Union (debating society). He was called to the Bar at Lincoln's Inn in November 1904 and by 1906 was living in suburban Manchester. From 1909 he made his home in Cecil Road, Hale, and his office was at 78 King Street in Manchester. He achieved considerable fame in the region over his work in defence of Cornelius Howard who was tried for the murder of George Harry Storrs on 1 November 1909.

Howard's trial took place after an appearance at the coroner's court when Nelson was his barrister; he was found not guilty in March 1910. Another man, Mark Wilde, was arrested for the same murder in August 1910 and his defence was brilliantly conducted by Nelson. To try two separate individuals for one murder was probably unique in English legal history, but the so-called Stalybridge murder did not get much attention in the London press in October 1910 as the trial of Dr Crippen was taking up a great deal of attention.

In 1913 Nelson was elected to Hale Council and served until his death in 1940 when he was in contact with the Manchester group within which Ras Makonnen was to move. In 1919 it was Edward Nelson who was employed by a group of black people in London to defend several Africans accused of rioting in Liverpool; the London group was the African Progress Union and the president of that organization from July 1921 was Dr John Alcindor, a medical practitioner of Trinidad birth who had lived in London since 1899.

Alcindor was born in Port of Spain in July 1873 and attended St Mary's College, the island's leading Catholic school. He was awarded one of the four Island Scholarships of 1892, which allowed him £150 a year for three years to study at a recognised institution in the British Empire (which generally meant Canada or Britain), and enabled him to travel to Britain in 1893. He studied at Edinburgh University for six years, and was often high on the list of marks awarded: first-class results in three chemistry examinations and second-class results in physiology and practical pathology. His practical work included clinical surgery at the Royal Infirmary and six months attending mental cases at Anderson's College in Glasgow.

He graduated in July 1899 and from October 1899 to April 1900 he was an anaesthetist at Paddington Infirmary in west London; he also worked in assisting John F. Little of Harley Street at a north London tuberculosis hospital from November 1899 to March 1901. The struggle for a living is also seen in that he was one of the three freshly qualified doctors to work as an assistant at St Mary's hospital for Women and Children in east London's Plaistow in 1900. His name appears in medical registers from 1905, with various addresses in the Paddington area from 1908 until he settled at 23 Westbourne Park Road.

John Alcindor had three papers published by the medical press: on influenza in the *General Practitioner* in 1907, on cancer in the *British Medical Journal* in 1908, and on tuberculosis in the *Practitioner* of 1913. He became a member of London's National Council for Combatting Venereal Disease and the American Anti-Tuberculosis Society. He established his practice at 201 Harrow Road, next to a dentist; he worked alone, dispensing his own medicines in the style of the era. His patients were largely the poor of the Paddington district, and he was recalled by two veterans as a generous and kindly man, with a high reputation among children for he often stopped in the streets, lifting a child into the air, and breaking down the distrust that a child would have of a black man and of a doctor. He also charged low fees and gave credit, most welcome in those pre-National Health Service days; and he took great care over details, insisting that his patients when hospitalised at the Paddington Infirmary had decent food and bedding. More than once he returned to his home and took the family dinner, saying 'My patient needs feeding, not doctoring'.

Alcindor played cricket, and had done so in Trinidad and at Edinburgh; he played for two different teams in the west London district of Acton, which suggests that he was working in that suburb between 1902 and 1908 when he is seen in Paddington. He was a wicket keeper and had his photograph published in the weighty *British Sports and Sportsman – Cricket and Football* in 1917 with a sightly inaccurate biography which included the fact that he 'was well known in West London cricket circles as an excellent wicket-keeper and a consistent batsman'. He married a Londoner in 1911 and there were three sons. He remained a staunch Catholic, and two of the boys went to Archbishop Vaughan's school and the oldest to the Jesuit Mounty St Mary's school in Derbyshire. He was a member of the Catholic doctors' society (the Guild of St Luke, St Cosmos and St Damian) and was a patron of the centenary celebrations of the Association of the Propagation of the Faith at Westminster cathedral in 1922. He took his sons to the local catholic church; his wife Minnie was a freethinker – where and how they met remains a mystery.

John Alcindor was known to others of African descent in Britain, much in the same way that Scholes and Nelson were, for the community was small. In July 1900 a group of black people with some interested whites gathered at the Pan-African Conference organized by Trinidad-born barrister Henry Sylvester Williams; this London meeting included John Alcindor; a Battersea photographer named John Richard Archer (born of a Barbados father in Liverpool in 1863); a composer named Samuel Coleridge-Taylor who had been born in London in 1875, the son of an African doctor from Sierra Leone; and an Afro-American professor of sociology William E.B. Du Bois. Coleridge-Taylor lived in Croydon, to the south of London, and had immense fame in Britain for his *Hiawatha* choral works. He had his father's African features and colouring, and as a successful black person attracted the attention of his kin. John Alcindor was an occasional visitor to his home, and when pneumonia struck the brilliant musician down in 1912 Dr Alcindor was present at the funeral. He remained a family friend and attended the wedding of the composer's daughter in 1922, where he is to be seen in the group photograph, between the composer's widow Jessie and his mother Alice. Alcindor's home at 31 Talbot Road was a base for Afro-American musical friends of Coleridge-Taylor in 1908 and 1909, and there are firm links to that address with singer Harry Burleigh White in 1910, and the doctor's letter remains in the White papers in New York.

Alcindor had other friends but no evidence has been located of specific black events until he became the head of the African Progress Union of London in July 1921; as his predecessor was John Archer (who had been mayor of Battersea in 1913, and active in support for women's rights candidate Charlotte Despard, in the 1918 general election), and others on the committee were not freshly arrived in London, we can presume continuation of contacts between the 1900 conference and his leadership of the African Progress Union. The African Progress Union voiced opinions on the affairs of black people to the imperial government and the metropolitan press; its members had a very wide range of experiece, and were quite capable of offering sound advice to younger men and women from the colonies freshly arrived to undertake studies in Britain. They were on hand to assist in the voicing of opinions by Africans and Caribbeans, in efforts to change the imperial system; they spoke out for black folk, tried to remedy injustice, and to adjust imbalances in the opinions of black people held by the larger society. Under John Alcindor they took a major part in the Pan-African Congresses held in London in 1921 and 1923.

These gatherings were largely financed by Afro-America; Du Bois participated in them all. They are usually seen as expressing New World black interest in the future of Africa and Africans, and those of 1921 and 1923 are regarded as the time when leadership of the black world passed from Americans to Africans and Caribbeans. Certainly the generation of leaders who fought imperialism and lived to see Africa and the Caribbean achieve political independence were influenced by men and women who were in Britain and the USA from the 1920s; but the role of Black Britain and the African Progress Union led by Dr John Alcindor is not well known. The Americans tended to link up with British liberals and self-appointed spokespersons for Africa and Africans such as John Hobbis Harris of the Anti-Slavery Society. Harris, who had done his best to thwart Sol Plaatje and the South African efforts to influence British public opinion in 1914 to 1917, had a great deal of influence, and so it was in August 1921 that Alcindor wrote to Harris to accept his invitation to meet Du Bois and the others on 27 August. The Congress was actually opened by John Alcindor who said that the battle for black rights must be fought with dignity and discretion, and that the public should be awakened and Africans galvanised into activity for Africa.

James Jackson Brown on holiday in the mid 1930s (Courtesy of Leslie Brown)

Two years later Du Bois and his US colleagues again arrived in London for a Pan-African Congress that was ill-prepared and needed to be rescued by Britain's African Progress Union led by John Alcindor. It is not to reduce the fame of Du Bois, who was truly a colossus of Afro-America, but to show the importance of Black Britons and established professions such as Alcindor, that we need to examine the documents relating to the London Pan-African Congress of November 1923. The Du Bois papers include a letter from Alcindor dated 23 August 1923 stating that it was from Audrey Jeffers in Trinidad that he had heard that the third Pan-African Congress was to be held in Trinidad around Christmas 1923. He continued that the Pan African Progress Union wanted to assist, and would make public any information in two London weeklies, the *African World* and *West*

Africa. Alcindor suggested that the British Empire Exhibition, scheduled for 1924, would be attracting many visitors and Trinidad in 1923 was not likely to attract men 'on this side of the Atlantic'.

Alcindor was in contact with Beton, the head of the Paris Pan-African Association, who had told him the conference was scheduled for Lisbon. Du Bois was in contact with Robert Broadhurst, a merchant of Euro-African descent and Sierra Leonean birth, active in Ghana (colonial Gold Coast); he had troubles with the French section, he advised Alcindor on 11 September. He wanted some fifty black people invited to the London meeting. Poor Alcindor had to reply asking the professor when he expected to be in London; he would arrange the annual meeting of the African Progress Union to be when the Pan-African Congress was held – but when was that? 'We shall have no difficulty in getting a good attendance of coloured people in London and Europeans interested in our cause'.

He called a meeting of the Union on 27 September and the London community backed Du Bois' efforts. There is a hint of discord amongst the Parisian group and a difference of opinion between the Francophone and the American folk; but practical matters remained – where did Du Bois want to hold his meeting in London? On October 4 Du Bois wrote to Alcindor to say that he would be in London from early November to 11 November, and suggested that 8 and 9 November would be the best dates for the meeting. The arrangements were in the hands of Alcindor now, although George Lattimore, the manager of a black orchestra in London, and recently employing the almost destitute Sol Plaatje as a spear carrier in a show, was indicated as being willing to loan the Philharmonic Hall in central London.

Two days later Du Bois cabled Alcindor to book a hall for 7 and 8 November. It was less than a month before the conference that Alcindor wrote to Du Bois asking him what the programme would be; but the Union meeting was arranged for 6 November. That his letter ends with regards to Du Bois' wife and daughter, who lived in England from 1914 to 1915 when Yolande Du Bois studied at Bedales School in Hampshire, suggests that they had made contact at that time. Du Bois sailed on 24 October and arrived in England on 4 November. Further evidence of a lack of full preparation is in the Alain Locke papers, for Du Bois wrote to Locke care of Thomas Cook and Son in London (as Locke was following his usual habit and was touring Europe that summer break from Howard University) on 5 October asking him to attend the conference and present a paper; he could be contacted via John Alcindor at 23 Westbourne Park Road.

The work of Alcindor and his colleagues was almost global. In the summer of 1922 he was attempting to establish a branch in the Cameroons (an ex-German colony by then occupied by France) and tried to appeal to the League of Nations in Geneva; in early 1923 he sent a copy of *Imperium* (a French language production) to John Harris; in early 1923 he was in contact with a delegation from Swaziland (here Pixley Seme and Sol Plaatje were of influence); he arranged a concert by the Afro-American singer Rohand Hayes in London in aid of Union funds; he was closely associated with black students in London, attending their new year's dance at the beginning of January 1922 as did committee colleagues John Alexander Barbour-James (a Guyanese civil servant who had worked for fifteen years in the postal service of Ghana; he had settled his family in Acton around 1904, and had participated in black affairs for years.) His Guyana-born daughter Muriel also attended (she eventually moved to Trinidad and worked with Audrey Jeffers in social work) and Dr Ojo Olaribigbe, a Sierra Leonean medical practisioner in London who qualified in 1915. Agatha Acham Chen, born in Martinique and married to the ethnic Chinese Trinidadian lawyer Eugene Chen (soon to be Foreign Minister of China), was also a committee member; her son Percy was present and his 1979 memoirs *China Called Me* contain interesting insights into life as a black person in London at this time (for Percy Chen showed his mother's complexion). Another student listed in *West Africa* was Joseph Agard, he qualified in law and moved to Mombasa in Kenya where, far from his Guyana birth place, he informed John Alcindor of events in east Africa that disturbed him in the middle of 1923.

An English settler in Kenya killed an African servant named Kitosh; Jasper Abraham was arrested and the news reached the London press. Questions were asked in parliament by Labour's Harry Snell. Agard sent cuttings from the *East African Standard* to Alcindor, and the medical evidence of the cuts, wounds, abrasions and swellings which were 'extensive and severe' indicating savage attack. Yet the jury, white settlers from the neighbourhood of Molo, brought in a verdict of 'grievous hurt' and Abraham was sentenced to two years. That the defence presented an argument that Kitosh had willed himself to die and that Karen Blixen immortalised this in a romantic racist account in her *Out of Africa* (written in 1937 and recently made into a movie) are aspects of European views of Africa that did not publicly concern Alcindor and his Union committee. They met in September 1923 and agreed that their president should write to the Secretary of State for the Colonies, the Duke of Devonshire.

Alcindor's letter was typed on 17 September 1923. Perhaps using the discretion and dignity he had recommended in 1921, he did not say that the Union was black, nor that he was a medical doctor. He did not challenge the defence argument: 'I would point out the utter inadequacy of the sentence on Abraham for this monstrous crime of murder'. He referred to the use of flogging by settlers 'for the purpose of extracting obedience from and terrorising the natives' and that Abraham has threatened to take away the servant's work ticket; the 'boy' had been flogged to death for insolence. Could three members of the African Progress Union discuss the matter with the Duke? No doubt the trio would have been the short 'black doctor of Paddington', the tall and somewhat pompous John Barbour-James with his tales of being the first guest of pure African descent to be invited by the governor of British Guiana in 1898, and Kwamina Tandoh, a chief from Cape Coast in Ghana who had developed many business and social contacts in Britain after nearly eighteen years in the country and was, like Barbour-James, an officer of the Union since 1918. Tandoh was soon to make Trinidad's governor tremble with fear. These were not callow youths nor inexperienced colonial subjects, but upper middle class Black Londoners.

The Colonial Office staff noted that the details in Alcindor's letter were correct, and acknowledged receipt of the document. The Duke of Devonshire wrote to the governor in Nairobi, and received a transcript of the trial. Shortly before handing over to his Labour successor J.H. Thomas, the Duke wrote to Nairobi on 20 December 1923. 'I must express my abhorrence at a crime which appears to me to offer no extenuating circumstances...my legal advisers...are of the opinion that a verdict of anything less than manslaughter is quite irreconcilable with the facts...the jury system can only be regarded...as on its trial'.

From now on any trial for alleged violence across racial lines had to have the transcript sent to London; juries were to be picked from regions distant from the site of the alleged crime. The liberals, returning to parliament in January 1924, asked Thomas about the trial, and he published the Duke's letter in *Hansard* on 26 February 1924. From there it was republished in *Kenya* by Norman Leys, a medical man who had served in Malawi and had attended the 1921 Pan-African Congress in London; his book was the first to suggest that white settlement in eastern Africa was not a matter that Britons could ignore. That Alcindor and his colleagues in London used the British parliamentary system to bring about a small change in colonialism in Africa and enabled Leys and others to publicize the nature of white settlement in Kenya not only places white liberals in less than centre spotlight, but suggests that black people in Britain had important contacts and influence in the affairs of their people. Settlers with professional status like the black doctors of inter-war London were well-placed to help the less fortunate members of their community in Britain and abroad.

Being in London, then the capital of the world's largest empire, also enabled Alcindor and others to assist in family matters, such as when the African merchant Charles Coussey expressed concern over the company his daughter Ann Marie Coussey was keeping in Paris in the summer of 1924. She and two Jamaicans had met Langston Hughes, a penniless sailor of promising literary talent (Du Bois alerted Locke to his European trip of 1924), and Coussey's concern led Alcindor to travel to Paris where he insisted that she returned to her studies. She did, and married Hugh Beresford Wooding, a lawyer from Trinidad active in black student circles in London; her sister Christine also married a London-based African from Mozambique who had studied in New York. There must have been many a middle class black family in the Caribbean and Africa grateful for such supervision of, and occasional interference in, the activities of their student children in Britain.

Yet another African link is seen in that Edward A. Renner of Sierra Leone was a witness to the will that John Alcindor made on 25 August, 1924. Two months later the doctor died, at St Mary's Hospital in Paddington. *West Africa* noted that 'Dr Alcindor was perhaps the best known practitioner in London amongst African people, though his professional skill was by no means limited to them'. The local paper said that he had been a

John Alcindor (second row) at the wedding of Gwendolen 'Avril' Coleridge-Taylor in 1922 (Courtesy of Marjorie Evans)

'familiar figure in the neighbourhood' and explained that Dr Alcindor was 'a man of colour, and widely known as the "Black Doctor". The funeral was attended by the two children of Samuel Coleridge-Taylor, by John and Edith Barbour-James (she was his second wife; from Barbados, she had worked as a teacher in Cape Coast for fourteen years), by the Red Cross in which Alcindor had been active after the British army refused his services as he was 'of colonial origin' back in 1917. Not that Alcindor had stepped away from his profession, for he had been one of Paddington's four medical officers under the poor law scheme, and indeed had fought to keep the system of home visiting when the district wanted centralisation. In fact John Alcindor was secretary of the Poor Law Medical Officers' Association, working with Sir Arthur Newsome, the pioneer tuberculosis expert. The *African World* noted 'the fact that a coloured man can earn the esteem and respect of all classes of the English people', and from New York Du Bois wrote to Minnie Alcindor to express regrets and sympathy, asking for biographic details for the *Crisis*.

For a quarter of a century the poor of London and members of Britain's black community had benefited from the colonial system which had removed, at Trinidad tax payers' expense, a valuable citizen and trained him to be a valued medical practitioner in London. He did not turn away from his people, but once established in his profession, spent much time and effort to assist others. In cricket he found a relaxing hobby; in his family he had joy, and surely would have welcomed his middle son Cyril's commission into the British Army in 1944; and in the respect of patients and colleagues in medicine he would have found comfort. That he died aged fifty-one was a tragedy for his young family and for the fight against racism and imperialism, for despite the magnitude of his achievements from his student years in Port of Spain, it is clear that John Alcindor, M.B., B.Ch. (Edinburgh), still had much to offer.

Present at the funeral was a Parsee named Bajana, and he was well known to another Caribbean doctor on the other side of London. James Jackson Brown was very different to John Alcindor in many ways. He was tall, had benefited from family wealth in Jamaica, had taken over ten years to complete his medical qualifications, had married whilst still a student, and was an egotist. Born on 9 October 1882 in the St Thomas region of Jamaica, the youngest of nine children, James Jackson Brown had claim on the family property which, after the deaths of his parents, was managed by a man named Hamilton. From private schooling in Jamaica he travelled to Canada where he started medical studies, possibly at McGill University in Montreal, although Dalhousie University in Halifax, Nova Scotia was also a likely place for black medical students at the turn of the century. He disliked the style of the tuition and returned to Jamaica; a legacy of those years in Canada was poor eyesight due to snow blindness. In 1905 Brown was in London, where he presented his credentials from Jamaica and Canada and, exempted in practical pharmacy, physics and chemisty, he started studies at the London Hospital in east London's Whitechapel Road on 22 September 1905. He passed the first part of his course in April 1906, and again with Canadian qualifications (in anatomy and examinations in 1907) after two abortive attempts. He had two years of study left, but he did not attempt his finals until 1911 and passed them in 1914, becoming: James Jackson Brown, M.R.C.S. Eng., L.R.C.P., Lond.

Brown had lodged at the home of a compositor on the *Jewish World* at 115 King Edward Road in Hackney, and he married Amelia 'Milly' Green, the landlord's daughter. Gerald was born in 1907 and Leslie in 1909, but his Jamaican relatives terminated his five pounds weekly allowance so Brown had to work as well as study. The Greens were a well-established Jewish family of Dutch origin, living in London for nearly a century, unlike many of the Jewish people in Hackney and Whitechapel at the time who had come from eastern Europe from the 1880s. These migrants and the local working class families were to be a loyal and supportive clientele for Dr Brown, but his student years were difficult. When Madan Lal Dhingra assassinated Williams Curzon Wyllie in 1909 'every coloured person had a hell of a time' and Brown was failed in the oral examinations. He complained to the authorities and passed the next examination. He worked as a dresser – assisting Jonathan Hutchinson from October to December 1909; Hutchinson was a well-known surgeon at the London Hospital who had a particular interest in venereal diseases (and identified incisor teeth deformities in congenital syphilis). From April to June the following year Brown assisted a Dr Dawson as his clinical clerk; Dawson was to become the personal physician to King George V and was later Lord Dawson of Penn. The hospital files note that Brown was graded as 'good' in both positions.

A family friend enabled Brown to start his practice at 96 Lauriston Road and after a spell in Brighton he settled in at 63 Lauriston Road in 1921. His working methods were chaotic, but in-laws helped him with paper work as the public health system required doctors to first supply medicines and claim back the costs later; Brown was excellent at the supply but hopeless at the claims, and he sometimes owed the drug supply companies more than the government were to pay him. He dispensed his medicines, again not without incident, for his son recalls an exploding bottle of medicine. Fortunately he had a substantial paying practice, encouraged by his skills, and by his acumen in placing a list of fees on the waiting room wall in both English and Hebrew.

He had a high opinion of his professional skills, and charged more than other doctors. His opinion was supported by the neighbourhood, for it would be Brown who would be called to a street accident in south Hackney. It was Brown who brought numerous babies into the world at a nearby private nursing home; and it was Brown who had regular calls for treatment from men suffering from venereal diseases.

His London Hospital training and the work with Hutchinson were the sources for his skills here, but there must have been an element of faith, in that white patients sought out black doctors who, to their British professional qualifications, added magic or *obeah*. Brown said he was a Maroon (the group of Jamaicans who had escaped slavery and established a semi-independent life style in the middle of the island, eventually tolerated by the British who had been unable to defeat them in battle), and he was proud of his blackness. To some patients this enhanced his abilities.

Brown's contacts with other black folk in Britain included that with Samuel Spencer Alfred Cambridge, a barrister from Guyana who visited Hackney around 1913 and is recalled today by Leslie Brown for Alfred Cambridge's three daughters were 'the first coloured girls we had ever seen'. Alcindor's name was recalled from this time; perhaps the first link was through cricket, for Brown played for the London Hospital team and, in response to the question 'Tell me Brown, why don't you find more than one or two niggers together?', he formed a team of black sportsmen which he name the Tropics. Bajana was a member until he split the group by taking the Indians to form the Indian Gymkhana team, whereupon Brown formed a team of African descent called the Africs. These men were largely Caribbean and included Percy Chen when they had a soccer team. Brown and Cambridge are named as the officials of the Afric Athletic Club in a publicity handout from 1919 which was used by the South African A.N.C. in England; a copy was given to the Nigerian nationalist Herbert Macaulay who was in England in 1920.

Brown's cricket team played all round London twice a week in the 1920s and 1930s, and set out to challenge whites and to beat them. It gave considerable enjoyment to the students and professionals who played, and for their families who watched. Many of these younger men were fed by Milly Green, whose home provided warmth and companionship after matches and on winter weekends, when bridge occupied the group which often numbered over twenty. The Leekam brothers from Trinidad, whose Chinese descent is seen in their name, were members of the group, although Harry Leekam settled in Trinidad in the 1930s after ten years in Euston. His brother Ferdie preferred cricket and music to study and finally qualified in 1941; he died in England in 1968.

Louis George Drysdale, a Jamaican who tutored singers including a number of Afro-Americans, but survived on his tailoring skills, was closely associated with the Browns. Drysdale had been involved in the African Progress Union back in 1918. Gerald 'Al' Jennings who was a musician from either Trinidad or St Kitts was involved in the group; the Jamaican musician Leslie Thompson first heard about 'the coloured doctor' from his landlady in the winter of 1919 and was soon made welcome at 63 Lauriston Road where he played duets with the doctor's wife. The London-educated son of Ghanaian lawyer and author J.E. Casely Hayford played for the cricket team, and Archie Casely Hayford persuaded Leslie Brown to travel to Ghana in 1934 where, having trained as an automative engineer, he planned to operate a garage for Archie Casely Hayford. Other Africans associated with Brown included H.O. Davies, a Nigerian lawyer and his daughters; Desmond Buckle, a left wing socialist and nephew of 'Boss' Bannermann of Ghana, also known to the Browns.

Caribbeans who lived in Africa were known to the Browns too, such as George James Christian from Dominica who had a valuable law practice in Sekondi, and architect named Phillips and the Guyanese legal family, the Abbensetts. Medical men of Caribbean birth included Eugene Escallier from Trinidad; Athelstan Da Costa Stoute from Barbados who had a practice in Chiswick and was an eye consultant in Harley Street; C. Gun Munro from Grenada who returned to England and established himself in Epsom where he was recalled with respect fifty years later; H.E. Bond fron Kingston who was eccentric but much loved; Alexander Dingwall who was well established in Sydenham in south London; and G.R. Marcano who worked in East Ham.

Some of these men were involved in an abortive effort to establish a residential centre for Caribbean students in London in 1924; so was Dr Harold Moody a Jamaican who had won considerable fame by the 1930s. He led the League of Coloured Peoples from 1931 to his death in 1947. Brown had little time for Moody, who he regarded as self-appointed, but the two Jamaican doctors had mutual friends including Ivan Shirley, another doctor. The cricket team and social group around Brown's Hackney home involved other professionals, including Adrian Date from Antigua who became a judge in Tobago, and Gerald Mair from Jamaica who was an accountant. The racing tipster and bogus 'African chief' Williams, then undergraduate at Oxford, later to be Prime Minister of Trinidad and Tobago, Arthur Lewis from St Lucia, an economist and officer of Moody's League of Coloured Peoples, visited; so did Parson Kamal Chunchie from the Coloured Men's Institute in the docks. He and Desmond Buckle were active in the 1945 Pan-African Congress in Manchester which involved Ras Makonnen, who was also known to the Lauriston Road community. James Alexander George 'Jags' Smith, a brilliant lawyer from Jamaica who represented the underdog in Kingston's legislative assembly, was taken ill during one visit and was nursed back to health in Dr Brown's home.

Milly Brown died in 1936 and Dr Brown married one of his patients. Gerald qualified as a doctor and set up in the district; Leslie returned from Africa and married his fiancé. They moved to Gloucester during the war when his engineering skills were valuable in the aircraft industry. He still recalls the shock of reading that his father had been struck off in February 1943. Brown had certified a man to be unfit for military service and when this decision was questioned, assumed that he would be seen to be correct. He took no legal advice and was genuinely surprised when his decision was judged incorrect. *The Times* and the *Hackney Gazette and North London Advertiser* reported the fact in mid-February 1943.

'J. J.', as he was known to many, made considerable efforts for the relief of bomb victims, working with the St John Ambulance Brigade. He was active in Freemasonry, heading the local Zetland Lodge. He was close to the local vicar, and it was at South Hackney parish church, just yards from his home and surgery at 63 Lauriston Road, that Dr Brown's funeral took place on 22 October 1953.

Thirty years later a letter to the *Jewish Chronicle* led to many veterans recalling the Jamaican doctor, 'the likes of which this generation has no knowledge', and another letter to the *Hackney Gazette* led to other recollections of the 'very kind, gentle and no matter how ill you were, just to see his smiling face and hear his voice, made you feel better immediately'. Brown had been replaced by Colin Franklin, from Barbados, whose elderly patients told him of their recollections of J.J. Brown. With such respect and loyalty, and with the strength of his family and friends, we can see why James Jackson Brown never returned to the Caribbean.

But why should Caribbeans trained in Britain have an obligation to the Westindies? There was Africa, where William Strachan had headed the Nigerian medical service in the 1900s (he died in Bromley in 1922) and fellow Jamaican Derwent Waldron had worked in Ghana before retiring to 1910's London and 1920's Brighton. Barbados-born Cedric Belfield Clarke had a substantial medical practice in 1930's south London and was a close associate of political writer George Padmore and Ghana's Kwame Nkrumah. There was the USA where Guyanese Philip Savory was active in New York and Jamaican Samuel Beckford headed a hospital in North Carolina for over twenty years. Peter Milliard had qualified in Scotland, worked in Panama, and settled in Manchester where he was helpful to fellow Guyanese Ras Makonnen; no doubt Caribbean medical men can be traced in South Africa (lawyer Henry Sylvester Williams worked there in the 1900s) and perhaps Kenya, for Lawyer Agard had a busy career there and in Uganda into the 1950s.

The medical profession allowed mobility and afforded levels of income that very much reflected the doctor's reputation and the recommendations of patients. The years of study and the struggle to get established meant that doctors were at least in their thirties, and most of the adult years of these young men would have been spent away from the Westindies. Marriage, property, professional obligations and research, children, and a sense of useful toil would hold down the doctor. The dream of returning, of visiting the islands was pleasant, but almost every year another young aspiring Caribbean would arrive and so the veteran had news of the home folk. And the years in England were so full – cricket, music, social events, conversation and discussion, charity work, children, politics and above all the sense of a job done to a fine standard. A professional standard might be a cause of trouble, for Brown just did not anticipate his decision being overruled, and Alcindor lost pension rights when in dispute with the poor law guardians in 1923. Bond had argued against the appointment of an inexperienced white to head the asylum in Kingston where he had spent years working with the patients. But a professional standard in medical training enabled these doctors to be free from other constraints and to have the financial and social independence to challenge conventional thinking as we have seen with Scholes and Alcindor. There was a price, and a high one, for John Alcindor was just fifty-one when he died, and Harold Moody was sixty-five when he died in 1947. David Vaughan's 1950 biography of Moody was entitled *Negro Victory,* and it is true that the Westindian doctors of Britain had triumphed and were victorious.

Further reading (available through the inter-library lending scheme): T.E.S. Scholes *Glimpse of the Ages* (London: 2 vols 1905, 1908); R.E. Lotz and I.L. Pegg (eds) *Under the Imperial Carpet: Essays in Black History 1780-1950** for Thomas Johnson and J.J. Brown; Jeffrey P. Green 'John Alcindor: A Migrant's Biography' *Immigrants and Minorities* (London) Vol 6 No 2 July 1987.
* (Crawley: 1986)

Jeffrey Green was born in England in 1944 and has written in several journals on black history, including *Musical Times, Journal of Caribbean History* and *New Community*.

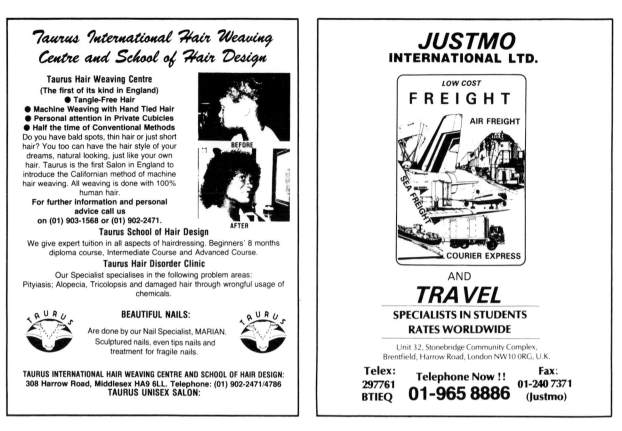

Black Heroes

Contributions to human civilisation

by Sam Yeboah

Africa is not only the birthplace of mankind but the continent where the torch of civilization was first lit. It is ironic that the continent which led Europe out of barbarism should have had its own civilization so brutally extinguished, and its people so mercilessly plunged into the darkest abyss by, and for the profit and development of, Europe.

Africa has suffered a twin-tragedy brought on her by Europe and from which she is unlikely to recover for several decades, if not centuries. This twin-tragedy was slavery and colonisation. Words are inadequate to describe the nature of the holocaust visited on Africa by Europe over the last five hundred years: the magnitude of the economic exploitation; the destruction of her economic infrastructure; the devastation of her social organisation and structures; the near obliteration of the history of her people; the appalling humiliation and degradation that her people have been, and continue to be, subjected to; and, above all, the shattering of the confidence and self-esteem of her sons and daughters.

The seed of this twin-tragedy was sown in 1441 when the Portuguese skipper Antam Goncalvez and his crew landed on the West African coast, attacked and captured two Africans – a man and woman. Goncalvez later teamed up with another Portuguese venturer, Nuno Tristao, and, together they attacked two African villages, killing four people and capturing ten more. The twelve African captives were brought to Prince Henry of Portugal who sought and obtained the Pope's blessing and forgiveness for future raids against those 'infidels'. In 1444 another 235 men, women and children were kidnapped in Africa, transported to Portugal and sold as household servants. In 1455, the Pope issued a papal bull authorising Portugal to reduce to servitude all infidel peoples.

Western Europe – Britain, France, Holland, Portugal, Spain – like vampires, tapped into the jugular vein of the continent and, what seemed like small bleeding in 1441, became a massive and almost terminal haemorrhage. In four centuries Africa lost what has been variously estimated to be 15-40 million of her young, healthy and strong sons and daughters. Five million more died during the 'purgatory' of the transatlantic voyage. At least hundreds of thousands, if not millions, died in the inter-tribal wars fought by African kings to procure slaves in exchange for European guns, alcohol and beads. This period marked the most shameful epoch in African history when African kings collaborated with European governments, slave traders, mercantile and industrial capitalists to bleed the continent of its most precious asset – its people.

By the mid nineteenth century, the debilitating effect of this savage slave trade had all but destroyed Africa's ability to defend itself against the second holocaust – the brutal European imperialist onslaught. By 1900 all of Africa except Ethiopia and Liberia was firmly under European colonial rule. There is little doubt that the most significant causal factor of black people's inferior status in the world today is slavery/colonialism.

In any analysis of Black Heroes then, the criteria for selecting which of the great sons and daughters of Africa to highlight as objects of emulation and inspiration to contemporary black youth must, in my view, be either those who contributed to the resistance against the twin-tragedy of slavery and colonialism and its contemporary effects or those who, prior to the twin-tragedy had shown by their achievements the heights to which black people can ascend. The history of black people is replete with great and courageous heroes and the following are but a tiny sample of those that I so much admire.

HARRIET TUBMAN

Conductor of the underground railway
Led many slaves to freedom

Menelik II
Hero of Anti-Colonialism

At the time of his birth in 1844, Africa had suffered from the holocaust of the European transatlantic slave trade for over three hundred years. Not only had this barbaric trade in human beings depopulated vast areas of West Africa, but the disgraceful wars fought between African tribes and kingdoms to secure captives for sale to the European slave traders had destroyed most of the previously powerful kingdoms. This had emboldened the European powers – Britain, France, Spain, Portugal, Germany and Italy – to seize large chunks of Africa.

In 1889, Sahala Mariem, as he was previously known before he changed his name to Menelik, became Negus Negusti (king of kings) of Ethiopia, having previously ruled Shoa, one of the four major kingdoms of Ethiopia, for twenty years. Internal strifes and struggles between the Gallo, Tigre, Shoa and Harar tribes had for years bedevilled the Ethiopian Empire. These internal strifes were aggravated by conflicts with the Madhists in the south and Somalis in the east.

When in 1885 the European powers signed the Berlin Treaty to regulate their conduct towards one another in the scramble for Africa, Menelik redoubled his efforts to take over and to unify the whole of Ethiopia for the inevitable struggle against the European imperialistic drive.

A highly intelligent and energetic man, Menelik was, unlike many of his contemporary African kings, a man of vision who put the independence and sovereignty of Ethiopia above everything else. Immediately after his ascension to the throne, he was pressured by the Italians to sign the Treaty of Uciallikl, under which the Italians were given complete control over Ethiopia's relations with foreign powers. The Italians sought this prize to frustrate Britain and France who were competing with the Italians in their machinations to colonise Ethiopia.

But Menelik was no fool! He had no intention of selling hiscountry's sovereignty to the Italians.His acceptance of the terms of the Treaty demanded by the Italians was based on a strategic calculation, for under the terms of the Treaty, the Italians gave Menelik 38,000 rifles and twenty-eight cannons and loaned him four million francs. Menelik quickly repaid the loan and began the process of uniting the various Ethiopian kingdoms and peoples and, without much fanfare, restructuring, modernising and training his armed forces.

The hypocrisy of the Italians' pretension of friendship soon became apparent when they seized the north-eastern part of the country and christened the area Eritrea. Menelik began mobilising the country, making peace with the troublesome kings and chiefs and building up his army and armaments.

The Italians meanwhile were moving men and equipment in readiness for the takeover of the country and by 1896 finally marched on Adowa, the Ethiopian holy city. Menelik had his men ready and waiting and engaged the 1,500 Italians on the plains of Adowa in a courageous and historic battle. By the time the battle was over, 12,000 Italian soldiers had been killed and over 1,000 had been captured. Menelik had demonstrated that the European powers were not invincible and that with foresight, strong determination to preserve the independence of his country, and intelligent and strategic planning, they could be thoroughly thrashed.

Looking at the agony of Africa today and the suffering of her daughters and sons scattered around the world, it is not too difficult to imagine a more positive history, if during the five centuries of the twin-tragedy of slavery and colonisation, the vision and leadership of Menelik had been the rule rather than one of the handful of exceptions.

Harriet Tubman
The courageous slave emancipator

Anyone reading the Anglo-Saxon rendition of the history of the slave trade and its abolition would gain the distinct impression that 'Great' Britain, out of pure altruistic motives decided (after three hundred years!) that slavery was morally indefensible and launched a crusade to abolish both the slave trade and, later, slavery itself.

From this Anglo-Saxon perspective of history, black people were helpless objects – commodities – purchased at first as much for their own beneift as for the owners' profit and Britain's economic development. Slaves were deemed to benefit from the European slavery system because they were assumed to have been purchased out of a life of savagery into a life in which they, hopefully, would not only be taught the rudiments of white civilisation, but also benefit from Christianity's spiritual redemption. Despite this benefit to the slaves, great Anglo-Saxon heroes such as Wilberforce and members of the Committee for the Abolition of the Slave Trade felt that enslaving human beings and subjecting them to a regime of such barbarity and terror was immoral and hence campaigned to stop it. White heroes, by definition therefore became the heroes that black people were expected to revere and to whom they were to be eternally grateful.

But *true* history is replete with great black heroes who courageously resisted the Europeans and valiantly fought to stem the tide of European slavery, capitalism, imperialism, colonialism, and their concomitant bestiality. Among these were the Angolan Queen Nzinga who for nearly 40 years in the seventeenth century fought against the Portuguese to prevent the extension of slavery to her territory; Pierre Dominique Tousaint (later nicknamed L'ouverture, the 'Opener'), Jacques Dessalines and Henri Christophe who led the revolt against their French masters in Saint Domingue in 1789 and created the republic of Haiti; the rebellion of Tacky (1760); the Sam Sharpe rebellion (1831-2); the Morant Bay uprising led by Paul Bogle; the Southampton (Virginia) rebellion led by Nat Turner and dozens of other uprisings in the Caribbean and the U.S., which demonstrated that in the most repressive and barbaric epoch of human history, there were great acts of resistance and heroism led by black people who were prepared to die in the attempts to destroy white enslavement of black people.

Among these great heroes was Harriet Tubman (1826-1913). Harriet was born into slavery in the early 1820s in Maryland. In 1849 she escaped from slavery to Pennsylvania. Her account of the first few moments of her freedom illustrates the utter hell of the emotional and physical conditions that all black slaves experienced: "I looked at my hands to see if I was the same person now I was free. There was such glory over everything; the sun came like gold through the trees and over the field, and I felt like I was in heaven."

She devoted the rest of her life to the cause of black emancipation. "Strong as a man, brave as a lion, cunning as a fox... Harriet Tubman who [was] unable to read or write, made nineteen journeys into the deep South and spirited over 399 slaves to freedom"* – a feat of which even the contemporary white fantasy hero, 'Rambo' cannot boast.

Harriet was a leading 'Conductor' of the *Underground Railroad* which was neither a railroad nor underground but an elaborate, highly organised, effective and efficient network of escape systems created to offer escape routes for black slaves to flee from the South to the North of the U.S. and into freedom. The network moved the escaped slaves "from one friendly hand to the next, from house to house, Church to Church; on foot, by horseback, wagons, trains, passing through slave state after slave state" till they reached the freedom of Ohio, New England or Canada. Literally thousands of black slaves were helped to freedom by the underground railroad.

The risks for the organisers and conductors were high as most slave states had severe penalties for those who aided and abetted other people's "property" to escape. Harriet became a living legend among black people and a target for the white slave-owners and their agents. She was pursued the length and breadth of the slave states by organised search parties, but through her ingenious devices and disguises, she eluded them all. Once when her train was boarded by the slave gangs who were searching for her, she pretended to be reading a newspaper, hoping that she held it right side up. Her pursuers overlooked her as they knew she could not read.

Totally disregarding her own safety, this intelligent and brave black leader brought freedom to over three hundred black people, outwitting their marauding white owners. Harriet served both as a nurse and spy for the Union during the American Civil War. She died in 1913 and was buried with military honours. She represents one of the hundreds of black women in history whose selfless devotion and unadulterated courage ought to serve as a shining example to all contemporary black people. Today, while black people in western multi-racial societies are nominally free, systematic racial discrimination has consigned most to a status of socio-economic inferiority, stultified their intellectual development, destroyed their confidence and alienated them from their true selves. We need to inculcate the spirit of Harriet Tubman in contemporary black youths so that they would hopefully help to shatter the chains of psychological slavery and emancipate black people from their white-imposed mental incarceration.

* Russel L. Adams, *Great Negroes Past and Present*, 3rd edition 1981 Afrom-Am Publishing Co. Inc. Chicago, Illinois.

Black scientists and inventors as heroes

One of the longest lasting effects of the enslavement and colonisation of black people of African origin is the 'myth' of black inherent inferiority. To justify and to excuse the most bestial treatment of human beings known to humankind, the Europeans developed the ideology of racism whose basic tenet was that black people are biologically inferior to white people. The proof of black inherent inferiority, as the race ideologues saw it, was: (a) that black people have never created a civilisation of their own without Caucasian intervention or direction; and (b) that no black individual has ever (nor could ever by definition) make any contribution to the development of science and technology.

Between the sixteenth and twentieth centuries, these propositions were elaborated with so many volumes of psuedo-scientific treatises that the doctrine gained the status of an 'axiom' – a self-evident truth. So thoroughly effective have the European race ideologues become in this venture that many, if not most, black people have come to accept privately, if not openly, the dual evidence of the doctrine. The reality, however, is that the Greeks – the originators of Western civilization, science and philosophy – proclaimed loudly and proudly that their civilization, science and philosophy was but a variant of the original created by the Egyptians who they described as being *black skinned* and *woolly-haired*.

The greatest triumph of European racism is that it suceeded in alienating black people from their true history and shattered the confidence and self-esteem of hundreds of millions of black people all over the world. One does not need a psychologist to postulate the effect that this lack of confidence can, and does, have on black people.

In spite of the falsification of black history, the destruction of black self-confidence, the almost non-existence for black people of the conditions necessary for scientific development through either the impoverishment of their economies by wanton Western exploitation or massive discrimination against black people in Western multi-racial societies, many black people have nevertheless distinguished themselves as inventors and made original and/or innovative contribution to the development of science and technology.* Let us take a look at three black heroes: the first of them, a man who prior to the twin-tragedy, earned the distinction of being the world's first known multi-genius; and the other two, more recent inventors who have greatly contributed to the enrichment of the quality of human life through the application of science.

Imoteph
The true father of scientific medicine

The achievement of medical science and its beneficial effect on the quality of human life is axiomatic. Some of the achievements we take for granted today would have been regarded as divine miracles a hundred years ago. The transplant of such vital organs as hearts, lungs, livers and kidneys have now become relatively routine procedures. The 'miracle' of life can be generated in a laboratory by taking an ovum from a woman, a sperm from a man and fertilising the former with the latter in a 'test-tube'. The fertilised 'egg' can then be implanted in the woman from whom it was taken or, even more miraculously, in another woman – surrogate motherhood is now a fact of life. Furthermore, fertilized ova (embryos) can be 'frozen' – held in a suspended state of animation as it were – for a number of years, unfrozen, and implanted in a woman who then produces a normal healthy baby. To most infertile couples today, children are no more the 'gift of the Gods' but the product of medical science.

Many human diseases which were fatal a few years ago, have either been more or less eradicated (at least in the rich industrialised countries) through effective vaccines, or else can be treated effectively and routinely. Accident victims can be brought back to life from the brink of what a few years ago would have been certain death. Most of these accident victims are saved through the use of respiratory machines which keep the body alive artificially while doctors undertake vital repairs to their 'shattered' bodies. But medical science can not only prolong life – it can, and does, improve the quality of human life in a way unthinkable to our ancestors two centuries ago.

The Eurocentric presentation of history informs the world that the person to whom humanity should be most grateful for initiating the

* for details on black scientists and inventors, see *The Ideology of Racism* by Sam Yeboah (Hansib 1988)

separation of medicine from superstition and thus establishing it on a scientific basis is the Greek physician, Hippocrates of Cos (460-377 BC). However, the Greeks, who should have wallowed in such marvellous recognition, knew better. They knew that 2,500 years before Hippocrates, a true genius – a black man – had originated scientific medicine from which they – the Greeks – became grateful beneficiaries and inheritors.

That man was Imoteph, the world's first multi-genius. Imoteph lived around of 2980BC during the reign of Pharoh Zoser of the Third Pharohnic Dynasty in the then Black Egypt. A member of the Pharoh's court, he was an accomplished architect, scribe, priest administrator and physician.

"Medical historians generally recognise the importance of Imoteph but do not comment on his race. According to Osler, he was 'the first figure of a physician to stand out clearly from the mists of antiquity'. Sigerist introduces Imoteph as the architect of the step pyramid of Saqqara: 'It is the oldest monument of hewn stone known to the world, and it was built by a man of genius, Imoteph, the first universal scholar, architect, engineer, statesman, sage and physician'. Ackerknect also acknowledges the priority and importance of Imoteph but, like Sigerist, makes no mention of his race."[1]

So great was his influence in the field of medicine that the ancient Egyptians erected shrines and temples in his honour to which Egyptians in need of healing flocked. By 525 BC he had become a full deity and an inscription to him read: "Turn thy face towards me, my lord Imoteph, son of Ptah. It is thou who dost work miracles and who are beneficient in all thy deeds."

By the time of Herodotus (480-420 BC), Egyptian knowledge of medicine was so advanced, thanks to Imoteph, that the former could state without equivocation: "Egyptians have discovered more prognostics than all the rest of mankind besides". Homer also stated in the *Odyssey*: "In medical knowledge, Egypt leaves the rest of the world behind".[2] Indeed it is a well known fact that the city-state of Athens as well as the kingdoms of the Near East used to import Egyptian physicians. Many medical historians clearly acknowledge the strong influence of Egyptian medicine on the development of Greek medicine.

The Greeks who knew Imoteph as Imouthes, later identified him with their god of healing, Aesclepios. Early Christian Rome also acknowledged his healing powers and identified him with Jesus, but unlike contemporary Western historians, acknowledged the fact that he was a black man. He was later replaced by Jesus as Massey writes: "Jesus, the divine healer, does not retain the black complexion of Iu-em-hetop in the canonical Gospels, but he does in the Church of Rome when represented by the little black bambino. A jewelled image of the child-Christ as a blackamoor is sacredly preserved at the headquarters of the Franciscan Order... to visit the sick, and demonstrate the supposed healing power of the Egyptian Aesculapius thus Christianised."[3]

Today, as we marvel at the achievements of scientific medicine, *true* history teaches us that Hippocrates is not the "Father of medicine", but Imoteph the black multi-genius who not only designed and built the first pyramid, but launched the world on the exciting path of scientific medicine which has benefited humankind so much. As the ten surviving medical papyri (the world's oldest medical textbooks written 5,000 years ago) show, it took thousands of years for Europe to rediscover and to reach the level of medical knowledge possessed by the Egyptians. Had Imoteph been white, he would without doubt be the hero of scientific medicine and not Hippocrates.

Great black heroes like Imoteph should not only inspire contemporary black people to aspire to the apogee of human achievement but should also remind us about how far we, as a people, have retrogressed since we were hit by the twin-tragedy of slavery and colonialism and also how high we can ascend. Let Imoteph serve as a beacon to guide us out of the abyss of inferiority into which white power and ideology have consigned us.

Elijah McCoy "The real McCoy" (1843-1929)

Eric Williams, Basil Davidson, Ronald Segal *et al* have demonstrated that the most significant factor of Britain's industrial revolution was the capital accumulation made possible by the transatlantic

[1]Newsome, Frederick, *Blacks in Science: Ancient and Modern* (1983) Edited by Ivan Van Sertima, Transaction Books, New Brunswick (U.S.A.) p. 129.

[2] Finch, Charles S., *Blacks in Science*, op. cit. p. 140.

slave trade and the plantation systems of the Westindies. Black labour and blood is, therefore, at the very heart of the origin and development of British industrialisation which soon spread through the other colonial European nations and the U.S.A.

The end of the American Civil War and the Reconstruction period brought a rapid growth in the exploitation of the massive natural resources of the U.S. The latter part of the nineteenth century saw a big boom in the manufacture of heavy machinery harnessing steam power. These complicated machines had many moving parts which had to be regularly oiled to reduce wear and tear caused by friction. Every time these machines needed oiling, they had to be stopped and production halted. This was a most inefficient way of lubricating moving parts of machines but the then available knowledge and technology failed to produce a more efficient method of oiling these complicated machines until McCoy came along with his revolutionary lubricating systems.

Elijah McCoy was born in Canada in 1843. Both his parents were slaves who fled from their owner in the State of Kentucky to Canada. As a boy, McCoy was fascinated with machines and tools, taking every chance to watch them in action and working on them whenever he could. He moved to the United States after the Civil War and settled near Ypsilanti, Michigan where he took up a job in a machine shop.

In 1870 his active and enquiring mind drove him to the challenge of developing a lubricating system for machines in motion. For two years McCoy worked on the problem and on July 12, 1872 received his first patent. This invention – the "drip cup" – was described as a key device in perfecting the overall lubrication system used in large industry today. It was quickly adopted by the major industries using heavy equipment.

In the spring of 1883, McCoy developed the small, oil-filled container with a stop cock to regulate the flow of oil to the innards of moving equipment. So popular did his lubrication system become that industrialists inspecting new equipment would enquire if it contained the *"real McCoy"*. This black inventor was eventually to receive fifty-seven patents, mostly for various kinds of steam cylinder lubricators. His inventions included twenty-three lubricators for different kinds of equipment, an ironing table, lawn sprinkler, steam dome and drip cup. He worked very hard, often receiving patents for two or three new devices a year. He set up the Elijah McCoy Manufacturing Company in Detroit, Michigan to manufacture and market his inventions.†

The measure of the significant contribution made by this black genius to industry is the fact that the phrase *"the real McCoy"* has become part of the English language and is symbolic of the genuine or original in contrast with cheap imitation. How many white people, or black people for that matter, who use the phrase "the real McCoy" know that they are affirming the inventive genius of a black inventor, a self-taught mechanic son of a fugitive slave couple?

George Washington Carver
One of the greatest scientists of all time

Our success in the task of reconstructing our shattered image and confidence and rediscovering our inventiveness and creativity as a race would be partly determined by how successful we are in recreating our distorted history and rediscovering and resurrecting our heroes whose work has not only helped to rebut five hundred years of white lies but has contributed to the enrichment of the quality of human life in general and *white* life in particular. I say white life in particular because, ultimately, white people have benefited more from the discoveries and inventions of black scientists than have black people.

George Washington Carver, like the great Imoteph who preceded him by 5,000 years, was a multi-genius in every sense of the word. Carver was born into slavery and suffered the most appalling catalogue of racial injustice, discrimination and humiliation. Despite his childhood craving for learning, he could not enter formal education until the age of 14 because of racial segregation, the U.S. version of apartheid. Yet he became a scientist of undisputed genius, one of the U.S.A.'s greatest biologists.

When at the age of 33, George received his long-sought Bachelor of Science degree, he took up a job with Iowa State University as an Assisant Botanist and was put in charge of the college's experimental station greenhouse. He concentrated on mychology, the branch of botany which deals

† On April 20 1915, McCoy received a patent for a 'Graphite Liberator' which he invented for use on railroad locomotives with superheated engines. This provided a continuous flow of oil without clogging the engine.

with fungus growth and soon his collection contained some 20,000 specimens. His skill at hybridising rendered whole families of fruits and plants resistant to fungus attack, and scientific journals began to cite Carver as their authority.

Around this time, Booker T. Washington, then the acknowledged spokesperson of black people in the U.S.A., set up the Tuskegee Institute for black people. He heard of Dr Carver and invited him to take up a teaching post with the Institute. When he arrived at Tuskegee, he found that the agricultural department he was supposed to be heading existed only on paper. There was a single room which had to serve as lecture hall as well as his living quarters. "Your laboratory", Washington told him, "will have to be in your head". George accepted the challenge and got down to work with his agriculture students.

When his experimental farms began to yield crops sometimes six times the usual harvest, Carver set up the wagon school which started a revolution in soil conservation, all but eradicated pellagra in the American South, and went on to become a worldwide institution. While teaching poor black and white farmers (in every piece of spare time he had from the College) on how to get the best yield out of their crops, he encouraged them (at first to no avail) to break from the tyranny of the cotton plantations.

In 1915 when the South suffered one of the worst plagues of the boll weevil, a rapacious beetle that feeds on cotton, the farmers began to pay attention to Carver's entreaty to diversify from cotton production. He had been experimenting with an odd little vine that produced peanuts which was considered at the time in the US to be worthless. Now on Carver's advice, whole communities abandoned cotton farming and planted acres upon acres of peanuts.

One October afternoon, an old woman came and complained to the professor that, having followed his counsel, she had had a bumper harvest and had hundreds of pounds of peanuts surplus to her requirements. "What could she do with them?" she asked. A hasty tour of the countryside revealed the enormity of his blunder; barns were piled up high with surplus and still more peanuts were rotting in the fields. He returned to his laboratory full of guilt. He had only thought the problem half-way through. Not only did the people have to be rescued from the tyranny of the cotton plantation but they also had to have an alternative cash crop.

Carver locked himself in his laboratory, shelled a handful of peanuts and literally tore the nuts apart, separating their fats and gums, their resins,sugars and starches. Spread before him were pentoses, pentosans, legumins, lysin, amido and amino acids. He tested these in different combinations under varying degrees of heat and pressure, and soon his hoard of synthetic treasures began to grow: milk, ink, dyes, shoe polish, creosote, salve, shaving cream and, of course, peanut butter.

From the shells, he made a soil conditioner, insulating board and fuel briquettes. Binding another batch with an adhesive, he pressed it, buffed it to a high gloss and held in his hands a light weatherproof square that looked precisely like marble and was every bit as hard. For two days and two nights he worked, dismissing his worried students who tapped at his door, enquiring if he was alright.

By the time the wearied professor stepped out into that chilly October morning in 1915, the world of *synthetics* and the discipline of agricultural chemistry were born! There are those who feel that this concept, still the subject of widespread research, was Carver's most important gift to humankind. Never before had anyone advocated the use of agricultural products for anything but food and clothing.

Carver had made it possible for farmers to use every peanut harvested. In 1981, the U.S. peanut production reached a staggering $1,069,526,000. By the time he died, there were well over 300 by-products, scores of factories had been built to make them and their range staggered the mind – mayonnaise, cheese, chili sauce, shampoos, bleach, axle grease, linoleum, metal polish, wood stains, adhesives and plastics.

Carver's inventive genius knew no bounds: he made paper from the southern pine – and 25 years later his process led to a major new paper industry. The synthetic marble he made from peanut shells and food wastes presaged the fabrication of plastics from all sorts of vegetable matter. Substituting cellulose for steel, U.S. car manufacturers were, in time, building 350 pounds of agricultural products into every car.

From the sweet potato, Carver devised 118 products, ranging from wartime flour to inexpensive gum for postage stamps and laid the foundation for still another industry. He discovered during the First World War that he could reduce 100 pounds of sweet potatoes to a powder that fitted in a compact carton, kept indefinitely, and could be instantly reconstituted by the addition of water. The multi-billion dollar dehydrated food industry owes his genius a debt of gratitude. From the Osage orange, he extracted a juice that tamed the toughest cut of beef – one of the first meat tenderisers. He showed that the giant thistle – ranted at by farmers – contained medical properties, as did 250 other weeds he examined. From the golden rod that covered the Georgia plantation Carver extracted a milky liquid that could be synthesised into a material with rubber-like characteristics, giving an exciting start to the long search for a synthetic substitute for rubber.

When chemists learned to synthesise rayon and other artificial fibres, it seemed that the era when Southern farmers could sell as much cotton as they could produce was over. But Carver's brilliant mind soon produced alternative solutions and in a few years the farmers were flourishing again, their markets spurred by the use of cotton in plastics, paving stones for roads, car tyres and fertiliser. He extracted paints and colour washes from the clay hills. Another Carver experiment led to the now-standard use of soya bean oil as the base for car spray paints. American industrialists used to import aniline dyes from Germany. Thanks to Carver, this no longer became necessary as he discovered 536 different dyes and gave the formula free to a dyestuffs firm.

He could have made a fortune, but spurned every offer of money. His inventions became freely available to U.S. industrialists, the overwhelming majority of whom were white. Whole factories were moved to Tuskegee so they could benefit from his free advice.

During the fortieth anniversary of Dr. Carver's arrival at Tuskegee, the college commemorated his work with an exhibition. The remarkable achievements of Carver's lifetime were truly a splendour. There were *thousands* of products shaped from peanuts, sweet potatoes and weeds. These were all gathered into a display that was later made permanent in a museum in a separate building, dedicated by Henry Ford and called the George Washington Carver Museum.

On January 5, 1943, Dr. Carver died at the age of eighty-two. The simple epitaph on his grave gave an eloquent testimony to a true intellectual giant and humanist in the truest meaning of the term:

"He could have added fortune to fame, but caring for neither, he found happiness and honour in being helpful to the world."

Today, there is hardly anybody in the industrialised world whose life is unaffected by the discoveries of Dr. Carver. He was not a product of "public school" or "grammar school"; not a product of Oxford, Cambridge, Harvard or Yale. There were no foundation scholarships for him, nor special grants for research; no finely equipped laboratores or well-stocked libraries – his initial laboratory was his head. He triumphed over the worst a racist society like the U.S. could throw at him. His brilliant intellect led him to a life-time of achievements that mark him out as one of the greatest scientists of all time.

Let Carver serve as a model to us as we resist the practice of teachers who routinely direct our children away from the study of the sciences and channel them into the pursuit of sports and music, at best, on the assumption that black people lack the intellectual capacity to make any meaningful contribution to science and technology.

EBONY DATE

Black inventors

Black people have made a major contribution to the development of science and technology in the USA. This list shows patented inventions by black Americans in the period, 1871-1900, and is taken from 'The Negro Almanac – a Reference Work on The Afro-American', published for the USA's bicentenary in 1976. It should be remembered that in the period in question black people were subject to pervasive legal and extra-legal discrimination in the USA.

Inventor	*Invention*	*Date*	*Patent*
Abrams, W. B.	Hame Attachment	Apr. 14, 1891	450,550
Allen C. W.	Self-Leveling Table	Nov. 1, 1898	613,436
Allen, J. B.	Clothes Line Support	Dec. 10, 1895	551,105
Ashbourne, A. P.	Process for Preparing Coconut for Domestic Use	June 1, 1875	163,962
Ashbourne, A. P.	Biscuit Cutter	Nov. 30, 1875	170,460
Ashbourne, A. P.	Refining Coconut Oil	July 27, 1880	230,518
Ashbourne, A. P.	Process of Treating Coconut	Aug. 21, 1877	194,287
Bailes, Wm.	Ladder Scaffold-Support	Aug. 5, 1879	218,154
Bailey, L. C.	Combined Truss and Bandage	Sept. 25, 1883	285,545
Bailey, L. C.	Folding Bed	July 18, 1899	629,286
Bailiff, C. O.	Shampoo Headrest	Oct. 11, 1898	612,008
Ballow, W. J.	Combined Hatrack and Table	Mar. 29, 1898	601,422
Barnes, G. A. E.	Design for Sign	Aug. 19, 1889	29,193
Beard, A. J.	Rotary Engine	July 5, 1892	478,271
Beard, A. J.	Car-coupler	Nov. 23, 1897	594,059
Becket, G. E.	Letter Box	Oct. 4, 1892	483,525
Bell, L.	Locomotive Smoke Stack	May 23, 1871	115,153
Bell, L.	Dough Kneader	Dec. 10, 1872	133,823
Benjamin, L. W.	Broom Moisteners and Bridles	May 16, 1893	497,747
Benjamin, Miss M. E.	Gong and Signal Chairs for Hotels	July 17, 1888	386,286
Binga, M. W.	Street Sprinkling Apparatus	July 22, 1879	217,843
Blackburn, A. B.	Railway Signal	Jan. 10, 1888	376,362
Blackburn, A. B.	Spring Seat for Chairs	Apr. 3, 1888	380,420
Blackburn, A. B.	Cash Carrier	Oct. 23, 1888	391,577
Blair, Henry	Corn Planter	Oct. 14,1834	
Blair, Henry	Cotton Planter	Aug. 31, 1836	
Blue, L.	Hand Corn Shelling Device	May 20, 1884	298,937
Booker, L. F.	Design Rubber Scraping Knife	Mar. 28, 1899	30,404
Boone, Sarah	Ironing Board	Apr. 26, 1892	473,653
Bowman, H. A.	Making Flags	Feb. 23, 1892	469,395
Brooks, C. B.	Punch	Oct. 31, 1893	507,672
Brooks, C. B.	Street-Sweepers	Mar. 17, 1896	556,711
Brooks, C. B.	Street-Sweepers	May 12, 1896	560,154
Brooks, Hallstead and Page	Street-Sweepers	Apr. 21, 1896	558,719
Brown, Henry	Receptacle for Storing and Preserving Papers	Nov. 2, 1886	352,036
Brown, L. F.	Bridle Bit	Oct. 25, 1892	484,994
Brown, O. E.	Horseshoe	Aug. 23, 1892	481,271
Brown & Latimer	Water Closets for Railway Cars	Feb. 10, 1874	147,363
Burr, J. A.	Lawn Mower	May 9, 1899	624,749
Burr, W. F.	Switching Device for Railways	Oct. 31, 1899	636,197
Burwell, W.	Boot or Shoe	Nov. 28, 1899	638,143
Butler, R. A.	Train Alarm	June 15, 1897	584,540
Butts, J. W.	Luggage Carrier	Oct. 10, 1899	634,611
Byrd, T. J.	Improvement in Holders for Reins for Horses	Feb. 6, 1872	123,328
Byrd, T. J.	Apparatus for Detaching Horses from Carriages	Feb. 6, 1872	123,328
Byrd, T. J.	Apparatus for Detaching Horses from Carriages	Mar. 19, 1872	124,790
Byrd, T. J.	Improvement in Neck Yokes for Wagons	Mar. 19, 1872	124,790
Byrd, T. J.	Improvement in Car-Couplings	Dec. 1, 1874	157,370
Campbell, W. S.	Self-Setting Animal Trap	Aug. 30, 1881	246,369

Inventor	*Invention*	*Date*	*Patent*
Cargill, B. F.	Invalid Cot	July 25, 1899	629,658
Carrington, T. A.	Range	July 25, 1876	180,323
Carter, W. C.	Umbrella Stand	Aug. 4, 1885	323,397
Certain, J. M.	Parcel Carrier for Bicycles	Dec. 26, 1899	639,708
Cherry, M. A.	Velocipede	May 8, 1888	382,351
Cherry, M. A.	Street Car Fender	Jan. 1, 1895	531,908
Church, T. S.	Carpet Beating Machine	July 29, 1884	302,237
Clare, O. B.	Trestle	Oct. 9, 1888	390,752
Coates, R.	Overboot for Horses	Apr. 19, 1892	473,295
Cook, G.	Automatic Fishing Device	May 30, 1899	625,829
Coolidge, J. S.	Harness Attachment	Nov. 13, 1888	392,908
Cooper, A. R.	Shoemaker's Jack	Aug. 22, 1899	631,519
Cooper, J.	Shutter and Fastening	May 1, 1883	276,563
Cooper, J.	Elevator Device	Apr. 2, 1895	536,605
Cooper, J.	Elevator Device	Sept. 21, 1897	590,257
Cornwell, P. W.	Draft Regulator	Oct. 2, 1888	390,284
Cornwell, P. W.	Draft Regulator	Feb. 7, 1893	491,082
Cralle, A. L.	Ice-Cream Mold	Feb. 2, 1897	576,395
Creamer, H.	Steam Feed Water Trap	Mar. 17, 1895	313,854
Creamer, H.	Steam Trap Feeder	Dec. 11, 1888	394,463
(Creamer also patented five steam traps between 1887 and 1893.)			
Cosgrove, W. F.	Automatic Stop Plug for Gas Oil Pipes	Mar. 17, 1885	313,993
Darkins, J. T.	Ventilation Aid*	Feb. 19, 1895	534,322
Davis, I. D.	Tonic	Nov. 2, 1886	351,829
Davis, W. D.	Riding Saddles	Oct. 6, 1896	568,939
Davis, W. R. Jr.	Library Table	Sept. 24, 1878	208,378
Deitz, W. A.	Shoe	Apr. 30, 1867	64,205
Dickinson, J. H.	Pianola	Mich., 1899	
Dorsey, O.	Door-Holding Device	Dec. 10, 1878	210,764
Dorticus, C. J.	Device for Applying Coloring Liquids to Sides of Soles or Heels of Shoes	Mar. 19, 1895	535,820
Dorticus, C. J.	Machine for Embossing Photo	Apr. 16, 1895	537,442
Dorticus, C. J.	Photographic Print Wash	Apr. 23, 1875	537,968
Dorticus, C. J.	Hose Leak Stop	July 18, 1899	629,315
Downing, P. B.	Electric Switch for Railroad	June 17, 1890	430,118
Downing, P. B.	Letter Box	Oct. 27, 1891	462,093
Downing, P. B.	Street Letter Box	Oct. 27, 1891	462,096
Dunnington, J. H.	Horse Detachers	Mar. 16, 1897	578,979
Edmonds, T. H.	Separating Screens	July 20, 1897	586,724
Elkins, T.	Dining, Ironing Table and Quilting Frame Combined	Feb. 22, 1870	100,020
Elkins, T.	Chamber Commode	Jan. 9, 1872	122,518
Elkins, T.	Refrigerating Apparatus	Nov. 4, 1879	221,222
Evans, J. H.	Convertible Settees	Oct. 5, 1897	591,095
Faulkner, H.	Ventilated Shoe	Apr. 29, 1890	426,495
Ferrell, F. J.	Steam Trap	Feb. 11, 1890	420,993
Ferrell, F. J.	Apparatus for Melting Snow	May 27, 1890	428,670
(Ferrell also patented eight valves between 1890 and 1893.)			
Fisher, D.	Joiners' clamp	Apr. 20, 1875	162,281
Fisher, D. C.	Furniture Castor	Mar. 14, 1876	174,794
Flemming, F., Jr.	Guitar*	Mar. 3, 1886	338,727
Forten, J.	Sail Control	Mass. Newspaper 1850	
Goode, Sarah E.	Folding Cabinet Bed	July 14, 1885	322,177
Grant, G. F.	Golf-Tee	Dec. 12, 1899	638,920

Inventor	*Invention*	*Date*	*Patent*
Grant, W.	Curtain Rod Support	Aug. 4, 1896	565,075
Gray, R. H.	Baling Press	Aug. 28, 1894	525,203
Gray, R. H.	Cistern Cleaners	Apr. 9, 1895	537,151
Gregory, J.	Motor	Apr. 26, 1887	361,937
Grenon, H.	Razor Stropping Device	Feb. 18, 1896	554,867
Griffin, F. W.	Pool Table Attachment	June 13, 1899	626,902
Gunn, S. W.	Boot or Shoe*	Jan. 16, 1900	641,642
Haines, J. H.	Portable Basin	Sept. 28, 1897	590,833
Hammonds, J. F.	Apparatus for Holding Yarn Skeins	Dec. 15, 1896	572,985
Harding, F. H.	Extension Banquet Table	Nov. 22, 1898	614,468
Hawkins, J.	Gridiron	Mar. 26, 1845	3,973
Hawkins, R.	Harness Attachment	Oct. 4, 1887	370,943
Headen, M.	Foot Power Hammer	Oct. 5, 1886	350,363
Hearness, R.	Detachable Car Fender	July 4, 1899	628,003
Hilyer, A. F.	Water Evaporator Attachment for Hot Air Registers	Aug. 26, 1890	435,095
Hilyer, A. F.	Registers	Oct. 14, 1890	438,159
Holmes, E. H.	Gage	Nov. 12, 1895	549,513
Hunter J. H.	Portable Weighing Scales	Nov. 3, 1896	570,553
Hyde, R. N.	Composition for Cleaning and Preserving Carpets	Nov. 6, 1888	392,205
Jackson, B. F.	Heating Apparatus	Mar. 1, 1898	599,985
Jackson, B. F.	Matrix Drying Apparatus	May 10, 1898	603,879
Jackson, B. F.	Gas Burner	Apr. 4, 1899	622,482
Jackson, H. A.	Kitchen Table*	Oct. 6, 1896	569,135
Jackson, W. H.	Railway Switch	Mar. 9, 1897	578,641
Jackson, W. H.	Railway Switch	Mar. 16, 1897	593,665
Jackson, W. H.	Automatic Locking Switch	Aug. 23, 1898	609,436
Johnson, D.	Rotary Dining Table	Jan. 15, 1888	396,089
Johnson, D.	Lawn Mower Attachment	Sept. 10, 1889	410,836
Johnson, D.	Grass Receivers for Lawn Mowers	June 10, 1890	429,629
Johnson, I. R.	Bicycle Frame	Oct. 10, 1899	634,823
Johnson, P.	Swinging Chairs	Nov. 15, 1881	249,530
Johnson, P.	Eye Protector	Nov. 2, 1880	234,039
Johnson, W.	Velocipede	June 20, 1899	627,335
Johnson, W. A.	Paint Vehicle	Dec. 4, 1888	393,763
Johnson, W. H.	Overcoming Dead Centers	Feb. 4, 1896	554,223
Johnson, W. H.	Overcoming Dead Centers	Oct. 11, 1898	612,345
Johnson, W.	Egg Beater	Feb. 5, 1884	292,821
Jones, F. M.	Ticket Dispensing Machine	June 27, 1939	2,163,754
Jones, F. M.	Air Conditioning Unit	July 12, 1949	2,475,841
Jones, F. M.	Two-Cycle Gasoline Engine	Nov. 28, 1950	2,523,273
Jones, F. M.	Starter Generator	July 12, 1949	2,475,842
Jones, F. M.	Thermostat and Temperature Control System	Feb. 23, 1960	2,926,005
(Jones also patented multiple devices related to gas engines and temperature control between 1939 and 1960.)			
Jones & Long	Caps for Bottles	Sept. 13, 1898	610,715
Joyce, J. A.	Ore Bucket	Apr. 26, 1898	603,143
Latimer, L. H.	Manufacturing Carbons	June 17, 1882	252,386
Latimer, L. H.	Apparatus for Cooling and Disinfecting	Jan. 12, 1886	334,078
Latimer, L. H.	Locking Racks for Hats, Coats and Umbrellas	Mar. 24, 1896	557,076
Latimer & Nichols	Electric Lamp	Sep. 13, 1881	247,097

Inventor	*Invention*	*Date*	*Patent*
Latimer & Tregoning	Globe Support for Electric Lamps	Mar. 21, 1882	255,212
Lavalette, W.	Printing Press*	Sept. 17, 1878	208,208
Lee, H.	Animal Trap	Feb. 12, 1867	61,941
Lee, J.	Kneading Machine	Aug. 7, 1894	524,042
Lee, J.	Bread Crumbing Machine	June 4, 1895	540,553
Leslie, F. W.	Envelope Seal	Sept. 21, 1897	590,325
Lewis, A. L.	Window Cleaner	Sept. 27, 1892	483,359
Lewis, E. R.	Spring Gun	May 3, 1887	362,096
Linden, H.	Piano Truck	Sept. 8, 1891	459,365
Little, E.	Bridle-Bit	Mar. 7, 1882	254,666
Loudin, F. J.	Sash Fastener	Dec. 12, 1892	510,432
Loudin, F. J.	Key Fastener	Jan. 9, 1894	512,308
Love, J. L.	Plasterers' Hawk	July 9, 1895	542,419
Love, J. L.	Pencil Sharpener	Nov. 23, 1897	594,114
Marshall, T. J.	Fire Extinguisher*	May 26, 1872	125,063
Marshall, W.	Grain Binder	May 11, 1886	341,599
Martin, W. A.	Lock	July 23, 1889	407,738
Martin, W. A.	Lock	Dec. 30, 1890	443,945
Matzeliger, J. E.	Mechanism for Distributing Tacks	Nov. 26, 1899	415,726
Matzeliger, J. E.	Nailing Machine	Feb. 25, 1896	421,954
Matzeliger, J. E.	Tack Separating Mechanism	Mar. 25, 1890	423,937
Matzeliger, J. E.	Lasting Machine	Sept. 22, 1891	459,899
McCoy, E.	Lubricator for Steam Engines	July 2, 1872	129,843
McCoy, E.	Lubricator for Steam Engines	Aug. 6, 1872	130,305
McCoy, E.	Steam Lubricator	Jan. 20, 1874	146,697
McCoy, E.	Ironing Table	May 12, 1874	150,876
McCoy, E.	Steam Cylinder Lubricator	Feb. 1, 1876	173,032
McCoy, E.	Steam Cylinder Lubricator	July 4, 1876	179,585
McCoy, E.	Lawn Sprinkler Design	Sept. 26, 1899	631,549
McCoy, E.	Steam Dome	June 16, 1885	320,354
McCoy, E.	Lubricator Attachment	Apr. 19, 1887	361,435
McCoy, E.	Lubricator for Safety Valves	May 24, 1887	363,529
McCoy, E.	Drip Cup	Sept. 29, 1891	460,215
(*In addition, McCoy also held 16 different patents for lubricators designed between 1873 and 1899.*)			
McCoy & Hodges	Lubricator	Dec. 24, 1889	418,139
McCree, D.	Portable Fire Escape	Nov. 11, 1890	440.322
Mendenhall, A.	Holder for Driving Reins	Nov. 28, 1899	637,811
Miles, A.	Elevator	Oct. 11, 1887	371,207
Mitchell, C. L.	Phoneterisin	Jan. 1, 1884	291,071
Mitchell, J. M.	Cheek Row Corn Planter	Jan. 16, 1900	641,462
Moody, W. U.	Game Board Design	May 11, 1897	27,046
Morehead, K.	Reel Carrier	Oct. 6, 1896	568,916
Murray, G. W.	Combined Furrow Opener and Stalk-knocker	Apr. 10, 1894	517,960
Murray, G. W.	Cultivator and Marker	Apr. 10, 1894	517,961
Murray, G. W.	Planter	June 5, 1894	520,887
Murray, G. W.	Cotton Chopper	June 5, 1894	520,888
Murray, G. W.	Fertilizer Distributor	June 5, 1894	520,889
Murray, G. W.	Planter	une 5, 1894	520,891
Murray, G. W.	Planter and Fertilizer Distributor Reaper	June 5, 1894	520,892
Murray, W.	Attachment for Bicycles	Jan. 27, 1891	445,452
Nance, L.	Game Apparatus	Dec. 1, 1891	464,035
Nash, H. H.	Life Preserving Stool	Oct. 5, 1875	168,519
Newson, S.	Oil Heater or Cooker	May 22, 1894	520,188

Inventor	*Invention*	*Date*	*Patent*
Nichols & Latimer	Electric Lamp*	Sept. 13, 1881	247,097
Nickerson, W. J.	Mandolin and Guitar Attachment for Pianos	June 27, 1899	627,739
O'Conner & Turner	Alarm for Boilers	Aug. 25, 1896	566,612
O'Conner & Turner	Steam Gage	Aug. 25, 1896	566,613
O'Conner & Turner	Alarm for Coasts Containing Vessels	Feb. 8, 1898	598,572
Outlaw, J. W.	Alarm for Coasts Containing Vessels	Feb. 8, 1898	598,572
Outlaw, J. W.	Horseshoes	Nov. 15, 1898	614,273

No. 795,243. PATENTED JULY 18, 1905.

G. T. & L. WOODS.

RAILWAY BRAKE APPARATUS.

APPLICATION FILED APR. 10, 1903.

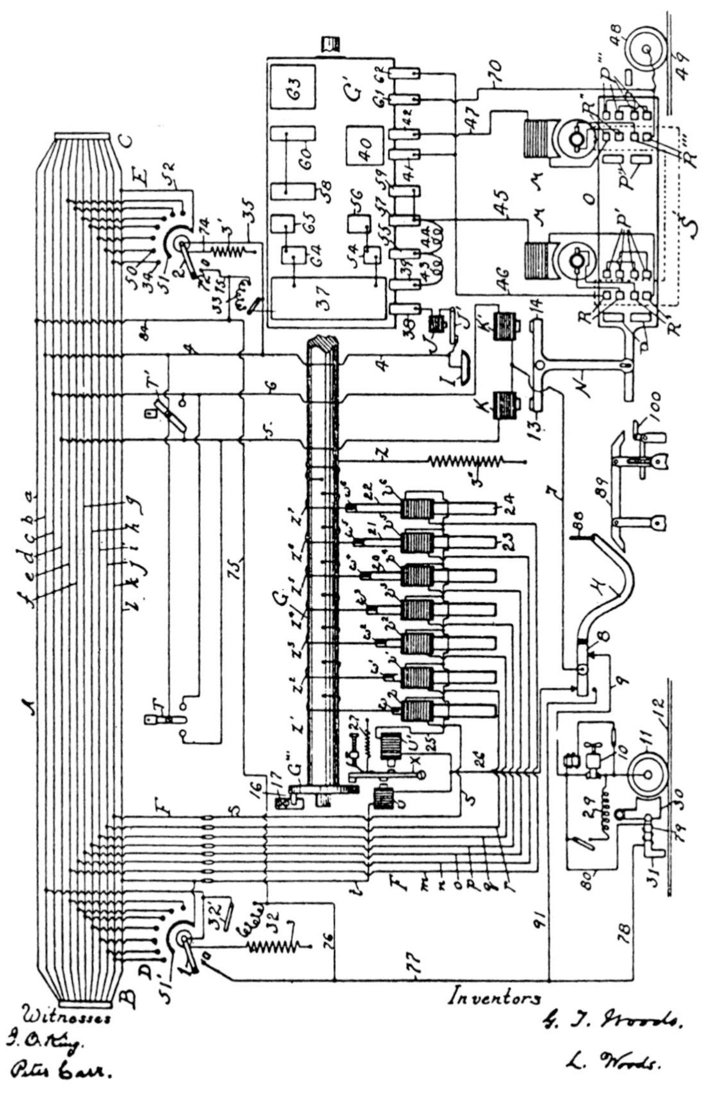

Inventor	*Invention*	*Date*	*Patent*
Perryman, F. R.	Caterers' Tray Table	Feb. 2, 1892	468,038
Peterson, H.	Attachment for Lawn Mowers	Apr. 30, 1889	402,189
Phelps, W. H.	Apparatus for Washing Vehicles	Mar. 23, 1897	579,242
Pickering, J. F.	Air Ship	Feb. 20, 1900	643,975
Pickett, H.	Scaffold	June 30, 1874	152,511
Pinn, T. B.	File Holder	Aug. 17, 1880	231,355
Polk, A. J.	Bicycle Support	Apr. 14, 1896	558,103
Pugsley, A.	Blind Stop	July 29, 1890	433,306
Purdy & Peters	Design for Spoons	Apr. 23, 1895	24,228
Purdy & Sadgwar	Folding Chair	June 11, 1889	405,117
Purdy, W.	Device for Sharpening Edged Tools	Oct. 27, 1896	570,337
Purdy, W.	Design for Sharpening Edged Tools	Aug. 16, 1898	609,367
Purdy, W.	Device for Sharpening Edged Tools	Aug. 1, 1899	630,106
Purvis, W. B.	Bag Fastener	Apr. 25, 1882	256,856
Purvis, W. B.	Hand Stamp	Feb. 27, 1883	273,149
Purvis, W. B.	Fountain Pen	Jan. 7, 1890	419,065
Purvis, W. B.	Electric Railway*	May 1, 1894	519,291
Purvis, W. B.	Magnetic Car Balancing Device	May 21, 1895	539,542
Purvis, W. B.	electric Railway Switch	Aug. 17, 1897	588,176
(Purvis also patented 10 paper bag machines between 1884 and 1894.)			
Queen, W.	Guard for Companion Ways and Hatches	Aug. 18, 1891	458,131
Ray, E. P.	Chair Supporting Device	Feb. 21, 1899	620,078
Ray, L. P.	Dust Pan	Aug. 3, 1897	587,607
Reed, J. W.	Dough Kneader and Roller	Sept. 23, 1884	305,474
Reynolds, H. H.	Window Ventilator for R. R. Cars	Apr. 3, 1883	275,271
Reynolds, H. H.	Safety Gate for Bridges	Oct. 7, 1890	437,937
Reynolds, R. R.	Non-Refillable Bottle	May 2, 1899	624,092
Rhodes, J. B.	Water Closets	Dec. 19, 1899	639,290
Richardson, A. C.	Hame Fastener	Mar. 14, 1882	255,022
Richardson, A. C.	Churn	Feb. 17, 1891	446,470
Richardson, A. C.	Casket Lowering Device	Nov. 13, 1894	529,311
Richardson, A. C.	Insect Destroyer	Feb. 28, 1899	620,363
Richardson, A. C.	Bottle	Dec. 12, 1899	638,811
Richardson, W. H.	Cotton Chopper	June 1, 1886	343,140
Richardson, W. H.	Child's Carriage	June 18, 1889	405,599
Richardson, W. H.	Child's Carriage	June 18, 1889	405,600
Richey, C. V.	Car Coupling	June 15, 1897	584,650
Richey, C. V.	Railroad Switch	Aug. 3, 1897	587,657
Richey, C. V.	Railroad Switch	Oct. 26, 1897	592,448
Richey, C. V.	Fire Escape Bracket	Dec. 28, 1897	596,427
Richey, C. V.	Combined Hammock and Stretcher	Dec. 13, 1898	615,907
Rickman, A. L.	Overshoe	Feb. 8, 1898	598,816
Ricks, J.	Horseshow	Mar. 30, 1886	338,781
Ricks, J.	Overshoes for Horses	June 6, 1899	626,245
Rillieux, N.	Sugar Refiner (Evaporating Pan)	Dec. 10, 1846	4,879
Robinson, E. R.	Electric Railway Trolley	Sept. 19, 1893	505,370
Robinson, E. R.	Casting Composite	Nov. 23, 1897	594,386
Robinson, J. H.	Life Saving Guards for Locomotives	Mar. 14, 1899	621,143
Robinson, J. H.	Life Saving Guards for Street Cars	Apr. 25, 1899	623,929
Robinson, J.	Dinner Pail	Feb. 1, 1887	356,852
Romain, A.	Passenger Register	Apr. 23, 1889	402,035
Ross, A. L.	Runner for Stops	Aug. 4, 1896	565,301
Ross, A. L.	Bag Closure	June 7, 1898	605,343

Inventor	*Invention*	*Date*	*Patent*
Ross, A. L.	Trousers Support	Nov. 28, 1899	638,068
Ross, J.	Bailing Press	Sept. 5, 1899	632,539
Roster, D. N.	Feather Curler	Mar. 10, 1896	556,166
Ruffin, S.	Vessels for Liquids and Manner of Sealing	Nov. 20, 1899	737,603
Russell, L. A.	Guard Attachment for Beds	Aug. 13, 1895	544,381
Sampson, G. T.	Sled Propeller	Feb. 17, 1885	312,388
Sampson, G. T.	Clothes Dried	June 7, 1892	476,416
Scottron, S. R.	Adjustable Window Cornice	Feb. 17, 1880	224,732
Scottron, S. r.	Cornice	Jan. 16, 1883	270,851
Scottron, S. R.	Pole Tip	Sept. 21, 1886	349,525
Scottron, S. r.	Curtain Rod	Aug. 30, 1892	481,720
Scottron, S. r.	Supporting Bracket	Sept. 12, 1893	505,008
Shanks, S. C.	Sleeping Car Berth Register	July 21, 1897	587,165
Shewcraft, Frank	Letter Box	Detroit, Mich.	
Shorter, D. W.	Feed Rack	May 17, 1887	363,089
Smith, J. W.	Improvement in Games	Apr. 17, 1900	647,887
Smith, J. W.	Lawn Sprinkler	May 4, 1897	581,785
Smith, J. W.	Lawn Sprinkler	Mar. 22, 1898	601,065
Smith, P. D.	Potato Digger	Jan. 21, 1891	445,206
Smith, P. D.	Grain Binder	Feb. 23, 1892	469,279
Snow & Johns	Liniment	Oct. 7, 1890	437,728
Spears, H.	Portable Shield for Infantry	Dec. 27, 1870	110,599
Spikes, R. B.	Combination Milk Bottle Opener and Bottle Cover	June 29, 1926	1,590,557
Spikes, R. B.	Method and Apparatus for Obtaining Average Samples and Temperature of Tank Liquids	Oct. 27, 1931	1,828,753
Spikes, R. B.	Automatic Gear Shift	Dec. 6, 1932	1,889,814
Spikes, R. B.	Transmission and Shifting Thereof	Nov. 28, 1933	1,936,996
Spikes, R. b.	Self-Locking Rack for Billiard Cues	around 1910	not found
Spikes, R. B.	Automatic Shoe Shine Chair	around 1939	not found
Spikes, R. B.	Multiple Barrel Machine Gun	around 1940	not found
Standard, J.	Oil Stove	Oct. 29, 1889	413,689
Standard, J.	Refrigerator	July 14, 1891	455,891
Stewart & Johnson	Metal Bending Machine	Dec. 27, 1887	375,512
Stewart, E. w.	Punching Machine	May 3, 1887	362,190
Stewart, E. w.	Machine for Forming Vehicle Seat Bars	Mar. 22, 1887	373,698
Stewart, T. W.	Mop	June 13, 1893	499,402
Stewart, T. W.	Station Indicator	June 20, 1893	499,895
Sutton, E. H.	Cotton Cultivator	Apr. 7, 1878	149,543
Sweeting, J. A.	Device for Rolling Cigarettes	Nov. 30, 1897	594,501
Sweeting, J. A.	Combined Knife and Scoop	June 7, 1898	605,209
Taylor, B. H.	Rotary Engine	Apr. 23, 1878	202,888
Taylor, B. H.	Slide Valve	July 6, 1897	585,798
Temple, L.	Toggle Harpoon	1848	
Thomas, S. E.	Waste Trap	Oct. 16, 1883	286,746
Thomas, S. E.	Waste Trap for Basins, Closets, etc.	Oct. 4, 1887	371,107
Thomas, S. E.	Casting	July 31, 1888	386,941
Thomas, S. E.	Pipe Connection	Oct. 9, 1888	390,821
Toliver, George	Propeller for Vessels	Apr. 28, 1891	451,086
Tregoning & Latimer	Globe Supporter for Electric Lamps	Mar. 21, 1882	255,212
Walker, Peter	Machine for Cleaning Seed Cotton	Feb. 16, 1897	577,153
Walker, Peter	Bait Holder	Mar. 8, 1898	600,241

The great Kings and Queens of Africa

compiled and written by Abiola Awojobi

Africa – nursery of civilisation, cradle of mankind, for centuries dubbed the dark continent and shrouded in mystery Africa is probably the oldest known civilisation in the world.

African civilisation certainly has a long history dating back to periods long before Christ was born. Evidence of this is shown in the findings of geographical and archaelogical research – a testament of Africa's heritage and of course in the existence of the great pyramids of Egypt with a history dating back to over 4000 BC.

Long before the coming of the Europeans, Africa administered and enjoyed a wide range of political formations, indeed traditional African kingdoms which can be equated to the state of today. Many countries of this, the second largest continent in the world, operated a centralised authority often manifested in the African empires, dynasties and of course the Royal Families. Even those known as stateless societies managed to build up powerful kingdoms on the basis of communication, co-operation and consensus.

For hundreds of years now there have been kings and queens in Africa, even before the days of Mena, the first historical monarch. The great kings and queens of Africa whose accomplishments were uncovered by extensive research often lasting several centuries, vary in their personal profiles but all share a common thread of heritage – their significant contributions to the civilised world. These accomplishments range from the gladitorial genius of Hannibal, the advancement and preservation of African culture by Queen Nefertiti, the great war strategist Queen Amina or the military might of Chaka – King of the Zulus.

This section presents a personal profile on some of the great kings and queens of Africa, men and women who may not be found in any Western history books but who have made enormous contributions to the expansion, development and survival of their empires.

Cleopatra – Great Queen of Egypt

Ancient Egyptian history is scattered with references to its famous dynasties, a succession of kings and queens who created and consolidated the whole majestic structure of Egyptian civilisation from infancy through to maturity. However, it is only recently that man has accepted that Egypt is indeed part of Africa.

Prior to the last century man found it hard to link this brilliant Egyptian civilisation with the rest of the continent. But today this group of people who have lived deep in the valley of the Nile for more than 1000 years are defined and indeed *refuse not to be defined in any other way than* African.

One of the special features of the ancient *Egyptian civilisation was the superiority given to a* reigning queen over the legitimate male heir. That is to say, when a King died, his widow the Queen would maintain her authority over the state. Hence when a Queen (the eldest daughter of the Royal family) was officially raised to the rank of a partner with the King in public acts, her right to the throne was permanent.

Many references have been made to the great Cleopatra – Queen of Egypt, but few of us realise that there were indeed several Cleopatras of Egypt. The most renowned and frequently referred to in literary and historical works is Cleopatra – Queen of Egypt 51-30 BC.

She was born around 69BC, the last of the Cleopatras, yet none the less endowed with the talent, beauty, ambition, even cruelty of her predecessors. On the death of her father, Ptolemy Auletes, Cleopatra, the eldest of his children along with the eldest of the male heirs, became Queen and King respectively of Egypt; that is Cleopatra VI and Ptolemy XV. However, in the fourth year of their 'joint reign' the young king's counsellors advised him to dispose of Cleopatra and take sole control of the kingdom's affairs. Cleopatra thus went into exile in Syria where she gathered an army and returned within a few months to attempt to reconquer her legitimate share of the throne.

In 48BC, Caesar, concerned that the affairs of Egypt were affecting Rome, intervened and came to Egypt to reinstate Cleopatra. He was immediately struck by her, not so much her beauty but her independence of character and striking spirit. In their brief time together, she gained an influence over him which was to follow him to the grave. Caesar decided that negotiation, not arms, was the only solution to the dispute, and, gathering a formal assembly together, he read to Cleopatra and her brother the will of their father. This directed them to wed and reign according to hereditary custom with the Romans as their custodians.

Under the agreement which he had instituted, Caesar returned to Rome, but not before the start of a love affair between he and Cleopatra. This affair resulted in the birth of Caesarian, Cleopatra's first son.

Three years later, Cleopatra's brother was murdered, it was rumoured, on Cleopatra's orders, and Caesarion was named as co-regent in his place. Cleopatra never failed to assert his royal privileges and decided never to live far from Caesar. Consequently sometime before Caesar was assassinated by Anthony in 44BC she came to Rome. Once her lover was dead she escaped secretly back to Egypt.

After her escape a great civil war ensued climaxing in 41BC after the decisive battle of Philippi. Anthony, Caesar's successor, sent an order to the Queen to come before him and explain certain suspicious conduct of hers throughout the war.

During her stay the Queen was somehow able to exert extreme influence over Anthony, not dissimilar to that which she displayed over Caesar – "she played at dice with him, drank with him, hunted with him, and let him escape her neither *by day nor by night" – she conquered him* completely.

When the beautiful siren eventually returned *forgiven, to Egypt, it was to be four years before* she and Anthony met again, this time in Syria. (During their four years apart she bore twins for her lover.)

No sooner had Anthony reached Syria than he fell once again under the influence of his Queen. In the words of Plutarch: "...the passion for

Cleopatra, which better thoughts seemed to have lulled and charmed into oblivion, upon his approach to Syria gathered strength once again, and broke into a flame."

Their reunion was to be brief. Anthony had a mission to carry out, battles to fight and wars to win. So after much dallying he sent Cleopatra home to Egypt to await his victorious return.

During this time there occurred one of the most spectacular scenes since the Queen of Sheba came to learn the wisdom of Solomon – Cleopatra arriving in state to Jerusalem to visit King Herod the Great. This time it was a very different kind of meeting: both were experts in the field of ambition and cunning and they absolutely detested one another.

It is rumoured that Cleopatra attempted to seduce Herod but failed to do so due to his devotion to his wife Mariamme. And it is said that Herod actually consulted with his council as to whether he should put her to death "for this attempt on his virtue". But he was dissuaded when he realised the vengeance Anthony would reap if he should hear of his great Queen's death.

The closing chapters of Cleopatra's life are a little harder to decipher, but we do know that a succession of battles, conquests and conflicts coloured her final years. And perhaps the most prominent was the battle that raged for years between Cleopatra and Anthony's long suffering wife Octavian.

In 36BC Cleopatra had prepared to meet the war-ravaged Anthony with clothes and provisions for him and his troops. He hence returned with her to spend the winter in Alexandria. So Cleopatra triumphed over Octavia as she snatched him yet again from his loyal wife who too had come from Rome to Athens, with, it is said, "succours even greater than those of Cleopatra".

Cleopatra died in 30BC, probably suicide after poisoning herself with the venom of a snake. She was a queen until the end. Even in death she was majestic: "They saw her stone dead, lying upon a bed of gold, set out in all her royal ornaments. Iras, one of her women, lay dying at her feet, and Charmion, just ready to fall, scarce able to hold up her head, was adjusting her mistress's diadem. And when one that came in said angrily: 'Was this well done of your lady, Charmion?' 'Perfectly well,' she answered, 'and as became the daughter of so many kings'; and as she said this she fell down dead by the bedside."

So died the great Queen of Egypt, the last of a dynasty which was one of a kind. A remarkable woman both in intellect and physique, she was exceptional in her own and indeed in any other age she might have been born.

References

Egypt Old and New Percy F Martin

Cook's Handbook for Egypt and the Sudan Wallis Budge

The Empire of the Ptolemies JP Mahaffy

Makeda, the Queen of Sheba

Ethiopia is an ancient independent kingdom in North Africa and it is from within its realms that there came one of the greatest black majesties of all time, Makeda, The Queen of Sheba. The story of the Queen of Sheba who undertook the arduous journey from Saba to Jerusalem in order to learn of the wisdom of King Solomon is told in *Kebra Nagast* – the cherished ancient Ethiopian book meaning *The Glory of Kings* and whose sources include a wealth of historical materials derived from the Old Testament, Ethiopian, Egyptian and Arabian writings.

Like most things of an historical nature there is a degree of scepticism about the story of the Queen of Sheba – fact or legend? Many eminent scholars have accepted the story as fact and it is believed by all classes in Ethiopia who regard Solomon as the first real king of their country, that their Royal House traces its origin to King Solomon and the Queen of Sheba. But there are some scholars/ historians who consider the Solomon and Sheba tale merely as a legend with no historical foundation. Some even believe it to be a legend of Arabian origin which has been borrowed by the Ethiopians and assimilated into their literature.

The Bible, however, makes reference to this Ethiopian Queen (Matthew 12, 4, 2, Luke 6, 31):

> The Queen of the South will rise at the judgement with the men of this generation and condemn, for she came from the ends of the earth to listen to Solomon's wisdom, and now one greater than Solomon is here.

It is hence difficult to believe that the story has no historical foundation. And suffice it to say that the origin of Haile Selassie, instigator of the Rastafarian movement, goes back to the time of Menelike I, son of Solomon and Makeda who became king in 975BC.

The visit of Makeda to Solomon

The First Book of Kings asserts:

> And when the Queen of Sheba heard of the fame of Solomon concerning the name of the Lord, she came to prove him with hard questions. And she came to Jerusalem with a very great train, with camels that bore spices, and very much gold and precious stones; and when she came to Solomon, she communed with him of all that was in her heart.

The Kebra Nagast relates that the merchants of the Queen of Sheba traded by land and sea from India to Asawan as well at to Palestine. The chief of these Ethiopian merchants was a man called Tamrin who is reputed as having possessed 520 camels and 370 ships. When Solomon heard of the Ethiopian merchant he instructed him to bring gold, ebony, sapphires and other precious stones for him to adorn the Temple of the Ark of the Covenant with.

Tamrin did as he was bid and Solomon paid him handsomely. Tamrin also rested in Jerusalem for several days. During his stay he was stunned by Solomon's wisdom, impartiality of justice, his splendour and wealth and the capacity with which he ruled his people and administered his empire. When he returned home Tamrin recounted to the Queen all that he had seen and learnt in Jerusalem probably exaggerated slightly as is typical of human nature. The more she heard the more the Queen wished to see this great man for herself although she dreaded undertaking such a long and arduous journey.

Finally her desire to go to Jerusalem became so great that she dispelled all apprehensions and announced to her people her desire for wisdom and understanding and began preparations for the journey. She hoped that a study of Solomon's wisdom might enable her own government to be as admirable and well administered as his. Indeed she is recorded as having said:

> I desire wisdom, and my heart seeketh to find understanding...for wisdom is far greater than treasure of gold and silver...it is a source of joy for the heart, and a bright shining lamp for the eyes; it is a teacher of those who are learned, and a consoler of those who are discreet and prudent...a kingdom cannot stand without wisdom.

The Queen then made ready to set forth with precious gifts for King Solomon – a caravan prepared by Tamrin consisting of over 700 camels, countless asses and mules as well as an extensive personal train.

As the Queen had predicted the journey was perilous – mountains and landscapes and the capital to the coast, then across the Red Sea and finally the long distance from Arabia to Israel.

The Queen was well received by King Solomon who placed part of his large palace and many of his servants at her disposal. She in turn was honoured by his graciousness and wisdom. He saw that she was well settled and attended to in the manner befitting a Queen. Over the weeks they always paid each other frequent visits conversing long and frequently and it was always 'the beauty of wisdom' that was the main subject on the agenda.

The Queen said of the King's teaching:

> "I went in through the doors of the treasury of wisdom and I drew for myself the waters of understanding."

Solomon explained that the wisdom God had given him was because he had asked neither for fame, riches nor triumph in battle, just wisdom. Eventually she consulted him about religion admitting that she was a sun worshipper but had heard of the God of Israel and the Ark of the Covenant. When the magnificence of the glory of God was revealed to her, the Queen abandoned her sun worship and became a follower of the Lord.

Makeda stayed in Jerusalem for six months during which time her knowledge of God increased greatly. At the end of this period she told King Solomon that it was time for her to return to her own country though she admitted there was still a large gap in her knowledge and so much more for her to learn. The virile King had now fallen for the beautiful Queen and he planned to ask her to wed him. He thus enquired of the Queen whether she intended leaving Jerusalem without seeing life at his quarters. He invited her to come and stay with him for a while so that he could complete her instruction in wisdom. The Queen graciously accepted and moved to his palace. Here she was well looked after – her chamber adorned with precious stones and spiced with aromatic fragrances. The king also prepared a banquet in her honour for which the food was highly salted and spiced. This was a deliberate attempt to ensure she would consequently have a great thirst.

When the Royal banquet ended Solomon said to the Queen: "Take thine ease here for love's sake until daybreak." She then replied: "Swear to me by thy God that thou wilt not take me by force. For if I, a maiden, be seduced, I should travel back home in sorrow and affliction and tribulation." Solomon then swore he would not take her by force as long as she swore that she would not take anything that was in his house by force. This oath was thus declared by both of them and they each returned to their separate chambers. During the night the Queen awoke parched with thirst – the peppery spices and acidic wine had done their job. She tried to resist her thirst without success and got up to go in search of some water. Finding none in her own room she crept to the King's chamber and therein spied a jug of water. Although she checked to see she was not being watched, unknown to her the king was not sleeping. Just as she lifted the jug to her lips she felt a hand on her shoulder – she had broken her oath. She was consuming something belonging to the King without his permission.

The King allowed her to finish the water and then the Queen, always a woman of honour, kept her pledge and surrendered herself to him. That night the future King of Ethiopia was conceived – Menelike I, founder of the Ethiopian royal dynasty.

After their night of love, the Queen awoke and begged permission to finally return to her own country. Solomon prepared to send her on her way with great pomp and ceremony, giving her gifts of ships, camels, jewels and cloths. Before he left he took her aside and, giving her the ring on his little finger said:

> "Take this so that thou mayest not forget me. And if it happen that I obtain seed from thee, this ring shall be sign of it, and if it be a man-child he shall come to me... and may the peace of God be with thee."

Like the story of Adam and Eve, the Solomon and Makeda tale has about it something that was forbidden – forbidden water rather than forbidden fruit. Solomon played his own Satan and his own Serpent engaging in both seduction and deception of Makeda – Eve. But in this royal tale of Solomon and Makeda the seduction scene did not lead to the beginning of death; it led to a new dynasty in the Horn of Africa.

References

The Africans – Ali A Mazrui

A History of Ethiopia – Sir Wallis Budge

Ethiopia – A Cultural History – Sylvia Pankhurst

Chaka – King of the Zulus

A profile on one of Africa's most ruthless yet respected leaders. He was responsible for the creation and consolidation of a mighty warrior nation, a man of 'iron resolve' and 'inflexible determination', a man who managed to build, out of nothing, an empire of honour and distinction in just twelve short years. His name was Chaka, Lord of Zululand.

Chaka was a descendant of the Zulus, an African tribe who lived in the north of what is now the great port of Durban. Born in a tiny village in the midst of Zululand, history books tell us that Chaka was an unwanted child and that his parents were unwed. His birth was the result of a lack of self-restraint on the part of his mother Nandi and his father Senzangakona while they were indulging in the Zulu practice of Uku-H'Obonga. This was a release in sexual tensions among the unmarried without conception resulting. When the head of Nandi's clan was told that she was pregnant he exclaimed that this was impossible and that she must be carrying an I-Chaka. An I-Chaka was an intestinal beetle believed by the Zulus to enter certain women causing severe menstrual disruption.

However, in 1787, a child was born and in contempt he was called U-Chaka. The boy's father Senzangakona, being a chief, was able to escape reprimand although it was considered a very serious crime to conceive a child out of wedlock among the Zulu people. As a consequence Nandi joined his household as a third wife.

Unfortunately, theirs was a stormy and turbulent relationship and eventually both Nandi and her son were driven out – compelled to seek refuge in her parent's home.

Although unknown at the time it was in this period of Chaka's life that the fundamental traits of his character as a future leader were being moulded. Chaka and his mother thrown back in disgrace to her family home were considered social outcasts and Chaka's childhood was thus not a happy one. Incessantly mocked and bullied by his playmates due to his insistence that he was the son of a chief while his mother suffered torment and ridicule it was within this climate that a child was growing up who would change the face of Southern Africa and much of central Africa.

Suffice it to say that Chaka's subsequent lust for power and dominance can almost undoubtedly be traced from a childhood overshadowed by torment and vindictiveness. These led to a strong feeling of hopelessness and inferiority, deep resentment and brooding, from which he may have developed the need to dominate his family, his tribe and eventually a vast empire.

In 1807, the head of Chaka's village died and his son Dingiswayo replaced him. Chaka's age group were called upon and he along with his peers found himself a soldier living in a military kraal (which was a normal procedure in the Zulu way of life). Chaka was now 20 years old, 6'3" and a man with a 'powerful body controlled by a ruthless and restless mind'. Under Dingiswayo's thumb he was inspired by many of the chief's ideas and was to implement some of them when, years later, he would become King of Zululand. He had many ideas to enhance an army but was unable to exercise these desires.

In 1817 Chaka's father died bestowing the chieftancy to the eldest son of his favourite wife. The new chief's reign, however, was short-lived – during a fight he was dethroned. Once again the throne sat empty. Chaka's time had come.

Dingiswayo, a man of similar aims and ambitions to Chaka's, sent him off with a batallion of his own regiment. Though he was not the rightful heir, armed with the might of Dingiswayo's regiment Chaka easily made himself the ruler of his father's people.

When he came to power Chaka's kingdom was ten miles by ten, his army barely numbered 500 men and was as yet untrained. He was to create and command an army of such energy and distinction that when many years later it came into combat with the armed forces of the British Empire, it was a highly organised force of some

30,000 men which was to return victorious. At this time the Zulu were a people who lacked a regular army or steadfast military organisation. Chaka began by calling up everyone capable of bearing arms and divided them into various groups depending on-age and status. He felt it imperative that his army was rearmed and for this task his blacksmiths were mobilised to work day and night on the lines of Chaka's new military strategy.

Chaka was now in a position to implement his ambitions as fully as possible – an opportunity he had long awaited. He began by giving his men a practical demonstration of his new methods. He split the force into two groups, one using traditional weapons and the other equipped with new improved equipment. He then arranged a simulated battle with the side using the older type weapons versus those using the new. The success of this experiment emphasised the superiority of Chaka's new methods and in doing so helped safeguard his position. Now ready and equipped with his new model army Chaka carried out what he has become notorious for – severe retribution for those who had ill-treated him and his mother so many years ago.

While Chaka was busy consolidating his empire the surrounding political climate was growing harsher and harsher. Each tribe in Zululand held strong political views and continual population growth brought frequent quarrels between clans. Three leaders were to emerge from this and carve for themselves powerful tribal empires. One of these was Sobhuza, the leader of the people who were to later become the Swazi. The second one was Zwide, chief of the Ndwandwe tribe – the largest and most powerful tribe in Zululand. Finally there was Dingiswayo the infamous chief of the Mthethwa people.

As long as Chaka remained subordinated to Dingiswayo his ambitions were under restriction but in this period of turbulence and expansion it was inevitable that sooner or later conflict would emerge.

In 1817 Chaka, blessed by his modern military equipment, military genius and political insight, was able to defeat the empires of the Sobhuza and Dingiswayo. The following year the momentous battle of the Mhatanze River occurred, a battle which brought about the collapse of the last remaining threat – the Zwide tribes.

As a result Chaka and the Zulu tribe in 1818 arose as the most dominant power in Zululand.

Now Chaka was able to fully implement his militaristic ambitions. All the same age groups whether from Zulu or conquered tribes were formed into separate regiments with a distinct regalia and placed in military towns. Each town also contained a section of royal women. Though Chaka claimed he never actually married these women, he did however make himself their guardian as they, in their hundreds, helped with the agricultural work needed for feeding the army and also participated in ceremonial dances. For this, they too were organised into age-regiments and when Chaka felt that a particular regiment should be released from service he would simultaneously release a female regiment so that these women would become the wives of the male regiment.

Through this system Chaka was able to develop a new attitude in the minds of his followers. The youths became trained into thinking of themselves 'first and foremost as followers of the king, secondly, members of particular regiments and only after that as members of a particular tribe or clan'.

It has been suggested that Chaka's rule was tyrannical and that his people were unhappy about the incessant wars in which they were engaged. His armies conquered and destroyed far and wide absorbing all the Nguni groups. And the upheavals he caused sent several groups into exile. Though Chaka had reduced the powers of the chiefs who, in traditional society, were usually the leaders of revolts, there were still several possible focuses of rebellion – the most prominent one being the misery of the people.

However, several of Chaka's brothers were still alive though they were not in positions of power. Sensing the misery and dissatisfaction of the people, two of his brothers Dingane and Mhlangana began to plot against Chaka with the chief of Mbhopa. Taking their opportunity during the absence of the bulk of the army, the conspirators made plans to assassinate the king.

One day Chaka was conducting an interview with some visiting ambassadors. The two brothers hid among some bushes, spears in hand ready for action. Dingane managed to divert Chaka's attention and suddenly Mhlangana lurched forward and stabbed the king in the back. Dingane reinforced the wound by another stab. It is held that Chaka staggered out of the enclosure crying 'Oh, Children of my father, what have I done to you?' But the assassins had no mercy and Chaka fell to the ground and died.

The great chief's reign was over. It had been short but it had, more importantly, left a permanent mark on African history. Chaka had organised a great kingdom from nothing, his army of 500 mushroomed to 50,000, and he was a chief of an area of 200,000 square miles. Often criticised for being ruthless and vindictive it is said that Chaka 'waded to power through blood'. However, in his few brief years as king he had brought together many different tribes to form a single kingdom. And unlike Dingiswayo's the great empire of Chaka the Zulu did not dissolve when he died but instead continued to play an important part in Southern Africa's history.

References

Leadership in Nineteenth Century Africa –edited by Professor Ikime

Shaka Zulu – The Rise of the Zulu Empire – E. A. Ritter

Nine Great Africans – Rex Niven

The Kingdom of Ashanti

Their whole existence was interlaced round a network of traditional modes which dictated the form of social conduct and the nature of artistic expression. Tutu made himself a crown of elephant skins which became the 'crown of Ashanti', worn by every successive king from then on.

She was the first black African country to obtain independence, a powerful ancient kingdom renowned for her vast resources of gold, cocoa and kola, flourishing agriculture and richly diverse arts and crafts; Ghana formerly the Gold Coast, is probably one of the most ancient of all the African domains.

Ancient Ghana was a country based on a collective of numerous independent kingdoms, each fighting for domination deep in the rainforests of Africa. The kingdoms of Accra, Fanti, Akwapim, Axim, Komanda and Afutu were some of the more prominent kingdoms which populated Ghana. And of these the most prominent was the Kingdom of Ashanti. No account of the early history of Ghana would be complete without reference to the Ashanti – the largest and most highly developed political body in West Africa.

The Ashantis originated from a race of people called the Akan whose exact origins remain unknown. It is certain, however, that like the other tribal groups along the Guinea coast, the Ashantis migrated southwards from the North coming from the direction of the Lake of Chad. However, to this day the Ashantis pride themselves with the belief of having originated from the 'soil of their country'.

The Ashantis also prided themselves on their rich degree of culture, indeed their whole existence was interlaced round a network of traditional modes which dictated the form of social conduct and the nature of artistic impression. Unfortunately historians have in the past, perhaps in their haste to emphasise the military might of the Ashantis, tended to overshadow the significance of the cultural qualities of the people.

Although Oti Akenten has been credited for founding the Ashantis as a military nation it was without doubt Osei Kofi Tutu who was the real founder of the Ashanti nation. Before Tutu the Ashantis lived in independent chiefdoms owing allegiance to no central body. But under Tutu all this changed. A powerful confederacy of chiefdoms was built by which the Ashanti nation was to slowly incorporate other tribes into their vastly growing domain to converge a single Ashanti nation.

While still a youth Tutu was sent to the court of his uncle, the King of Denkara. But while there he fell in love with the King's sister. She became pregnant then when she realised Tutu was the father helped him to flee and seek refuge in a nearby town called Akwanu.

While there, Tutu heard the news that his uncle Obiri had died and as a result he was summoned by the nobles of Ashanti to return and take the reins of government. Tutu obeyed and made ready for the journey. On the way, tradition goes, he made himself a crown of elephant skins which was to become the 'crown of Ashanti' (Denchemche) and worn by every successive king. The King also wore it when addressing chiefs on the eve of a campaign, imposing upon them, by oath, their duty to defeat the enemy or sacrifice their lives. And it was upon this oath that all chiefs had to swear proclaiming that they would return victorious or die.

Tutu was warmly welcomed by the people who, though grieved by their King's death, were looking forward to the enstoolment of a new one. And as Reindorf wrote in *History of the Gold Coast and Ashanti* (1895), "with his advent a new era began in the history of the Ashantis".

Tutu, now King, soon formed a friendship with an Akwapi priest – Komfo Anotchwi. Their alliance was to have immeasurable consequences for the Ashanti people. Confidential adviser and righthandman to the King, together Tutu and Anotchwi founded the customs and laws of the Ashanti confederacy which was to eventually unite the kingdom into a single powerful unit.

Anotchwi began his service by planting a *Kuma Tree,* prophesysing that as it grew, so would Titu's power and henceworth the name of the capital became Kum-Ase (under the Kum Tree.

Anotchwi also decided to provide a stool which would represent the unity of the Ashanti nation by revealing that this stool had aesthetic unity in the same way as the people of Ashanti. And this, the Golden Stool of Ashanti, has become one of the deepest elements in Ashant cultural history.

According to Ashanti legend, during a great gathering at Kumasi, Anotchwi produced from the sky a wooden stool adorned with gold, from a pillar of cloud. It's great seat was shaped like a half-moon and it was decorated with intricately designed impressions. Then Anotchwi told the people that the stool was the *sunsum* (soul) of the nation, the embodiment of the spirit, unity and greatness of the Ashanti people. All its power, health, bravery and greatness were vested in the stool and, the Ashantis believed, (and still do to this day), that if the stool was seized or destroyed the Ashanti nation would crumble just as a man may sicken and die. Thus both mystically and constitutionally, the other chiefs of the Ashanti alliance were subservient to Tutu – the cement for a new nation had been set and now Tutu truly was Ashantehene, ruler of a new empire.

Once settled on the throne, Tutu, with the unanimous support of his nobles prepared to avenge his late uncle's death against Oama Kwessi. Mission accomplished, gradually neighbouring kingdoms such as Amokum and Ofinso became incorporated into the rapidly expanding Ashanti empire. One feature that was prevalent in the Ashanti's internal affairs was that all conquered tribes were given full rights as Ashanti citizens and beyond certain obligations they experienced no interference from the Ashantis. And gradually, through this policy the conquerer and conquered kingdoms were able to become friends.

Another feature of the internal affairs of the kingdom was that the king could not himself make laws. The supreme authority was the Ashante State Council of which chiefs from neighbouring states were members. In this council the King was neither first among equals nor a dictator. He had to work in conjunction with the chiefs and the Council dealt not only in matters of war and peace but also the Supreme Court of the realm before which even the King could be tried. Through this system the Ashantis emerged a strong, confident and united people.

The Ashantis were the conquerers of many enemies and undoubtedly their brilliant military co-ordination and organisation lent them an immense superiority over neighbours and raised their country to the proud position of the paramount power among the surrounding states for the space of two hundred years.

But though the Ashantis conquered enemies they never in effect governed them. One such enemy was the Akim tribe. This tribe boldly managed to evade their financial obligations until finally in 1717 they openly rebelled. The source of the problem was the non-payment of *Atenve* on Ashanti oaths by the Akim people. *Atenve* was the fee paid for breaking an oath, The Akims persisted in refusing to pay these fees and finally Tutu and his chiefs lost patience and prepared to attack. They drove the Akims across the river Prah and invaded. But the Akims discovered where Tutu was to cross the river, laid an ambush for him and Osei Tutu fell, face downwards in the water before before being swept away by the strong current. His body was never recovered. The Ashantis maintain that his death was kept secret so as not to discourage the army and they indeed did not return until Akim had been conquered, during which time *Opoku Ware* whom Tutu had named his heir represented the deceased monarch.

And so died Osei Tutu, founder of a dynasty and first King of Ashanti. He had created and consolidated a powerful warrior nation based on organisation, respect and military strategy. And it was not until 1896 when the British captured and seized the Ashanti Empire that the power of this, the vanished dynasty of Ashanti, was broken.

Osei Tutu – Basil Freestone
Ghana Resurgent – Michael Dei Anang
A vanished Dynasty (Ashanti) – Fuller

Keep alive the memory of the leaders of liberation

A perspective and a proposal

by E.S. Reddy, former Assistant Secretary-General of the United Nations

The main current in the flow of history in the twentieth century has been the struggle of the majority of humanity not only for its freedom but for a new world order of justice and peace.

The warning and prophecy of the Pan African Conference in 1900 – when it declared that the "problem of the twentieth century is the problem of the colour line" – has been more than confirmed. National movements against colonial and racist oppression became part of a larger international movement, each supporting and benefiting from the other, and espousing common aspirations for a new world.

Mahatma Gandhi – apostle of Indian freedom and non-violence

The victory of the long struggle for freedom by India shook the British empire and facilitated the independence of other nations. The defeat of French colonialism in Indo-China and Algeria, at the cost of four million lives, enabled other nations in the French empire to gain independence with fewer casualties. Nasser's Egypt suffered and resisted a triple invasion in 1956 for Algeria's freedom, and since then many other nations have emulated that example. The black people's movement in the United States helped the movement to end the Vietnam war.

This historic struggle has given rise to great leaders with courage and determination, with faith and vision, who have moved the masses of men, women and children to resistance against brutal and desperate forces, which, armed to the teeth, showed no hesitation about massacring millions of people. Many men and women in the metropolitan countries shared the vision of a world without oppression, power politics and war and have courageously stood by the oppressed people.

Mahatma Gandhi and Martin Luther King, Jr., Patrice Lumumba and Jean Paul Satre symbolise the spirit of the twentieth century – not their jailers, nor the generals and admirals who have carried on unending wars against the people.

For these leaders national independence was not

Paul Robeson – artist and activist

an end in itself, nor even solely a means to overcome poverty, illiteracy and disease in their countries. They sought to restructure the world order. They played a significant role, as their nations attained independence, in pressing for action on global concerns such as disarmament, the banning of nuclear weapons, equitable economic relations, and international co-operation for economic and social progress.

As they began to succeed in uniting not only the peoples of the Third World but large segments of opinion in the privileged nations, they came under attack by forces wedded to power politics who sought to replace one form of domination by another. Many of them were assassinated, exiled and paralysed.

Homage to these great leaders and martyrs is not only a duty of our generation, it is an essential means to educate and inspire the people, especially the young, in the Third World as well as in Europe and North America, in order to complete the unfinished struggle. This is true not least because the vision of a community of humankind remains unfulfilled; the newly-independent nations remain victims of distant and unseen forces and of a vicious international economic order; popular governments have been overthrown by neo-colonial mercenaries; and corruption has become endemic in a number of countries.

Ten years ago, as head of the Centre against Apartheid in the United Nations, I had the privilege, in association with Ambassador Leslie Harriman of Nigeria, of organising, though in the limited context of solidarity with the South African people, a series of international tributes to Mahatma Gandhi and Dr. W.E.B. Du Bois, Paul Robeson and Martin Luther King, Jr., Marcus Garvey and George Padmore, Jawaharlal Nehru and Gamal Abdel Nasser, Franz Fanon and José Marti, and many others – great leaders who were persecuted and vilified by the imperialists, and who could not even petition the United Nations in its early years, were honoured in the United Nations Headquarters and at special sessions and events in Atlanta, Kingston, Accra and New Delhi.

We were able to secure a resolution by the United Nations General Assembly on January 24,

"Showboat", filmed in the 1930s, shot Paul Robeson to world fame. Playing alongside an actress whose stage name was "Princess Kouka", Paul Robeson starred in "Jericho". It was renamed "Dark Sands" for showing in the United States

1979 – resolution 33/183 C – calling on the United Nations and UNESCO to honour the memory of leaders of the oppressed peoples in their struggles against apartheid, racial discrimination and colonialism and for peace and international co-operation, as well as those who have made significant contributions to solidarity with the struggles of oppressed peoples. Governments and organisations were invited to co-operate in making the contributions of these leaders widely known for the education of world public opinion, especially of youth.

We hoped to organise world-wide tributes to the leaders, as a continuing programme through TV and radio features, books, pamphlets, postage stamps, naming of institutions etc. We hoped to break the walls of separation created by colonial rule and facilitate a concert of people toward a new world as envisaged by the leaders of liberation and renaissance.

If African nations issue postage stamps of Pandit Nehru and if India does the same for Eduardo Mondlane, if Latin American nations honour Ho Chi Minh and Japan honours Marcus Garvey, and so on, a meaningful first step would have been taken towards real human solidarity.

Though our plans received a warm welcome from many organisations I was unable to see to the effective implementation of the resolution before my retirement from the United Nations. Meanwhile, I am distressed that many great leaders of people who have inspired us are now being treated even in the Third World as "non-persons" because of coups and neo-colonial settlements.

Mohamed Ali Jinnah – founder of Pakistan

Marcus Garvey – his centenary underlined his continuing relevance

That is particularly true of Africa where a false sense of protocol prevails among the Heads of State. In the observance of the 25th anniversary of the founding of the Organisation of African Unity (OAU) this year not only are there few references to the great Pan African leaders who laid the groundwork for the OAU but many of the leaders of the African struggle are deliberately and totally ignored. The name of Diallo Telli, the first Secretary-General of OAU and a great African patriot, is not even mentioned. Fighters and martyrs like Patrice Lumumba of the Congo (now Zaire), Sylvano Olympio of Togo, Felix Moumié of the Cameroon, Prince Louis Rwagasore of Burundi are virtually banned. Others are treated as merely national, rather than African and international, leaders. It appears that only Gamal Abdel Nasser and Kwame Nkrumah cannot be confined to oblivion or to national boundaries.

Somewhat of a similar situation has developed in Asia. Sukarno and Mohamed Hatta of Indonesia, U Aung San of Burma, Mossadegh of

Marcus Garvey Junior – committed to the ideals of his illustrious father

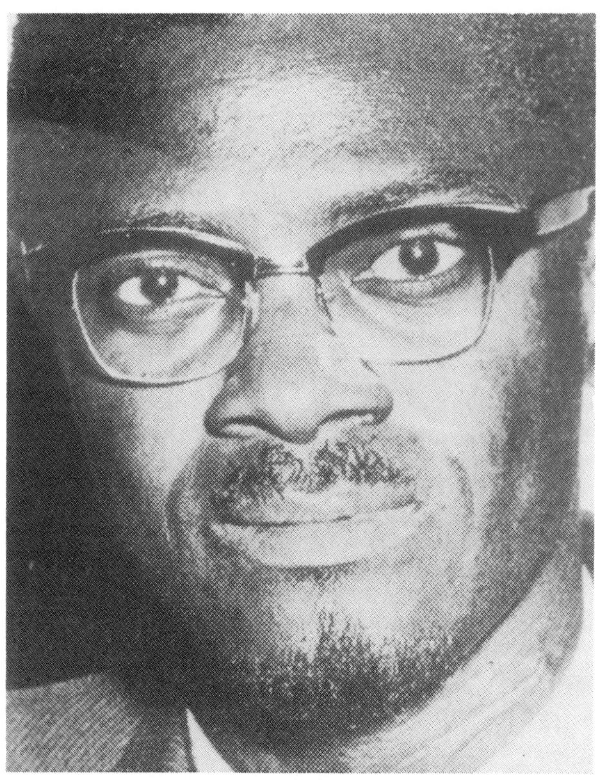

Patrice Lumumba – his martyrdom was a tragedy that exposed the reality of neo-colonialism

Martin Luther King, Jr. – civil rights leader in the USA

Iran and Mujibur Rahman of Bangladesh have been sentenced to become non-persons. Mere lip service is paid to Mohamed Ali Jinnah, the founder of Pakistan, hailed by Mahatma Gandhi as "incorruptible", while corruption seems to have engulfed the country he created.

Another tragedy has been the tendency of some to form sects around their favourite saints and defame others. The followers of Marcus Garvey who attack Dr Du Bois, and the admirers of Martin Luther King, Jr., who denounce Malcom X do no service, except to the common enemies of emancipation.

We must find ways to reclaim the spirit of the great struggle of this century and to publicise the lives and aspirations of the true leaders of humanity in the light of the United Nations resolution. With the present crisis in the United Nations and UNESCO, the initiative will need to be taken by public organisations, educators and the media. The observance of the centenary of Marcus Garvey can, I hope, be the beginning of the movement and the forthcoming centenaries of Jawaharlal Nehru and Lord Fenner Brockway may provide a fillip.

Lord Fenner Brockway

"None so fit to break the chains as those who wear them." It is only natural that the work of liberation should be primarily executed by those who are oppressed. But there have always been those who have made a lifelong commitment to the cause of the oppressed and thereby won their trust and affection. Such a person was Lord Fenner Brockway who passed away on April 28 1988 – as this book was going to press and just six months short of his 100th birthday.

Born in Calcutta, India, on November 1 1888, Brockway became a socialist in 1907 and from then up to his last days did not waver in his commitment to the cause of peace, national liberation and the freedom of working people.

Imprisoned for refusing to serve in the First World War, he was the last survivor of the 1927 Brussels World Conference Against Imperialism, in which Jawaharlal Nehru of India and freedom fighters from South Africa, China and Ireland and elsewhere participated. In 1948 he set up the People's Congress Against Imperialism and was personally known to the leaders of many new emerging former colonial states, many of whom honoured him with their countries' highest decorations and awards. In 1954 he founded the movement for Colonial Freedom – now Liberation – and was its President until his death. He was an active opponent of the war in Vietnam and a stalwart of the Campaign for Nuclear Disarmament (CND). In 1972 he was on the platform of a civil rights march in the Irish city of Derry when British soldiers fired into the crowd killing 13 people on what became know as 'Bloody Sunday'.

On his 99th birthday the Indian High Commissioner in London presented him with personal gifts from Prime Minister Rajiv Gandhi. It was surely a foretaste of what the people of the world would have been preparing for his centenary.

Sixty Glorious Years of Westindian Test Cricket

by Bridgette Lawrence

(L-R) Frank Worrell, Everton Weekes, Sonny Ramadhin and Clyde Walcott at a reception at the start of the Westindies tour of England in 1957

In 1988 Westindian cricket celebrates its Diamond Jubilee of Test match status. Since taking their first tentative steps at Lord's in 1928, they have evolved from a bunch of talented and unpredictable individuals into a magnificent fighting unit which has dominated the cricketing landscape since the mid-1970s.

In the early years their batting revolved around the masterful George Headley and their bowling around the prodigious Manny Martindale; but, on the few occasions that several players fired together, they proved a dynamic combination as at Georgetown, Guyana, in 1930, when they won their first match against England, and at Sydney, Australia, in 1931, when they beat the hosts. Against England, Headley became the first Westindian to score two centuries in the same Test, while Clifford Roach weighed in with the first double hundred by a Westindian; and, in the bowling department, the irrepressible Learie Constantine took nine wickets in the match. At Sydney, Frank Martin supported Headley with the bat, while attacking captaincy from Jackie Grant inspired his bowlers, Martindale, Herman Griffith and George Francis, to gel together and lift the visitors to success.

Westindies won their first Test series against England in the Caribbean in 1935. Their two outstanding pre-World War II players, Headley and Martindale, clinched the rubber for the home side in the last match at Kingston. Headley scored a majestic 270 not out, while Martindale's four for 28 in the tourists' second innings, was instrumental in dismissing England for their lowest score of 103 against Westindies.

On their own soil, however, the English were still too strong for Westindies and the most notable feat of the 1939 rubber in England was Headley's two centuries in the opening Test at Lord's, as he became only the second man ever to score two hundreds in the same Test on two separate occasions.

After the Second World War, the three "W"s arrived on the scene to provide Test cricket with a unique triumvirate of batting talent. Having been weaned in the competitive nursery of domestic cricket in the Caribbean, Clyde Walcott, Everton Weekes and Frank Worrell became central figures on the world stage in the 1950s. On Westindies' first visit to India in 1948-49, Weekes set a world record of five successive Test hundreds and seemed to be heading for a sixth before he was controversially run out for 90 in the fourth Test at Madras.

Meanwhile, the bowlers dominated the headlines in England in 1950. Sonny Ramadhin and Alf Valentine appeared from nowhere to sweep Westindies to their first victory on English soil, as they entranced the home batsmen with their spin. However, in Australia the following year, Westindies were themselves entranced by the overwhelming speed of Ray Lindwall and Keith Miller; while Australia's own powerful batting line-up proved equal to most that the Westindies could put up against them. Clyde Walcott headed the counter-attack in the return rubber in the Caribbean four years later by scoring five centuries in just three Tests, including two in the match at Kingston.

Westindian cricket reached a new peak against Pakistan in 1958, due to the efforts of one man. In the third Test at Kingston, having played four series without a Test hundred to his name, Gary Sobers set new standards of batsmanship with a world record 365 not out. He followed that up with two hundreds in the fourth match at Georgetown, and was soon recognised as the best batsman of his generation. In India later that year, Sobers' all-round ability, together with the pummelling power of Roy Gilchrist and Wes Hall, crushed the home side. The trip was the making of Hall, who took a fifth of all his Test wickets on that twin tour to India and Pakistan, including a hat-trick in the final Test in Pakistan at Lahore. For good measure, Rohan Kanhai, who was to become another giant of Westindian cricket, revealed his true potential by scoring a brilliant maiden double century against India at Calcutta; and at Lahore helped himself to another 217 runs – more than the combined total of any other Westindian on that part of the tour.

Frank Worrell, the first black man to be appointed captain of Westindies on a long-term basis

In Australia in 1960-61, Frank Worrell, the first black player to be appointed captain of Westindies on a long-term basis, raised the team's standards even higher with an attacking approach that laid the groundwork for their later triumphs.

Sonny Ramadhin, who helped to spin Westindies to success against England in 1950

His leadership qualities were most explicitly revealed in the remarkable tied Test at Brisbane. With six runs required off the last (eight-ball) over, to be bowled by Wes Hall, Worrell implored his big fast bowler to keep a good line and length. Richie Benaud, who had shared in what appeared to be a match-winning stand of 134, was caught off the second ball and Wally Grout was run out off the sixth. Then, Lindsay Kline, the last man in, somehow managed to lay his bat on a blistering delivery from Hall and raced toward the bowler's end. Joe Solomon picked up the ball and threw down the stumps to run out the non-striker, Ian Meckiff, and bring off the most famous result in the history of cricket: the first tied Test.

Besides Hall, Lance Gibbs proved to be another bowling sensation in Australia. After playing in three Tests, he found himself heading the bowling averages, aided by a hat-trick taken in the fourth match at Adelaide. To give the Westindies attack even more depth, Sobers established himself as the best all-rounder in the world on that trip. Besides his masterful batting and the support he gave Valentine as the slow left-armer, Sobers shared the new ball with Hall and, to underline his phenomenal gifts, treated the Australian crowds to some spectacular catching.

Despite these splendid individual performances, the visitors still lost the series by the narrowest of margins due, in no small measure, to some dubious umpiring decisions. Even so, Worrell must have been comforted by the fact that success could not be far away, as, at last, Westindies were playing as a team. They crushed India 5-0 in the Caribbean in 1962 and enjoyed a triumphant series in England the following year. In that series Charlie Griffith hit the headlines as, in partnership with Wes Hall, he subdued the home side by capturing 32 wickets in the Tests. Their 3-1 triumph over the "old country" was a suitable epitaph for Worrell, who had led Westindian cricket to its highest peak of excellence yet.

Thereafter, they improved with every match and completed their first series victory over Australia in 1965, thanks largely to some brilliant bowling by Gibbs. He took 18 wickets in the rubber, including the remarkable figure of six for 29 in front of his home crowd at Georgetown.

Rohan Kanhai, one of the finest batsmen ever produced by Westindies

Clive Lloyd, the greatest Test captain of all time, and a master batsman

Sobers dominated the series against England in 1966. Leading from the front, he orchestrated the visitors' win by scoring 722 runs from five Tests. He also took 20 wickets at 27.25 each, 10 catches and, for good measure, won the toss on each occasion. He was dominant in the return rubber in the Caribbean in 1968, but ran into trouble after his "infamous" declaration at Port-of-Spain, which eventually decided the series in favour of England.

By this time, however, the wheel of fortune was already starting to turn against Westindies. Although they won the opening Test of the subsequent series against Australia, there were to be another 24 matches before they were to taste victory again – apart from their success against New Zealand at Auckland in 1969. It was a transitionary phase that all world class teams have to suffer, as some of the great players retire, and before their successors are fully established. Indeed, during those years, Westindies cricket was nurturing the players who were to set the 1970s and 1980s ablaze, as they prepared to dominate the world cricket scene with unprecedented success. In particular, Clive Lloyd was revealing himself to be a batsman of the highest calibre, before taking over the reins of captaincy for the series against India in 1974-75, at the start of what was to be the most successful tenure in the history of Test cricket.

Westindies returned to their winning ways in England in 1973, under the auspices of Rohan Kanhai, who, in his 13 Tests as captain, instilled the killer instinct into the Westindies team that Lloyd was to put to such good use. Meanwhile, other gifted individuals had begun to make their presence felt: Alvin Kallicharran announced himself as a batsman of outstanding ability by scoring a century on his Test debut, against New Zealand at Georgetown in 1972, and went on to

Gary Sobers, whose prolific batting helped him to the world record individual score of 365 not out

become an important component in Westindies' rennaissance; while Lawrence Rowe enjoyed the most successful debut in Test history, when he scored 214 and 100 not out in the first match of that series and, against England at Bridgetown in 1974, became only the second Westindian to score a triple Test century.

To complement the batsmen, Andy Roberts had emerged as a world class fast bowler, and, in 1974-75 took a record 32 wickets from five Tests in India and collected another 12 from the two in Pakistan. By the time of the following tour to Australia, he was partnered by the promising but, as yet, erratic Michael Holding. But in spite of this individual excellence, Westindies were comprehensively beaten by Australia as they faltered against the pace of Dennis Lillee and Jeff Thomson.

Even though the series was lost, the seeds of success had already started to flower: Viv Richards

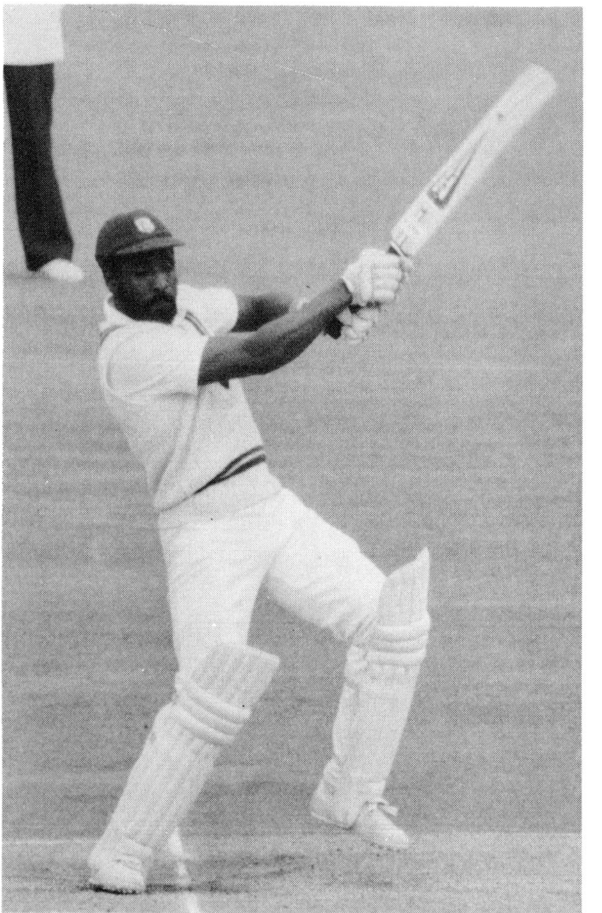

Viv Richards – proud owner of the fastest hundred in Test cricket

Gary Sobers, whose various styles of bowling made him cricket's greatest all-rounder

began his sequence of scores that was to establish him as the finest batsman of his era and catapult Westindies to the top of world cricket. In eight unforgettable months he pillaged first Australia, then India and England for 1,710 runs. *Wisden* wrote of his feats in 1976: "If he fails to make another run in Test cricket his performance in this single year will always be a source of conversation for the enthusiasts and inspiration to young batsmen."

Gordon Greenidge also emerged as a batsman of rare quality by becoming only the second Westindian batsman after George Headley to score a hundred in each innings of a Test in England, when he achieved the feat at Old Trafford in 1976. Altogether, his match aggregate was 38 more than the whole England team. While Richards nd Greenidge mesmerised the world with their battin, Holding and Roberts were causing havoc with the ball. In that vintage summer, Holding gave one of the finest displays of quick bowling ever seen in Test cricket, when he coaxed pace out of a lifeless

Alf Valentine, who took eight English wickets on his first day in Test cricket

Oval wicket, and collected a record 14 wickets for 149 runs to take Westindies to a comprehensive victory.

The Westindies juggernaut continued on against Pakistan in 1977 as, this time, Colin Croft re-wrote the record books by returning the sensational figures of eight for 29 at Port-of-Spain. After the 'Packer' interlude, the Westindies players returned to the official Test match fold and embarked on a victorious campaign culminating in their record 11 successive Test wins under Clive Lloyd beginning in the Westindies, when they beat Australia at Bridgetown in 1984. Westindies had won their first Test series in Australia in 1979-80 aided by some splendid performances from Joel Garner, who went on to harangue batsmen the world over. Against England in 1980, Westindies ruled supreme and were similarly dominant in the return rubber which saw the first Test played in Antigua. There, Richards predictably celebrated the use of his home ground as a Test match venue by scoring a majestic century.

The disappointment of losing the World Cup to India in mid-1983 only seemed to fuel Westindies desire to be the best and they exacted their revenge when they toured the subcontinent later that year.

They won the one-day series 5-0 and the Tests 3-0, aided in large part by some magnificent bowling from Malcolm Marshall, who finished the series with 33 wickets.

Westindies went on to beat Australia by the same margin in 1984 and completed an unprecedented 5-0 victory over England later that summer. Then, finally, came retribution in Australia over a full five-match rubber in 1984-85. Appropriately, it was Clive Lloyd who, in his last Test series, set the scene for victory when he thrashed 114 in the second Test at Brisbane to give his side an unassailable lead in the series. After the debacle in Australia nearly a decade earlier it was fitting that Lloyd, who was instrumental in making Westindies the dominant force in world cricket, should enjoy his crowning moment on Australian soil.

In his retirement speech to the Westindies Board of Control in 1985, Lloyd said that he looked on his career as "the continuation of the revolution started by Sir Frank Worrell". Now Viv Richards finds himself the protector of that revolution. He began his career auspiciously by beating New Zealand (one of the few feats to elude Lloyd) and then emulated the Guyanese by defeating England 5-0 in the Caribbean in 1986. Since then the passage has been less smooth, with a great team again entering a transitionary phase. As ever, there is not shortage of talented batsmen or bowlers waiting in the wings and, having establish himself as one of the greatest batsmen of all-time, like Lloyd and Worrell before him, Richards now has to turn his attention to leading Westindies to even greater success.

Fuller details of the history of Westindian Test Cricket can be found in 100 Great Westindian Test Cricketers, from Challenor to Richards *by Bridgette Lawrence with Reg Scarlett, published by Hansib Publishing.*

The prodigious Alvin Kallicharran, who made a century on his Test debut

The Sports Scene

Britain's visible minority communities have made and are making an enormous contribution to the development of sports nationally and internationally. It is an area of outstanding achievement.

But as with all such areas of achievement it has been one where we have had to fight tooth and nail for opportunities and recognition – whether for the facilities to train at the start or to be selected for a national team. Even when this is achieved there remains the insidious pressures from sections of the establishment and the loutish racism of the terrace lobby. Black footballers, in particular, still have to contend with vile abuse every time they take to the pitch. Their restraint in response to this behaviour is an example of professionalism and superiority that is an example to the sporting world and to the whole of society.

If better sports facilities – many of the ones that were achieved are falling victim to the new era of local authority cutbacks – were available and if the general socio-economic situation of the visible minority communities was not so strained, a far greater number of truly brilliant sportspeople – men and women – would surely be nurtured and would surely capture the top awards nationally and in the top international arenas.

But congratulations are still in order to a host of outstanding achievers such as athletes Tessa Sanderson and Fatima Whitbread and numerous footballers such as Garth Crooks and John Barnes, as well as Brian Stein, who in April 1988 secured Luton's victory over Arsenal. In other sports Desmond Douglas has led English table tennis for many years whilst Laurie Francois, international Wushu champion is a rising star. It is significant that the black community is not being ghettoised into any one sport or group of sports – as can be seen in the new achievements in rugby and lawn tennis.

Many sportspeople from the indigenous community are taking a stand against racism – in sport and society, and this positive example to the young people of Britain needs to be put to more systematic use. The fight is certainly not against individual sportspeople, in the main, but against the sporting and wider establishment.

In the following sections, compiled by Rolando Vitale, we highlight some of the achievers and rising stars. We ask the forgiveness of those we may have ommitted.

American Football

Victor Ebubedike

Nigerian Victor Ebubedike is an athlete in the true sense of the word. At 6ft 2in and built like a bodybuilder, he can sprint the 60 metres dash faster than most sprinters. He is one of a few British-based American footballers with real aspirations of making the grade in the United States NFL (National Football League).

The 22-year-old London Ravens running back helped his team, Britain's most successful outfit over the past five years, capture the 1987 Budweiser Bowl with three superb touchdowns rushing over 170 yards. His speed and power have gained him national honours for Britain.

The African sportsman will be attending Harper College in Chicago to further his studies in the hopes of becoming a sports journalist after his playing career. His other interests include Rap music and socialising.

Arm-Wrestling

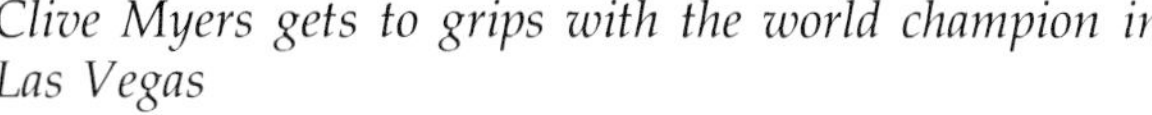

Clive Myers gets to grips with the world champion in Las Vegas

Clive Myers

Britain played host to the seventh World Arm-Wrestling Championships in November 1987 which attracted global interest. Over fifteen countries were represented in several categories.

Organiser and participant Clive "Ironfist" Myers, in association with the BAF (British Arm-Wrestling Federation) oversaw the administrative and financial headaches accompanying the international occasion in Gillingham, Kent.

Clive Myers is a former World Arm-Wrestling champion, better known for his wrestling exploits inside the ring. As a wrestler he clinched the European middleweight championship, Over The Top middleweight crown, as well as six British titles.

Furthermore the strong athlete assisted and instructed multi-millionaire actor Sylvester Stallone, famed for his roles as Rocky and Rambo, during the film *Over The Top* which features numerous arm-wrestling sequences.

Dola Akanmu

It is Dola Akanmu's dream to become the world's best female arm-wrestler in this male dominated sport. The articulate and intelligent Dola, known as "Dynamite D" on the circuit, though only 5ft 3" tall, revels in the physical exertion of notching victory after victory over her male counterparts.

The south-London based Nigerian has obtained a degree in bio-chemistry and her favourite pastimes include teaching children and keeping fit.

Born on July 20, 1964, Akanmu notched up her greatest success when she picked up a bronze medal in the 55kg weight category at the November World Championships. She made her debut in the sport in Manchester 1986 and since then she has acquired regional titles in the Midlands, Lambeth, the UK and the Caribbean, finishing runner-up in the 1987 British Championships. She extends admiration to the great Muhammad Ali.

Athletics

1987 marked the World Championship year in athletics and in retrospect conjures up vivid memories of Africa's domination in the men's middle and long distance events and the splendid 100m world record effort by Jamaica-born sprinter Ben Johnson, who runs for Canada.

By comparison Britain's presence in the championships was overshadowed, and in medal terms proved mediocre with only javelin thrower Fatima Whitbread striking gold. Britain will be hoping to reverse the situation with fine successes in forthcoming international events and among the national representatives a significant proportion are of ethnic minority background.

Derek Redmond (400m)

The Birchfield Harriers athlete has broken the 400m British record twice and re-set the new mark during the 1987 World Athletics Championships in Rome with a time of 44.50. In a fiercely competitive line-up Redmond finished fifth in the final, won by East German one-lap-king Thomas Schoenlebe. Redmond was born in September 1965. He trains with his athletics club in Birmingham and lives outside Northampton. He is a committed member of the British 4x400m relay squad which contains reputed athletes such as Roger Black, Phil Brown, Kriss Akabusi, Brian Whittle and Todd Bennett. He relaxes by listening to all types of music ranging from classical to soul. His own interests include experimenting with musical sounds.

Joyce Oladapo (Long Jump)

Joyce Oladapo is of Ghanaian origin and was born on February 11, 1964. She trains for the Bromley Ladies Club. Joyce took an astonishing gold medal in the 1986 Edinburgh Commonwealth Games. Her personal best long jump is a wind assisted 6.80 metres. She has been forced to change and restructure her take-off stance due to a niggling injury in her right leg. After months of severe training she is approaching a certain degree of normality. The south London-based athlete now leaps from her left leg. She has cleared 6.56 metres and is still pushing for greater distance. Ms Oladapo is studying for a Movement Studies degree.

Barrington Williams (Long Jump)

Born in Jamaica on September 11, 1955, this veteran representative of the British team is a preacher from Cannock. He is the 1987 Amateur Athletics Association indoor long jump champion. Williams, who was granted British citizenship in early 1988 after a long wait, works as a building control officer for the Cannock Chase District Council.

His personal best for the 100m sprint is 10.5 secs. and for the long jump is 7.83 metres.

Colin Jackson (110m hurdles)

The Cardiff-born hurdler has propelled his senior international fortunes to the forefront of world athletics. He gained a bronze medal in the 1987 World Championships behind Greg Foster of the United States and team mate Jon Ridgeon. The 6ft 7in Cardiff-based athlete was born on February 18, 1967 and en route to the top has established impeccable credentials at junior level. He was second in the 1985 European Junior Championships, won a gold medal in the 1986 World Junior Championships, and in the same year, took silver in the Commonwealth Games and silver in the 1987 European Cup.

His personal best for the 110m hurdles is 13.37. He has also run the 100m in 10.49. Jackson also holds the 60m British indoor record of 7.52.

Eric McCalla (Triple Jump)

Eric McCalla is about the most courageous person in world athletics. Hampered by kidney trouble, which almost cost him his life in 1985, the triple jumper has returned to the forefront of his discipline unperturbed by his previous painful experiences.

Thanks to a timely kidney donor and successful surgery, the Birmingham-based electrician is competing at the top level once again with more determination than ever before. McCalla's best achievement to date is making the 1984 Olympic final. In the qualifying heats of the same event he set a personal best of 17.01. He joined his club, Birchfield Harriers, in 1976 and, in early 1988, was awarded the 1987 Birmingham Sportsman of the Year trophy.

Tessa Sanderson (Javelin)

Born in Jamaica, on March 14, 1956, Tessa Sanderson made her senior England debut in 1973. She participated in the 1976 Montreal and 1980 Moscow Olympics and capped all her national and international achievements with a gold medal in the 1984 Los Angeles Olympic Games with a tournament record throw.

Ms Sanderson became the first British athlete to win a gold in a throwing event. Soon afterwards she was awarded an MBE (Member of the Order of the British Empire) medal in recognition for her services to sport. In the 1986 Commonwealth Games staged in Edinburgh, she pipped her great rival, Fatima Whitbread, for the gold.

Marcus Adams (Sprinter)

A young sprinter with a bright future. In 1987 he received the Rotary Watches Sports Male Athlete of the Year award for his outstanding performances in the European Junior Championships, staged in Birmingham, England. He is the ninth recipient of the honour. Other winners have included Linford Christie, Steve Cram and Fatima Whitbread. Adams won the 200m gold and ran the anchor leg in the gold medal winning 4x100m relay for Britain.

Ernest Obeng (Sprinter)

The 32-year-old Ghanaian student has been running at the top flight of athletics for over a decade. He arrived in England in 1976 from west Africa and in that time has studied agriculture at London and Reading Universities, and is currently completing a doctorate at Loughborough University. Obeng has been denied the chance to compete in the last two Olympics, the 1980 and 1984 games, because of boycotts and a personal dispute with Ghana's selection officials. The former African 100m record holder is currently hoping that the Home Office will grant him British Citizenship before the September Olympics. The self-coached athlete ran the second fastest time for a Briton in 1987 with a wind assisted time of 10.14.

Daley Thompson (Decathlon)

Born in London in 1959 of a Nigerian father and a Scottish mother, some have labelled him as arrogant and pompous; others have hailed him as the supreme athlete of modern times. One thing is for sure, Daley Thompson cannot be ignored, for his achievements speak volumes for his perseverance and dedication in reaching the apex of his chosen discipline. He has gained respect from his colleagues and arch-rivals and has won every major honour in the sport.

His nine-year unbeaten streak came to an end in the 1987 Rome World games when he relinquished his world title to Torsten Voss of the German Democratic Republic. In that time Thompson had broken the world record four times. His personal best and highest score in the ten events is 8847 points. He has won two Olympic golds in 1980 and 1984, one world title in Helsinki in 1983, three European Championship golds and three Commonwealth golds in 1978, 1982 and 1986 respectively. The articulate athlete has nine 'O' levels and two 'A' levels, and is married with a daughter.

Linford Christie (Sprinter)

Born in St Andrews, Jamaica, in 1960, Linford Christie is the most successful male British sprinter since Allan Wells. He has dominated the European circuit for the last two years. In 1987 he set a new 100m British record of 10.03 seconds in Hungary, the third fastest time of the year behind Ben Johnson and Carl Lewis. In the 1987 European Games in Prague, Czechoslovakia, the Harlesden-based kingpin became the first sprinter since Eugen Ray of the German Democratic Republic to do the double, clinching the 100m and 200m gold.

Christie, who is coached by Ron Roddan, finished fourth in the historic Rome 100m which saw Ben Johnson set new figures for the event in the Stadio Olimpico.

John Regis (Sprinter)

The powerfully-built 200m sprinter raised a few eyebrows in the 1987 World Championships when he raced away to a bronze medal in the 200m. In the same effort Regis, cousin of famous footballer Cyrille, smashed the seven-year-old British record of 20.21, held by Allan Wells, lowering it by three hundredths of a second. The Belgrave Harriers sprinter lives in south London and works as a sports shop assistant in central London and is trained by coach John Isaacs.

Judy Simpson (Heptathlon)

The 1986 Commonwealth gold medallist is the British queen of the seven disciplines which make up the heptathlon. The Birmingham-based athlete has obtained a degree in sociology, and had it not been for a cruel quirk of fate in her preparations for major events, Judy Simpson could well have been crowned world champion. Ms Simpson is trained and supervised by coach John Anderson. She competed in the 1984 Los Angeles Olympic Games and made her first appearance in the endurance event almost four years ago. Ms Simpson is the current British and Commonwealth record holder.

Badminton

Though very few black badminton players have made it to the higher echelons of the sport in Britain, badminton remains nevertheless a very popular sport amongst the ethnic minority communities. Stanley White, far left, runs the George Sylvester badminton club in Hackney, east London and has helped stage many tournaments in the London area. The former trainer and talent scout for West London club Queens Park Rangers set up a ladies tournament in 1987 in an attempt to find the best female badminton players in the region. The photograph illustrates the lucky winners of the various categories.

Henry Terry Gaspard

Born on January 21, 1960, in St Lucia, the 5ft 6" badminton enthusiast devotes much of his time to coaching club members of the Tottenham "Black Arrows" in north London, one of Britain's leading black badminton clubs.

In competition, Gaspard has won over 30 Open tournaments and has represented London and Essex County. His most important career point came in the Metropolitan District Cup when he led Hackney Council's NALGO (National Association of Local Government Officers) team to victory in 1986/87, only the second time since 1928. His future aims include the positive projection and promotion of badminton participation amongst the black community. His hobbies include sports photography.

Prakash Padukone

Prakash Padukone is one of India's most successful badminton players. He has been on the professional circuit for a long time and won the British Airways sponsored British Open Masters at the Royal Albert Hall in 1979. The Bangalore-born badminton player tried to regain the title in 1987 but was ousted in the semi-final of the competition by Britain's Stephen Baddeley.

Christine Magnusson

The Uganda-born Christine Magnusson, who now lives in and competes for her adopted country, Sweden, is in a unique position. She is the sole black badminton player in the top echelons of a white dominated sport.

The affable and much travelled player is a member of the prosperous Swedish first division side Carlskiona and, at the age of 13, was introduced to the sport at a secondary school in Taby.

She has come a long way since then. She is rated in the world's top ten in both the ladies singles and doubles. Along with her partner Maria Bengtsson they achieved the greatest victory to date when they won the All England Open championships in 1986. Badminton is set to become an Olympic sport in 1992 and when it does the 23-year-old Ms Magnusson will be setting her sights on the ultimate triumph.

Basketball

Basketball as a sport has endured many years of dwindling resources and limited sponsorship. However, the upward surge in recent years towards profit and publicity has reaped numerous benefits. In the period of 1980-1985 a 400 per cent increase in spectators was recorded. And at the start of the regular 1987/88 NBL (National Basketball League) season the sport received another boost, firstly securing a sponsorship deal with the Carlsberg Brewers and secondly an assurance by the BBC of coverage of the championship finals. While it is true that many players from the United States have been drafted over to add their expertise and arouse public interest, several talented home-grown players, in particular from the black community, have responded and excelled at the challenge.

Karl Tatham (Portsmouth)

The 6ft 2in basketballer is an England international who has been a valuable member of the Portsmouth side which has won national honours in recent years. The versatile and experienced individual can play small forward or guard. He has quick hands and scores points at vital stages of matches.

Alan Cunningham (Portsmouth)

The skilful court specialist is a former Harlem Globetrotter who played college basketball in Colorado State, USA. The 6ft 8in player with dual nationality is Portsmouth's captain. He plays the captain's role to the full and has great presence as a forward who can thrill and rebound effectively. In the 1986 NBL season Cunningham finished up with 592 points, notching his highest score of 39 against Solent.

Alton Byrd (Manchester United)

Alton Byrd is recognised as one of the most accomplished players ever to play in the NBL. He has held a position of pre-eminence in the sport for almost ten years, firstly with Crystal Palace, then with Livingston (Scotland) and now with Manchester United. Success has attended his team throughout this period, and there has never been a season when he has failed to win at least one national honour. Frequently dwarfed on the court of play by human pillars the 5ft 9in Byrd is able to impose his authority on the game by a combination of athleticism, invention and width of vision which stamps him as a player of rare ability. He is a graduate of Columbia University in New York and is currently a stockbroker in Manchester.

He was born November 3, 1957 in San Francisco, USA. The highly-active individual also had a successful spell as a television basketball commentator with Channel 4. Byrd is married with a small daughter and lives in Gatley. He enjoys travelling and playing racquetball and tennis, and one of his aims is to achieve financial independence by the age of 40.

Colin Irish (Portsmouth)

Full name. Colin Brian Irish. The 6ft 6in forward, known as the "smiling assassin" on the court, was born on March 3, 1961 in Hendon, north London. He spent his childhood partly in England, Trinidad and in the United States. Irish attended the Cathedral Latin High School in Ohio, USA, and later went to the Bowling Green University in the same state. The England international has silky skills and is surprisingly mobile for a tall athlete. Among his many achievements he rates the Manchester United victory over Kingston in the 1985 Wembley final with Portsmouth capturing the league title in 1986 as his greatest moments in the game.

Dan Davis (Kingston)

The 6ft 9in Dan Davis played college basketball for North Carolina in the United States. He is a favourite with the crowds and players alike. A great rebounder, he possesses remarkable pace for such a tall man. In the 1986 NBL season, Davis netted 483 points, top-scoring against Birmingham with 37. He is an established member of the England team and he inspired Kingston to the 1986 Prudential National Cup triumph over Portsmouth at the Royal Albert Hall, central London.

Kevin Penny (Manchester United)

Kevin Penny was born on April 18, 1962 in Birmingham and as a basketballer, has acquitted himself capably in all the England national sides. He has gained caps at schoolboy, under 19 and senior levels. The 6ft 4in utility player has made 11 full international appearances for England. Penny is married with a son. He enjoys cooking and spending time with his family and is currently a member of the Manchester police force pursuing a future ambition of becoming an inspector. He is an admirer of Daley Thompson.

Kevin Michael Cadle (Kingston coach)

Kevin Cadle is one of the youngest and most ambitious basketball coaches in the NBL – and the most successful. Born in Buffalo, USA, he has managed Falkirk, the Scotland national team, Manchester and Kingston. His list of achievements include two cup triumphs for Falkirk and two cup victories for Kingston. He is the assistant coach for the 1988 Great Britain Olympic basketball team. In his spare time he enjoys watching American football and snooker. His other pastimes include reading the Bible and listening to jazz music. He would like to meet Reverend Jesse Jackson.

Tony Balogun (Leicester)

The 6ft 6in England international forward is a first class player who possesses superb leaping ability and positional sense in offensive movements. Born of Nigerian parents, Balogun has switched his playing fortunes to a number of NBL clubs. In September 1984 he was sold from Bracknell to Hemel Hempstead for £6,000. A year later he moved from Hemel to Manchester for a fee of £9,000. In the 1987/88 season, having spent a loan period to Hemel from Manchester, he was eventually sold to Leicester for £2,000. The African has won 23 England caps and first represented the country against Czechoslovakia in 1984.

Clive H. Vaughan (Leicester)

Born on January 30 1962 in Paddington, north London, he made his debut in basketball in September 1984. Vaughan was the league's leading scorer in 1986/87. The 6ft 5in, 210lbs. athlete has gained 24 England caps. He graduated from Pittsburgh University in the United States. Clive extends his admiration to Muhammad Ali as his favourite sports personality.

Boxing

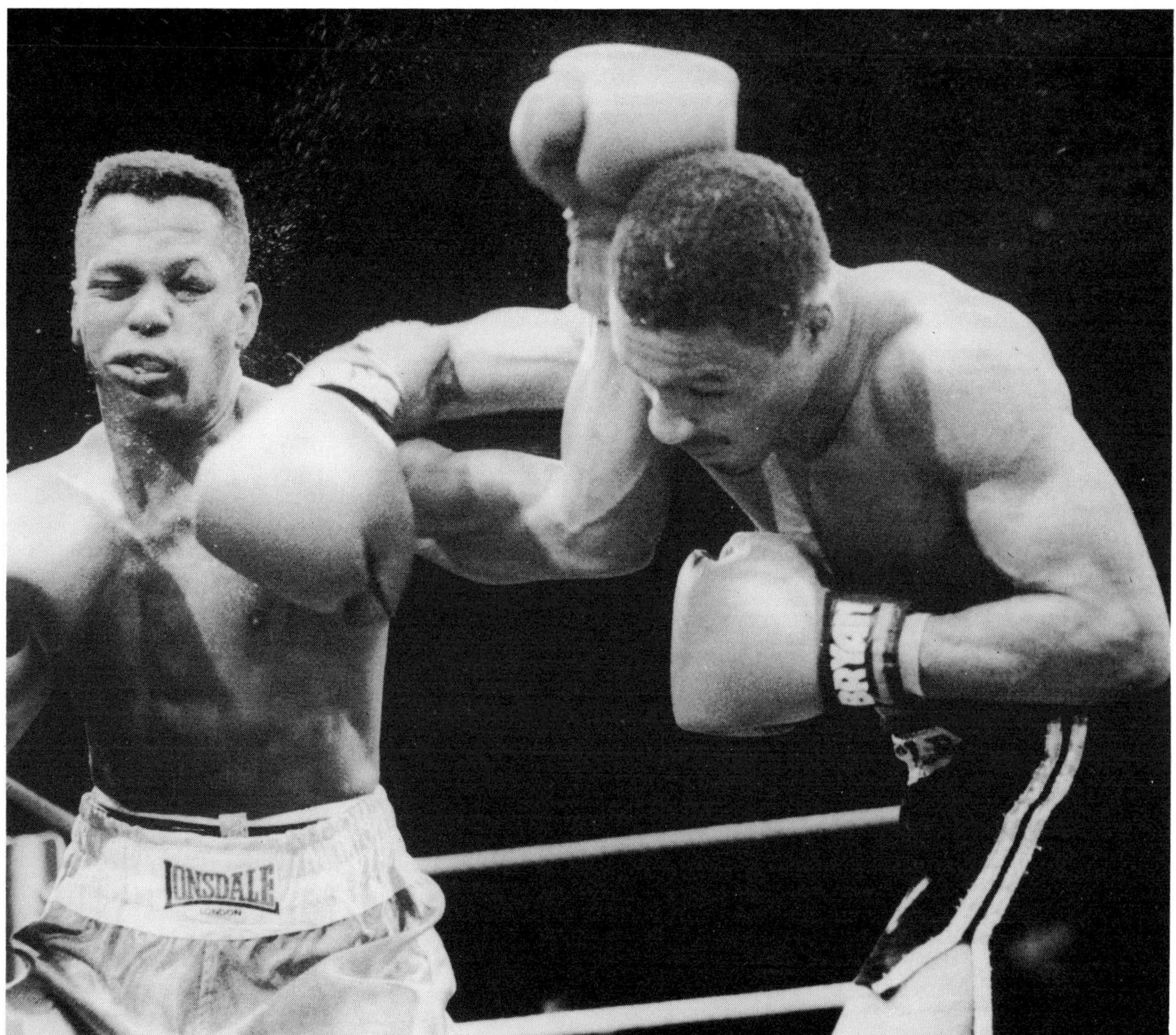

Michael Watson sweeps through with a jaw-breaking right against Kenny Styles of the United States

Michael Watson (Middleweight)

The Islington-based middleweight boxer served out his apprenticeship in the professional ranks in February 1988 when he stopped world ranked Don Lee of the United States in the fifth round at the Wembley Grand Hall, north west London. The 23-year-old has won seventeen of his eighteen fights. His only defeat came to the durable James Cook in 1986. His manager Mickey Duff believes his boxer can go all the way to a world title shot.

Gary Mason (Heavyweight)

Gary Mason completes a trio of heavyweights under the wings of Britain's most successful boxing manager, Terry Lawless. Like Bruno, Mason comes from Wandsworth in south London and has won all of his 26 professional contests, halting 25 of them before the final bell. Nine of them have lasted only one round to the merciless Mason. In the January 1988 WBC (World Boxing Council) ratings, Mason was placed at number 15.

Lloyd Honeyghan (Welterweight)

Born in Jamaica on April 22, 1960. Nobody gave Honeyghan a realistic chance of dethroning Don Curry, the undisputed welterweight champion, in September 1986. But the determined Bermondsey-based boxer proved the experts wrong with a sixth round stoppage.

In boxing Lloyd has displayed a moral and defiant stand against the evils of apartheid, relinquishing his World Boxing Association belt in 1986 rather than contest his first defence against South African Harold Volbrecht. Honeyghan successfully defended his two other belts on three occasions defeating Johnny Bumphus, Maurice Blocker and Gene Hatcher before coming unstuck against Mexican Jorge Vaca. The Jamaican was controversially denied glory by a technical decision after the two pugilists had clashed heads in round eight in October 1987. Despite the setback Honeyghan made amends when he became the first Briton to regain a world crown in seventy years by stopping Vaca in the third round of a re-match at the Wembley Arena in March 1988. Honeyghan's record reads 32 wins in 33 fights.

Tom Collins (Light-heavyweight)

Curacao-born boxer Tom Collins is a courageous sporting individual who, despite being a professional for the past eleven years, still remains a figure of anonymity in boxing circles. However, he made headlines in 1987 when he captured both the British and European titles with impressive stoppage victories over John Moody and Alex Blanchard. The 32-year-old, who now lives in Yorkshire, won his first British title in 1982 when he outpointed Dennis Andries, who later went on to become world champion. Collins has fought Andries four times in his professional career winning only once.

Lloyd Christie (Light-welterweight)

Born in London on February 28, 1962, Lloyd Christie is the other half of the Christie boxing clan. While his brother Errol Christie was given the media attention when he turned professional after a supreme amateur record, Lloyd learned his trade the hard way, boxing in all corners of the world to earn a living.

But situations have changed drastically with Lloyd enjoying the present swing in fortunes. The Wolverhampton-based boxer wrested the British title from Tony McKenzie in January 1987 in three rounds. In a topsy turvy career Christie has fought many hostile battles against class opposition. The list includes Terry Marsh, Clinton McKenzie, Said Skouma and Judas Clottey.

Chris Pyatt (Light-middleweight)

Leicester's Chris Pyatt is potentially Britain's strongest candidate for a world title. His aggressive style and sharp punching make him a formidable opponent. In 1986 he earned Britain's Best Young Boxer award from the Boxing Writers' Club for his ring exploits, winning the British and European title from Prince Rodney and John Van Elteren respectively. However, things went wrong for him in 1987 when he lost his European title in his first defence to Gianfranco Rosi of Italy, who later went on to win the WBC Light-middleweight championship. He has recorded 21 wins in 23 fights and, at 23-years-old, still has enough time to achieve his career goal.

Kirkland Laing (Welterweight)

The Jamaican-born pugilist is a rare artisan of his sport. His ring finesse and self-belief are admirable traits in a sport where all too often the boxers disregard their craft and engage in slugging battles. The 33-year-old 5ft 9in current British welterweight champion is best remembered for his ten rounds points victory over Panamanian ring legend Robert Duran in Detroit, USA, six years ago. In a professional career spanning over 13 years Laing is on the verge of a first world title fight.

Frank Bruno (Heavyweight)

Born November 16, 1961. Frank Bruno is Britain's most popular boxer who has won the hearts of millions with his famous catchphrase, "Yeh – now what I mean 'arry!" The South Londoner is a hard-hitting heavyweight who has won 31 out of his 33 contests. His two defeats have been to former world heavyweight champions, James "Bonecrusher" Smith and Tim Witherspoon.

The Wandsworth boxer is managed by Terry Lawless and is currently awaiting his second world title shot having lost to Witherspoon in July 1986 at Wembley by an eleventh round stoppage. For the record, Bruno had won the ABA (Amateur Boxing Association) heavyweight title in 1980 and captured the European title in 1985, when he stopped Anders Eklund of Sweden in four rounds.

Najib Daho (Super-featherweight)

Born in Morocco on January 13 1959. Najib Daho reached the pinnacle of his 54 fight career when he dispatched the two-time world title challenger Pat Cowdell in one round of non-stop punishment in May 1986. In his next fight in August 1986 Daho challenged Barry Michael for the IBF (International Boxing Federation) super-featherweight title, and after twelve gruelling rounds, lost a points decision to the Australian. The Manchester-based African is a favourite among supporters with his aggressive fight-style and, despite surrendering his British title to Pat Cowdell in October 1987, is now on the comeback trail.

Nigel Benn displays awesome power on his way to a knock-out stoppage over Ronnie Yoe of the United States in 1987

Nigel Benn (Middleweight)

Nigel Benn has healthy career prospects. He is an Eastender with a fearsome reputation. His explosive style has already created quite an impact on the international boxing scene and the 24-year-old is heading for major honours.

Benn has won all seventeen of his professional contests inside the distance and has been labelled by his manager Frank Warren as a "mini Mike Tyson". Benn, who sports a distinct haircut, has set his sights on the British, and European titles before the close of 1988, having captured the Commonwealth title with a second round stoppage over Umaru Sanda of Ghana at Alexandra Palace in April 1988.

Known as the "Dark Destroyer", Benn made the switch from amateur to paid ranks in January 1987 after acquiring the ABA middleweight title in 1986. The West Ham fighter was voted the 1987 Best Young Boxer of the Year by the Boxing Writers' Club.

Taju Akay (Cruiserweight)

Taju Akay, better known in British boxing circles as Tee Jay, captured the British cruiserweight title in only his seventh contest when he disposed of the champion Roy Smith in 90 seconds of the first round in Battersea, in May 1987. The Clapham-based boxer who trains at the famous All Stars Amateur Boxing Club in Paddington is managed by his father, Isola Akay, Britain's only black boxing manager.

Boxing as a light-heavyweight, Taju Akay represented his native Ghana in the 1984 Los Angeles Olympics when he was eliminated from the tournament by Evander Holyfield, the current ruler of the cruiserweight division. Akay lost his British title in December 1987 to Glenn McCrory, the Commonwealth champion by a mere half a point and is expected to return with thoughts of avenging his defeat.

Duke McKenzie (Flyweight)

Duke McKenzie is an accomplished boxer, who won the European title from former world champion Charlie Magri in May 1986. He is a member of the successful McKenzie boxing family based in Croydon and, at 5ft 7in, he is one of the tallest flyweights in the world. McKenzie is undefeated in 19 fights and is patiently awaiting his opportunity for a world title challenge.

Horace Notice (Heavyweight)

Whilst Frank Bruno has gained all the recognition from the British media, this 30-year-old Midlander has steadily built up an impressive record. He is the holder of the British and Commonwealth titles and remains unbeaten in 16 fights. The Jamaican is managed by Terry Lawless and, in 1982, Notice won the ABA heavyweight title.

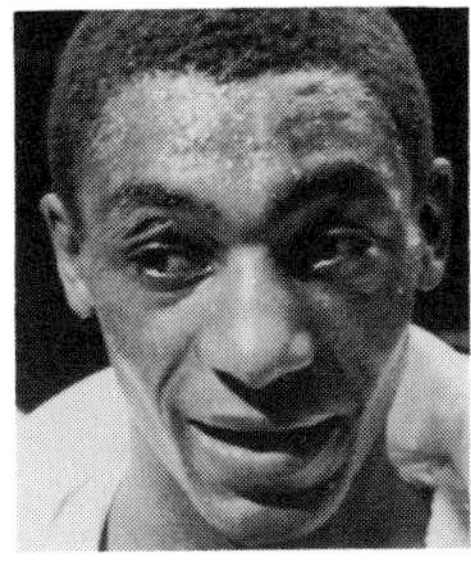

Herol Graham (Middleweight)

Herol Graham is a middleweight with outstanding ability. His illusive defensive movements have made him one of the most difficult boxers in the sport to hit. As an amateur Graham swept a great many accolades. In the 'pro' ranks Graham has successively gained the British, Commonwealth and European titles.

The Nottingham-born Graham, now based in Sheffield, has been trained and managed by Brendan Ingle for the major part of his career. He is now under the wing of Barney Eastwood, the Irish millionaire who guided Barry McGuigan to world honours. Graham's world title ambitions took a U-turn in May 1987 when he was out-pointed by Italy-based African, Sambu Kalambay, losing the European title in the process. The defeat is Graham's only blemish in a 40-fight track record.

Dennis Andries (Light-heavyweight)

The Guyana-born former world champion, who once turned up at a press conference with his championship belt inside a shopping bag, is boxing again, seeking a second world title shot. Not much has been heard of Andries since he lost his WBC (World Boxing Council) title to Tommie Hearns in Detroit in March 1987.

Andries split with manager Greg Steene after the boxer claimed that he had been mismanaged. The former British champion has teamed up with revered United States trainer Emmanuel Steward at the Kronk Gymnasium in Detroit and has scored a couple of successes in that time.

Cricket

Cricket is a sport which has been followed almost religiously by many of the Third World communities and their strengths and obvious devotion have shone at international level. Great strides have been made in the game with Third World countries no longer the students of this most traditional of English games, but placed rather firmly at the helm.

Moreover these progressive leaps forward have not only enriched the success of the Westindies and Asian countries in the international arena, they have had the effect of enabling a growing number of individuals from minority ethnic backgrounds to excel in the fields, parks and county cricket grounds of England. And today a great number of Third World-rooted players figure prominently in the future of British cricket. Listed below are just a few of the British-based black Britons who have achieved success at various levels.

19-year-old Mark Alleyne

Mark Alleyne

Mark Alleyne created a little piece of history in 1986 when he became the youngest ever Gloucestershire player to score a century in county cricket. The 19-year-old Barbadian-born cricketer has gained honours at England under-19 level as well as having played for South England Schools. He also helped Haringey Cricket College to victory in the 1986 *Caribbean Times*/Viv Richards cricket knockout cup competition.

Hareen Marcelline

Full name, Hareen Anthony Marcus Marcelline, he was born on March 7, 1968 in the Sri Lankan capital of Colombo. An admirer of the great Indian batsman Sunil Gavaskar, Marcelline is the proud owner of several records in the game. He became the first Sri Lankan to win the Wetherell award for the 1987 leading all-rounder in English schools cricket. In the same year he became the first student cricketer for Bishop's Stortford College to score over a 1,000 runs. And his score of 1,166 runs broke a 91-year-old college record. Marcelline hopes to represent Sri Lanka at Test level one day.

Damian Basil D'Oliveira

A Worcestershire right-hand batsman, born on October 19, 1966, in Cape Town, South Africa, he made his county debut in 1982. He has scored four first class centuries. His highest score of 146 came against Gloucestershire. A member of the English Counties XI, D'Oliveira toured Zimbabwe in 1985. He is married with a child. His famous father also played for Worcester and represented England at Test level.

Gladstone Small

The 26-year-old Warwickshire fast bowler is an England international. He has played four Test matches and 20 one-day internationals. The Barbados-born Small was sidelined for most of the 1987 season due to an injury incurred during the Sharjah tournament, and as a result missed all of England's home commitments. The cheerful fast bowler helped England retain the Ashes with an heroic display in the Melbourne Test with a five wicket haul and a final catch. Small possesses an unwanted claim to fame having bowled an 18-ball over including eleven no balls in 1982.

John Abrahams

A Lancashire batsman, born on July 21, 1952 in Cape Town, South Africa, he has lived in England since 1962. Abrahams has scored over 1,000 runs in a season on four occasions. He was a substitute for England in the fifth Test against the Westindies at Headingley in August 1980. After cricket he hopes to become a physiotherapist.

David Lawrence

24-year-old David Valentine Lawrence was born in Gloucester. The 6ft 3in right hand batsman and fast bowler made his Gloucester county debut in 1981. He toured with the England B team to Sri Lanka in 1986 and came close to selection into the senior Test side. Scarborough CC, Perth and Western Australia are all overseas teams that Lawrence has played for. In the 1985/86 season the powerfully-built cricketer was offered terms to play professional rugby league but turned down the proposal.

Norman Cowans

A Middlesex and England right-arm fast-medium bowler, born in Enfield, St Mary, Jamaica, Norman George Cowans made his England Test debut in the 1982-83 season on the Australia/New Zealand tour. In total he has so far appeared in 19 Tests. The 6ft 3in bowler has taken 50 wicket hauls in a season on three separate occasions. Educated at Stanmore, Middlesex, outside cricket he is a glassblower with White Friars hand made glass. In his spare time he relaxes with friends listening to reggae music and watching Arsenal football club on Saturdays.

Phillip De Freitas

Born in Dominica on May 18, 1966, the Leicestershire all-rounder made a name for himself in the England Test side during the 1986/87 winter tour of Australia. His performances with the ball were exceptional, assisting England in retaining the Ashes and clinching the Sharjah Cup. He left the Caribbean and came to England in 1975. As a cricketer he progressed from the Marylebone Cricket Club (MCC) ground staff to Leicestershire. He is an established member of the England Test set-up.

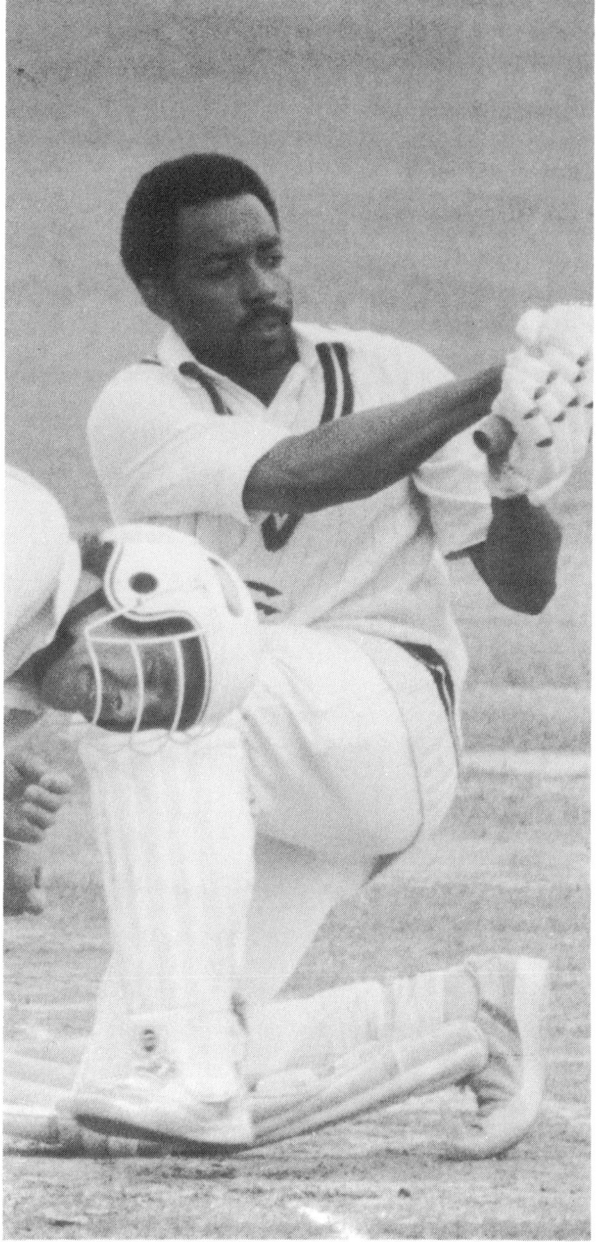

Roland Butcher

Full name, Roland Orlando Butcher, he is a right-hand batsman for Middlesex who made headlines in 1980-81 by becoming the first black player to represent the England Test side. He was born on October 14, 1953 at East Point, St Philip, in Barbados. In all, he has played three one-day internationals and three Test matches for England. Butcher came to England at the age of 13. He is married with two children. His highest score in county cricket is 197, scored against Yorkshire at Lord's in 1982. Outside cricket Butcher is an insurance salesman.

Gary Headley

Hopeful Gary Headley is a young cricketer with sound prospects. He has played for the MCC ground staff – a traditional breeding ground of many top British cricketers. Headley has received encouragement and financial assistance from the *Caribbean Times* to boost his career chances. The youngster spent five winter months in 1987/88 in Australia, co-sponsored by Hansib Publishing, acquiring experience and adjusting to play conditions for the Melbourne-based Werribee Cricket Club in the Sub District League. Headley is hoping to make a breakthrough into the English county game. The all-rounder is shortlisted for 1988 trials with Gloucestershire, Glamorgan and Derbyshire.

Allan Warner

Allan Esmond Warner is a Derbyshire utility player. He was born on May 12, 1959 in Birmingham. Warner was educated at the Tabernacle school in St Kitts, Westindies. He made his county debut in 1982 for Worcestershire and, at the end of 1984, joined Derbyshire. His best bowling figures are 5-27 against Glamorgan in 1984.

Wilfred Slack

A Middlesex left-hand batsman, Wilfred Norris Slack is an England international. Born on December 12, 1954 in Troumaca, St. Vincent, Slack appeared in three Tests and two one-day internationals during the 1985-86 season. He is the scorer of 1,000 runs in a season six times. Outside cricket Slack is a digital electronics test engineer. His highest score in county cricket came against Leicestershire in 1981, when he notched 248.

Neil Williams

A Middlesex fast bowler, born on July 2, 1962 in St. Vincent, he made his county debut in 1982 and has taken 50 wickets in county cricket on two occasions. He has attained six 'O'-levels and one 'A'-level. He likes relaxing to reggae, soul and soca music. His best bowling performance was against Zimbabwe XI for the English Counties XI in 1984/85 with figures of 7-55.

Mark Ramprakash

A Middlesex batsman, born in Bushey, Hertfordshire, on September 5, 1969 of an English mother and Indo-Guyanese father, Mark has quickly established himself a future place in the England senior ranks. He marked his first class county debut with Middlesex in April 1987 with a score of 63 against Yorkshire.

Currently studying for 'A'-levels in politics and economics, Mark has represented England Schools and MCC, and was a member of the England under-21 side which lost in the semi-final to Australia, the eventual winners of the 1988 World Youth Cricket Cup.

His highest score in county cricket is 71. He is contracted to Middlesex till 1989.

Rehan Kebal Alikhan

Rehan Alikhan was born on December 28, 1962 in London. The Sussex right-hand batsman made his county debut in 1986. He has notched seven first class 50s in cricket. Educated at King's College School, he obtained eight 'O'-levels and two 'A'-levels. Outside cricket he is an insurance broker.

Field Hockey

Imran Sherwani, England's experienced player rounds a Pakistani marker in an international match

Imran Sherwani

Full name Imran Ahmed Khan Sherwani, he was born in Stoke-on-Trent on April 9, 1962. The 5ft 9in field hockey player was one of the star England representatives in the 1986 World Cup when England captured a silver medal.

He has gained 69 England caps and 23 caps for Great Britain. In 1987 he was a member of European Cup silver medallist England team. In the same year he was voted Bovril Men's Player of the Year.

Sherwani is a dedicated sportsman who also likes the odd game of cricket. He longs for the day when field hockey players can devote all their concentration and energies to first class competition. When he is not playing, he works in a newsagents shop, from 5am-6pm. Sugar Ray Leonard figures prominently in his list of admired personalties. 1988 is an important year for Sherwani; the Olympics loom in September and more significantly his wedding day presents itself in October.

Kulbir Singh Bhaura

Kulbir Singh Bhaura, born in India, but now based in west London, is a multi-capped international England and Great Britain player who helped Great Britain take the bronze medal in the 1984 Los Angeles Olympic Games.

As well as fulfilling obligations on the national level, Bhaura captains the renowned Indian Gymkhana hockey team which won the South Premier title for the first time in the club's history in 1986/87. In the same year the team narrowly missed out in the Hockey Association Cup.

Football

The emergence and impact of black footballers in domestic competition is a remarkable phenomenon and one that was not easily seen until a decade ago. In factual terms black Britons made their mark during the 1950s. Though limited, the figure increased slightly by the early seventies and gathered refreshing momentum in the late seventies. In retrospect it would appear that Viv Anderson's selection into the England team in 1978 sparked off substantial growth in the percentage of black individuals translating their apprenticeship status to the paid ranks.

Almost all 92 clubs in the four league divisions have a black player registered on their books, and the first division plays host to more players of Third World origin than ever before. Though the player gains at domestic level have not in relative terms been reflected in the England senior team, the England under 21, youth and schoolboy sides, project an optimistic picture for the foreseeable future. The positive contribution of black footballers is impressively mirrored at the non-league level, which has provided a solid platform for so many of the league's supreme protagonists.

Football fanaticism has grown in all parts of the world, not least in Third World countries where the game is seen as a possible escape route from poverty.

In recent years Africa has produced world class players who rank alongside the best. Midfield player Mohammed Timoumi of Morocco and Algerian striker Rabah Madjer, both winners of the African Footballer of the Year Award, offer their services to avaricious European clubs. However, challenging the role of the world's best footballer is Holland's dreadlocked Ruud Gullit. The 25-year-old of Surinamese origin, a vociferous anti-apartheid campaigner and the world's most expensive footballer at £5.7 million, is looking to launch Third World football into a new era. Those who succeeded before him include the Moroccan-born Juste Fontaine, who netted 13 times during the 1958 World Cup, which is still a tournament record and the Mozambique-born Eusebio who played for Portugal, helping them to a third place in the 1966 World Cup, their best ever placing. His goal scoring exploits propelled his club Benfica to the forefront of European football in the sixties. And of course Edson Arantes Do Nascimento, better known as Pelé, stunned the world as a 17-year-old in the 1958 World Cup with his superb individualism and pace. His score of over a thousand goals makes him the greatest forward of all time. The tall, athletic, cheerful and charismatic Gullit, who plays his club football in the Italian first division for AC Milan, will be aspiring to emulate his Third World-rooted predecessors with grand performances, assisting the Dutch to rekindle the form which took them to two World Cup finals in the seventies.

Ruud Gullit, Holland's influential playmaker

John Barnes (Liverpool & England)

The all-conquering wing forward, John Barnes, is regarded by many national and international soccer observers as the most exciting and creative talent in the English Football League. He has won 36 caps for England and has scored six goals. He joined Liverpool in June 1987 from Watford for a fee of £900,000. His previous clubs have included non-league Sudbury Court, signing for Watford in July 1981. He made his professional league debut in September of the same year against Oldham. Born in Kingston, Jamaica, on November 7, 1963, Barnes has quickly reached his best form for the Merseysiders, developing a useful understanding with team mate and England striker, Peter Beardsley. Barnes' best goal for England still remains the exceptional solo effort scored against Brazil in the Maracana Stadium, Rio de Janeiro, in 1984.

Viv Anderson (Manchester United & England)

A quietly effective and capable right back with a knack of scoring vital goals for his club, Anderson was born in Nottingham on August 29, 1956. He reserved himself a place in the record books in November 1978 when he became the first black footballer to play for England against Czechoslovakia at Wembley. To date he has won 29 caps and scored twice. Anderson, who began his football career with Nottingham Forest under the guidance of Brian Clough, was a member of the triumphant 1977/78 League Championship team. He also gained two European Cup winners medals, and two League Cup winners medals. In July 1984 he ended his stay at Forest, signing to London giants Arsenal for a fee of £250,000. In his two seasons at Highbury he assisted a young side to the Littlewoods Cup victory over Liverpool in the 1986/87 final with a 2-1 win at Wembley. He left the north Londoners in July 1987 for a place in the multi-talented Manchester United team at a price of £250,000.

Cyrille Regis (Coventry City & England)

A powerfully-built, mobile and athletic striker, this French Guiana-born striker was Coventry's top scorer in the 1986/87 season with a total of 16 goals. He was a vital member of the Coventry City side which won the Football Association Cup in 1986/87 for the first time in the club's 104-year history, beating Tottenham 3-2 in the final. Regis joined Coventry from neighbours West Bromwich Albion in October 1984 for a fee of £300,000. The 30-year-old striker won the last of his four England caps against West Germany in 1982. However a revival in his fortunes brought him back into contention for an England place in 1986/87. He made his entrance into professional league football in March 1978 when he was signed from Isthmian league side, Hayes. The former electrician has gained honours at England 'B' level.

John Fashanu wins the ball against a Newcastle defender

John Fashanu (Wimbledon)

Born of Nigerian parents in the Kensington district of west London on Setember 18, 1963, John Fashanu has developed a high profile for his scoring exploits in recent years and is on the verge of an England full cap. The centre forward is a well conditioned athlete with an amazing appetite for success. Since joining Wimbledon from Millwall in March 1986 for a fee of £125,000 Fashanu has finished as the club's top scorer each year. He netted 16 in 1986/87 and has notched 20 in 1987/88. His league football career began with Norwich at the age of sixteen. He joined Lincoln in 1983 before signing for second division Millwall for £55,000. The articulate Nigerian, who was brought up in a Dr Barnados' home, does a lot of promotional work for the childrens' foundation. He is also brother to Justin Fashanu, Britain's first black million pound player.

Paul McGrath (Manchester United)

A world class defender, his versatility in defence and in midfield is an asset to club and country. Born in Ealing, west London, McGrath joined Manchester United from the Dublin-based St Patrick's Athletic in April 1982. The 27-year-old made his senior debut in a pre-season match that year against Aldershot and his first league game was against Tottenham in November. The composed and stout figure at the heart of the Manchester United defence is a reassuring sight for colleagues and club supporters alike. He has won over 15 caps for the Republic of Ireland, and under the Ireland manager Jack Charlton, is set for a long and rewarding international career.

Des Walker (Nottingham Forest)

An exciting defender, Walker looks destined to add full England honours to the seven England under-21 caps he already has. Born in Enfield, north London, he signed as an apprentice to Forest in July 1982 and was upgraded to full professional in December 1983. He made his league debut at home to Everton in March 1984.

Franz Carr (Nottingham Forest)

A winger with scintillating pace, the former Blackburn Rovers player was transferred to Nottingham Forest in August 1984 for a meagre £25,000 in another of Brian Clough's astute scoops. Carr spent the 1985 season being groomed in Forest's reserves and was introduced to first team action in the 1985/86 season. Carr was born in Preston in September 1966.

Mark Chamberlain (Sheffield Wednesday)

A wing forward, he joined the Yorkshire club from Stoke City in September 1985 and made his debut for the club as substitute, coming on against Arsenal at Highbury. The Stoke-born footballer made his name with Port Vale, for whom he signed as an apprentice. When transferred to Stoke in August 1982, the fee was a record for a fourth division player. He has won full England caps at senior and under-21 level.

Mark Stein (Luton Town)

An agile forward, the younger brother of Brian Stein was recruited by the club on the Youth Opportunities Programme. He turned professional in 1984, making his first team debut against Everton in April. He is a reglalr member of the Luton Town squad and sometimes partners his brother in the frontline. He also spent a loan period at Aldershot.

Chris Hughton (Tottenham Hotspurs)

An effective full back, Christopher William Gerrard Hughton was born at Forest Gate on December 11, 1958 of a Guyanese father and an Irish mother. He joined Tottenham as a part time professional in June 1977, completing his apprenticeship as a lift engineer before signing full professional forms in June 1979. He made his league debut against Manchester United in 1979. Hughton has made over 260 appearances for the club, scoring 18 goals and was a member of the Tottenham team which won two FA Cups in 1981 and 1982 and the 1984 UEFA Cup. In addition to his successes at club level, Hughton has represented the Republic of Ireland over 30 times. Married with three children, Hughton lives in Hertfordshire. Listening to soul music, in particular to Stevie Wonder are among his favourite pastimes.

Garth Crooks (Charlton Athletic)

An ex-Stoke and Tottenham Hotspurs centre forward, during his stay at White Hart Lane, Crooks' pairing with Steve Archibald was among the most lethal striking partnerships in world football. Crooks was a member of the Tottenham 1981 FA Cup winning team against Manchester City, scoring in the 3-2 replay win. He also scored the precious goal which saved Charlton from relegation to the second division in the 1986/87 season against Leeds United in the last play-off match. In July 1980 he was signed from Stoke to the north London club for a fee of £600,000. Crooks is now an active member for Sickle Cell Anaemia Research (S.C.A.R.) and is the Director of Overseas Projects for the Calderpier Sports Company.

Ricky Hill (Luton Town)

Born in west London, Ricky Hill rose from the apprenticeship ranks to make his league debut in 1976. It took the graceful midfield player a couple of years to earn a regular place but he now looks proudly over 350 league appearances for the club. Hill has also won three England caps. Injuries have cruelly deprived Hill of a sustained international presence in the England set-up.

David Rocastle (Arsenal)

A promising midfielder, and a player with real quality. He assisted Arsenal in their Littlewoods Cup triumph over Liverpool in 1987. Rocastle scored the crucial winner against Tottenham in the semi-final which put the Gunners on the road to Wembley. He has won seven caps at England under-21 level. In 1986 he was voted Arsenal's Player of the Year by the Supporters Club. Rocastle made his debut against Newcastle in September 1985. Born in Stockwell, south London, he first joined the club on schoolboy forms in May 1982 and become a full time professional in December 1984.

Carlton Fairweather (Wimbledon)

A very tall wing forward, the 26-year-old Chingford-based footballer suffered a severe setback in January 1988 when he broke his leg in a league match against Watford. He is a committed member of the enthusiastic team under the guidance of Bobby Gould and Don Howe. Born in Dulwich, south London, he joined Wimbledon from Tooting and Mitcham. He made his league debut against Oldham on New Year's Day, 1985.

Wimbledon's Carlton Fairweather solidly challenged by Arsenal defender Gus Caesar in a first division encounter

Brian Stein (Luton Town)

A sharp and hard-working striker, the South African-born footballer was bloodied in Luton's first team in 1977 and led their scoring list for the first time in 1980-81 with 19 goals. The following year he netted 21 when Luton won promotion. Stein won his only England cap against France in Paris in 1984. He also gained three England under-21 caps. He played non-league football for Edgware before turning professional status.

Clive Wilson (Chelsea)

A right back, born in Manchester, he signed for Manchester city as a non-contract player in October 1979. The Jamaican first appeared in City's league team at home to Wolverhampton in December 1981. He spent the 1982/83 season on loan to Chester. In 1986/87 season Wilson moved to London, joining Chelsea for a fee of £250,000.

Laurie Cunningham (Wimbledon)

A great dribbler of the ball, the wing forward recently returned to British football after a long absence. He joined Wimbledon in 1988 on a free transfer from Belgian club, Charleroi. Cunningham also had a term in Spain where he played for Real Madrid. However it was with Orient and West Bromwich Albion (WBA) that he made his name. Born in Archway, north London, the slender athlete began league football with the east London club. He left Orient for WBA in March 1977 and went on to win England under-21 honours, prior to winning his senior cap against Wales in 1979.

George Lawrence (Millwall)

A winger, George Lawrence joined the east London club Millwall from Southampton in July 1987 for a transfer fee of £150,000. Lawrence had previously played for Oxford United and left after helping them to win the third division championship. The tall striker signed for the Saints for a £60,000 fee. He was born in London of Grenadian parents on September 14, 1962.

Remi Moses (Manchester United)

A spirited combatant with exceptional ball control, Moses' career has been dogged by frustrating injuries. He made it to the professional ranks with West Bromwich Albion. The Manchester-born footballer was signed in a joint deal with England captain Bryan Robson worth £2,400,000 in September 1981. Moses has won honours at England under-21 level. He made his league debut for WBA away to Crystal Palace in January 1980.

Worrell Sterling (Watford)

A winger, born in Bethnal Green, east London on June 6, 1965. He signed as an apprentice for Watford in July 1981 and turned professional in May 1983, making his debut against Manchester United in April 1983. He is a potential an England international player.

Paul Parker (Queens Park Rangers)

A central defender who, despite standing at only 5ft 6¾in, finds that holding the defensive unit together gives him few problems, Paul Parker is an outstanding athlete with commanding aerial ability. The 23-year-old signed to Loftus Road for £250,000 in the 1986/87 season from Fulham. Parker is a London-born player who developed through the apprentice ranks at Craven Cottage, making his league debut in April 1981. He has won England youth honours.

Chris Fairclough (Tottenham Hotspurs)

A composed centre back, formerly of Nottingham Forest, he became a Tottenham Hotspurs player in the summer of 1987, signing for £350,000. An England under-21 international, Fairclough likes to join the attack using his heading ability to good effect. He scores frequently.

Leroy Rosenior (West Ham United)

The distinctively-named forward made his league appearance for Fulham in 1983 playing away to Leicester. The former pupil of the Furzedown school in Streatham signed for West Ham United in March 1988 and marked his debut with a winning goal against Watford. He spent a fruitless period at QPR in the intermediate period. The 23-year-old marksman has great potential for the future.

Dave Bennett (Coventry City)

A skilful wing forward, this Manchester-born footballer made his league debut in April 1979. He was instrumental in Coventry's historic FA Cup win over Tottenham in 1987, scoring first and inspiring a remarkable comeback. He was also a member of the Manchester City team who were 1981 FA Cup losing finalists. He had a brief spell at Cardiff City before moving to the Midlands.

Gus Caesar (Arsenal)

An adaptable defender and England under-21 player, Gus Caesar has been unable to establish a regular place in the north London team's first eleven but has every hope of achieving his goal. He is sharp and possesses a good soccer brain.

Mitchell Thomas (Tottenham Hotspurs)

An attack-minded full back, Thomas joined Tottenham from Luton Town in July 1986 for £250,000. Born in Luton of Jamaican parents on October 2, 1964, Thomas joined the professional ranks via the Youth Training Scheme. He has gained three England under-21 caps and represented the England youth team. Thomas was also selected into the full England squad for a number of friendlies in 1987.

Michael Thomas (Arsenal)

A defender midfield, Michael Thomas has been a revelation in the Arsenal midfield in the 1987/88 season. The Lambeth (south London) born footballer first caught the eye of the Arsenal scouts when playing for the South London Boys'. He is a former captain of the England schoolboys and has won caps at under-21 level.

Emeka Nwajiobi (Luton Town)

A skilful wing forward born on May 25, 1959 in Anambra State, Nigeria, Nwajiobi was snapped up for a bargain fee of £5,000 from Isthmian league side Dulwich Hamlet by Luton scout John Moore who later went on to become Luton Town manager. He marked his league debut against Nottingham Forest with a goal. A former England schoolboy international who migrated to England in 1970 due to the politically sensitive situation in Nigeria, Nwajiobi is also a qualified pharmacist, graduating with honours from the Cardiff Institute of Science and Technology. He is another professional whose career has been scarred by horrendous injury problems.

John Chiedozie (Tottenham Hotspurs)

Born in Owerri, Nigeria, John Chiedozie has been absent from first team action for the best part of two years. The stylish winger gained a reputation for being one of the fastest footballers in English league football. He began his career with Orient in 1977. He moved on to Notts County for a fee of £600,000 in 1981 and linked up with Tottenham in 1984 for £375,000. Chiedozie came to England at the age of twelve and attended the St. Bonaventure's secondary school. Chiedozie is a Nigerian international player.

Paul Davis (Arsenal)

A tenacious and gifted midfielder, Davis is a former England under-21 player. Born in London of Jamaican parents, he has established himself in the engine room of the Arsenal side after terrible luck with injuries. He made his league debut for the Gunners against Tottenham in the local derby match at White Hart Lane in April 1980. The Stockwell-born player served an impressive career with the South London Boys' soccer team. He was upgraded to full professional status in July 1979.

Luther Blissett (Watford)

A loyal goal scoring machine, Blissett has notched over 120 league goals for Watford in over 350 league appearances. He was a part of Watford's meteoric rise from the fourth division to the first under the chairmanship of Elton John and management of Graham Taylor. In 1983/84 Blissett was transferred to crack Italian club AC Milan for £1 million. He failed to justify his stay, with only six goals. The Jamaican-born striker returned to Watford the following season for £550,000. Blissett made his league debut in Division 4 against Swansea in April 1976. He was capped at England senior level, scoring a hat-trick on his England debut against Luxemburg.

Danny Wallace (Southampton)

An enterprising forward, born in London, Wallace was signed by Southampton as an Associated Schoolboy. He graduated to apprentice ranks in July 1980 and made his league debut in the number seven shirt away to Manchester United. Wallace stands at 5ft 4½in and is one of the shortest strikers in the first division. Has been capped at England under-21 level.

Dalian Atkinson (Ipswich)

Born on March 21, 1968 in Shropshire, Atkinson made his professional debut in March 1986 against Newcastle. The most important moments in his brief career to date have been to help his club to a youth tournament victory in France and scoring two goals against Barnsley in the 1987/88 season. He extends great admiration to the Brazilian soccer legend Pele.

Ian Wright (Crystal Palace)

Born in London of Jamaican parents, this highly-rated 24-year-old striker is the focal point of transfer talk among top clubs. In the 1987/88 season Wright scored 22 goals in a 45 goal partnership with Mark Bright. He joined the south Londoners as an apprentice. He first caught the eye at amateur level during the 1985 *Caribbean Times* football knockout competition.

Jason Neil Beckford (Manchester City)

Born in Manchester, the 5ft 9in player has become a full professional making his first senior appearance in April 1988. He has gained caps at England under-15/16/17 level. His other sporting interests include American football, cricket and basketball.

Bob Hazell (Port Vale)

This volatile defender was born in West Kingston, Jamaica. Bob Hazell has played at England under-21 and 'B' level and was a member of the Queens Park Rangers (QPR) team which reached the FA Cup final in 1982. He began his league football career with Wolverhampton and moved to QPR for a fee of £240,000 in September 1979. He has since played for Leicester City and Port Vale. The imposing figure of Hazell masterminded the biggest upset in FA Cup competition in recent years when lowly placed third division side Port Vale knocked out Tottenham in the fourth round of the 1987/88 competition with a 2-1 win.

Mark Bright going for goal in a league match against Plymouth in the 1986/87 season

Mark Bright (Crystal Palace)

A prolific goalscorer, he joined the paid ranks at Port Vale in the lower reaches of the third division in 1983. He moved to Leicester City before signing for the south London club nicknamed the Eagles. He was born in Stoke-on-Trent in 1962 of a Gambian father and English mother.

Devon Winston White (Bristol Rovers)

A tall striker with superb heading ability who was born in Nottingham on March 2, 1964, he played for Lincoln City before moving south and joining the Eastville side. His achievements include reaching the Lincolnshire Cup final with his team and making the 3AAAs (Amateur Athletics Association) 800m final. He is married with three sons and his ambition is to play in the first division. Among the many personalities chosen he would dearly like to meet Terry Venables with a suitable contract.

Gary Bennett (Sunderland)

Central defender and Sunderland captain, he left Cardiff City for the Tynesiders in July 1984. He made 87 appearances for the Ninian Park side before moving to Sunderland. Bennett has been instrumental in guiding Sunderland back to the second division.

Paul Elliott (Pisa)

A smart and fearless defender, London-born Paul Elliott signed for Italian first division club Pisa from Aston Villa for a fee of £400,000 in July 1987 on a three-year contract. The former England under-21 player has played for Charlton Athletic and Luton Town. He joined the Bedfordshire club from Charlton for £145,000 in March 1983.

Mark Walters (Glasgow Rangers)

A pacey winger, Birmingham-born Walters made his league debut for Aston Villa against Leeds United in April 1982. He signed for the club originally as an Associate Schoolboy and then became an apprentice in July 1980. A former England youth and under-21 international the footballer signed for Graeme Souness's spendthrift Glasgow Rangers during the 1987/88 for a large fee.

Garry Thompson (Aston Villa)

An aggressive striker, he joined Villa from Sheffield Wednesday in the 1986/87 season. Born in Birmingham, Thompson developed in Coventry City's apprentice ranks. He was upgraded to full professional rank in 1977 and made his league debut for the Midlands club in March 1978. He left Coventry for West Bromwhich Albion in February 1985. He has been capped for the England under-21 team.

Victor Peter Kasule (Shrewsbury)

A midfield striker, born in Glasgow on May 28, 1965 of Ugandan parents, Kasule has the distinction of being Scotland's only professional black footballer and was, until Mark Walters signed for Rangers, the only black individual in the Scottish football league divisions. A jovial character with a taste for victory, his previous clubs have been Albion Rovers and Meadowbank Thistle. He joined the second division Shrewsbury from Meadowbank for £30,000. He made his professional debut at 17. Kasule has also gained four Scottish youth caps. His other sporting interests include tennis and basketball.

Golf

Allan Jarrett

Jamaican-born Allan Jarrett aims to become the first black British golfer to make the breakthrough onto the PGA (Professional Golf Association) circuit. The 32-year-old British Airways employee is fast improving on his present handicap of plus two. His highest accolade to date is being voted the Best Overseas Player in the 1985 Jamaican Open. The smart and sensible individual, who extends his admiration to black American golfer Calvin Peete for having achieved his career goal late in life, is inspired by this. Allan Jarrett is a member of the Surrey-based Home Park golf Club.

Snooker

Don Watson

South London-based Jamaican Don Watson is another sportsman with his sights firmly fixed on the record books – becoming the first black snooker professional. The 21-year-old professional/amateur player has captivated packed national venues with his placid and calculated destruction of opponents. To date he has accumulated twelve tournament victories making two breaks of 144. A member of the Stockwell Snooker Club in South London, who form part of the Green King sponsored London league, Watson is hot on the heels of the lucrative paid ranks set-up. Television coverage is guaranteed to make Don Watson a household name in the future.

Judo

L-R: Britain's three top judo exponents sit side by side patiently contemplating the future. On the extreme left is British heavyweight champion Elvis Gordon, a community worker for Action Sport in Wolverhampton. The bespectacled Kerrith Brown and Denzine White are both business partners in a health and fitness project based in Wolverhampton. The trio are all members of the successful area judo club.

Martial Arts

Martial Arts is a generalised term given to illustrate and incorporate various fighting styles in most cases reach back to China, Korea and Japan. According to the Martial Arts Commission, Britain's overall ruling body, there was a 36 per cent increase in the number of practitioners participating in the sport in 1986 and, by and large, many of those were black aspirants. Featured below are just a few of the top achievers from the ethnic minority communities in Britain.

Keinosuke Enoeda demonstrates a strike technique to student Caesar Andrews

Keinosuke Enoeda (Karate)

Karate is not just a sport, it is a way of life for Keinosuke Enoeda who was appointed the official representative to Great Britain and Europe in 1968. In that time the Master has built the Karate Union of Great Britain which accommodates 30,000 members and 450 clubs. Enoeda was born in Fukuoka, Japan, in 1935. He adds a new dimension to his technical ability with a superior literary knowledge of the artform. He won the International Karate title in 1965, today's equivalent of the world championships. He has written many books on Shotokan Karate and instructed many film actors and actresses on stances and fighting styles including Sean Connery, Ingrid Pitt and Edward Fox.

Neville Wray (Kickboxing)

Born October 2, 1955, in Portland, Jamaica. The 6ft 1in competitor made his debut in kickboxing in 1972. His list of achievements to date reads impressively. He has won one world title, two world team titles, six European semi-contact titles, seven British titles and five European 'Kung Fu' championships. He has represented Britain at international level since 1978 and captained Britain and England from 1981. Away from the competition rigours, Wray is an enthusiastic gardener who enjoys tranquil restaurants. He is married with a son.

Kashmir Singh Gill (Kickboxing)

Born in Birmingham on July 2 1966, the Midlander has won championship honours in his sport, including the 1986 world kickboxing middleweight title and the 1986 European title. He carved an opening into the sport at the tender age of 14. In that time he has received the best possible guidance from Howard Brown and has gained 14 England caps. Gill is now a full-time Karate instructor. His aim is to win a world professional title and to retire undefeated.

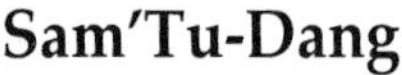

Sam'Tu-Dang

The Sam'Tu-Dang Martial Arts Society has emerged from humble beginnings and grown into an internationally acclaimed organisation, integrating and harnessing the basics of physical excellence with mental strength. The founder member and Master of the society is the Guyana-born Laurie Theophilus Ince. The Wandsworth-based organisation has conducted several tour exhibitions to the Caribbean, Canada, Europe and the United States. Branches of the Society are also found in several countries in the Westindies as well as in Ghana, West Africa.

Kevin Brewerton (Kickboxing)

Kevin Brewerton, now a professional 'Lau Gar' and 'Kung Fu' instructor was born in Miami, Florida, on September 9, 1962. The expatriate, who now lives in and competes for England, made his debut appearance in the sport in 1976. Since then he has won numerous England caps, collecting the World, European and British light-heavyweight Kickboxing titles. The personable and articulate artist has said that he would like to pursue a career in films. He is currently putting the final touches to a book relating to the psychological approach to martial arts competition.

Laurie Francois (Wushu)

The Grenada-born Laurie Francois is among Britain's leading exponents of the ancient Chinese artform Wushu (war art). Francois led the British team to 17 medals in the 1987 international championships staged in China. He gained three medals, two bronze and a gold in the three-man combat routine.

The ILEA (Inner London Education Authority) social worker who works at the Four Feathers club in north west London is a former gold medallist at the 1985 European Kung Fu Championships staged in Sweden. Francois is a professional Kung Fu and Wushu instructor.

Albert Blissett (Tae-Kwon-Do)

The 6ft, 14 stone martial arts enthusiast, Albert Blissett, is one of Britain's leading exponents in the ancient Korean art of self-defence, Tae-Kwon-Do. Blissett, whose famous brother plays football for Watford, won two gold medals at the April 1988 World Tae-Kwon-Do championships staged in Budapest, Hungary.

Blissett has been practising the art for over ten years and achieved his most important moment in a long career when he first struck gold in the hyperweight category in the Male Individual Power Test. He then helped Britain take the team event in the Team Power Test. Born on September 3, 1956 in Jamaica, Blissett is a part-time martial arts and fitness instructor at the Gladstone Centre, north west London.

Crypt Association members. On the extreme right is Mike Sailsman. Leslie Fairclough is in the middle with a successful colleague on the far left

Crypt Association (Karate)

The Crypt Association, one of Wolverhampton's leading black community organisations, has proved to be a winner with martial arts. The group can boast of two British Karate champions in Leslie Fairclough and Mike Sailsman. In the 1988 British Karate championships they both struck gold at the Crystal Palace Sports Centre in south London.

Sailsman won the gold medal in the heavyweight division and Fairclough acquired his in the light-heavyweight section, retaining the title he won in 1987. The talented individuals are both members of the strong British Karate squad.

Howard Patrick Brown (Kickboxing)

Howard Brown known as "The Hawk" for his sharp and instinctive speed inside the ring was born in Birmingham on December 30, 1957. Brown is the current world junior-featherweight champion who first made his appearance in kickboxing at the age of 19. Brown, of Jamaican background, has through his championship exploits gained notoriety and fame in the United States. This is due largely to a sports cable television network, ESPN, which has screened most of his fights. Brown, a former karate practitioner, won the world amateur kickboxing championship in 1979 and the world professional title in 1987. The Midlander made the WKA (World Kickboxing Association) title his outright possession in March 1988 when he KO'd Japan's Kazuma Saiki in the eighth round. The 30-year-old is married with two sons and hopes to become a film scriptwriter in the future. He has already written a film part for actor/singer Phil Collins.

Netball

Jeanne Bailey shoots the Westindies into the lead in the international match against England at Wembley

The 1987 touring Westindies netball team proved too formidable an obstacle for England when they came over and played two Test matches, winning one and drawing the other.

The star of the two matches was Jeanne Bailey – her sharp and instinctive goal-shooting skills ensured her 31 goals in the Westindies second match 45-40 victory at Wembley, north west London.

This was all achieved in a year when Trinidad and Tobago were runners-up in the World Netball Championships in the August event staged in Glasgow, Scotland. The tournament, narrowly won by Australia, figured strong Caribbean participation and Jamaica finished fifth overall with Barbados and the Cook Islands placed equal sixth.

Netball is catching on rapidly amongst female members of the minority ethnic communities. Several representatives in the England national team are black and this growing interest seems, in particular, to have been triggered off by the perennial achievements of the Caribbean countries at top international level. Hansib Sports Association sponsor a national knockout netball competition each year.

Street Hockey

Street Hockey is a forty-year-old sport that was rediscovered six years ago. It is played on roller skates using an ice hockey type stick, a plastic non-bouncing ball, and rules that have evolved through the course of time.

The game is a fast moving, physically demanding, body-contact sport. There are more than 250 teams spread throughout Britain with hundreds more in six European countries. Players are divided into four categories – Seniors are aged 16 and over, Juniors between 13 and 16, Pee Wees between 10 and 13 and Minnows are between 5 and 10 years of age.

Street Warriors

Most members of the cult team, Street Warriors, live and work across south London stretching between Battersea in the south west to Bromley in the south east. They were formed in March 1982 after six founder members met while studying for an engineering course at South East London Technical College, Lewisham.

The team, guided and inspired by manager Winston Douglas and captain Robert Williams, have won an impressive array of trophies: 1983 League Cup, 1984 and 1985 Bauer Shield, 1984 and 1987 National Champions, and undisputed winners of the London League Division One Championship for the sixth successive time.

The Street Warriors are searching for a major team sponsor as they strive towards maintaining their grip on the major prizes in the sport. Among future hopes, the Street Warriors would like an inter-city league set-up or a full scale national league. The establishment of a European league championship is fully supported by the south London street hockey club.

Enforcers 'A'

The Enforcers 'A' team all live and work around Stoke Newington in north east London in the Borough of Hackney. The team belongs to the Enforcers Club which comprises an A and B Senior team, C and D Junior teams and up-and-coming Pee Wee and Women's teams. They were formed in April 1985 at the Stamford Hill Youth Centre in north London.

The Enforcers 'A' team, managed by Terry Sommers, has risen rapidly to the top flight of the sport in London. In 1987 they won the London League Division II Championship, gaining promotion to Division I where, after their first season, they finished in second place. In the same year they reached the quarter-finals of the British Street Hockey Association's National Championship. The Enforcers hope that 1988 will be their year as they go in search of glory in the National Championships at the Granby Halls, Leicester in July. The team is pitted against fifteen other top teams from around Britain.

Squash

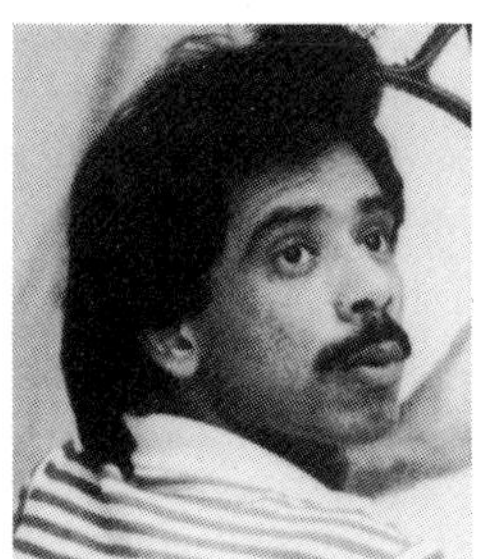

Jahangir Khan

Jahangir Khan stands alone as the most revered and outstanding exponent of his sport. Born into a powerful squash playing family in Karachi, Pakistan, on December 10, 1964, Jahangir quickly learnt the ropes and went about conquering. He received the best tuition possible from his father Roshan, who won world honours. He began playing at the age of ten and won the Pakistani Junior Championships at 14. By this time his brother Torsam was established in the world's top ten and at the age of 15 came to England and trained with him. Things just got better and better for Jahangir. He became the youngest ever World Amateur champion. After his brother's tragic death he joined forces with his cousin Rahmat Khan in December 1979. At the age of 17 he became the youngest ever senior world champion.

In his time at the top, Jahangir has won five World Men's Singles Championships and six British Open Championships among an array of other titles. Indeed Jahangir notched up an unbeaten five-and-a-half year streak before he was defeated in the World Open in Paris by New Zealander Ross Norman in 1986. Jahangir, a frequent visitor to these shores, is based at his family home in Karachi. According to his coach, Rahmat Khan, Jahangir, which translates as "Conquerer of the world", has pocketed more money than most of the world's top ten tennis players.

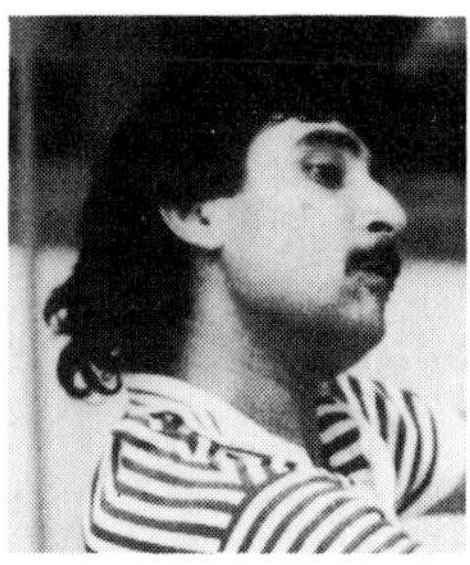

Umar Hayatt Khan

Umar Hayatt Khan is another member of the proficient squash playing Khan dynasty. The tall and well-built individual aided Pakistan to capture the World Team Championship at the Royal Albert Hall, central London, in 1987, along with Jahangir and Jansher Khan. The stocky player is currently ranked at number seven in the world ratings.

Jansher Khan

Jansher Khan is no relation to the great Jahangir, but the young protege stepped out of his idol's shadow in 1987 when he swept to victory in most of the season's open tournaments. His list of acquisitions for 1987 include The Perrier Open in April, Malaysian Open, Singapore Open, Hong Kong Open in September, Pakistan Open, and World Open in October.

In November the 19-year-old captured the United States Open, Swiss Masters, Pakistan International Airways Masters and the Al Falaj Master in Oman. The battle for the number one position between the Khans is one of the most intriguing developments in sporting duels.

Rugby Union/League

It is said that the origins of rugby union stem from a game of football in 1823 when a gentleman called William Webb Ellis decided to transfer his skills from foot to hand and run with the ball. This prompted years of active discussion and administrative headaches. Various clubs were formed and regulations and codes set-up, but it was not until 1871, the year of inception of the RFU (Rugby Football Union), that things really started to move.

Archival papers show that minority ethnic involvement in rugby union, one of Britain's oldest organised sports, dates back to the early 1900s. In fact one James Peters broke many barriers, becoming the first black individual to play for England in 1906. He gained five caps, with his last coming two years later. Born in Salford in 1880 he enhanced his rugby playing reputation in the West Country. He represented several provincial clubs before serving Bristol in the 1900-02 seasons. Like so many other of his amateur counterparts he joined the paid ranks, signing for Barrow rugby league club in 1913. Though talented black individuals emerged over the next decades, an ensuing eighty year gap had to be filled in February 1988 when Chris Oti represented England against Scotland at Murrayfield.

Christopher Oti is congratulated by England team mates after scoring his third try against Ireland on his home debut in March 1988

Christopher Oti

In 1988 an emerging star confirmed his unquestionable potential with selection into the England senior side. He has to date represented England twice and celebrated his home debut against Ireland at Twickenham in March 1988 with a hat-trick of tries in a spell of eleven minutes to inflict on the Irish team their heaviest defeat by England in a century.

The affable and articulate Oti has gained honours for the England students, England universities and the England 'B' team. Born of Nigerian parents, Oti is currently studying for his final exams in the two-year Land Economy course at St Edmund's College, Cambridge University.

The England left wing has dazzling skills and pace. He was born on June 16, 1965. He attended Millfield school in Devon and Durham University where he obtained a General Arts degree. He plays his club rugby for Nottingham. In 1987 he assisted Cambridge to triumph in the 'varsity' encounter against Oxford when he scored two superb tries in the 15-10 result. His favourite pastimes include listening to soul music and night clubbing.

The Reading Westindians are one of a number of minority ethnic community clubs scattered over the country who play competitive rugby in their respective regions. Rugby is also seen as a means of uniting various people of the same cultural background on a recreational basis.

Glen Webbe

Glen Webbe is a Wales international player who entered the world scene during the 1987 five-nations championships. The adaptable Bridgend winger made quite an impact during the 1987 Rugby World Cup, won by New Zealand. Webbe scored twice in Wales' 29-16 demolition of Tonga. He was concussed during the match and returned to Britain.

Ralph Knibbs

Ralph Knibbs made his debut in first class rugby at the age of 17 and since then he has played over 220 games for his club, Bristol. His high point came in 1983 when Bristol came from behind to topple Leicester 28-22 in the John Player Cup final. The darty centre-back was born in Bristol of Jamaican parents and attended Whitefield Comprehensive School. He moved to the top junior club, Whitehall, in the Bristol combination system. His list of honours include appearances for the England 'B' Under-23, sevens' and South West Division. Outside rugby he is a qualified draughtsman who recently changed his profession to that of an estate agent.

In the summer he finds time to play wide receiver for the local American football team, Bristol Packers.

Victor Ubogu

Victor Ubogu is unique for he occupies a prominent position in the scrummage. The strong and burly prop forward is agile and fast with amazing instincts for try-scoring.

Born in the Nigerian capital, Lagos, Ubogu has already been capped at England schoolboy and Under 19 level. The 23-year-old, who made his 'varsity debut in 1987, is studying for his post graduate diploma in politics and economics at St Anne's College, Oxford. His ambition is to work for the International Monetary Fund (IMF) in Washington, USA.

Everton Davis

The 6ft 8in rugby wing is one of the tallest rugby union players in the world. He has represented Leicester at under-15, county and under-19 level, and in 1981 he narrowly missed out on selection to the England under-19 side. His skills, sought after by several top English clubs, were eventually snapped up by the London-based Harlequins side. The articulate and academically-minded individual has obtained 8 'O' levels and 3 'A' levels.

World Rugby

The inaugural 1987 World Rugby Cup tournament enabled 16 of the game's top nations to have an opportunity of testing each other out in a bid to lift the top prize in the sport. Spearheading the challenge from the Third World countries was Fiji, South Pacific neighbours, Tonga, and African representatives, Zimbabwe.

Grouped with favourites New Zealand, Argentina and Italy, the Fijians acquitted themselves admirably. Their fluent and adventurous brand of rugby paid dividends in their opening game defeating the Argentine Pumas 28-9. And, although they lost their next two successive games, against Italy and New Zealand, they did just enough to merit a place in the quarter-finals scoring more points. Their historic entrance had done much to enhance the country's position in world terms and answered the critics who doubted Fiji's selection for the World Championships. She went down to the eventual finalists, France, 31-16 in the quarter-final. (The Fiji Rugby Union was formed in 1913 and, although it participated in regional challenges, it only significantly stepped up in terms of quality opposition during the late 'sixties and early 'seventies.) And during this period it achieved notable success over the Barbarians and the British Lions in 1970 and 1977. Six hundred clubs and 12,500 members are affiliated to the union.

Fijian winger Senivalati Laulau

Rugby League

Rugby league is an offshoot of the original rugby union, the sport's ruling body. However, due to the failure to agree on certain administrative issues, a rebel group broke away from the union and formed the rugby league in 1895. This resulted in fundamental changes in all aspects of the sport. Different rules and playing conditions evolved which have made the sport independent of union activity.

The game, which has attracted an abundance of talent from the minority ethnic communities, has gained in popularity on all fronts. The rugby football league recorded 2,153,300 spectators attending games in the 1984/85 season. Statistics also show that due to media coverage and television exposure, clubs affiliated to the league have increased to 36. Though still concentrated in the three original counties of Lancashire, Yorkshire and Cumbria it is spreading outwards. Giving the game a high profile have been several talented black individuals who are idolised in their given areas for their exploits.

Hussein M'Barki

Hussein M'Barki is a Moroccan rugby union international who began his rugby league career in England playing for Warrington and Fulham. In 1985 he signed for Oldham. He made over 60 appearances for them in a two-year-period before given a free transfer to the Humberside Club, Hull, in September 1987. The Moroccan international is a versatile defensive player who can occupy many positions. He is a good catcher of the ball and very sharp and incisive when running with it.

Martin Offiah

Martin Offiah was born in London on December 29 1965. The 6ft 1in, 13 stone former rugby union player, who wore the Rosslyn Park and Ipswich jersey, is now a successful rugby league player with the renowned Cheshire side, Widnes. Offiah signed to Widnes in the summer of 1987 making his debut in August. In his first season, Offiah has captured the public's imagination with his try-scoring feats. He has surpassed the club's 30-year-old record of 36 tries in a season. He scored in eleven successive games equalling the first division record of New Zealander Gary Prohm a few years ago, and was in sight of Eric Harris's 51 year-old-record of having scored in 17 consecutive matches. Offiah has also gained a full England cap in his first season, scoring in his debut against France in the first Whitbread Trophy Test. Great Britain won 28-14 in Avignon. Offiah, son of a Nigerian magistrate, had represented England students, the Barbarians and the London Division before moving up north to the professional ranks. His performances for England and Widnes have attracted widespread interest, indeed as far as Australia, where clubs in the premier Sydney League, such as Manly-Warringah and Brisbane Broncos are preparing their cheque books. Offiah, the new star of northern rugby league, is currently studying for a BA in business studies at Liverpool Polytechnic.

Brimah Kebbie

Speed king Brimah Kebbie is yet another rugby union player making the switch to the paid ranks. Widnes signed him in March 1988 and the Manchester-based 22-year-old will begin the 1988/89 season in the competitive first division. Kebbie is an undergraduate at the North Staffordshire Polytechnic. Salford also expressed an interest but were beaten to the signature.

Des Drummond

Des Drummond was born in Sauannah-la-Mar, Jamaica, on June 17 1958. Drummond is one of the most exciting and prolific try-scorers in the English rugby league and is currently with Warrington. He was signed by them from Leigh in February 1987 for a fee of £45,000. 1975 was the year Drummond's involvement in the game ignited. Since then he has gained 24 Great Britain caps and 5 England caps. His highest number of tries in one season is 29.

Ellery Hanley

Ellery Hanley is undoubtedly the most popular and talented individual in the game today. His tackling, sense of direction, leadership qualities and belligerent running ability make him unquestionably supreme. The Great Britain captain, who plays for Wigan, was transfer-listed for a world record fee of £225,000 during a February 1988 dispute with his club coach, Graham Lowe. The disagreement was subsequently solved and Hanley has scored over 30 tries in the 1987/88 season.

Table Tennis

Desmond Douglas

Desmond Douglas

At 32, Desmond Douglas is still Britain's number one table tennis player. Perched at the top of his game for over 14 years, Douglas received honorary recognition in 1987 when he was presented with an MBE (Member of the British Empire) by the Queen at Buckingham Palace.

The Jamaican-born protagonist has won a record ten ETTA (English Table Tennis Association) titles and achieved his best tournament victory in the Europa/Stiga Top Twelve competition staged in Switzerland in January 1987, when he toppled Europe's number one Jan Ove Waldner of Sweden. In the same year, in the New Delhi world championships dominated by China, Douglas reached the last 16. The Walsall-based player, whose cat-like reflexes, nimble movements and dogged characteristics have made him into one of Britain's most celebrated sportsmen, he first represented England at international level at the age of 18. Douglas has played for Steelstock Wolverhampton and for Bath in the British league. However, because of the paltry financial returns, Douglas signed a contract with the German Bundesliga side, Borussia Dusseldorf, in 1985. A great ambassador for the sport, he is the most successful British player since Johnny Leach in the 1950s.

Skylet Andrew

Skylet Andrew is Britain's under-study to Desmond Douglas. Andrew, based in London, has threatened on a number of occasions to break the champion's hold on British table tennis but has yet to succeed. In the January 1987 British rankings, Andrew was slotted in at number three. Andrew is the winner of many junior titles and has achieved victory at the ETTA championships in the doubles section. He has also represented England at senior international level.

Tennis

When Arthur Robert Ashe, the black American tennis player won the Wimbledon Men's singles title in 1975, he quashed all myths that tennis could only be played proficiently by the white bourgeoisie. In the event his input resulted in an upsurge of minority ethnic participation in the sport. It is worthy of note that his achievement was not unprecedented in that Althea Gibson of the USA was the first black woman to win at Wimbledon way back in 1957. She is now a professional golfer in the USA.

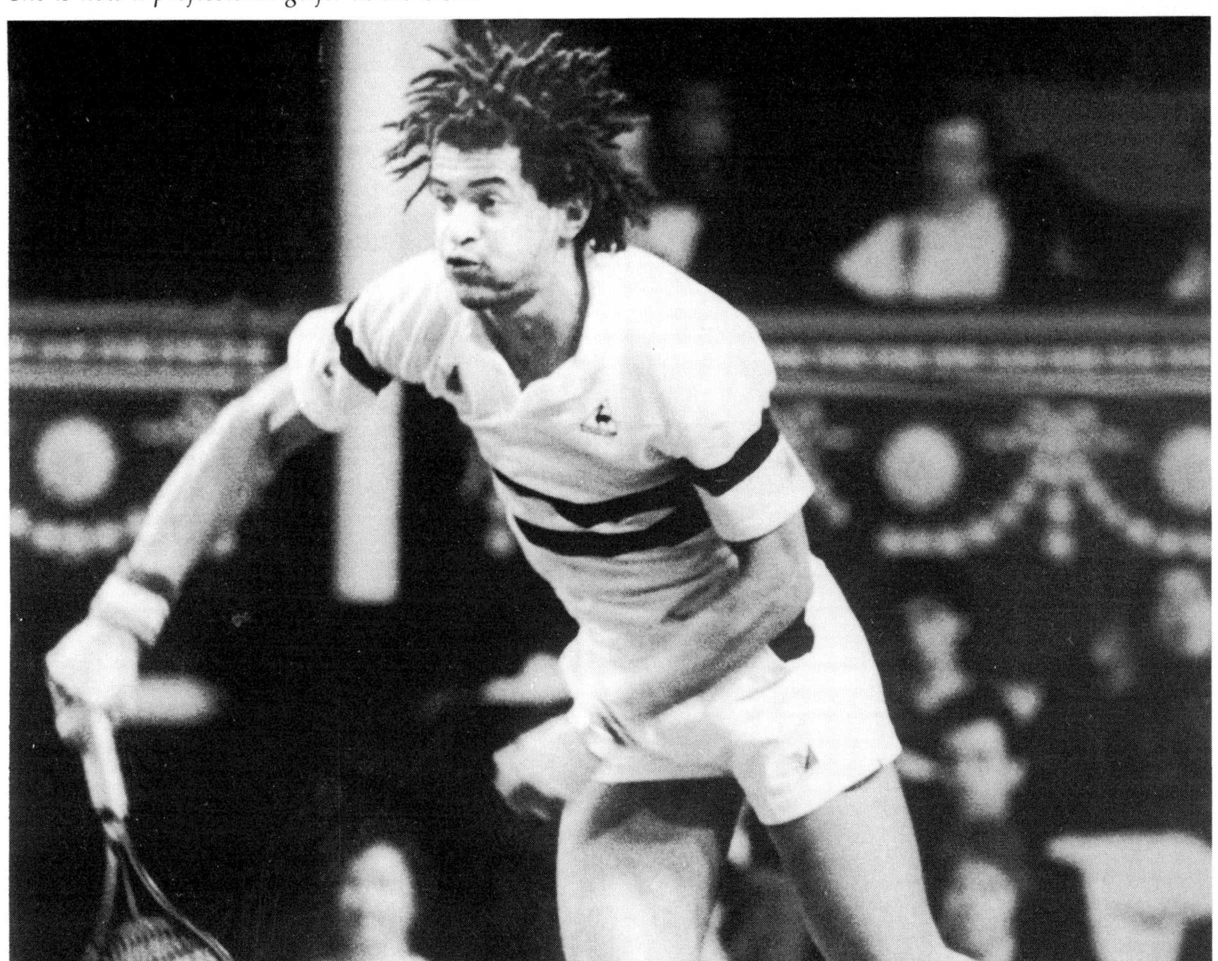

The swashbuckling Yannick Noah

Yannick Noah

Born in Sedan, France, on May 18 1960, Yannick Noah is easily identifiable through his spikey dreadlocks and is unquestionably the most exciting and charismatic court specialist in the game today.

Noah, whose father is from the Cameroons, has won over three million US dollars in career prize money and his most remarkable achievement to date has been winning the French Open in 1983. He became the first French citizen in 37 years to achieve such a feat. A year later he won the French Open doubles title. In 1985 he captured the Italian Open. In all Noah has won over 15 tournaments since turning professional in 1978. He has residences in Paris and New York, and is divorced with two children.

Ramesh Krishnan

The 5ft 7in Madras-born Ramesh Krishnan comes from a solid tennis family background. His father assisted India to the 1966 Davis Cup final whilst young Krishnan himself was the world top junior in 1979, winning the French Open and Wimbledon, but as a professional he has not fulfilled his potential. His elegant stroke play and balance are just some of the features of a varied repertoire. He inspired India to a 1987 Davis cup final encounter with Sweden, the first in 13 years.

Anthony Mmoh

Anthony Mmoh has been a tennis professional since 1983. His tenacious qualities backed up with a strong service make him a very difficult opponent to play. He is a member of the Nigerian Davis Cup squad. The 30-year-old lives in Kingston, Jamaica, and trains on the United States circuit.

Floyd Williams

London-born Floyd Williams heads a crop of black British individuals with hopes of reaching the higher echelons of tennis. His ambition is to make a breakthrough into the world's top 100. The 24-year-old made his debut in 1984. In 1987 he won two professional/amateur tournaments. His most admired sportsman and woman are Carl Lewis and Martina Navratilova.

Vijay Amritraj

The charming and popular tennis star has represented India in Davis Cup competitions since 1970. He achieved his highest world ranking of 16 in 1980. A superb grasscourt player, he has served his sport with great distinction and dignity. Tennis is no longer number one on Vijay's list of priorities as he has set up a film production company with his brother in the United States. The Los Angeles-based Amritraj has also appeared in 007 films such as *Octopussy*. The 34-year-old was the brain behind in launching India's first tennis school, in an attempt to help India discover prospective talents.

Who's Who of the Visible Minority Community in Britain

This section has been organised alphabetically by surname. Please note that profiles on contemporary sportsmen and women can be found in the Chapter on Sport immediately before this section.

ABBOTT, Diane Julie, MP

was born in London on September 27, 1953. Ms Abbott is the Labour Member of Parliament for Hackney North and Stoke Newington. She is single. Ms Abbott holds an M.A. degree in History from Cambridge University. Before her election, she headed the Press Office of Lambeth Borough Council. She previously worked for the Home Office, National Council for Civil Liberties, Thames TV, TV AM, the Greater London Council and a trade union. Diane Abbott received a *Caribbean Times* community award in 1987. She hopes to unite all of Hackney's many communities, building on the "traditional anti-fascism and anti-racism" of the area.

ABBOTT-BUTLER, Pauline, Ms.

works as a Race Relations Adviser, with responsibility for women, in the east London area. Ms Abbott-Butler is widowed. She holds a Bachelor of Education (B.Ed.) degree and formerly worked as a nurse and then as a teacher. She is the President of two community-based organisations, the Afro-Caribbean Educational Project and the National Council for St. Vincent and Grenadines Women (UK). Ms Abbott-Butler aims to contribute to the establishment of a National Council for Women of African Descent and more generally to ensure that the needs and rights of the black community, particularly in Waltham Forest and Hackney, are fully catered for.

ABRAMS, Joseph, Cllr

represents Graveney Ward in the London Borough of Merton for the Labour Party. Resident in Britain since 1960, Joseph Abrams obtained a Bachelor of Arts degree with Honours in Law at the University of London and is now Head of Pastoral Care at Bow Boys School in east London. A councillor since 1982, Joseph Abrams is presently deputy leader of the Labour group in Merton. On a local level his main concern is education. He sits on the Education Committee, the School Special Sub-Committee for the appointment of teaching staff and the local Manpower Services Committee. Outside of his council work, Joseph Abrams is busy with voluntary work at numerous youth clubs in the borough. He is also the chair of the National Association of Community Relations Councils. He is married with four children, one of whom also became a councillor in Merton in May 1986.

ABRAMS, Kingsley Joseph, Cllr

represents Trinity Ward in the London Borough of Merton for the Labour Party. Born in Britain in 1962, Kingsley Abrams was brought up in Guyana. Upon his return he graduated from South Bank Polytechnic with a B.Sc. degree in Social Sciences and worked as an insurance salesperson and then as an advice worker at Mitcham Citizens Advice Bureau, a position he relinquished after his election as a councillor. He is a member of the Wimbledon Labour Party, chair of Wimbledon Young Socialists and Assistant Secretary of his local Black Section. Elected to Merton Council in May 1986, he became its youngest member and joined his father, Joseph Abrams, who was re-elected to represent Graveney Ward. Cllr Abrams is secretary of Merton Afro-Caribbean Organisation and an executive committee member of Merton Community Relations Council. He is also a governor of Richards Lodge School. His hobbies are cricket, football and table tennis.

AFZAL, Muhammad, Cllr

represents the Ashton Ward on Birmingham City Council for the Labour Party. Born in Pakistan in 1945 and resident in Britain since 1969, Muhammad Afzal is an Accountant by profession with a Bachelor of Science degree. He has been active in the Labour Party for fifteen years and is presently Treasurer of the Small Heath Constituency Labour Party and a member of the party's Birmingham District Committee. Cllr Afzal's spare time activities include social work and he is trustee and treasurer of the Birmingham Central Mosque. He is currently chair of the Urban Renewal Committee on the City Council. Cllr Afzal is married with two children.

AGWUNA, Ben, Chief

was born in Nigeria. He is married with two teenage children and has made his home in Liverpool. Over the years he has given a lot of time and energy to the black community of Liverpool. Chief Ben Agwuna has been instrumental in ensuring that the Charles Wooton Centre continues to provide education for the local black community. Many of the former students have gone on to higher education and have gained degrees. When the Labour council in Liverpool tried to close the centre, Ben Agwuna led a successful campaign to retain this important facility. He is a member of the Federation of Black Organisations, a leading member of the Nigerian Union and chair of World Promotions Ltd.

AHMED, Sadique, Cllr

represents St. Katharine's Ward in the London Borough of Tower Hamlets for the Labour Party. Born in Bangladesh in 1954 and resident in Britain since 1968, Sadique Ahmed completed his higher secondary education in Bangladesh. After moving to Britain he ran his own small business for ten years before deciding to pursue his interest in social work in a full-time capacity. He is now employed as a Social Worker. Cllr Ahmed has been a member of the Labour Party since 1978 and is currently a member of Labour's Ethnic Minority Group. Sadique Ahmed is associated with a number of local community groups, including Bangaldesh Youth Solidarity, the Federation of Bangladeshi Youth Organisations, the Bangladesh Welfare Association, Tower Hamlets Training Forum and the Inner London Education Authority's Multi-Ethnic Consultative Committee. He is also a governor of two schools. Sadique Ahmed has been a councillor since May 1986 and is a member of the Housing Sub-Committee, the Housing and Advisory Group, the Policies and Resources Committee and he is also chair of the Wapping Neighbourhood Committee.

AHUJA, Raj Kumari, Dr

was born on October 17, 1938 and currently works as a General Practitioner (Principal) in Wigan, Lancashire. Dr Ahuja is married with a son and a daughter. She was educated at Vikram and Liverpool Universities. Dr Ahuja arrived in Britain from India in November 1965 and is a member of the British Medical Association (BMA), the Indo-British Association, and the Family Planning Association, the National Executive of the Overseas Doctors Association, of which she is the chair of its Wigan Branch. She lists her recreations as music, cookery and sports.

AHUJA, Satish Kumar, Dr

was born in Quetta, the capital of Baluchistan, Pakistan, on April 16, 1936. He is a Principal General Practitioner in Wigan, Lancs. Dr Ahuja is married with one son and a daughter. He was educated at Lucknow and Liverpool Universities and the Royal College of Surgeons in London. From 1987-1988 he was President of the Wigan Division of the British Medical Association (BMA), and he has been Director of Wigan Metropolitan Medical Services since its inception in 1978. He is an active member of the overseas Doctors Association. A keen sports enthusiast, Dr Ahuja was the Honorary Medical Officer of Wigan Athletic Football Club (1979-1983).

AJEEB, Mohammed, Cllr

is currently the chair of the Race Relations Committee of Bradford City Council. He is married. Now self-employed, Cllr Ajeeb has previously worked as the Manager of the Bradford Council of Mosques and in various posts connected with the provision of housing. An active member of the Labour Party, Ajeeb became a Bradford councillor in 1979 and in 1985 became the first Asian Lord Mayor in Britain. He plays a prominent role in numerous Pakistani community organisations and received an *Asian Times* Community Award in 1987. The previous year he received an honorary MA from Bradford University. Cllr Ajeeb hopes to become an MP.

AKHTAR, Jamil, Cllr

represents Newsome Ward in the Metropolitan Borough of Kirklees for the Labour Party. He worked as the Branch chair of the Transport and General Workers' Union (T&GWU) for 6 years before becoming Branch Secretary, a position he has held for the last two years. Cllr Akhtar was elected in May 1987, and is vice-chair of the Highway Sub-Committee, the Further Education Sub-Committee and the Road Safety Sub-Committee, as well as being a member of the Social Services and Peace Committees. Cllr Akhtar is also involved as a Trustee in two local Community Associations. He is married with three children and has lived in Huddersfield for the last twenty years.

ALAM, Jahangir, Cllr

represents St. Dunstans Ward in the London Borough of Tower Hamlets for the Labour Party. Born in Bangladesh in 1949 and resident in Britain since 1970, Jahangir Alam, known as Jan, has worked as a Restaurant Manager, Housing Officer and Social Services Liaison Officer. Since 1983 he has been a Social Worker. He has a degree in Sociology and Social Work from Oxford and has published several articles on racism and social work with the Asian community. An active Labour Party member since 1970 Alam has served as chair of the Ward and Assistant Secretary of the Bethnal Green and Stepney Constituency Party. He is now Deputy Leader of the Labour group in Tower Hamlets and represents the Greater London Labour Party on the National Executive Committee's Black and Asian Advisory body. Jahangir Alam was General Secretary of the Bangladeshi Youth League UK from

1970 to 1978, vice-chair of the Federation of Bangladeshi Youth Organisations from 1982 to 1983 when he also took over as Press Officer for the Association of Asian Social Workers. He has also been chair of the Social Services Committee, Tower Hamlets Association for Racial Equality since 1985. He was elected as a local councillor in May 1986 and is an active member of the Campaign for Nuclear Disarmament (CND) and the Anti Apartheid Movement (AAM) and is the vice-chair of Stepney Neighbourhood Committee.

ALAN, Misli, Ms

gained her Diploma in English Literature and Dramatic Arts from J.L Forster High School. She specialised in Dramatic Arts at the University of Windsor, Canada. She has also attended Summer Short Courses organised by the Second City Improvisation Workshop and The Refrigerator Theatre Company. Misli is an up and coming young stage, film and video star. She has played the lead roles in: *The Young And Fair* staged by the University Players; *Plaza Suite* by Attic Theatre; and *See How They Run* by Windsor Light Players. Her Film and Video performances include parts in: Neil Simon's *Boeing Boeing* screened by the Turkish Films Int.; *Guilt* by The Refrigerator Theatre Company; and *A Man I Never Knew* by Star Productions. She was also in the cast of the stage version of this production. Her recent work includes *The Birthday Party* by Ravi Randhawa; and *And The Name of the Daughter Was Rose* by Roxanne Shafer staged by ACT and The Royal Court Theatre Upstairs respectively.

ALEXANDER, Juliet, Ms

is the presenter of BBC 2's Ebony, a programme designed to attract Britain's black community. Juliet has worked in the media for the past 11 years, first as a reporter with the *Hackney Gazette* and later at the *Sunday Times*. She has been a reporter/presenter at BBC Radio and TV, Central TV and Thames TV, and has worked on programmes such as *Black Londoners, John Craven's Newsround* (BBC TV) and *Caribbean Links* (BBC Radio 4). To coincide with "Caribbean Focus '86", Juliet is currently working on a couple of half-hour documentaries for Radio 4 to be broadcast this summer.

ALI, Ashek, Cllr

represents St. Katharine's Ward in the London Borough of Tower Hamlets for the Labour Party. Born in Bangladesh in 1933 and resident in Britain since 1964, Ashek Ali gained a Bachelor of Science and L.B at Dhaka University before becoming a Barrister-at-Law at Lincoln's Inn in London. He held a number of government posts in Pakistan before joining the Britiish civil service as a Clerical Officer in 1973 where he still works. Cllr Ali has been a councillor since 1982. He is a member of Amnesty International and chair of 'Dishari Shilpi Gosthi', a Bangladeshi cultural organisation.

ALI, Naqi, M.A., P.D.M., M.A.I.E, Mr

is a Journalist and Writer from Hyderabad, India. After several years in advertising he is currently working as Head of Publications in the Public Relations Department at the post office headquarters. He is a regular contributor to the *Asian Times* and other publications and has published many short stories and a novel in Urdu which has been hailed as an outstanding experimental work in Urdu fiction.

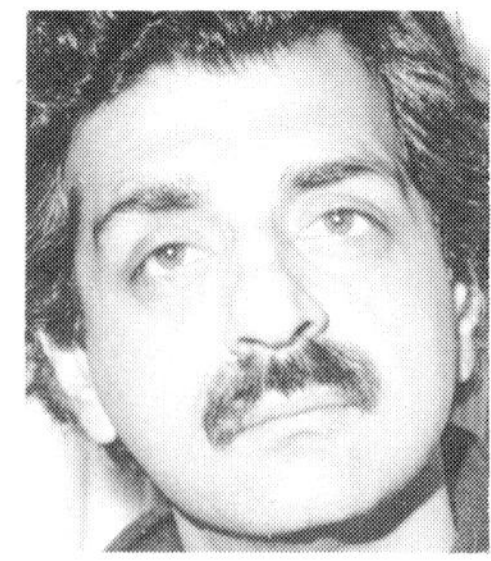

ALI, Tariq, Mr

Writer and Political Analyst, Tariq Ali was born in Lahore (now in Pakistan) in 1943. In 1963 he came to Oxford University where he studied Politics and Philosophy. He was the first Pakistani to be elected President of the Oxford Union and played a major role in the student upheavals of 1968. In recent years he has confined his work to writing and is the author of several books on world history and politics, his most recent being *The Nehrus and the Gandhis: an Indian Dynasty* published by Chatto and Windus. He was one of the founder directors of Bandung Productions and one of the two programme editors of the Bandung File, a current affairs magazine programme for the ethnic minorities shown on Channel 4. He recently published an autobiography entitled *Street Fighting Years* and serves on the Editorial board of the Veno Publishing Company.

ALLAN, Vincent, Cllr

represents Westbourne Ward in the City of Westminster for the Labour Party. Educated at Hammersmith Technical College, he has lived in Paddington for the last thirty three years. He is a bricklayer by trade. An active trades unionist, for over twenty years, Cllr Allan has served on the Hammersmith and Kensington Trades Council. He is also a member of the Board of Governors of the Edward Wilson County School and St. Georges Roman Catholic School. A councillor since May 1982, he is particularly concerned with education and would like to see a complete shake-up in the whole education system.

AMEEN, Bilal, Mr

is director of Caribbean Development Foundation. Mr Ameen has worked as a Community Development worker, a cultural officer with the Westindian Women's Association and was Founder of the Caribbean Development Foundation – London. He is also a member of the Community Youth Exchange Council; the Black Youth Exchange National Executive Collective; and an executive member of the St. Vincent Support Committee.

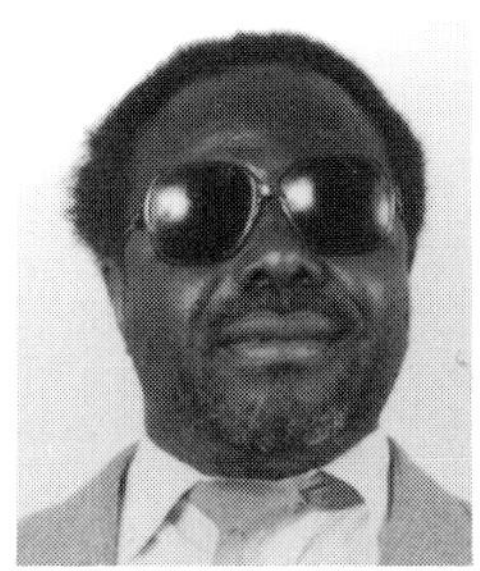

AMIN, Joshua, Cllr

represents Ferndale Ward in the London Borough of Lambeth for the Labour Party. Born in Ghana in 1944 and resident in Britain since 1974, Cllr Amin is a qualified Social Worker with an honours degree in Sociology. Before coming to this country he was employed in Ghana as a Public Relations Officer. One of his main concerns is community welfare, particularly for the elderly and the disabled. He is a member of the 'Outsiders Club' for the elderly and the National Society for the Blind. Cllr Amin is chair of the Lambeth Board for the Employment of Disabled People and is a member of the Economic Activities and Employment Committee, the Amenities and Community Affairs Committee and the Inner City Programme Committee. He is also presently involved with the development of a women's agency to look at the needs of black women locally and nationally. Interests outside the council include the theatre, swimming, listening to the radio and travelling.

AMOO-GOTTFRIED, Hilda, Ms

was a Barrister between 1972-82 and since then has been practising as a Solicitor. She is the Principal of Amoo-Gottfried Solicitors, a firm which she founded in February 1986. She is also a member of the Law Society, the Law Society Race Relations Committee – of which since 1986 she has been vice-chair – and the Law Society Women's Careers Working Party. Ms Amoo-Gottfried is married with three sons.

ANIONWU, Elizabeth Nneka, Ms

is the Head of the Brent Sickle Cell and Thalassaemia Centre in north London. Before taking up full-time responsibilities with the Sickle Cell Centre, Ms Anionwu, who is single, worked in the local area as a Health Visitor and a Community Nurse Tutor. Ms Anionwu was made a Churchill Fellow (1981), received a CRE Bursary in 1979, a Health Service Association Scholarship in 1975 and a Kings Fund Scholarship, 1977-9. Her ambitions centre on greater recognition of the needs of Sickle Cell and Thalassaemia sufferers and the creation of a federation of voluntary groups.

ANUP, Singh, Choudry, Mr

a solicitor, was born in Uganda in 1949. He arrived in Britain in 1969 where he obtained his B.Sc. at London University and his LL.B. and LL.M. at Cambridge University. Mr Choudry, who is married, enjoys golf in his spare time. He is also the author of several books.

ANWAR, Choudhury Mohammad Nurul, Mr

was born in Calcutta, India, on April 1, 1935 and since November 1986 he has been employed as the Principal Community Relations Officer of Waltham Forest CRC. He is married with one daughter and holds an M.A. in Political Science. He arrived in Britain from Bangladesh in June 1965. Since 1971 he has worked in the field of community relations, in Oxford, Croydon, Enfield and Waltham Forest. Mr Anwar is a Member of the Institute of Public Relations and is the Secretary General of the Federation of Bangladeshi Associations in the UK and Europe. His recreations are gardening and community work.

ANWAR, Muhammad, Dr

was born in Pakistan on April 4, 1945. He arrived in Britain in 1970. He is the Principal Research Officer of the Commission for Racial Equality (CRE). He holds an MA degree from Manchester University and a Ph.D. from Bradford University. He is a member of the BBC General Advisory Council and other working, steering and advisory groups and is the author of a number of books and articles on ethnic minorities and their interventions in British politics. Dr Muhammad lists his recreations as reading and gardening.

APPIAH, Kofi, Cllr

represents Weaver's Ward in the London Borough of Tower Hamlets for the Liberal Party. Born in Ghana in 1943, Cllr Appiah is a Barrister-at-Law. He obtained his Law degree from the University of London in 1973 and was called to the bar in 1974. He is a member of Inner Temple and once served as Assistant State Attorney in Ghana. At present he is employed by Islington Council. He has been a Councillor in Tower Hamlets since 1982, is currently vice-chair of the Bethnal Green Standing Neighbourhood Committee, a member of the Decentralisation Committee and the Borough's African Community Organisation. Councillor Appiah is married with two sons.

ARAIN, Ashtaq Chaudry, Cllr

represents the Pepys Ward in the London Borough of Lewisham for the Labour Party. Born in Kenya in 1958 and resident in Britain since 1971, Ashtaq Arain is a self-employed businessman who has been actively involved in local government issues for a number of years. Cllr Arain was vice-chair of the East Lewisham Party from 1985-86 and was a co-founder of the Black Section movement in east Lewisham. He currently holds the position of Secretary. Arain became a councillor in May 1986 with the aim of encouraging participation of the black community in politics both locally and nationally. His main concern is to represent black people in areas that have so far been neglected by government and he will be looking to co-opt members on to various committees. He is currently vice-chair of the Race Relations Committee. Councillor Arain is a keen sportsman and particularly enjoys playing squash and cricket.

ARIF, Mohammed, Mr

Mohammed Arif was born in India on November 15, 1939 and came to Britain in 1962. He graduated from Karachi University and was the President of Raza Ali College Students Union. After coming to Britain he obtained a B.Sc. degree in Economics from London University and then undertook post graduate work at Reading University. Helping to estalbish the Pakistan Student Federation (GB) he served as its vice-president and secretary. Mohammed Arif is a Senior Lecturer in Economics at Kingston Polytechnic in Surrey and has published articles in numerous journals as well as giving visiting lectures on international relations. Active in political and community affairs, Mohammed Arif is the secretary of the British Afro-Asian Solidarity Organisation and the Friends of Afghanistan Society. He was a delegate at three conferences of the National Union of Students (NUS) and has participated in many international conferences in the Soviet Union, India, Afghanistan, the German Democratic Republic, West Germany and other countries. He is constantly in demand for radio interviews and remains very active in the affairs of the Pakistani community in Britain. Mohammed Arif is married and has one son.

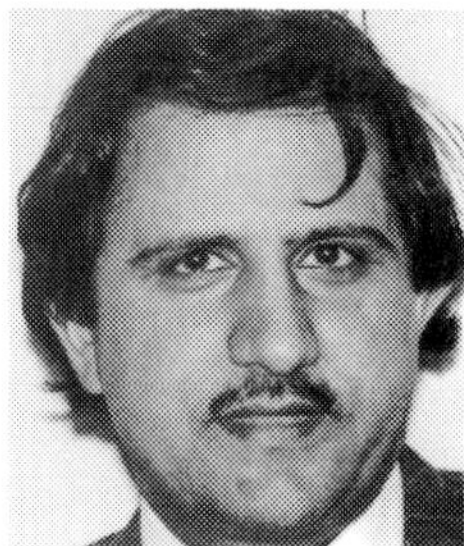

ASLAM, Muhammad, Cllr

represents Upton Ward in the London Borough of Newham for the Labour Party. Born in what is now Pakistan in 1945 and resident in Britain since 1970, Cllr Aslam graduated from Punjab University in Pakistan where he studied English, Chemistry and Biology. Upon arrival in England he studied Computer Programming and Automobile Engineering. He currently works as a Booking Officer Clerk for London Transport. A Labour Party member for the last six years, he was elected to Newham Council in May 1986. He is at present a member of the Housing and Education Committees and the Police and Race Relations Sub-Committees. Cllr Aslam is founder and President of the local Muslim Welfare Association and is on the board of Newham Council for Racial Equality. He is married with two children and has been living in Newham for sixteen years.

ATKIN, Sharon, Ms

was born on September 4, 1951 of a Jamaican father and English mother. Married with one son, Ms Atkin has been a Labour Party member and committed socialist since the age of 15. She has worked in a number of jobs, including as a journalist, nurse and social worker and has always been an active trades unionist and anti-racist. Active in the Black Section movement, which she joined in 1984, Ms Atkin was their National chair (1985-86) and National Womens' Officer, elected at conference in 1988. Elected as a councillor in the London Borough of Lambeth in 1984 she chaired a number of committees but was surcharged and removed from office, along with numerous colleagues, in April 1986. The previous month Nottingham East Constituency Labour Party adopted her as their parliamentary candidate but she was summarily removed by the Labour Party National Executive Committee two weeks before the calling of the 1987 general election. A founder member of Women for Socialism, Ms Atkin is currently writing a number of books.

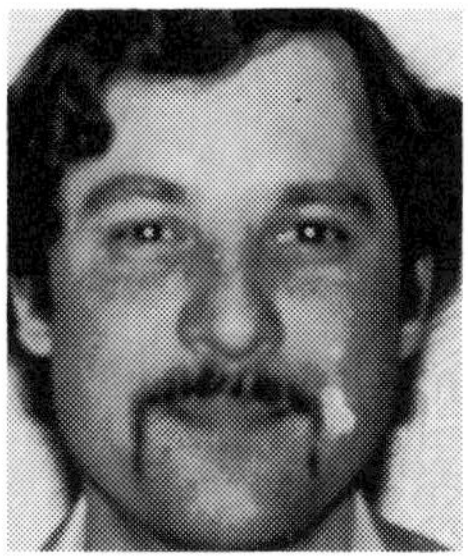

AUGLEY, Ronald, Cllr

represents Forest Gate Ward in the London Borough of Newham for the Labour Party. Cllr Augley is a driver by trade and was first elected to Newham Council in 1982. He is currently a member of the Race Equality Sub-Committee and chair of the Continuing Education Sub-Committee. Cllr Augley is married. He is a member of Animal Aid, the Anti-Apartheid Movement and the Campaign for Nuclear Disarmament (CND).

AYODHYA, Roy, Mr

was born in Guyana on April 9, 1938. He is married and lives in Streatham, south London. Roy Ayodhya is a property dealer and jeweller and is also the president and founder of the South London Indian Cultural Centre. He says that he wants to continue fighting for equal opportunities in society and continue to be a strong advocate for his religion.

BAINS, Jaswant Singh, Cllr

is married and plays an active role in the life of his local community in the Northampton area. He is the president and trustee of the Siri Guru Singh Sabha, vice-president of the Northampton Community Relations Council, a councillor of the Northampton Borough Council, a member of the Northampton District Health Authority, a member of the Manpower Services Commission Area Board Northamptonshire, of the county's Age Concern and its Race Relations Joint Consultation Group, a governor of Spencer Middle School and a member of the Police Central Consultative Committee.

BAIRD, Hazel, Cllr

represents Mapesbury Ward in the London Borough of Brent for the Labour Party. British-born Hazel Baird is a lawyer by profession and is currently chair of the Brent Women's Committee. She is also chair of the governing body at Willesden College of Technology.

BAKHSH, Qadir, Mr

was born in Peshawar, in what is now Pakistan on January 5, 1944. He has had a varied and extensive education, and holds a string of degrees ranging from Urdu to Psychology and a Certificate in Statistics. He has worked as a lecturer and journalist in Pakistan, before coming to Britain in 1968. He continued his education at London University where he gained an M.Sc. in Social Pyschology in 1975. He is a member of the British Psychological Society. Since 1981 he has been a Trustee of the Barking Mosque, and a governor of Barking College of Technology. Qadir Bakhsh is an author and the Managing Editor of Cheetah Books. He has worked for many years in the field of Race Relations and is currently Head of the Race Relations Unit for the London Borough of Waltham Forest. He is married with one daughter and lives in Barking, Essex.

BARBER, Ramanbhai, Mr

was born in 1946 and works in the field of administration and management. He is married with four children. Mr Barber arrived in Britain from Kenya in 1964 and in 1970 became a founder member of the Shree Sanatan Mandir. He was its assistant secretary from 1971-77 and its secretary from 1977 to date. He is also the secretary of the National Council of Hindu Temples (UK), vice-president of the Indian Education Society (Leicester) and a former assistant secretary of the Gujarat Hindu Association (Leicester). He is a governor of schools and colleges and the president of the Shree Surat District Limbachia H. Mandal (UK).

BARROW, Jocelyn, O.B.E, Ms

was born in Trinidad, but has lived in England for many years. She was awarded an O.B.E in 1972 for her services to the community and her contribution to Education. Jocelyn Barrow married Henderson Downer, Barrister of Lincoln's Inn and the Jamaican Bar in 1970. She graduated from London University with a degree in English and subsequently studied for a post–graduate degree in Education. At present she is working on her Ph.D. Her community work has been long and varied. She is a former vice-president of the National Union of Townswomen's Guild (1980) and is currently chair of East London Housing Association, a post she has held since 1977. She was made a governor of the BBC in 1981. Jocelyn Barrow is on secondment to London University's Institute of Education.

BART, Delano Frank, Mr

is a Barrister-at-Law, having been called to the bar in 1977. He is married. Mr Bart has been an executive member of the Society of Black Lawyers since 1985. He is also a member of the South Bank Polytechnic Minority Access to the Legal Profession Project, a member of the Westindian Standing Conference and a legal adviser to, and executive member of, the Afro-Caribbean Medical Society. He is a holder of the Higgs Hill Centenary Award. Mr Bart's hobbies are squash, music and going to the theatre.

BEDI, Mohinder Paul Singh, Prof

was born in Uttar Pradesh, India, on July 16, 1936. Arriving in Britain from Delhi in September 1965, Professor Bedi, a specialist with mentally handicapped children, is married with two sons and three daughters. Professor Bedi holds degrees in education, philosophy and child psychology from Punjab, Delhi and Birmingham Universities. Since 1986 he has been the National chair of the Anglo-Asian Conservative Society and he is also the general secretary of the United Association for Asians. Professor Bedi lists his recreations as politics, entertainment and culture.

BELLOS, Linda, Cllr

represents Larkhall Ward for the Labour Party and was the Leader of the London Borough of Lambeth until her resignation in April 1988. Raised in Brixton, south London, and with a background in finance, Cllr Bellos previously worked for the Greater London Council. A member of the Labour Party since 1984 she was vice chair of the Black Section National Committee and of her local Labour Party Black Section when elected council leader in May 1986. She became one of two black women council leaders in the country. Cllr Bellos received a *Caribbean Times* Community Award in 1987.

BENJAMIN, Floella, Ms

was born in Trinidad. She had been a bank clerk before becoming an actress, singer, musical and dramatic writer, editor and consultant for children's books. Floella can be seen regularly on programmes for children's television. She is a member of the Women of the Year Association and was awarded the Eivan Health Award in 1985.

BERESFORD, Randolph, B.E.M. M.B.E., Mr

was born in the then British Guiana in 1914 and came to Britain in 1953. Now retired, Mr Beresford was a carpenter by trade and during his working life was an active trades unionist. He was elected to the council of the London Borough of Hammersmith and Fulham in 1964. Since 1967 he has played a prominent role on the Hammersmith Council for Community Relations. For five years he was the chair of his local Labour Party ward and Mayor of Hammersmith (1975-76). Randolph Beresford has been appointed a Member of the British Empire and was awarded the British Empire Medal and a *Caribbean Times* Community Award.

BERNARD, Jean, Cllr

represents West Thornton Ward in the London Borough of Croydon for the Labour Party. She also represents the Bethnal Green and Stepney Ward in the London Borough of Tower Hamlets on the Inner London Education Authority (ILEA). Born in Jamaica and resident in Britain since 1961, Jean Bernard first worked in catering and local government before taking on her present post as a qualified Social Worker in the London Borough of Southwark. She has been an active member of the Labour Party since 1973 at ward and constituency level, has been a delegate to the Greater London Labour Party on the Anti-Racist Standing Conference and has served on the Lambeth, Southwark and Lewisham Health Authorities. For some years Cllr Bernard was actively involved with the community in Lambeth, with tenant associations, youth clubs, day centres, a day nursery, law centres and a campaign group. Since moving to Croydon in 1981 she has continued her work with various community groups and the black community. She is a member of Croydon Community Relations Council, the Campaign for Nuclear Disarmament and Amnesty International. She has been a governor of three schools and of Peckham Art College and now serves as vice-chair of the ILEA Schools Sub-Committee with responsibility for over 1,100 schools.

BERRY, James, Mr

was born in Jamaica and has lived in England for over 30 years. He has worked in television and radio, and has published several poems, short stories and articles in magazines, newspapers and anthologies in Britain, the USA and the Caribbean. His publications include *Lucy's Letter* (1975), *Bluefoot Traveller* and *Fractured Circles* (1979) – selections of his poems. Berry has served on the Community Arts Committee of the Arts Council and the Literature Panel of the GLA – Greater London Arts. He has also received a Minority Rights Group Art Award for his writing (1979) and his poem *Fantasy of an African Boy* was awarded first prize in the National Poetry Competition, 1981.

BHANOT, Basheshar Nath, Mr

is a Teacher with the London Borough of Redbridge. He is married with one son and three daughters. Mr Bhanot received an M.A from Punjab University, a Post Graduate Diploma in Education from Sheffield University and a Certificate in Multi Cultural Education from Waltham Forest College. He was previously a Teacher in Kenya government high schools. Having the ambition to serve Hindu organisations and temples, Mr Bhanot has been the Secretary of the Vishwa Hindu Parishad Ilford since 1986.

BHARGAVA, B.N., Dr

was born in India and is now a retired teacher. After acquiring a B.Sc. degree he took part in the Indian freedom struggle. Having worked in the family business of textiles and local agricultural produce he farmed his own land in the early 1950s. Arriving in Britain in 1962 he went on to acquire further academic qualificatons, including a PhD. After working as an industrial chemist and then as a lecturer in the north of England, Dr Bhargava moved to London to become a teacher in 1975 and took early retirement in 1985. However, he has carried on work in the community.

BHARGAVA, Rameshwar Nath, Mr

was born on June 2, 1936 and is Managing Partner of the Suman Marriage Bureau. He is married with a son and daughter. He holds a B.A. degree from Punjab University. Mr Bhargava is the chair of the Anglo-Asian Conservative Association in Southall and is a school governor. He is a trustee of the Vishwa Hindu Temple, Southall; executive member of Institute of Sikh Studies; member of International Punjabi Society; Hindu Centre, London; and Arya Samaj London. He is president of the Bhargave Sabha. He received the Shiromani Award 1986 from the President of India.

BHATTI, Ashiq Hussain, Mr

graduated from the University of Punjab, Lahore, and is an associate member of the Institute of Cost and Management Accountants, London. Previously an Auditor to the Pakistan Army he is now established in business in the Nottingham area. Since 1964 he has also been actively involved in social and community work, holding a number of posts in various organisations and ten years ago was one of the founders of the Nottingham Islamic Centre and he has been chair, for the last ten years.

BINDRA, Narendra Kumar, Mr

was born on July 6, 1935 in Quetta, which is now in Pakistan. He is a Teacher and Freelance Translator of a number of Indian languages. He is married and has one son and one daughter. He holds B.A. and M.Ed. degrees and is a fellow of the Royal Society of Arts. Mr Bindra is an affiliate of the Institute of Linguists and of the Translators' Guild. Arriving in Britain from India in May 1965 he is now the secretary of the Association of Teachers of English to Pupils from Overseas (ATEPO) and the public relations officer of the Young Indian Association.

BLACKS, Sonny, Mr

born in Trinidad, is an impresario who came to Britain in 1961 after having promoted a series of successful concerts in Trinidad and throughout the Caribbean. His concert promotion and management have taken him throughout Europe. In the late 1970s he organised the first Reggae Festival in Munich, West Germany, and in 1981 he originated the concept of the Copenhagen Carnvial and acted as Consultant. The next year he advised and assisted on the Oslo Carnival. He has served on the Panel of Judges of the Notting Hill Carnival. In 1987 he organised the *Black Stalin* Trinidad Calypso King '87 European Tour, with appearances in many countries, including at the Helsinki Festival.

BOATENG, Paul, MP

is the Labour MP for Brent South. Although his parents are from Ghana, West Africa he was born in in the east London Borough of Hackney in June 1951.He is a Solicitor who has acted for the families of Cherry Groce and Cynthia Jarrett after the Brixton and Broadwater Farm uprisings and also for the police attack victim, Clinton McCurbin's family. He joined the Labour Party as a Young Socialist and was elected to the GLC for Waltham Forest in 1981 where he became the GLC Police Committee's chair. He fought Hemel Hempstead parliamentary seat for Labour in 1983 and was elected MP for Brent South in 1987. Paul describes himself as "a radical Christian socialist and Pan-Africanist."

BORLAND-KELLY, Lorna May, Cllr

represents Norwood on the Inner London Education Authority (ILEA) for the Labour Party. Born in Jamaica in 1952 and resident in Britain since 1959, Lorna Boreland-Kelly is a Social Worker in Lambeth and was a co-opted member of the Inner London Education Authority for two years before her election in May 1986. She is presently chair of the Authorities Equal Opportunities Sub-Committee. Councillor Boreland-Kelly is a member of the British Association of Social Workers and vice-chair of the governing body of South London College. She has five children and says her favourite hobby is looking after her plants.

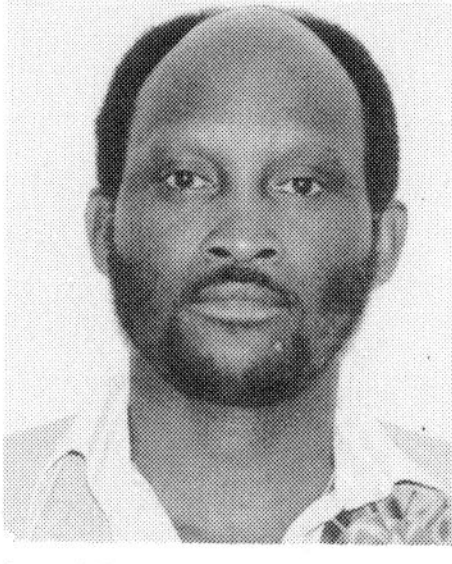

BOYCE, Lewis, Cllr

represents Monega Ward in the London Borough of Newham for the Labour Party. Born in 1944, he has lived in the London Borough of Newham for 22 years and he is a railway supervisor. He was elected a member of the borough council in 1982 and was chair of the Race Equality Sub-Committee for two years, 1984-86. Since May 1986 he has been a member of two major committees – the social services and leisure committees and is currently the Majority Party Chief Whip.

BROWNE, Lincoln, Mr

a Television Producer, was born in Montserrat in 1952. He has worked as a Reporter/Presenter of London Weekend Television's *Skin* programme (1980); Assistant Producer/ Director of BBC's *Ebony;* and Producer/Director of LWT's *Black on Black.*

BROWNE, Ronald, Cllr

represents White City and Shepherds Bush Ward in the London Borough of Hammersmith and Fulham for the Labour Party. Born in Nevis, Ronald Browne is an Electrician by trade. He was elected as a local councillor in May 1986. Cllr Browne is Secretary of the Chiswick branch of the EETPU (Electrical Engineers Technicians and Plumbing Trade Union) and treasurer of a local cultural welfare association. He is currently the vice-chair of the housing committee.

CAESAR, Imruh, Mr

was born in St. Kitts-Nevis, and came to England in 1966 where he attended Leeds Central High School (1966-67). He obtained a diploma with distinction in Film, Theatre and Television Studies from Bradford College of Art in 1975. In 1982 he graduated as a Film Director from the National Film and Television School. In 1981 he wrote, directed and produced a documentary entitled *Riots and Rumours of Riots*. He worked as an assistant producer on *Ebony* (BBC2) in 1984. In 1987 he wrote and produced the first full-length film study of Aubrey Williams, the great Caribbean artist. Imruh's book of poems *Secret Lives*, was published by Bogle L'Overture in 1986.

CAESAR, Petula, Dr

was born in Britain on August 19, 1957. On leaving school she studied at the University of Aston where she gained a B.Sc. Hons. In 1984 she completed her Ph.D., also at Aston University, on artificial liver support and related systems. She is at present working at Southampton General Hospital on a research project in Foetal Human Lung Disorders. She recently saved her money to visit Dominica in order to discover her roots, as both her parents were born there. Dr Caesar is married and says that her ambition is to become a University Lecturer heading a research team. She would like to work in the Caribbean in the future.

CAMPBELL, Betty, Ms

headmistress of Mount Stewart primary school. Ms Campbell was born in Cardiff and trained as a teacher between 1960 and 1963. In 1971 she obtained a diploma in education and followed that up with an Honours degree in education in 1977. In 1973 she was appointed headmistress of her present school. She continued with her studies and obtained a masters degree in multicultural curriculum. Her main concern as an educationalist is to see the advancement of a multicultural curriculum. She believes black children can achieve more if given encouragement at home and at school. Married with 4 children, Ms Campbell is interested in art, literature and doing voluntary community work.

CAMPBELL, Kenneth Theophilus, Mr

has, apart from a short period of employment in Jamaican government service, been a writer and journalist for over three decades in both Jamaica and Britain. Amongst the many publications on which he has worked are the Jamaican weekly *Public Opinion*, *Westindian Review*, as the Assistant Editor of *The Welfare Reporter* and for the book publishing division of the Gleaner Company, *The Pioneer Press*. Originally coming to Britain on a British Council bursary, he then undertook journalistic work for the British Medical Association as an editor of the pictorial monthly *Flamingo*, and later as the co-ordinator for SWAPO's *Namibia Today*. Ken is also a member of the Management Committee of the Community Education Trust and is the author of *The Caribbean* (1980). He has been Editor of *Westindian Digest* for the last five years. A founder member of Caribbean Labour Solidarity and a member of the governing board of Acton College, Ken is also a former vice-chair of Ealing Community Relations Council.

CARNEGIE, Andrew, Cllr

represents Herne Hill Ward in the London Borough of Lambeth for the Labour Party. Born in Jamaica and resident in Britain since 1967, Andrew Carnegie obtained a Bachelor of Arts degree in Psychology and Philosophy before going on to obtain a Certificate of Education. Presently employed as a Lecturer, he has also worked as a Youth Worker in Brixton and Balham and as a Teacher at two London colleges. Cllr Carnegie was elected in May 1986 on a manifesto which stressed the need for improved arts, recreation and leisure activities and better housing in the borough. He is currently chair of the Amenities Services Committee. As a councillor, Andrew Carnegie hopes to bring recreation in Britain to the prominence it enjoyed prior to the abolition of the Greater London Council (GLC) and to extend communications between the black community and the council with a view to involving ordinary people in its machinery. He is a keen sportsman and also enjoys travelling and international politics, with particular reference to Third World countries.

CARTER, Trevor, Mr

is an educational adviser employed by the Inner London Education Authority (ILEA) and a member of the National Union of Teachers (NUT). Aged 45, and originally from Trinidad, he has been a member of the Communist Party of Great Britain (CPGB) since 1964. At the 40th Congress of the CPGB in 1987 Trevor Carter was elected to the Executive Committee. He is also secretary of his local party branch. Trevor Carter is also a member of the Executive Committee of the Westindian Standing Conference and the chair of the board of directors of the Black Theatre Co-op. His first book, 'Shattering Illusions – Westindians in British Politics', was published by Lawrence and Wishart in November 1986.

CHADHA Singh, Balwant, Mr

is a Social Worker attached to the Social Work Department in Airdrie, Scotland. Having twice fought district elections, he is a candidate for the 1989's local government elections. His career has to date encompassed many aspects of the social sphere. He served as a Clerk to the Supreme Court of Kenya in 1955, and in 1962 became a Supervisor with the Scottish Co-operative Society. In 1974 he became a Social Worker for Strathclyde Regional Council – a position he held until 1987. A member of the National Black Members Co-ordinating Committee of NALGO and the NALGO Equal Opportunity Committee, in 1972 Mr Chadha was appointed the first Indian-born Justice of the Peace (JP) in Scotland.

CHARLES, Faustin, Mr

was born in Trinidad and educated there. He came to England in 1962 and read English at Kent University. Upon graduation he started to publish poetry and fiction, and is the author of three volumes of poetry (the most recent title, *Days and Nights in the Magic Forest,* published by Bogle L'Ouverture, in 1986) and two novels, as well as two edited collections of folk tales from the Caribbean. Faustin teaches Caribbean Literature and History in a variety of institutions on a part-time basis. He has also worked as a Visiting Lecturer for the Commonwealth Institute in London.

CHARLES, Sebastian, Reverend Canon

was born in India in 1932 and educated at Madras University and Lincoln Theological College. Canon Charles was a Curate and Teacher in Burma before moving to Britain. In 1966 he became curate of St. Thomas', Heaton Norris, Stockport, and a member of the Industrial Mission Team. He was made Canon of Westminster Abbey in 1978. He is a member of the Central Advisory Committee of the BBC and the Independent Broadcasting Authority (IBA); member, Board of Governors, Westminster School; member, Advisory Council, Charities Aid Foundation; trustee and director of Inner City Aid a charitable Trust targeting inner city deprivation and a patron of Black Rights (UK).

CHATTERJEE, Debjani, Dr

was born in India and educated in Bangladesh, Japan, India, Hong Kong, Egypt and Britain. She came to Britain in 1972 and since 1984 has been Principal Community Relations Officer with Sheffield Council for Racial Equality. Dr Chatterjee, who has been a Lecturer in comparative religion at Didsbury College of Education and Teacher in two Sheffield secondary schools, is presently a school and polytechnic governor and a member of several community groups in Sheffield. She is author of *The Role of Religion in a Passage to India* and co-editor of an anthology of children's poetry *Peaces: Poems for Peace.* Dr Chatterjee has also contributed to several anthologies of black women's writing.

CHAUHAN, Husenmiyan, Dr

was born in India in 1924. He arrived in England in May 1967 and after a short period of hospital work qualified as a GP in 1968. His interest in the medical world has spanned over two decades and he is a member both of the British Medical Association and the Indian Medical Association. Dr Chauhan is well-travelled. He received distinctions in all his subjects in M.B.B.S. and achieved a proficiency certificate in anatomy. He is also a member of the Overseas Doctors Association. After his retirement he looks forward to devoting his life to charitable work.

CHEEMA, Hussain Muhammed, Captain

was born in what is now Pakistan in 1916. A retired Army Officer, he joined the Royal Mountain Artillery in April 1935. In 1954 he retired as King Commissioned Officer; arriving in Britain in March 1957. He is the holder of several awards and medals including the War Medal, Indian Service Medal, Pakistan Medal and was awarded the Jangi Inam for life during Active Service in World War Two. Captain Cheema, who is married with six children, holds dual citizenship of Britain and Canada, and is currently studying religious philosophy.

CHIN, Henry Ivan, Mr

was born in Guyana on September 3 1923. He served in the Royal Air Force from 1945-47. He is a member of the Westindian Ex-Servicemens Association. Ivan Chin has served in the diplomatic service and has maintained and developed strong community links. He was a founder of the Guyana Circle and is also a member of the Carib Housing Association, where he has held the positions of treasurer and chair. Ivan now works as a part-time Musician and Bandleader, of the *Ivan Chin Steel Combo.* He promotes tourism for the Westindies in all the main cities of Europe with his band.

CHUPRA, Singh, Amarjit, Dr

has been a Principal in General Practice in Barking since 1968. Between 1959-61 he worked in the Professional Medical Unit, Patna Medical College, India and after his move to Britain in 1972 became a hospital Medical Practitioner specialising in Rheumatology. Mr Chupra, who is married, is a member of the Sikh Doctors Association, the British Medical Association and has been on his local Medical Committee since 1977. He also holds Honours in Medical Jurisprudence.

CLARE, Neville, Mr

is a sickle cell sufferer and a pioneer of sickle cell research in Britain. He founded the Organisation for Sickle Cell Anaemia Research (OSCAR) in 1975, and now manages the project. He is a member of the Haringey Community Health Council and the Haringey Disablement Association. Mr Clare has been awarded trophies by OSCAR for work carried out in the sickle cell field.

CLARKE, Cedric, Cllr

represents Chapel Allerton Ward on Leeds City Council for the Labour Party. He is self-employed in the building industry, has been a member of the Labour Party for eight years and a local councillor for six. He has been chair of the Equal Opportunities Sub-Committee for the last two years and sits on the Education, Personnel and Nursery Committees. He is also a member of the West Yorkshire Police Authority. Cllr Clarke's major concerns are young people and provision for the elderly. He is married with three children and lives in Leeds.

CLEGHORN, Henry, Cllr

represents New Town Ward in the London Borough of Newham for the Labour Party. Born in Trinidad in 1935 and resident in Britain for some twenty years, Cllr Cleghorn studied for his nine 'O' levels in Britain and is currently studying for a degree in Law with the Open University. He is a Section Supervisor with British Rail. Cllr Cleghorn has been a keen member of the Labour Party and active Trade Unionist for a number of years. He has held a number of positions with the N.U.R (National Union of Railwaymen) at district level including those of vice-president and auditor. He is currently on the executive committee and chair of his local branch. Cllr Cleghorn is also a member of the Department of Health and Social Security (DHSS) Tribunal and the Mental Health Tribunal. Elected in May 1986, he is vice-chair of the Chatsworth Community Centre Committee and sits on the Housing, Environmental Services, Planning and Development and Race Equality Committees.

CLEMENTS, Vernon Lanceford, Mr

is a member of the Police Complaints Authority, married with 3 children. His qualifications include that of Pharmacist and state Registered Mental Nurse. Previously he has held the positions of nursing administrator at Nottingham Hospital, Magistrate, Assistant CRO Nottingham, Senior CRO at Coventry and principal CRO at Brent. His interests include football & travel.

COFIE, Edmund, Mr

is a Barrister-at-Law and is currently serving as a Barrister in the Chambers of Edmond Alexander. Mr Cofie, who is single is an active member of the Society of Black Lawyers, where he is executive member. He is also on the management committee of the North Kensington Law Centre.

COTTER, Hercules Emmanuel, Mr

was born in St. Lucia and has lived in Britain for the past twenty six years. He is an industrialist both in Britain and the Caribbean and to this end he is pioneering the first black financial institution in Britain, the First Partnership Bank. Manny Cotter has received a number of scholarships to study economic development in the United States of America. He was one of the first Business Advisors to look at why so few black businesses existed in Britain. As a result of his employment with Hackney's Economic Development Unit he was able to advise and help in the establishment of hundreds of black businesses. Recently he was instrumental in persuading the City of London Polytechnic to establish a management training unit to cater for black entrepreneurs. Manny Cotter is a leading figure in the movement for black and minority economic regeneration of the inner cities.

CRICHLOW, Frank, Mr

was born in Trinidad and Tobago and came to Britain in the early fifties. For more than twenty years, Frank Crichlow has been an active campaigner on behalf of the black community in the Notting Hill area of London. In the late sixties he established the Mangrove restaurant which quickly became a focal point for the black community. He was acquitted of the charge of causing an affray in the notorious Mangrove Trial, one of the first black political trials in modern Britain. He is a lynchpin in the *Caribbean Times* Mangrove Steel Band. As an acknowledged community leader he is actively involved in the Notting Hill Carnival.

CRICHLOW, Victor, Mr

is currently working as the Co-ordinator of the Carnival and Arts Committee (CAC). One of the leading black promoters in London in the sixties and early seventies, he organised the very first Queen of the Band competition. He was one of the leading lights in setting up the first Carnival Development Committee (CDC). He has been the Treasurer of the CAC and for the past 28 years has been involved in some aspect or other of Carnival. He is chairman of the Kensington and Chelsea Mode B Network training scheme and is also a voluntary Social Worker in the Notting Hill area.

CRITCHLOW, Irma, Cllr

represents Vauxhall Ward in the London Borough of Lambeth on the Inner London Education Authority (ILEA) for the Labour Party. A Community Worker and former member of Lambeth Council, she was elected to the Inner London Education Authority in May 1986. She is a member of the ethnic minority section and the black supplementary schools movement, as well as the black social workers groups and the Black Education Action Group. Cllr Critchlow is also member of the local ILEA consultative group for tertiary education, the education committee of the local Community Relations Council and a member of Lambeth M.I.N.D (National Association for Mental Health). She is also vice-chair of the staff sub-committee.

CRUICKSHANK, Ray, Mr

is currently an Administrative Officer (Personnel) for the London Borough of Brent. He is a professional Sociologist. He has worked in the community relations field in the boroughs of Hammersmith and Brent. From 1977-1985 he was the Specialist Careers Adviser (Ethnic Minorities) in Brent before taking up his present position. He is a member of the

Labour Party and is active in its Northfields ward. He is also member of the Fabian Society and is the chair of the Black Workers Support Group (Brent). His ambitions lie in developing educational, social and economic programmes for black people in Britain as well as in the Caribbean and South America.

DABYDEEN, David, B.A., Ph.D.

was born in Guyana and is a lecturer in the Department of Caribbean Studies of the University of Warwick. He was a fellow in Residence, Yale University (1983-88). As an undergraduate at Cambridge University, Dr Dabydeen took the English Prize (1978) and went on to win the Commonwealth Poetry Prize (1984) as well as the GLC Literature Prize (1985). His published work includes *Slave Song* (1984), *Hogarth's Blacks* (1985), *The Black Presence in English Literature* (1985), *Hogarth, Walpole and Commercial Britain* and *Coolie Odyssey*, both published in 1987.

DALAL, Maneck Ardeshir Sohrab, Mr

was born in Bombay, India on December 24 1918. He studied at Trinity College Cambridge and was called to the Bar, Middle Temple, in 1945. Mr Dalal is currently Managing Director of Tata Limited, London and Group Director of Tata Industries Bombay. Prior to that he was regional Director of community groups and educational organisations. He is married and lives in Hampton, Middlesex. Mr. Dalal lists his hobbies as Tennis and Squash; as an undergraduate at Cambridge he captained the Tennis team. He is a Trustee of the Zoroastrian Association and member of the Board of the Royal Commonwealth Society for the Blind.

DALEY, Rudolph, Cllr

represents the Thornton Ward in the London Borough of Lambeth for the Labour Party. Born in Jamaica and resident in Britain since 1958, Rudolph Daley is an administrator and a Justice of the Peace. He was elected as a councillor in May 1986. Cllr Daley is a member of St. John's International Club in Brixton and of a local Parent-Teacher Association. He is also a governor of Brixton College. His main responsibilities on the Council are as acting Chair of the Town Planning and Economic Development Committee and Chair of the Town Planning Applications Sub-Committee.

DANIELS, Neville, Cllr

represents the Bedford Ward in the London Borough of Wandsworth for the Labour Party. Born in Guyana and resident in Britain since 1960, Neville Daniels is a self-employed builder. Elected as a councillor in May 1986, he sits on the Policy and Finance Committee and the Housing Improvement Sub-Committee and is Labour Party spokesperson on race issues. Councillor Daniels' main aims as a councillor are to see the implementation of equal opportunities in the areas that directly affect the black community.

DAS GUPTA, Provat Tapan, Cllr

represents the Seven Kings Ward in the London Borough of Redbridge for the Labour Party. Born in Britain in 1930, councillor Das Gupta went to India where he grew up and completed his education with a Bachelor of Arts degree from the University of Calcutta. He then worked as a medical representative for a number of years before returning to England to further his career in the same field. He is now a Regional Manager for Hoechst UK Ltd. A committed member of the Labour Party, Cllr Das Gupta has held a variety of offices including secretary of his Constituency Labour Party (CLP), Political Education Officer and secretary of the Cranbrook Valentines branch. He represented his constituency at the 1987 Labour Party Conference. Councillor Das Gupta was elected in May 1986 on a manifesto that gave priority to housing, library services and environmental health. He is involved with matters affecting his own ward such as better street lighting and road safety for children.

DAVE, Bhupendra, Cllr

represents the Latimer Ward on Leicester City Council for the Labour Party. Born in Uganda and resident in Britain since 1970, Bhupendra Dave obtained a B.Sc. honours degree in Economics from Bristol University and then continued his education with a diploma in Social Administration, a diploma in Applied Social Studies at the University of Southampton, a diploma in Management Studies at Leicester Polytechnic and a Certificate of Social Work. Bhupendra Dave has been a councillor since 1983 and is currently chair of the Employment and Urban Policies Sub-Committee and Chair of the Low Pay campaign. His special interests are employment, welfare benefits, low pay, contract compliance and equal opportunities. Councillor Dave is a founder member of ASRA (Asians Sheltered and Residential Accommodation) Housing Association Ltd, the first and largest association of its kind in Britain. He lives in Leicester with his wife, Usha and their two children.

DAVID, Frank Matthew, Mr

is a Shipping and Travel Consultant who is actively involved in the sporting, social and cultural life of the black community in Britain. He is chair of the Caribbean Sports and Social Club, manager of BWIA Cricket Team, captain of Trinidad and Tobago All Fours, and chair of Sound of the Caribbean Association.

D'CRUZE, Kenneth, Cllr

was born in Calcutta, West Bengal, India, on October 20 1924. During the Second World War, Kenneth D'Cruze saw active service and was subsequently decorated. He is the recipient of the Star Defence Medal, General Service Medal, and Burma Star. He made his home in London in 1953. Kenneth is now retired, following a successful career in Local Government. He employs his experience as a local Government Official as the Conservative Party spokesperson on the Housing and Race Relations Committees for the London Borough of Lewisham. He is also a member of the London Valuations Panel and a school governor. He is father of six children and is married to Rosemary.

DELANO, Abdul Malik de Coteau, Mr

born in Grenada, 1940, the year Marcus Garvey died. Lived in Trinidad since the age of 2. Jailed for 7 months for his part in the Black Power uprising in Trinidad in 1969-70. Developed into one of the most powerful poet-performers to emerge from the Caribbean. Published 'Black Up' (1972) and 'Revo' (1975). latest poetry work 'The Whirlwind' 1988 received critical acclaim. Influenced by the Bible & Marcus Garvey. Interest is to see the "Caribbean consciousness" freed from foreign domination.

DESAI, Meghnad Jagdishchandra, Dr

is a prominent economist who has published the work *Marxian Economic Theory* (1974). He married Gail Wilson in 1970, and he has two daughters and one son. He was born in the Gujarat state in India on July 10, 1940 and was educated at Bombay University where he gained a B.A. Hons, (1958) and M.A. (1960). He came to London via the USA in September 1985 after being awarded a Ph.D. from the University of Pennsylvania. Dr Desai is an active member of the Labour Party and served as Chair of Islington and Finsbury Labour Party from 1986 to 1987.

DENMAN, Sylvia, Mrs

An Academic Lawyer, Mrs Denman is the Pro-assistant Director at the South Bank Polytechnic in London. Born in Barbados, she settled in the UK some 25 years ago and studied Law at the University of London. Between 1976 and 1982 she lectured in Barbados before taking up a one year Fellowship at the New York University. Mrs Denman has been active in community affairs and served on the Race Relations Board which preceded the Commission for Racial Equality. A resident of Camden, she is involved in the borough's community issues. Married with one daughter, she lists music, walking and visiting the Caribbean as her main interests.

DEU, Amerjit, Mr

is best known for his role as Dr Singh in the immensely popular programme, *Eastenders*, shown twice weekly on BBC TV. He was recently cast in the lead role for the feature film *Caught*, which is due to be released in Britain in 1988. Amerjit has been the recipient of many awards for speech and drama. He holds diplomas in Electronics and Drama. In his spare time he plays and watches sport and is also a member of the British Academy of Fencing. He says his ambition is to be successful in everything he does, particularly in the field of drama.

DEVGUN, Amarjit, Cllr

represents the St. James' Street Ward in the London Borough of Waltham Forest for the Labour Party. Born in Kenya in 1950 and resident in Britain since 1963, Amarjit Devgun is an Electrical Engineer by profession. He was first elected as a councillor for the London Borough of Waltham Forest in 1979 and was one of the first three black councillors in the history of the borough. Prior to his election he was actively involved with a number of Asian and Afro-Caribbean groups, the local Community Relations Council and various campaigning groups. He is presently a member of the Labour Group Executive Committee. Concerned with economic development, resource strategies and decentralisation, Amarjit Devgun seeks to involve wider community participation in the decision making process of the council through co-options.

DHAVAN, Rajeer, M.A., B.A., LL.B., Ph.D.

born in Uttar Pradesh in India in August 1946, Dr Dhavan is a Barrister-at-law. He arrived in Britain from India in June 1968 and lectured at Queen's University in Belfast between 1972-73. He was the visiting professor to Delhi University in 1979, to the Indian law Institute 1977-78, 1980, 1981, to University of Wisconsin 1987 and to University of Texas 1985. He is also the author of several books and articles.

DHEER, Ranjit, Cllr

represents the Dormers Wells Ward in the London Borough of Ealing for the Labour Party. Born in India and resident in Britain since 1966, Ranjit Dheer has been a councillor since 1982. He became chair of the Race Equality Committee in 1986 and is chair of the Association of London Authorities Race Committee and a Justice of the Peace on the Middlesex Commission. He is also a member of the Policy Committee, the Education Committee and the Equal Opportunities Joint Consultative Working Party. Cllr Dheer's main aim is to develop the race relations strategy through the borough's new Race Equality Unit – providing improved services for the ethnic minorities.

DHILLON, Arjan Singh, Cllr

represents the Hounslow West Ward in the London Borough of Hounslow for the Labour Party. Born in Malaysia in 1934 and resident in Britain since 1964, Arjan Singh Dhillon gained his Bachelor of Science degree in Agriculture from Punjab University in India. Upon arrival in Britain he became an active member of the Labour movement and has been involved in trades union organisations, particularly among ethnic minority workers. Since 1964 he has worked for London Transport, Air India and the Southern British Road Service. A member of the Labour Party since 1969, Cllr Dhillon was chair of his local ward Labour Party from 1983 to 1985 and has been a member of the Transport and General Workers' Union since 1967. He is currently a member of the General Management Committee of the Heston and Feltham Constituency Labour Party, serves on Hounslow Community Relations Council, is a member of the Indian Workers' Association, the Sikh Art and Culture Centre and Hounslow Anti-Apartheid Movement. Elected for the first time in May 1986, Dhillon says he will strive for a harmonious and peaceful multi-racial society and is committed to achieving equal opportunities for all. He is currently chair of the Careers Service Advisory Committee and a council representative to the Association of London Authorities on Race. Councillor Dhillon lives in Hounslow with his wife and children. His spare time interests are community service and travelling.

DHILLON, Gurdip Singh, Cllr

represents the Woolwich Common Ward in the London Borough of Greenwich for the Labour Party. Born in India in 1938 and resident in Britain since 1963, Cllr Dhillon was born and educated in the Punjab, north India. Since arriving in Britain he has been a community activist, involved as a founding member of the Indian Cultural Society and as a member of the Asian Resource Centre. Gurdip Dhillon is the current chair of the Greenwich Action Committee against Racist Attacks and the local CND (Campaign for Nuclear Disarmament) branch. He was instrumental in establishing a day centre for the Asian elderly and is currently involved with building an Asian community and Sports Centre. A councillor since 1978 he is presently chair of the Race Committee.

DHOLAKIA, Navnit, JP, Mr

was born in Tabora, Tanzania, in 1938. He settled in the United Kingdom in 1956. Since that time he has been extremely active in the field of race relations, community politics and local government. In the early sixties, Navnit Dholakia, served as a county councillor in Brighton. In the late Sixties he was appointed Senior Development Officer for the Community Relations Commission. Since 1984 he has been a Principal Officer for the Commission for Racial Equality. He specialises on policing and judicial matters and is now a member of the Parole System Review, and a prison visitor. Since 1977 he has been a Justice of the Peace.

DIVINE, David, Mr

was born in Scotland in 1953. His professional background is in social work. He was the National Secretary of the Association of Black Social Workers and Allied professionals. David Divine is the Managing Director of the British Fostering and Adoption Agencies. He was formerly the Principal Social Worker with Hackney council and subsequently became Assistant Director for Hackney Social Services. David Divine is now the Director of Social Services for the London Borough of Brent. He has published many articles on the subject of transracial adoption.

DORDI HOMI, Edalji, Ervad (Rev)

was born in India and served in the Royal Indian Air Force from 1939 to 1945. As a result of his active service during the war years, he was awarded the Burma Star. He is married and was a Warranty Manager with the Ford Motor Company for over twenty years until his retirement. Since retirement he has served the Parsee community through his work with various inter-faith groups both in Harrow and Surrey.

DRAKE, Boyce, Mr

is a picture restorer and retailer of artists' materials based in Gloucester. He is single. He studied Fine Art at Gloucester College of Art from 1955 to 1960. From 1963 to 1963 he did teacher training at St. Pauls College, Cheltenham, and from 1966 to 1969 studied picture restoration in Bristol and London. During 1979-80 he obtained a scholarship to study picture restoration techniques in Stuttgart, West Germany. He took up his present position in 1986. He has been the branch chair of the International Friendship League in Gloucester since 1985.

DRYDEN, George Dudley, M.B.E., Mr

was born in Jamaica and emigrated to Britain where he established a successful hair care business. He is the recipient of many awards and has been an influential member of a number of community groups, particularly the Westindian Standing Conference, the Hackney Council for Racial Equality and the Association of Jamaicans (U.K.). Mr Dryden received the Caribbean Times Award in 1982 for services rendered to the black community, and the M.B.E. in 1985. Mr Dryden's aim is to offer assistance to those in need.

DUTTA, Amal, Dr

was born in Rangoon, Burma, on August 10, 1939 and is a Consultant Psychiatrist at a Merseyside hospital. He is married with two sons. Dr Dutta holds a number of degrees and diplomas in the fields of medicine, law and psychiatry. He arrived in Britain from India in October 1972. Prior to taking up his present position at Rainhill Hospital, Dr Dutta was a Registrar in Psychiatry and Medical Sub-normality at hospitals in the north-west of England, and from 1983 to 1985 he was the Senior Registrar for the Mersey Regional Rotational Training Scheme. He is a member of the Royal College of Psychiatrists, the British Medical Association and the Liverpool Psychiatric Society, as well as the Overseas Doctors Association. Dr Dutta was the Debating Champion at Calcutta University (1963-1965) and stood first in Biological Sciences at City College, Calcutta, (1961-62). His recreations are photography, chess and cycling. He aims to contribute to medical science through his research.

EDWARDS, Mark Berisford, Mr

was born in Guyana in 1930 and worked as a printer in Manchester in the 1960s. He has a long history of service to the black community including organising summer schools, youth clubs, conferences and self-help projects. Mr Edwards is Treasurer of the Moss Side People's Association and works as a Warden/Youth and Community Worker with the Westindian Centre in Manchester.

EDWARDS, Yasmine Lorraine, Cllr

represents Church End Ward in the London Borough of Brent for the Labour Party. Born in Britain in 1958 of an English mother and Jamaican father, Yasmine Edwards was brought up in Brent. She was educated in the borough and took up a career in dental nursing before returning to full-time education at Kilburn Polytechnic. She is currently pursuing her studies for an Open University degree whilst working as a Play Group Leader. A member of the Labour Party since the age of 17, Cllr Edwards is now chair of her Ward party and vice-chair of the Constituency Labour Party. She is also a member of Brent Women's Council and Women's Section. Her various community activities include involvement with Brent Visually Handicapped Group and elderly support groups. She is a member of the local Campaign for Nuclear Disarmament (CND) branch, Brent Voluntary Services Council, the National Council for One Parent Families and she is also a school governor. Yasmine Edwards was elected as a local councillor in May 1986. As well as being chair of the Special Education Committee, she sits on fifteen other committees and is the Council's representative on the London Boroughs' Ecology Committee and the London Boroughs' Joint Committee for the Under Fives.

ELLIS, Barrington, Mr

was born in London on November 18, 1961. He studied Business Management for four years in London. Barrington Ellis is married and has one son. He now runs a successful car phone and office system company.

ENGLAND, Carmen, L.T.C.L., Ms

was the first black woman in Britain to establish a hairdressing salon in 1948. She is equally well known as a pianist and accompanist. Carmen England later studied hair and beauty culture in London, New York and Paris. Since 1984 Carmen England has received numerous awards and was in 1987 the recipient of a *Caribbean Times* award. Carmen England worked with the late Claudia Jones. She was also the chair of West Indian Carnival Queens Committee from 1959-62 and a founder member of CASH (Caribbean and African Society of Hairdressers). Now retired, she is the widow of the late Paul England, the theatrical producer and impressario who died in 1977.

EYO, Peter, Mr

has been the principal Race Equality Adviser to the London Borough of Southwark since 1983. He has had a long career working on behalf of the community. Peter Eyo is very interested in the arts and serves on a number management committees, including Oval House Theatre, the Minority Arts Advisory Service and is an executive director of the Sass Theatre Company. He lives in Forest Hill, south east London.

FISHER, Laris, Ms

was born in Jamaica on September 2, 1946. Laris Fisher first came to Britain in 1967 for three years to undertake general nursing training at Ipswich and East Suffolk General Hospital. After spending one year in Jamaica, she returned to Britain to continue her nursing studies in Midwifery and Health Visitor training and became a Health Vistior for Haringey from 1974 to 1984. Laris is a trained Sickle Cell Anaemia Counsellor with experience in assisting sickle cell sufferers and was in 1985 appointed Britain's first full-time Sickle Cell Social Worker.

FLATHER, Paul, Cllr

represents Tooting on the Inner London Education Authority (ILEA) for the Labour Party. Born in Britain in 1959, he is a freelance Journalist and is currently working on a Ph.D. on Indian Politics at Oxford University. An active member of the Labour Party, he is a member of the Tooting Black Members Group and sits on the Further and Higher Education Sub-Committee. Councillor Flather was elected as a representative to the Inner London Education Authority in the May 1986 elections and his priority is to extend access into further and higher education, particularly for women and black people. Outside work his main interests are running, reading and cooking.

FLATHER, Shreela, Cllr

represents the St. Mary's Ward in the Royal Borough of Windsor and Maidenhead for the Conservative Party. She obtained her Law degree from University College, London, and was called to the Bar at Inner Temple. She has worked as an Infant Teacher and as a Teacher of English as a second language. Cllr Shreela Flather was a member of the Committee of Inquiry, Rampton Swann Committee, into the Education of Children from ethnic minority groups and the Duke of Edinburgh's Committee of Inquiry into British housing. She is a member of the Conservative Women's National Committee. She has been a Justice of the Peace since 1971 and was a founder member and vice-chair of Maidenhead Community Relations Council as well as secretary/organiser of Maidenhead Community Relations Council and secretary/organiser of Maidenhead Ladies Asian Club. She started the New Star Boys Club for Asian Boys, a summer school project for Asian children in Maidenhead, and also prepared an English teaching scheme for Asian adults. Her past appointments include membership of the Commission for Racial Equality, the Police Complaints Board and West Metropolitan Conciliation Committee of the Race Relations Board. Cllr Flather is president of Cambs. Chilterns and Thames Rent Assessment Panel and a member of the Lord Chancellor's Legal Aid Advisory Committee. Her new appointments include the Social Security Advisory Committee, BBC's South East Regional Council and Broadmoor Hospital Board. Elected as Mayor in 1986, she is the first Asian woman mayor in Britain.

FRANCIS, Jenni, Ms,

is founder and Managing Director/Public Relations Executive of Networking PR. With Networking PR, Ms Francis offers advertising, copywriting, press releases and biographies, photocalls and photographic sessions as well as a wide range of other skills necessary in developing and maintaining a profile. Currently a member of the Institute of Public Relations and the Institute of Directors, Ms Francis has considerable experience in the business/management field from her years as in-house consultant to Cannons Sports Club and as a vibrant freelancer in the business, media, fashion, music and sporting worlds.

FRANCIS, Les, Cllr

represents Eltham on the Inner London Education Authority (ILEA) for the Labour Party. Born in Jamaica in 1931 and resident in Britain since 1961, Les Francis was brought up in Jamaica where he qualified and worked as a Teacher. He is currently working as a Driver/Attendant for Greenwich Social Services but has, over the last twenty-five years, been employed as an Engineer, Welder, Railway worker and Bus Conductor. Over the years he has been involved with numerous community organisations including Youth Projects, Age Concern and Greenwich Employment Resource Unit. He is the governor of five ILEA schools and two colleges. As a councillor, Mr Francis is strongly committed to defending the existing education system against cuts and aims to ensure that the service is not only maintained but improved. Les Francis is a member of the Race Relations Sub Committee of the Community Affairs Committee (CAC) in Greenwich. Councillor Francis has lived in Greenwich with his wife, Edna, and their family for over twenty years. He enjoys music and plays the guitar, banjo and harmonica. His main hobby is photography.

FRASER, Flip, Mr

has a remarkable track record in the fields of music, entertainments and journalism. Brought up in Jamaica, he studied Media and communications at Tennessee State University and then worked in London as the inspiring force behind such burgeoning labels as Harvest, Virgin and Mountain. During this time, he also co-produced the innovative *Double Vision*, a twin packaged doubled sleeved 12", which included two self-penned songs. Promotions manager for Ashanti Record and Bamboo Music and later Vulcan Records, he later wrote for *Sounds* magazine, promoting a positive image for reggae music in Britain. A well respected figure in the black community, Flip became Assistant/Music Editor of the newly launched *Caribbean Times* newspaper, and provided a unique coverage of both the local and international entertainments scenes, including his popular talent competition "Search for a Star". In 1982, Flip left CT and was invited to become the first Editor of a new black newspaper *The Voice*. He went on to launch *Black Beat International*, an international magazine for black music. He has since presented guest spots on national TV and radio, including Channel 4's *Black on Black*, *Radio Horizon* and *Specials* on Radio 1. In 1984, Flip recorded his debut song *Babylove*, the first in a collection of his own compositions. His latest brainchild "Talent Discoveries" has been set up to provide back up and promotional services for new discoveries.

FORD, Amos Adolphus, Mr

was born in Belize in 1916 and came to Britain during the Second World War to serve with the Ministry of Supply in Scotland. Settling in Britain after the war, he worked as a civil servant in the Department of Health and Social Security from 1947 until his retirement in 1980. Mr Ford now devotes his time exclusively to writing on the black experience. His published work includes *Telling The Truth*, which looks at the experience of workers from Belize in the Scottish forestry industry during the war. Mr Ford is also an accomplished guitarist and has taught Spanish and Classical guitar music. He was the recipient of a *Caribbean Times* award in 1986.

FORBES, Everton Uriah, Mr

was born on March 22, 1933, in St. Elizabeth, Jamaica. He emigrated to Britain in 1955 and studied at the London School of Printing and Graphics, where he gained certificates in Printing and Book-Binding. He was the first person to organise cheap charter flights to the Caribbean in 1968, until charters were stopped in 1974. Since that time he has run a successful travel agency in Finsbury Park, north London, as well as a Shipping Company and has added a show room that sells tropical equipment and tax-free furniture for export to the Caribbean. He is married with three children and lists his hobbies as dominoes, boxing, cricket and photography. Mr Forbes is currently chair of the Caribbean Travel Action Group (CATAG)

GADHIA, Anisha, Ms

is a full-time Law Student and part-time Model. She is a member of the Law Society and the Pat Keeling Model Agency. Anisha also trained for Kathak –Indian classical dancing, as well as jazz/contemporary dance forms. She is interested in astrology and music, plays badminton and does a spot of weight-lifting. Anisha has worked in Asian Youth Projects in Leicester and keeps a keen eye on Race Relations.

GAZEN, Issam, Cllr

represents Trent Ward where he is also chairman of the Nottingham East Labour Party branch. Cllr Gazen, who works as a social worker for the Nottingham County Council, was born in Pakistan in 1959 and settled in the UK in 1963. He studied Business Studies at the Polytechnic of Lancashire and worked in the family business after leaving college. Cllr Gazen joined the Labour Party in 1985 and served as a member's secretary in his local branch before he became chairman. Married with one child, Cllr Gazen's main concern is with economic development and equal opportunities for all races. Cricket is his favourite sport and he also enjoys doing voluntary work for the community.

GEORGES, Franklyn, Cllr

represents Leytonstone Ward in the London Borough of Waltham Forest for the Labour Party. Born in Dominica and a Fitter by trade, Franklyn Georges is a keen member of N.U.P.E (National Union of Public Employees) and was a member of its national Committee. Cllr Georges was elected to Waltham Forest Council in May 1986.

GHAI, Yash, Professor

a Kenyan citizen, read Law at Oxford and Harvard Universities. He trained as a Barrister-at-Law at the Middle Temple and was called to the Bar in 1962. Prof Ghai has taught at universities in Africa, Australia, Sweden, Britain and the USA, and is currently a Professor of Law at Warwick University. He has published numerous books, monographs and articles, many on subjects relating to Law in developing countries. He has worked as a consultant/adviser to the governments of Papua New Guinea, Solomon Islands, New Hebrides and Western Samoa, and international bodies such as the United Nations. Professor Ghai is a member, Editorial Board, *African Legal Studies*; Trustee, International Centre for Law in Development; Trustee, Foundations for the Pacific Peoples; and member, Commonwealth Legal Education Association. Professor Ghai has been awarded the Independence Medal (Papua New Guinea), the Queen's Medal for Distinguished Service (New Hebrides) and the CBE (UK).

GIFFORD, Zerbanoo, Ms

a politician, was born in Calcutta in 1950. She came to Britain in 1953 and was educated at Watford College of Technology and the Open University. She was a Harrow Councillor from 1982-86 and the Parliamentary Candidate for the then SDP/ Liberal Alliance in Harrow East in 1987. She was also chair of the Liberal Party's Community Relations Panel, 1985, in succession to Lord Avebury; chair of the Commission looking into Ethnic Minority Involvement 1985-86; and was also a member of the Status of Women's Commission, 1984-86. Ms Gifford, who is married with two children, is president of the Harrow Zoroastrian Association and editor of *Libas International* magazine.

GILKES, Michael, Dr

is a Senior Lecturer in English at the University of the Westindies (Barbados) and has been living in Britain since 1976 when he went to the University of Warwick to take up a Lever Hulme Fellowship in Caribbean Studies. He was born in Guyana and educated at the University of the Westindies and the University of Kent where he obtained his doctorate. Dr Gilkes is the author of several books and articles on Caribbean Literature, including *The West Indian Novel* (1981).

GILL, Karamjit, Mr

is the Principal Lecturer in Artificial Intelligence at Brighton Polytechnic. He obtained an M.A. in maths, M.Sc. in computer science and a D.Ph. in comparative science. He is at present Director of the SEAKE Centre at Brighton Polytechnic and is Editor of the *AI and Society Journal*, Service Editor of AI Foundations of the Future and a member of the South East Arts General Panel. Mr Gill is married with three children.

GILL, Satnam Singh, Cllr

represents Camden Ward in the London Borough of Camden for the Labour Party. Born in India in 1955, Satnam Singh Gill obtained his B.Sc. degree in Social Administration and a Teaching Certificate in Social Sciences. He is currently employed as a Personnel Officer having also worked as a Teacher and Immigration Adviser. He is an active member of N.A.L.G.O (National Association of Local Government Officers) and was elected as a local councillor in May 1986. Cllr Gill is chair of the Policy and Resources Committee.

GORDON, Rhodan, Mr

is a Community Development Worker with the Black Peoples Information Centre in London. His job mainly entails running the centre, a project in which he has been actively involved for the last twenty-five years. Mr Gordon is also a member of the Unity Association, the Carnival Industrial Project and the Notting Hill Carnival and Arts Committee. In 1983 and 1986 he won the Community Awards for Justice.

GOSWAMI, Sham, Cllr

is a Social and Liberal Democrat Party elected representative in London Borough of Richmond-Upon-Thames. Born in 1940, Sham Goswami has lived in Whitton for over 10 years where he has developed his interest in community work. He is an accountant and holds various qualifications including a degree in Political Science and a certificate in Management Studies from the British Institute of Management. Cllr Goswami has been involved for many years with charitable organisations including the Westminster Disablement Association, Commonwealth Deaf Society and is currently a member of the committee for 'The Friends of the Annexe' Centre for the Disabled. He is married with one daughter, Nina, who attends the local state school. Cllr Goswami and his wife Joy were active members of the local Liberal Party for many years, holding positions including vice-chair and membership secretary.

GRAHAM, Aubyn, Cllr

represents Lyndhurst Ward in the London Borough of Southwark for the Labour Party. Resident in Britain since 1962, Aubyn Graham took up his seat on Southwark Council after the local elections in May 1982. As a councillor he is very concerned with the promotion of black business and arts in the area. He plans to be instrumental both in securing accessibility of advice and grants to black business and in encouraging increased involvement in the arts. He is chair of the Leisure and Recreation Committee. Outside working hours Councillor Graham enjoys football, running and helping with his local youth club.

GRAHAM, Clifton George, Cllr

represents Drake Ward in the London Borough of Lewisham for the Labour Party. Born in Jamaica in 1943 and resident in Britain since 1966, Clifton Graham is a qualified Electrical Engineer and has lived and worked in Deptford, south London for the last twenty years. He is a strong socialist and has held a number of positions as a member of the Labour Party including Postal Vote Officer and Fundraising Officer. He has also been chair of his branch Labour Party. In a 1983 by-election Cllr Graham was first elected to Lewisham Borough Council. He was re-elected in May 1986 and in the same year stood for selection as Parliamentary Candidate for Deptford – a position he lost by a narrow margin to Joan Ruddock, vice-chair of CND (Campaign for Nuclear Disarmament), who was subsequently elected to Westminster.

GRANT, Bernie, MP

was elected as Member of Parliament for Tottenham in June 1987. He also represents Bruce Grove Ward in the London Borough of Haringey for the Labour Party. Born in Guyana in 1944 and resident in Britain since 1963, Bernie Grant completed his education with three 'A' levels at Tottenham Technical College and two years of a degree course in Mining Engineering at Heriott-Watt University in Edinburgh. He has worked as a British Rail Clerk, a Telephonist, an Area officer for N.U.P.E (National Union of Public Employees), and as an Equal Opportunities Officer in the London Borough of Newham. Bernie Grant has been very active in the Labour Party for twelve years and in that time has held most positions at local level in the Bruce Grove and Coleraine Wards and in Tottenham and Wood Green Labour Parties. Elected as a councillor in 1978 he became Deputy Leader of Haringey Council in 1982 but did not stand for re-election. In April 1985 he was elected as Council Leader. He is involved with a range of anti-racist and anti-fascist activities in London. He is a founder member of the Haringey Labour Movement Anti-Racist and Anti-Fascist Campaign and of the All-London Campaign Against Racism and Fascism. Bernie Grant is closely involved with a number of black community groups, youth groups in particular. These include the Westindian Leadership Council, the Young Single and Homeless Project and the Haringey/Grenada Youth Exchange.

GRANT, Cy, Mr

qualified as a barrister in 1951 but is perhaps more well known as an actor/singer. He has appeared in several films, including *Shaft in Africa* and *At the Earth's Core*. He was chair/co-founder of Drum Arts Centre in 1974 and has been Director of the Concord Festival Trust, an organisation that exists to offer information, advice and services which enable towns or cities to stage prestigious multi-cultural festivals of national importance.

GRAY, Icelyn Amanda,JP, B.Sc. (Soc), M.Sc. (Man St), Ms

is head of the Business Unit of Ealing College in west London. In 1981 she became an Executive Officer at British Telecom, a post she maintained until 1985 when she became Business Development Manager for the UK Caribbean Chamber of Commerce. Ms Gray is former vice-president of Lignum Vitae Club, former chair of Stardust Youth Club and Founder Member of both the Norman Manley Foundation and the Norman Manley Committee. She is also a member of the Latchmere Remand Centre Board of Visitors. Amongst her ambitions Ms Gray expresses a desire to return to Jamaica to fly a light aircraft.

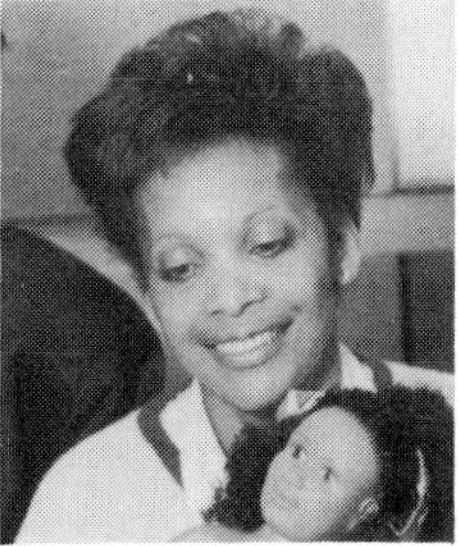

GREY, Ann-Marie, Ms

was born in Jamaica and lived for several years in Tehran, the capital of Iran. She has been working in the media as an interviewer and programme presenter for the past nine years. She began by freelancing with LBC on the London Programme with Hylton Fyle and also had a regular slot on Radio One as well as co-presenting *Black Londoners*. She narrated the BBC television documentary for the 50th Anniversary of the Apollo Theatre in Harlem and is 'the voice' on several TV commericals. Ann-Marie Grey is currently presenter of the BBC *Topical Tapes* programme *Caribbean Magazine*, a programme which is transmitted to nearly all the Caribbean countries. Ann-Marie, who enjoys bodybuilding, is also an avid poetry writer and hopes to have a book of her work published in the future.

GRIFFITH, Eddie, Cllr

represents South Hornsey Ward in the London Borough of Haringey for the Labour Party. Born in Barbados, Eddie Griffith has a Bachelor of Science degree and a Teaching Certificate. He is currently Head of Politics and Social Education at a school in Newham, east London. He is a member of the NUT (National Union of Teachers), the British Caribbean Association, and Newham Afro-Caribbean Association. Cllr Griffith is chair of the governing body of Highgate Wood Secondary School and a member of Finsbury Park Community Trust Management Committee. He is also chair of several council committees such as the Youth Services Sub-Committee, Youth Affairs Committee, the Health Committee and the Further Education Sub-Committee, as well as being the vice-chair of the Education Committee. His interests outside politics are cricket, volleyball, radio-presenting, writing and travel.

GUJRAL, Gurdip Singh, Mr

a businessman, was born in Sargodha, Punjab in 1935. He was educated in Rawalpindi and Ambala and arrived in Britain in 1965. Since 1970 he has been involved in the garment importing business and is Managing Director of Gujral Bros. Ltd. He is President of the Punjabi Society of the British Isles and is the present chair of the Indian Clothing Imports Association. In 1985 he received the Shiro Mani Award from the President of India. Mr Gujral, who lists travelling among his interests, is married with two children.

GULATI, Ramesh Kumar, Dr

was born in the North West Frontier Province on November 24, 1942. He has a medical general practice and is married with two sons and one daughter. Having gained Medical qualifications at Lucknow University, Dr Gulati acquired further specialised qualifications from Liverpool and London. He arrived in Britain from India in 1968 and is a member of the British Medical Association, the Overseas Doctors Association and various other organisations. Dr Gulati's recreational interests are badminton, bridge and boating. He currently lives in the Preston area.

GUMBITI-ZIMUTO, Andrew, Mr

is a Barrister-at-Law, and was admitted to Chambers in 1984. Born in Zimbabwe, he was educated in England at the St. William of York School and later attended the University of Sussex and graduated from the Inns of Court School of Law. He is a member of the Society of Black Lawyers and is currently an adviser to Black Rights (UK).

GUNN, Richard, Mr

was born in St. Vincent and the Grenadines on January 19, 1936. He is the High Commissioner in London for the Eastern Caribbean States and is married with one son and two daughters. Mr Gunn has studied for diplomas in Architecture and Business Administration. He has previously worked for Hazells Ltd. in a management capacity and has been the Director of the Caribbean Association of Industry and Commerce (1985-1987), chair of the National Broadcasting Corporation of St. Vincent and the Grenadines and chair of the country's National Shipping Company. Mr Gunn has been active in the St. Vincent Jaycees since the early 1960s and later in the Westindies Jaycees (vice-president (1966-67)) and Jaycees International, being appointed a Senator in 1968. From 1985-86 he was president of the St. Vincent Chamber of Industry and Commerce and in 1987 was Secretary-General of European/Caribbean Contacts II. He was appointed High Commissioner in London in 1987.

GURTATA, Balwant Singh, JP, Mr

was born in India in 1948. He came to Britain in January 1960 and in 1984 was appointed Justice of the Peace. He is also the present chair of an hotel group. Mr Gurtata, who enjoys reading, walking and travel, is married with two sons.

GUPTA, Chaman Lall, Dr

is currently based at his surgery in Welling, Kent. He has been a GP since 1977. He has worked as a Registrar of Psychology, a Medical Officer for Northern Railways and as a Civil Assistant Surgeon for the Punjab Government (1961-63). Mr Gupta is an Executive Member of the Overseas Doctors Association (south London); a member of the Medical Practitioners Association; and Executive Member of the Indian Association, London. As well as being a member of the BMA (British Medical Association) he is also chair of the Indian Association UK (Kent). Mr Gupta is married with two sons.

HABGOOD, Yvonne Veronica, Ms

is a self-taught artist who lives in Wiltshire. Here she is fully able to express her creative instincts producing work that has been described as owning "a high degree of mature stylistic integration...and a consistent intensity of vision given impetus by landscape, or rather, the spirit". She has had her work exhibited at several exhibitions including the Mall Galleries, National Society of Painters and Sculptors, at Manchester Academy Annual Exhibitions and at the Commonwealth Institute. She was also instrumental in organising the first Swindon Caribbean Carnival. As well as continuing to develop and expand her creative inspirations Ms Habgood also does some acting in her spare time.

HAFEEZ, Bashir ul, Cllr

represents the Wall End Ward in the London Borough of Newham for the Labour Party. Born in 1934, Bashir ul Hafeez was educated in Britain and obtained a diploma in Automobile Engineering in London. He is now employed as a Senior Local Government Officer in the London Borough of Tower Hamlets. Councillor Hafeez was elected in May 1986. He is the vice-chair of the Works and Supplies Sub-Committee and a member of Education and Environmental Services.

HALL, Ian, Mr

a Guyanese, was the first black music graduate from Oxford. Since his graduation he has been involved in several spheres of his profession – from composition and teaching to performing and presenting. He was the first black person to present a major television series in the UK – *Songs that Matter* (1972). In 1970 he founded the Bloomsbury Society in a bid to advance international inter-ethnic understanding. His musical compositions, which generally reflect cultural ambivalence, are usually dedicated to an event or to a particular personality. Several of his essays and verse have also been published.

HALL, Trevor, Mr

is a Home Office Community Relations Consultant. A pioneer in multi-racial youth exchanges to European Community countries, Hall's experience in the educational sector spans 20 years. In 1968 he served on the Church of England Board of Education and was the Rugby Community Relations Council Youth Advisor between 1971 and 1975 and became the Rugby Community Relations Council's Senior Community Relations Officer. Mr Hall, who is married, is also a council member of the Royal Commonwealth Society, and in 1987 was made vice-chair of the National Youth Bureau.

HALLWORTH, Grace, Ms

who was born and brought up in Trinidad, is well-known for her magical stories based on the folktales and way of life in the Westindies. As a little girl there was nothing Grace liked more than listening to and reading stories, especially those which were part of the island's customs, folklore and humour. In her books she has captured all the vitality and magic of those stories. Among the works she has written are *Listen to This Story* – a wonderful collection of traditional stories, illustrated by Dennis Ranston. Other books include *The Carnival Kite* and *Mouth Open Sorty Jump Out* – a collection of chilling supernatural stories based on the folklore of Trinidad and Tobago. One of Grace's main interests is the role of language in education, and her writing gives a vivid impression of the way people speak in Trinidad and Tobago.

HAMID, Peter, Cllr

represents Ponders End Ward in the London Borough of Enfield for the Labour Party. Peter Hamid and his family have lived in Enfield for over fourteen years. He first stood for an Enfield Council election in May 1982 when he took the Ponders End Ward. He is actively involved in a number of trade union activities and is a member of MSF (Manufacturing, Science and Finance). This activism extends to his political and community work. Amongst the posts he has held are Labour Group delegate to the Association of London Labour Oppostition Groups as well as membership of a number of policy groups on housing, social services and anti-racism. He is also a member of the Steering Committee of the Standing Conference of Afro-Caribbean and Asian Councillors and founder/director of the Ethnic Minorities Information Exchange.

HAMILTON, Al, Mr

was born in Jamaica. He is a sports writer and organiser of the Commonwealth Sports Awards, which are now in their ninth year. He was the first sports editor for the *Caribbean Times* and has also written for a number of other publications. Al Hamilton is the publisher of the monthly journal, *Sports Scene*. His first book was published in 1982 and is entitled *Black Pearls of Soccer*. In 1987 he took a football team 'Sons of Jamaica' to Jamaica for the Garvey Centenary and the twenty-fifth anniversary of Jamaica's independence. Al Hamilton also arranges sports exchanges with the Jamaican government.

HANSON, Kenrick, Cllr

represents Homerton Ward in the London Borough of Hackney for the Labour Party. Born in Jamaica, Kenrick Hanson is currently employed as a Progress Supervisor with London Regional Transport. Cllr Hanson is a member of the National Union of Railwaymen (NUR) and held the position of secretary of Kingsmead Teachers' Association for a period of ten years. He has been a school governor since 1970.

HARRIS, Wilson, Mr

from Guyana, is a writer of English fiction. His first novel *Palace of the Peacock* was published in 1960 to critical acclaim, and is now a set text at several universities around the world. He has published a dozen novels and two books of literary criticism. In 1979 he was appointed a visiting lecturer at Yale University. Between 1980 and 82, he was a visiting Professor at the University of Austin, Texas. He is presently an Associate Fellow at the University of Warwick's Centre for Caribbean Studies.

HARTE, Joe, Mr

is at present the principal training officer in the Directorate of Economic Development and Estates in Lewisham, south east London. He is the co-chair of Black Rights (UK). Joe Harte read a diploma in Social Studies at Ruskin College, Oxford and went on to gain an honours degree from London University. He is now studying for his doctorate on organisational behaviour at Warwick University. Joe Harte was the legal officer with the Westindian Standing Conference and Editor of the journal *Teamwork*.

HASAN, Ayse, Cllr

represents Mildmay Ward in the London Borough of Islington for the Labour Party. Born in Cyprus in 1958 and resident in Britain since 1960, Ayse Hasan studied for a diploma in Business in London before reading Law at Leicester Polytechnic. She is now employed as a Development Worker for the Union of Turkish Women in Britain. Elected as London's first Turkish-speaking councillor in May 1986, she sits on the Race Relations and Committee, Recreation, Finance and Expenditure, and Policy and Resources Committees. She is involved with many issues affecting the Turkish and other ethnic minority communities, including anti-deportation campaigns. In her spare time Cllr Hasan enjoys reading and the theatre.

HASHMI, Siyar Farrukh, Dr

has had a long and distinguished career in the Health Service. He is a Consultant Psychiatrist working in the Birmingham District. In 1974 he was awarded the O.B.E. Dr Hashmi served on the Home Office Parole Board from 1981 to 1985 and he was also a commissioner for the Commission for Racial Equality from 1980 to 1986. He is married and lives in Edgbaston, Birmingham.

HASSAN, Ahmed, Cllr

represents St Anne's Ward for Nottingham East constituency for the labour party which he joined in 1980. Cllr Ahmed has been chairman of his ward for the last 4 years and also served as vice-chairman in 1987. Cllr Ahmed was born in Pakistan in 1951 and obtained a degree in political science. He was involved in the Trade union movement in Pakistan and was arrested and detained for three years. He settled in the UK in 1978 and has worked as a bank clerk and community centre education officer in Nottingham. Cllr Ahmed's main concern is for equal opportunities for all races and economic development in areas that have been hit by unemployment. He is married with 2 children and his main interests are cricket and reading.

HAYNES, Aaron, Dr

is a Principal at the Community Roots College of which Lord Pitt of Hampstead is President. Dr Haynes, who holds a certificate in Medical Technology, a Teachers Certificate, a B.A. in Biology, M.A. in Sociology and a Ph.D. in Sociology, worked as a Science Teacher, Medical Technologist and Senior Community Relations Officer before his present appointment. He was also Regional Principal and Chief Executive in the Commission for Racial Equality. Dr Haynes, who feels he can make a definite contribution to creating an effective black leadership, is a Fellow of the British Institute of Management and of the Royal Society of Arts.

HERBERT, Donald Peter, Mr

is a Barrister-at-Law called to the Bar in 1982. In 1983 he became a Tenant at Stone Buildings in Lincoln's Inn. He is the vice-chair of the Society of Black Lawyers and an Executive Officer with Lawyers Against Apartheid. He is hoping to help produce a Directory of Black Lawyers, Probation and Social Workers and to establish an umbrella group for this. He is at present involved in campaigning for the introduction of anti-racist training for all judges and magistrates and for the eventual elimination of the disparity of sentencing and treatment between black and white offenders in the criminal justice system.

HERBERT, Vince, Mr

a broadcaster, was born in St. Kitts and Nevis in 1950. He trained at Mount View Drama School and Amos Rep in New York. He entered radio journalism in 1975 with BBC Radio Manchester and moved to Radio London in 1979 working as a presenter on *Black Londoners*. He was a presenter on BBC's TV's programme *Ebony* for three years. Mr Herbert is a member of Artist Exchange USA.

HINDS, Donald Lloyd, B.A., M.A., P.G.C.E.,Mr

a former Bus Conductor, he is Head of the History department at Geoffrey Chaucer School, and a writer of considerable merit. He was the principal reporter on Claudia Jones' *West Indian Gazette*, and several of his short stories and articles have appeared in anthologies, newspapers, and journals. He has a "bulging drawer" of unpublished novels. As an historian he contributed to Tulse Hill School's world famous, *World History Course*, and is on the management committee of *Oral History*.

HOTHI, Sukhvinder S., Cllr

represents the Mount Pleasant Ward in the London Borough of Ealing for the Labour Party. Born in India in 1940 and resident in Britain since 1962, Sukhvinder Hothi is a wine merchant with two outlets, in Bayswater and in Kensington. A Labour Party member for the last ten years, he is Branch Secretary of Mount Pleasant Ward and a member of Ealing and Southall Constituency Labour Party. He was elected as a councillor in May 1986. Cllr Hothi was a Senior Shop-Steward of the T&GWU (Transport and General Workers Union) for six years, has been a supporter of CND (Campaign for Nuclear Disarmament) since the early 1960s and was an active member of the Vietnam Solidarity Campaign. He is also a veteran of Mangrove Community Centre in west London. Cllr Hothi's main concern as a councillor is with housing and he is a member of the Housing Committee, the Community Services Committee and the Housing Management Committee on Ealing Borough Council. He is married with three children.

HOWE, Darcus, Mr

born on the Caribbean island of Trinidad and Tobago in 1942, Darcus Howe is regarded as a respected journalist and political activist. In the early 60s he was appointed editor of the Trinidadian newspaper *Hustler*. After arriving in Britain he became involved with two of the early English black publications – *Black Dimension* and *Flambeau*. In 1970 Darcus Howe successfully defended himself in the historic *Mangrove Nine* trial, in which he was charged with riotous affray, a charge which had not been brought before a British court for several decades. Darcus became editor of the political and cultural journal *Race Today* in 1974 and in 1985 was made Managing Editor of Race Today Publications, which has so far published 15 titles.

In 1985 Darcus co-founded Bandung Production, the makers of *Bandung File*, a magazine programme for the Asian and Afro-Westindian communities, broadcasted by Channel 4 television. Recipient of 1987 Caribbean Times Award.

HOWELLS, Rosalind Patricia, Ms

is a Community Liaison Officer and Deputy Director in south London. Trained in welfare and counselling she was formally the Deputy High Commissioner for Grenada and an Equal Opportunities Director with Greenwich Commission for Racial Equality. She has also served on the executive of several voluntary bodies including Fullemploy, Family Forum, National Playboard Association and City Parochial. She is vice-chair of the London Voluntary Service Commission and the Afro-Caribbean Education Resource Centre. Ms Howells is also a governor on Avery Hill and Thames Polytechnic Committee of Governors and chair of the Charlton Consortium.

HUNTLEY, Jessica, Ms

is a publisher and bookseller being a Director of Bogle L'Ouverture. She was also responsible for the opening of one of the first black bookshops in Britain – the Walter Rodney Bookshop – and was the first to publish the poet Linton Kwesi Johnson. Ms Huntley is a keen political, cultural and community activist associated with several organisations including the Peter Moses Saturday Supplementary School. She is married with two children of whom one, her daughter Accabree, is a poet.

HUSSAIN, Mian Farrukh, Dr

is a Consultant Psychiatrist at St. Augustine's Hospital in Canterbury, Kent. Born in what is now Pakistan in 1940, Mr Hussain came to Britain in 1967. A member of the British Medical Association, he has previously worked in the psychiatry department of Tooting Bec and Lonsgrove Hospitals. Mr Hussain is a member of the Royal Society of Medicine and is also affiliated to the Society of Clinical Psychiatrists. He is the vice-chair of SCAO and has been honoured by Rotary International for his work in refugee camps in the Philippines. Mr Hussain, who is married with three children, enjoys badminton and chess in his spare time.

INCE, Laurie Theophilus, Mr

was born in Guyana and has lived in Britain since the early 1960s. A martial arts expert, he is Master Founder of the Sam' Tu-Dang Society of Martial Arts. The Sam' Tu-Dang Society has given exhibition performances in Europe, the Caribbean, Canada and the USA.

INDRAKUMAR, Vijayambigai, Ms

is a talented Indian classical dancer, a Choreographer and Teacher who began teaching in Colombo in Sri Lanka, 1972. Since then she has been praised as a highly versatile dancer and choreographer of Indian and South Asian Performing Arts. She has given more than 200 performances, perhaps one of the most noteworthy being her (adaptation) of the Bolshoi Theatre's *Swan Lake* performed in the USSR, India and Sri Lanka. In Britain she has performed, amongst others, for the Bharatiya Vidya Bhavan – London, London Sri Murugan Temple and the Hackney Hindu International Cultural Society. Vijayamigai, who is married to Dr Indrakumar, was described by the *Ceylon Observer* in 1972 as "not only a talented dancer, but she has the right mixture of showmanship, and physical beauty to make her performance a delight."

IRANI, Ruston, Mr

was born in London, of Zoroastrian ancestry, and read Theology at the University of Cambridge, graduating in 1984. He went on to study for a postgraduate diploma in Journalism at City University, London. Between 1985 to 1987 he worked as a Freelance Journalist for BBC Radio, conducting interviews for the World Service's *Caribbean Magazine*. In 1987 he was appointed by BBC television as a Researcher in current affairs, working for the *Kilroy* and *Panorama* programmes. His first book of poems is due to be published in 1988.

JACKMAN, Frank Irvine, JP

a garage inspector, has worked with London Transport since 1958. An active trade unionist, he joined the Labour Party in 1966 and was elected as a councillor in the London Borough of Newham in 1982. He was appointed a Justice of the Peace in 1982. Mr Jackman was born in Barbados in 1931.

JACKSON, Anthony Carl, Mr

is a Music Teacher and Organist. He was educated at the Royal Academy of Music, Downing College, Cambridge, and the University of London, Goldsmith's College. He teaches at the Whitgift School, Croydon, Surrey, and is an organist at the Croydon Parish Church. He is a Fellow of the Royal College of Organists and is a member of the Incorporated Society of Musicians.

JACKSON, Elaine, Ms

is a Lecturer in Nursing and has been a voluntary community worker in Harrow for the last 15 years. Elaine moved from student nurse in 1952 to her present position as Nurse Tutor. During those years she held the posts of Ward Sister, Domiciliary Midwife Teacher, Health Visitor and Nursing Officer. A Justice of the Peace since 1984, Elaine holds membership of several organisations, including Nurses Association of Jamaicans, Caribbean Teachers' Association and Harrow Police Counsultative Committee. Since 1974, Elaine was given permission by the Bishop of Willesden to administer the chalice at Holy Communion.

JAMES, C.L.R., Mr

was born in Trinidad in 1901 and must be considered as one of the leading political figures of the century. His work spans continents and subject matters in a quite unprecedented way. His published works include fiction, political theory, philosophy, historical analysis, cricket, etc. The Caribbean, Africa, Britain, Europe and the USA have all come under his critical gaze. A life-long Marxist, he has also struggled against what he saw as anti-democratic trends within the Marxist tradition. A man who has never forgotten the special oppression endured by the black race, he has followed and participated in the liberation struggle in Africa and of the African diaspora all his life. In 1960 he went to Ghana to work with Kwame Nkrumah. His analysis of the Haitian revolution led by Toussaint L'Ouverture, which led to the creation of the first black republic in history, *The Black Jacobins* is unanimously regarded as a classic. Since 1981 he has lived on Brixton's 'Frontline' where he continues to be involved, passing on his wealth of knowledge and experience to new generations of strugglers. In 1987 he received the *Caribbean Times* Award and in 1988 he was honoured by the government of Trinidad and Tobago.

JAMES, Valda Louise, Cllr

represents Highview Ward in the London Borough of Islington for the Labour Party. Born in Jamaica in 1927 and resident in Britain since 1961, Valda James worked in the fields of catering and dress-making before taking up her present position as a Community Nursing Auxiliary with the Bloomsbury Health Authority. In May 1986 she became the first black woman to be elected to Islington Council. She was not entirely new to the work because for two previous years she had been a co-opted member of the Development and Planning and Women's Committees. Cllr James is an active member of the tenants' association where she lives in Finsbury and is the only black governor at three local primary schools. She currently holds the position of Deputy Mayor of Islington. Her main concern as a councillor is the continuing fight against housing and health service cuts. Since her divorce in 1971 she has brought up her six children alone and is now the proud grandmother of five grandchildren. Most of Cllr James' work is concerned with the social services, dealing particularly with children.

JAMU, Amrik Singh, Mr

is a supervisor at the Ford Motor Company Ltd, Dagenham, Essex. He was born in Jawana-Wala-Lyallpur, Punjab, India in October 1937 and obtained a B.Sc. in Agriculture from Khalsa College in Amritsar in 1959. He became an Agricultural Inspector in Punjab in 1960 before migrating to England in 1966. He joined the Ford Motor Company in 1970 and became a supervisor seven years later. Jamu joined the Labour Party in 1976, and since then has been an active member of the River Ward. A married man, he was awarded a BEM (British Empire Medal) in 1986.

JASSAR, Sham Singh, Cllr

represents Hounslow Central Ward in the London Borough of Hounslow for the Labour Party. Born in India in 1938 and resident in Britain since 1968, Sham Singh Jassar graduated from Punjab University in India with a Masters degree in Economics and taught for a number of years at two secondary schools. After arriving in Britain he worked in the Customs Department before joining the Post Office where he is now a Postal Officer. An active trade unionist, Sham Jassar has been an executive member and organiser of his district of the UCW (Union of Communication Workers). In 1972 he joined the Labour Party and has served as representative of Hounslow Central Ward in the Constituency Labour Party and held the position of vice-chair and executive committee member for the last two years. Elected as a councillor in May 1986, Sham Jassar is vice-chair of the Education Committee and serves on the Finance, Employment and Police Liaison Committees. He is also the Deputy Chief Whip on the Executive Committee. Cllr Jassar is a member of his local Law Centre and Hounslow Community Relations Council.

JAVED, Muhammed, Cllr

represents Loxford Ward in the London Borough of Redbridge for the Labour Party. Born in Pakistan in 1951 and resident in Britain since 1967, Muhammed Javed studied Social Sciences with the Open University, has a Housing diploma from Hackney College and is a member of the Institute of Housing. He is currently employed full time as a Housing Officer and continues this special interest in his council work. A committed member of the Labour Party, Muhammed Javed was Secretary of the Ilford South Labour Party from 1980 to 1982 and is presently serving as Secretary of the Redbridge Labour Group. He has been vice-president of the Pakistan Welfare Association and an executive member of Redbridge Community Relations Council. First elected as a councillor in 1982, Muhammed Javed is spokesperson both on the Highways Committee and the Housing Committee and serves on the Grants and the Environmental Health Committees. His main concerns are with housing and transportation. He wants to encourage the council to fund more Housing Associations and has been a strong campaigner against the closure of local bus routes. Cllr Javed is married with children and serves as a school governor.

JEFFERY, Pansy, Ms

is organiser of the Community Service of the Citizens Advice Bureau in Kensington. A trained Nurse, Pansy has worked as a Sister with the National Temperance Hospital, a Health Visitor at the Kentish Town Health Centre and a Health Education Specialist in Brent. She is a founder member of the Pepper Pot Club for senior Westindian citizens and of the North Kensington Law Centre, the first law centre in England, the Notting Hill Housing Trust and also holds membership of various associations including the Royal Commonwealth Society and Woman of the Year Association. Pansy received an award in the Queen's Jubilee Honours in 1977 and received a *Caribbean Times* Award in 1985.

JOHNSON, Amryl, Ms,

is a writer and lecturer who was born in Trinidad. She is well known for her poetry as well as her works on her early life in the Caribbean. As a poet she has travelled around Britain, assisting pupils in schools with their creative writing. Her latest book, *Sequins for a Ragged Hem*, has just been published by Virago and quickly climbed into the Top Ten Book list. Her previous works include *Watchers and Seekers* (Womens' Press), and *With a Poets Eye* (Tate Gallery Publication). She is currently working on her first novel. Amryl Johnson lives in Coventry.

JOHNSON, Nkechi B. Ms

is a professional Social Worker. She is founder of the African Women's Welfare Association, founder and President of the Brent African Women's Council and founder of Brent African Youth Organisation and President of Brent African Action Group. Her interests revolve around promoting the welfare and justice of Africans in Brent, particularly of African women and their children. She has two children.

JOHSI, Nimmi, Ms

is a well known Broadcaster and Radio Presenter. She has won many awards for her radio work and linguistic abilities. Many people will know her as an author following the successful publication of a cookery book and her series on food which was broadcast on LBC radio. Nimmi Joshi is currently a presenter on *Sangeet Sarita* on Mercia Sound and is also the presenter for *Jhankar* on Beacon Radio. Nimmi is married and resides in Birmingham.

JOSEPH, Bertha, Cllr

is one of the Labour Party's representatives on the London Borough of Brent. She is the present chair of the Leisure Services Committee, being the first black woman to hold that position. Before becoming a councillor she had a long history of community work. In 1977 she became secretary to the Carnival and Arts Committee and from 1981-84 she was secretary of the Stonebridge Ward Labour Party. Bertha Joseph has two sons and says that her ambition is to enter parliament, either in Britain or the Caribbean.

JOSHI, Suresh, B.Sc., M.B.K.S., Mr

produced the first Asian programme on ILR radio and was also the first newscaster to present regular bulletins in Hindustani. A well-known Broadcaster, he is also an accomplished Radio Presenter. Suresh is responsible for the highly acclaimed *Geet Mala* on LBC Radio and *Jhankar* on Beacon Radio. He was named radio personality of the year by the Asian Listeners and Viewers Association for both 1983 and 1984/85. He is also the recipient of the Co-op Award in 1982 for Asian topics on Beacon Radio. Suresh does not confine his activities to radio, he is the ITN News Correspondent for Sri Lankan affairs and is also a member of the Independent Producers Association for Channel 4. Suresh Joshi is married and lives in Birmingham.

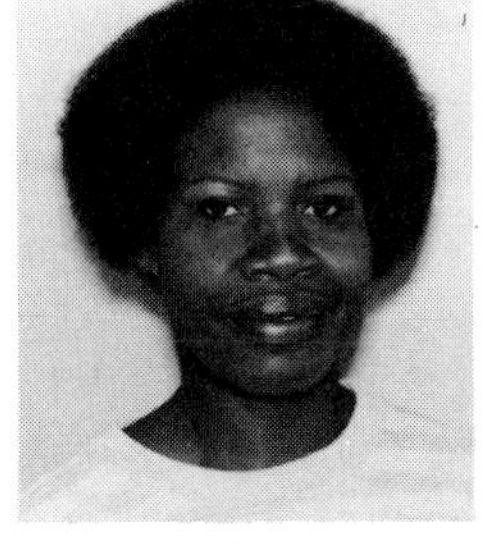

JORSLING, Judy, Cllr

represents Custom House and Silvertown Ward in the London Borough of Newham for the Labour Party. Born in 1949 and elected as a councillor in May 1986, Judy Jorsling is currently chair of the Docklands Joint Sub-Committee and chair of the Policy and Resources, Planning and Development and Housing Committees.

KABIR, Mahmuda, Ph.D. M.A., M.S.C., Dr,

is a Local Government Official with the Social Services Department. She formerly worked as a Lecturer and Senior Social Worker before her current employment. Exceedingly active in community affairs, Ms Kabir is treasurer of the Bangladesh Women's Association (UK), secretary of the Asian Forum and member of both the Bangladesh Centre and the South London Bangladesh Association. Among her ambitions she lists a desire to be a 'successful mother to her two sons', to establish herself as a writer and to serve the community overall on a larger level.

KALICHARAN, Neville, Mr

a Travel Agent and active community worker, was born in Guyana on April 17, 1930. In Guyana he was a popular musician and singer running the Indian Hotshots Orchestra, hosting programmes on local radio stations, and issuing records. He was badly injured during riots in 1963 and was flown to Moorfields Hospital for treatment. Continuing both his music and his penchant for community work in Britain, Neville Kalicharan formed the Maha Sabha (London) – a religious and social organisation which is still active. He also runs a cricket team and organises coach outings. Until 1978 he worked as a Civil Servant in the British Museum and then set up in the travel business. Neville Kalicharan is now the proprietor of Skyglobe Travel, based in Walthamstow, north east London.

KALYAN, Chaman, Cllr

represents Delapre Ward on Northampton County Council for the Labour Party. He was born in Punjab, India, and graduated from Punjab University. Since he settled in Britain he has been involved in the Trade Union and Labour movements. Cllr Kalyan is a member of the Education, Planning and Transportation committees, and is also shadow spokesperson for the Careers Services Advisory Sub-Committee. A shop steward for two years for the 5/83 Branch of the TGWU (Transport and General Workers' Union), he was also chair of the Northampton South Constituency Labour Party in 1981 and chair of the Northampton District Labour Party in 1982. He was also the National Delegate at the annual Labour Party Conference in 1981 and has been chair of Northampton Council for Community Relations since 1984 and a member of Northamptonshire Family Practitioner Committee since 1985. He serves on the Executive Committee of the Council for Voluntary Service of Northampton District and County Council. Cllr Kalyan is a governor of Nene College Upper School and Delapre Middle School in Northampton.

KANODIA, Jai Prakash, Dr

is a GP. Born in India in 1943 he came to Britain in July 1968. He is a member of the British and Indian Medical Associations and the Overseas Doctors Association. He was secretary of the Indian Medical Association, 1969-79. He hopes one day to orchestrate a project which will facilitate more 'good hospitals' in India. Dr Kanodia, who enjoys antique collecting and restoration in his spare time, is married with three children.

KANWAL, Harbans Singh, Cllr

represents Cranford Ward in the London Borough of Hounslow for the Labour Party. Born in India and resident in Britain since the 1960s, Cllr Kanwal now owns and manages an hotel, after being a proprietor of a newsagent's shop and an employee with British Airways. Educated in India, he obtained a B.A. degree. Cllr Kanwal was first elected in 1982. His main concerns lie with the Asian community with particular emphasis on the elderly, welfare and education. He has always been heavily involved in community development and at present is an executive committee member of the Indian Workers' Association (Southall) and of the Indian Social and Welfare Society, as well as being a member of Hounslow Community Relations Council. One of Cllr Kanwal's latest projects is a day centre for the Asian elderly and more sheltered accommodation in the borough. He is married with no children.

KAPOOR, Sukhbir Singh, Dr

is the Director Principal of Khalsa College, London, since 1984. He is the chair of the Board of Studies BTEC Higher National Awards, at the Faculty of Accounting and Finance London Polytechnic. In 1966-68 he was the president of the Indian Association (Glasgow) and since 1970 has been the secretary general of the Indo-Scottish Friendship Club. Mr Kapoor is the author of several books including a few on accounting, economics and Sikh history, as well as research articles in several British Accounting journals.

KARADIA, Chotu, Mr

a Media Consultant, was born in India in 1936 and grew up in Kenya. He has worked as a Journalist on newspapers in Kenya, India and Britain. He was a member of the India Press Council and one of the founding Editors of the OPEC News Agency in Vienna. He holds a B.A. Degree in International Relations from Sussex University.

KARIM, Ashraf, Mr

is a senior partner in the firm of Karim Laxman Solicitors. He is also an executive member and legal advisor of Black Rights (UK). Mr Karim, who was a founding member of the Society of Black Lawyers, is also the chair of the steering committee of the Asian Lawyers Conference, 1988. He would like to see an increase in the number of black and ethnic minority people joining the legal profession, taking senior positions in the Bar and the Law Society. Mr Karim is a member of the Law Society and of the Camden Chamber of Commerce. He is married with two children.

KARIM, Talal, Cllr

was born on December 5, 1953. He is a graduate of the University of Warwick and has a B.A. in Politics. Cllr Talal was first elected to Islington Borough Council in May 1982 and at various times has served on a number of key committees. He is the former chair of Labour Party Black Sections in Islington. An active trades unionist Talal Karim has been a delegate to national union conferences. He is currently employed by the London Borough of Haringey to work in the Community Advice section. His hobbies include reading, travelling, music, cooking and football.

KATHIRAVELOE, Indra Kumar, Dr

is a Registrar in Psychiatry and a specialist in acupunture. He has a Diploma of Membership in Acupuncture, is a Fellow of the International Laser Therapy Association, and an overseas member of the Scandinavian Acupuncture Foundation. Dr Indra Kumar is currently executive director of Vijayanarthanalaya (Academy of Indian Arts, UK). He won the Sri Lanka President's Sahitya (Literary) Award for writing the book *From Earth to Space*, written in Tamil in 1972. He is married to Vijayambigai, an Indian dancer, Choreographer and Dance Teacher of international fame.

KAUSHAL, Jagdish Mitra, Dr

was born in India. After obtaining a medical degree from Banaras Hindu University he arrived in Britain in 1966. He worked for four years as a Research Officer at the National Hospital. After his resignation, he started the first Hindi Magazine *Amar Deep*, a move which was appreciatively acknowledged by several MPs in the Indian Parliament. Mr Kaushal is the president of the Hindi Kendra (UK) and the Hindi Mission (UK). He is also the general secretary of Hindi Sahitya Sabha (UK).

KHAIRA, Ram Singh, Mr

is the managing director of Golden Finance Ltd. He came to Britain in 1965 and three years later started a business in travel, insurance and brokerage. After this was sold in 1983 he founded Golden Finance Ltd. Previously a governor at Handsworth Technical College in Birmingham Mr Singh has been the president of the Federation of Indian Organisations since 1976. He is also a trustee of the Asian Traders Association. Mr Singh who enjoys reading and social activities in his spare time is married with four children.

KHAN, Imran Ahmad Niazi, Mr

a world class cricketer known both for his right hand bat and as a right arm fast bowler, he is considered one of the best all-rounders in the sport. He is the current captain of the Pakistan Test side. Born on November 25, 1952 in Lahore, Pakistan, Imran Khan is single. He was educated at Keeble College, Oxford, where he obtained a B.A. in Politics and Economics. He made his debut for Lahore A (1969-70) and for Worcestershire in 1971. In the same year he won an Oxford Cricket Blue and made his Test debut in the same year. He was a Test Captain for the first time, 1982 to 1983. Imran Khan has scored over 25 first class centuries and over 65 five wicket innings. He has played world series cricket and in the MCC Centenary match at Lord's in 1987. His interests include squash, swimming and listening to eastern and western music. A boyhood injury prevents the full extension of his left arm.

KHAN, Lily, Ms

was born in Baghdad, Iraq, in 1926. She came to Britain from Dakkar, Senegal, in 1971. She is an Education Co-ordinator with the Homeless Families Project of the Inner London Education Authority. Ms Khan is also a commissioner for the Commission for Racial Equality, a member of the BBC *Asian Magazine*, and of Save the Children Fund. In 1968 she won the Gold Medal for her 'outstanding contribution to education' in Pakistan. Ms Khan, who is hoping to write a book about her experiences in coping with the British system, is the mother of two daughters. She enjoys embroidery, knitting, travelling and tapestry in her spare time.

KHAN, Mohammed, Cllr

represents Grovegreen Ward in the London Borough of Waltham Forest for the Labour Party. Born in India in 1936, Mohammed Khan qualified as an Accountant in Gujarat, India, before coming to Britain where he worked in the same field for a number of years. He now runs a sub-post office with his wife in Leytonstone. Cllr Khan joined the Labour Party in 1968 believing it to be the only political party that was at least thinking about the black community. He was elected Mayor of Waltham Forest in May 1986. Actively involved with the Asian community in the borough for a number of years, Cllr Khan was instrumental in setting up the local Community Relations Council and a number of religious and community organisations. He is also the chair of the Police Committee and president of the Indian Muslim Federation which is an organisation campaigning for the rights of Muslim people in India.

KHAN, Mahmood Shafi, M.A., LL.B., D.I.L.L., M.W.I., Mr

was born in India in 1928. He came to Britain in 1964 and today works as a Local Government Officer with the London Borough of Lewisham. He was formerly attached to the solicitors J. Esner and Co. and was a Community Relations Officer in Luton, Beds., before his current appointment. He is a founder member of several institutions and is a member of the Institute of Welfare Officers, the Institute of Legal Executives and the Institute of Training and Development. Mr Khan, who is married with two children, has recently completed an M.A. in Social Policy and Public Administration.

KHAN-CHEEMA, Mohammed Akram, M. Phil., Mr

is a member of the Directorate of Educational Services (Bradford) where he is one of three Senior Advisors. His responsibilities include the preparation and administration of specialist curricula as well as direct responsibility for a number of individual schools and institutions. He is further expected to carry management responsibilities for a team of general advisors within the middle school sector. Mr Khan-Cheema, who holds a diploma in the Advanced Study of Education and a degree of Master of Philosophy, is a member of the Union of Muslim Organisations (UK and Eire), the Council of Mosques (UK and Eire) and since 1986 has been the chair of the National Association of Local Education Authorities Advisory Officers. He is married with three children.

KHANGURA, Jagpal Singh, Cllr

represents Cranford Ward in the London Borough of Hounslow for the Labour Party. Born in India and resident in Britain since 1963, Cllr Khangura has a Bachelor of Arts degree in English and Politics and works as a Hotel Consultant. A Labour Party member for over twelve years and a councillor since May 1986, his main interests in the borough are with housing and issues affecting the ethnic minorities. Cllr Khangura has been a member of the Indian Workers Association (Southall) since 1968, and vice-president since 1981. He has been vice-chair of Hounslow Community Relations Council for a period of five years. Cllr Khangura's hobbies include walking his dog and gardening.

KHANNA, Balraj, Mr

a painter and novelist, is the chair of the Indian Arts Council (UK). He was born in India in 1940 and has lived in both India and France. He worked as a foreign correspondent during the India-Pakistan War of 1971-72 and in the following year lectured on Indian Art and Culture for the Commonwealth Institute. His work has been exhibited in India, Britain, France, and the USA, including at the Punjab University, the Serpentine, London, the Galerie Transposition-Paris, and the Herbert Benevy Gallery in New York. His work has been described as 'refining...flowing...sophisticated illusion.' He was awarded the Mahatma Gandhi Prize for Fiction by the Greater London Council for his unpublished novel *Partition* in 1985.

KHOTE, Hajra, Cllr

represents Northwold Ward in the London Borough of Hackney for the Labour Party. Born in South Africa and resident in Britain since 1976, Hajra Khote began her career as a community worker in South Africa, and in Britain, she has worked for a number of community groups. She is currently chair of the Hackney Muslim Women's Project and has been active in campaigns against rate-capping. Cllr Khote was elected in May 1986. One of her main aims is to remedy the under-representation of black people and women in the borough Council. She is currently chair of the council's Community Development Committee and vice-chair of the Social Services Committee.

KIHORO, Wanjiru, Ms

studied Economics at Columbia University, New York, and has just completed an M.A. in Development Studies at Leeds University. Since 1984 she has been the Education and Programme Officer of the Africa Centre in London. She has been involved in several organisations engaged in democratic activities and is a member of Akina Mama wa Afrika – an African women's voluntary development organisation. Her interests include film, drama, writing, reading and singing. A mother of three, Ms Kihoro's husband and comrade, Mr Kihoro, has been detained without trial in Kenya since July 1986.

KING, Lloyd, Cllr

represents Westdown Ward in the London Borough of Hackney for the Labour Party. Born in Jamaica in 1949 and resident in Britain since 1965 Lloyd King qualified as an Electrical Engineer before gaining an Honours Degree in Education at the Polytechnic of North London. He is now head of training at Camden Social Services. A member of N.A.L.G.O. (National Association of Local Government Officers) and highly active in local community politics for a number of years, Cllr King is a founder member of the Hackney Education and Development Society (HEADS) where he has spent much time helping black children to cope with their education in schools. He also helped to set up one of the first projects for elderly black people in the London Borough of Hackney. In 1979 he personally spearheaded a campaign for better library facilities and has been involved with building an Afro-Caribbean centre in the borough. He has been chair of Hackney Council for Racial Equality since 1982. Elected as a councillor in May 1986, Lloyd King's main concerns are with equal opportunities in housing, education and the social services.

KIRWAN, Glenda, Ms

is a State Registered Nurse S.R.N. and a National District Nurse. She is also a former Afro-Caribbean Liaison Health Worker. Ms Kirwan was the chair of Hackney Council for Racial Equality, 1986-88, and was an executive member on the same body 1985-86. She is also a main committee member of the Tenants Association within her area. A member of OCSAR, the sickle cell research organisation, Ms Kirwan aspires to continue making a positive contribution to the development of health care amongst ethnic minority people.

KOTECHA, Kishor Champaklal, Mr

LL.B(Hons), M.B.B.G.S., F.B.I.M., F.B.S.C., F.S.C.T., is a Solicitor and Senior Management Consultant based in London. He qualified as one of the youngest fellows of the Society of Commercial Teachers and the British Society of Commerce. His articles have appeared in numerous professional journals and newspapers in England and overseas. In 1982, Mr Kotecha was appointed as an Examiner in Law by the British Society of Commerce. He is a member of the International Bar Association, the Commonwealth Lawyers Association, the International Arbitration Commission and the Union Internationale Des Advocats.

KUMAR, Surjit, Colonel, Retired,

is a Financial Executive with an investment company. Born in India in 1937 he was commissioned as a Second Lieutenant from the Indian Military College in 1958. In 1974 he rose to the rank of Lieut. Colonel but was later to take early retirement. He first arrived in Britain in 1970 but only settled here in 1980. Mr Kumar is a Fellow of the British Institute of Management, holds a Diploma of the Institute of Management Research and Development (India) and is a member of the Royal Commonwealth Society. He won several service medals from the Indian Army and the Silver Medal Literary Award (Punjab University) in 1980. Mr Kumar, who enjoys oil painting, gardening and photography in his spare time, is married with two sons.

LALL, Dharam Bir, Mr

was born in Bannu, Pakistan, and was educated at the University of Calcutta, where he graduated with a B.Sc. in Accountancy. In 1958 he moved to Britain making his career in Finance. Mr Lall is a Fellow of the Institute of Chartered Accountants and an Associate of the Institute of Cost and Management Accountants. He lists his hobbies as golf and reading. He and his family reside in Chigwell, Essex.

LAYNE, Ken Hugh, Cllr

represents High Cross Ward in the London Borough of Haringey for the Labour Party. Born in Barbados and resident in Britain since 1961, Ken Layne is a qualified Building Services Engineer and worked as an Electrician until taking up his present position as a Postal Engineering Officer with the Post Office in 1967. An active voluntary community worker, Cllr Layne was a founder member of the Haringey Community Relations Council and the Caribbean Teachers Association. He also serves as an executive member of the borough's Community Relations Committee. Cllr Layne's main commitment lies in education. He is an executive member of the National Anti-racist Movement in Education (N.A.M.E) and speaks on behalf of the organisation on various educational issues for teachers, community groups, education officers and local authorities. He is also a school governor. A Labour Party member for the last three years and an active trade unionist, he is a committee member and Education Officer for the National Communications Union. Ken Layne was elected as councillor in May 1986 and as well as serving on Haringey's Education Committee he is vice-chair of the Council's Community Affairs Committee. Cllr Layne has lived in Haringey for twenty five years. He is married with two children.

LE-KIN, Ermine, Ms

was born in Trinidad. She has been working in Britain since 1965 as a Social Worker. Her speciality has been childrens' issues and to that end she has served on a number of committees concerned with fostering and adoption, including the working party in 1975 and headed the 'Soul Kids' campaign, 1974 to 1975. The purpose of the 'Soul Kids' Campaign was to encourage black families to adopt and foster black children. At the present time Ermine Le-Kin is Deputy Director of Social Work and Education, for the Inner London Education Authority. She is deeply concerned that black children are suffering because of the cuts in social security allowances and the lack of free school milk and worries that, with the proposed abolition of ILEA, black children will be exposed to greater suffering. Ermine Le-Kin says her greatest achievement was to raise a black child who is now 18 and well adjusted. In her spare time she enjoys making soft furnishings and working with children, through the Thomas Coram Foundation as a Trustee and the National Childrens' Bureaux.

LINTON, Eric Lloyd, BEM, Mr

born in Jamaica in 1928, is a director of MSB Travel and Shipping. He is chair of Coventry West Indians Community Centre; member of the Board of Visitors HM Youth Custody Glen Parva Prison, Leicester; executive member Coventry CRC. Mr Linton was awarded the British Empire Medal (BEM) in 1986.

LONG, Dorman, Cllr

Brent Council leader and Race Relations Adviser to Lambeth Housing. He was born in St. Lucia in 1937 and educated there before settling in the UK in 1960. Worked for London Transport and the Post Office. Cllr Long joined the Labour Party in 1968 and later became secretary and chairman of his local branch of Roundward. His priorities as councillor are to tackle problems caused by a shortage of funds in social services and education. Cllr Long is married with four children and enjoys reading.

LUTHERS, Vibert, Cllr

represents Tooting Ward in the London Borough of Wandsworth for the Labour Party. Born in Guyana in 1932 and resident in Britain since 1952, Vibert Luthers holds a certificate and a diploma in social work and is presently employed as a social worker by Merton Borough Council. He has been a member of the Labour Party since 1956 and also a member of N.A.L.G.O (National Association of Local Government Officers). First elected as a councillor in 1973, he has represented Tooting Ward since then and is currently Labour Party spokesperson for the Housing Improvement Sub-Committee. He has been married for thirty three years, has three adult sons and is a drummer and musician who now only gets time to perform in the odd charity show. He also enjoys boxing, cricket and football.

MCCALLUM, Mavis, Cllr

represents Leabridge Ward in the London Borough of Hackney for the Labour Party. A Child Care Worker in Hackney, Mavis McCallum was elected to the council in May 1986. She has a special interest in the Social Services and wants to see a better representation of black people including women at council level. She is currently vice-chair of the Women's Committee. Cllr McCallum considers herself to be a family woman. She has a son and a daughter.

MCDONALD, Trevor, Mr

was born and educated in the Westindies. He came to England in 1969, to work first for *BBC's World Service* after a broadcasting career in the Westindies, which included working for radio and television as well as writing for newspapers. He joined ITN in 1973 as a general reporter and covered, among other things, Northern Ireland. He was for a time sports correspondent, covering cricket tours of Australia and the sub-continent, before becoming diplomatic correspondent for ITN and travelling throughout the world. In 1982 he joined ITN's Channel Four News as diplomatic correspondent and co-presenter of the award winning programme, and in 1987 he was made diplomatic editor for Channel Four News and weekend news presenter for ITN bulletins. In the last few years he has travelled extensively throughout Europe, America, India, Pakistan, South Korea, the Philippines, Southern Africa and the Soviet Union.

MAGLOIRE, Michael, Cllr

represents Manor Ward in the London Borough of Brent for the Labour Party. Born in St. Lucia in 1948 and resident in Britain since 1965, Michael Magloire is a practising Barrister specialising in criminal and family law, industrial relations and housing law. He joined the Labour Party in 1974 and since then has held most offices at constituency level including those of chair and treasurer of the Brent South Labour Party. First elected to Brent Council in 1982, he is currently chair of the Housing Committee. Cllr Magloire is a member of the Society of Labour Lawyers, a member of the Haldane Society of Socialist Lawyers and is also a member of the St. Lucia Bar.

MAKANJI, Narendra, Cllr

represents Noel Park Ward in the London Borough of Haringey for the Labour Party. Born in Malawi in 1952 and resident in Britain since 1973, Narendra Makanji was brought up in Zimbabwe. He came to Britain to study for a degree in Textile Chemistry at Bradford University. Since graduating he has worked as an Industrial Chemist, a Community Relations Officer, a Project Development Officer with the Greater London Council and is now an Employment Officer with Islington Borough Council. Cllr Makanji first joined the Labour Party in 1975 and has been a general committee and executive committee member of Hornsey and Wood Green Constituency Labour Party. He has been an executive member of the Greater London Labour Party and was national secretary of the Labour Party Black Section (1985-87). An active trades unionist, he was a member of the ASTMS (Association of Scientific and Technical Management Staff) and NALGO (National Association of Local Government Officers) until 1982 when he joined NUPE (National Union of Public Employees). Since joining the Labour Party Narendra Makanji has been in major political campaigns – for anti-racism, peace, jobs, and local democracy. Narendra Makanji has been a councillor in the London Borough of Haringey since 1982. He was secretary of the Labour Group (1985-86). Cllr Makanji's special interests outside the council are with economic development and restructuring the welfare state. He is a member of the Campaign for Nuclear Disarmament (CND).

MAMBU, Yomi, Cllr

represents Rusholme Ward on Manchester City Council for the Labour Party. Born in Sierra Leone and resident in Britain since 1968, Yomi Mambu is a Nurse by profession and has been an active trades unionist for several years. She has held several positions of responsibility in NUPE (National Union of Public Employees) which include: Steward, Health and Safety Representative, Union Delegate to the Central Manchester Constituency Labour Party, Union Delegate to the City Labour Party, to the Divisional Area Committee, and to the Divisional Nurses Advisory Committee. Cllr Mambu was elected as a Labour councillor in 1986. She sits on the Education, Social Services, Equal Opportunities and Race Committees and is also Deputy Chair for Central Manchester Education Sub-Committee. She holds the women's seat on the North West Divisional Council. Cllr Mambu is also governor of two primary schools and of Central Manchester College.

MANDAIR, Tarlok Singh, Mr

a Chartered Accountant, was born in India in 1940. A Fellow of the Institute of Directors (London), he arrived in Britain from Kenya in 1958. He is General Secretary of the India UK (Grays and Southend Branch). From 1971-87 he was a partner in the Tree and Son Chartered Accountant Company and then in the Morrison Stoucham Chartered Accountants. Mr Mandair enjoys sport in his spare time and to this end is vice-president of the London-Indian Hockey Club, the treasurer of Southend Hockey Club and a member of the Essex Hockey Umpire Association. He is married with two children.

MANGAR, George Edward Mr

was born in 1937 in Guyana. He came to Britain in 1959. In Guyana he was a Policeman for three years and later joined the Royal Army Medical Corps for six years. On leaving the Royal Army Medical Corps, Mr Mangar worked in the Department of Orthopaedics at Guy's Hospital, London. Whilst in the Army he obtained a Fellow of the Institute of Technologists in Venereology and is a member of the Royal Society of Health. His spare time activities have included being a Sergeant of the Special Metropolitan Police Constabulary, based at Heathrow Airport. He is now a member of the Board of Prison Visitors at Brixton Prison. Thirteen years ago Mr Mangar established the first Community Relations Council in Wales. He is currently employed as a Grants Officer with the Commission for Racial Equality. He is married with two daughters.

MANGAR, Harold, Mr

is the Director of Black Rights (UK), a position which he has held since October, 1987 when he was seconded from the Commission for Racial Equality. Born in Guyana, Mr Mangar was educated at Central High School. He also obtained a certificate in Industrial Relations and Trade Union Law from the London School of Economics. From 1969 to 1977 he held the position of Conciliation Officer Secretary to the South Metropolitan Conciliation Committee at the Race Relations Board which later became the Commission for Racial Equality. Mr Mangar has been with the Commission for Racial Equality for 10 years and before secondment to Black Rights (UK) he held the position of Senior Projects and Training Officer.

MANI, Sinna, Cllr

represents Crofton Park Ward in the London Borough of Lewisham for the Labour Party. Born in Sri Lanka and resident in Britain since 1960, Sinna Mani is an Economics Teacher and Journalist. He is currently Education Liaison Officer with the Inner London Education Authority (ILEA) and is heavily involved in creating educational and employment opportunities for black people. He is the director of several educational projects. Elected to Lewisham Council in 1985, he is currently vice-chair of the Finance Committee, chair of the Computer Sub-Committee and chair of the Voluntary Sector Committee. Sinna Mani is actively concerned with a number of environmental issues and is an executive member of the Socialist Countryside group and director of the League Against Cruel Sports. He has also held the position of president of the Overseas Indian Association since 1979. Cllr Mani's interests outside work include national liberation, nature conservation, wildlife and animal welfare.

MANKU, Gurdev Singh, Cllr

represents Sandwell Ward on Birmingham City Council for the Labour Party. Born in India in 1948 and resident in Britain since 1966, Gurdev Singh Manku is a Community Advice Worker by profession. He was elected to Birmingham City Council in May 1986. Cllr Manku has been a member of the Labour Party for six years and in that time he has held a number of offices. These include vice-chair of his ward party, treasurer of the ward and Constituency Labour Party and delegate to the Birmingham District Labour Party for four years. He has also taken part in a number of regional conferences. Cllr Manku is involved with local community work in Birmingham and finds that his ability to converse in Punjabi, Urdu, Hindi and Swahili is useful when dealing with the city's multi-racial community. His interests outside council work are sports, music and films.

MARGAI, Mameisia, Cllr

represents South Defoe Ward in the London Borough of Hackney for the Labour Party. Resident in Britain since 1968, Mameisia Margai studied midwifery in Dublin, Ireland, and is now a Community Worker in Hackney where she has lived for most of the twenty years she has spent in Britain. Elected as a councillor in the May 1986 elections, Cllr Margai has a keen interest in child care, promoting the role of women in society, housing and economic development. She currently holds the position of chair of the Race Relations Committee. Cllr Margai is married with two children.

the twenty years she has spent in Britain. Elected as a councillor in the May 1986 elections, Cllr Margai has a keen interest in child care, promoting the role of women in society, housing and economic development. She currently holds the position of chair of the Race Relations Committee. Cllr Margai is married with two children.

MARK, Constance, Ms

popularly known as 'Connie' is a retired Medical Secretary. She was born in Kingston, Jamaica, 63 years ago. After leaving college she enlisted in the Forces and was attached to the Royal Army Medical Corps. After working there for ten years she was awarded the War Medal. Although now retired Connie keeps busy through tutoring in Caribbean history, cooking and teaching Caribbean dancing in schools. Among the many community associations she is involved in are the British Caribbean Association, the Anti-Racist Committee, Founder Friends of Mary Seacole and the Westindian Ex-Servicemens' Association. Connie is at present working on her first book "Experiences of a black girl in a White Army" and is preparing an exhibition of her own photographs.

MARTIN, Abdul, Mr

is an Information Officer at the Commission for Racial Equality (CRE). Born in what is now Bangladesh in 1924 he was educated and obtained his degree at Dacca University. He worked as the correspondent of an Indian news agency in Dacca before coming to Britain in 1960 as a correspondent of a Bengali newspaper – *Azad*. In 1967 he joined the National Committee for Commonwealth Immigrants as Assistant Information Officer and retained this post when the National Committee was absorbed into the CRC. He was later promoted to Press and Information Officer. Mr Martin enjoys photography in his spare time and is also the author of three books including a collection of short stories.

MARTINDALE, Kenneth Gaspar, Cllr

represents Wormholt Ward in the London Borough of Hammersmith & Fulham for the Labour Party. Born in St. Lucia and resident in Britain since 1958, Kenneth Martindale has been involved in community work since his arrival and was a Community Development Worker in Notting Hill for ten years and a Child Care Officer in Ealing from 1975-79. He is currently working as a self-employed Photographer but finds time to continue his community involvement. An active participant in borough affairs, he is a member of Hammersmith & Fulham Community Relations Council, the area Youth Committee and has been an active organiser and co-ordinator for the borough's Caribbean Focus since 1985. He was also a founder member of the Black People's Information Centre based in Ladbroke Grove and the Dashiki Housing Association in 1973. A councillor since May 1986, he is chair of the Ethnic Minorities Committee and a member of the Planning and Applications, Leisure and Recreations, Social Services and Community Organisations Support Committees. His special interests are in equal opportunities and economic development and his various leisure activities include travel and sport.

MARTIN-DEL-BURGO, Patricia Ms

was born in Trinidad on May 14, 1942. A Psychiatric Nursing Sister, Patricia Martin-del-Burgo had been actively nursing for ten years (1962-72). In 1964 she was awarded a prize for the Theory and Practice of Nursing. She has also held the position of activator of the Aylesbury Vale Council for Racial Equality and as part-time voluntary worker for various agencies. She is now closely involved in community projects and is member of such associations as Aylesbury United Westindian Association, and Aylesbury Professional and Business Women's Group. Ms Martin-del-Burgo is also the present co-ordinator of Aylesbury "Caribbean Focus '86". Much of her time is spent writing poetry and a book on the Westindian Community in Aylesbury.

MASSEY, Reginald, Mr

Author and Journalist, is current editor of *An Indian Bookworm's Journal*, which is published quarterly by the Institute of Indian Studies. His journalistic work spans two continents. In India he worked as a journalist and here in Britain is continuing in that mould whilst expanding into film-making where he is the producer of *Bangladesh I Love You* starring Muhammed Ali, *The Greatest*. Reginald Massey is a member of the National Union of Journalists (NUJ) and a Fellow of the Royal Society of Arts. He is also the author of several books which are a mixture of poetry, fiction, academic study and travel.

MATHAROO, Nrinder Singh, Cllr

represents Lloyd Park Ward in the London Borough of Waltham Forest for the Labour Party. Born in India in 1936 and resident in Britain since 1964, Nrinder Singh Matharoo obtained his post graduate diploma in Primary Education at Leeds University in 1967 and since then has been teaching. As head of Mathematics and Computers at a school in Newham, east London, he is actively involved with his union and with the school governing body. He is also secretary of his local Asian Youths and Parents Association. Cllr Matharoo has been a member of the Labour Party for fourteen years, is vice-chair of Chingford Constituency Labour Party (CLP), the Fund Raising Committee, and executive member of the Local Government Committee. He is also Chingford's delegate to the Waltham Forest Community Relations Council. He is chair of the Race Relations Committee as well as being active on a number of other boards and committees. A resident of Waltham Forest for twelve years, Cllr Matharoo is married with three daughters.

MAVI, Dilbagh Singh, Mr

was born in Fateh Garh, Punjab, on February 2 1936. He is a Home/School Liaison Officer employed by the Birmingham Education Authority and is married with two sons. Mr Mavi acquired two degrees at Punjab University and subsequently did post-graduate teacher training at Nottingham University. A councillor in Walsall from 1974-76 and a commissioner of the Commission for Racial Equality from 1978-84, from 1982-84 he also chaired the Regional Committee on Race Relations in the West Midlands and has chaired the West Midlands region of the Sikh Study Circle since 1970. He arrived in Britain in May 1965.

MEERAN, Gulam, Mr

is one of the leading practioners at the Bar, specialising in racial discrimination cases. He was previously employed at the Commission for Racial Equality as a Principal Officer in charge of the Complaints Section. In 1983 he was promoted to head the Directorate of Education, Housing and Services Division, a position which he held until he was called to the Bar in 1986. Gulam Meeran was a founder member of Black Rights (UK) and was a pioneer in ensuring that black solicitors and barristers became involved in fighting race discrimination cases. He holds degrees from Manchester University and the London School of Economics. He is a member of the Society of Black Lawyers, a school governor and a Justice of the Peace in Kingston, Surrey.

MELVILLE, Pauline, Ms

was born in Guyana and is an Actress by profession. She studied at Brunel University, obtaining an honours degree in Psychology, Sociology and Economics in 1974, and a postgraduate certificate in Education from London University in 1975. Between 1966 and 1970 she was a Drama Lecturer in Adult Education for the Inner London Education Authority (ILEA), and an Assistant Director in the National Theatre. She has also worked with the Sistren Theatre Company in Jamaica. Pauline Melville's special interest is in Caribbean theatre, its origin and development, as well as in the folk myths of the region.

MENDEZ, Greta, Ms

was born in Trinidad and Tobago. In 1972 she was awarded a Trinidad and Tobago government scholarship to study at the London School of Contemporary Dance. Greta Mendez has also studied choreography. She has taught dance at Middlesex Polytechnic, the National Youth Festival of Dance and in Athens, Greece. As a performer her work includes Scottish Ballet Moveable Workshop, November 1976-1977, Samson and Delilah Royal Opera House, Covent Garden, London. From 1984 to 1985 Greta Mendez was the Carnival Co-ordinator for the Roundhouse. She is currently director of the Battimal Theatre Company.

MENON, Kuttan, Mr

a Barrister, is part-time chair of the Social Security Tribunal. Formerly the Principal Complaints Officer at the Commission for Racial Equality (CRE) Mr Menon has had wide experience in issues of race discrimination, employment, immigration, crime, personal injuries, civil liberties, medical negligence and public law cases. He is also a member of the Haldane Society of Socialist Lawyers and of the Society of Black Lawyers.

MENZIES, Vida, Ms

a prominent female member of the Afro-Caribbean community in Britain. She is the president of the Association of Jamaicans (UK) and is also involved in various other community organisations. Ms Menzies, who was born in Jamaica, settled in Britain 20 years ago. She was awarded the First Order of Distinction by the Jamaican government in recognition of her voluntary services for the country. She also received a *Caribbean Times* Award in 1983. She lists her love of people, reading and theatre as her main interests.

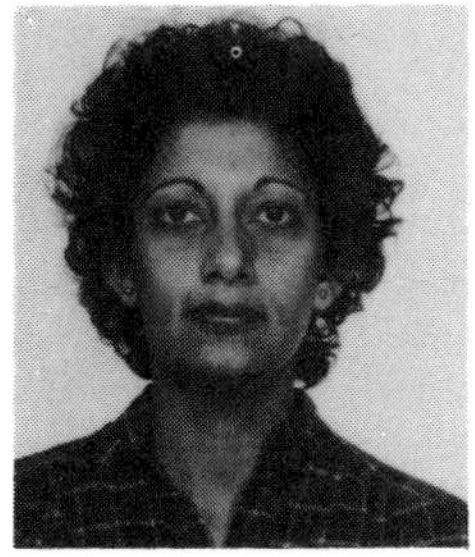

MINHAS, Rehana, (B.A. Hons. PGCE), Ms

an Educationalist is at present the Director of the Inner London Education Authority (ILEA) Centre for Urban Education Studies. She arrived in Britain from Uganda in 1972. In 1978 she became a social sciences Teacher at Skinner Company's School, Hackney, and was involved in the establishment of the school's anti-racist policy. Rehana Minhas was vice-president of the National Union of Teachers in 1986 and chair of the Independent Inquiry into the Recruitment and Promotion of Ethnic Minority Teachers in Ealing. She is also the author of several publications including *"An Introduction to ILEA Handbook on Classroom Practice Primary/Secondary Matters"* and is a co-author of *"Just a Bunch of Girls"* and has published several reviews in educational journals.

MITCHELL, Brenton B. Mr

was born in Jamaica. He worked as a businessman from 1954 to 1972 before setting up practice as a Barrister-at-Law. Mr Mitchell has served on many public bodies and black organisations. They include the Parole Board (1982-85), Police Complaints Board (1982-85), Rent Tribunal (1984), Westindian Standing Conference, Society of Black Lawyers, Joint Committee Against Racialism, and the High Cross Youth Hostel Management Committee. He is a member of the British Society of Criminology and the Institute of Marketing.

MOGHAL, Manzoor Elahi, Mr

a Financial Consultant, was born in Pakistan in 1936. He was educated at the Punjab University and arrived in Britain from Uganda in 1972. He is a former vice-president of the Uganda Evacuees Association and chair of Leicestershire County Council's Race Relations Committee. He was an SDP parliamentary candidate for Bradford West in 1987 and in the current (1987-88) session is vice-chair of Leicestershire County Council Race Relations Committee. Mr Moghal was a recipient of the Uganda Independence Medal in 1962. He is married with three children.

MOGHAL, Nasrullah Khan, Cllr

represents Longsight Ward on Manchester City Council for the Labour Party. Born in Pakistan in 1947 and resident in Britain since 1966, Nasrullah Khan Moghal spent his formative years living with his parents in Kenya before returning to study for a short time in Pakistan. He passed three 'A' levels at Loughborough Technical College in Britain and then graduated from Manchester University in 1970 with an honours degree in Engineering. He is currently employed as a Software Quality Consultant with ICI in Manchester. An active trades unionist, he has been a member of ASTMS (Association of Scientific and Technical Management Staff) now MSF (Manufacturing, Science, Finance) for the last eleven years and has served as both a representative and convenor. He has played an active role in negotiations with management over a number of issues such as health and safety and relocation packages. Since leaving school Cllr Moghal has been involved in community work and in Manchester has helped to establish a number of group facilities for the Asian community with particular emphasis on support for the elderly and on the cultural and educational needs of the young. He is also secretary of the Pakistan Community Centre in Longsight. Cllr Moghal is a firm supporter of the Manchester Labour Party and has been instrumental in formulating policies in the area of anti-racism, equal opportunities and police accountability. Cllr Moghal was elected to Manchester City Council in May 1986 and is deputy-chair of the Equal Opportunities Committee. He is married with one daughter.

MOHAN, Man, Cllr, Dr

represents the Grinling Gibbons Ward in the London Borough of Lewisham for the Labour Party. Born in India and resident in Britain since 1954, Dr Man Mohan is an eminent sociologist. He has worked for the United Nations in New York and has lectured at the University of the Westindies in Trinidad and also in Singapore. He is currently at the University of Oxford. Dr Mohan is a member of the National Committee of Black Sections and convenor of the Deptford Constituency Labour Party Black Section. He aims to encourage black political participation and active involvement on a much larger scale both locally and nationally. A councillor in the London Borough of Lewisham since May 1986, Cllr Mohan is mainly concerned with the problems of housing, immigration and economic development. He is presently examining ways of encouraging businesses to move into his Deptford area and create jobs. Cllr Mohan is eager to be seen working for the development of the whole community with equal emphasis on all disadvantaged groups.

MOHINDRA, Sunil, Mr

is a Solicitor of Indian origin and was born in Kenya. He came to Britain in 1967 and obtained a B.Sc. in Physics and an A.R.C. at Imperial College, London University. In 1978 he qualified as a Solicitor receiving distinctions in parts 1 and 2 of the Law Society Finals. In 1980 he set up his own practice of solicitors in Manchester. The former vice-president of the Indian Association, Manchester, Mr Mohindra is a current member of the Manchester Law Society Council and is chair of the Manchester Society of Ethnic Lawyers.

MOODIE, Hyacinth Maud, SRN, SCM, Ms

is Director/Founder of the Caribbean Progressive Association and the present chair of OSCAR, the sickle cell research organisation. In the past she has worked as a Youth Officer Researcher in the adoption society as well as a SRN and Midwife. She is currently involved in a range of voluntary work mainly in the field of community ventures such as organising travel clubs, a senior citizens club and an advisory centre. In 1977 she received the Badge of Honour for meritorious services (Jamaica), the *Caribbean Times* Award in 1986 and the Asian Artist Award for Waltham Forest in 1986.

MOODLEY, Parimala, Ms

a Psychiatrist and Senior Registrar at the Maudsley and Bethlem Royal Hospitals. She is also an executive member of the Transcultural Psychiatry Society and a member of the Special Committee of the Royal College of Psychiatry on psychiatric practice and training in British multi-ethnic society. She is a consultant at the Fanon Day Centre for blacks in Britain. Parimala Moodley wishes to further her career in psychiatry with a particular interest in the needs of, and service delivery to, black people and other ethnic minorities in Britain.

MORRIS, William (Bill), Mr

was born in Jamaica in 1938. Bill Morris has been extremely active in the Labour and Trades Union Movements. He was one of the first black trades union officials and previously worked as the Area Organiser for the Transport and General Workers' Union (T&GWU) in Nottingham. He was subsequently promoted to become Head of Passenger Services nationally on the retirement of Alex Kitson, Bill Morris was elected Deputy General Secretary of the (T&GWU). He is a former Commission for Racial Equality Commissioner. In 1988 Bill Morris was the union's representative on the TUC General Council. Mr Morris is married and lives with his wife in Hertfordshire.

MORRISON, Lionel, Mr

was born in Johannesburg, South Africa. Lionel Morrison became an activist in the nationalist movement from an early age. He stood trial with Chief Albert Luthuli, Nelson Mandela and 153 other leaders in the famous treason trial. Mr Morrison was later incarcerated for his participation in the campaign against the pass laws. He began his journalistic career in South Africa and formed the South African Union of Journalists, a multi-racial journalists' organisation. He escaped from South Africa in 1960, visiting the socialist countries on the invitation of various journalist unions and became the African Secretary of the Afro-Asian Journalists' Association stationed in Djarkata, Indonesia for the next seven years. He travelled extensively in Africa, Asia, Europe and Latin America. In Britain where he settled from 1969, he worked for most Fleet Street papers while helping to launch papers of the black community such as *Westindian World*. Currently employed as the Principal Information Officer for the CRE, Mr Morrison is chair of the Trustees/Management of the Tiverton Youth and Community Centre. In 1987/88 Mr Morrison was elected as the first black president of the National Union of Journalists (NUJ).

MTHETHWA, Jim, Cllr

represents Peckham on the Inner London Education Authority (ILEA) for the Labour Party. Born in Zimbabwe and resident in Britain since 1966, Jim Mthethwa is a Teacher by profession and taught for ten years in Zimbabwe and Zambia. He has a B.A. Honours degree in Sociology and Education from Middlesex Polytechnic, a M.A. degree in Government and Politics from the City of London Polytechnic and a Certificate of Education. He worked for fourteen years in the British Civil Service before taking early retirement in 1984. He is a member of the Socialist Education Association, treasurer for Southwark Council for Community Relations and a member of the Consumer Council. First co-opted onto the Ethnic Minorities Committee of the Inner London Education Authority (ILEA) in 1983, he became an elected member in May 1986. He is Deputy Chief Whip of the Majority Party and active on a number of committees. He is also an authorised member for Rural and Urban (Education) Centres and for Community and Voluntary Initiatives within the inner London area. Cllr Mthethwa is married with children. In his spare time he enjoys reading and study of African languages.

MUKHERJEE, Tara Kumar, Mr

was born on December 20 1923. He came to Britain in 1949. He is married with one son and a daughter and currently lives in Brentwood, Essex. He is a Branch Manager of the Guardian Royal Exchange PFM. Mr Mukherjee has been president of the Confederation of Indian Organisations (UK) since 1975.

MULLA, Abdul Gafoor, Cllr

represents Leabridge Ward in the London Borough of Hackney for the Labour Party. Born in India, Abdul Mulla has lived for the past twenty years in Hackney. As councillor he is committed to fight racism and to strive to improve housing, education and immigration with the aim of building harmonious community relations. A devout Muslim, Cllr Mulla is very proud of his religion, culture and identity. He is married with four children.

NANDY, Dipak, Mr

is chief executive of Intermediate Technology Development Group. Born in Calcutta, on 21 May 1933, he was educated in St. Yavier's College, Calcutta and the University of Leeds, where he obtained a B.A. (Hons.) Class 1 in English Literature. He arrived in Britain from Indian in 1956 and lectured at the University of Leicester 1962-66 and the University of Kent 1966-68. The Founder Director of The Runnymede Trust 1968-73; he became a consultant at the Home Office in 1975 and was Deputy Chief Executive of the Equal Opportunities Commission between 1976-86. He was chair of the BBC Asian Programmes Advice Committee in 1983 and also on the BBC's General Advice Council. Between 1984-87, he was governor of the British Film Institute; and awarded a Gold Medal for an English Essay in 1952. He lists his recreations as photography, opera and collecting records. He is married to Louise Byers and has two daughters, Francesca and Lisa.

NARAYAN, Rudy, Mr,

is a Barrister of great repute who is considered by many, including Judges, to be outstanding in his profession. At present he is practising at Temple Chambers EC4. Born in Guyana, Mr Narayan came to further his studies in Britain in the late 50s. He has been involved with some extremely important political cases and his brilliance in handling them has won him great admiration. A former Labour Councillor in Lambeth, Mr Narayan is the author of a book entitled *Barrister for the Defence* which was published in 1985. Mr Narayan founded the Society of Black Lawyers and spearheaded the foundation of Black Rights (UK), the leading civil rights organisation. He is married and has two daughters.

NASTA, Susheila Mary, Ms

was born on October 16, 1953, and is a Writer and a Lecturer in Literary Studies at Portsmouth Polytechnic. She obtained a Combined Honours Bachelor of Arts degree in English and History at the University of Kent in 1975, a Post Graduate Certificate of Education in Teaching of English and Drama from London University in 1976 and a Master of Arts degree in English from the Uiversity of Kent in 1981. Ms Nasta has held various posts as a Teacher, and has also been a Literary Agent for Samuel Selvon and a Literary Consultant to Heinemann Educational Books and Longmans Caribbean. Ms Nasta is the treasurer of ATCAL (Association for the Teaching of African, Caribbean and Associated Literatures) and was an Assistant Examiner for the Oxford and Cambridge Joint Examination Board as well as an Advisor on multicultural texts for the Joint Matriculation Board. Since 1984 she has been the Editor of the twice yearly educational journal *Wasafiri*. Among several books she is the author of *Mothers and Mirrors*, on black women's writing, and books and articles on the works of Sam Selvon.

NATH, Aruna, Dr

is a Senior Medical Officer for the Department of Health and Social Security. She was born in India and came to Britain in 1966 in order to study medicine. Dr Nath is chair of the South East Division of the Overseas Doctors' Association. She is both a member of South London Indian Council and a member of the southern branch of the Womens' Medical Federation. She has published a number of papers on Cervical Cancer and the effects of prolonged oral contraceptive steroid use on enzyme activity and vitamin status. Her hobbies are the study of comparitive religion and music.

NG, Mee Ling, Cllr

represents Evelyn Ward in the London Borough of Lewisham for the Labour Party. Born in Malaysia in 1952, Mee Ling Ng is a Braille Transcriptor with the Royal National Institute for the Blind. She holds a Bachelor of Science degree in Biological Chemistry and a Masters degree in Environmental Resources. She is a member of the Deptford Labour Party of which she was vice-chair from 1984-5, and is also a member of the N.U.J (National Union of Journalists) and was a mother of the Chapel. She was one of the founder members of the Lewisham Anti-Apartheid Movement and Arts for Labour. Elected as a councillor in May 1986, Mee Ling Ng is currently chair of Lewisham's Women's Committee.

NIJHAWAN, Krishan Kumar, Mr

is a Consultant Ceramist who was born in India and arrived in England via Germany in 1963. He was a member of the Institute of Ceramics, Stoke on Trent, and a fellow of the Royal Microscopical Society, Oxford. Kumar Nijhawan was granted patents in the United States of America, Britain and Australia in 1971 for the purpose of research in ceramics, for the manufacture of synthetic bone china. He is a member of the Brahma Kumari World Spiritual University, Mount Abu, India. The spiritual University is engaged in the advancement of world peace and is affiliated to the United Nations. Kumar Nijhawan is interested in philosophy, metaphysics and yoga. He is married with four children and resides in Northholt, Middlesex.

NILES, Douglas Sylvester Eddie, Cllr

was born in Barbados and, since settling in Britain, he has established himself in both the Trade Union Movement and the Labour Party. He is a local council member for the London Borough of Islington and is currently deputy chief whip. Eddie Niles was the first black branch secretary for the National Union of Public Employees (NUPE) in local authority. He has been a delegate to national NUPE conferences and also to London divisional conferences of the union. In 1983 he was elected chair of Islington North Constituency Labour Party, a position that he held until 1985. Since then he has been the vice chair of Islington North's Fundraising Committee.

NISCHAL, Paul, F.C.E.A., F.P.C.S., Mr

was born in India. He is married with three children and lives in Small Heath, Birmingham. He is an Estate Agent and Insurance Consultant. Paul Nischal is a keen community worker, helping the old and disabled in the Asian community. He takes a keen interest in education and served for many years as a member of Birmingham Education Committee. He was elected chair of Birmingham, Small Heath Traders Association and general secretary of the Asian Peoples Welfare Society. In 1983 and 1987 Paul Nischal unsuccessfully contested Birmingham Small Heath at the General Election for the Conservative Party. In 1984 he was elected chair of the Anglo-Asian Conservative Society.

NOON, G K, Mr

is the managing director of Bombay Halwa Ltd, a famous sweets firm. Mr Noon was born in Bombay, India and came to Britain in 1973. In India he was appointed to the bench and served as a JP from 1969 to 1973. He enjoys sports, particularly swimming, shooting and cricket. Mr Noon is married and has two daughters.

OBAZE, David Ewemade, Cllr

represents Little Venice Ward in the City of Westminster for the Labour Party. Born in Nigeria and resident in Britain since 1960, David Obaze came to Britain to further his education. He has since qualified as a Doctor of Naturopathy and Osteopathy in London and is a specialist in the alternative treatment of bone, back and head problems. He is a member of the British Naturopathic and Osteopathic Association. Cllr Obaze's first position with the Labour Party was as a co-opted school governor. He is now chair of his local Labour Party Branch Section. New to the political scene, he was elected to Westminster Council in May 1986 taking a traditionally Conservative seat by a safe margin. He is a member of the Social Services, Grants and Licence Committees. Cllr Obaze's main aim is to encourage Africans in Britain to be more political. He is married with four children.

O'CONNOR, Bill, Cllr

represents Queensbridge Ward in the London Borough of Hackney for the Labour Party. Born in Jamaica Bill O'Connor works as a Civil Servant and has lived in Hackney for the past twenty years. Throughout this time he has been an active voluntary worker with a number of community organisations. Stressing that he is a councillor for the whole community, Cllr O'Connor is primarily concerned with the issues of housing and leisure, both of which cut across the spectrum of race, colour and culture. He is vice chair of the Race Relations Committee and chair of the District Office 5 Housing Committee. Cllr O'Connor is a single parent with two sons.

OLAFISOYE, Venisawelah, Mrs

was born and educated in Barbados. She came to England in 1958 to train as a Nurse and qualified as a S.E.N. in 1960. In 1966 she was awarded The Clifford Morrison award for proficiency in surgery. In addition she augmented her skills with an advanced City and Guilds for Dressmaking. Venisawelah has lived in the borough of Hammersmith and Fulham since 1972 with her husband and three children. She was recently elected treasurer of a new organisation called Hammersmith and Fulham African Link (HAFLO). She is secretary of a local social club and a representative on the Hammersmith and Fulham Council for Racial Equality.

OSAMOR, Martha, Cllr

represents Bruce Grove Ward in the London Borough of Haringey for the Labour Party. Born in Nigeria and resident in Britain since 1963, Cllr Osamor is a Legal Adviser at the Tottenham Neighbourhood Law Centre where she specialises in matters involving young people and immigration. She is also a mother and houseperson. A resident in Haringey for the last twenty three years, she has been instrumental in forming the United Women's Action Group, Haringey Black Pressure Group on Education, Haringey Black Women's Centre, the Broadwater Farm Youth Association and the Farm's Day Centre and Mother's Project. In 1982 Martha Osamor became chair of the Haringey Independent Police Committee and has fought hard to make the police more accountable to the community and for a better Police Complaints Authority and procedure. Cllr Osamor was elected as a local councillor in May 1986, and has been deputy leader of the council.

OUSELEY, Herman, Mr

is possibly the most senior black local government official in Britain. Herman Ouseley has always had a strong community base and he still finds time to serve on many voluntary management committees, including the Ujima Housing Association where he is chair, on the Editorial Advisory Board for the Equal Opportunities Review and as a council member for the Institute for Race Relations. Herman Ouseley has published several works on local government and social policy. He was a member of the Inquiry into the uprisings in Handsworth, Birmingham in 1985, which produced the report, *A Different Reality*. Herman Ouseley has been working in local government since 1983. He has held many senior positions, including Principal Race Advisor and Head of the Ethnic Minorities Unit for the Greater London Council. He returned to work in Lambeth as Assistant Chief Executive and in 1986 left Lambeth to take up the post of Director of Education for ILEA (Inner London Education Authority). In March 1988 he was appointed Chief Executive of I.L.E.A.

PADMORE, Stephen, Cllr

represents Marlowe Ward in the London Borough of Lewisham for the Labour Party. Born in Guyana in 1939 and resident in Britain since 1965, he completed his schooling at Tutorial High School in Georgetown, Guyana, after which he joined the police force where he stayed for four years. He came to England with the idea of studying law but graduated instead with a B.Sc. degree in Social Sciences from the Polytechnic of the South Bank. Employed as a Community Relations Officer in employment for the last seven years by the Greenwich Council for Racial Equality, Cllr Padmore has been a member of the Labour Party for five years. He was elected in May 1986 and sees his role as a servant of the whole community, saying that he cannot ignore or marginalise the needs of the white working class. Councillor Padmore is a member of Equity, the actors' union, and has written a number of plays. He has lived in New Cross for the last fifteen years.

PAJWANI, Kishor Shamlal, Dr

has been a Medical Practitioner since 1967. Born in India in 1932 Dr Pajwani came to Britain in September 1959. He has been a Trainer since 1981 and is an Honorary Adviser in General Practice Studies at Mangalore University, India. Mr Pajwani who enjoys theatre, golf and classical music in his leisure time, is married with a son.

PAL, Arya Raj, Dr

is a Consultant Psychiatrist with Mersey Regional Health Authority. He has also worked at the Royal College of Physicians and the Royal College of Psychiatrists. Dr Pal is a member of several social, cultural and medical organisations and is a former chair of Merseyside Asian Social and Cultural Organisation and a Fellow of the Overseas Doctors Association. A member of the World Federation of Mental Health, Dr Pal was the president of the Liverpool Psychological Society in 1986.

organisations and is a former chair of Merseyside Asian Social and Cultural Organisation and a Fellow of the Overseas Doctors Association. A member of the World Federation of Mental Health. Dr Pal was the president of the Liverpool Psychological Society in 1986.

PANTON, William Dwight, Mr

is a Barrister. He was the chairperson of the Society of Black Lawyers in 1984-87 and in the same period the chairperson of Lewisham Way Youth and Community Centre. Mr Panton, who hopes one day to open a successful legal practice in Jamaica, is the present treasurer of the Afro-Caribbean Education Research Project.

PAREKH, Bikhu, Prof

Professor Bikhu Parekh was born in a small village in the Indian state of Gujarat and did not start learning English until the age of 11. From then on his academic career flourished. He graduated from the University of Bombay with a degree in Economics and a masters in Politics and came to Britain in 1959 where he left the London School of Economics with a Ph.D. He has been a lecturer in Political Science at the University of Hull since 1964 and became a Professor in 1982. In 1981 he returned to the University of Baroda in India where he lectured briefly before coming to London, this time as vice-chancellor for a three-year spell. Eighteen months ago Bikhu Parekh became part-time deputy chair of the Commission for Racial Equality and commutes regularly between London and Hull where he still lectures and conducts his academic research. He is the author of several books and over thirty five professional articles.

PARIKH, Ashok, Prof

has been a Professor of Economics since 1980. He formerly worked as a research statistician at the Institute of Economic Growth, New Delhi and a Reader in Economics at the Grokhale Institute of Politics and Economics. He is also a former Lecturer in Economics at the University of Sussex and a former researcher in Economics at the International Monetary Fund, Washington. He is a member of the American Economic Association, The Royal Economic Society and a Fellow of the Royal Statistical Society

PARSHOTAM, Nitinkumar, Cllr

represents Wembley Central Ward in the London Borough of Brent for the Labour Party. Born in Mozambique in 1956 and resident in Britain since 1973, Nitinkumar Parshotam obtained a combined honours degree and postgraduate diploma in Management Studies after which he went on to become a Business Studies Lecturer – a position he still holds. A Labour Party member since 1976, he has been actively involved in a number of political activities, campaigning at election times and with membership drives in Alperton Ward. Cllr Parshotam is involved in a number of community organisations including the Parent-Teacher Association at a local school and the management committee of a local youth club. He is a member of the National Association of Teachers in Further and Higher Education (NATFHE) and is presently chair of the Education Committee in Brent.

PASCALL, Alex, Mr

was born in Grenada, where he became involved from an early age in the cultural life of the Caribbean, forming and teaching percussion groups all over the island and accompanying Grenada's first folk group, The Bee Wee Ballet Troupe. He migrated to England in 1959 and continued to develop his talents as a drummer, singer and songwriter becoming a resident compere at one of London's leading night clubs for several years. In 1969, he founded the Alex Pascall Singers linking the songs and rhythms of Africa and the Caribbean in their performances. In later years he advised on TV programmes for schools, recorded *Anansi Stories* for broadcasting in BBC Radio schools programmes, and composed songs for TV documentaries such as *A Question of Numbers*. In 1974 Alex was invited to host the first black radio programme in Britain, *Black Londoners*, on Radio London. He is a trustee of the Maurice Bishop Memorial Fund and a member of the Maffleborne Rotary Club. He is chairperson of the Notting Hill Carnival and Arts Committee and vice-chair (UK) of the European Foundation of Carnival Cities.

PATEL, Jayantilal Chhotabhai, Mr

was born in Chaklashi, Gujarat, India, on March 20 1939, and is a Pharmacist and Company Director. He married Mrudula Ambalal Patel in 1964 and has three sons, Shiten, Sandip and Maneesh. Qualifying in 1964 he holds three academic awards: B. Pharm (Hons), M.P.S. and F.Inst.D. He arrived in Britain from Kenya in September 1957.

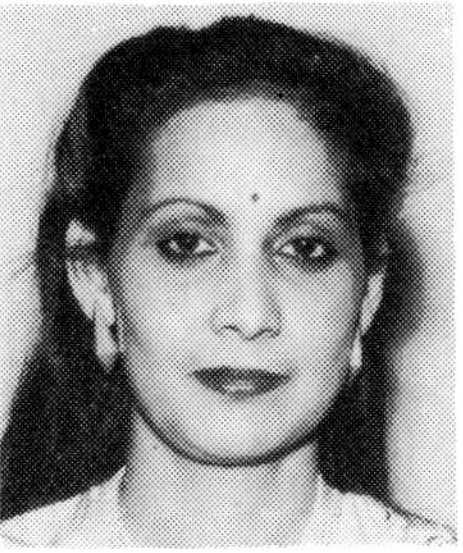

PATEL, Lata, Ms

born and educated in India and Uganda, is a Business Woman. Married to a well-known businessman Lata is a mother of a seven-year-old daughter. She has been selected by the Labour Party to fight the forthcoming council elections in the London Borough of Brent. She strongly believes in equality and is interested in fighting crime against women.

PATEL, Maganbhai, Cllr

represents Plashet Ward in the London Borough of Newham for the Labour Party. A resident of Newham for twenty two years, Cllr Patel is on the committee of both the Newham Monitoring Project and the Newham Council for Racial Equality. He held the position of shop steward for the TGWU (Transport and General Workers Union) while working at Fords and is now self-employed. Cllr Patel is president of the Shree Mandhata Youth Community Centre and a governor of two comprehensive schools in Newham.

PATEL, P.A., (Jyotishi Anand), Mr

is an Astrologer, Palmist and Numerologist. He is a widower. Having taught accountancy and commercial studies, as well as astrology in both Uganda and India, Mr Patel took up full time astrological activities in London in 1979. He is the founder and president of the Hindu Astrological Society (UK) and founded similar organisations in India and Britain. He is a member of the Astrological Lodge of England and the Astrological Association in England. Other organisations he has been associated with include the World Astrology Society, Dhaka, and the International School of Astrology. He is the author of two books and numerous articles.

PATEL, Raj, Mr

was born in India and is a seasoned Professional Actor, Producer, and the Director and Founder of Star Productions. He is the Artistic director of the British Asian Theatre Company which he formed in 1982 as a project of Star Productions. The company trains and encourages young actors and technicians to develop an Asian perspective which they feel is lacking in the British media. Mr Patel is vice chair of the Afro-Asian Committee of Equity, the actors' trade union.

PATEL, Ramesh, Mr

a Chemist, was born in India in 1938. He came to Britain from Uganda in 1972. He is a member of Patidar Samaj, Bhartiya Vidhya Bhavan, and the Anand Overseas Brotherhood (UK). Mr Patel enjoys stage shows, drama, ballet and 'Ras Gurba' and was the producer of Gujarah ballet *Narsaiyo Bhakt Harino.* He is married with three children.

PATIL, Anand, Cllr

represents Plaistow Ward in the London Borough of Newham for the Labour Party. Born in India in 1927 and resident in Britain since 1954, Anand Patil has been an employee of London Regional Transport for the last twenty years. He was first elected as a councillor in 1982. He is a member of the Labour Party's Local Government Committee. As a member of Newham Commission for Racial Equality for four years, it follows that his main concerns as a councillor are with equal opportunities and anti-apartheid policies. He is also concerned particularly with education, social services, housing, the docklands, sport and recreation. He is a member of the Social Services and Housing Committees. As the only major source of help for Asians in his ward he has been offering considerable assistance with immigration problems. Cllr Patel is married with one son and three daughters.

PATIL, Madhav, Cllr

a trades unionist, was born in India. He began his trade union activities in India amongst sugar workers and has been active in the British labour movement since 1962, having held various positions – from Shop Steward to Branch Secretary – with NALGO, GMWU and the CPSA. A member of the Labour Party since 1964, he is a fervent supporter of the Black Sections Movement and chair of the Southall Black Section.

PATKA, Mohammed Yaqub, Mr,

is the acting chair of the Waltham Forest Islamic Association and has for some time been actively involved with a number of Muslim organisations including the Bait-ul-Mall Organisation (UK & Eire), Memon Jamaat (UK) and the Union of Muslim Organisations. He is the press secretary to the International Muslim Movement (UK) and a lecturer on Islam at Sunday classes. Currently employed as a British Telecom Technical Engineer he was previously self-employed in a handicrafts business. In the late 1950s he was an active trades unionist at the Naval Dockyards at Bombay, India.

PARMAR, Gordon Devraj, Cllr

represents Abbey Ward on Leicester City Council and Leicestershire County Council for the Labour Party. Born in Bhanvad, India, in 1938 and resident in Britain since 1966, Gordon Parmar also spent some time in Tanzania where he sat his Cambridge exams. He is now working as a Senior Clerk for British Gas in the East Midlands and has been employed there for the last seventeen years. A member of the Labour Party for sixteen years, Cllr Parmar was first elected as a representative on the council for St. Margaret's Ward in 1977 and as a city councillor in 1979. Currently Lord Mayor, Ethnic Minority Officer for Leicester West and High Bailiff of Leicester, on the county council he has served on the Library, Manpower and Urban Policy Committees and is a governor of a local school. Cllr Parmar is particularly interested in immigration and nationality issues and housing, with particular emphasis on the ethnic minority communities and their problems. He aims to encourage black people to join the Labour Party and play an active role in local politics. Cllr Parmar is married with five children. He enjoys listening to music and watching football and cricket.

PAUL, Swraj, Dr

was born in Jalandhar City, India, in 1931. He graduated from Punjab University in 1949. In 1966 he came to Britain. He holds an Honorary Doctorate of Philosophy from the American College of Switzerland and was named the first 'Asian of the Year' in Britian in October 1987. In 1983/84 he also won the United Nations Council of Indian Youth (UNICY) Award and the *Asian Times* Award in May 1987. He is the author of *Indira Gandhi* – a pictorial biography, and is the chair of the Caparo Group Ltd. The founder-chair of the Indo-British Association, he is married with four children.

PHILLIPS, Mark Trevor, B.Sc., Mr

a journalist, is a former Researcher and Producer with London Weekend Television. He has also worked on Thames Television as a Presenter and Editor of current affairs programmes. Trevor Phillips is perhaps most famous to date for his work on the programmes – *Skin, Black on Black, Club Mix, The Making of Britain, This Week* and *The London Programme.* He is a former president of the National Union of Students.

PILLAYE, Jayshree, Dr

is a Harley Street Medical Practitioner. She qualified in South Africa in 1972 and worked in Hamburg before coming to London. She has also worked as a family planning Doctor and a sessional Doctor with BUPA. Dr Pillaye is a member of the British Acupuncture Society, The National Association of Family Planning Doctors, The Royal Society of Medicine and the Indian Women's Association.

PITT, David, Lord (of Hampstead)

was born in Grenada in 1913 and came to Britain in 1938 to study Medicine at Edinburgh University. A political activist since those student days, he took up employment in Trinidad and Tobago after he qualified as a Doctor. In 1943 he was one of the founders of the Westindian National Party. He returned to live in Britain in 1947, and resumed his membership of the Labour Party which he had first taken out in 1936. Working as a General Practitioner whilst sustaining his political activities Lord Pitt unsuccessfully stood for parliament twice – in Hampstead (1959) and Clapham (1970). He served on the Greater London Council, including a period as its chair. His long service and struggle was acknowledged with the award of a life peerage in 1975. However, he regards his greatest achievement as his Presidency of the British Medical Association (BMA) in the period, 1985-86. Lord Pitt is married with three children. He enjoys reading, going to the theatre and watching football and cricket.

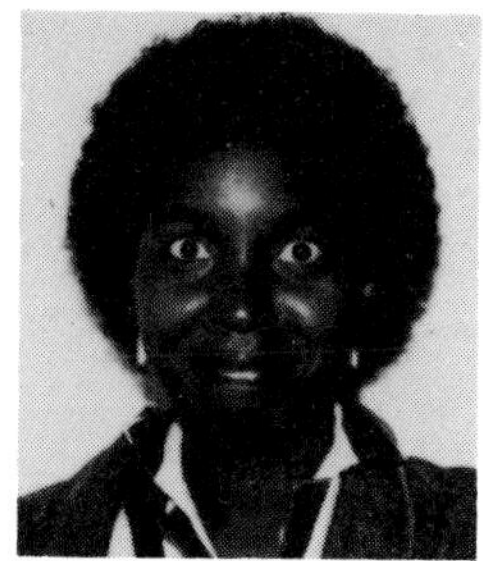

POWELL, Jennifer Maxine, Ms

works in the advertising and publicity sector. In 1976-83 Ms Powell was the advertising manager for Cable Wireless PLC and is a former Advertising Manager for London Regional Transport.

PRASHAR, USHA, Ms

was born in Nairobi, Kenya, in 1948. She came to Britain in 1964, where she attended the Wakefield Girls' High School, Yorkshire. In 1970 she obtained a B.A. hons degree, Political Science, University of Leeds, and in 1971, a diploma in Social Administration, University of Glasgow. From 1972 to 1975 she was a Conciliation Officer with the Race Relations Board. In 1976 she joined the Runnymede Trust as its Assistant Director and from 1977 to 1984 was its Director. From 1984 to 1986 she was a Fellow with the Policy Studies Institute, where she looked at primary health care in inner London, and the equal opportunity programmes of local authorities. In 1986 she was appointed as the Director of the National Council for Voluntary Organisations (NCVO). Currently she is a member of the London Food Commission, Anti-Racism Consortium, BBC Educational Broadcasting Council, Independent Broadcasting Telethon Trust. She is a trustee of the Charities Aid Foundation, Academy of Indian Dance, Director of the Roundhouse Trust, on the main board of Project Fullemploy, and on the advisory council of the Open College. She also has had articles published in numerous journals.

PROFITT, Russell, Mr

was born in Guyana. He came to Britain at an early age and was educated at Goldsmiths College, London University, where he studied for a Bachelor of Education degree and Teaching Diploma. From 1971-1980, Russell Profitt held various teaching positions, before he became Principal Race Advisor to the London Borough of Brent. He has had a long association with the Labour Party, was one of the first black Aldermen to be appointed to serve on Lewisham Council and went on to be elected as a councillor for Deptford. Russell was a deputy leader of Lewisham Council before his resignation in 1986. He unsuccessfully contested Lewisham East, for Labour at the last election. Russell Profitt is a former national chair of the Labour Party Black Section. He received a *Caribbean Times* award in 1986. Russell Profitt is married with two daughters and lives in Lewisham, London.

PUI, Joe Pui B.A. M.A, Mr

is a fashion and textile designer, is involved in the promotion of Art and Design from the Third World and the setting up of craft centres and art colleges. He is a member of the Textile Institute and the Association of Illustrators. He was born in Malaysia in 1955.

PURI, Gopal Singh, Professor

was born in August 1915. He was educated at the Punjab, Lucknow and London Universities and holds Doctorate degrees in Botany and Ecology. He has lectured at universities worldwide including Punjab, Lucknow, Agra, Ibadan and Kumasi. Prof Puri is a member of the Mersyside Asian Social and Cultural Organisation and of The World Federation of Healing. He has also published numerous research papers and several books. He is married with three children.

PURI, Kailash, Ms

was born in 1926. She is the former editor of *Roopvati Monthly* and the author of several books. She has travelled worldwide including in Canada, the USA, Africa, the Middle East and east and west Europe. She has worked as a Civil Servant, taught Punjabi, appeared on television and radio and is president of the UK Asian Women's Association. She is also founder-director of the Asian Women's Centre and in 1984 won the Woman of the Year Award as well as in 1987, the Literary Award. Ms Puri, who is married with three children, is also an 'agony aunt' and counsellor on social, cultural and marital problems to numerous Asian families.

QURESHI, Muhammad Younus, Dr

is a Scientist, who came to Britain in the late Sixties from Pakistan. He eventually settled in Scotland. He is very actively involved in community work and was the president of the Islamic Association of North Scotland. Muhammad Qureshi has served as an executive member of the Grampian Community Relations Council since 1984. He states that his ambition is to be a great scientist.

RABBANI, Mushtaq, Cllr

represents Handsworth Ward on Birmingham City Council for the Labour Party. Born in what is now Pakistan in 1928 and resident in Britain since 1967, Mushtaq Rabbani completed his studies at Punjab University in Pakistan and worked as an Inspector on the anti-smuggling staff for the Food Department of Pakistan before coming to Britain. Upon arrival he immediately became active in voluntary social work and now works full time as a Social Worker in Birmingham. One of Cllr Rabbani's major contributions in Handsworth has been as chair of the Handsworth and Aston Welfare Association. Mushtaq Rabbani has been a councillor since May 1986.

RAFFERTY, John Victor Mr

a senior Community Relations Officer, has been involved in community work in Britain since the early sixties. He has worked with organisations such as Recidivists Anonymous, Notting Hill Neighbourhood Centre, Marcus Garvey Memorial Trust, Black Business Development Association Hammersmith, and West London College where he currently serves as a governor. Born in Guyana in 1932, Mr Rafferty qualified as a teacher before migrating to England in 1955.

RAHI, Piara Singh, Cllr

represents Plumstead Common Ward in the London Borough of Greenwich for the Labour Party. Born in India in 1941 and resident in Britain since 1961, Piara Singh Rahi began his career as a Draughtsman and Quality Engineer for the Ministry of Defence after gaining O.N.C. and H.N.C. qualifications in Mechanical Engineering and a postgraduate qualification in Industrial Administration and Works Management at the Polytechnic of South Bank. He is now employed as a full time Community Development Officer for the ethnic minorities section by Kent County Council. A founder member of the local Community Relations Council which started in Greenwich fourteen years ago, Cllr Rahi has also played a leading role in an advisory council set up by the Inner London Education Authority (ILEA) six years ago with the aim of promoting equality in education. Cllr Rahi has also been personally responsible and closely involved with establishing improved facilities for the Asian community in his borough over a number of years, including a centre for Asian youth, an Asian senior citizens club and the Greenwich Action Committee Against Racial Attacks (GACARA). A member of the Labour Party for twelve years he stood as a candidate for the local election in May 1986 and was returned with a substantial majority. He now serves on the Race Committee, Community Affairs Committee and Social Services Committee; and feels that in all these areas he will be able to promote racial equality and achieve positive action. Cllr Rahi has lived in Greenwich for the last twenty-five years.

RAHMAN, Abdur Mohammad, Dr

is a General Practitioner Originally from Bangladesh, he came to Britain after qualifying as a Doctor of Medicine in 1962 at Dacca University. From 1983 to 1986 Dr Rahman served as the general secretary of the Bangladesh Medical Association. He is currently president of the Bangladesh Cultural Society. Dr Rahman is married with one daughter and two sons. His hobbies include reading, politics and the theatre.

RAIT, Satwant Kaur,M.Phil. J.P, Ms

has been the Race Relations Officer, Libraries, at Derbyshire County Council since 1986, having been School Librarian in Delhi (1961-67), Library Assistant in Leeds (1974-75) and Assistant Librarian in Kirklees (1983-86). In March 1986 Ms Rait was sworn in as a Justice of the Peace. She has published a number of books, reports and articles including a dictionary of Punjabi names and a leisure orientated cookery book. In her spare time Ms Rait likes to stroll, cook, knit and read.

RAMADHIN, Sonny, Mr

became an overnight sensation when he spun Westindies to their first victory on English soil in the Test series of 1950. He took 26 wickets in the Tests, including 11 in the match at Lord's. This stunning success in partnership with Alf Valentine, prompted calypsos sung in praise of the two spinners: *We want Ramadhin on the Ball*. Back in England seven years later, he bowled a record number of overs in the opening Test and headed the overall first-class bowling averages, with 119 wickets. After many years playing cricket in the Lancashire League, Ramadhin appeared for the county in 1964 and 1965. He also turned out for Lincolnshire and Commonwealth XIs and, even in his fifties, still played in the Bolton Association. Mr Ramadhin has made his name in England and now runs a pub in Lancashire.

RAMDEEN, Leela, Ms

was born in Trinidad and is currently Assistant Chief Education Officer in the London Borough of Haringey. She obtained a Bachelor of Education degree at Digby Stuart College, London, in 1976, and a Masters Degree in Education in 1980. She was later appointed Director of ILEA's Primary Curriculum Development Project for pupils of Caribbean origin, and then Inspector of Multi-ethnic Education. She sees her future as continuing working in a senior capacity in the field of education. Additionally, since 1987 Leela has been chairperson of Cardinal Hume's Committee for the Caribbean Community.

RAMDHANIE, Bob, Mr

was born and educated in Trinidad. His education has been diverse and full. Bob has undertaken post graduate work and also gained a Certificate of Qualification in Social Work. As an arts administrator with a strong community bias, he developed the C.A.V.E. arts project in Birmingham. He currently directs two dance companies as well as the Black Dance Development Trust. To complement the art background, Bob produces a weekly local radio programme in Birmingham. He is married with two children and his hobbies include travelling and food.

RAMPHAL Shridath, Mr

is Secretary-General of the Commonwealth. Born in 1928 in Berbice, Guyana, he is fiercely Westindian though his name points to his Indian ancestry. After his early education in Guyana, he graduated with an LL.B hons and gained an LL.M with distinction from King's College, London University. He was called to the Bar at Gray's Inn and later spent a year at the Harvard Law School on a Guggenheim fellowship. After serving in legal posts in the Federal Government of the Westindies between 1958-62, he returned to Guyana to become Attorney-General at the invitation of Prime Minister Forbes Burnham and drafted the Country's Independence Constitution of 1966. In 1972, he became Minister of Foreign Affairs and in 1973 was made Minister of Justice as well. In June 1975 Shridath Ramphal was unanimously elected Secretary-General of the Commonwealth by the Heads of member Governments. They elected him to a second term of five years from July 1980 and a third term commencing July 1985. He is the holder of many awards, including a CMG in 1966 and made a Knight Batchelor in 1969 (he chooses not to use title 'Sir'). In 1982 he was made Honorary Companion of the Order of Australia (AC) and in 1983 received his country's highest honour, the Order of Excellence (OE). He has been awarded honorary degrees by Universities in the Commonwealth and beyond and sits on a number of international Boards and Committees. Mr Ramphal is the only person to have been a member of all five Independent International Commissions of the 1980s concerned with global issues. He is also the author of numerous publications.

RAMROOP, Andrew Mr

is the Managing Director of Maurice Sedwell Ltd. of Saville Row. He has also been a Lecturer at the London College of Fashion for the past ten years. He was born in Trinidad in 1952.

RAMSEY, Dudley Claude, Mr

was born in Barbados. During the Second World War he saw active service and was awarded a medal. In the middle fifties Claude Ramsey worked as a reporter on the *Barbados Recorder* and subsequently as the sports editor of the newspaper. In the fifties he emigrated to Britain and has since published books. A founder member of the Westindian Standing Conference and a Community Worker, Claude Ramsey is at present the chair of the Thamesmead Multi-Cultural Funfield Association and a co-optee on Greenwich Council Race Equality Committee. Since 1985 he has served as vice-chair of the Thamesmead Moorings Labour Party.

RANA, Jogindar Singh, Mr

was born in India and came to England in 1965. In August 1987 he accepted early retirement from his position with the Inner London Education Authority (I.L.E.A). He is a widower. Holding an M.A. degree in History from Punjab University, Rana was head of his village Panchayat from 1953-61. He took up a teaching post in London in 1972 and moved to the West Midlands upon retirement. Active in developing policies for multi-racial education, in the Indian Workers' Association, Lewisham Council for Community Relations and Lewisham Council's Race Relations Committee, he plans to return to India to further his community work.

RANA, Satvinder, Mr

was born in India and educated in Britain. He is a radio presenter and has recently won awards for the presentation of Punjabi music. His programme, Aaj-kal was voted best programme in the East Midlands (1988). Satvinder Rana is also a Local Government Officer, currently working for Derby City Council as an Equal Opportunities Co–ordinator. He has been very active in Race Relations and lists as his unfulfilled ambitions, to be part of the 'Black Political movement in the House of Commons' and to present an Asian programme on Radio One for the BBC.

RASHID, Mirza Abdul, Mr

a Barrister-at-Law at Temple Chambers, was born in Pakistan in 1947. He is a former president of the Inns of Courts Pakistan Society and is the current president of the Ealing Muslim Society. Mr Rashid devotes a great deal of his time to working for the Pakistani community.

RATTAN, Harmegh Singh, Cllr

represents Kensington Ward in the London Borough of Newham for the Labour Party. Born in India in 1940 and resident in Britain since 1965, Cllr Rattan is a Civil Servant by profession. He lived in Kenya for eight years where he was employed in government service and was seconded to the United Nations Economic Commission for Africa (UNECA)and the Organisation of African Unity (OAU). He has been a member of the Labour Party for eight years and has held trade union membership since 1975. Cllr Rattan has held various offices in the London area and takes a keen interest in welfare organisations in Britain. He has also served as a representative on the UK Immigrants Advisory Service. Elected as a councillor in May 1986, he is a member of the Housing and Leisure Committees and is former chair and vice-president of Newham Commission for Racial Equality. He is also a member of on the governing body of a local school in the Kensington Ward. He is married with two children and has lived in the London Borough of Newham for seven years.

RIAZ, Mohammed, Cllr

represents University Ward on Bradford Metropolitan Council for the Labour Party. Born in Pakistan in 1952 and resident in Britain since 1960, Cllr Riaz holds a B.Sc. honours degree in Economics from the University of London and also undertook a post graduate course in Computer Science at Bradford University. During his studies he was actively involved in the student movement and over the years has become a leading member of the Community Relations Council (C.R.C) in Bradford. Elected as a councillor in February 1985 after a by-election in his ward, he is now chair of the Employment and Environment Services Committee and was the first visible minority councillor to be elected as head of a major committee on Bradford Council. He is also the first to be elected as chair of the West Yorkshire Police Authority's Complaints Committee.

RICE, Anstey, Cllr

represents Lewisham East on the Inner London Education Authority (ILEA) for the Labour Party. He is a Social Services Race Equality Adviser with the London Borough of Southwark. A Labour Party member for over six years, he is a delegate to Peckham General Committee and has been vice-chair and press officer of the Peckham Labour Party. He is also a member of a number of black community groups in Southwark and is active in his trades union, N.A.L.G.O. Cllr Rice was a member of the Advisory Committee of Warwick Park School and a governor of Walworth School. As an elected member of the Inner London Education Authority since May 1986 Cllr Rice is working to secure universal education for the under 5s, the integration of children with special educational needs in ordinary schools and the improvement of the child-teacher ratio.

ROBERTSON, Patsy, Ms

was born in Jamaica and educated at the Wolmers, Jamaica's oldest girls school. She worked as a Journalist on the national *Daily Gleaner* and studied History, English and Journalism at the University of New York. In 1962, when Jamaica gained independence, Patsy Robertson was one of the first women to be recruited into the country's Foreign Service. She joined the Commonwealth Secretariat shortly after it was established in 1965. After 13 years with the Secretariat, Ms Robertson has been promoted to Assistant Director, with responsibility for media and public relations. She is married with three children.

ROBINSON, Earle, M.B.E., Mr

has been with the Leicester Education Department as a Community Adviser on behalf of the Caribbean community since 1974. His contribution and work on behalf of the black community has been acknowledged by many, and subsequently rewarded by the number of awards he has received over the years. In 1980 he received an M.B.E. and in the same year a *Caribbean Times* Community Award. Clearview College bestowed an award on Earle Robinson in 1987 for his significant contribution to community life over the past twenty five years. Earle Robinson is a graduate of both Leicester Polytechnic and Leicester University and a member of the Society of Jamaicans.

RODRIGUES, Ferdinand, K.C.S.G., F.C.I.S., M.B.I.M., Mr

was born in Busoga, Uganda on 10th December 1933. He married Blanche Carlos in 1960 and they have two sons. The family emigrated to Britain from Uganda in 1972. He is currently employed as a Company Secretary for Guinness PLC. Amongst the many positions he has held are former Town Councillor, Entebbe 1964-1972, and former president of the Entebbe Institute. He is holder of both the Queen's Uganda Independence Medal, 1962, and the Uganda Republic Medal, 1972. His many interests include education and he has been chair of governors of St. Stephens's School since 1985.

ROY, Nirmal Chandra, Cllr

represents South End Ward in the London Borough of Camden for the Labour Party. Born in India in 1935 and resident in Britain since 1967, Cllr Roy was educated in India and Britain. He holds an M.Sc. degree and completed field work for his Ph.D. thesis at London University. He is a member of the British and International Sociological Association and their Research Committee on 'Race, Ethnic and Minority Relations'. He has worked as a Polytechnic Lecturer, a Community Relations Officer and as a Team Leader in Housing. He is presently employed as a Principal Policy Adviser (Ethnic Minorities) for the London Residuary Body. He held a similar position under the Greater London Council. He has been a member of the Labour Party for over twenty one years, and has held the positions of branch chair and constituency vice-chair of St. Pancras Labour Party. He represents Camden Council at the National Executive Committee of Local Government Against Apartheid and is a member of the I.L.E.A/L.R.B/N.A.L.G.O (National Association of Local Government Officers) Branch Executive. Cllr Roy is a member of the Hampstead Health Authority, governor of Kingsway-Princeton College, London College of Printing, Central Institute of Adult Education and Edith Neville Primary School. A councillor since May 1986, Cllr Roy is vice-chair of the Policy and Resources Committee and a member of the Housing Development Committee.

ROUSSEL-MILNER, David, Mr

is a Freelance Journalist and Arts Consultant. He is the son of Carmen England, who is famed for being the first black hairdresser in Britain. David Roussel-Milner has had a diverse career. At various times he has been an Articled Clerk to chartered accountants, a Commando with the Royal Marines, a pop singer and a Senior Finance Officer at the Arts Council of Great Britain. Over the years he has been a regular contributor to *Caribbean Times*.He lists his community experience as being a founder member of the Martin Luther King Foundation, the Notting Hill Carnival Finance Committee and a former vice-chair of ASTMS trades union group (now MSF) at the Arts Council. David Roussel-Milner says that, although he is semi-retired, his ambition is to become a successful novelist. He is married to Jean, a Nurse from Jamaica, and he has three sons, Nicholas, Tschaka and Paul.

SAAKANA, Amon Saba, Mr

was born in Port -of-Spain, Trinidad, and came to Britain in 1965. He is married. He is a Writer and Publisher and has been the director of Karnak House since 1977. He is the author of a number of books and is also responsible for a number of anthologies, as well as articles in journals and magazines. Mr Saakana has also prepared programmes for radio and television and has lectured extensively. He is the editor of the journal *Frontline*. Mr Saakana has served as a member of the Greater London Arts Association, Music Panel; the Greater London Council, Ethnic Arts Sub-Committee; and is a former Public Relations Officer for the Carnival and Arts Committee, responsible for the Notting Hill Carnival. Since 1979 he has been the secretary of the Carnival Industrial Project.

SACHA, Gurinder Singh, Mr

is an Advisor Teacher in Community Languages for the Inner London Education Authority (ILEA). Born in India in 1936 he came to Britain in 1967 where he became a Principal Examiner in the Punjabi Institute of Linguists. Between 1975-85 he was the vice-chair of Barking Commission for Racial Equality. He is also an assessor for the Diploma in Community Languages-Royal Society of Arts and is very actively engaged in community and voluntary work. To this end he is a member of the World Congress of Faiths-Sikh Missionary Society UK and the former vice-president of the Singh Sabha London East. Mr Sacha is also the author of *The Sikhs and Their Way of Life* as well as a number of papers on Punjabi language and culture. He is married with three children.

SAFIULLAH, Major General, K. M., His Excellency

has been High Commissioner for Bangladesh in Britain since July 1978. Born in Dhaka in 1935, he graduated from the Pakistan Military Academy with a regular commission in the infantry. In 1955 he was awarded the second highest gallantry award of Bangladesh (Bir Uttam). In 1972 he was appointed Chief of Army Staff and in 1973 Major General. He has also served as High Commissioner in Malaysia, 1976, Canada in 1981 and as Ambassador to Sweden in 1986. Among his recreations he lists sports, golf, photography and gardening. He is married with three children.

SAHOTA, Bachitter Singh, Cllr

represents Glebe Ward in the London Borough of Ealing for the Labour Party. Born in India in 1930 and resident in Britain since 1965, Cllr Sahota qualified as a Teacher in India and worked in a higher secondary school in the Punjab for ten years. Before coming to Britain he was elected as Commissioner for his home town municipality, a position he held for four years. He is now a Warden in a residential hostel for elderly Asian people in London. A member of the Labour Party for a number of years, Cllr Sahota acted as treasurer of his ward's Labour Party from 1978 to 1983, is currently Ward Secretary and has been a delegate to the management committee of the Constituency Labour Party for the last eight years. He says that he is firmly committed to the Labour Party manifesto and will continue to carry out his role as councillor in accordance with party policy. A councillor with considerable experience, he first served on Ealing Council from 1970 to 1974 and was re-elected in 1978, 1982 and 1986. His particular interests lie in welfare, education and the problems of unemployment. He is a member of the Personnel Committee, the Social Services Committee, and the Police, Emergency and Public Services Committee. Cllr Sahota is a family man, he has a daughter aged 21 and a son aged 20.

SAKSENA, Jonathan H, Cllr

represents Brookfield Ward on Preston Borough Council for the Labour Party. Cllr Saksena holds a Bachelor of Arts degree from Keele University and a Diploma of Librarianship and he is currently employed as a Librarian. He was elected to Preston Borough Council in May 1984. Cllr Saksena is currently a member of the Policy and Resources and Equal Opportunities Committees and is also vice-chair of the Housing Committee. He was a council representative of the Farringdon Park Peoples Centre Association and also of the Lancashire Fields Association from May 1984 to 85. One of his main aims as a councillor is to improve equal opportunities and to see members of the ethnic minorities achieve better representation. Cllr Saksena is unmarried. In his spare time he is interested in music and reading.

SAMBRANO, Joseph, Cllr

represents Plashet Ward in the London Borough of Newham for the Labour Party. Resident in Britain since 1962, Joseph Sambrano is currently studying full-time for a diploma in Higher Management. He has been a member of the Labour Party for the last six years and is a member of the TGWU (Transport and General Workers Union) and of the NUS (National Union of Students). Elected as a councillor in May 1986, he is a member of the Education and Social Services Committees and Race Sub-Committee. He also represents the council on the government funded Homeless Young People's Project – something which he feels is vital to the needs of the large number of black homeless in the country. Cllr Sambrano is governor of a college in Newham and of St. Anthony's Roman Catholic School in the borough and is a member of its affiliated Caribbean Association. He is married with two children and lives in Newham.

SAMUEL, Lee, M.B.E., Ms

was born in Guyana. She is a voluntary worker in the field of community relations, specialising in housing for the black elderly. Lee Samuel was founder member and former chair of the Carib Housing Association, and she serves on the management committee of the Marsha Phoenix House in Lewisham, south east London. In 1985, Lee Samuel was awarded the M.B.E. and has also been a recipient of a *Caribbean Times* Community Award. She is a trustee and honorary secretary of the Urban Trust. Her ambition is to see elderly black people rehoused with the comforts and dignity they deserve.

SANDERS, Ron, Mr

was appointed Visiting Fellow at Oxford University in January 1988 to undertake a study of small states in the international system. A former elected member of the executive board of UNESCO (1985-87), Sanders, who was born in Guyana, served as Antigua and Barbuda High Commissioner in London (1984-87), Ambassador to UNESCO (1983-87), and Deputy Permanent Representative to the United Nations (1982-83). The former diplomat also held several senior media positions in the Caribbean. He was general manager of the Guyana Broadcasting Service (1973-76), president of the Caribbean Broadcasting Union (1974-76) and a member of the Caribbean newsagency (1976-77). He is the author of several publications including a study of broadcasting in Guyana which was published in London in 1978 by Routledge and Kegan Paul.

SAWH, Roy, Mr

was born in Guyana in 1934 and came to live in Britain in 1958. Working in a variety of occupations and getting involved in the life and struggles of the black community, Roy Sawh developed a penchant for speaking at Hyde Park's Speaker's Corner, where he has long been considered one of the most impassioned, articulate and controversial orators. Speaking through the eyes of Britain's visible minorities he has long elucidated national and international matters for the benefit of all those who care to listen. He was one of the initiators of the Free University for Black Studies in the sixties, and pioneered the formation of the Racial Adjustment Action Society. In that capacity he played an important role in the early industrial struggles of the black working class in Britain. He has lectured at universities and elsewhere in Britain, various European countries, and India. Early in 1973, Sawh returned to Guyana at the request of the then Prime Minister Forbes Burnham and served as manager of the Guyana Wholesale Co-operative Society. On his return to Britain he once again involved himself in community activities. He recently completed a period as director of Black Rights (UK) and remains honorary secretary of the organisation. Roy Sawh is currently employed as the Financial Director of Hansib Publishing Limited. His biography has been published under the title *From Where I Stand*.

SCARLETT, Reginald Osmond, Mr

played Test cricket for Westindies in the early 1960s, having been the youngest player ever to appear for Jamaica. The off-spinner spent 15 years playing league cricket in Scotland and the north of England and is a leading figure in charity cricket in England. Scarlett returned home to Jamaica in 1975 for four years and was given special responsibilty for youth development by the Jamaican Cricket Board of Control. He also commentated on Shell Shield and Test matches played in Jamaica. He re-settled in England in 1979 and became a driving force in many sporting activities promoted by the Greater London Council (GLC). A Staff Coach with the National Cricket Association, he is cricket consultant with the London Community Cricket Association and Chief Coach at Haringey Cricket College, two organisations set up to promote cricket, especially among young people and deprived groups. He also acted as the consultant on *100 Great Westindian Test Cricketers*, published at Hansib Publishing.

SELVARAJAH, Sam, Mr

was born in Sri Lanka where he studied for his 'A' levels. In 1969 he came to Britain to continue his education. He joined the Wilson, Green and Gibbs, accountancy practice in the City and remained there until 1974. In the same year he and his brother established their own accounting firm in Hampstead. Sam Seeborajah is a member of the Institute of Administrative Accountants and a member of the British Institute of Management. He is married and says his ambition is to become a millionaire.

SENGUPTA, Ram Prasad, Dr

is a Consultant Neuro-Surgeon. In 1961 he obtained his M.B.B.S. from Calcutta University and in 1976 was certified by the Royal College of Surgeons of England as a fully trained Neuro-Surgeon. Dr Sengupta, who was awarded a medal for proficiency in Biochemistry (1975) and the Dickson Research Prize – Regional Hospital Board (1973), is also a member of The Society of India and The Congress of Neuro-Surgeons USA. He has published numerous scientific presentations in neuro-surgical conferences and journals.

SETHI, Mul Raj, Mr

is a Teacher. He has taught in both Kenya and Britain and between 1953 and 1971 served as a Teacher and Deputy Head Teacher in Nairobi. Since 1972 he has been teaching in the London Borough of Brent. He is secretary of the Middlesex Branch of Ama Samaj and of the Arya Pratindha Sabha (UK). Mr Sethi is also president of the Hindu Cultural Society (UK).

SHAH, Abrar Husain, Mr

was born in what is now Pakistan on March 25, 1938. He works as a Co-ordinator of translations for Brent Council and is married with one son and two daughters. He holds an M.A. degree in Fine Arts from Lahore University. Considering himself a professional Artist, Mr Shah has previously worked in textile mills in Pakistan, as a researcher in Multi-cultural Education Materials at Manchester Polytechnic and as Community Arts Officer for the National Association for Asian Youths. Mr Shah won a prize for graphic arts whilst at university in Pakistan and his paintings have been widely exhibited. He is the chair of the Association of Translation and Interpretation (London), the organiser of the Oriental Writers Forum and a member of Southall Arts.

SHAH, Atia, Ms

Was born and educated in Britain. She did a course in performing arts as well as in tap and modern dancing. She is an outstanding film, television and stage star. She has worked in Yorkshire Television's *Boxwalla*, BBC's *It Ain't Half Hot Mum*, Television South's *Catseyes* and LWT's *Mitch & Winter's Break*. Atia has also acted in *Octopussy* (Eon Film Productions), *Cricketer* (East End Film Production), *Good & Bad at Games* (Quinted Productions), *Indiana Jones and the Temple of Doom* (Lucas Film Productions). But she is noted for her roles in various community plays both, in the lead as well as supportive roles. Apart from her general interests in sports of all kinds, Atia enjoys dancing.

SHAH, Syed Sultan Ali, Mr

is a Civil Servant, Publisher and Editor. Born in Kashmir State in 1930, he came to Britain in 1958. Founder of the Kashmir Independence Movement (UK) and the Imamia Mission UK (a registered charity), Mr Shah has had tremendous experience in the Asian welfare and social sphere. A former executive member of the Labour Party in West Ham North and a member of its management committee since 1964, he is also an executive member of the Asian Welfare and Cultural Association. One of his lifetime ambitions is to secure provision and welfare for senior citizens especially those of Asian origin.

SHARIF, Khalid, Mr

a Company Director, was born in Pakistan in 1936. He came to Britain in 1956. A member of the Local Rate Court, and Arbitration Tribunals, Mr Khalid is the Chairman of the Board of Governors of Ivydale School and Robert Browning School. He is also on the Local Parole Review Committee. A Fellow of the Property Consultants Society and the British Institute of Management, Mr Khalid has recently been appointed Vice-President of Southwark Borough Race Equality Sub-Committee, and a member of the Social Security Appeals Tribunals.

SHARMA, Jagdish Rai, Cllr,

represents Hounslow Heath Ward in the London Borough of Hounslow for the Labour Party. Born in India in 1937, Jagdish Sharma is a teacher and has lived in Hounslow for over twenty years. A Labour Party member since 1967, he has been an Executive Committee member of Feltham and Heston Constituency Labour Party for a number of years and a member of the Local Government Committee. Cllr Sharma was first elected in 1974 and since then has been a member of a number of committees. He has served on the Leisure Services Committee for two years and has been chair of the Ethnic Police Liaison Committee. Cllr Sharma was the first Asian to become a Mayor in Britain, holding office 1979-1980. He has been a JP for the Middlesex Commission area since 1975, and he is the Governor of three local primary and secondary schools and Kings College, London. He is also the chair of the Ethnic Minorities Liaison Sub-Committee and a member of the Sub-Committee of Hounslow Community Police Consultative Group.

SHARMA, Virendra Kumar, Cllr,

represents Dormers Wells Ward in the London Borough of Ealing for the Labour Party. Born in India, Virendra Sharma has a Bachelor of Arts degree in Political Science and a diploma in Industrial Relations. He has worked as a Bus Conductor, a Booking Clerk, a Community Relations Officer, a Race and Immigration Adviser and has been general secretary of Brent Voluntary Action. He is presently employed as the National Ethnic Minorities Officer of the Labour Party. Cllr Sharma is also a member of the Indian Workers' Association (Southall), Ealing Community Relations Council, the Fabian Society, the Anti-Apartheid Movement, the National Council for Civil Liberties and Amnesty International. Cllr Sharma is a member of various council committees, including the Nuclear Issues Working Party, the Housing Committee and the Race Equality Committee.

SHETH, Pranlal, Mr

is a Barrister, Director and Company Secretary of Abbey Life Assurance Co. Ltd. Before his appointment in 1980 Mr Sheth worked as a Journalist in Kenya and was the chair of Navanza Farmers Co-operative Society. In 1962 he was called to the Bar at Lincoln's Inn. He is an active member of several groups and associations, including the director of Roundhouse Arts Centre, a member of the BBC Asian Programmes Advisory Committee, a trustee of the Runnymede Trust (1987), member of Board of Governors Polytechnic N. London, member of BBC Consultative Group on Industry and Business Affairs. He is chief Editor of Gojaret Samachar.

SHILLINGFORD, Lennin Bernard, Cllr

represents Normanton Ward on Derby City Council for the Labour Party. Born in Dominica in 1942 and resident in Britain since 1960 , Cllr Shillingford's interest in local government politics has been apparent ever since his arrival in Britain. It was not, however, until 1982 that he was elected as a councillor. Since that time he has been concentrating on increasing the participation of black people at a local level. Currently chair of the Equal Opportunities Committee on the council, Cllr Shillingford is attempting to ensure, through co-operation with other councils, that equal opportunities exist throughout the Midlands. His one frustration with council work is the slow speed at which the bureaucratic system operates. In his spare time Cllr Shillingford is a keen sports player.

SHIWCHARAN, Clem, Mr

was born in Berbice, Guyana, where he obtained his 'O' and 'A' levels before taking up an appointment in 1968 as a teacher at the Berbice Educational Institute. He went on to McMaster University in Canada where he obtained a B.A. Honours degree in Social Anthropology in 1974 and a Masters degree in 1977. He returned to Guyana in 1978 and taught English, politics and history at a private secondary school, whilst researching the early history of East Indians in the region. He is presently doing a doctoral dissertation on the subject at the University of Warwick. Clem has a passion for cricket and in 1988 published a book entitled *Indo-Caribbean Cricket* (Hansib Publishing Ltd).

SHOWMAN, Mitch, Mr

has been described as a 'sensational vocalist entertainer'. He has worked in Europe, Canada, the USA and England. He sings popular songs as well as writing most of his own material. And his magnificent voice is matched by a "great personality".

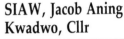

SIAW, Jacob Aning Kwadwo, Cllr

represents Dalston Ward in the London Borough of Hackney for the Labour Party. Born in Ghana and resident in Britain since 1968, Jacob Aning Kwadwo Siaw was elected as a councillor in May 1986. He is currently employed as a Lawyer. Past appointments have included that of Headteacher and Teacher. His main interest as a local councillor is to assist and help deprived members of the community. Outside of work, Cllr Siaw's interests include community and voluntary activities.

SIDANA, Sangat Singh, Dr

is a GP specialising in Ophthalmology. Formerly a medical officer for the Kenyan government, Dr Sidana was also a medical officer at Mulago Hospital, Kampala, Uganda. Dr Sidana is chair of the Indian Association (UK) and vice-president of the Sikh Forum-UK. He is also a life time member of the International Punjab Society, the Institute of Sikh Studies and the Indian Medical Association.

SIDDIQUI, Nilofar, Cllr

represents Harpurhey Ward on Manchester City Council for the Labour Party. Cllr Siddiqui was born, in Kanpur, India. Before coming to Manchester in 1965, she took a Masters degree in social work after which she studied for a Diploma in Community Development at Manchester University. Cllr Siddiqui is currently employed as a community worker. Cllr Siddiqui had been a member of the Labour Party for twelve years before her election as a councillor in May 1982. She is the deputy chair of the Highways Committee and Assistant Whip. Cllr Siddiqui takes a special interest in issues concerning women, young people, child care, career progression and retraining in skilled professions. She hopes that women will soon be included in all aspects of decision making in the community. She is a member of the Greater Manchester Passenger Transport Authority. Cllr Siddiqui has two children – a boy and a girl.

SIHERA, Elaine, Ms

Born in Kingston, Jamaica in 1948, Elaine Sihera was educated at the Convent of Mercy Academy in Kingston and later gained a B.A. in Sociology and Education from the Open University. She then acquired a Post Graduate Certificate in Education from Cambridge University and undertook an external diploma course at London University. For four years she was an Information Officer with the Royal Air Force at Brize Norton and then spent ten years as an English Teacher, her last position being as Head of Year in an Oxford secondary school. A Freelance Writer as well as a broadcaster and newsreader on independent radio, Ms. Shihera is a member of Women in Management and the Institute of Journalists. Her hobbies include travelling and solving problems of logic.

SIMMONS, Lydia Emelda, Ms

was born in Montserrat and came to England in the early 50s. She lived in London until 1960 before moving to Slough where she became involved in the promotion of race and community relations. Lydia became a councillor in 1979, deputy mayor 1983-84 and eventually mayor for the term 1984-85. She received a *Caribbean Times* Award in 1985 in honour of her being appointed the first black mayor in Slough. Lydia's present occupation is as a Compositor and Paste-up Artist.

SINGH, Amarjit, Cllr

represents Manor Park Ward in the London Borough of Newham for the Labour Party. Born in what is now Pakistan in 1946 and resident in Britain since 1958, Amarjit Singh is a Systems Design Engineer. He was first elected to Newham Council in 1978. He has been a Labour Party member for some years and is an executive member of Newham North East Constituency Labour Party and his local government committee. Cllr Singh is concerned with actively encouraging black people to attend political meetings and, as a councillor, his main concerns are with race relations, policing, social and economic affairs, education and industrial relations. He is a member of the Policy and Resources, Education, and Planning and Development Committees.

SINGH, Gurcharan, Cllr

represents Waxlow Ward in the London Borough of Ealing for the Labour Party. Born in India and resident in Britain since 1972, Gurcharan Singh gained a Masters degree in Mathematics in India before coming to Britain where he now owns and manages an off-licence business. Elected as a councillor in May 1986 his main interest is housing in the borough. He is chair of the Property Sub-Committee and a member of the Planning and Economic Committee. He is married with three children – two girls and a boy.

SINGH, Harbhajan, Cllr

represents Erith Town Ward in the London Borough of Bexley for the Labour Party. Born in India in 1939 and resident in Britain since 1966, Harbhajan Singh is head of the Community Outreach Department in a large comprehensive school in the London Borough of Newham and has been teaching in this country since 1968. He has an M.A. degree in Sociology and was a Lecturer in Humanities at an engineering college in the Punjab, India, before coming to England. Closely involved with community affairs in his borough for a considerable time, Cllr Singh was presented with a local paper annual award in 1983 for his community work. One of his main contributions is as secretary to the Anglo-Asian, Afro-Caribbean Friendship and Cultural Association in Bexley, Newham and Greenwich. He is the only Asian councillor in the borough which has a 93 per cent white population. He has gained himself the nicknames of 'Mr Petition' and 'the Fighting Councillor'. His main concerns are with education, employment and equal opportunities. Cllr Singh is married with three children.

SINGH, Krishan Kumar, Mr

an author and writer, is at present Director of Park Publications. Born in India in 1915 he came to Britain in March 1947. In 1984 he was the General Secretary of the Punjab Unity Forum and a Trustee of the Hindi Centre, London. He has had several works published including *'Money Does Grow on Trees'*, *'Destination UK'*, *'I've been here before'* and *'India Home and Abroad'*. Mr Singh is married with three children.

SINGH, Mota, Q.C.

Born in Kenya 26 July 1930. He was educated at the Duke of Gloucester School Nairobi until 1947. He was a solicitor's clerk from 1948-1954 in Kenya. He came to Britain in 1954 where he qualified as a Barrister called to the Bar in 1956. He is a member of the Honorary Society Lincolns Inn. He returned to Kenya in 1957, started his own practice, and was Advocate, High Court, Kenya, from 1957. He was the first Indian Secretary to the Law Society 1963-1964. He entered the political arena as the youngest Asian elected to the Kenyan parliament and he was Alderman from 1958-1963. In 1964 he returned to Britain where he's permanently settled. At the British Bar he specialised in landlord and tennant cases, and in 1965-1967 was chair of the rent assessment panel. In 1968 he was appointed to the Race Relations Board where he remained until 1977. During 1976 to 1982 he served as a Deputy Judge then Recorder in the Crown Court, he also took Silk and became a QC in 1978. He has an Hon. LL.D. Guvunannak Dev University Amritsar 1981. He then became a Circuit Judge in 1982. Judge Singh is married with 2 sons and for recreation he likes reading and cricket (he formerly represented Kenya).

SINGH, Rajinder, Mr

was born in Jullundur, India, on 15th July 1954. By training he is a Computer Systems Engineer and he is currently the owner of RS Computer Systems, of Coventry and Birmingham. He is married with two young sons. Mr Singh holds two degrees, B.Sc. and M.Sc., as well as a diploma in Computer Systems Engineering. He arrived in Britain from India in August 1976 and is a member of various organisations. He lists his recreations as reading and swimming, and currently lives in Leamington Spa.

SINGH, Ranjit, Mr

is a Teacher specialising in Mother Tongue Teaching. He was born in India in 1939 and came to Britain in 1964. A former general secretary of Sri Guru Singh Sabha, Southall, since 1981 he has been its president. He is the chair of the joint governing body of Hounslow Heath Junior and Infants Schools. Mr Singh is also vice-chair of the Ethnic Minorities Police Liaison Sub-Group Hounslow and a member of the executive committee of Hounslow Community Relations Council. He has been appointed to the Panel of Lay Visitors Hounslow Police Station by the Home Secretary. He is married with two children.

SINHA, Aswinee Kumar, Dr

was born in India in 1933. He came to Britain in 1959 and since then has held several medical posts in various hospital departments. For example he was the Medical Registrar for the Edgware Group of Hospitals and Principal General Medical Practitioner in Southend-On-Sea. He also actively practices in several organisations including social, medical and sporting ones. These range from being a member of the British Medical Association, a Licentiate of the Royal Photographic Society and an Honorary Medical Officer with Southend United Football Club. Mr Sinha, who enjoys photography, gardening, driving and sports, is married with two children.

SLOAN, John Mr

trained in journalism at British Press International has had a great deal of experience as a Journalist. He has worked in Italy, France and Scandinavia as a freelance reporter before returning to Britain to work for the Kent Messenger Group of papers. He has worked on the Weekly Gleaner and as a reporter and was promoted to News Editor. Deciding on a career change to television journalism, in 1985 John Sloan worked for the BBC programme *Brass Tacks* as a Researcher/Reporter. He currently works on the *Cooke Report*, for Central Television. Since 1986 John Sloan has been the Equalities Officer for the freelance branch of the National Union of Journalists. His ambitions are to complete a book on the Changing Nature of Police Powers and to produce for Independent Television.

SMITH, Kingsley, Cllr,

represents Tulse Hill Ward in the London Borough of Lambeth for the Labour Party. Born in Jamaica, Kingsley Smith is a Senior Youth and Community Worker with the Inner London Education Authority (ILEA). He holds a certificate in Youth and Community Work and a diploma in Social Legal Studies. A founder member of the Afro-Caribbean Youth Movement in Camden, Cllr Smith was for five years secretary of the Standing

Conference of London Youth Workers. In 1986 he was vice-chair of his local Labour Party Black Section and Vice-Chair of Tulse Hill Ward Labour Party. Elected as a councillor in the by-election of 1985, be became Mayor of the Borough in 1986-87 and is now Vice-Chair of the Community Affairs Committee.

SMITH, Pamella Elaine, Ms

is a Development and Social Worker. Ms Smith formerly worked with Youth, was a Personal Secretary, as well as a Co-ordinator and Black Development Social Worker. She was chair of the Black Elderly Group, Southwark, and was previously chair of Southwark Council's Women's Committee. Among her aspirations Ms Smith expresses a political ambition – possibly to become an MP, and fight for equality of service particularly in education. Ms Smith has one daughter.

SODHI, Mahinder, Dr

is a medical practitioner and surgeon. He was born in West Bengal, India, in 1933. A member of the British Medical Association, the Royal Society of Medicine and a Fellow of the Royal College of Surgeons, Dr Sodhi received his surgical hospital training in Britain. His Urology training was obtained in New York. He is a member of the Rhodes Boyson Parliamentary Club and the Stone Watersports/ Boat Club (Essex). In his spare time Dr Sodhi enjoys shooting, snooker and photography. He is married with one son.

SOHPAL, Rajinder, Cllr

represents Redlands Ward on Reading Borough Council for the Labour Party. Born in India in 1956 then emigrating to Britain in 1965, Cllr Sophal was educated in Birmingham where he attained seven 'O' levels and two 'A' levels, before going on to study biological science for three years at Wolverhampton Polytechnic. He failed to re-sit his final year examinations but is presently studying an Open University Degree course in education to be completed in 1988. His work experience includes employment as a Boiler Attendant, a Project Worker for the Boy Scouts Association and a Playleader. He became a community relations officer in Swindon in 1981 and is currently employed by the Reading Council for Racial Equality. He is also a part-time Lecturer in the London Borough of Newham. As an active trade union member, Cllr Sohpal was a member of the executive committee of the Students union at Wolverhampton Polytechnic for two years. He has held several representative positions with the former ASTMS (Association of Scientific and Technical Management Staff) since 1980. Elected as a councillor in May 1986, he captured his seat from the conservative party and represents a Ward comprised mainly of white voters. He is chair of the Economic Promotion Sub-Committee. Cllr Sohpal has been involved in running a number of courses with the Community Roots Trust. He is married with two children and lives in Reading.

SONI, Ramesh Kumar, Mr

a Journalist, was born in India in 1938. After graduating with a B.A. at Punjab University he came to Britain in 1963. He subsequently became chair of the Hindi Parent Group and an executive member of GEME. Mr Soni is the publisher and editor of *Milap* (an Urdu weekly) and *Navin Weekly* – a Hindi Publication. He is married with three children.

SPRINGER, Samuel Massiah, MBE, Mr

was born in Barbados in 1934 where he was educated. He began his career as a Deep Sea Diver and Wet Dock Contractor. He also owned and managed a Small Tourist Business in Barbados. He came to England in 1955. His Trade Union and Political work started in 1958 during the London Transport Bus Strike. From 1967 he served as a member of a number of statutory and voluntary bodies; 1971 to 1986 member of Hackney Borough Council, serving on the Economic Development Staff and Equal Opportunities Committees, North Metropolitan Conciliation Committee of the Race Relations Board; founder member Hackney Committee against Racism; The Home Secretary's Advisory Council on Race Relations; member of the Industrial and Employment Appeal Tribunals; 1978 appointed additional Commissioner to investigate employment policies of the National Bus Company – during the same period he led Social and Economic Delegations to France, Germany and Moscow. In 1982 he became the first black Mayor of Hackney and, during his term of office, he recognised the need to develop a Black Financial Institution and led a delegation to USA to research the possibility. He is now chair of the Project Committee. In 1986 Sam Springer led a delegation to Dallas to discuss exchange trading between minorities in USA and UK and to promote Black Business development in Dallas. He was given the Key to the City of Dallas. In 1976 he was awarded the M.B.E. for his services in Race Community Relations, in 1984 admitted to the Freedom of the City of London and in 1986 appointed Deputy Lord Lieutenant of Greater London. He was the first recipient of a *Caribbean Times Community Awards*. He now manages his own firm of Consultants. Special Interests: the development of a financial institution (BANK) owned and controlled by the black community, to work in partnership with the whole community and underpin the economic development of the Black & Ethnic minority Communities'; cultural, business and educational participation in developing measures to tackle unemployment, race and sex discrimination.

STENNETT, Enrico Alphonso, Mr

was born in Jamaica in 1928, he came to Britain in the late 1940s and is now a Youth and Community Worker with the Wolverhampton Council for Community Relations. A former Hyde Park orator, he published the *African Voice* between 1950 and 1956 and was joint secretary of the Movement for Colonial Freedom (1954-58). He is the founder of the African Club (1950) and the African League (1952). Part of Mr Stennett's memoirs have been serialised in the *Caribbean Times*. He continues to write as a columnist in the *Coventry Challenge* newspaper.

STEPHENSON, Paul, Mr

was born in Essex. In April 1963, as a youth development worker in St. Pauls, Bristol, Mr Stephenson led a successful campaign to end racist employment policies of the Bristol Omnibus Company. In 1974 he was appointed the first black member of the British Sports Council and in 1975 founded the Mohammed Ali Sports Development Association (MASDA) in Brixton, of which he is presently an honorary member. In 1981 he resigned from the Sports Council over the Prime Minister's attitude towards South Africa, in particular over continued British sporting links. He is presently a member of the Press Council and a Senior Executive Officer at the Commission for Racial Equality (CRE). Mr Stephenson is married with two children.

STEPHENSON, Steve, Mr

formerly one of the best known black Social Workers in Luton, Steve Stephenson recently moved to the Handsworth area of Birmingham to take up work in the fostering and adoption field. In Luton he was chair of a youth football team, the treasurer of a youth cricket team and an executive member of the local Community Relations Council. He was also the leader of the town's Starlight Youth Club. He holds a B.A. degree in Applied Social Studies from Hatfield Polytechnic and a Certificate of Qualification in Social Work. He was a cultural adviser to BBC Radio Bedfordshire.

STEWART, Cordella, Ms

born in Jamaica on January 4, 1958, Ms Stewart was admitted as a Solicitor in March 1987. She is a founder member of the Society of Black Lawyers and she is a member of the Minority Access to the Legal Profession Project, based at the South Bank Polytechnic; as well as being a Management Committee member of the Hackney Legal Defence Campaign. Ms Stewart acts as Legal Adviser to the Broadwater Farm Defence Committee, the Extended Family Housing Association, and the Caribbean Hospital Support Group. Ms Stewart enjoys going to the theatre when she has the time, particularly to see black productions.

STEWART, Daphne Ethelrosa, JP, Ms

born in Guyana. Daphne is the Divisional Careers Officer of the ILEA careers service in Hackney. She began her career in 1955 as a primary school teacher in Guyana, where she worked until 1961 after which she migrated to England. She held various clerical appointments until 1967 when she received a diploma in vocational guidance. After working in Division 9 in Brixton as a C.O., she became Officer in charge of the Kings Cross careers office until 1975. She then moved to Hackney and held the position of Deputy Divisional Careers Officer until 1980 when she was promoted to her present office. In 1976, Daphne was presented to the Queen and the Duke of Edinburgh at Buckingham Palace, and was appointed a Justice of the Peace in 1980. Daphne is the first black female Careers Officer to have been appointed by ILEA, and the only black woman at senior management level in the census service in England. Memberships include trustee of Community

Roots Trust; co-opted member of African-Caribbean Medical Society; founder member of the Association of Black Careers Staff and council member of British Caribbean Association.

ST HILL, Crispin, Mr

is Race Relations Advisor for the London Borough of Brent. He has had considerable experience in the political sphere and has played a major and influential role in Caribbean political and social development, for example in his role as Director of the St. Lucia Youth Development Programme 1980-83. Mr St. Hill, who has had previous experience as a magistrate, was also chair of the Catholic Commission for Racial Justice in England and Wales from 1974-78. He believes that his future lies in the political sphere and, to this end, was the Labour Party parliamentary candidate for the Mid-Staffordshire constituency in the June 1987 general election, where he took the Labour Party position from third to second place and increased the party's share of the vote by over 2000.

STUART, Moira, Ms

is currently a presenter of BBC television's hourly news summaries and weekend news programmes. She joined BBC Television News in 1981, and over a period of five years presented *News Afternoon,* the early evening *5.40 News,* and Sixty Minutes. Moira first came to the BBC in 1973 and for four years worked in talks and documentaries – first as a Secretary, then as a Production Assistant. In 1977, she became a Radio 4 newscaster and in February 1980 joined Radio 2 as a Newscaster and Presenter. Moira, who is a regular panellist on *Call My Bluff,* has also presented various Further Education programmes, and co-presented the Open University's *Open Forum* monthly magazine. In addition, she has presented several other radio programmes including *Moira Stuart Presents* and *The Georgie Fame Concert.* Jazz and classical music, the theatre, cinema, yoga, literature, and dance – modern and classical ballet – are among Moira's interests.

STRAKER, Ralph, JP, Mr

is a Community Relations Officer, who was born in Barbados in 1936. Having previously worked as a bus conductor and a post office worker, Ralph Straker was appointed as a Justice of the Peace in 1982. He is well-known for his work as a 'Master of Ceremonies' at a range of functions. He received a *Caribbean Times* Award in 1985.

SULLIVAN, Brian, Mr

is Assistant Director, of Polytechnic of North London. Mr Sullivan, who was born in Cardiff interrupted his education at an early age and joined the R.A.F. in 1961. He spent three years in the R.A.F. before resuming his studies at night school. Later he studied at Hull University where he obtained a degree in Economics, before he came to London to study for an M.Sc. at the London University. He became a Lecturer in 1972 and was promoted to Senior Lecturer in 1976. The following year he went to lecture in Nigeria where he also researched on small scale industry. He returned to Britain in 1979 and was appointed Senior Lecturer at Huddersfield Polytechnic. In 1984 he was appointed Head of Department at Ealing college of Higher Education. In 1987 he was appointed to his present post. He is currently on the North London Branch of Full-employ.

SYED, Nasrullah, Cllr

represents Brownswood Ward in the London Borough of Hackney for the Labour Party. Resident in Britain since 1964, Nasrullah Syed has been actively involved in community work since his arrival in Britain from Pakistan. He also worked for some time as a monitoring officer on the Race and Housing Action Team in Tower Hamlets. Elected as a councillor in May 1986, one of his main aims is to see the decentralisation of social services in the Borough. He currently holds the position of Mayor of Hackney. Cllr Syed is a single man and has lived in Hackney since 1975.

SYED, Shahid Hussain Shah Bokhari, Dr

was born in Buchakalan, Punjab, now Pakistan, on October 25 1934. He came to Britain in 1971. He is employed as Senior Clinical Medical Officer, concerned with Adult Health. As a former secretary of the British

Medical Association he was able to utilise his skills and knowledge when he subsequently served on the Rochdale Area Health Authority. Dr. Syed was a Liberal Councillor in Rochdale from 1973-1975 and says now that he would like to be a Conservative Parliamentary Candidate at the 1991 general election. He is married with six children and lives in Rochdale, Lancashire.

THEA, Dan, Mr,

is the Principal Race Relations Adviser for the London Borough of Hackney. He became the first Race Relations Adviser in the country when he was appointed to the post in Lambeth in 1978. Born in Kenya, he is the Deputy Chairman of the Committee for The Release of Political Prisoners in Kenya and is on the Executive Committee of the Anti-Apartheid Movement.

THOMPSON, Angus, Mr

is a Photographer who worked for Edward Briscoe Associates for ten years, before leaving to establish his own company. For the past two years, Angus Thompson has specialised in still life photography. His clientele include British Airways, Rank Xerox, Dyke and Dryden, the Co-op and the Trustee Savings Bank. Apart from being a successful Photographer, Angus Thompson finds time to enjoy basketball, tennis and travelling.

THOMPSON, Valerie, Ms

was born in Nottinghamshire on March 16, 1958. She is currently Assistant Manager of an Afro-Caribbean Centre. Valerie's education has been predominated by art and graphic design which has prepared her for a part -time freelance career in graphics between full-time employment. She is a member of the Afro-Caribbean National Artistic Centre, the Westindian Nationals and was vice-chair of the Caribbean Focus '86 Executive Committee (Nottingham).

THUKRAL, Pritam, Mr

a businessman, was born in India in 1939. After obtaining a B.A. at Punjab University he came to England in 1963. He is an active member of the Ealing Acton Business Club and in his spare time enjoys swimming, tennis and golf. Married with three children Mr Thukral presently works at P and S Motors Ltd, specialists in Mercedes Benz.

UDDIN, Abbas, Cllr

represents Spitalfields Ward in the London Borough of Tower Hamlets for the Labour Party. Born in Bangladesh in 1960 and resident in Britain since 1972, Abbas Uddin has a diploma in Youth and Community Work and is employed as a Youth Liaison Officer in Tower Hamlets. He has been extremely active in the borough, an area with a large Bangladeshi community since the 1970s, and is particularly concerned with the problem of housing. He was an active member of the Bengali Housing Action Group and played an important role in the occupation of Camden Town Hall by homeless families in December 1985. He was also chair of Spitalfields Housing Co-operative from 1982 to 1985 and treasurer from 1985 to 1986. Abbas Uddin became a councillor in July 1985 at the age of twenty four and was the youngest Asian ever elected to a council in Britain. He sits on the Bethnal Green Neighbourhood Committee, the Policy and Resources Committee, and the Policy Sub-Committee.

UPPAL, Balbir Singh, Mr

is a community Development Worker based in West Yorkshire. Mr Uppal, who is married, began his career after completing a course in Electrical and Electronic Engineering. He then trained as a Project Co-ordinator and is a school governor and an executive member of Kirklees Community Relations Council. He is also current vice-president of the Sikh Social centre in Huddersfield, a member of the Police Forum and treasurer and founder member of Sadeh-Lok Housing Association, and treasurer of Kirklees Black Workers Group.

VAISH, Ashok, Mr

was born in India on December 12, 1935. He graduated from New Delhi University with a Master of Arts degree in Economics in 1958. Ashok Vaish is married with a daughter and a son. In 1961 he joined the staff of Air India, as Sales and Marketing Manager and later became a Commercial Manager. He was responsible for sales to Eastern Europe, Hong Kong and Japan. In 1986 he transferred to London to take up an appointment as Regional Manager for Air India in the United Kingdom, Ireland and Scandanavia. Mr Ashok Vaish lists his hobbies as golf and music.

VAZ, Keith, MP, Mr

was born in Goa, India, and spent his early life in Aden, South Yemen. He was educated in Britain and graduated from Cambridge University. In 1982 Keith Vaz worked for Richmond Council as a Solicitor. Between 1983 to 1985 he was employed by Islington Council firstly as a Solicitor and then as a Senior Solicitor. In 1985 he was selected as a Labour Party candidate to fight the Tory-held marginal Constituency of Leicester East. Keith Vaz had previously fought as a Labour candidate in Richmond and Barnes in 1983 and then as the 'Euro' candidate for Surrey West in 1984. He was a former chair of Richmond and Barnes Constituency Labour Party. Since his historic victory in Leicester East in 1987, Keith Vaz has become a very hard working Member of Parliament. He currently serves on the following committees:– Home Affairs Select Committee, Immigration Bill Standing Committee, secretary of the Footwear and Textiles All Party Committee and secretary of the Indo-British Parliamentary Group. He is a National Union of Public Employees sponsored MP and the president of the Leicester-based Thurnby Football Club.

VAZ, Valerie, Cllr

is a Local Government Lawyer with Brent Council and Labour Party Councillor for Elthorne Ward in the London Borough of Ealing. Valerie Vaz was born in South Yemen in 1954 and has been resident in the UK since 1965. After arriving in Britain from Goa with her family she gained an Honours Degree in Bio Chemistry before deciding upon law as her career. An active member of the Labour Party she is also a keen member of the Campaign for Nuclear Disarmament, Amnesty International, War on Want, the National Council for Civil Liberties, the Socialist Education Association and Asian Solicitors Association.

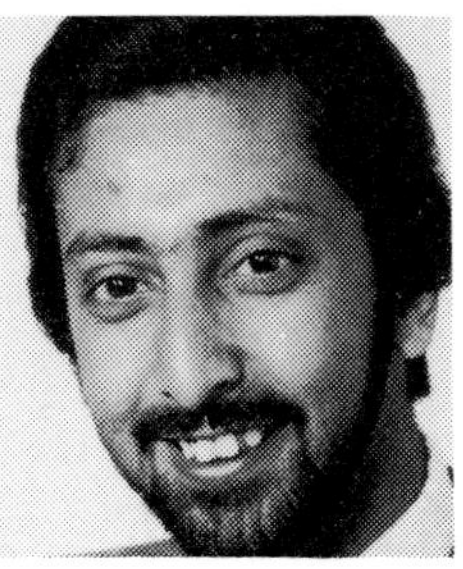

VEDI, Sanjiv, Cllr

represents Heston West Ward in the London Borough of Hounslow for the Labour Party. Born in Kenya and resident in Britain since 1970, Sanjiv Vedi completed his education with a Bachelor of Science degree in Law and Politics at University College, Cardiff. He is now a Race and Immigration Community Worker at a Law Centre in Hillingdon, north-west London. A Labour Party member since 1979, Cllr Vedi is vice-chair of his constituency Labour Party and a delegate to various organisations and bodies. He is also secretary of the Hounslow Black Section. Sanjiv Vedi was elected to Hounslow Council in the 1986 local elections and is currently chair of the Equal Opportunities Committee. He is actively involved with various committees and organisations, such as CND (Campaign for Nuclear Disarmament), AAM (Anti-Apartheid Movement), the Immigration Law Practice Association and the Socialist Education Association. He is also a member of the National Executive of the Law Centre Federation and National Immigration Co-ordinator for the Labour Party's Black Section movement. Cllr Vedi's interests outside work include current affairs, badminton and football.

VERMA, Chand Mehar, Mr

is an Educational Psychologist. He was born in India on August 15, 1931 and came to Britain in May 1967. He successfully completed his studies for B.A., B.T., M.Ed., M.A. and for a Psychology diploma in Educational Guidance counselling. Mehar Verma is a former chair of West Glamorgan Community Relations Council. He was the founding chair of the India Society of West Wales in 1985. In 1987 he was awarded an Educational Fellowship at the Moscow Institute of Psychology. Mehar Verma is married with two adult sons and currently resides in Swansea, Wales.

VIR, Parminder, Ms

was born in India and educated in England. She gained her B.Ed. (Hons) from Dartford College of Education and specialised in Physical Education and Geography. In the early part of her career she worked with the London Minorities Arts and Advisory service and the Commonwealth Institute. She was one of the first black women to be appointed as a senior administrator in the Greater London Council. She was the head of the GLC's Race Equality Unit, Arts and Recreation Department.

WADE, Anthony E S, M.B.E. M.B.I.M., Mr

is the Managing Director of Dyke and Dryden Limited and he is married. Mr Wade is also chair of the North London Business Development Agency and Director of the Haringey Enterprise Board (HEB) Limited and HEB Investments Limited. Mr Wade is a Member of the British Empire (M.B.E.) and a Member of the British Institute of Management (M.B.I.M.). He is also a member of the Governing Council of Business in the Community.

WADOODI, Arshad, Ali, Mr

is a consultant on Asian and Middle Eastern affairs and on British Economic and Community Development affairs. Presently Director of Politik-Plus and Spectrum Consultancy Services, Mr Wadoodi has also worked as a Research Assistant to a Labour MP and a Senior Research and Development Officer at Kala Ujama Ltd. As a Labour Party activist he worked at the Labour headquarters in the Targeting Unit during the 1987 election campaign. He is also acting chair of 'Gulab', a parliamentary lobby group. Mr Wadoodi, who in 1984 was awarded a prize by 'The City' for his essay on Financial Institutions, aspires to one day become a Professor of Peace. In his spare time he enjoys music, poetry and travelling and is also fluent in Urdu and Arabic.

WADSWORTH, Marc, Mr

was born in November 1955. After leaving school he trained as a Journalist, working on several local newspapers. He is a regular contributor to *Campaign News, New Statesman* and *Root Magazine*. He now works as a Senior Reporter for Thames TV. Marc is an active member of the National Union of Journalists (NUJ) and currently serves as the Father of the Chapel for Thames TV and is co-chair of the NUJ's Ethics Council. For the past two years, Marc has been the national chair of Labour Party Black Sections. He recently stood down as chair and took over the role of Campaign Officer for the National Executive. Marc is actively involved in the work of Black Action for Liberation of Southern Africa (BALSA). In 1986 he edited the Catholic Church report on black people, *With You in Spirit*.

WALAYAT, Choudry Mohammed, Cllr

represents Darnall Ward of Sheffield City Council for the Labour Party. Born in Pakistan and resident in Britain since 1962, Cllr Walayat is employed as the Chief Adviser to the Pakistan Welfare Association in Sheffield and is chair of the Ethnic Minorities Advisory Project. A Labour Party member for some years, Cllr Walayat has been a member of the TGWU (Transport and General Workers Union) since 1962. Between 1979 and 1985 he was the founder chair of the Police Liaison Panel in Sheffield, a member of the Conciliation Committee of the Race Relations Board for Yorkshire and the North East and an initiator of the Ethnic Minority Advisory Project in Spittal Hill. He is also a member of the Social Security Tribunal and a governor of Park House School in Sheffield. Elected to Sheffield City Council in May 1986, Cllr Walayat's main concerns are with inner city deprivation and housing.

WATSON, Pauline Alison, Cllr

represents Clapham Town Ward in the London Borough of Lambeth for the Labour Party. Born in Jamaica, Pauline Watson became a councillor in May 1986 on a manifesto which prioritised the need for more money to be injected into housing and for greater equality within the educational system. Cllr Watson is vice-chair of the Amenity Services Committee. A Nurse by profession, Cllr Watson's main leisure interests are reading, socialising, watching television and cooking.

WEBB, Rene, Mr

was born in Jamaica in 1921. A Youth Worker with ILEA, he is also Director of the Melting Pot Foundation, chair of Lambeth CRC and general secretary, National Federation of Self Help Organisations. In 1976, Mr Webb was awarded the Badge of Honour by the Jamaica government for services to the black community in Britain.

WESTCOMBE, Shaheen Choudhury, Ms

is an Architect and Community Development Officer in the London Borough of Hackney. Born in Calcutta in 1945, after studying at Kyoto University, Japan, she came to Britain in 1979. She has worked as a Lecturer in the Department of Architecture as well as an Architect in several British architectural firms. A member of several community based organisations, Ms Westcombe was general secretary of the Bangla Education Cultural Centre in 1986. She has been a member of the steering group, Multi Ethnic Women's Health Council since 1982. She is also a member of South Islington Law Centre. The mother of a young son, she hopes to write a book on her experiences in the future and continue with her work on women's issues.

WILLIAMS, Aubrey, Mr

is an Artist and was born in Guyana in 1926. He worked for several years in the Guyanese Civil Service, where he lived among Warrav Indians in the jungle, before coming to London in 1954 where he studied at St. Martins College of Art. Williams is a Lecturer in Fine Art (painting) at Exeter College of Art, Devon, and the

Camden Arts Centre, London. He is considered to be one of the greatest contemporary painters to emerge from Guyana and has won several leading awards for art including the considerable inspiration from pre-Columbian cultures. His paintings have been purchased by the Arts Council, the Commonwealth Secretariat, York Art Museum, the BBC and Oxford University.

WILLIAMS, Jerry Haldane, Cllr

represents Castlehaven Ward in the London Borough of Camden for the Labour Party. Born in Barbados and resident in Britain since 1957, Cllr Williams is a Supervisor with British Rail. He has been a school governor, chair of ILEA's Appeal Committee, a member of the National Union of Railwaymen (NUR) North London District Council, Guard and Shunter Grades Secretary. Elected as a councillor in May 1986 he is currently Mayor of Camden.

WILTSHIRE, Bernard, Cllr

represents Hackney North and Stoke Newington on the Inner London Education Authority (ILEA) for the Labour Party. Born in Dominca, he is a Barrister and Lecturer with particular experience in educational matters. During his career he has taught at universities in New York, Jamaica and Dominica. He is vice-chair of governors at Hackney Downs School, which he also attended, and chair of the governors at Hackney College, as well as being chair of the borough's Black Governor's Collective. In 1984 he carried out a research project into the achievement of black pupils at Hackney Downs School and he also pioneered the first supplementary school in the borough. Cllr Wiltshire was elected Deputy Leader of ILEA in May 1986.

WONG, Ansel, M.Ed., Mr

is Special Projects Officer for the Chief Executive of the London Borough of Ealing. Born in Trinidad he studied at Hull, London and Brunel Universities, specialising in English and Education. He has held the positions of Principal Race Relations Adviser to the Greater London Council (GLC) and Principal Race Equality Adviser to the London Strategic Policy Unit (LSPU). Mr Wong is married with six children and is interested in modern dance and cricket.

WOOD, Wilfred E. Denniston, Rt. Reverend, Dr

has been Bishop of Croydon in the Diocese of Southwark since 1985. He was born in Barbados in 1936. He was ordained Deacon at St. Michael's Cathederal, Barbados, and in 1962 was ordained Priest of St. Paul's Cathedral. Since then he has served as Vicar of St. Lawrence, Catford, Canon of Southwark Cathedral. A former JP for Inner London and Doctor of Divinity, chair of the Martin Luther King Foundation, a member of the Royal Commission on Criminal Procedure 1978 to 1980, Archbishop of Canterbury Commission on Urban Priorities, a member of the World Council of Churches Programme to Combat Racism. He is also the founder member of a number of black self-help organisations including Shepherds Bush social and Welfare Association, Berbice Housing Association Co-op, member of the Housing Corporation and the Martin Luther King Memorial Trust. He has also contributed to several publications including *The Vicious Circle* (with John Downing) (1968) *The Committed Church* and *Black Britain White Media*. Dr Wood, who claims to be 'an armchair follower of most sports', is married with five children.

WORRELL, Maxwell, Cllr

represents Goldborne Ward in the Royal Borough of Kensington and Chelsea. Born in Trinidad in 1947, Maxwell Worrell was elected as a councillor in the May 1986 elections. He is currently a member of the Policy and Resources, Health and Housing Committees.

WYNTER, Alphonso C., Mr

is a Solicitor presently in private practice. He was admitted as a Solicitor in 1984 and practised for a year with a Brixton-based firm. In 1985 he joined the Hallmark, Charter and Atkinson Law Company. This later became the Hallmark, Carter and Wynter Partnership. A member of the Law Society and the Society of Black Lawyers, Mr Wynter is married with one child.

YEBOAH, Samuel Kennedy, Mr

was born in Ghana in 1949. He is Principal Personnel Officer of Equal Opportunities, Staff Planning and Information with the London Borough of Hackney. His active involvement in the struggle for racial equality and justice began with a research study he undertook in part-fulfilment of an M.A. course into the policy and practice of equal employment opportunities. He is also a corporate member of the Institute of Administrative Management. He has made a substantial contribution to policy development in Hackney particularly in terms of implementation and monitoring. He is also the author of *Ideology of Racism* to be published by Hansib, which traces the origin and development of Western racism and the ideology which underpins it.

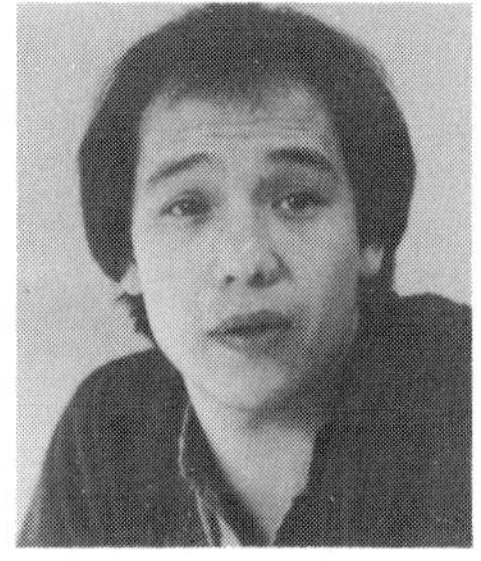

YIP, David, Mr

David Yip is 36 years old and was born in Liverpool of a Chinese father and an English mother. After leaving drama school he furthered his acting career with appearances in the West End and at the Young Vic. After a number of television appearances, David Yip shot to fame in the starring role of Detective Ho in the *Chinese Detective* (BBC), a series hailed as something of a breakthrough in the portrayal of Britain's Chinese community. The most prominent actor in Britain's Chinese community, he is steadily increasing his role in films, having starred in *Ping Pong*, the first full-length feature film made entirely by members of the Chinese community in Britain, and was also involved in the production of Steven Speilberg's *Empire of the Sun*. His latest film role is in *Hawks*, which stars Timothy Dalton and is scheduled for release next year. David Yip is also a committed campaigner for progressive causes and is a former vice-chair of the Afro-Asian Committee of the actors' union, Equity. He is involved with a number of organisations, including Arts for Labour, Campaign for Equal Opportunities in the Arts and Amnesty International. David Yip supports many groups and activities within the Chinese community itself in Manchester, Liverpool, Birmingham, London and elsewhere.

YOUSUF, Abba Ali, Mr

a Company Secretary and Insurance Executive,was born in India in 1943. Presently company Secretary of CCL Finance Group PLC he has formerly worked as executive officer of EFU Agencies Ltd and Office manager of Slate Life Corporation of Pakistan. Mr Yousuf, who came to Britain in 1969, is also a member of several organisations including being general secretary of Memon (UK and Eire) (1980-84) and is an executive member of Memons International. In 1968 he was awarded the Gold Medal by the Sind Muslim Law College for the first position he secured in his LL.B. from Karachi University. Mr Yousuf, who enjoys reading and writing and hopes one day to publish a quarterly, is married with three children.

ZAIWALLA, Sarosh Ratanshaw, Mr

is a Solicitor and was born in Bombay, India in 1947. He came to Britain in 1975. He is a member of the Law Society and a supporting member of the London Maritime Arbitrators Association. In November 1987 he was nominated for election to the Court of Arbitration, International Chamber of Commerce, Paris. He enjoys cricket and reading in his spare time and is married with two children.

They made the Third World

Stephen Bantu Biko
1946 – 1977

Steve Biko was a formidable black student leader and political thinker.

He founded the Black Consciousness Movement when he led black students away from a white-controlled students' union and formed the South African Students Organisation. A few years later Biko formed the Black People's Convention, but, soon after he was put under a banning order by the South African government and was restricted to his hometown of King Williams Town. He was detained without trial on a number of cases.

During one such detention in 1977, Biko suffered fatal injuries at the hands of the South African secret police – these were consistent with torture. Fluid and blood were found in his spinal column. Before he died he was driven naked and unconscious on a 600 mile journey on the back of a land rover.

Biko's death caused a lot of international outrage and for the first time, the United Nations Security Council voted to ban exports of arms to South Africa by any UN member state.

Maurice Bishop
1947 – 1983

Maurice Bishop, a barrister, was Prime Minister of revolutionary Grenada who shot right into the forefront of history by masterminding one of the world's socialist revolutions.

In a classical Marxist fashion, and in a style that the old masters, particularly Lenin and Mao, would have appreciated, he seized power in a comparitively bloodless revolution which was to enjoy the overwhelming support of the Grenadian people. The revolution ended the tyrannous and repressive regime of dictator Sir Eric Gairy, who ruled with the help of a brutal and lawless private army, and whose delusions of grandeur led him to believe that he was not only one of the world's foremost authorities on Unidentified Flying Objects (UFOs), but was the true successor to the kings of medieval Europe with a divine right to preside over the affairs of Grenada.

Bishop was murdered by the Grenadian militia, and not a day passed without some act to undermine it, often directed and financed by external secret service agents.

Bishop was murdered by the Grenadian militia allegedly at the order of some of his leading cabinet members who had turned against him for ideological reasons. A few days before his murder, they put him under house arrest and declared that they were now in charge of running the country. But within two days, Grenadian masses marched to the Prime Minister's residence and rescued him and then marched to nearby Fort Rupert. As they arrived, the militia opened fire on them and isolated Bishop and some of his government colleagues. A few minutes later they were shot cold-bloodedly and Bishop's remains have still not been discovered.

Following Bishop's murder, the United States army, with the backing of some of the Caribbean states, invaded and occupied Grenada – something which the American administration had been craving for throughout the Grenadian revolution.

Simon Bolivar
1783 – 1830

Bolivar, widely known as "The Liberator", is a leading figure in the Latin American history of liberation. A statesman of vision, extraordinary thinker, ideologist of freedom, rights, peace and international understanding, Bolivar wished to unite all Latin America under one nation. Countries like Venezuela, Colombia, Ecuador, Peru, Bolivia and Panama – all of which jointly cover an area of over five million square miles with a population of nearly 70 million – owe their freedom to Bolivar. Costa Rica, Dominican Republic, Cuba and Puerto Rico wanted to be included in the programme of his struggle for independence.

Lord Learie N. Constantine
1902 – 1971

Learie Constantine is said to have come into contact with cricket at the age of five, mainly because his father was an established cricketer himself. From very early in his career Learie showed tremendous potential with both bat and ball as well as with his exploits in the field. On the 1923 tour of England, Learie was chosen as one of the talented youngsters.

When the Westindies team toured England in 1928 for the very first Westindies Test Series, Learie was again selected. Although not very impressive in the Test matches, he achieved the double of 1,000 runs and 100 wickets on the tour.

In a three-day game against Middlesex on the 1928 tour of England, Constantine took charge of the match so much that he became a cricket superstar overnight with fans everywhere.

Middlesex batted first and scored 352 for 6. When Constantine went to the wicket the score was 79 for 5. In twenty minutes he had scored 50 and top scored with 86 as the Westindies made 230. No other batsman before Constantine had taken 7 for 57, including a spell of 6 for 11 in 6 overs. In the match he so badly damaged one of his opponent's fingers that it still had not healed by the end of the season.

Constantine was the first High Commissioner for Trinidad and Tobago in Britain but, in spite of the restrictions placed on a diplomat, he spoke out against racism in Britain. As Lord Constantine he was the first Afro-Caribbean peer in the House of Lords.

W.E.B. Du Bois
1868 – 1963

Du Bois was America's first black sociologist and also the most important black protest leader in the first half of the twentieth century. While teaching at Atlanta University, he gradually came to the conviction that only agitation and protest could challenge the racism of the US.

In 1905, Du Bois formed the Niagara Movement, whose main purpose was to speak against Booker T. Washington, whose philosophy was that black people should accomodate white supremacy. The Movement became the forerunner of the National Association for the Advancement of Coloured People (NAACP). Du Bois became the NAACP's director of research and editor of its magazine, *Crisis*.

Powerful with his words, Du Bois once wrote about the characteristic dualism of black Americans: "One ever feels twoness – an American, a Negro; two souls, two thoughts, two unreconciled strivings, two warring ideals in one dark body, whose dogged strength alone keeps it from being torn asunder... he simply wishes to make it possible for a man to be both a Negro and an American, without being cursed and spat upon by his fellows, without having the doors of opportunity closed roughly in his face".

Du Bois advocated pan-Africanism, a philosophy that all people of African descent have common interests and should work together in the struggle for their freedom. He was one of the organisers of the Pan-African Conference held in London in 1900. In 1934, he resigned from the NACCP because he felt that the association was serving the interests of the black bourgeoisie and was ignoring the black masses.

A Marxist by ideology, Du Bois took part in pro-Soviet Union activities. In 1951, he was arrested and charged with being an unregistered agent of a foreign power. After his acquittal through a judge's direction, Du Bois became more disillusioned than ever about the US. In 1961 he joined the Communist Party and left to live in Ghana, renouncing his American citizenship a year later.

Frantz Fanon
1925 – 1961

Frantz Fanon is one of the outstanding heroes of the African revolution, and, like Che Guevara, he gave his life to the spirit of genuine internationalism. Hailing from the French colony of Martinique in the Caribbean, he was one of the most prominent leaders of the Algerian struggle against French colonialism, although he tragically passed away from leukaemia a few months before Algeria's historic victory.

Fanon made two outstanding contributions to

black people's ideology of struggle. Firstly, he exposed how the colonialists helped to perpetuate their rule by convincing the colonised of their supposed inferiority. In works such as *Black Skins White Masks,* Fanon stressed that self respect was essential for a people who wanted to be free.

Secondly, he broke with 'classical' (or more accurately dogmatic) Marxism in evaluating the role of the urban working class. As well as recognising the privileged position of white workers in the metropolitan countries he considered the working class to be a relatively privileged stratum in those countries where the vast majority were tied to the land. Accordingly, Fanon saw the most oppressed as the vanguard of the struggle. Just as the centre of world revolution was in the oppressed nations, so the centre of the revolution in those nations lay in the countryside. In many ways, therefore, Fanon's ideas paralleled those of the great Asian communist leaders such as Mao Zedong, Ho Chi Minh and Kim Il Sung. In turn, Fanon's ideas have inspired many of the successful liberation struggles in Africa.

Marcus Garvey
1887 – 1940

Garvey, born in Jamaica, travelled extensively throughout many countries observing the poor working conditions of black people. In 1916 he formed the Universal Negro Improvement Association, an international organisation. Its main objects were the encouragement of self-government for black people worldwide, self-sufficiency and self-help in their economic projects and it protested vigorously against race discrimination and cultural deprivation.

In 1921 Garvey went to the US where he began teaching principles of Black Freedom. For this, he was arrested and deported back to Jamaica where he continued his political activities and founded the People's Political Party in 1929.

Garvey left Jamaica again for England where he died in 1940 due to ill-health. His body was taken back to Jamaica in 1964 where he is buried in the National Heroes' Park

Mohandas Karamchand Gandhi
1869 – 1948

Mahatma Gandhi first became involved in politics in South Africa when he challenged that country's laws of racial segregation which humiliated Indians. He founded the Natal Indian Congress and led Indians in peaceful defiance campaigns against the racist laws between 1893 and 1914.

On his return to India, Gandhi led the non-violent protests against the British Raj and was arrested many times. He refashioned the 35-year-old Indian National Congress into an effective political instrument. Fasting was one of Gandhi's major weapons in his struggle for justice. In 1932, while serving a prison sentence for sedition, he embarked on a fast to protest against the British government's decision to segregate the untouchables by alloting them separate electorates in the new constitution. In 1934, Gandhi resigned not only as the leader but also a member of the Congress Party because he had come to believe that its leading members had adopted non-violence as a political expedient and not as the fundamental creed it was for him.

On 30 January 1948 while on his way to an evening prayer meeting, Gandhi was shot down by a Hindu fanatic.

Ernesto 'Che' Guevara
1928 – 1967

"Che" Guevara was a prominent figure in the Cuban revolution of the 1950s. An Argentinian by birth, Guevara went to Guatemala in 1953 where Colonel Jacobo Guzman led a progressive government, which particularly through land reform attempted to bring about a social revolution.

In 1954, Guzman's regime was overthrown in a coup that was backed by the Central Intelligence Agency (CIA). This convinced Guevara that the US would always overthrow progressive governments in Latin America. He left for Mexico where the Cuban brothers, Fidel and Raul Castro, who were political exiles, were preparing the overthrow of Cuba's dictator, Fulgencio Batista. Che joined Castro's forces and trained them in guerilla warfare. During the years of guerilla warfare that followed, Guevara exhibited great courage and skill in combat and soon became one of Castro's trusted men. He was made a Major and appointed leader of the liberation army's second column.

After victory in 1959 and the establishment of a revolutionary government, Guevara became a Cuban citizen and a prominent member of the government, travelling widely to represent Cuba in delegations to Asia, Africa and Eastern Europe.

In 1965 he dropped out of public life altogether and vanished. Later that year Castro revealed a letter written to him by Guevara some months before his disappearance in which Che reaffirmed his solidarity with the Cuban Revolution but added that "other nations are calling for the help of my modest efforts", and that, having "always identified with the world outcome of our Revolution", he had decided to go and fight as a guerilla in other liberation struggles.

For the next two years Guevara's movements remained a secret. In 1966 he went to Bolivia in disguise and then began training freedom fighters there and fighting with them. In 1967 his detachment was encircled by the Bolivian Army. Guevara was captured after being wounded and was shot dead soon afterwards.

George Alphonso Headley
1909 – 1984

Commonly known as the "Black Don Bradman", George Headley chalked up a number of firsts in cricket. He became the first black man to be appointed captain of the Westindies team, and the first Westindian to score two centuries in the same Test match. He was one of the longest-serving Test players, and certainly the oldest ever to play for the Westindies. He remains one of the best batsmen of the 20th century. He set the stage for Westindian batsmanship, for he was an artist in every sense of the word.

Headley's feats of batsmanship stand out all the more prominently when it is considered that while he played, the Westindies were never quite able to field their strongest teams. In 1939, when the Westindies toured England, Headley scored 106 runs in the first Test at Lord's. In the second innings he scored an unblemished 107, thus becoming the second man in the history of the game to score two centuries in the same Test match on two separate occasions.

After World War II, Headley was made captain of the Westindies for the 1948 M.C.C. tour of the Westindies. This was an historic moment in itself: he had become the first black man to lead the Westindies. However, he now suffered from damaging injuries and clearly could not rekindle the old fire of pre-war years. He made an unsuccessful trip to India in 1948-49 where he played in the first Test but, as a result of his injury, missed most of the rest of the tour.

In 1953/54, when the M.C.C. toured the Westindies, he was recalled for the first Test at Sabina Park, thus becoming the oldest Westindian ever to play Test cricket. Sadly, the great man was unwell and truly past his prime at the age of almost 45, and made 16 and 1.

Ho Chi Minh
1890 – 1969

Ho Chi Minh, who was born Nguyen That Thanh, and was known to millions as Uncle Ho, is remembered not simply as the leader of the Vietnamese revolution but also as an outstanding figure in the international communist movement and an inspiration to liberation fighters everywhere.

Leaving Vietnam in his youth, he travelled extensively, working in a variety of menial jobs, including washing dishes in a London hotel. Inspired by the Russian revolution he became a communist as well as a Vietnamese patriot and spent a number of years working for the Communist International in the Soviet Union and China.

In 1930 he played the leading role in founding the communist Party of Indochina and from then until his death he was involved in the armed struggle to liberate his country from the French, Japanese and United States aggressors.

He proclaimed the Democratic Republic of Vietnam in 1945 and, following their defeat at Dien Bien Phu, the French were forced to negotiate in 1954.

In the 1960s Ho struggled to prevent a deterioration in relations between the Soviet Union and China and to ensure their continued aid to Vietnam. His struggle not only inspired other Third World people but also caused a profound crisis in the USA. Although he did not live to see Vietnam's victory in 1975 it belonged to him above all. He is best remembered by his saying: "Nothing is more precious than independence and freedom."

Mohammed Ali Jinnah
1876 – 1948

Jinnah first entered politics in the 1906 Calcutta session of the Indian National Congress and was elected to the Imperial Legislative Council four years later. Thus began a long and distinguished parliamentary career.

Jinnah's eagerness to raise the international status of India and to develop a sense of Indian nationhood among the peoples of India were the chief elements of his politics.

In the beginning, Jinnah looked upon the Muslim interest in the context of Indian nationalism. His attempts to bring about a political union between Hindus and Muslims earned him the title of "the best ambassador of Hindu-Muslim unity". In 1906, the All-India Muslim League was formed mainly to safeguard Muslim interest, but Jinnah stayed out of it until 1913, and joined it only after being assured that the League was as devoted as the Congress to the political progress of India. He was instrumental in organising the Home Rule League and was elected as the president of its Bombay Branch.

Jinnah opposed Gandhi's non-cooperation movement and his 'Hindu approach' to politics. He withdrew from the Home Rule League and Indian National Congress due to Gandhi's growing influence over the two organisations. The emergence of the Hindu revivalist movement led to bitter feuds between the Hindus and Muslims. But Jinnah continued to work for the good of India, and felt that the settlement of Hindu-Muslim conflict was a necessary pre-requisite to India's political emancipation. He continued to work towards this end within the legislative assembly and at the Round Table Conference in London from 1930-32. He failed, however, to get even minor amendments in the Nehru committee proposal over the question of a separate electorate and reservation of seats for Muslims in legislatures.

In 1937, the Congress obtained an absolute majority in the six provinces of India and decided not to include the League. This ignited Muslim discontent.

Although Jinnah worked towards co-operation between the Muslim League and the Indian National Congress and for coalition governments in the provinces right to the end, the elections in 1937 proved to be a turning point in the relationship of the two organisations.

Jinnah emerged as the leader of the renascent Muslim national movement and, soon after the resignation of the provincial Congress ministries in December 1939, called upon all Muslims to observe a "Day of Deliverance". Three months later, on March 22-23, 1940 in Lahore, the League adopted a resolution to form a separate Muslim State, Pakistan. At first the Congress opposed the idea but Jinnah led his movement with "such skill and tenacity" that ultimately, both the Congress and the British government agreed to the partitioning of India. Pakistan emerged as an independent state in 1947.

Jinnah became the first head of the new state and tackled its problems with authority. He was revered as the father of the Nation. He died in Karachi on September 11, 1948

Claudia Jones
1915 – 1964

Buried in a grave next to Karl Marx in London's Highgate Cemetery, Claudia Jones was a fighter against racial oppression and class exploitation of international significance.She was born in Port-of-Spain, Trinidad, and was active in the USA from where she was deported because of her political beliefs and activities.

From there she came to Britain where she was active on the Left and amongst the minority communities – and from this base she travelled to the Soviet Union and the People's Republic of China.

Claudia's mother died in 1927 – a machinist in a clothing factory in the USA, she collapsed at her machine from overwork. It was a memory that Claudia never allowed to leave her. By the age of 18 she adopted Marxism-Leninism as "the philosophy of her life" and joined the Young Communist League. She was engaged in full-time political work for the rest of her days.

Particularly after the Second World War, she concentrated on issues relating to anti-racism and black liberation, the special oppression of black women and the national liberation movements against imperialism. In 1948 – at a time of right-wing hysteria in the USA – she was arrested and charged with seeking "the overthrow of the government by force and violence". Years of persecution followed which ended with Claudia arriving in London to live in 1955. In 1958 she launched the *Westindian Gazette and Afro-Asian Caribbean News* and was active in organising opposition to racism, including state racism, supporting freedom struggles and defending the socialist countries. Although she was ill, Claudia drove herself tirelessly. She died in her sleep over the 1964 Christmas holiday.

Seretse Khama
1921 – 1980

Sir Seretse Khama was a Botswana administrator and President. He was also at one time chief of the Bamangwato tribe and while he was still a minor his uncle administered the tribe for him.

In 1948 Khama married Ruth Williams, an English woman, at a time when marriage across the colour line was still unheard of in Africa. This caused a dispute between Khama and his uncle over the succession to the chieftainship, which resulted in Khama being banished from Botswana in 1950.

Six years later there was a reconciliation between Khama and his uncle and, when Khama returned home, he renounced all claims to the chieftaincy and entered local politics. He became President of the Bechuanaland Democratic party which won a sweeping victory in Bechuanaland's first general election held under universal suffrage in 1965. He became the country's first Prime Minister and later executive President. He was knighted in 1966.

Under Khama, Botswana became one of the few countries in Africa that tolerated open political opposition.

Rev. Dr. Martin Luther King, Jnr
1929 – 1968

King was a US non-violent campaigner for black civil rights and was an ardent follower of the teachings of Mahatma Gandhi. During the years he campaigned, King was arrested and jailed on numerous occasions, while many of his followers had dogs set on them by the police.

King joined other civil rights leaders in organising the historic March on Washington. On August 28, 1963, a multi-racial crowd of more than 200,000 people gathered peaceably in the shadow of the Lincoln Memorial to demand equal rights for black people. It was on this occasion that King made his famous speech, "I have a dream". In 1964 Dr King was awarded the Nobel Peace Prize for his work for civil rights.

On April 4, 1968 King was killed by a sniper's bullet while standing on the balcony of the motel where he was staying. The following year, a white Southerner, James Earl Ray, who had confessed to the assassination, was sentenced to 99 years in prison.

Toussaint L'Ouverture
DoB Unknown – 1803

L'Ouverture was a leader of the slaves in Haiti and sought an honourable place for the black population. In 1789 he was one of the people who led a slave uprising in the French colony of St. Domingue, now known as Haiti. On August 9, 1789 the French territory reverberated to the rhythm of hundreds of drums and the white people were extremely terrified. With a great sweep, the black people moved from village to village, putting the torch to everything that would burn and killing every white encountered.

After the uprising had ended in 1791, L'Ouverture led the takeover of St. Domingue and successfully repulsed a British invasion from Jamaica which had resulted in the deaths of 40,000 English soldiers.

In 1802, Napoleon Bonaparte's soldiers attempted to restore French control over St. Domingue. They captured L'Ouverture and he died in a French prison, but his success as a revolutionary is symbolised the his continued fame.

Patrice Lumumba
1925 – 1961

Lumumba was a leading nationalist politician of the Belgian Congo, now Zaire. In the first national elections before the Congo became independent in 1960, Lumumba's party – the Congolese National Movement (MNC) – swept the polls and Lumumba formed his first government.

A few days after, there was a mutiny by some units of the army led by a Belgian commander. Soon after that, the mineral-rich province of Katanga announced that it was seceding. Belgium sent in troops, claiming that it was protecting its nationals but these troops landed in Katanga where they sustained the secessionist regime of Moise Tshombe. Lumumba appealed to the United Nations which responded by sending in a peace-keeping force to the Congo, but the secession did not end.

Lumumba was dismissed by President Kasavubu, but the legalities of this act were soon questioned by Lumumba because there were two groups now claiming to be the central government. While Lumumba was travelling from the capital city, he was captured by the rebel forces and murdered.

Albert John Mvumbi Luthuli
1898 – 1967

Albert Luthuli, a traditional South African chief, was the first African to be awarded the Nobel Prize for Peace in recognition of his non-violent struggle against apartheid. He was president of the African National Congress (ANC) from 1952 until its banning by the South African government in 1960.

In 1952, the ANC led a campaign against apartheid laws and 8,500 men and women went voluntarily to prison. The government demanded that Lutuli resign from the leadership of the ANC or abdicate his chieftainship. He refused to do either saying: "The road to freedom is via the cross". He was put under a banning order and was prohibited from leaving his village. He was struck by a train and died as he was crossing a railway bridge near his sugar cane farm.

Malcolm X
1925 – 1965

In his teenage days Malcolm X, born Malcolm Little, led a life of crime and delinquency which culminated with him in prison for burglary. It was between 1946 and 1952, while he was still serving his sentence, that he acquainted himself with the teachings of the Black Muslim movement and its leader Elijah Muhammad. In 1953 Malcolm X became an assistant minister of the Detroit mosque and was later assigned to Philadelphia and Harlem.

In 1963, having overshadowed his superior Elijah Muhammad, Malcolm X was suspended as a minister. During his attempt to form the Organisation of Afro-American Unity, he travelled widely throughout the US and Africa preaching the message of black manhood and independence. In the process he made many enemies, both black and white.

On 21 February 1965 Malcolm X was assassinated in New York as he was about to address a meeting.

Mao Zedong
1893 – 1976

Mao Zedong will be remembered above all as the man who led the "sick man of Asia" to become a great and respected power in the world, and in so doing became a source of pride and inspiration to all Third World peoples.

Coming from a reasonably prosperous peasant background, he could be said to have begun to make revolution at the age of 13 when he ran away from home as a protest against the bullying attitude of his father. He spent his youth trying to find a way for China to overcome its poverty and oppression by foreigners. Under the inspiration of the October Revolution in Russia, he accepted Marxism and became one of the founders of the Communist Party of China in 1921.

Mao's most important contribution to Marxism was his analysis that, in "backward" countries like China, the most important revolutionary force was not the small industrial working class but the vast mass of bitterly oppressed peasants. This position, which is now widely accepted, had to be established in the teeth of opposition from more rigid and unimaginative Marxists.

Mao was also an outstanding military strategist, the Long March of 1935 being an epic where a routed army regrouped and created a base from where the liberation war was carried out to victory. In 1949 Mao stood in the centre of Peking and proclaimed the founding of the People's Republic of China.

Whilst noboby can seriously deny the enormous progress made in the People's Republic, it is arguable that Mao was not so good at building the new world as he was destroying the old. Increasingly preoccupied with the idea that the revolution might go astray, he launched a series of political campaigns that culminated in the chaos of the Cultural Revolution in the late 1960s. These campaigns are now considered to have held back China's development. But Mao will undoubtedly continue to inspire all those in the Third World who long to throw off domestic and foreign exploiters. In 1949 he said: "The Chinese people have stood up. Nobody will ever humiliate us again." So far his words have held true.

Robert Nesta 'Bob' Marley
1945 – 1982

Perhaps the greatest reggae musician, Bob Marley, was without doubt the Third World's first musical superstar who brought the music of the working people of Jamaica into the mainstream of world culture.

The son of a Jamaican mother and an English army captain from Liverpool, Marley grew up in the urban village of Trench Town, the area he was later to make famous. In 1962, together with the late Peter Tosh, he founded 'The Wailers'. Marley signed to the Island record label in 1972, and in 1975 he established himself as a figure in the wider rock scene – filling a void that had existed since the tragic death of Jimi Hendrix.

Marley's importance extends far beyond musical confines, and he is a crucial figure in the rise of the Third World and the struggles of black people. He did more than any other individual to establish the religious legitimacy of Rastafarianism. He played a prominent role in Jamaican politics, being seriously wounded when right wing gunmen opened fire during a 1976 rally of the People's National Party, where he was due to play. At the invitation of Robert Mugabe he played at Zimbabwe's independence celebrations in 1980. Above all, with albums such as *Uprising* and songs such as *I Shot the Sheriff* and *Get Up, Stand Up,* he captured the defiant spirit of rebellion amongst a generation of young black people.

Jamaica awarded him its Order of Merit in April 1981. Bob Marley died of cancer and he is buried in Kingston, Jamaica, where he is a National Hero.

Jose Julian Marti
1853 – 1895

Marti was a Cuban writer and patriot. He is Cuba's greatest hero and, like Simon Bolivar, is a symbol of liberty throughout Latin America.

In his early age, Marti made the acquaintance of Rafael Maria de Mendive who became Marti's source of inspiration as well as his teacher and benefactor. In 1869 Mendive was part of an uprising as a result of which he was imprisoned and his school closed. Marti was also detained and was deported to Spain after serving six months of hard labour.

While living in New York, he began writing a regular column for *La Opinion Nacional* of Caracas and *La Nacion* of Buenos Aires, and his articles in these publications made him famous.

In 1892 Maria was elected "delegado" of the new Partido Revolucionario Cubano, which he had helped to form – he refused to be called president. On 29 January, 1895, the movement decided to go on the offensive. Marti left New York two days later and went to Santo Domingo, accompanied by other revolutionary leaders. He was killed in a skirmish that took place shortly after he landed in Cuba.

Claude McKay
1890 – 1948

McKay was born in Jamaica but left for the United States in 1912 to pursue formal education. A few years later he cut short his studies and went to live in New York where he pursued his interests in Bohemian circles, supporting himself with a variety of jobs.

He wrote a lot of poetry about Harlem and the black community and came to be widely regarded as perhaps the most blunt and outspoken black poet of that period. Commenting on the race riots of 1919, McKay wrote:

> If we must die, let it not be like hogs,
> Hunted and penned in an inglorious spot,
> While round us bark the mad and hungry dogs,
> Making their mock at our accursed lot.
> If we must die; O let us nobly die...

McKay's first book of verse was *Songs of Jamaica,* published in 1911. This was followed by *Spring in New Hampshire* (1920) and *Harlem Shadows* (1922). In 1928 he wrote *Home to Harlem,* his first novel. This was followed by *Banjo* (1929) and *Banana Bottom* (1933) which was set in Jamaica.

He lived in many parts of the world including France, Morocco and the Soviet Union. He enjoyed living among the masses, for he regarded them with high esteem.

Omar al Mukhtar
1858 – 1931

Omar Al Mukhtar may be little known outside the borders of the Libyan Jamahiriya, but the record of his 20 years of resistance, from 1911 to 1931, against the Italian invaders of his country puts him in the forefront of the African continent's struggles against colonial rule.

Born in 1858, to the family of a minor clan of chieftains in Libya, Omar al Mukhtar spent the first half century of his life as a simple man, without political ambition or military experience, teaching among his people. Widely respected for his devout Muslim faith and upright character, he seemed destined to make little long-term impact upon the history of his country.

In 1911, however, the Italians invaded Libya, seeing in this far-flung appendage of the Ottoman Empire an easy prize to add to their existing African colonies. Certainly the Italians were right in their assessment of the Turks, who capitulated within a year. They were, however, badly mistaken in believing that the Libyan people would accept colonial occupation lying down.

As soon as the Italians landed, patriotic Libyans flocked to join the struggle against the invader. Amongst those who did so was Omar al Mukhtar, then in his fifty-third year, and without any experience of warfare. He proved himself to be a natural commander, and soon gathered around him a small body of guerilla fighters, whose raids from out of the desert wreaked havoc on the Italian supply lines and patrols.

In 1922, Omar al Mukhtar, then over 60, was appointed leader of all resistance forces in eastern Libya, to face the genocidal policy adopted by the new fascist regime of Benito Mussolini in Italy. During the decade that followed, the Italians used mass bombing, concentration camps and long barbed wire fences along the borders to pen in the Libyan population, and to attempt to cow their resistance. Yet, armed only with the few light weapons that they were able to purchase secretly, or which they captured from the invaders, Omar al Mukhtar and his men fought on.

He never had more than 700 fighters under his direct command in any stage of the struggle, but, like a will-o'-the-wisp, struck almost at will against the Italians throughout the whole of eastern Libya.

Despite pouring up to 100,000 men into Libya at the height of the resistance campaign, it was not until September 11th, 1931 that the Italians were eventually able to capture the Libyan resistance leader, seizing him and a few followers in an ambush laid by more than 5,000 troops.

Wounded, and in chains, Omar al Mukhtar, then in his seventy-fourth year, was taken to Benghazi, to be taunted by the architect of Italy's genocidal policies, General Rodolfo Graziani, before being taken to the small town of Soluk, 50 kilometres south-west of Benghazi, where he was hanged on September 16th, 1931.

In a film by Mustapha Akkad in 1981, Omar al Mukhtar was immortalised by Anthony Quinn's portrayal of him as 'The Lion of the Desert', and for the first time, something of the courage and drama of the resistance struggle which he led was introduced to an international audience. Within the Libyan Jamahiriya, however, the memory has always remained vibrant and inspiring, of this proud, loyal and determined patriot who, in his old age, fought for 20 years against the overwhelming force of the Italian invader.

Gamal Abdul Nasser
1918 – 1970

While serving in the Egyptian army in the Sudan, Nasser founded the Free Officers, a secret revolutionary organisation whose objective was to oust the British and the Egyptian royal family. In 1952 he and 89 other officers removed the monarchy in a bloodless coup. A Revolutionary Command Council of 11 officers was established under the leadership of Nasser.

A few years later Nasser emerged as the Prime Minister. In 1954 a fanatic of the Muslim Brotherhood tried to assassinate him. In 1956 Nasser announced the nationalisation of the Suez Canal and promised that the tolls Egypt collected in five years from the canal would be used to finance the Aswan High Dam project. Two days later French and British planes attacked the Egyptian airfields and, at the same time, the Israeli army was attacking the Sinai Peninsula which it later occupied.

Although the Egyptian Air Force was virtually destroyed during the siege, Nasser emerged from the brief war with undiminshed prestige throughout the Arab world.

An internationalist, Nasser joined Tito of Yugoslavia, Nehru of India and Nkrumah of Ghana as an advocate of non-alignment and a founder of the movement. He died from a heart attack.

Mbuya Nehanda
DoB unknown – 1898

Nehanda was the first Zimbabwean freedom fighter. She led a revolt against white settlers and was captured together with her associate, Kaguvi. They were executed in Harare, then Salisbury, in 1898.

Nehanda's leadership in the struggle formed the backbone of the liberation war which was to be revived years later and which culminated in Zimbabwe's independence in 1980.

Jawaharlal Nehru
1889 – 1964

Nehru was the first Prime Minister of independent India. During the independence struggle he differed widely with Gandhi over political strategy.

Nehru became general secretary of the Congress Party for two years from 1923 and again in 1927 for another two years. As he travelled widely through India he became exposed for the first time to the poverty and degradation of the peasants, something that had a profound influence on his political analysis. He was arrested on a number of occasions by the British authorities. Hindu – Muslim antagonism made the struggle for independence difficult. In 1946 alone, clashes between the two groups made the partition of India inevitable. In 1947 India and Pakistan were declared two separate states. Nehru remained an idol of his people throughout his leadership, and later died from a stroke. He was one of the founders of the Non-Aligned Movement.

Agostinho Neto
1922 – 1979

Neto began his career by working in Angola for the Portuguese health service. He later studied in Lisbon, qualifying as a medical doctor in 1957. While he was in Lisbon he was arrested for his stand against Portuguese colonialism on a number of occasions – in 1951, 1952, 1955 and was released in 1957. In 1959 he returned to Angola where he established a private practice which provided cover for his underground work for the Popular Movement for the Liberation of Angola (MPLA).

In 1960 he was arrested and deported to Lisbon. He was later transferred to a house arrest, from which he escaped to Kinshasa. A military coup in Portugal accelerated the liberation process in its colonies.

In 1975 there was an attempt to set up a provisional government in Angola under the auspices of Portugal but this failed when the counter-revolutionary National Front for the Liberation of Angola (FNLA) and UNITA began to oppose the line set by the MPLA. A civil war ensued with the counter-revolutionaries being backed logistically by the US government, the Central Intelligence Agency (CIA) and South African troops.

Under the leadership of Neto, and with fraternal help from Cuban troops, the MLPA was able to repel the aggression and form a government.

Lilian Masediba Ngoyi
1911 – 1980

Lilian Ngoyi is regarded as a symbol and inspiration of the liberation movement amongst the women of South Africa. Right up to her death she retained confidence in the inevitable victory of the liberation movement.

Lilian is particularly remembered for her participation in the campaign against the extension of the pass laws to women. As President of the Federation of South African Women and President of the African National Congress' Women's League she led more than 20,000 women in the historic march on 9 August 1956 to protest against the pass laws. She continued to fight against oppression although faced with increasing restrictions and banning orders.

At a conference in 1954 held to organise against rent increases, Lilian asked: "Why must we be afraid of being ejected? We are used to living in shelters in Moroka shacks, in tents. Let us not be disgraced by fear of poverty." Lilian was one of the 155 Treason Trialists in 1956 and was placed in solitary confinement for 19 days. She died from heart trouble and hypertension.

Kwame Nkrumah
1909 – 1972

Nkruma intensively studied literature of socialism and nationalism, especially that relating to Marcus Garvey, the Jamaican leader who in the 1920s struggled to promote unity among black people of the world. In 1947 Nkrumah published his first major book, *Towards Colonial Freedom*, in which he outlined an ideological blueprint for the anti-colonial struggle.

He became general secretary of the United Gold Coast convention (before the country became Ghana) and was detained by the British in 1948 when he led the anti-colonial movement and riots broke out. During the first general election in 1951, Nkrumah was elected into parliament and was released from prison. He became leader of the government and later Prime Minister. Nkrumah embarked on the policy of Africanisation and took a leading role in the formation of the Organisation of African Unity (OAU). He was invited to Hanoi by President Ho Chi Minh to present proposals for the ending of the Vietnam War. While Nkrumah was in Peking, however, the army in Ghana seized power on 24 February 1966.

Nkrumah found asylum in Guinea and that country's President appointed him co-head of state. He continued to articulate an ideology of contemporary significance until his death in Bucharest, Romania, in 1972 from cancer.

Sheikh Mujibur Rahman
1920 – 1975

Rahman is popularly known as 'the father of Bangladesh'. His political outlook was greatly influenced by H.S. Suhrawardy, who had been Prime Minister of a united Bengal in the last days of the British Raj. Suhrawardy had also founded the Awami League, whose slogan was "United Bengal for the Bengalis".

Rahman's separatist politics led him into trouble with successive Pakistani regimes. In 1966 he was arrested for allegedly plotting against Pakistan but was released two years later after popular agitation had threatened the government. He became even more popular when Bengalis claimed that the Pakistan authorities had reacted with indifference to their plight following a cyclone in November 1970. A month later the Awami League took all but two of East Pakistan's seats in the general election and gained an absolute majority in the National Assembly. A war broke out between Bengalis, supported by India, and Pakistan, ending in the defeat of Pakistan.

Rahman resigned as President and became Prime Minister. In an effort to avoid retaliatory bloodshed, he ordered Bengali guerillas to turn in their weapons. After a period in office he became increasingly authoritarian, declaring a one party state. In 1975 he was assassinated together with members of his family.

Paul Robeson
1898 – 1977

Robeson became internationally known for his baritone voice that sang spirituals like *Go Down Moses, Sometimes I Feel Like a Motherless Child, Joshua Fit the Battle of Jericho* and *Ol' Man River*.

Robeson was a tireless fighter against black oppression in America. He showed a great admiration of socialism after making a concert tour of the Soviet Union. In January 1947 he said he would give up his career for two years to "talk up and down the nation against prejudice". Soon after, the House of Representatives Committee on un-American activities accused him of supporting 'Communist front' organisations. He testified that he was not a member of the Communist Party but reiterated his love for the Soviet Union, saying that when he was there he had experienced no prejudice from the people.

Walter Rodney
1942 – 1980

Guyanese Dr Walter Rodney was already a writer and academic specialising in African history when an incident in Jamaica pushed him into the political spotlight. While working on the Mona campus of the University of the Westindies, he extended his extramural activities to lecturing to poor working people about their African heritage. For this, the government of Jamaica dubbed him a subversive and declared him persona non grata.

Rodney subsequently vowed to contribute to the political development of his native Guyana. He became leader of the Working People's Alliance (WPA) on its formation in 1979. It started as a loose coalition of small left-wing groups before formally declaring itself a political party with a multi-racial leadership and Marxist orientation.

Rodney was assassinated in strange circumstances when his car was damaged by a bomb blast which is believed to have been planted by his political enemies. The incident provoked strong international focus, particularly in the Caribbean, Africa and Canada.

Mary Seacole
1805 – 1881

Mary Seacole, born Grant, is known as the "black Florence Nightingale" for her work in the Crimean War, Jamaica and England. From an early age she acquired from her mother, herbal remedies and other skills in dealing with diseases such as cholera, yellow fever and malaria to which European medicine could bring little more than inspired guesses.

She travelled widely to England, Cuba, Haiti, Central America and the Bahamas. She was active in relief work during the 1850 cholera epidemic in Jamaica. In that year she joined her brother in Curces, on the Isthmus of Panama, then "the great high road" to the gold fields of California where she had gone to open a store. Grimly, within days of her arrival, an outbreak of cholera demanded her energies.

Back in Jamaica in 1853, she was called upon on her arrival to help in a yellow fever epidemic. In 1854, hearing that British soldiers in the Crimea were dying in great numbers from diseases well known to her, she felt that she could be useful as a nurse to the troops. She came to England and offered her services to the War Office.

Officialdom laughed and cold-shouldered her, but undeterred, she decided to take her services to the war zone at her own expense. The help she gave both on and off the battlefield earned her the affection and gratitude of thousands of soldiers and officers.

Ahmed Sekou Toure
1922 – 1984

Ahmed Sekou Toure was one of the most formidable leaders Africa has produced. He never gained much formal education but taught himself after he was expelled from school for joining a strike.

When Toure was elected to represent Guinea in the French National Assembly, he seized the opportunity to fight against French colonialism. In 1958 he led his country to independence through a national referendum that overwhelmingly supported him. He ordered the nationalisation of the French-owned power plants and water supplies. In November 1965, Toure accused France and other NATO countries of plotting against the Guinean revolution. This led to a breach of relations between Guinea and France and the arrest of a number of French citizens on charges of conspiring against the Guinean government. The NATO powers tried to use different forms of international subversion to overthrow Toure and organised a powerful fifth column among politicians and the military, which was, however, broken up after an abortive mercenary invasion against the Republic in 1970. It took less than 96 hours to defeat the mercenaries.

Toure, together with Nasser, Haile Selassie and Nkrumah took part in the formation of the Organisation of African Unity which aimed at solving African problems peacefully.

Eric Williams
1911 – 1981

Eric Williams was not only one of the creators of Caribbean history, but one of its chroniclers. He combined a lifetime of political activity and leadership, together with being – along with Walter Rodney – one of the greatest Caribbean historians. Having worked as an academic in the USA, Williams founded the People's National Movement in 1956. He became Trinidad's first chief minister that year, and its first Premier in 1959. He led the independence talks in 1961, becoming Premier of Trinidad and Tobago after independence later in the same year. Williams held the post of Premier until his death.

Amongst the important works authored by Williams are: *Capitalism and Slavery; History of the People of Trinidad and Tobago;* and *From Columbus to Castro: The History of the Caribbean, 1491-1969.*

Sir Frank M.M. Worrell
1924-1967

While still at school, Worrell played his first cricket match for Barbados at the age of 18. At this stage he was considered a left-arm spinner and batted at number 11.

The following year, while playing in an inter-territorial game against Trinidad, young Frank was sent in to bat at number four as a nightwatchman, a wicket having fallen with just a few minutes to go to close of play. The next day he continued his innings and managed to score 64 runs. It was decided to keep him at number four for the rest of the series.

In the very next match of the series, Worrell scored the first century of his career, 188 runs. The young man's talents with the bat were now fully recognised.

His opportunity came during the 1947/48 tour of the Westindies when he was selected to play his first Test match in that series. He missed the first match through illness, but in the second he scored

97 in the first innings, thereby falling short by three runs to score a Test century on his debut.

Around this time Worrell went to live in Jamaica, following a public furore in Barbados. Many statements made against him, calling him conceited and arrogant, annoyed and hurt him deeply. It was an experience which he never forgot.

For the remainder of that series, Worrell's contribution was a revelation. At Port-of-Spain he scored 97 and then 38 not out in the final Test. His courage and conduct were beyond reproach throughout his career. He once refused to tour India in the 1948/49 series when he had a dispute with the Cricket Board of Control over wages.

In 1964, Worrell was knighted. He was appointed Warden at the University of the Westindies, besides being elected a senator in the Jamaican parliament. When he died from leukaemia, flags flew at half mast in Jamaica and Barbados.

Worrell will always be remembered for his words after his final tour of England in 1963 when he said: "I have had a great run and, as I have satisfied my greatest ambition in the last two years, I have no complaints. My aim was always to see Westindies moulded from a rabble of brilliant island individualists into a real team – and I've done it".

Zhou Enlai
1898 – 1976

Zhou Enlai was the first Premier of the People's Republic of China, a post which he held from 1949 until his death in 1976.

Born into a wealthy family he was one of the leaders of the Communist movement in China from its foundation. He was known as a superb administrator and diplomat with a tremendous capacity for detail, diplomacy, tact and hard work. He was also modest, urbane and had great personal charm.

Although very different from Mao Zedong in temperament the two men were lifelong friends and comrades and to a large extent they functioned as a team. Whilst Mao was a great visionary, Zhou attended to the practical details and made sure that the ship of state stayed afloat while Mao was steering it through stormy waters. It was largely thanks to him that the Chinese economy remained reasonably healthy during the chaotic Cultural Revolution.

Zhou was well known as a diplomat attending the Bandung and Geneva conferences in the 1950s as well as being involved in major events in the Soviet Union and Eastern Europe. In the early '60s he toured Africa where he made his famous statement: "Africa is ripe for revolution." In the 1970s he played a large part in China's opening to the United States.

To the end of his days Zhou always wore a small lapel badge of Chairman Mao bearing the words, "Serve the people."

Africa

The vast continent of Africa, with immense human and mineral wealth and enormous strategic significance, is today made up of 50 independent states each with their unique and distinctive features. A number of countries have populations of under one million (Seychelles has just 66,000) whereas Zaire has more than 30 million people and Ethiopia has more than 40 million.

The real place of Africa in world history and world politics is only starting to be written but scientists agree that human life began on the continent – some studies even suggest that the Biblical Garden of Eden may be found in Ethiopia. Africa has also made a signal contribution to the development of world civilisation. The wonders of Ancient Egypt are well-known but the fact that this was a *black African* civilisation is all too frequently glossed over. Only recently have some scholars been at pains to point out that the civilisation of Ancient Greece (itself the root of western civilisation, notions of democracry, etc.) was of Egyptian derivation, a fact acknowledged by the Greeks themselves. Later contributions included the universities of medieval Mali and the stone ruins of Great Zimbabwe.

However no people on earth can have suffered as much as the peoples of Africa, save for the original peoples of North, Central and South America who were virtually wiped out, in an act of almost total genocide. The centuries-long slave trade was the greatest and most protracted genocide in history. It destroyed societies, generated the wealth that built up western industrial capitalism and exacted a price that can never be fully calculated.

A glance at a map of Africa shows up a number of unusually straight lines cutting across the latitude and longitude of the continent. This is the legacy of the way, at the end of the last century, European powers divided Africa amongst themselves in the most arbitrary and self-seeking manner, bequeathing problems that persist to this day.

At the dawn of the century there were just two states in Africa that could be said to be independent – Liberia and Ethiopia. The collapse of a series of colonial empires like so many packs of cards in a matter of a couple of decades was a great chapter in the history of the struggle for human freedom, which was begun with the independence of Ghana (formerly the British colony of the Gold Coast) under the leadership of Osagyefo Kwame Nkrumah, a leader with a continental and global vision of Pan-African liberation that is still a source of inspiration to many freedom fighters.

Despite these great victories a central task remains on the agenda. The struggle against the apartheid regime in South Africa and Namibia is in a very real sense the cause of humanity uniting people of every conceivable viewpoint. Apartheid not only maintains the majority of the people within its borders in a state akin to slavery – it attacks its neighbours directly and covertly and, by sustaining wars in Angola and Mozambique, cripples the developments of those countries. The South African regime has attacked countries as far afield as the Seychelles and its nuclear alliance with Israel means that no country in Africa is safe from its predatory interests. Assassins and bombers believed to be in its pay have also struck in Western Europe.

In the sense that apartheid is a creation of imperialism it is linked to the other problems of the continent. The southward advance of the Sahara desert and the cycle of famines are not mysterious acts of God. It is clear that the famine in Mozambique would not exist without the South-African instigated and fuelled war. However this is just the most extreme example – the imposition of mono-crop economies and the crippling weight of foreign debt are more responsible for starvation than any periodic rain failure.

Knowledge of this reality is gaining ground – in 1987 the Ethiopian capital Addis Ababa hosted two conferences on Africa's foreign debt – one organised by the Organisation of African Unity and the other by the Organisation of African Trade Unity with the World Federation of Trades

Osagyefo Kwame Nkrumah – Pan-African visionary who still inspires

Unions.

Despite the difficulties, Africa is displaying a sense of hope for the future and her millions of people in the diaspora could yet organise themselves to play a major part in the continent's regeneration and liberation.

Africa

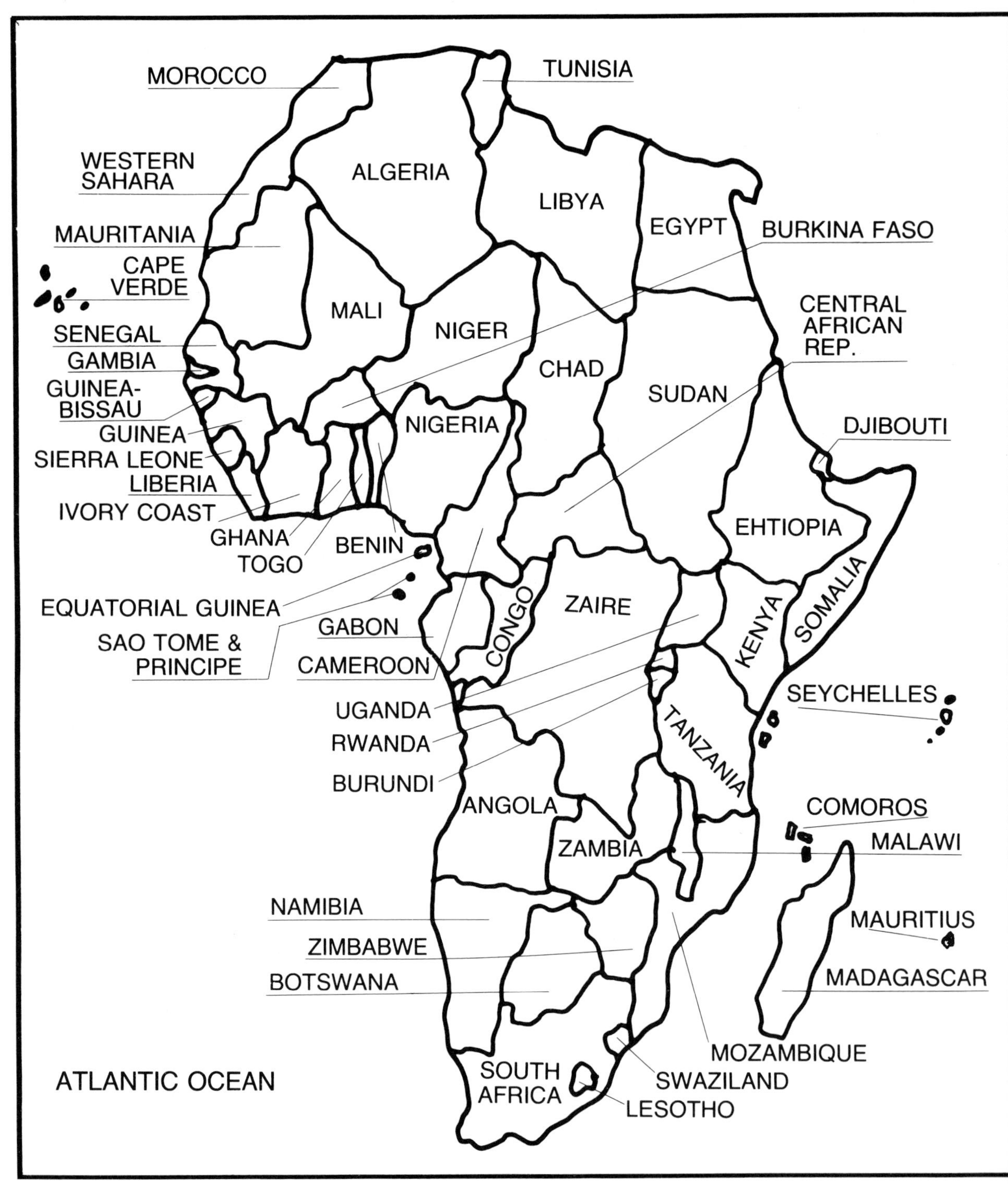
MOROCCO
TUNISIA
WESTERN SAHARA
ALGERIA
LIBYA
EGYPT
BURKINA FASO
MAURITANIA
CAPE VERDE
MALI
NIGER
CENTRAL AFRICAN REP.
SENEGAL
GAMBIA
CHAD
SUDAN
GUINEA-BISSAU
NIGERIA
DJIBOUTI
GUINEA
SIERRA LEONE
LIBERIA
IVORY COAST
EHTIOPIA
GHANA
BENIN
TOGO
SOMALIA
EQUATORIAL GUINEA
ZAIRE
CONGO
KENYA
GABON
SAO TOME & PRINCIPE
CAMEROON
SEYCHELLES
UGANDA
RWANDA
TANZANIA
BURUNDI
ANGOLA
COMOROS
ZAMBIA
MALAWI
NAMIBIA
MAURITIUS
ZIMBABWE
BOTSWANA
MADAGASCAR
MOZAMBIQUE
SOUTH AFRICA
SWAZILAND
ATLANTIC OCEAN
LESOTHO

Algeria

Popular Democratic Republic of Algeria
Head of State: President Chedli Benjedid
Ruling Party: National Liberation Front (FLN) Party of Algeria
Land Area: 2,381,741 (sq. km.)
Capital City: Algiers
Population: 21.86 million (1983)
Population Growth Rate: 3.1%
Infant Mortality: 111
Life Expectancy: 60
Gross National Product (GNP): 55,230 (Million US Dollars)
GNP Per Head: $2,530
Language: Arabic
Religion: Muslim
Currency: Dinar
Membership of International Organisations: United Nations, Organisation of African Unity (OAU), League of Arab States, Organisation of Petroleum Exporting Countries, Non Aligned Movement.

Angola

People's Republic of Angola
Head of State: President Jose Eduardo Dos Santos
Ruling Party: Popular Movement for the Liberation of Angola (MPLA) . Workers' Party
Land Area: 1,246,700 (sq. km.)
Capital City: Luanda
Population: 8.75 million (1983)
Population Growth Rate: 3.1%
Infant Mortality: 165
Life Expectancy: 43
Gross National Product (GNP): n/a
GNP Per Head: n/a
Language: Portuguese, Ovimbundu, Kimbundu, Bakongo, Chokwe
Religion: Christian, Pantheist
Currency: Kwanza
Membership of International Organisations: United Nations, Organisation of African Unity (OAU), Non-Aligned Movement.

Benin

People's Republic of Benin
Head of State: President Mathieu Kerrekou
Ruling Party: People's Revolutionary Party of Benin
Land Area: 112,622 (sq. km.)
Capital City: Cotonou
Population: 4.04 million (1983)
Population Growth Rate: 2.9%
Infant Mortality: 117
Life Expectancy: 49
Gross National Product (GNP): 1,080 (Million US Dollars)
GNP Per Head: $270
Language: French, Bariba, Fulani, Fon, Yoruba
Religion: Muslim, Christian, Pantheist
Currency: CFA Franc
Membership of International Organisations: United Nations, Organisation of African Unity (OAU), Signatory of the Lome Convention, Non-Aligned Movement.

Botswana

Republic of Botswana
Head of State: President Quett Masire
Ruling Party: Botswana Democratic Party
Land Area: 582,000 (sq. km.)
Capital City: Gaberone
Population: 1.07 million (1983)
Population Growth Rate: 4.3%
Infant Mortality: 80
Life Expectancy: 58
Gross National Product (GNP): 900 (Million US Dollars)
GNP Per Head: $840
Language: Setswana, English
Religion: Christian
Currency: Pula
Membership of International Organisations: United Nations, Organisation of African Unity (OAU), the Commonwealth, Signatory to the Lome Convention, Non-Aligned Movement.

Burkina Faso

Head of State: Captain Blaise Campaore
Ruling Party: Popular Front Council
Land Area: 274,200 (sq. km.)
Capital City: Ouagadougou
Population: 7.88 million (1983)
Population Growth Rate: 2.3%
Infant Mortality: 157
Life Expectancy: 45
Gross National Product (GNP): 1,080 (Million US Dollars)
GNP Per Head: $140
Language: French, Mossi
Religion: Pantheist, Muslim, Christian
Currency: CFA Franc
Membership of International Organisations: United Nations, Organisation of African Unity (OAU), Signatory to the Lome Convention, Non-Aligned Movement.

Burundi

Republic of Burundi
Head of State: Major Pierre Buyoya Bagaza
Ruling Party: Party of National Union and Progress
Land Area: 27,834 (sq. km.)
Capital City: Bujumbura
Population: 4.69 million (1983)
Population Growth Rate: 2.3%
Infant Mortality: 123
Life Expectancy: 47
Gross National Product (GNP): 1,110 (Million US Dollars)
GNP Per Head: $240
Language: Kirundi, French, Kiswahili
Religion: Christian
Currency: Burundi Franc
Membership of International Organisations: United Nations, Organisation of African Unity (OAU), Signatory to the Lome Convention, Non-Aligned Movement.

Cameroon

United Republic of Cameroon
Head of State: President Paul Biya
Ruling Party: People's Democratic Movement of Cameroon
Land Area: 475,442 (sq. km.)
Capital City: Yaounde
Population: 10.19 million (1983)
Population Growth Rate: 3.2%
Infant Mortality: 92
Life Expectancy: 54
Gross National Product (GNP): 8,300 (Million US Dollars)
GNP Per Head: $810
Language: French, English, Bali, Bamileke, Bassa, Douala, Fulani, Hausa.
Religion: Christian, Muslim, Pantheist
Currency: CFA Franc
Membership of International Organisations: United Nations, Organisation of African Unity (OAU), Signatory to the Lome Convention, Non-Aligned Movement.

Cape Verde

Head of State: President Aristides Pereira
Ruling Party: African Party for the Independence of Cape Verde
Capital City: Praia
Land Area: 4,033 (sq. km.)
Population: 327,000 (1983)
Population Growth Rate: 1.6%
Infant Mortality: 78
Life Expectancy: 64
Gross National Product (GNP): 140 (Million US Dollars)
GNP Per Head: $430
Language: Portuguese
Religion: Christian
Currency: Cape Verde Escudo
Membership of International Organisations: United Nations, Organisation of African Unity (OAU), Non-Aligned Movement.

Central African Republic

Republic of Central Africa
Head of State: General Andre Kolingba
Ruling Party: Democratic Rally of Central Africa
Land Area: 622,984 (sq. km.)
Capital City: Bangui
Population: 2.58 million
Population Growth Rate: 2.3%
Infant Mortality: 119
Life Expectancy: 49
Gross National Product (GNP): 700 (Million US Dollars)
GNP Per Head: $270
Language: Sango, French
Religion: Pantheist, Muslim, Christian
Currency: CFA Franc
Membership of International Organisations: United Nations, Organisation of African Unity (OAU), Signatory to the Lome Convention, Non-Aligned Movement.

Chad

Republic of Chad
Head of State: President Hissen Habre
Ruling Party: National Union for Independence and Revolution
Land Area: 1,259,200 (sq. km.)
Capital City: N'djamena
Population: 4.98 million (1983)
Population Growth Rate: 2.1%
Infant Mortality: 161
Life Expectancy: 44
Gross National Product (GNP): n/a
GNP Per Head: n/a
Language: French, Arabic
Religion: Christian, Muslim, Pantheist
Currency: CFA Franc
Membership of International Organisations: United Nations, Organisation of African Unity (OAU), Signatory to Lome Convention, Non-Aligned Movement.

Comoros

Head of State: President Ahmed Abdallah
Ruling Party: Comarian Union for Progress
Land Area: 2,236 (sq. km.)
Capital City: Moroni
Population: 395,000 (1983)
Population Growth Rate: 2.7%
Infant Mortality: 89
Life Expectancy: 55
Gross National Product (GNP): 110 (Million US Dollars)
GNP Per Head: $280
Language: Arabic, Comorian, French
Religion: Muslim
Currency: Comoros Franc
Membership of International Organisations: United Nations, Non-Aligned Movement, Organisation of African Unity (OAU).

Congo

People's Republic of the Congo
Head of State: President Denis Sassou Nguesso
Ruling Party: Party of Labour of the Congo
Land Area: 342,000 (sq. km.)
Capital City: Brazaville
Population: 1.87 million (1983)
Population Growth Rate: 3.1%
Infant Mortality: 68
Life Expectancy: 57
Gross National Product (GNP): 1,910 (Million US Dollars)
GNP Per Head: $1,020
Language: French
Religion: Christian, Pantheist
Currency: CFA Franc
Membership of International Organisations: United Nations, Organisation of African Unity, Signatory to the Lome Convention, Non-Aligned Movement.

Djibouti

Head of State: President Hassan Gouled
Ruling Party: Popular Rally for Progress
Land Area: 21,783 (sq. km.)
Capital City: Djibouti
Population: 362,000 (1983)
Population Growth Rate: 5.7%
Infant Mortality: 30
Life Expectancy: 48
Gross National Product (GNP): n/a (Million US Dollars)
GNP Per Head: n/a
Language: Arabic
Religion: Muslim
Currency: Djibouti Franc
Membership of International Organisations: United Nations, Organisation of African Unity (OAU), Non-Aligned Movement.

Egypt

Arab Republic of Egypt
Head of State: President Hosni Mohammed Mubarak
Ruling Party: National Democratic Party of Egypt
Land Area: 997,738 (sq. km.)
Capital City: Cairo
Population: 47.10 million (1983)
Population Growth Rate: 2.6%
Infant Mortality: 104
Life Expectancy: 60
Gross National Product (GNP): 32,220 (Million US Dollars)
GNP Per Head: $680
Language: Arabic
Religion: Muslim
Currency: Egyptian Pound
Membership of International Organisations: United Nations, Organisation of African Unity (OAU), the League of Arab States (membership suspended), Non-Aligned Movement.

Equatorial Guinea

Republic of Equatorial Guinea
Head of State: President Obiang Nguema Mbasogo
Ruling Party: n/a
Land Area: 28,051 (sq. km.)
Capital City: Malabo
Population: 373,000 (1983)
Population Growth Rate: 1.7%
Infant Mortality: 138
Life Expectancy: 43
Gross National Product (GNP): n/a

GNP Per Head: n/a
Language: Spanish, Fang, Bubi
Religion: Christian
Currency: CFA Franc
Membership of International Organisations: United Nations, Organisation of African Unity, Signatory to the Lome Convention, Non-Aligned Movement.

Ethiopia

People's Democratic Republic of Ethiopia
Head of State: President Mengistu Haile Mariam
Ruling Party: Workers' Party of Ethiopia
Land Area: 1,223,600 (sq. km.)
Capital City: Addis Ababa
Population: 42.27 million (1983)
Population Growth Rate: 2.7%
Infant Mortality: 122
Life Expectancy: 44
Gross National Product (GNP): 4,630 (Million US Dollars)
GNP Per Head: $110
Language: Amharic, Tigrinya, Oromo, Arabic
Religion: Christian, Muslim, Pantheist
Currency: Ethiopia Birr
Membership of International Organisations: United Nations, Organisation of African Unity (OAU), Signatory to the Lome Convention, Non-Aligned Movement.

Gabon

Head of State: President El-Hadj Omar Bongo
Ruling Party: Democratic Party of Gabon
Land Area: 267,667 (sq. km.)
Capital City: Liberville
Population: 997,000
Population Growth Rate: 1.5%
Infant Mortality: 113
Life Expectancy: 50
Gross National Product (GNP): 3,330 (Million US Dollars)
GNP Per Head: $3,340
Language: French
Religion: Christian, Pantheist
Currency: CFA Franc
Membership of International Organisations: United Nations, Organisation of African Unity (OAU), Organisation of Petroleum Exporting Countries, Signatory to the Lome Convention, Non-Aligned Movement.

Gambia

Head of State: President Dawda Jawara
Ruling Party: People's Progressive Party
Land Area: 11,295 (sq. km.)
Capital City: Banjul
Population: 737,000 (1983)
Population Growth Rate: 3.4%
Infant Mortality: 194
Life Expectancy: 42
Gross National Product: $170 (Million US Dollars)
GNP Per Head: $230
Language: English, Mandinka, Woloff, Fula, Jola
Religion: Muslim
Currency: Dalasi
Membership of International Organisations: United Nations, Organisation of African Unity (OAU), the Commonwealth, Signatory to the Lome Convention, Non-Aligned Movement.

Ghana

Republic of Ghana
Head of State: Flight Lieutenant Jerry Rawlings
Ruling Party: **Committee for the Defence of the Revolution**
Land Area: 238,537 (sq. km.)
Capital City: Accra
Population: 12.71 million (1983)
Population Growth Rate: 2.7%
Infant Mortality: 86
Life Expectancy: 53
Gross National Product (GNP): 4,960 (Million US Dollars)
GNP Per Head: $390
Language: English, Akan, Ga, Mole Dagbeni, Hausa, Ewe
Religion: Christian, Muslim
Currency: New Cedi
Membership of International Organisations: United Nations, Organisation of African Unity (OAU), the Commonwealth, Economic Community of the West African States, Signatory to the Lome Convention, Non-Aligned Movement.

Guinea

Head of State: President Lansana Conte
Ruling Party: n/a
Land Area: 245,857 (sq. km.)
Capital City: Conakry
Population: 6.4 million (1983)
Population Growth Rate: 2.0%
Infant Mortality: 190
Life Expectancy: 38
Gross National Product (GNP): 1,950 (Million US Dollars)
GNP Per Head: $320
Language: French, Soussou, Manika
Religion: Muslim
Currency: Franc Guineen
Membership of International Organisations: United Nations, Organisation of African Unity (OAU), Signatory to the Lome Convention, Non-Aligned Movement.

Guinea Bissau

Head of State: President Joao Bernardo Vieira
Ruling Party: African Party for the Independence of Guinea Bissau and Cape Verde
Land Area: 36,125 (sq. km.)
Capital City: Bissau
Population: 886,000 (1983)
Population Growth Rate: 3.7%
Infant Mortality: 144
Life Expectancy: 38
Gross National Product (GNP): 150 (Million US Dollars)
GNP Per Head: $170
Language: Portuguese
Religion: Muslim, Pantheist
Currency: Peso de Guine Bissau
Membership of International Organisations: United Nations, Organisation of African Unity (OAU), Signatory to the Lome Convention, Non-Aligned Movement.

Cote d'Ivorie

Republique de Cote d'Ivorie
Head of State: President Felix Houphouet-Boigny
Ruling Party: Democratic Party of Cote d'Ivorie
Land Area: 322,462 (sq. km.)
Capital City: Abidjan
Population: 9.31 million (1983)
Population Growth Rate: 4.0%
Infant Mortality: 119
Life Expectancy: 48
Gross National Product (GNP): n/a
GNP Per Head: n/a
Language: French
Religion: Muslim, Christian, Pantheist
Currency: CFA Franc

Membership of International Organisations: United Nations, Organisation of African Unity (OAU), Signatory to the Lome Convention, Non-Aligned Movement.

Kenya

Republic of Kenya
Head of State: President Daniel Arap Moi
Ruling Party: Kenya African National Union
Land Area: 580,367 (sq. km.)
Capital City: Nairobi
Population: 20.35 million (1983)
Population Growth Rate: 4.0%
Infant Mortality: 77
Life Expectancy: 54
Gross National Product (GNP): 5,960 (Million US Dollars)
GNP Per Head: $290
Language: Swahili, English, Kikuyu, Luo, Luhya
Religion: Christian, Pantheist, Hindu, Muslim
Currency: Kenya Shilling
Membership of International Organisations: United Nations, the Organisation of African Unity (OAU), the Commonwealth, Signatory to the Lome Convention, Non-Aligned Movement.

Lesotho

Kingdom of Lesotho
Head of State: King Moshoeshe II
Ruling Party: n/a
Land Area: 30,355 (sq. km.)
Capital City: Maseru
Population: 1.51 million (1983)
Population Growth Rate: 2.4%
Infant Mortality: 94
Life Expectancy: 54
Gross National Product (GNP): 730 (Million US Dollars)
GNP Per Head: $480
Language: Sesotho, English
Religion: Christian
Currency: Loti
Membership of International Organisations: United Nations, Organisation of African Unity (OAU), the Commonwealth, Signatory to the Lome Convention, Non-Aligned Movement.

Liberia

Republic of Liberia
Head of State: Samuel Kanyon Doe
Ruling Party: National Democratic Party
Land Area: 111, 369 (sq. km)
Capital City: Monrovia
Population: 2.19 Million
Population Growth Rate: 3.3%
Infant Mortality: 91
Life Expectancy: 50
Gross National Product (GNP): 1,040 (Million US Dollars)
GNP Per Head: $470
Language: English
Religion: Muslim, Christian, Pantheist
Currency: Liberian Dollar
Membership of International Organisations: United Nations, Organisation of African Unity (OAU), Non-Aligned Movement.

Libya

Great Socialist People's Libyan Arab Jamahariya
Head of State: Mu'ammar al-Qathafi
Ruling Party; n/a
Land Area: 1,775,500 (sq. km.)
Capital City: Tripoli
Population: 3.60 million (1983)
Population Growth Rate: 4.0%
Infant Mortality: 95
Life Expectancy: 59
Gross National Product (GNP): 27,000 (Million US Dollars)
GNP Per Head: $7,500
Language: Arabic
Religion: Muslim
Currency: Libyan Dinar
Membership of International Organisations: United Nations, Organisation of African Unity (OAU), League of Arab States, Non-Aligned Movement, Organisation of Petroleum Exporting Countries.

Madagascar

Democratic Republic of Madagascar
Head of State: President Didier Ratsiraka
Ruling Party: Malagasy Vanguard of Revolution
Land Area: 587,041 (sq. km.)
Capital City: Antananarivo
Population: 10.21 million
Population Growth Rate: 2.9%
Infant Mortality: 116
Life Expectancy: 52
Gross National Product (GNP): 2,510 (Million US Dollars)
GNP Per Head: $250
Language: Malagasy, French, Hova
Religion: Muslim, Christian, Pantheist
Currency: Franc Malagasy
Membership of International Organisations: United Nations, Organisation of African Unity (OAU), Signatory to the Lome Convention, Non-Aligned Movement.

Malawi

Republic of Malawi
Head of State: President Hastings Kamuzu Banda
Ruling Party: Malawi Congress Party
Land Area: 118,484 (sq. km.)
Capital City: Lilongwe
Population: 7.04 million (1983)
Population Growth Rate: 3.1%
Infant Mortality: 137
Life Expectancy: 45
Gross National Product (GNP): 1,160 (Million US Dollars)
GNP Per Head: $170
Language: Chichewa, English
Religion: Muslim, Christian, Pantheist
Currency: Kwacha
Membership of International Organisations: Organisation of African Unity (OAU), the Commonwealth, Signatory to the Lome Convention, Non-Aligned Movement.

Mali

Republic of Mali
Head of State: General Moussa Traore
Ruling Party: People's Democratic Union of Mali
Land Area: 1,240,000 (sq. km.)
Capital City: Bamako
Population: 7.51 million (1983)
Population Growth Rate: 2.5%
Infant Mortality: 132
Life Expectancy: 46
Gross National Product (GNP): 1,070 (Million US Dollars)
GNP Per Head: $140
Language: French, Bambara, Fulfulde, Sonari, Tamashek, Soninke, Dogon
Religion: Muslim, Christian, Pantheist
Currency: Mali Franc
Membership of International Organisations: United Nations, Organisation of African Unity (OAU), Signatory to the Lome Convention, Non-Aligned Movement.

Mauritania

Islamic Republic of Mauritania
Head of State: President Ould Sid' Ahmed Taya
Ruling Party: n/a
Land Area: 1,030,700 (sq. km.)
Capital City: Nouakchott
Population: 1.69 million (1983)
Population Growth Rate: 2.1%
Infant Mortality: 138
Life Expectancy: 46
Gross National Product (GNP): 700 (Millions US Dollars)
GNP Per Head: $410
Language: Arabic
Religion: Muslim
Currency: Ougujia
Membership of International Organisations: United Nations, Organisation of African Unity (OAU), League of Arab States, Signatory to the Lome Convention, Non-Aligned Movement.

Mauritius

Head of Government: Prime Minister Aneerood Jugnauth
Ruling Party: Socialist Movement of Mauritius
Land Area: 2,040 (sq. km.)
Capital City: Port Louis
Population: 1.03 million (1983)
Population Growth Rate: 1.4%
Infant Mortality: 32
Life Expectancy: 66
Gross National Product (GNP): 1,110 (Million US Dollars)
GNP Per Head: $1,070
Language: English, French, Hindi, Creole
Religion: Hindu, Muslim, Christian
Currency: Mauritius Rupee
Membership of International Organisations: United Nations, Organisation of African Unity (OAU), the Commonwealth, Signatory to the Lome Convention, Non-Aligned Movement.

Morocco

Kingdom of Morocco
Head of State: King Hassan II
Ruling Party: n/a
Land Area: 458,730 (sq. km.)
Capital City: Rabat
Population: 21.92 million (1983)
Population Growth Rate: 2.4%
Infant Mortality: 125
Life Expectancy: 59
Gross National Product (GNP): 13,390 (Million US Dollars)
GNP Per Head: $610
Language: Arabic
Religion: Muslim
Currency: Dirham
Membership of International Organisations: United Nations Organisation of African Unity (currently boycotting because of the dispute over Western Sahara), the League of Arab States, Non-Aligned Movement.

Mozambique

People's Republic of Mozambique
Head of State: President Joaquim Alberto Chissano
Ruling Party: Mozambique Liberation Front (FRELIMO) Party
Land Area: 799,380 (sq. km.)
Capital City: Maputo
Population: 13.7934 million (1983)
Population Growth Rate: 2.6%
Infant Mortality: 111
Life Expectancy: 46
Gross National Product (GNP):n/a
GNP Per Head: n/a
Language: Portuguese, Ronga, Shangaan, Muchope
Religion: Christian, Pantheist
Currency: Metical
Membership of International Organisations: United Nations, Organisation of African Unity (OAU), Non-Aligned Movement.

Niger

Republic of Niger
Head of State: Colonel Ali Seibou
Ruling Party: n/a
Land Area: 1,267,000 (sq. km.)
Capital City: Niamey
Population: 6.39 million
Population Growth Rate: 3.0%
Infant Mortality: 132
Life Expectancy: 43
Gross National Product (GNP): 1,250 (Million US Dollars)
GNP Per Head: $200
Language: French, Fulani, Hausa, Songhui, Tuareg
Religion: Muslim
Currency: CFA Franc
Membership of International Organisations: United Nations, Organisation of African Unity (OAU), Signatory to the Lome Convention, Non-Aligned Movement.

Nigeria

Federal Republic of Nigeria
Head of State: President Babangida
Ruling Party: n/a
Land Area: 923,768 (sq. km.)
Capital City: Abuja
Population: 99.66 million (1983)
Population Growth Rate: 2.8%
Infant Mortality: 109
Life Expectancy: 50
Gross National Product (GNP): 75,940 (Million US Dollars)
GNP Per Head: $760
Language: Hausa, Ibo, Yoruba, English
Religion: Muslim, Christian, Pantheist
Currency: Naira
Membership of International Organisations: United Nations, Organisation of African Unity (OAU), Economic Community of West African States, Organisation of Petroleum Exporting Countries, the Commonwealth, Signatory to the Lome Convention, Non-Aligned Movement.

Rwanda

Head of State: President Juvenal Habyarimana
Ruling Party: National Revolutionary Movement for Development of Rwanda
Land Area: 26,338 (sq. km.)
Capital City: Kigali
Population: 5.83 million (1983)
Population Growth Rate: 3.3%
Infant Mortality: 126
Life Expectancy: 47
Gross National Product (GNP): 1,730 (Million US Dollars)
GNP Per Head: $290
Language: Kinyarwanda, French
Religion: Christian, Pantheist
Currency: Rwanda Franc
Membership of International Organisations: United Nations, Organisation of African Unity (OAU), Signatory to the Lome Convention, Non-Aligned Movement.

Sao Tome and Principe

Head of State: President Manuel Pinto Da Costa
Ruling Party: Liberation Movement of Sao Tome and Principe
Land Area: 964 (sq. km.)
Capital City: Sao Tome

Population: 108,000 (1983)
Population Growth Rate: 2.2%
Infant Mortality: 62
Life Expectancy: 63
Gross National Product (GNP): 30 (Million US Dollars)
GNP Per Head: $310
Language: Portuguese
Religion: Christian
Currency: Dobra
Membership of International Organisations: United Nations, Organisation of African Unity (OAU), Non-Aligned Movement.

Senegal

Head of State: President Abdou Diof
Ruling Party: Socialist Party of Senegal
Land Area: 196,192 (sq. km.)
Capital City: Dakar
Population: 6.37 million (1983)
Population Growth Rate: 2.8%
Infant Mortality: 155
Life Expectancy: 46
Gross National Product (GNP): 2,400 (Million US Dollars)
GNP Per Head: $370
Language: French, Wolof, Diola, Bambara, Peul
Religion: Muslim, Christian
Currency: CFA Franc
Membership of International Organisations: United Nations, Organisations of African Unity (OAU), Signatory to the Lome Convention, Non-Aligned Movement.

Seychelles

Republic of Seychelles
Head of State: President France Albert Rene
Ruling Party: Seychelles People's Progressive Movement
Land Area: 433 (sq. km.)
Capital City: Victoria
Population: 66,000 (1983)
Population Growth Rate: 1.3%
Infant Mortality: 51
Life Expectancy: 69
Gross National Product (GNP): 140 (Million US Dollars)
GNP Per Head: $2,400
Language: Seychellois, English, French
Religion: Christian
Currency: Seychelles Rupee
Membership of International Organisations: United Nations, Organisation of African Unity (OAU), the Commonwealth, Signatory to the Lome Convention, Non-Aligned Movement.

Sierra Leone

Republic of Sierra Leone
Head of States: President Joseph Saidu Mommoh
Ruling Party: All People's Congress
Land Area: 72,325 (sq. km.)
Capital City: Freetown
Population: 3.74 million (1983)
Population Growth Rate: 2.1%
Infant Mortality: 190
Life Expectancy: 38
Gross National Product (GNP): 1,380 (Million US Dollars)
GNP Per Head: $370
Language: English, Krio, Mende, Temne, Limba
Religion: Muslim, Christian, Pantheist
Currency: Leone
Membership of International Organisations: United Nations, Organisation of African Unity (OAU), the Commonwealth, Signatory to the Lome Convention.

Somalia

Democratic Republic of Somalia
Head of State: President Mohammed Said Barre
Ruling Party: Somali Revolutionary Socialist Party.
Land Area: 637,657 (sq. km.)
Capital City: Mogadishu
Population: 5.38 million (1983)
Population Growth Rate: 2.8%
Infant Mortality: 184
Life Expectancy: 46
Gross National Product (GNP): 1,450 (Million US Dollars)
GNP Per Head: $270
Language: Somali, Arabic, Italian, English
Religion: Muslim
Currency: Somali Shilling
Membership of International Organisations: United Nations, Organisation of African Unity (OAU), League of Arab States, Signatory to the Lome Convention, Non-Aligned Movement.

Sudan

Republic of Sudan
Head of State: President Ahmad Ali Al-Mirghani
Ruling Party: Ummah Party and Democratic Unionist Party
Land Area: 2,505,813 (sq. km.)
Capital City: Khartoum
Population: 21.93 million (1983)
Population Growth Rate: 2.9%
Infant Mortality: 119
Life Expectancy: 48
Gross National Product (GNP): 7,350 (Million US Dollars)
GNP Per Head: $330
Language: Arabic
Religion: Muslim, Christian, Pantheist
Currency: Sudanese Pound
Membership of International Organisations: United Nations, Organisation of African Unity (OAU), League of Arab States, Signatory to the Lome Convention, Non-Aligned Movement.

Swaziland

Kingdom of Swaziland
Head of State: King Mswati III
Ruling Party: n/a
Land Area: 17,363 (sq.km.)
Capital City: Mbabane
Population: 758,000 (1983)
Population Growth Rate: 3.5%
Infant Mortality: 130
Life Expectancy: 54
Gross National Product (GNP): 490 (Million US Dollars)
GNP Per Head: $650
Language: Siswati, English
Religion: Christian, Pantheist
Currency: Lilangeni
Membership of International Organisations: United Nations, Organisation of African Unity (OAU), the Commonwealth, Signatory to the Lome Convention, Non-Aligned Movement.

Tanzania

United Republic of Tanzania
Head of State: President Ali Hassan Mwinyi
Ruling Party: Chama Cha Mapinduzi (Revolutionary Party of Tanzania)
Land Area: 945,087 (sq. km.)
Capital City: Dar-es-Salaam
Population: 22.24 million (1983)
Population Growth Rate: 3.4%
Infant Mortality: 98
Life Expectancy: 52
Gross National Product (GNP): 5,840 (Million US Dollars)
GNP Per Head: $270
Language: Swahili, English
Religion: Muslim, Christian, Pantheist
Currency: Tanzanian Shilling
Membership of International

Organisations: United Nations, Organisation of African Unity (OAU), the Commonwealth, Signatory to the Lome Convention, Non-Aligned Movement.

Togo

Republic of Togo
Head of State: General Gnassingbe Eyademma
Ruling Party: Rally of the Togolese People
Land Area: 56,785 (sq. km.)
Capital City: Lome
Population: 3.03 million
Population Growth Rate: 2.8%
Infant Mortality: 122
Life Expectancy: 51
Gross National Product (GNP): 750 (Million US Dollars)
GNP Per Head: $250
Language: French, Kabiye, Ewe
Religion: Christian, Muslim, Pantheist
Currency: CFA Franc
Membership of International Organisations: United Nations, Organisation of African Unity (OAU), Signatory to the Lome Convention.

Tunisia

Republic of Tunisia
Head of State: President Zine Al-Abidine Ben Ali
Ruling Party: Destour Socialist Party
Land Area: 163,610 (sq. km.)
Capital City: Tunis
Population: 7.14 million (1983)
Population Growth Rate: 2.4%
Infant Mortality: 65
Life Expectancy: 62
Gross National Product (GNP): 8,730 (Million US Dollars)
GNP Per Head: $1,220
Language: Arabic
Religion: Muslim
Currency: Dinar
Membership of International Organisations: United Nations, Organisation of African Unity (OAU), League of Arab States, Non-Aligned Movement.

Uganda

Republic of Uganda
Head of State: Yoweri Museveni
Ruling Party: National Resistance Movement
Land Area: 236,036 (sq. km.)
Capital City: Kampala
Population: 15.47 million (1983)
Population Growth Rate: 3.2%
Infant Mortality: 120
Life Expectancy: 51
Gross National Product (GNP): 5,000 (Million US Dollars)
GNP Per Head: $230
Language: Swahili, English, Luganda, Lwo, Ateso
Religion: Muslim, Christian, Pantheist
Currency: Uganda Shilling
Membership of International Organisations: United Nations, Organisation of African Unity (OAU), the Commonwealth, Signatory to the Lome Convention, Non-Aligned Movement.

Zaire

Republic of Zaire
Head of State: President Mobutu Sese Seko
Ruling Party: National Revolutionary Movement
Land Area: 2,344,885 (sq. km.)
Capital City: Kinsasha
Population: 30.55 million (1983)
Population Growth Rate: 3.0%
Infant Mortality: 106
Life Expectancy: 51
Gross National Product (GNP): 5,220 (Million US Dollars)
GNP Per Head: $170
Language: French, Kiswahili, Kiluba, Kikongo, Lingala
Religion: Christian, Pantheist
Currency: Zaire
Membership of International Organisations: United Nations, Organisation of African Unity (OAU), Signatory to the Lome Convention, Non-Aligned Movement.

Zambia

Republic of Zambia
Head of State: President Kenneth David Kaunda
Ruling Party: United National Independence Party
Land Area: 752,614 (sq. km.)
Capital City: Lusaka
Population: 6.64 million (1983)
Population Growth Rate: 3.2%
Infant Mortality: 105
Life Expectancy: 51
Gross National Product (GNP): 2,620 (Million US Dollars)
GNP Per Head: $400
Language: English, Bemba, Lozi, Lunda, Tonga, Nyanja
Religion: Christian, Pantheist, Muslim
Currency: Kwacha
Membership of International Organisations: United Nations, Organisation of African Unity (OAU), the Commonwealth, Signatory to the Lome Convention, Non-Aligned Movement.

Zimbabwe

Republic of Zimbabwe
Head of State: President Robert Mugabe
Ruling Party: Zimbabwe African National Union (ZANU) . Patriotic Front
Land Area: 390,759 (sq.km.)
Capital City: Harare
Population: 8.40 million (1983)
Population Growth Rate: 3.2%
Infant Mortality: 83
Life Expectancy: 57
Gross National Product (GNP): 5,450 (Million US Dollars)
GNP Per Head: $650
Language: Shona, Ndebele, English
Religion: Christian, Pantheist
Currency: Zimbabwe Dollar
Membership of International Organisations: United Nations, Organisation of African Unity (OAU), Southern African Development Co-ordination Conference, Non-Aligned Movement, the Commonwealth, Signatory to the Lome Convention.

Asia

The Asian continent, which contains the majority of the population of the world, grouped in vastly different countries, is in many ways the continent that analysts expect to set the global pace in the approaching 21st century. Asia contains the world's two most populous nations – India and China – as well as other important states with huge and growing populations, such as Pakistan, Bangladesh, Japan and Indonesia. Furthermore it is often forgotten that more than half of the territory of the Soviet Union is contained within Asia.

Historically the site of ancient civilisations and the birthplace of great world religions, Asia is today a home to thriving economies, technical innovations, huge markets and great potentials. To believe certain politicians and labour leaders in the United States of America even such tiny states and regions as Singapore and Taiwan now pose an economic threat to the superpower US. But Asia's economic advance is set not just to embrace Japan and the statelets of the Far East. It is often forgotten that India has long been amongst the world's top ten industrial nations, whilst China is engaged in a huge modernisation programme, Indonesia and other countries are rising powers and Japanese investment, amongst other factors, may yet transform the face of the Soviet Far East.

Stories of economic success and potential are not the only face of Asia. After Europe it was the second continent on whose soil the socialist system became consolidated. But it has also been Asia that has seen the most determined and vicious attempts to roll back the new social system. Aside from the continuing Iran/Iraq war this has been the context for the major wars in the post World War II period – those waged against Korea and against Vietnam and the other Indochinese countries. It is also in Asia that atomic weapons have been used in wartime for the first, and hopefully only, time – against the Japanese cities of Hiroshima and Nagasaki in 1945.

The consequences of those atomic strikes and wars are still with us. Many are still dying from the effects of radiation. The national division of Korea persists with its attendant dangers for world peace whilst the contradictions in Indochina continue to make Kampuchea a 'killing field'.

Elsewhere in Asia a host of old and new problems – many of them directly or indirectly the legacy of the imperialist practice of 'divide and rule' – continue to hold back steady progressive development. In a number of countries military or quasi-military dictatorships are in power, and against them an increasingly consistent democratic struggle is being waged.

Other acute problems essentially revolve around an aspect of the national question. They bring in their wake not only democratic struggles but also terrorism, divisions, foreign intervention and internationalisation. The Tamil question in Sri Lanka and the conflict in India's Punjab are cases in point. Also falling within this broad context is the situation in Afghanistan, whose long-running civil war has been exacerbated by the involvement of foreign forces, whilst the prospects for its end centre on the exclusion of foreign interference.

In addition to such problems of political democracy, national independence and integrity, many countries face acute social problems which centre around questions such as the oppression of women or the stigma of 'untouchability' and the caste system generally in India. Such anachronisms not only cast a shadow over the lives of those immediately affected, they place in question the progressive credentials of the country concerned and prevent the full mobilisation of the human resources of the country concerned for its national development.

Overhanging everything is Asia's enmeshing in the nuclear race. Whilst some missiles in the region are to be destroyed as a result of the agreement reached by the leaderships of the United States and the Soviet Union at the end of 1987, the continent is still under a nuclear threat – both from weapons held on foreign military bases – as in the Philippines and in South Korea – and from Asian countries that have joined the nuclear club, such as China. This latter status, it is constantly speculated, could easily be reached by India, Pakistan and some other countries.

Asia will continue to progress but it will certainly not be plain sailing – not least because outside forces can grasp the potential of the region.

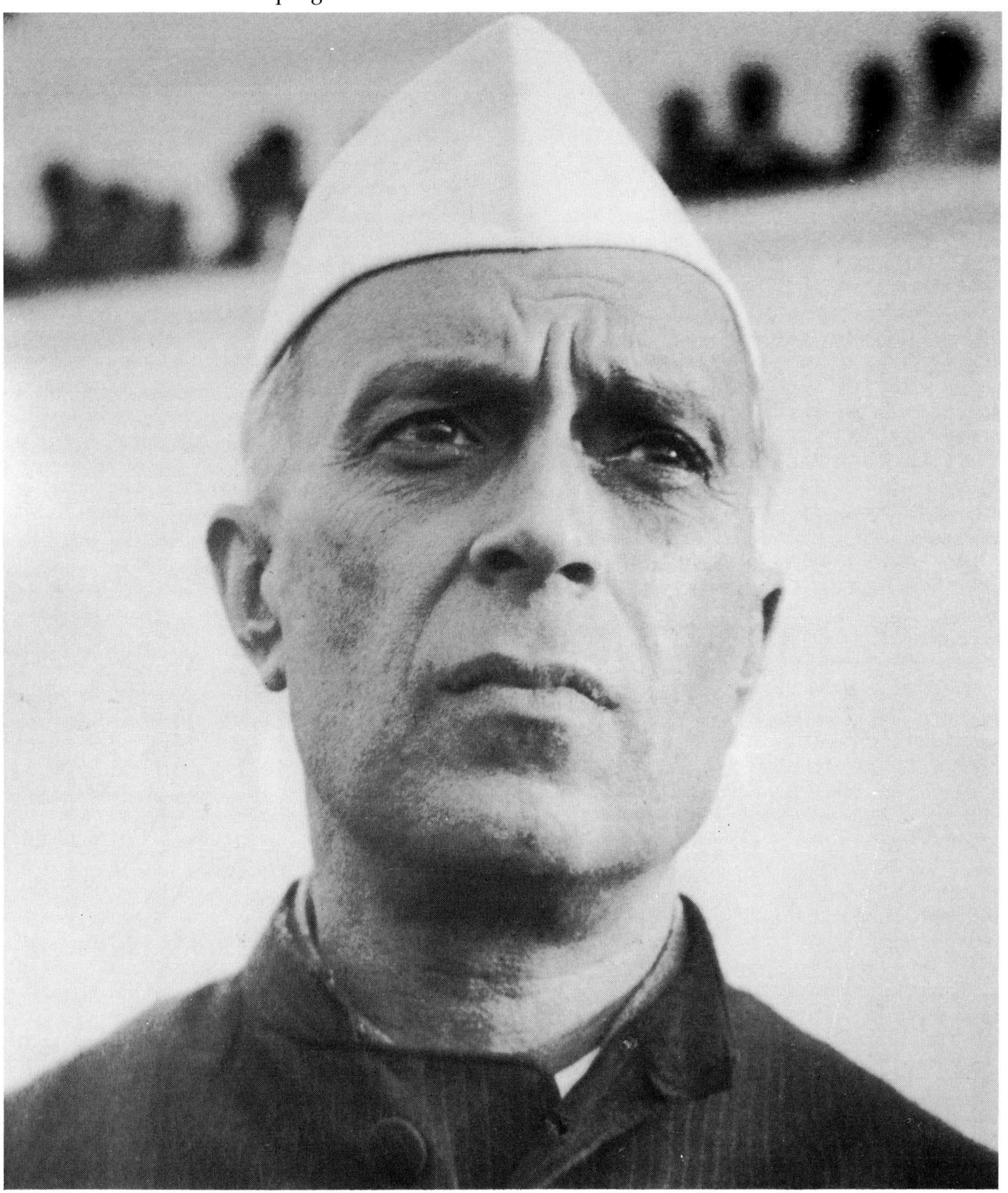

1989 marks the centenary of Jawaharlal Nehru's birth. The first leader of independent India would not have envisaged the turmoil which continues four decades after Independence

Asia

MONGOLIA
AFGHANISTAN
CHINA
PAKISTAN
NEPAL
BHUTAN
BURMA
INDIA
BANGLADESH
SRI
LANKA
MALDIVES
MALAYSIA
SINGAPORE

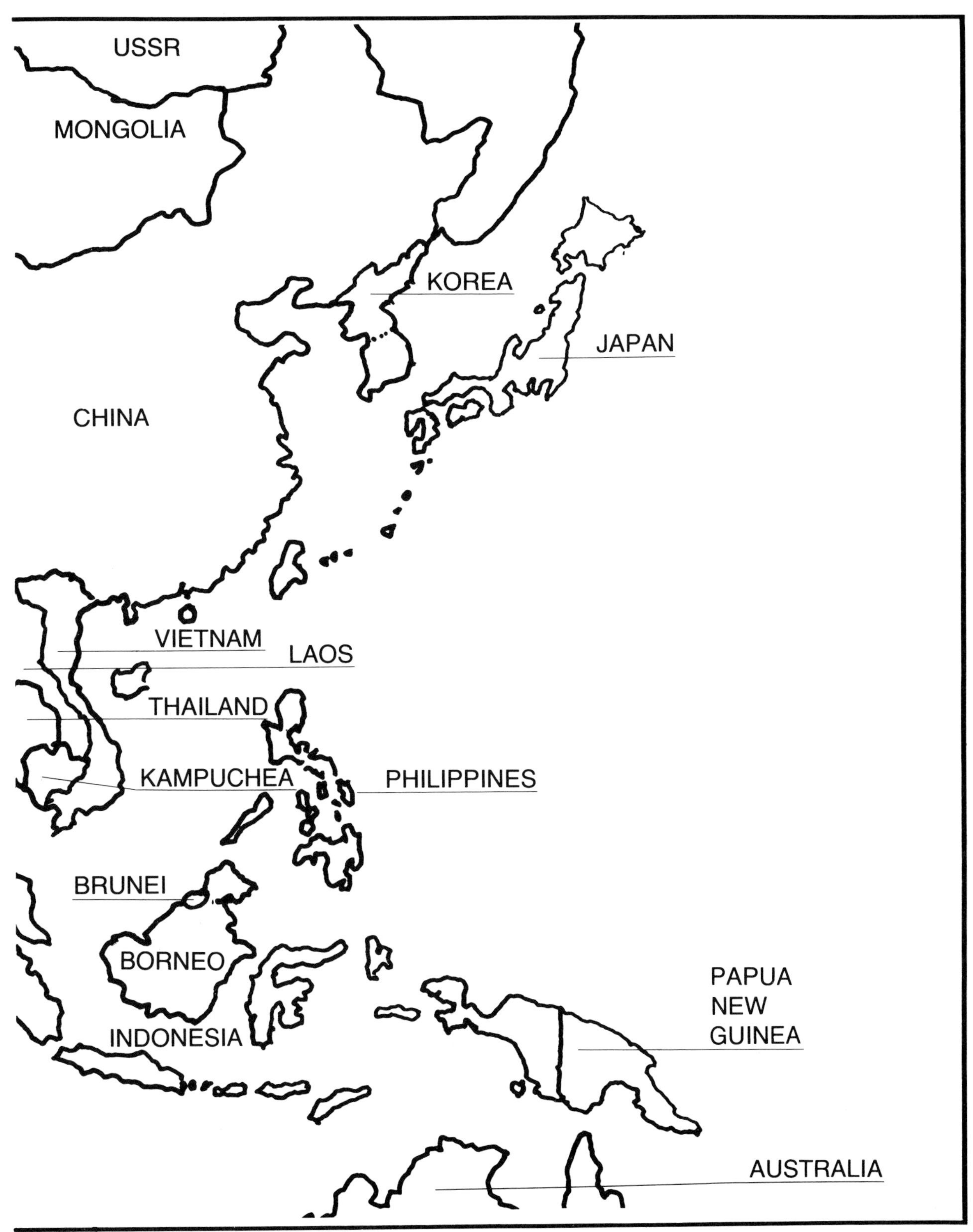
USSR
MONGOLIA
CHINA
KOREA
JAPAN
VIETNAM
LAOS
THAILAND
KAMPUCHEA
PHILIPPINES
BRUNEI
BORNEO
INDONESIA
PAPUA
NEW
GUINEA
AUSTRALIA

Afghanistan

Republic of Afghanistan
Head of State: President Dr. Najibullah
Ruling Party: People's Democratic Party of Afghanistan
Land Area: 647,497 (sq.km)
Capital City: Kabul
Population: 17.72 Million (1983)
Population Growth Rate: 2.6%
Infant Mortality: 205
Life Expectancy: 36
Gross National Product (GNP): n/a**GNP Per Head:** n/a
Language: Dari, Pushtu
Religion: Muslim
Currency: Afghani
Membership of International Organisations: United Nations, Non-Aligned Movement

Bangladesh

People's Republic of Bangladesh
Head of State: General Mohammed Ershad
Ruling Party: Jatiya Party
Land Area: 143,998 (sq. km)
Capital City: Dhaka
Population: 100.59 million (1983)
Population Growth Rate: 2.5%
Infant Mortality: 133
Life Expectancy: 50
Gross National Product (GNP): 14,770 (Million US Dollars)
GNP Per Head: $150
Language: Bengali
Religion: Muslim
Currency: Taka
Membership of International Organisations: United Nations, South Asian Regional Co-operation Council, Non-Aligned Movement, the Commonwealth

Bhutan

Kingdom of Bhutan
Head of State: King Jigme Singye Wangchuk
Ruling Party: n/a
Land Area: 47,000 (sq.km.)
Capital City: Thimpu
Population: 1.24 million (1983)
Population Growth Rate: 2.0%
Infant Mortality: 163
Life Expectancy: 43
Gross National Product (GNP): 190 (Million US Dollars)
GNP Per Head: $160
Language: Dzongkha
Religion: Buddhist
Currency: Ngultrum, Indian Rupee
Membership of International Organisations: South Asian Regional Co-operation
Council, Non-Aligned Movement, United Nations

Brunei

Sultanate of Brunei
Head of State: Sultan Muda Hassanal Waddaulah
Ruling Party: n/a
Land Area: 5,765 (sq.km.)
Capital City: Bandar Seri-Begawan
Population: 224,000
Population Growth Rate: 3.7%
Infant Mortality: 18
Life Expectancy: 74
Gross National Product (GNP): 3,940 (Million US Dollars)
GNP Per Head: $17,580
Language: Malay
Religion: Muslim
Currency: Brunei Dollar
Membership of International Organisations: Association of South East Asian Nations (ASEAN), the Commonwealth

Burma

Socialist Republic of the Union of Burma
Head of State: President U San Yu
Ruling Party: Burma Socialist Programme Party
Land Area: 676,552 (sq. km)
Capital City: Rangoon
Population: 36.83 million (1983)
Population Growth Rate : 2.0%
Infant Mortality: 96
Life Expectancy: 58
Gross National Product (GNP): 7,080 (Million US Dollars)
GNP Per Head: $190
Language: Burmese
Religion: Buddhist, Christian, Muslim
Currency: Kyat
Membership of International Organisations: United Nations

China

People's Republic of China
Head of State: President Yang Shungkun
Ruling Party: Communist Party of China
Land Area: 9,571,300 (sq.km.)
Capital City: Beijing (Peking)
Population: 1041 million (1983)
Population Growth Rate: 1.4%
Infant Mortality: 67
Life Expectancy: 69
Gross National Product (GNP): 318,920 (Million US Dollars)
GNP Per Head: $310
Language: Chinese, Tibetan, Uyghur
Religion: Buddhist, Muslim, Christian
Currency: Yuan Renminbi
Membership of International Organisations: United Nations

India

Republic of India
Head of State: President Ramaswamy Venkataraman
Ruling Party: Indian National Congress (Indira)
Land Area: 3,287,263 (sq.km.)
Capital City: New Delhi
Population: 765.147 million (1983)
Population Growth Rate: 2.2%
Infant Mortality: 94
Life Expectancy: 56
Gross National Product (GNP): 194,820 (Million US Dollars)
GNP Per Head: $250
Language: Hindi, Bengali, Gujarati, Punjabi, Tamil, Malayalam, Urdu, Telugu, Assamese, Kannada, Kashmiri, Marathi, Oriya, Sindhi, English
Religion: Hindu, Muslim, Buddhist, Christian
Currency: Rupee
Membership of International Organisations: United Nations, South Asian Regional Co-operation Council, Non-Aligned Movement, the Commonwealth

Indonesia

Republic of Indonesia
Head of State: President Suharto
Ruling Party: Sekber Gologan Karya GolkarLand Area: 1,919,270 (sq.km.)
Capital City. Djakarta
Population: 162.21 million (1983)
Population Growth Rate: 2.3%
Infant Mortality: 102
Life Expectancy: 55
Gross National Product (GNP): 86,590 (Million US Dollars)

GNP Per Head: $530
Language: Bahasa, Indonesian, Javanese
Religion: Muslim, Hindu, Buddhist, Christian
Currency: Rupiah
Membership of International Organisations: United Nations, Association of South East Asian Nations, Non-Aligned Movement

Japan

Head of State: Emperor Hirohito
Ruling Party: Liberal Democratic Party
Land Area: 377,748 (sq.km.)
Capital City: Tokyo
Population: 120.58 Million
Population: Growth Rate: 0.9%
Infant Mortality: 7
Life Expectancy: 77
Gross National Product (GNP): 1,366.04 (Million US Dollars)
GNP Per Head: $11,330
Language. Japanese
Religion: Shintoism, Buddhist
Currency: Yen
Membership of International Organisations: United Nations, Organisation of Economic Co-operation and Development (OECD)

Kampuchea

People's Republic of Kampuchea
Head of State: President Heng Samrin
Ruling Party: People's Revolutionary Party of Kampuchea
Land Area: 181,035 (sq.km.)
Capital City: Phnom Penh
Population: 8.2 Million
Population Growth Rate: Not Available
Infant Mortality: Not Availble
Life Expectancy: Not Available
Gross National Product (GNP): n/a
GNP Per Head: n/a
Language: Khmer
Religion: Buddhist. Muslim and Christian minorities
Currency: Riel
Membership of International Organisations: n/a

Korea

Democratic People's Republic of Korea
Head of State: President Kim II Sung
Ruling Party: Workers' Party of Korea
Land Area: 120,538 (sq.km)
Capital City: Pyongyang
Population: 20.35 million (1983)
Population Growth Rate: 2.6%
Infant Mortality: 32
Life Expectancy: 74
Gross National Product (GNP):n/a
GNP Per Head: n/a
Language: Korean
Religion: None
Currency: Won
Membership of International Organisations: Non-Aligned Movement

Laos

People's Democratic Republic of Laos
Head of State: President Souphvanouvong
Ruling Party: Lao People's Revolutionary Party
Land Area: 236,800 (sq.km.)
Capital City: Vientianne
Population: 3.62 million (1983)
Population Growth Rate: 1.6%
Infant Mortality: 159
Life Expectancy: 45
Gross National Product (GNP): n/a
GNP Per Head: n/a
Language: Lao, Meo
Religion: Buddhist
Currency: New Kip
Membership of International Organisations: United Nations, Non-Aligned Movement

Malaysia

Kingdom of Malaysia
Head of State: Almutawakkil Alallah Sultan Ishkandar Yang Bi-Pertuan Agong
Ruling Party: National Front Coalition
Land Area: 332,632 (sq.km.)
Capital City: Kuala Lumpur
Population: 15.61 million (1983)
Population Growth Rate: 2.4%
Infant Mortality: 29
Life Expectancy: 69
Gross National Product (GNP): 31,930 (Million US Dollars)
GNP Per Head: $2,050
Language: Bahasa Malay, Tamil, Chinese, English
Religion: Muslim, Christian, Buddhist
Currency: Malaysian Ringgit
Membership of International Organisations: United Nations, Association of South East Asian Nations (ASEAN), Non-Aligned Movement, the Commonwealth

Maldives

Republic of Maldives
Head of State: President Abdul Gayoom
Ruling Party: n/a
Land Area: 298 (sq.km.)
Capital City: Male
Population: 178,000
Population Growth Rate: 2.9%
Infant Mortality: 88
Life Expectancy: 53
Gross National Product (GNP): 50 (Million US Dollars)
GNP Per Head: $290
Language: Dhiveni
Religion: Muslim
Currency: Rufiyaa
Membership of International Organisations: United Nations, South Asian Regional Co-operation Council, Non-Aligned Movement, the Commonwealth

Mongolia

People's Republic of Mongolia
Head of State: President Jambyn Batmonh
Ruling Party: Mongolian People's Revolutionary Party
Land Area: 1,565,000 (sq. km.)
Capital City: Ulan Bator
Population: 1.90 million (1983)
Population Growth Rate: 2.8%
Infant Mortality: 51
Life Expectancy: 63
Gross National Product (GNP): n/a
GNP Per Head: n/a
Language: Mongolian
Religion: Buddhist
Currency: Tugrik
Membership of International Organisations: United Nations, Council for Mutual Economic Assistance (COMECON)

Nepal

Kingdom of Nepal
Head of State: King Birendra

Ruling Party: n/a
Land Area: 140,797 (sq. km.)
Capital City: Kathmandu
Population: 16.52 million
Population Growth Rate: 2.6%
Infant Mortality: 145
Life Expectancy: 47
Gross National Product (GNP): 2,610 (Million US Dollars)
GNP Per Head: $160
Language: Nepali
Religion: Hindu, Buddhist
Currency: Nepalese Rupee
Membership of International Organisations: United Nations, South Asian Regional Co-operation Council, Non-Aligned Movement.

Pakistan

Islamic Republic of Pakistan
Head of State: General Mohammed Zia ul Haq
Ruling Party: n/a
Land Area: 828,453 (sq km)
Capital City: Islamabad
Population: 94.93 million (1983)
Population Growth Rate: 3.0%
Infant Mortality: 211
Life expectancy: 51
Gross National Product (GNP): 36,230 (Million US Dollars)
GNP Per Head: $380
Language: Urdu, Sindi, Baluchi, Pushtoon, English
Religion: Muslim
Currency: Rupee
Membership of International Organisations: United Nations, South Asian Regional Co-operation Council, Non-Aligned Movement.

Philippines

Republic of the Philippines
Head of State: President Corazon Aquino
Ruling Party: Coalition including New Society Movement (KBL), United Nationalist Democratic Organisation (UNIDO)
Land Area: 300,000 (sq km)
Capital City: Manila
Population: 54.72 Million (1983)
Population Growth Rate: 2.7%
Infant Mortality: 51
Life Expectancy: 63
Gross National Product (GNP): 32,630 (Million US Dollars)
GNP Per Head: $600
Language: Tagalog, Cebuano, Iloco
Religion: Christian, Muslim
Currency: Peso
Membership of International Organisations: United Nations, Association of South East Asian Nations (ASEAN)

Singapore

Republic of Singapore
Head of State: President Wee Kim Wee
Ruling Party: People's Action Party
Land Area: 618.1 (sq km)
Capital City: Singapore
Population: 2.55 Million (1983)
Population Growth Rate: 1.3%
Infant Mortality: 11
Life Expectancy: 72
Gross National Product (GNP): 18,970 (Million US Dollars)
GNP Per Head: $7,420
Language: Chinese, Malay, Tamil, English
Religion: Buddhist, Muslim, Hindu, Christian
Currency: Singapore Dollar
Membership of International Organisations: United Nations, Association of South East Asian Nations (ASEAN), the Commonwealth, Non-Aligned Movement.

Sri Lanka

Democratic Socialist Republic of Sri Lanka
Head of State: President Junius Richard Jayewardene
Ruling Party: United National Party
Land Area: 65,610 (sq km)
Capital City: Colombo
Population: 16.41 Million (1983)
Population Growth Rate: 1.8%
Infant Mortality: 32
Life Expectancy: 69
Gross National Product (GNP): 5,980 (Million US Dollars)
GNP Per Head: $370
Language: Sinhala, Tamil
Religion: Buddhist, Hindu, Muslim, Christian
Currency: Rupee
Membership of International Organisations: United Nations, South Asian Regional Co-operation Council, the
Non-Aligned Movement, the Commonwealth.

Thailand

Kingdom of Thailand
Head of State: King Bhumibol
Ruling Party: Coalition
Land Area: 513,115 (sq km)
Capital City: Bangkok
Population: 50.95 Million (1983)
Population Growth Rate: 2.2%
Infant Mortality: 51
Life Expectancy: 63
Gross National Product (GNP): 42,100 (Million US Dollars)
GNP Per Head: $830
Language: Thai
Religion: Buddhist, Muslim
Currency: Thai Baht
Membership of International Organisations: United Nations, Association of South East Asian Nations.

Vietnam

Socialist Republic of Vietnam
Head of State: President Vo Chi Cong
Ruling Party: Communist Party of Vietnam
Land Area: 329,566 (sq km)
Capital City: Hanoi
Population: 61.64 Million (1983)
Population Growth Rate: 2.6%
Infant Mortality: 53
Life Expectancy: 65
Gross National Product (GNP): n/a
GNP Per Head: n/a
Language: Vietnamese
Religion: Buddhist, Christian
Currency: Dong
Membership of International Organisations: United Nations, Non-Aligned Movement, Council for Mutual Economic Assistance (COMECON).

The Caribbean

Fourteen countries are detailed in this section with the main body of them consisting of English-speaking members of the Commonwealth. They are predominantly island states with small populations – for example Antigua and Barbuda has a population of 79,000. Other countries have slightly bigger populations, for example there are some two-and-a-half million people in Jamaica and six-and-a-quarter million in the Dominican Republic.

The Caribbean states were essentially created as a result of the slave trade and the resultant plantation economy. Their relative stability and, in certain cases, prosperity, are a tribute to the peoples' ingenuity that belies the tragedy and trauma of the birth of their nations.

In contrast to their South American neighbours the majority of Caribbean states achieved national independence – overwhelmingly by peaceful means – comparitively recently. In the case of Antigua and Barbuda, independence came in 1981.

In most of the countries there is a basic tradition of parliamentary democracy, although the revolutionary upheavals elsewhere in the area have not been without their positive and negative impact on the Caribbean, and this factor may grow to be of increasing importance. The tragedy of Grenada shows this overlap in an all-round way. The revolution lied by Maurice Bishop with his charismatic personality inspired many; they were disgusted by the manner of his death and that of his comrades; these killings provided the pretext for introducing the Caribbean Commonwealth states to the familiar routine of US marines wading ashore to impose their will on other peoples.

One problem that is growing progressively more acute in the region is that of tension between and discrimination against people of varying national and ethnic backgrounds. Although people of Asian (largely Indian) background form the largest ethnic group in Guyana and in Trinidad and Tobago there is a widespread feeling that they have been denied a proper share of political power and that their contributions to the development of the region have been slighted. This criticism is focussed particularly on successive administrations led by the People's National Congress of Guyana.

The late Maurice Bishop – a symbol of revolutionary triumph and tragedy

Other problems increasingly affecting both developed and developing socieities have not left the Caribbean immune. These include political violence, drug addiction and drug smuggling and the foreign debt. Whilst it is true that a country like Haiti has long fallen victim to some of the worst afflictions – internal and external – that are held by many to be characteristic of the Third World this is fortunately far from typical of the region. In stating that it is indisputably part of the Third World we do so largely in a positive sense – the Caribbean states, especially Guyana, have been amongst the staunchest supporters of the anti-apartheid struggle in South Africa.

Caribbean

BAHAMAS
TURKS &
CAICOS
CUBA
DOMINICAN
REPUBLIC
PUERTO
RICO
HAITI
JAMAICA
VIRGIN IS.
ANGUILLA
BARBUDA
ST KITTS-NEVIS
ANTIGUA
MONTSERRAT
GUADELOUPE
DOMINICA
MARTINIQUE
BARBADOS
ST LUCIA
ST VINCENT
GRENADINES
GRENADA
TOBAGO
TRINIDAD
VENEZUELA
GUYANA
SOUTH AMERICA

Antigua and Barbuda

Head of Government: Prime MinisterVere Bird
Ruling Party: Antigua Labour Party
Land Area: 441.6 (sq.km)
Capital City: St. Johns
Population: 79,000
Population Growth Rate: 1.2%
Infant Mortality: 32
Life Expectancy: 72
Gross National Product: 160 (Million US Dollars)
GNP Per Head: $2,030
Language: English
Religion: Christian
Currency: Eastern Caribbean Dollar
Membership of International Organisations: Caribbean Community (CARICOM), Organisation of American States, United Nations, the Commonwealth.

Bahamas

Head of Government: Prime Minister Sir Lynden Pindling.
Ruling Party: Progressive Liberal Party.
Land Area: 13,939 (sq.km)
Capital City: Nassau
Population: 234,000.
Population Growth Rate: 2.1%
Infant Mortality: 32
Life Expectancy: 69
Gross National Product (GNP): 1670 (Million US Dollars)
GNP Per Head: $7,150
Language: English
Religion: Christian
Currency: Bahamian Dollar
Membership of International Organisations: United Nations,Organisations of American States,the Commonwealth, Signatory to the Lome Convention, Non Aligned Movement.

Barbados

Head of Government: Prime Minister Erskine Sandiford
Ruling Party: Barbados Democratic Labour Party
Land Area: 430 (sq. km)
Capital City: Bridgetown
Population: 252,000
Population Growth Rate: 0.3%
Infant Mortality: 26
Life Expectancy: 72
Gross National Product (GNP): 1,180 (Million US Dollars)
GNP Per Head: $4,680
Language: English
Religion: Christian
Currency: Barbados Dollar
Membership of International Organisations: United Nations, Organisation of American States, Caribbean Community (CARICOM), the Commonwealth, Signatory to the Lome Convention , Non Aligned Movement.

Belize

Head of Government: Prime Minister Manuel Esquivel
Ruling Party: United Democratic Party
Land Area: 22,965 (sq.km)
Capital City: Belmopan
Population: 159,000
Population Growth Rate: 1.9%.
Infant Mortality: 45
Life Expectancy: 66
Gross National Product (GNP): 180 (Million US Dollars)
GNP Per Head: $1,130
Language: English, Spanish, Creole, Carib, Maya
Religion: Christian
Currency: Belize Dollar
Membership of International Organisations: Caribbean Community (CARICOM), the Commonwealth, Non-Aligned Movement.

Dominica

Commonwealth of Dominica
Head of Government: Prime Minister Mary Eugenia Charles
Ruling Party: Dominica Freedom Party
Land Area: 750.6 (sq. km)
Capital City: Roseau
Population: 78,000
Population Growth Rate: 0.7%
Infant Mortality: 20
Life Expectancy: 74
Gross National Product (GNP): 90 (Million US Dollars)
GNP Per Head: $1,160
Language: English
Religion: Christian
Currency: Eastern Caribbean Dollar
Membership of International Organisations: Caribbean Community (CARICOM), Organisation of American States, the Commonwealth.

Dominican Republic

Head of State: President Joaquin Balaguer
Ruling Party: Revolutionary Social Christian Party
Land Area: 48,072 (sq.km)
Capital City: Santo Domingo.
Population: 6.26 Million (1983)
Population Growth Rate: 2.4%
Infant Mortality: 65
Life Expectancy: 64
Gross National Product (GNP): 5,050 (Million US Dollars)
GNP Per Head: $810
Language: Spanish
Religion: Christian
Currency: Peso
Membership of International Organisations: United Nations, Organisation of American States.

Grenada

Head of Government: Prime Minister Herbert Blaize
Ruling Party: New National Party
Land Area: 344 (sq.km)
Capital City: St. Georges
Population: 96,000 (1983)
Population Growth Rate: 1.8%
Infant Mortality: 15
Life Expectancy: 69
Gross National Product (GNP): 90(Million US Dollars)
GNP Per Head: $970
Language: English
Religion: Christian
Currency: Eastern Caribbean Dollar
Membership of International Organisations: Caribbean Community (CARICOM) Organisation of American States, the Commonwealth, Non-Aligned Movement.

Guyana

Co-operative Republic of Guyana
Head of State: President Desmond Hoyte
Ruling Party: People's National Congress
Land Area: 214,969 (sq.km)
Capital City: Georgetown
Population: 700,000 (1983)
Population Growth Rate: 1.1%.
Infant Mortality: 33.6
Life Expectancy: 66
Gross National Product (GNP): 460 (Million US Dollars)

GNP Per Head: $570
Language: English, Creole, Hindi,Urdu, Amerindian.
Religion: Christian, Hindu, Muslim.
Currency: Guyana Dollar
Membership of International Organisations: United Nations, Non Aligned Movement, Caribbean Community (CARICOM), the Commonwealth, Signatory to the Lome Convention.

Haiti

Republic of Haiti
Head of State: General Henri Namphy
Ruling Party: n/a
Land Area: 27,750 (sq.km)
Capital City: Port-au-Prince
Population: 5.41 Million (1983)
Population Growth Rate: 1.7%
Infant Mortality: 110
Life Expectancy: 55
Gross National Product (GNP): 1,900 (Million US Dollars)
GNP Per Head: $350
Language: Creole, French.
Religion: Christian, Voodoo
Currency: Gourde
Membership of International Organisations: United Nations, Organisation of American States.

Jamaica

Head of Government: Prime Minister Edward Seaga
Ruling Party: Jamaica Labour Party
Land Area: 10,991 (sq.km)
Capital City: Kingston
Population: 2.32 Million (1983)
Population Growth Rate: 1.1%
Infant Mortality: 10
Life Expectancy: 73
Gross National Product (GNP): 2,090 (Million US Dollars)
GNP Per Head: $940
Language: English
Religion: Christian
Currency: Jamaica Dollar
Membership of InternationalOrganisations: United Nations,Organisation of American States, the Commonwealth, Signatory to the Lome Convention, Non-Aligned Movement, Caribbean Community (CARICOM)

St. Christopher (St. Kitts) & Nevis

Head of Government: Prime Minister Kennedy Simmonds
Ruling Party: People's Action Movement
Land Area: 261.6 (sq.km)
Capital City: Basseterre
Population: 43,000
Population Growth Rate: 0.0%
Infant Mortality: 53
Life Expectancy: 63
Gross National Product (GNP): 70 (Million US Dollars)
GNP Per Head: $1,520
Language: English
Religion: Christian
Currency: Eastern Caribbean Dollar
Membership of International Organisations: Caribbean Community (CARICOM), theCommonwealth

St. Lucia

Head of Government: Prime Minister John Compton.
Ruling Party: United Workers Party
Land Area: 616 (sq.km.)
Capital City: Castries
Population: 136,000 (1983)
Population Growth Rate: 2.1%
Infant Mortality: 30
Life Expectancy: 69
Gross National Product (GNP): 160 (Million US Dollars)
GNP Per Head: $1210
Language: English
Religion: Christian
Currency: Eastern Caribbean Dollar
Membership of International Organisations: United Nations, Caribbean Community (CARICOM), Organisation of American States, the Commonwealth, Signatory to the Lome Convention

St. Vincent & the Grenadines

Head of Government: Prime Minister James Mitchell
Ruling Party: New Democratic Party
Land Area: 389.3 (sq.km)
Capital City: Kingstown
Population: 119,000 (1983)
Population Growth Rate: 1.9%
Infant Mortality: 45
Life Expectancy: 70
Gross National Product (GNP): 100 (Million US Dollars)
GNP Per Head: $840
Language: English
Religion: Christian
Currency: Eastern Caribbean Dollar
Membership of International Organisations: United Nations,Caribbean Community (CARICOM),Organisation of American States, the Commonwealth, Signatory to the Lome Convention.

Trinidad & Tobago

Head of Government: Prime Minister A.N.R. Robinson
Ruling Party: National Alliance for Reconstruction Movement
Land Area: 5,128 (sq.km)
Capital City: Port of Spain
Population: 1.18 Million (1983)
Population Growth Rate: 1.6%
Infant Mortality: 26
Life Expectancy: 69
Gross National Product (GNP): 7,140 (Million US Dollars)
GNP Per Head: $6,010
Language: English
Religion: Christian, Hindu, Muslim.
Currency: Trinidad & Tobago Dollar
Membership of International Organisations: United Nations, South Pacific Forum, the Commonwealth, Signatory to the Lomé Convention

Middle East

The Middle East area is made up of 15 countries (the majority of them belonging to the Arab world) in West Asia and the Mediterranean region. The area includes small sheikhdoms such as Bahrain and Qatar, as well as Saudi Arabia which has a population of less than 2 million but a huge area of more than two million square kilometres. In contrast Turkey has some 50 million people and Iran some 45 million.

Historically the area can be said to have avoided some of the worst excesses of the heyday of European colonialism as compared to other parts of the Third World, but today, with the settler state of Israel in its midst, the Middle East is the scene of one of the most difficult and bitter of contemporary struggles for national liberation.

People who were still under some illusion regarding the nature of Zionism and the regime it has created will surely have been enlightened by the mass popular uprising of the Palestinian people in the occupied West Bank and Gaza Strip that began at the end of 1987 and continued for months without respite.

Several key lessons emerged from that uprising – the fascist nature of the denial of the Palestinians' national rights, the heroism of the ordinary people, and their ability to change history – as shown in their effective scuppering of the plan of United States Secretary of State George Schultz to stabilise the area without taking due account of Palestinian national rights.

The Palestinian question is central to the struggles of peoples in the Middle East but it is not the only contradiction they must face. This explains why some Arab rulers required the Palestinian peoples' uprising to stay their hand regarding the Shultz plan. Historically Jordan and other countries have bloodily suppressed the Palestinian people and nearly all have attempted to use them in a politically opportunist fashion.

The Middle East is also identified with its main export, oil. The discovery of vast oil reserves and the explosion in oil prices, particularly in the early 1970s, certainly injected great wealth into the region. But the income from this strictly finite resource has been used wisely and fairly only in a very few countries. In general there persists the contrast between the ancient and the modern – the culture of the veil coexisting with the culture of the Mercedes. Nor can it be said that the new found affluence in the Middle East was always of benefit to the rest of the Third World. Many were forced to pay the infinitely higher oil prices while their own raw material exports were retailed at stagnant or even declining prices. This impeded their development and helped bring on the colossal Third World debt crisis.

However the most criminal use of oil wealth has to be the way it has sustained the war between Iran and Iraq, which has now continued for more than twice as long as World War I and has been fought largely according to the same inhuman rule book. This has been a war full of atrocities, including the widespread use of poison gas particularly in areas inhabited by the Kurdish people whose lack of a national homeland is ignored by the world.

Even when this terrible war eventually ends, it will leave two decimated younger generations, a vast reservoir of enmity, ruined economies and huge debts. It is little wonder that great powers, whilst piously calling for peace, have done so much to stoke and fuel the war. It is also a great irony of our times that whilst the Palestinian people continue to suffer at the hands of the Zionists two of the world's most stridently anti-Zionist nations continue to rip each other apart.

Sadly, crisis in the the Middle East may be expected to continue being part of the international scene for the foreseeable future.

Palestinians in struggle. Their courage has amazed the world and provides universal lessons

Middle East

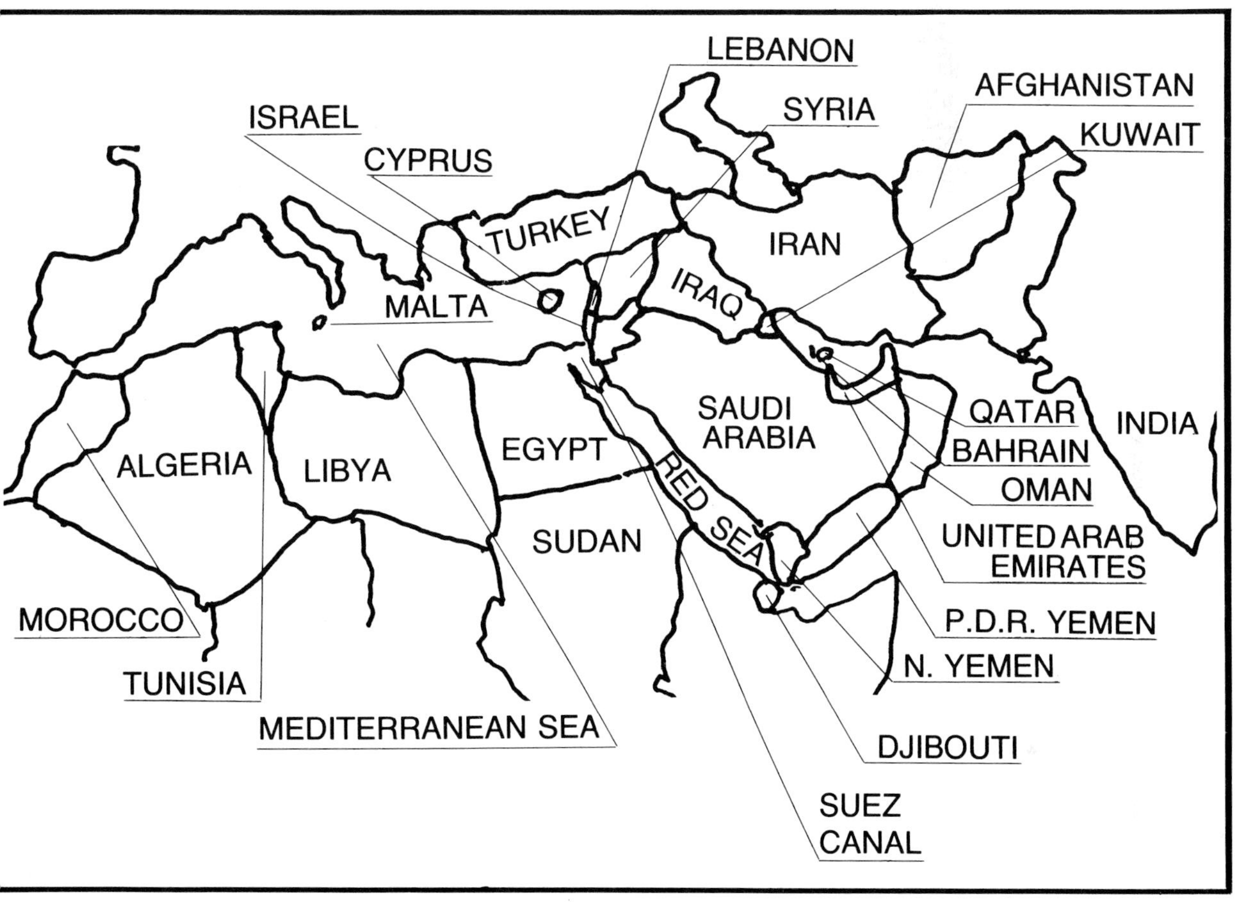

LEBANON
AFGHANISTAN
SYRIA
ISRAEL
KUWAIT
CYPRUS
TURKEY
IRAN
IRAQ
MALTA
SAUDI ARABIA
QATAR
INDIA
EGYPT
BAHRAIN
ALGERIA
LIBYA
RED SEA
OMAN
SUDAN
UNITED ARAB EMIRATES
MOROCCO
P.D.R. YEMEN
N. YEMEN
TUNISIA
MEDITERRANEAN SEA
DJIBOUTI
SUEZ CANAL

Bahrain

Head of State: Amir Sheikh Isa Bin Sulman Al-Khalifa
Ruling Party: n/a
Land Area: 677·9 (sq. km.)
Capital City: Manama
Population: 423,000 (1983)
Population Growth Rate: 4.6%
Infant Mortality: 50
Life Expectancy: 69
Gross National Product (GNP): 4,040 (Million US Dollars)
GNP Per Head: $9,560
Language: Arabic
Religion: Muslim
Currency: Bahrain Dinar
Membership of International Organisations: United Nations, the League of Arab States, Organisation of Petroleum Exporting Countries, Non-Aligned Movement.

Cyprus

Republic of Cyprus
Head of State: President Spyros Kyprianou
Ruling Party: Democratic Party
Land Area: 9,251 (sq. km.)
Capital City: Nicosia
Population: 660,000 (1983)
Population Growth Rate: 0.7%
Infant Mortality: 20
Life Expectancy: 75
Gross National Product (GNP): 2,650 (Milllion US Dollars)
GNP Per Head: $3,790
Language: Greek, Turkish
Religion: Christian, Muslim
Currency: Cyprus Pound
Membership of International Organisations: United Nations, the Non-Aligned Movement, the Commonwealth, the Council of Europe.

Iran

Islamic Republic of Iran
Head of State: President Ali Khameinei
Ruling Party: Islamic Republican Party of Iran
Land Area: 1,648,000 (sq. km.)
Capital City: Tehran
Population: 45.16 million (1983)
Population Growth Rate: 3.1%
Infant Mortality: 102
Life Expectancy: 61
Gross National Product (GNP):n/a
GNP Per Head: n/a
Language: Farsi
Religion: Muslim
Currency: Rial
Membership of International Organisations: United Nations, Non-Aligned Movement, Organisation of Petroleum Exporting Countries.

Iraq

Republic of Iraq
Head of State: President Saddam Hussein
Ruling Party: Arab Ba'ath Socialist Party
Land Area: 438,317 (sq. km.)
Capital City: Baghdad
Population: 15.65 million (1983)
Population Growth Rate: 3.6%
Infant Mortality: 73
Life Expectancy: 60
Gross National Product (GNP):n/a
GNP Per Head: n/a
Language: Arabic
Religion: Muslim
Currency: Iraqi Dinar
Membership of International Organisations: United Nations, League of Arab States, Non-Aligned Movement, Organisation of Petroleum Exporting Countries.

Kuwait

Head of State: Sheikh Jaber Al-Ahmad Al-Sabah
Ruling Party: n/a
Land Area: 17,818 (sq. km.)
Capital City: Kuwait
Population: 1.73 million
Population Growth Rate: 5.7 (1983)
Infant Mortality: 32
Life Expectancy: 72
Gross National Product (GNP): 30,290 (Million US Dollars)
GNP Per Head: $24,760
Language: Arabic
Religion: Muslim
Currency: Kuwaiti Dinar
Membership of International Organisations: United Nations, the League of Arab States, the Organisation of Petroleum Exporting Countries, Non-Aligned Movement

Lebanon

Republic of Lebanon
Head of State: President Amin Gemayel
Ruling Party: Falange (as part of coalition)
Land Area: 10,452 (sq. km.)
Capital City: Beirut
Population: 2.65 million (1983)
Population Growth Rate: 0.3%
Infant Mortality: 39
Life Expectancy: 65
Gross National Product (GNP): n/a
GNP Per Head: n/a
Language: Arabic
Religion: Muslim, Christian
Currency: Lebanese Pound
Membership of International Organisations: United Nations, League of Arab States, Non-Aligned Movement.

Malta

Republic of Malta
Head of State: Acting President Paul Xuereb
Ruling Party: Malta Nationalist Party
Land Area: 316 (sq. km.)
Capital City: Valetta
Population: 360,000
Population Growth Rate: 1.2%
Infant Mortality: 14
Life Expectancy: 73
Gross National Product (GNP): 1,190
(Million US Dollars)
GNP Per Head: $3,300
Language: Maltese, English
Religion: Christian
Currency: Maltese Pound
Membership of International Organisations: United Nations, Non-Aligned Movement, the Commonwealth, Council of Europe.

Oman

Sultanate of Oman
Head of State: Sultan Qaboos
Ruling Party: n/a
Land Area: 212,457 (sq. km.)
Capital City: Muscat
Population: 1.18 (1983)
Population Growth Rate: 4.4%
Infant Mortality: 123
Life Expectancy: 53
Gross National Product (GNP): 8,360

(Million US Dollars)
GNP Per Head: $7,080
Language: Arabic
Religion: Muslim
Currency: Rial Omani
Membership of International Organisations: United Nations, League of Arab States, Non-Aligned Movement.

Qatar

Head of State: Sheikh Khalifa Bin Hamad Al-Thani
Ruling Party: n/a
Land Area: 11,437 (sq. km.)
Capital City: Doha
Population: 320,000 (1983)
Population Growth Rate: 6.8%
Infant Mortality: 50
Life Expectancy: 72
Gross National Product (GNP): 5,110 (Million US Dollars)
GNP Per Head: $15,980
Language: Arabic
Religion: Muslim
Currency: Qatar Riyal
Membership of International Organisations: United Nations, League of Arab States, Organisation of Petroleum Exporting Countries, Non-Aligned Movement

Saudi Arabia

Kingdom of Saudi Arabia
Head of State: King Fahd
Ruling Party: n/a
Land Area: 2,149,690 (sq. km.)
Capital City: Riyadh
Population: 11.52 Million (1983)
Population Growth Rate: 4.8%
Infant Mortality: 108
Life Expectancy: 62
Gross National Product (GNP): 102,120 (Million US Dollars)
GNP Per Head: $8,860
Language: Arabic
Religion: Muslim
Currency: Saudi Riyal
Membership of International Organisations: United Nations, the League of Arab States, Organisation of Petroleum Exporting Countries, Non-Aligned Movement.

Syria

Syrian Arab Republic
Head of State: President Hafez Al Assad
Ruling Party: Arab Ba'ath Socialist Party
Land Area: 184,050 (sq. km.)
Capital City: Damascus
Population: 10.48 million (1983)
Population Growth Rate: 3.4%
Infant Mortality: 58
Life Expectancy: 63
Gross National Product (GNP): 17,060 (Million US Dollars)
GNP Per Head: $1,630
Language: Arabic
Religion: Muslim, Christian
Currency: Syrian Pound
Membership of International Organisations: United Nations, League of Arab States, Non-Aligned Movement.

Turkey

Republic of Turkey
Head of State: General Kenan Evren
Ruling Party: Anathavan Partisi (Motherland Party)
Land Area: 779,452 (sq. km.)
Capital City: Ankara
Population: 49.40 million (1983)
Population Growth Rate: 2.2%
Infant Mortality: 83
Life Expectancy: 64
Gross National Product (GNP): 56,060 (Million US Dollars)
GNP Per Head: $1,130
Language: Turkish
Religion: Muslim
Currency: Turkish Lira
Membership of International Organisations: United Nations, Organisation of Economic Co-operation and Development (OECD), North Atlantic Treaty Organisation (NATO), Council of Europe, European Economic Community (EEC . application submitted).

United Arab Emirates

Head of State: Sheikh Zayed Bin Sultan Al-Nahayan
Ruling Party: n/a
Land Area: 83,600 (sq. km.)
Capital City: Abu Dhabi
Population: 1.38 million (1983)
Population Growth Rate: 10.0%
Infant Mortality: 50
Life Expectancy: 72
Gross National Product (GNP): 26,400 (Million US Dollars)
GNP Per Head: $19,120
Language: Arabic
Religion: Muslim
Currency: UAE Dirham
Membership of International Organisations: United Nations, League of Arab States, Non-Aligned Movement, Organisation of Petroleum Exporting Countries

N. Yemen

Yemen Arab Republic
Head of State: President Ali Abdullah Saleh
Ruling Party: n/a
Land Area: 195,000 (sq. km.)
Capital City: Sanaa
Population: 7.95 million
Population Growth Rate: 2.8%
Infant Mortality: 163
Life Expectancy: 45
Gross National Product (GNP): 4,140 (Million US Dollars)
GNP Per Head: $520
Language: Arabic
Religion: Muslim
Currency: Yemeni Rial
Membership of International Organisations: United Nations, League of Arab States, Non-Aligned Movement.

S. Yemen

People's Democratic Republic of Yemen
Head of State: President Haydar Abu Bakr Al-Attas
Ruling Party: Socialist Party of Yemen
Land Area: 332,968 (sq. km.)
Capital City: Aden
Population: 2.08 million
Population Growth Rate: 2.3%
Infant Mortality: 140
Life Expectancy: 47
Gross National Product (GNP): 1,130 (Million US Dollars)
GNP Per Head: $540
Language: Arabic
Religion: Muslim
Currency: Yemen Dinar
Membership of International Organisations: United Nations, League of Arab States, Non-Aligned Movement.

South and Central America

The geopolitical area of South and Central America is made up of 19 independent countries which, with the exception of Surinam, have either Spanish or Portuguese as their first language (Belize and Guyana have been included in the Caribbean section). Whilst the Central American isthmus contains a number of small states, such as Honduras and El Salvador, the area is also straddled by a sub-continental giant, namely Brazil with its approximate population of 140 million and its land area of 8,511,965 square kilometres, making it the third largest country in the world.

The modern history of the region (constantly shadowed by its more powerful neighbour to the north) is a graphic illustration for people around the world that the question of imperialism cannot be reduced solely to the question of direct colonialism. The armies of Simon Bolivar ('The Liberator') freed numerous South American countries from the Spanish colonialists at the beginning of the nineteenth century, ie. long before many parts of the Third World even came under the colonial yoke. But it would be a grave mistake to think that these countries have enjoyed centuries of free and unfettered development. The rising power of the United States of America – apart from asserting itself in the westward expansion that led it to take its current national form – saw the countries to its south as a natural sphere of influence and domination.

Under the 'Monroe Doctrine' the United States proclaimed that the 'old world' had no business interfering in the affairs of the 'new', although for some reason this principle did not apply to Britain's 1982 war with the Argentina over the Malvinas 'Falklands'. It is easy to view this principle from an anti-colonial and progressive angle, but, seen through the eyes of those directly affected, more a case of the USA announcing its exclusive 'rights' to the region.

Following the Spanish-American war at the turn of the century Cuba became a virtual American colony – a situation that was only ended by the revolution of 1959. US marines and troops intervened in the region on numerous occasions up until the 1960s – they may yet do so again in Panama. In Nicaragua the United States waged a war in the 1920s against the popular leader Augusto Sandino (who gave his name to today's Sandinistas) and installed the corrupt Somoza dynasty with the immortal phrase, "He may be a son of a bitch but he's our son of a bitch."

Throughout this period Britain was also active in the region – being for long the dominant power in Argentina until the rise of the nationalist Juan Peron.

The foreign domination of South and Central America could not survive without its internal base – this is in the nature of neo-colonialism. This base has historically been provided by a section of the military, the oligarchy and the *latifundista*, who control the great estates and plantations. This in turn has a racial aspect – the ruling class has been drawn overwhelmingly from those of European descent whilst the labouring people of town and country are often of Amerindian or African origin.

It was above all the Cuban revolution that broke the cycle of poverty and dependency and therein lies the reason for the attempts to isolate and crush it. Its 'threat' is one of example. Likewise tiny Nicaragua is absurdly held to be threatening the mighty United States. An important difference from the early days of the Cuban revolution is that then only Mexico would or could take a stand against the United States. Today the majority of countries in the region are defending Nicaragua and maintaining independence from the USA – a trend that is related to the collapse of many of the continent's military dictatorships.

This process of independence and democratic unity is also being expressed in attempts to find a way to tackle the problem of the foreign debt – a monstrous and self-perpetuating burden that was not incurred by the people and is responsible for misery, starvation and death, blighting all real development prospects.

General Augusto Sandino – an anti-imperialist symbol through the generations

South America

GUYANA
VENEZUELA
SURINAM
FRENCH GUYANA
COLOMBIA
ECUADOR
PERU
BRAZIL
BOLIVIA
PARAGUAY
CHILE
URAGUAY
ARGENTINA
FALKLAND ISLANDS

Central America

U.S.A.
GULF
OF
MEXICO
CUBA
JAMAICA
MEXICO
BELIZE
HONDURAS
GUATEMALA
CARIBBEAN SEA
EL SALVADOR
NICARAGUA
PANAMA
CANAL
COSTA
RICA
PANAMA
COLOMBO
SOUTH
AMERICA

Argentina

Republic of Argentina
Head of State: President Raul Alfonsin
Ruling Party: Radical Civil Union
Land Area: 2,766,889 (sq.km)
Capital City: Buenos Aires
Population: 30.53 million (1985)
Population Growth Rate: 1.6%
Infant Mortality: 44
Life Expectancy: 70.
Gross National Product (GNP): 65,080 (Million US Dollars)
GNP Per Head: $2,130
Language: Spanish, Italian
Religion: Christian
Currency: Argentinian Peso
Membership of International Organisations: United Nations, Organisation of American States, Non-Aligned Movement

Bolivia

Republic of Bolivia
Head of State: Dr. Victor Paz Estenssoro
Ruling Party: National Revolutionary Movement Historic
Land Area: 1,098,581 (sq.km)
Capital City: La Paz
Population: 6.38 Million (1983)
Population Growth Rate: 2.7%
Infant Mortality: 126
Life Expectancy: 53
Gross National Product: 3,010 (Million US Dollars)
GNP Per Head: $470
Language: Spanish, Quechua
Religion: Christian
Currency: Peso
Membership of International Organisations: United Nations, Organisation of American States, Andean Group, Amazon Pact, Non-Aligned Movement.

Brazil

Federal Republic of Brazil
Head of State: President Jose Eduardo Sarney
Ruling Party: Social Democratic Party
Land Area: 8,511,965 (sq.km)
Capital City: Brasilia
Population: 135.54 million (1983)
Population Growth Rate: 2.3%
Infant Mortality: 73
Life Expectancy: 64
Gross National Product (GNP): 222,010 (Million US Dollars)
GNP Per Head: $1,640
Language: Portuguese
Religion: Christian
Currency: Cruzado
Membership of International Organisations: United Nations, Organisation of American States

Chile

Republic of Chile
Head of State: General Augusto Pinochet
Ruling Party:-
Land Area: 755,626 (sq.km)
Capital City: Santiago
Population: 11.99 million (1983)
Population Growth Rate: 1.7%
Infant Mortality: 70
Life Expectancy: 70
Gross National Product: 17,230 (Million US Dollars)
GNP Per Head: $1,440
Language: Spanish
Religion: Christian
Currency: Peso
Membership of International Organisations: United Nations, Organisation of American States.

Colombia

Republic of Colombia
Head of State: President Dr Virgilio Barco Vargas
Ruling Party: Liberal Party of Colombia
Land Area: 1,138,914 (sq. km.)
Capital City: Bogota
Population: 28.41 million
Population Growth Rate: 1.9%
Infant Mortality: 54
Life Expectancy: 64
Gross National Product (GNP): 37,610 (Million US dollars)
GNP Per Head: $1,320
Language: Spanish
Religion: Christian
Currency: Peso
Membership of International Organisations: United Nations, Organisation of American States, Andean Group, Non Aligned Movement.

Costa Rica

Republic of Costa Rica
Head of State: President Oscar Arias Sanchez
Ruling Party: National Liberation Party
Land Area: 51,060 (sq. km.)
Capital City: San Jose
Population: 2.67 million (1983)
Population Growth Rate: 2.8%
Infant Mortality: 18
Life Expectancy: 73
Gross National Product (GNP): 3,340 (Million US Dollars)
GNP Per Head: $1,240
Language: Spanish
Religion: Christian
Currency: Colon
Membership of International Organisations: United Nations, Organisation of American States.

Cuba

Republic of Cuba
Head of State: President Fidel Castro-Ruz
Ruling Party: Communist Party of Cuba
Land Area: 114,524 (sq. km.)
Capital City: Havana
Population: 10.09 million (1983)
Population Growth Rate: 0.8%
Infant Mortality: 17
Life Expectancy: 75
Gross National Product (GNP): n/a Available
GNP Per Head: $1,270
Language: Spanish
Religion: Christian
Currency: Peso
Membership of International Organisations: United Nations, Non Aligned Movement, Council for Mutual Economic Assistance (COMECON).

Ecuador

Republic of Ecuador
Head of State: President Leon Ferbes Cordero
Ruling Party: Social Christian Party
Land Area: 283,561 (sq. km.)
Capital City: Quito
Population: 9.36 million (1983)
Population Growth Rate: 2.9%
Infant Mortality: 78
Life Expectancy: 65

Gross National Product (GNP): 10,880 (Million US Dollars)
GNP Per Head: $1,160
Language: Spanish, Quechua
Religion: Christian
Currency: Sucre
Membership of International Organisations: United Nations, Organisation of American States, Organisation of Petroleum Exporting Countries, Non Aligned Movement.

El Salvador

Republic of El Salvador
Head of State: President Jose Napoleon Duarte
Ruling Party: Christian Democratic Party
Land Area: 21,073 (sq. km.)
Capital City: San Salvador
Population: 5.56 million (1983)
Population Growth Rate: 3.0%
Infant Mortality: 72
Life Expectancy: 65
Gross National Product (GNP): 3,940 (Million US Dollars)
GNP Per Head: $710
Language: Spanish
Religion: Christian
Currency: Colon
Membership of International Organisations: United Nations, Organisation of American States.

Guatemala

Republic of Guatemala
Head of State: President Marco Vinicio Cerezo
Ruling Party: Christian Democratic Party of Guatemala
Land Area: 108,429 (sq. km.)
Capital City: Guatemala City
Population: 7.963 million (1983)
Population Growth Rate: 2.8%
Infant Mortality: 66
Life Expectancy: 60
Gross National Product (GNP): 9,890 (Million US Dollars)
GNP Per Head: $1,240
Language: Spanish
Religion: Christian
Currency: Quetzal
Membership of International Organisations: United Nations, Organisation of American States.

Honduras

Republic of Honduras
Head of State: President José Simon Azcona
Ruling Party: Liberal Party of Honduras
Land Area: 111,888 (sq. km.)
Capital City: Tegucigalpa
Population: 4.36 million (1983)
Population Growth Rate: 3.5%
Infant Mortality: 83
Life Expectancy: 61
Gross National Product (GNP): 3,190 (Million US Dollars)
GNP Per Head: $730
Language: Spanish
Religion: Christian
Currency: Lempira
Membership of International Organisations: United Nations, Organisation of American States

Mexico

United States of Mexico
Head of State: President Miguel De La Madrid
Ruling Party: Institutional Revolutionary Party
Land Area: 1,972,547 (sq. km.)
Capital City: Mexico City
Population: 78.82 million (1983)
Population Growth Rate: 2.8%
Infant Mortality: 53
Life Expectancy: 66
Gross National Product (GNP): 163,790 (Million US Dollars)
GNP Per Head: $2,080
Language: Spanish
Religion: Christian
Currency: Mexican Peso
Membership of International Organisations: United Nations, Organisation of American States.

Nicaragua

Republic of Nicaragua
Head of State: President Daniel Ortega
Ruling Party: Sandinista National Liberation Front
Land Area: 130,000 (sq. km.)
Capital City: Managua
Population: 3.26 million (1983)
Population Growth Rate: 3.1%
Infant Mortality: 86
Life Expectancy: 60
Gross National Product (GNP): 2,760 (Million US Dollars)
GNP Per Head: $850
Language: Spanish, English
Religion: Christian
Currency: Cordoba
Membership of International Organisations: United Nations, Non Aligned Movement, Organisation of American States.

Panama

Republic of Panama
Head of State: President Eric Arturo Del Valle
Ruling Party: Democratic Revolutionary Party
Land Area: 77,082 (sq. km.)
Capital City: Panama City
Population: 2.18 million (1983)
Population Growth Rate: 2.3%
Infant Mortality: 33
Life Expectancy: 71
Gross National Product (GNP): 4,400 (Million US Dollars)
GNP Per Head: $2,020
Language: Spanish
Religion: Christian
Currency: Balboa
Membership of International Organisations: United Nations, Organisation of American States, Non Aligned Movement.

Paraguay

Republic of Paraguay
Head of State: General Alfredo Stroessner
Ruling Party: Partido Colarado
Land Area: 406,752 (sq. km.)
Capital City: Asuncion
Population: 3.38 million (1983)
Population Growth Rate: 2.5%
Infant Mortality: 45
Life Expectancy: 66
Gross National Product (GNP): 3,180 (Million US Dollars)
GNP Per Head: $940
Language: Spanish, Guarani
Religion: Christian
Currency: Guarani
Membership of International Organisations: United Nations, Organisation of American States.

Peru

Republic of Peru
Head of State: President Alan Garcia

Peres
Ruling Party: American Popular Revolutionary Alliance (APRA)
Land Area: 1,285,216 (sq. km.)
Capital City: Lima
Population: 18.65 million (1983)
Population Growth Rate: 2.4%
Infant Mortality: 83
Life Expectancy: 59
Gross National Product (GNP): 17,830 (Million US Dollars)
GNP Per Head: $960
Language: Spanish, Quechua
Religion: Christian
Currency: Sol
Membership of International Organisations: United Nations, Non-Aligned Movement, Organisation of American States.

Surinam

Republic of Surinam
Head of State: President Ramsewak Shankar
Ruling Party: 26 February Movement
Land Area: 163,265 (sq. km.)
Capital City: Paramaribo
Population: 393,000 (1983)
Population Growth Rate: 0.2%
Infant Mortality: 119
Life Expectancy: 65
Gross National Product (GNP): 1,010 (Million US Dollars)
GNP Per Head: $2,570
Language: Dutch, English, Hindi, Javanese, Sranang Tongo, Chinese, Spanish
Religion: Hindu, Muslim, Christian
Currency: Surinam Guilder
Membership of International Organisations: United Nations, Non-Aligned Movement, Organisation of American States.

Uruguay

Republic of Uruguay
Head of State: President Julio Sanguinetti
Ruling Party: Colarado Party
Land Area: 176,215 (sq. km.)
Capital City: Montevideo
Population: 3.00 million (1983)
Population Growth Rate: 0.6%
Infant Mortality: 34
Life Expectancy: 73
Gross National Product (GNP): 4,980 (Million US Dollars)
GNP Per Head: $1,660
Language: Spanish
Religion: Christian
Currency: Peso
Membership of International Organisations: United Nations, Organisation of American States.

Venezuela

Republic of Venezuela
Head of State: President Jaime Lusinchi
Ruling Party: Democratic Action
Land Area: 912,050 (sq. km.)
Capital City: Caracas
Population: 17.32 million (1983)
Population Growth Rate: 3.3%
Infant Mortality: 39
Life Expectancy: 69
Gross National Product (GNP): 53,800 (Million US Dollars)
GNP Per Head: $3,110
Language: Spanish
Religion: Christian
Currency: Bolivar
Membership of International Organisations: United Nations, Organisation of American States, Organisation of Petroleum Exporting Countries, Andean Group.

South Pacific

Eight independent Third World countries are to be found in the South Pacific region, a vast area made up of scattered island states with tiny populations. Only Papua New Guinea has a population in excess of one million, whilst, according to the lastest available figures, Tuvalu has a population of just 8,729.

A region that has lent its name to a famous 'musical', the South Pacific is traditionally presented as a backwater or an idyll, but this belies the reality. The people of the South Pacific have not escaped the brutalisation that the white nations have inflicted on the Third World, and today it is the centre of imperialist and superpower strategic contention. Many are the voices in the United States and elsewhere that proclaim that the 21st century will be that of the Pacific – but this is a promise that holds out mixed blessings. At present the small states have to take into account the presence in their region of relatively large developed countries, Australia and New Zealand; the continued presence of French colonialism and nuclear testing; and the rival attentions of the United States, Japan, the Soviet Union and China, as well as some rising regional powers like Indonesia.

The South Pacific is the last region in the Third World to have witnessed the rise of the national liberation movement, with most of the countries gaining their national independence only in the last decade or so.

A number of countries are still under direct colonial rule, in particular New Caledonia and Tahiti, held by France, and Micronesia, under the control of the United States of America. The area has been the most consistent victim of the nuclear arms race, and in particular France persists in its programme of atmospheric nuclear tests. The results have been catastrophic with generations being born with the most horrendous deformities and the promise only of more to come. It is often recalled that, when a group of western peace women met a delegation of women from the South Pacific some years ago, they were told that, whilst they were worried about the prospect of nuclear war in the future, the women of the South Pacific have lived and died with it for the last four decades.

In such a situation the South Pacific countries and peoples are getting together to try and build a better life for themselves free from outside interferences. Inspired by other regional alliances they have formed the South Pacific Forum, which in turn has put forward the Rarotonga Treaty, aiming to turn the region into a nuclear-free zone. Of the five recognised nuclear powers, the Soviet Union and China have signed the relevant protocols, whilst the United States, Britain and France have not. In contrast the USA has exercised immense pressure on Micronesia to delete the anti-nuclear clause that was formerly in its constitution.

Vanuatu is the only country in the region that is a member of the Non-Aligned Movement, but the attraction of non-alignment is undoubtedly growing. In 1987 there were two coups d'état in Fiji – the first ones in the region. An immediate cause may be found in the tensions between ethnic and national groups that are so commonly inherited by post-colonial societies. But external disquiet at the professed support for non-alignment on the part of the democratically elected government of Dr Bavadra was also a factor. It is notable that even slight assertions of independence on the part of South Pacific countries meet with a heavy-handed response – when Kiribati (with a population of under 70,000) signed a fisheries agreement with the Soviet Union, it was forced to rescind it the following year.

Events in the South Pacific do not make the headlines as often as those elsewhere in the world. But a 'Third World pattern' is still discernible – despite all difficulties the peoples of the South Pacific are emerging onto the stage of history as independent actors.

Dr Timoci Bavadra – his programme for a non-aligned Fiji made him powerful enemies

South Pacific

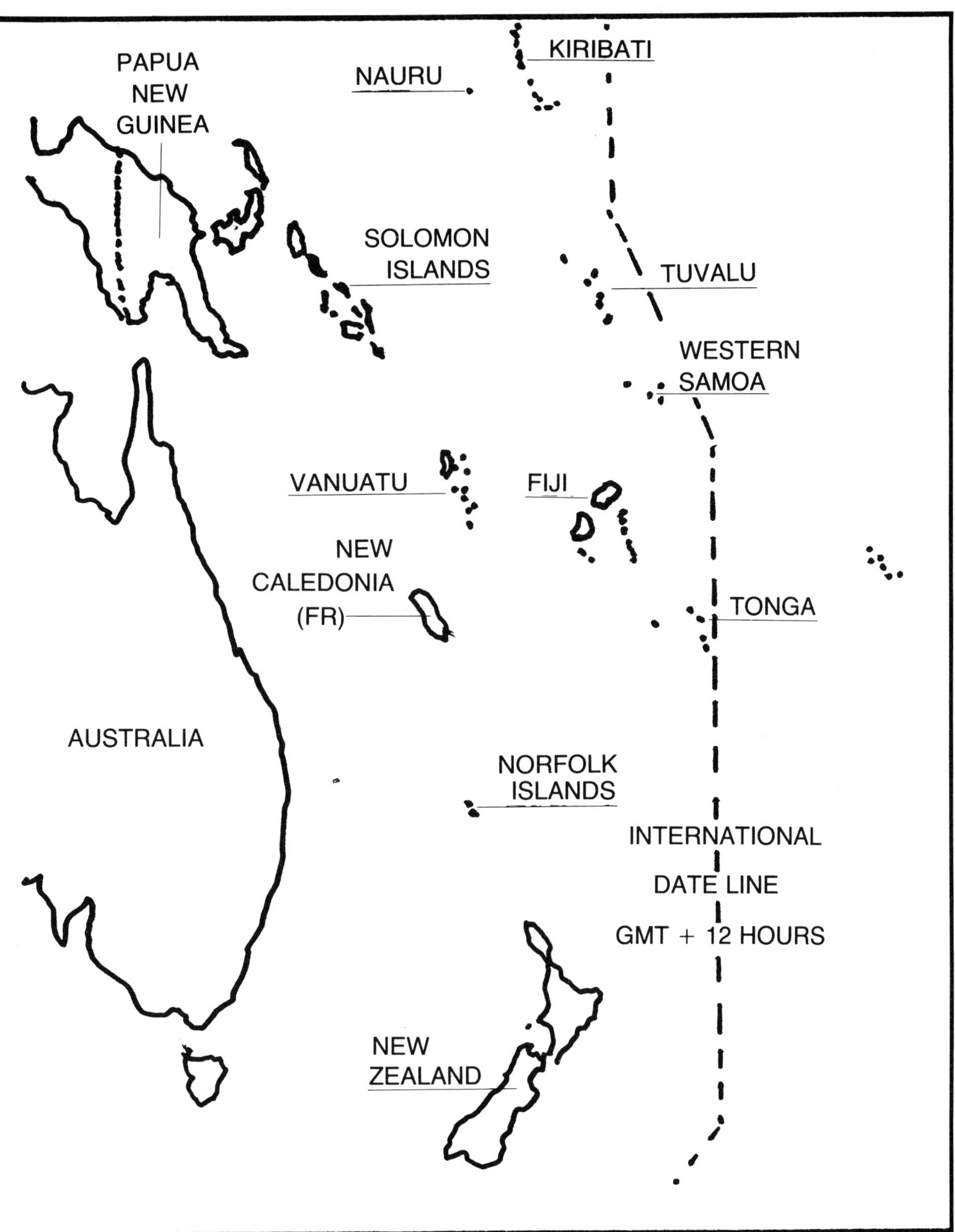
KIRIBATI
PAPUA
NEW
GUINEA
NAURU
SOLOMON
ISLANDS
TUVALU
WESTERN
SAMOA
VANUATU
FIJI
NEW
CALEDONIA
(FR)
TONGA
AUSTRALIA
NORFOLK
ISLANDS
INTERNATIONAL
DATE LINE
GMT + 12 HOURS
NEW
ZEALAND

Republic of Fiji

Head of State: President Ratu Penaia Ganilav
Ruling Party: Alliance Party
Land Area: 18,376 (sq. km.)
Capital City: Suva
Population: 702,000 (1983)
Population Growth Rate: 2.0%
Infant Mortality: 34
Life Expectancy: 65
Gross National Product (GNP): 1,190 (Million US Dollars)
GNP Per Head: $1,700
Language: Fijian, Hindi, Chinese, English
Religion: Hindu, Muslim, Christian
Currency: Fiji Dollar
Membership of International Organisations: United Nations, South Pacific Forum, Signatory to the Lomé Convention

Kiribati

Head of State: President Ierema T. Tabai
Ruling Party: .
Land Area: 754 (sq. km)
Capital City: Bairiki
Population: 64,000 (1983)
Population Growth Rate: 1.8%
Infant Mortality: n/a
Life Expectancy: 52
Gross National Product (GNP): 30 (Million US Dollars)
GNP Per Head: $450
Language: Kiribati, English
Religion: Christian
Currency: Australian Dollar
Membership of International Organisations: South Pacific Forum, the Commonwealth

Papua New Guinea

Head of Government: Prime Minister Paias Wingti
Ruling Party: Coalition
Land Area: 462,840 (sq. km.)
Capital City: Port Moresby
Population: 3.49 million (1983)
Population Growth Rate: -2.6%
Infant Mortality: 99
Life Expectancy: 52
Gross National Product (GNP): 2,470 (Million US Dollars)
GNP Per Head: $710
Language: Pidgin, Hirimotu, English
Religion: Christian, Pantheist
Currency: Kina
Membership of International Organisations: United Nations, the Commonwealth.

Solomon Islands

Head of Government: Prime Minister Ezekiel Alebua
Ruling Party: Solomon Islands United Party
Land Area: 29,800 (sq. km.)
Capital City: Honiara
Population: 267,000 (1983)
Population Growth Rate: 3.3%
Infant Mortality: n/a
Life Expectancy: 57
Gross National Product (GNP): 140 (Million US Dollars)
GNP Per Head: $510
Language: English, Pidgin
Religion: Christian
Currency: Solomon Island Dollar
Membership of International Organisations: United Nations, South Pacific Forum, Signatory to the Lome Convention, the Commonwealth

Tonga

Head of State: King Taufa'ahau Tupou IV
Ruling Party: .
Land Area: 748 (sq. km.)
Capital City: Nuku'alofa
Population: 97,000 (1983)
Population Growth Rate: 0.07%
Infant Mortality: 21
Life Expectancy: 63
Gross National Product (GNP): 70 (Million US Dollars)
GNP Per Head: $730
Language: English, Tongan
Religion: Christian
Currency: Pa'anga
Membership of International Organisations: South Pacific Forum, the Commonwealth, Signatory to Lome Convention.

Tuvalu

Head of Government: Prime Minister Tomasi Puapua
Ruling Party: .
Land Area: 26 (sq. km.)
Capital City: Funafuti
Population: 8,729
Population Growth Rate: 2.8%
Infant Mortality: 42
Life Expectancy: 59
Gross National Product (GNP): 5 (Million US Dollars)
GNP Per Head: $680
Language: Tuvaluan, English
Religion: Christian
Currency: Tuvaluan Dollar, Australian Dollar
Membership of International Organisations: The Commonwealth, South Pacific Forum.

Vanuatu

Republic of Vanuatu
Head of State: Father Walter Lini
Ruling Party: Vanuaaku Parti
Land Area: 14,800 (sq. km.)
Capital City: Port Vila
Population: 134,000
Population Growth Rate: 2.8%
Infant Mortality: 97
Life Expectancy: 56
Gross National Product (GNP): 90 (Million US Dollars)
GNP Per Head: $700
Language: Bislama, English, French
Religion: Christian
Currency: Vatu
Membership of International Organisations: South Pacific Forum, Non-Aligned Movement, the Commonwealth

Western Samoa

Head of State: King Malietoa Tanumatili II
Ruling Party: Human Rights Protection Party
Land Area: 2,831 (sq. km.)
Capital City: Apia
Population: 163,000 (1983)
Population Growth Rate: 0.9%
Infant Mortality: 13
Life Expectancy: 65
Gross National Product (GNP): 110 (Million US Dollars)
GNP Per Head: 660
Language: Polynesian, English
Religion: Christian
Currency: Tala Dollar
Membership of International Organisations: United Nations, South Pacific Forum, the Commonwealth, Signatory to the Lome Convention.

Selected International Organisations

ADB	Asian Development Bank
AfDB	African Development Bank
AIOEC	Association of Iron Ore Exporting Countries
ANRPC	Association of Natural Rubber Producing Countries
ANZUS	ANZUS Council treaty signed by Australia, New Zealand and United States of America
ASEAN	Association of Southeast Asian Nations
ASPAC	Asian and Pacific Council
ASSIMER	International Mercury Producers' Association
BENELUX	Belgium, Netherlands, Luxembourg Economic Union
BLEU	Belgium-Luxembourg Economic Union
CACM	Central American Common Market
CARICOM	Caribbean Common Market
CARIFTA	Caribbean Free Trade Association
CCC	Customs Co-operation Council
CDB	Caribbean Development Bank
CEAO	West African Economic Community
CEMA	Council for Mutual Economic Assistance
CENTO	Central Treaty Organisation
CIPFC	Intergovernmental Council of Copper Exporting Countries
DAC	Development Assistance Committee (OECD)
EAMA	African States Associated with the EEC
EC	European Communities
ECOWAS	Economic Community of West African States
EFTA	European Free Trade Association
EIB	European Investment Bank
ELDO	European Space Vehicle Launcher Development Organisation
EMS	European Monetary System
ENTENTE	Political-economic Association of Ivory Coast, Dahomey, Niger, Burkina Faso and Togo
ESRO	European Space Research Organisation
G-77	Group of 77
GCC	Gulf Co-operation Council
IADR	Inter-American Defense Board
IATP	International Association of Tungsten Producers
IBA	International Bauxite Association
IBEC	International Bank for Economic Co-operation
ICAC	International Cotton Advisory Committee
ICCAT	International Commission for the Conservation of Atlantic Tuna
ICCO	International Cocoa Organisation
ICEM	Intergovernmental Committee for European Migration
(ICES	International Co-operation in Ocean Exploration
ICO	International Coffee Organisation
IDB	Inter-American Development Bank
IDB	Islamic Development Bank
IEA	International Energy Agency (associated with the OECD)
IHO	International Hydrographic Organisation
IIB	International Investment Bank
INRO	International Natural Rubber Organisation
INTELSAT	International Telecommunications Satellite Organisation
IOOC	International Olive Oil Council
IPU	Inter-Parliamentary Union
IRC	International Rice Council
ISO	International Sugar Organisation
ITC	International Tin Council
IWC	International Whaling Commission
IWC	International Wheat Council

LAIA	Latin America Integration Association
NAM	Non-aligned Movement
NATO	North Atlantic Treaty Organisation
OAPEC	Organisation of Arab Petroleum Exporting Countries
OAS	Organisation of American States
OAU	Organisation of African Unity
ODECA	Organisation of Central American States
OECD	Organisation for Economic Co-operation and Development
OECS	Organisation of Eastern Caribbean States
OIC	Islamic Conference Organisation
OPEC	Organisation of Petroleum Exporting Countries
PAHO	Pan American Health Organisation
SADCC	Southern African Development Co-ordination Conference
SPC	South Pacific Commission
UDEAC	Economic and Customs Union of Central Africa
UEAC	Union of Central African States
UPEB	Union of Banana Exporting Countries
WEU	Western European Union
WFTU	World Federation of Trade Unions
WPC	World Peace Council
WSG	International Wool Study Group
WTO	World Tourism Organisation

Selected UN Organisations

Principal Organs

GA	General Assembly
SC	Security Council
ECOSOC	Economic and Social Council
TC	Trusteeship Council
ICJ	International Court of Justice Secretariat

Other organs

UNCTAD	UN Conference on Trade and Development
TDB	Trade and Development Board
UNDP	UN Development Programme
UNICEF	UN Children's Fund
UNIDO	UN Industrial Development Organisation

Regional Economic Commissions

ECA	Economic Commission for Africa
ECE	Economic Commission for Europe
ECLA	Economic Commission for Latin America
ECWA	Economic Commission for Western Asia
ESCAP	Economic and Social Commission for Asia and the Pacific

Specialised agencies and other autonomous organisations within the system

FAO	Food and Agriculture Organisation
IBRD	International Bank for Reconstruction and Development (World Bank)
ICAO	International Civil Aviation Organisation
IDA	International Development Association (IBRD affiliate)
IFAD	International Fund for Agricultural Development
IFC	International Finance Corporation (IBRD affiliate)
ILO	International Labour Organisation
IMF	International Monetary Fund
IMO	International Maritime Organisation
ITU	International Telecommunication Union
UNESCO	UN Educational, Scientific and Cultural Organisation
UPU	Universal Postal Union
WFC	World Food Council
WHO	World Health Organisation
WIPO	World Intellectual Property Organisation
WMO	World Meteorological Organisation
GATT	General Agreement on Tariffs and Trade
IAEA	International Atomic Energy Agency

Directory of Organisations

The names and addresses of over 2,000 community organisations can be found in this comprehensive directory. In order to facilitate easy reference, entries have been divided into sections and listed alphabetically.

The purpose of these listings is not only to provide information but to contribute to the development of the community, to assist the work of the organisations and to facilitate the link between them.

Third World Impact is published every two years and these lists are subject to constant revision. If you are active in an organisation that has not been listed here, of if you know of such a group, then please send the details to: *Third World Impact*, Hansib Publishing, Tower House, 139/149 Fonthill Road, London N4 3HF. We will include it in the ninth edition to be published in 1990. Inclusion in these listings is free.

A – Z of Community Organisations

Ashton

Shree Bharatiya Mandal, 103 Union Road, Ashton, Lancashire

Barking

Gurdwara Singh Sabhac, London East, 100 North Street, Barking, Essex
Tel: 01 594 3940

League of British Muslims (UK), 37 Webber House, North Street, Barking, Essex 1G1 8JG

Basingstoke

Sikh Temple, 4 Kingshill Road, Basingstoke, Hants. RG21 3JE

Bedford

Bedford Westindian Cultural and Social Club, 2 Woburn Road, Bedford
Tel: 0234 52298

Caribbean and Afro Society of Hairdressers, (C.A.S.H.), 27 Park Road West, Bedford MK41 7SB,
Tel: 0234 53922

Pakistan Christian Welfare Organisation (UK), 68 Rosamond Rd, Bedford MK40 3UQ

Birmingham

ACAFESS Ltd, 198-200 Moseley Rd, Highgate, Birmingham B12 ODG
Tel: 021 440 5288

Advice Bureau, 238-240 Stratford Road, Sparkbrook, Birmingham B11, (7pm . 10pm Fridays)

Afro Caribbean Co-operative Society, 24 Porchester Drive, Newtown, Birmingham 19
Tel: 021 632 4544
Con. Mr M Warner . Secretary

Afro Caribbean Co-ordinating Council, 212 Winson Green Road, Winson Green, Birmingham B18
Tel: 021 554 2594 or 551 4015
Con. Mr L Blake

Afro Caribbean Resource Centre Limited, 339 Dudley Road, Winson Green, Birmingham B18 4HB
Tel: 021 348 3351

Afro Caribbean Self Help Organisation, 104 Heathfield Road, Lozells, Birmingham
Tel: 021 554 2747
Con. Mr B Brown

Afro Caribbean Teachers Association, The Broadway Annexe, Canterbury Road, Perry Barr, Birmingham
Tel: 021 356 4006
Con. Mr R K Frater

Afro Caribbean Teachers Network, Bordesley Centre, Stratford Road, Birmingham B11 1AR
Tel: 021 772 7676

Asian Resource Centre, 101 Villa Road, Handsworth, Birmingham B19 1NH
Tel: 021 523 0580/021 551 4518

Association of Muslim Youth, 31 Farm Road, Birmingham 11
Tel: 021 771 3339

Associated Translation & Typesetting, 5 Durham Road, Sparkhill, Birmingham B11 4LG
Tel: 021 773 7081

Babbar Khalsa International, 153 Winson Street, Winson Green, Birmingham 16
Tel: 021 454 2996

Bangladesh Centre UK, 97 Walford Road, Birmingham 11
Tel: 021 772 8839

Birmingham Anjumanha Islam, 23 Arden Road, Aston, Birmingham B6

Birmingham Community Association, The Institution, Jenkins Street, Small Heath, Birmingham B10 OQH
Tel: 021 384 3830

Birmingham Westindian Commonwealth Social Club, 37 Rodney Close, Birmingham 16
Tel: 021 454 6964
Con. Mr A Hamilton

The Black Development Trust, 34-35 Clarence Chambers, 4th Floor, 39 Corporation St, Birmingham B2 4SL
Tel: 021-631-3808

Black Expression Theatre, 32 Elmhurst Road, Handsworth, Birmingham B21 9QB
Tel: 021 554 4915
Con. Hermin McIntosh

Black Workers Association, 5 Oak Drive, Erdington, Birmingham B23 5DQ
Tel: 021 384 3830
Con. Mr A R Burnett

British Association of Muslims, Mount Pleasant Centre, Balsall Heath Road, Birmingham B12 9DS

Canterbury Cross Youth Club, Canterbury Road School, 359 Birchfield Road, Perry Barr, Birmingham B20 3BJ
Tel: 021 356 0656
Con. Mr D L Griffiths

Caribbean Women's Association, Advice & Training Centre, For Black Women, 12 Bell Barn Shopping Centre, Cregue Street, Lee Bank, Birmingham B15 2D2

C.H.A.S., City and Handsworth Alternative Scheme, 23 Hamstead Rd, Handsworth, Birmingham B19 1BX
Tel: 021-523-4181

Community Roots, 84 McDonald Street, Highgate, Birmingham B5 6TN
Tel: 021 622 1981
Con. A Glasford

Community Roots Resource Centre, 177 Barsord St, Highgate, Birmingham B5 7ET
Tel: 021 622 3432

Community and Village Entertainment, (C.A.V.E.), 516 Moseley Road, Balsall Heath, Birmingham B12 9AH
Tel: 021 440 3742

Cultural Centre, 326/328 Hampstead Road, Handsworth, Birmingham
Tel: 021 551 4263/4

Ethnographic Resources For Art Education, Dept of Art, Birmingham Polytechnic, Margaret Street, Birmingham B3 3BX
Tel: 021 359 6721 Ext. 247
Con. Dr N Stanley

Faith & Confidence Social Club, 178 Soho Hill, Handsworth, Birmingham
Tel: 021 554 7989
Con. Mr D Johnson

Gordon House Residential Home, (for Black Elderly), 38-40 Livingstone Rd, Perry Barr, Birmingham B20 3LL
Tel: 021-356-3871

Gujarati Language Service, Educational Translating Interpreting, 24 Lincoln Street, Balsall Heath, Birmingham B12 9EX

Gurdwara Bhatra Singh Sabha, 221 Mary Street, Balsall Heath, Birmingham 12
Tel: 021 554 1879/7987

Guru Nanak Gurdwara, South Birmingham, 629-631 Stratford Road, Sparkhill, Birmingham
Tel: 021 771 0092

Gurdwara Singh Sabha, Somerset Road, Handsworth Wood, Birmingham 20

Gurdwara Bebe Nanaki, Rookery Road, Handsworth, Birmingham 21
Tel:021 551 3489

Gurmat Missionary College, 276 Soho Road, Handsworth, Birmingham 21

Guru Nanak Nishkam Sewak Jatha, 14-20 Soho Road, Handsworth, Birmingham
Tel: 021 551 1124

Handsworth Employment Scheme Ltd, 143 Lozells Road, Birmingham 19 2TP
Tel: 021 554 1879/7987

Harambee Housing Association, 27/39 Grove Lane, Handsworth, Birmingham 21
Tel: 021 554 8479
Con. Mr F M Andrews

Head Heart & Hand Westindian Progressive Association, 22 Highfield Road, Saltley, Birmingham
Tel: 021 327 2787
Con. Mr C Clarke

Indian Overseas Youth Congress, 24 Westbourne Road, Handsworth, Birmingham B21 8AL

Indian Workers Association, 346 Soho Road, Handsworth, Birmingham 21

Khalsa Welfare Trust, Khalsa House, 4 Hollyhead Road, Handsworth, Birmingham 21
Tel: 021 554 8034

Kokuma Performing Arts, 163 Gerrard Street, Lozells, Birmingham, (Afrikan Dance Co.)
Tel: 021 554 9635

Lane Neighbourhood Centre, 422 Ladypool Road, Balsall Heath, Birmingham 12
Tel: 021 449 0438
Con. Shamshev, Evone, Sue or Dave

Link Information Centre, 74 Dalten Street, Birmingham B4 6PH
Tel: 021-233-1508

Midlands Community Growth & Support Association, Muhammed Ali Centre, Icknield Street, Hockley, Birmingham
Tel: 021 554 9721
Con. Mr J Hunte

National Association Of Black Businessmen, 44 Coventry Road, Small Heath, Birmingham
Tel: 021 771 0719

Opportunities Industrialisations Centre UK Ltd, 198/200 Moseley Road, Highgate, Birmingham B12 ODG, (Afro/Carib)
Tel: 021 440 5288
Con. Mr H Coore

Osborne House, Rest Home for Ethnic Minority Elders, 38 Livingstone Road, Perry Barr, Birmingham 20

Pakistan Pukhtoon Association, 48 Denbeigh Street, Bordesley Green, Birmingham

Pakistan Welfare Association, 32 Malmesbury Road, Small Heath, Birmingham B1 0J0
Tel: 021 772 4253

People's National Party, 1 Vimy Road, Billesley, Birmingham B13 OUA
Tel: 021 444 0243/021 455 6382
Con. Mr S C Batchelor

P.R.E.W., Project for Religious, Education & Welfare, Wesleyan Holiness Church, Holyhead Rd, Birmingham B21 0LA
Tel: 021-551-0519

The Punjabi Guardian and Multi Lingual Publishers Co. Ltd, 125 Soho Rd, Handsworth, Birmingham
Tel: 021-554-3995

Ramgarhia Sikh Temple, Graham Street, Handsworth, Birmingham 1
Tel: 021 236 5435

Rookery Road Westindian Youth Club, 49 Hallewell Road, Edgbaston, Birmingham

Sanhota Dancers, 1-7 Gower Street, Holte School Annexe , Lozells, Birmingham 19
Tel: 021 554 9915
Con. Ms M Turner/Ms M Crawford

Servol Trust, 235 Dudley Road, Winson Green, Birmingham
Tel: 021 454 3081
Con. Mr L Burke

Sharomani Akali Dal Welfare and Sikh Centre, Khalsa House, 535-537 Park Road, Hockley, Birmingham 18 4EZ

Singh Sabha Bhatra Gurdwara, 221 Mary Street, Balsall Heath, Birmingham

Spade Hammer & Pen Society, 202 Slade Road, Erdington, Birmingham B23 7RJ
Tel: 021 384 5329
Con. Mrs P Tulloch

Sri Dasmesh Sikh Temple, 305 Wheeler Street, Lozells, Birmingham
Tel: 021 440 2358

Tamaduni Creative Arts Ltd, 326-328 Hanstead Road, Handsworth, Birmingham B20 2RA
Tel: 021 551 4273/5

Tree of Life, Culture Shop, 147a Heathfield Road, Handsworth, Birmingham B19 1HL
Tel: 021 554 4736

Unemployed Youth Activities, Holte School Annexe, 1-7 Gower Street, Lozells, Birmingham 19
Tel: 021 554 4915
Con. Ekyla Char/Audrey Seymore

Westindian Federation Association, 212 Winson Green Road, Winson Green, Birmingham 18
Tel: 021 554 2594/021 551 4015
Con. Mr L Blake or Mr G Adamson

Westindian Federation Association Community Centre, 212 Winson Green Road, Winson Green, Birmingham B18 4BA
Tel: 021 554 6726

Westindian Chaplaincy, 46 Little Oaks Road, Aston, Birmingham B6 6JX
Tel: 021 326 6964/021 328 9626
Con. Rev K Dunn,

West Midlands Ethnic Minority Arts Service, Holyhead School/Community Centre, Florence Road, Handsworth, Birmingham B12 OH
Tel: 021 523 7544
Con. L Jamdagni

World Sikh Students Federation, PO Box 514, Aston, Birmingham B6 6SB

Bolton

The Islamic Culture Centre, c:o Zakaria Mosque, 20 Peace Street, Bolton, Lancaster
Tel: 0204-35002

Bolton Westindian Centre, Queens Park, Mayor St, Bolton
Tel: 0204 394 944

Bradford

Abu-Bakar Mosque, 36 Gladstone Street, Bradford BD3 9PL

Ahmadiyya Muslim Association, 393 Leeds Road, Bradford BD3 9LY

A.K. Muslim Association, 11 Farcliffe Place, Bradford BD8 8QD

Al-Falah Islamic Youth Mission, Al Saleh Buildings, Richmond Road, Bradford BD7 1DH

All Stars Volley Ball, 85 Halstead Place, Bradford BD3 8HY

Amrik Parchar Dharmic Diwan, 20 Thornbury Avenue, Bradford BD3 8HY

Anglo Asian Conservative Association, 25 Branksome Crescent, Bradford BD9 5LD

Anjuman-e-Hadeira, 13 Arnold Place, Bradford BD8 8NH

Asian Cultural Centre, c/o Scout's Hut, St Paul's Road, Bradford BD8 7LP

Asian Women's & Girl's Centre, c/o Scout's Hut, St Paul's Road, Bradford BD8 7LP

Asian Youth Movement/Saathi Project, 2 Hallfield Road, Bradford BD1 3RQ

Asian Tuition Association, 130 Asbourne Way, King's Park, Bradford

Asian Workers' Support Group, 45 Leylands Lane, Bradford BD9 5PX

Association for Asian Ladies in Distress, 31 Brantwood Road, Bradford BD9 6QJ

Azad Kashmir Muslim Association, 11 Farcliffe Place, Bradford, West Yorkshire BD8 8QD
Tel: 0274 498 677

Bangladesh Association, Keighley, 4 Park Grove, Keighley, Bradford

Bangladesh People's Association, 9 Cornwall Terrace, Bradford BD8 7JS

Bangladesh Youth Association, 9 Cornwall Terrace, Bradford BD8 7JS

Bangladesh Youth Committee, 9 Cornwall Terrace, Bradford BD8 7JS

Bangladesh Youth Organisation, 5 Cornwall Terrace, Bradford BD8 7JS

Bangladesh Youth Organisation, 17 Acres Street, Keighley, Bradford

Bazm-E-Urdu, 5 Sherborne Road, Bradford BD7 1RB

B'Nal B'Rith, c/o 260 Bradford Road, Shipley, Bradford BD18 3AE

Bradford Khalifa Muslim Society, 2 Oakfield Grove, Bradford BD9 4PY

Bradford Labour Party, 83 Buchanan Towers, Radwell Drive, Bradford BD5 OQT

Bradford Muslim Welfare Society, 5 Kirkham Road, Bradford BD7 2DJ

Bradford Sikh Parents' Association, 24 Oakwood Grove, Bradford BD8 8QB

Council for Mosques, 6 Claremont Road, Bradford BD7 1BQ

Commonwealth Women's Association, 53 Ashwell Road, Bradford BD9 4A

Difewan Bookseller & Cultural Centre, 22 Hallfield Road, Bradford BD1 3RQ
Tel: 0274 725745

Dominica Association Bradford, 4 Hallfield Rd, Bradford 3RQ
Tel: 0274-394490

El Hadith Masjid (Salfia) Comm, 9 Hampden Place, Bradford BD5 OJZ

Federation of Bradford Sikh Organisations, 7 Sunny Bank Lane, Thornbury, Bradford BD3 7DG
Tel: 0274 666659

Frizinghall Community Association, 6 Hilton Drive, Shipley, Bradford BD18 2AL

Grange Interlink Community Association, 44 Wheatlands Drive, Bradford BD9 5JJ

Gujarkhan Burial Society, 18 Easby Road, Bradford BD7 1QX

Gurdwara Amrit Parchar Dharmak Diwan, Harris Street, (Off Leeds Road), Bradford 3
Tel: 0274 724853

Guru Govind Singh Sikh Temple, 2 Redmire Street, Bradford BD3 8LY

Guru Nanak Charitable Trust, 64 Avenue Road, Bradford BD5 8DS

Guru Nanak Sikh Temple, 5 Flockton Drive, Bradford BD4 7LL

Guru Nanak Sikh Temple, Wakefield Road, Bradford BD4 7AH
Tel: 0274 723557/0274 725849

Hanfia Mosque, Carlisle Road, Bradford BD8

Hussainia Islamic Mission, 154 Folkstone Street, Bradford BD7 3AF

Indian Federation, 22 Roslyn Place, Bradford BD7 3AF

Indian Workers' Association, 9 Fernbank Road, Bradford BD3 OPJ

Indo-Pakistan International Society, 5 Selborne Terrace, Bradford BD9 4NJ

Islamic Culture Centre, Roxy Building, Barkerend Road, Bradford BD3 9AP

Islami Madressa, 41 Woodview, Bradford BD8 7AJ

Jamiyat-ahl-Hadith, 120 Lower Rushton Road, Bradford BD3 8PZ

Jamiyat Tabligh-ul-Islam Mosque, 21 Aberdeen Place, Bradford BD7 2HG

Jamiya Tabligh-ul-Islam Mosque, 13 Mannham Road, Bradford BD9 5DX

Jamiyat Tabligh-ul-Islam Mosque, 18 Southfield Square, Bradford BD8 7SL

Karamand Centre, Barkerend Road, Bradford BD3 8QX

Keighley Muslim Association, 77 Devonshire Street, Keighley, Bradford BD21

Madressa Tabligh-ul-Islam, 114 Lumb Lane, Bradford BD8 7RS

Muslim Association of Bradford, 30 Howard Street, Bradford BD5 OBP

Muslim Girls School, 15 Woodville Terrace, Bradford BD5 OJH

Nusrati Islam Mosque, 5 Archibald Street, Bradford BD7 1LR

Oriental Arts Bradford, 9 Wool Exchange, Market Street, Bradford BD1 1LN

Pakistan Medical Society, 53 Ashwell Road, Bradford BD9 4BA

Pakistan Women's Group, 73 Whitehall Road, Bradford BD1 29L

Pucktoon Society, 30 Pearson Street, Bradford BD3 8EU

Ramgarhia Sikh Temple, Bolton Road, Bradford 2
Tel: 0274 632761

Shree Prajapati Samaj, 466 Great Horton Road, Bradford BD7 1QJ

Sikh Temple, 20 Newburn Street, Bradford 7
Tel: 0274 75916

Surti Muslim Khalifa Society, 2 Oakfield Grove, Bradford BD9 4PY

Tablighul Islam, 84 Beamsley Road, Bradford BD18 2DP

Tawakulia Islamic Society, 48 Cornwall Road, Bradford BD8 7JN

Tehriq-istaq-Ial, 37 Hampden Street, Bradford BD5

The Bradford Sikh Parents Association, 2 Luther Way, Kings Park, Bradford BD2 1EK
Tel: 0274 44932/0274 390069

UK Islamic Mission, 67 Glenrose Drive, Bradford BD7 2QQ

United Sikh Association, Guru Gobind Singh Sikh, Temple, Malvern Ventnor Street, (Off Lees Road), Bradford 3
Tel: 0274 727928

West Bowling Islamic Mission, 44 Woodroyd Road, Bradford BD75 8EL

Westindian Community Centre Association, (Checkpoint), 45 Westgate, Bradford BD1 2QR

Westindian Parents Association, 17 Claremont, Bradford BD7

Y.M.H.A., 1 Bowling Hall Rd, Bradford BD4 7LE, West Yorkshire
Tel: 0274-734600

Brierley Hill

Sikh Parents Association, 20 Ravensitch Walk, Brierley Hill, West Midlands

Bristol

Adrinka Dance Company, 15a Albany Road, Montpelier, Bristol 6
Tel: 0272 555972

Anti-Apartheid Movement, 4 Rookfield Road, Cotham, Bristol BS6 5PW
Tel: 0272 40344

Arts Opportunity Theatre, (St Pauls YTS), 98-100 Grosvenor Road, St Pauls, Bristol 2
Tel: 0272 557660

Asian Women's Association, 40 Bredon, Yate, Bristol

Asian Youth Club, 46 Alfred Place, Kingsdown, Bristol 2
Tel: 0272 41652

Bangladesh Association, 257 Ashley Down Road, Bristol BS7 9BW
Tel: 0272 422185

Barbados & Caribbean Friends Association, 11 Holton Road, Horfield, Bristol 7
Tel: 0272 691181

Bhangra Dance Group, (Punjabi), 54 Sandbed Road, St. Werburghs, Bristol 2
Tel: 0272 554955

Black Social Workers'Association, 2 Elmgrove Avenue, Easton, Bristol
Tel: 0272 542211

Bristol Caribbean Community Enterprise Ltd, Trinity Church, Trinity Road, Bristol, Avon BS2 ONW

Bristol Council of Churches, Race Relations Group, 23 Charlton Mead Court, Westbury-on-Trym, Bristol
Tel: 0272 505444

Bristol Mosque Committee, Green Street, Totterdown, Bristol
Tel: 027 770944

Bristol Performing Arts, (Promotions), 26 Alfred Place, Kingsdown, Bristol 2
Tel: 0272 41652

Bristol Resource Centre, 62 Bedminster Parade, Bedminster, Bristol
Tel: 0272 667933

Bristol Sikh Cultural Centre, 114 St Marks Road, Easton, Bristol 5
Tel: 0272 521318

Bristol Westindian Parents and Friends Association, c/o 58 St. Nicholas Road, Bristol BS2 9LH

Bristol Sikh Temple, 71-75 Fishponds Road, Eastville, Bristol 5
Tel: 0272 511609

Campaign Against Racism in Education, (CARE), 62 Bedminster Parade, Bristol 3
Tel: 0272 667933
Con. Tony Gomez

Campaign Against Racist Laws, (CARL), 29 North Street, Downend, Bristol
Tel: 0272 570534

Community Growth & Support Association, (mainly Westindian), 14 Badminton Road, St Agnes, Bristol 2
Tel: 0272 554181

Dockland Settlement, City Road, St Pauls, Bristol
Tel: 0272 49873

Easton Community Association, 104 Bloy Street, Easton, Bristol BS5

Easton Islamic Darasgah, St Mark's Road, Easton, Bristol

Ekome Dance Group, 36 Argyle Road, St Pauls, Bristol
Tel: 0272 426475

Guru Nanak (Sikh Temple), 1-7 Fishponds Road, Eastville, Bristol 5
Tel: 0272 511609

Guru Nanak Prakash Sikh Temple, 8 St Marks Road, Bristol 5
Tel: 027 552447

Indian Association, 218 Stapleton Road, Easton, Bristol 5
Tel: 0272 510505

Indian Women's Association, 2 Melrose Road, Clifton, Bristol 8
Tel: 0272 735949

Inkworks Community Centre, 22 Hepburn Road, St Pauls, Bristol
Tel: 0272 421870

Islamic Darasgah, 109 Lower Cheltenham Place, Montpelier, Bristol

Jatha N.S. Sikh Temple, 11 Summerhill Road, St George, Bristol 5
Tel: 0272 559333

Maternity Links, 42 Chelsea Road, Easton, Bristol
Tel: 0272 541487

Multi-Lingual Advice Project, 36 Chelsea Road, Easton, Bristol
Tel: 0272 540350

Multi-Racial Youth Hostel, 97 Ashley Road, St Pauls, Bristol
Tel: 0272 559303

Muslim Women's Association, 46 Arnos Street, Totterdown, Bristol

Pakistan Association, 10 Tewkesbury Road, St Werburgh's, Bristol 2
Tel: 0272 558102

Pioneer House (Hostel for Young Men), 112 York Road, Bedminster 3, Bristol 3
Tel: 0272 634131

Ramgharia Sikh Temple, 81 Chelsea Road, Easton, Bristol 5
Tel: 0272 554929

Rastafarian Brethren, 22 Hepburn Road, St Pauls, Bristol 2
Tel: 0272 421870

Sanatan Deevya Mandal, (Hindu Temple), 163b Church Road, Redfield, Bristol BS5 9LA

Sangat Singh Sabha Gurdwara, 11 Summers Hill Street, St George, Bristol 5

Sikh Community Council, 2 Normanby Road, Easton, Bristol 5
Tel: 0272 515010

Sikh Cultural Centre, 114 St Marks Road, Easton, Bristol
Tel: 0272 512377

St Pauls Advice Centre, 146 Grosvenor Road, St Pauls, Bristol 2
Tel: 0272 552981

St Pauls Area Community Enterprise Ltd, City Road, St Paul's, Bristol 6

St Pauls Community Association, St Barnabas Community Centre, 82 Ashley Road, St Pauls, Bristol
Tel: 0272 554497

St Pauls Neighbourhood House, 15 Brighton Street, St Pauls, Bristol 2
Tel: 0272 421918

St Pauls Youth Council, BCRE Offices, Colston House, Colston Street, Bristol 1
Tel: 0272 24221

St Werburghs Community Centre, Horley Road, St Werburghs, Bristol

Star Domino Club, 1-5 Meadow Street, Bristol

Westindian Parents & Friends Association, 58 St Nicholas Road, St Pauls, Bristol 2
Tel: 0272 551917

Broadstone

Shree Kadwa Patidar Samaj UK, 148 West Way, Broadstone , Dorset, BH18 9LN
Tel: 0202-671212 ext 2512

Burton-on-Trent

Burton Caribbean Association, 1 Westwood Park, Newhill, Burton-on-Trent

Pakistan Welfare Association, 62 Victoria Road, Burton-on-Trent, Staffordshire DE14

Cambridge

Cambridge University Pakistan Association, Peterhouse, Cambridge CB2 1RD

Chatham

Bangladesh Welfare Association, 26 Chatham Hill, Chatham, Kent ME5 7AA

Chorley

Chorley Muslim Society, 30 Cunliffe Street, Chorley, Surrey

Coventry

Afro-Asian Teachers Association, 31 Walton Close, Eynesford Garage, Coventry CU3 2LT

Centre for Caribbean Studies, University of Warwick, Coventry CV4 7AL
Tel: 0203-523443

Community Friendly Society, Coventry Cathedral, 7 Priory Row, Coventry
Tel: 0203 689 760

Coventry Westindian Association, 90 St Raphael Close, Coventry CV5 8LS
Tel: 0203 70662, Secretary Mr J Hylton
Tel: 0203 552929 (Club), Spon Street, Coventry CV1 3BB

Gurdwara Ajit Darbar, 396 Stoney Stanton Road, Coventry

Gurdwara Guru Nanak Parkash, Harnell Lane West, Coventry
Tel: 0203 20960

Indian Overseas Congress, 399 Amsty Road, Coventry CU2 3BQ

Minority Craft Workshop, Boston Place, Off Lockhurst Lane, Holbrooks, Coventry
Con. Ms Evett Hutchinson

OSABA Womens Centre, 43 Primrose Hill Street, Hillfields, Coventry
Tel 0203-21816
(Black Women's Group Challenge Newspaper)

Punjab Language Association, 22 Haselbech Road, Coventry CV3 2HT

Ramgarhia Missle, Khalsa House, 19 St Lukes Road, Holbrooks, Coventry CV6 4JA
Tel: 0203 661442

Ramgarhia Sikh Temple, 1103 Foleshill Road, Coventry CU6 6EP
Tel: 0203 88208

Sikh Temple, Tree Tops, Foleshill Road, Coventry

Supreme Council of Sikhs, 70-72 Humber Road, Coventry CV3 1BA
Tel: 0203 448876/0203 29688

Tamara Productions, 43 Primose Hill St, Hillfields, Coventry
Tel: 0203 715471
(Wakiyl Al Ansaari) (Makeda Sauda)

Unity Organisation, c/o 43 Primrose Hill Street, Hillfields, Coventry
Tel: 0203 21816
Con. E. Best./V.Cummins

Cranford

The Sikh Art and Culture Centre, 93 Waye Avenue, Cranford, Middlesex TW5 9SQ
Tel: 01 759 0639

Crawley

Gurdwara Sri Guru Singh Sabha, 27-29 Spencer Road, West Green, Crawley, Sussex
Tel: 0293 30163

Croydon

Black Parents Association, 47 Wellesley Road, Croydon, Surrey CRO 2AJ

Croydon Race & Community Organisation, 47 Wellesley Road, Croydon, Surrey CR0 2AJ

The Sikh Temple Croydon, 4 Edit Road, Croydon, Surrey CRO

Dagenham

Asian Welfare Association, 24 First Avenue, Dagenham, Essex RM10 9AT

Darlington

Sikh Temple Darlington, Louisa Street, Darlington, Co. Durham DL1 4ED
Tel: (0325) 461 2525

Derby

Association of Teachers of Ethnic Minorities, 28 Tilton Drive, Derby

Derby Westindian Association, Community Centre, Carrington Street, Derby DE1 2ND
Tel: 0332 371529/381320
Secretary: Miss C Wright

Indian Community Centre, Rawdon Street, Derby
Tel: 0332-42892

Guru Nanak Istri Sabha, 158 Pear Tree Street, Derby 8

Guru Arjan Dev Gurdwara, Cromwell Road, Derby
Tel: 0332 32539

Dewsbury

Savile Town Muslim Jamaat, 57/9 Savile Grove, Savile Town, Dewsbury, West Yorks

Dorset

Shree Kadwa Patidar Samaj, 148 West Way, Broadstone, Dorset BH18 3LN
Tel: 0202 671212 ext. 2512

Dudley

Dudley Mosque and Muslim Community Centre, Birmingham Street, Dudley, West Midlands

Dudley and Sandwell Bengali Speaking Organisation 34 Beeches Road, Rowley Regis, Warley, Dudley B63 OAT

Dudley Sikh Temple, 118 Wellington Road, Dudley, West Midlands
Secretary: Mr K.S. Judge

Dudley Westindian Community Association, 28 Kilburn Place, Dudley, West Midlands

Eve Hill Community Organisation, Eve Hill Youth and Community Centre, Salop Street, Dudley, West Midlands

Indian Workers Association, 56 Spring Parklands, Dudley, West Midlands

Markazi Jamiat Ahl-E-Hadith, 29 Queens Cross, Dudley, West Midlands

Muslim Youth Association, 16 North Street, Dudley, West Midlands

Shree Gujarati Hindu Centre, Shree Krishna Temple, Hope Street, Off Churchfield Street, Dudley, West Midlands

Shromani Akali Dal (UK), 12 Molyneux Road, Netherton, Dudley, West Midlands

Sikh Educational and Cultural Association (UK), Sat-Nam Cottage, Compton Gardens, Kinver, Nr. Stourbridge

Sri Guru Nanak Singh Sabha Temple, 26 Wellington Road, Dudley, Worc.
Tel: 0384 53054

United Defence Committee, 6 Russell Street, Dudley, West Midlands

Edgware

The Sikh Cultural Society of Great Britain, 88 Mollison Way, Edgware, Middlesex HA8 5QW
Tel: 01 952 1215

Erith

Gurdwara Guru Nanak Darbar, 31 Crabtree Manerway, Belvedere, Erith, Kent
Tel. 03224 32847

Farnham

Indian Ground Work, 58 Ridgway Road, Farnham, Surrey GU9 8N3 (Management/Training)
Tel: 0252 713643

Filey

New Eden Society, P.O. Box 2, Filey, North Yorkshire YO14 9HJ

Gravesend

Asian Welfare Society, 14c Lennox Road, Gravesend
Tel: 0474 50999

Gravesend & Dartford Muslim Association, 59 Old Road West, Gravesend, Kent
Tel: 0474 51996

Kshatrya Sabha, 77 High Street, Gravesend, Kent

Shiromani Akali Dal, 49 Milton Road, Gravesend, Kent

Sikh Gurdwara Committee, Sikh Temple Management Committee, Clarence Place, Gravesend
Tel: 0474 65121-

Sikh Missionary Society, 20 Peacock Street, Gravesend, Kent
Tel: 0474 61834

Grays

Gurdwara Grays, 6 Maidstone Road, Grays, Essex
Tel: 0375 76086

Halifax

Asian Defence Committee, c/o Mr Ghani, 23 Woodbine Terrace, King Cross Road, Halifax
Tel: 0422 68581

Bangladesh Muslim Association, c/o Mr W Uddin, 23 Westgrove Terrace, Hopwood Lane, Halifax
Tel: 0422 59360

Calderdale Asian Youth Movement, c/o Mr Hussain, 74 Hopwood Lane, Halifax
Tel: 0422 44558

Calderdale Indian Welfare Association, 17 Harrison Road, (Buttoo & Sons), Halifax
Tel: 0422 66709

Elland Mosque, 26/34 Elizabeth Street, Elland, Halifax
Tel: 0422 75297

Hanson Lane Mosque, (Jamiat-Ahle-Hadith), 124 Hanson Lane, Halifax
Tel: 0422 41012

Islamic Mission, 122/124 Gibbet Street, Halifax
Tel: 0422 42366

Madni Mosque, c/o Mr Lal Din, 140 Gibbet Street, Halifax
Tel: 0422 65607

Muslim Youth Sports Club . Elland, c/o Mr Aslam, 4 Dean Street, Elland, Halifax
Tel: 0422 75297

Neighbourhood Information & Advice Centre, (Rhodes Street Advice Centre), 2 Rhodes Street, Halifax
Tel: 0422 41908

Queens Road Muslim Cricket Association, c/o Mr Seraj, 18 Grosvenor Terrace, Halifax
Tel: 0422 65082 .

Pakistan Peoples Party, c/o Mr Ata, 128 Gibbet Street, Halifax
Tel: 0422 60236

Rhodes Street Central Mosque, 49 Rhodes Street, Halifax
Tel: 0422 52039

Todmorden Mosque, Islamic Centre, Eagle Street, Todmorden

Welfare Association for the Peoples Republic of Bangladesh, c/o Mr Hussain, 11 Milton Place, Halifax
Tel: 0422 43043

Halsowen

U.K. Islamic Mission, Blackheath Islamic and Community Centre, 314-318 Long Lane, Halesowen, West Midlands

Harrow

Brent Sikh Community Centre, 37 Sudbury Court Drive, Harrow, Middlesex
Tel: 01 904 2189

Hatfield

Indian Cultural Association, 84 Cherry Way, Hatfield, Herts AL10 8LD
Tel: 0707 269964

Ramgarhia Sikh Temple, Bearton Avenue, Hitchin, Herts

Sri Guru Singh Sabha Gurdwara, Radcliffe Road, Hitchin, Herts
Tel: 0462 2993

High Wycombe

Afro-Westindian Association, 82 Armison Avenue, High Wycombe, Bucks

Caba Association, 11 Jubilee Road, High Wycombe, Bucks

Carib Domino Club, 79 Queen Road, High Wycombe, Bucks

Carib Peoples Association, 1 Tamar House, Hicks Farm Rise, High Wycombe, Bucks

Cultural Resource Centre, 205 Desborough Road, High Wycombe, Bucks
Tel: 0494 21655

Khandan Child Support Scheme, 4 Ridgeside, Bledlow Ridge, High Wycombe, Bucks.

Sharomani Akali Dal, 80 Totteridge Road, High Wycombe, Bucks.

Sikh Temple, 27 Kingston Road, High Wycombe, Bucks.

3 W's International Youth Organisation, c/o Ms J.A. Roberts, 8 Sharrow Vale, High Wycombe, Bucks.
Tel: 0494 22814

Hillingdon

World Sikh Welfare Organisation, (G.B.), 14 Temple Park, Hillingdon, Middlesex
Tel: 0895 32121

Hounslow

Ahmadiyya Muslim Association, 327 Martindale Road, Hounslow, Middlesex TW4 7HG
Tel: 01 572 4055

Bangladesh Welfare Association, 70 Barrack Road, Hounslow, Middlesex TW4 6AN

Gurdwara Sri Guru Singh Saba, Hibemia Road, Hounslow, Middlesex
Tel: 01 577 2793

Guru Nanak Nishkam Sewak Jatha, 142 Martindale Road, Hounslow, Middlesex TW4 7HQ
Tel: 01 570 4774

Huddersfield

Gurdwara Sri Guru Singh Sabha, Hill House Lane, Fartown, Huddersfield
Tel: 0484 42982

Guru Nanak Sikh Temple, Prospect Street, Huddersfield
Tel: 0484 23773

Ilford

Asian Senior Citizens Welfare Association,
82 Green Lane, Ilford, Essex 1G1 1YH
The Muslim Welfare Association, 54/56 Albert Road, Ilford, Essex IGI 1HW

Sikh Study Forum, 85 Inglehurst Gardens, Ilford, Essex IG4 5HA
Tel: 01 550 5778

Ipswich

Ipswich Caribbean Association, 17 All Saints Road, Ipswich

Ipswich & Suffolk Indian Association, c/o Tourist Info Office, Town Hall, Princess Street, Ipswich

Kettering

Sri Guru Singh Sabha Gurdwara, 1 Wavil Close, Kettering, Northants

Lancaster

Hindu Community, 1/3 De Vitre Street, Lancaster LA1 1QU

Leamington Spa

Ahmaddiya Muslim Community, Mr. R. Ahmed, 9, Woodway Avenue, Hampton Magna, Warks, Leamington Spa
Tel: 0926 498629

Association of Indian Communists, 24 Claremont Road, Leamington Spa
Tel: 0926 24818
Mr. K.S. Atwal

Hindu Religious Association, 21 Clemens Street, Leamington Spa
Tel: 0926 22077
Mr. Y.P.Tara

Indian National Association, Warwick District Commonwealth Club, 3 Church Street, Leamington Spa
Mr. B.S. Dhesi, Tel: 0926-27896

Indian Overseas Congress, 6 Freshwater Grove, Sydenham Estate, Leamington Spa

Indian Workers Association, 24 Claremont Road, Leamington Spa
Tel: 0926 24818

Life (Save the Unborn Child), 118-120 Warwick Street, Leamington Spa, Warwickshire CV32 4QY
Tel: 0926-21587/311667

Mary Seacole Society, Mrs Dorrette McAuslan, Chairperson, 2 Lillington Road, Leamington Spa, Warwickshire CU32 5YR

Pakistani Welfare Association, Mr. A.Ghafoor, 153 Rugby Road, Leamington Spa
Tel: 0926-20498

Shromani Akalidal UK, 89 Willes Road, Leamington Spa
Tel: 0926-37774

The Sikh Temple, 96-100 New Street, Leamington Spa, Warwickshire
Tel. 0926 24297

Westindian Association, 23 St. Mary's Crescent, Leamington Spa
Tel: 0926-26562

Leeds

Almadina Jamia Mosque, Muslim Council, 33 Brudenell Road, Leeds 6

ASHA, Bengali Women's & Welfare Centre, 24 Stratford Street, Leeds 11

Bangladesh United Association, 17 Hilton Road, Leeds 8

Bhatra Nirman Jatha, 203 Harrogate Road, Leeds 7

Captive Nations Committee, 121 Hawksworth Road, Leeds LS18

Caribbean Cricket Club, 72 Francis Street, Leeds 7

Chapeltown Neighbourhood Council, Chapeltown Community Centre, Reginald Terrace, Chapeltown, Leeds 7
Tel: 0532 625 444

Federation of Indian Organisations, 377 Street Lane, Leeds 17

Guru Nanak Sikh Temple, 62 Tong Road, Armley, Leeds 12
Tel: 0532 636525

Hindu Charitable Trust, 11 Green View, Meanswood, Leeds 8

Hindu Garba Group, 7 Hill Top Mount, Leeds 8

The Hindu Samaj, 68 Manor Drive, Leeds 17

Indian Welfare Society, 134 Street Lane, Leeds 8

Indian Women's Association, 6 Ederoyd Crescent, Pudsey, Leeds LS7

Indian Workers Association (Leeds), 283 Harrogate Road, Leeds LS17 6PR/A
Tel: 0532 686615

Indian Workers Association, 185 Wetherby Road, Leeds 17

Indian Workers Association, 25 Carr Manor Parade, Leeds 17

Islamic Centre, 20 St Martins View, Leeds 7

Kashmir Muslim Welfare Association, 21 Wickham Street, Leeds LS11 7AR

Lawisha, 99 Roundhay Road, Leeds LS8 5AJ

Leeds Caribbean & Domino & Social Club, 12 Mexborough Drive, Leeds 7

Leeds Harambee Association, 60/6A Cowper Street, Leeds LS7 4DS

Leopold Street Mosque, 24 Birchwood Avenue, Leeds 17

Mandela Centre, Chapeltown Road, Leeds LS11 6JF

Muslim Association of Leeds 11, 278 Dewsbury Road, Leeds LS11 6JT

Muslim Association Mosque, 25 Stratford Street, Leeds 11

Muslim Community Centre, 69 Woodsley Road, Leeds LS3 1DU

Muslim Commonwealth, 18 Winston Mount, Leeds 8

Muslim Council, 19 Model Avenue, Leeds 12

Muslim Council, 165 Town Street, Armley, Leeds 12

Muslim Cultural Society, 71 Elford Grove, Leeds 8

Muslim Youth Centre, 61 Spencer Place, Leeds 7

Muslim Welfare Centre, 4 Brooklyn Terrace, Armley, Leeds 12

Namahari Sangat, 48 Ederoyd Crescent, Pudsey, Leeds 28
Tel: 0532 623718

Pakistan Muslim Association, 118 Street Lane, Leeds 17

Palace Youth Project, 173 Spencer Place, Leeds LS7

Punjabi Sabha, 38 Whinmoor Avenue, Leeds 14

Ramgharia Ladies Circle, 55 Kingswood Gardens, Leeds 8

Ramgarhia Sikh Temple, 138 Chapeltown Road, Leeds 7
Tel: 0532 625 427

Ramgharia Sports Club, 41 The Avenue, Leeds 17

Shah Jahal Masjid Mosque, 27 Ellers Road, Leeds LS8 4HJ

Shepherds Lane Language Centre, Harehills Primary School, Shepherds Lane, Leeds 7

Sikh Study Centre, 560 Scott Hall Road, Leeds 7

Sikh Temple, 281 Chapeltown Road, Leeds 7

Sikh Temple, 25 Carr Manor Parade, Leeds 17

Springboard, 24 Hamilton View, Leeds 17

Sri Guru Nanak Sports Club, 26 Silver Royde Drive, Leeds 12

Sri Guru Nanak Sikh Temple, 62 Tong Road, Armley, Leeds 12

Talash, c/o Mr G Hussain, 67 Bayswater Grove, Leeds 8

Tunstall Road Community Centre, Tunstall Road, Leeds 11
Tel: 0532 774820

Uganda Asians Association, 39 Willow Garth Close, Leeds 16

United Caribbean Association, 12 Hall Lane, Leeds 17

Westindian Family Councillor, Mrs M Saddler, 16 Baldovan Terrace, Leeds 8

Leicester

The Ajani Centre, 3 Mill Hill Lane, Highfields, Leicester LE2 1AH
Tel: 0533-556796

Business Development Unit, Business Advice Centre, 30 New Walk, Leicester LE1 6TF
Tel: 0533-554464

Charnwood Community Relations Council, 43 Church Gate, Loughborough, Leicester LE11 1VE
Tel: 0509-261651

The Concorde Festival Trust, 10 St Pauls Road, Leicester LE3 9DE
Tel: 0533 539410
(Multi Cultural Arts Promotions & Festivals)

Highfields & Belgrave Law Centre, 6 Seymour Street, Highfields, Leicester LE2 OLB
Tel: 0533 532 928

Highfields Girls Venture, 3 Mill Hill Lane, Highfields, Leicester
Tel: 0533 556796
(Self Help)

Guru Nanak Sikh Temple, 5 New Walk, Leicester LE1 6DE
Tel: 0533 540101

Gurdwara Sri Guru Teg Bahadur, 23 East Park Road, Leicester LE5 4QD
Tel: 0533 760517

The Jain Samaj, Mr. M.Z. Shah, 3a Loughborough Road, Leicester

Leicestershire Museums, Art Galleries and Records Service, 96 New Walk, Leicester LE1 6TD

Leicester Black Women's Group, c/o 30 Westleigh Road, Leicester LE3 0HH
Tel: 0533 552011

Leicester Indian Art Circle, 60 Essex Road, Leicester

Leicester United Caribbean Association, 72 Rutland Street, Leicester 8

Ramgarhia Board, 51 Maynell Road, Leicester
Tel: 0533 760765

Shree Sanatan Mandir, Weymouth Street, off Catherine Street, Leicester 11 1E

Sikh Parents Association, 88 Evington Drive, Leicester LE5 5PE
Tel: 0533 738836

Spectrum Organisation, 13 Midland Street, Leicester LE1 1TC

Liverpool

Black Linx, c/o Merseyside CRC, 64 Mount Pleasant, Liverpool L3 5SH
Tel: 051-709 9698

Charles Wooten Education Centre, 248 Upper Parliament Street, Liverpool 8
Tel: 051 708 9698

Gurdwara Sikh Community Centre, Wellington Avenue, Liverpool 15
Tel: 051 773 0076

Jamaica House, 42 Upper Parliament Street, Liverpool 8
Tel: 051 708 6881

Liverpool 8 Law Centre, 34-36 Princes Road, Liverpool 8
Tel: 051 709 7222

Merseyside Caribbean Council, Amberley Street, Liverpool 8
Tel: 051 708 9790

Merseyside Caribbean Council, Merseyside Caribbean Centre, Amberley Street, Liverpool 8
Tel: 051 708 9790

Merseyside Chinese Community Service, 10 St George Square, Liverpool 1
Tel: 051 236 0990

Merseyside Somali Community Association, 22 Princes Road, Liverpool 8
Tel: 051 709 7704

Pakistan Liverpool Association, 60 Mulgrave Street, Liverpool L8 2TF

Racism Awareness Network, c/o Merseyside C.R.C., 64 Mount Pleasant, Liverpool L35 SH

LONDON

Abeng Youth Centre, 7 Gresham Road, Brixton, London SW9
Tel: 01 737 1628/274 5261

Academy of Indian Arts, 23 East Avenue, London, E12 6SG
Tel: 01-471-2039

Academy of Indian Dances & Performing Arts, Trinity Centre, East Avenue, London E12 6SJ
Tel: 01 472 8947

Academy Social Club, 44 Highcroft Gdns., London NW11 0LX

Acton Asian Association, 2 Vincent Rd, London, W3
Tel: 01-993-6096

Advice Centre, Association of Sangam Asian Women, 235-237 West Hendon Broadway, London, NW9
Tel: 01-202-4629

A.D.V.O., Aid for Destitute Victims of Oppression, c/o 330 Copley Close, Hanwell, London W7 1QF
Tel: 01 575 6591

Africa Centre, 38 King Street, London WC2 E8JT
Tel: 01 836 1973

Africa Heritage Trust (Trade), I.O.R.U.M., 204a North Gower Street, (Entrance) Starcross St. Euston, London NW1
Tel: 01 387 4308

African Peoples Historical Monumental Foundation, (Black Cultural Archives), 378 Coldharbour Lane, Brixton, SW9
Tel: 01-733-3044

African Refugee Housing Action Ltd, 2nd Floor , St Margarets, 25 Leighton Rd, London, NW5
Tel: 01-482-3829

African Women's Association, (Akoya Project), (P.O. Box 115), c/o Celestial Church of Christ, Stratford Parish Hall, Arcadia Street, E14
Tel: 01-987-0371

The Afrikan Study Programme, 82 Tynemouth Rd, Tottenham, London, N15 4AX
Tel: 01-885-5392

Afro-Asian Advisory Service, Cambridge House, 137 Camberwell Road, London SE5
Tel: 01 701 0141

Afro-Asian Artistes, 34 Grafton Terrace, London NW5
Tel: 01 485 9338

Afro-Asian Solidarity Organisation, 366 York Rd, London, SW18 5GX
Tel: 01-874-6295

Afro-Caribbean Community Association, Community Centre, 5 Mayall Road, London SE24
Tel: 01 326 1028

Afro-Caribbean Cultural Association, 192 Uxbridge Road, Southall, Middlesex, UB1 3DX
Tel: 01-574-4879

Afro-Caribbean Cultural and Social Foundation, 43 Warbeck Road, London W12
Tel: 01 740 4831

Afro-Caribbean Educational Project, (Self Help/Education), 593 High Road, Leyton, London E10 6PY
Tel: 01 558 2285

Afro-Caribbean Educational Resource Project, Wyvil Road School, Wyvil Road, London SW8 2TJ
Tel: 01 627 2662

Afro-Caribbean Elderly Group Fairhazel Luncheon Club, 8 Fairhazel Gardens, London NW8
Tel: 01 328 4311

Afro-Caribbean Group, Hardie Close, London NW10
Tel: 01 451 6564

Afro-Caribbean Organisation, 335 Grays Inn Road, London WC1
Tel: 01 837 0396

Afro-Caribbean Project, 107 Kingsgate Road, London NW6
Tel: 01 328 4656

Afro-Caribbean Project, 422 Seven Sisters Road, London N4
Tel: 01 800 9052

Afro-Caribbean Supplementary Education Service, 192 Marlowe Rd, Walthamstow, London, E17 3HG
Tel: 01-521-0983

Afro-Caribbean Voluntary Help Association, (National HO), 48 Eastlake Road, London SE5
Tel: 01 737 3603

Afro-Global Progressive Organisation, Acton College, Mill Hill Road, Acton, London W3 8UX
Tel: 01 993 2344 ext. 2396

Ahmadiya Movement in Islam, 67 Cardington Square, Hounslow, Middlesex

Albany, 179 Deptford High Street, London SE8
Tel: 01 092 0231

All London Teachers Against Racism and Facism, A.L.T.A.R.F., Panther House, Room 216, 38 Mount Pleasant, London WC1X OAP
Tel: 01 278 7856

Aman Arts, (specialist in Oriental, Pakistani, Arab, Islamic Art & Archaeology), 24 Gloucester Road, London E12 5JU
Tel: 01 478 4256

Andhra Association, UK, 45 Fairbourne Road, Tottenham, London N17

'Ankur' Harlesden Asian Youth Project, 19 Nicoll Road, London NW10

Arya Samja London, 69A Argyle Road, West Ealing, London W13

Asian Affair, 46 Parsons Green Lane, London SW6
Tel: 01 736 6096

Asian Action Group (AAG), Annexe B, Tottenham Town Hall, Approach Road, London N15
Tel: 01 801 1431

Asian Centre, 17-19 Dalston Lane, London E8 3DF
Tel: 01 254 4898

Asian Community Action, Youth Group, 322a Brixton Road, London SW9
Tel: 01 733 7494

Asian Community Centre, 239 Uxbridge Road, London W12
Tel: 01 740 6940

Asian Drama & Dance Group, Fellowship House, St Bartholomew Road, London E6
Tel: 01 552 6198

Asian Education Advisory Service, 15 New Road, London E1
Tel: 01 247 9546

Asian Elderly Milap Group, c/o 48 Lillyville Road, London SW6

Asian Mother and Baby Campaign, Save the Children Fund, Mary Datchelor House, 17 Grove Lane, Camberwell, London SE5 8RD
Tel: 01 703 5400
Ms Veena Bahl

Asian Pensioners Group, The Oak Tree Community Centre, Osborne Road, South Acton, London W3
Tel: 01 992 5566

Asian Project Community Development, Youth Centre, Tulse Hill, London SW2

Asian Resource Centre, LEB Buildings, McBean Street, London SE18
Tel: 01 854 1188

Asian Sheltered Residential Accommodation, 5a Westminster Bridge Road, London SE1
Tel: 01 928 9379

Asian Sheltered Residential, Accommodations Ltd, 42 Kempshott Road, London SW16
Tel: 01 764 4695

Asian Studies Centre, Tower Hamlets Institute, Myrdle Street, London E1 1HL
Tel: 01 247 6363

Asian Unemployment Outreach Project, Montifiore Centre, Deal Street, London E11

Asian Women's Forum Co. Ltd, 2nd Floor, Nursery Premises, Wood Green Shopping City, Wood Green, London N22
Tel: 01 888 2446

Asian Women's Organisation, 48 Knowles Hill Crescent, Lewisham, London SE13 6DG
Tel: 01 318 4440

Asian Youth Council, 30 Haroldstone Road, Walthamstow, London E17 7AN, (Youth Services)
Tel: 01 509 1871

Asian Youth Project, 583 Commercial Road, London E1
Tel: 01 790 4406

Association of Black Social Workers & Allied Professions (ABSWAP), c/o Consortium of Ethnic Minorities, 403 Brixton Road, London SW9
Tel: 01 703 1089

Association of Sangam Asian Women, 235-237 West Hendon Broadway, London NW9
Tel: 01 202 4629

Balham & Tooting Outreach Centre, 1 Letchworth Street, Tooting, London SW17 8SX
Tel: 01 767 0246

Balham and Tooting Sports and Social Club, 94 Balham High Road, London SW12 9AA
Tel: 01 673 5968
Secretary: Mr N Williams
Tel: 01 689 7058

Bangladesh Association, 5 Fordham Street, London E1

Bangladesh Education Association, 192 Hanbury Street, London E1
Tel: 01 247 3972

Bangladesh Educational & Cultural Centre, 91 Highbury Hill, London N5,
Tel: 01 359 5836

Bangladesh Welfare Association, 39 Fournier Street, London E1
Tel: 01 247 6093

Bangladesh Youth Approach Community Centre, Duckett Street, London E1
Tel: 01 790 9733

Bangladesh Youth Front, Spitalfield Centre, 192/196 Hanbury Street, London E1

Bangladesh Youth Movement, 21-23 Henriques Street, London E1 1NB
Tel: 01 488 1831

Bangladesh Youth Movement For Equal Rights, Ponler Street, London E1
Tel: 01 488 1831

Battersea Black Elderly Group, c/o York Gardens, Lavender Road, London SW11
Tel: 01 223 7561

The Belizean Association (UK), 28 Barret Ave, Wood Green, London N22
Tel: 01 888 0216

Bengali International, 242 Francis Road, London E10 6NJ

Bengali Workers Action Group, 1 Robert Street, London NW1
Tel: 01 388 7313

Bharatiya Vidya Bhavan, Castletown Road, London W14
Tel: 01 381 3086/4608

Black Action Group (Advice/Training), 53 Bedford Hill, London SW12 9EC
Tel: 01 673 3445/6

Black Advisory Group on Post Abortion, Post Abortion Centre, Interchange Building, 15 Wilkin Street, London NW5 3NG
Tel: 01 284 0555

Black Amalgamated Self-Help Co-operative, 7 Gayford Road, London W12
Tel: 01 740 6752

Black Art Gallery, 225 Seven Sisters Road, London N4
Tel: 01 263 1918

Black Audio Film Collective (Film Prod.), 89 Ridley Road, London E8
Tel: 01 254 9536/254 9527

Black Business Development Association, c/o 50 Hugon Road, London SW6
Tel: 01 736 8329

The Black Cultural Archives Foundation U.K., c/o Cold Harbour Works, 245a Coldharbour Lane, London SW9 8RR
Tel: 01 274 7700

Black Cultural Centre, St Pauls Court, Gliddon Road, London W14
Tel: 01 741 7119

Black Education Unit, 59 Goldolphin Road, London W12 8JF

Black Gospel Association, 4 Acre Lane, Brixton, London SW2
Tel: 01 281 2340

Black Health Workers & Patients Project, 259a High Road, Tottenham, London N15
Tel: 01 809 0774

Black Independent Record Labels Association (BIRLA), Ventura House, 176-188 Acre Lane, London SW2 5UL
Tel: 01 733 7012

Black Information Unit, 50 St Stephens Avenue, London W12
Tel: 01 743 7893

Black Ink Collective, 258 Coldharbour Lane, London SW9
Tel: 01 733 0746

Black Insight Community Organisation, 146 Manor Park Road, London NW10
Tel: 01 961 4168

Black Londoners' Action Group, South Bank House, Black Prince Road, London SE1
Tel: 01 587 0330

Black Mental Health Project, Afro-Caribbean & Asian
Tel: 01 453 0243

Black Parents Association, B.P.A., 8 Camberwell Green, London SE5
Tel: 01 761 0387

Black Parents Action Group, 63 Durban Road, Tottenham, London N17 8ED
Tel: 01 801 5060

Black Parents Education Group, 190 Evelyn Street, Deptford, London SE24
Tel: 01 692 7568

Black Pensioners Group, c/o Lord Morrison Community Centre, Chestnut Road, London N17

Black Peoples Information Centre, 301 Portobello Road, London W10
Tel: 01 969 9825

Black Rights UK, 221 Seven Sisters Road, Finsbury Park, London N4
Tel: 01 281 2340

Black Roof Housing Co-op, 19a Groveway, Stockwell, London SW9 OAH
Tel: 01 582 4436

Black Theatre Co-op, 67-71 Colliers Street, London N1
Tel: Admin 01 833 3785

Black Women's Centre, Former Somerset Lower School, Lordship Lane, London N17
Tel: 01 808 7973

Black Youth & Community Workers Group, Bishop Creighton House, Lillie Road, London SW6
Tel: 01 385 9689

Body Torque, Community Dance and Workshop Co., B.C.M. Body Torque, London WC1N 3XX
Tel: 01 692 1732

Brent Asian Elders Group, 9 Nicoll Road, Harlesden, London NW10

British Asian Theatre Co, The Basement, 61 Thistlewaite Road, London E5 0QG
Tel: 01 986 4470

Brixton Art Gallery, 21 Atlantic Road, Brixton, London SW9 8HX
Tel: 01 733 7757, (Black & European Artists)

Brixton Association for Development, 77 Atlantic Road, Brixton, London SW9
Tel: 01 733 0077

Brixton Neighbourhood Association, 1 Mayall Road, London SE24
Tel: 01 737 3504

Brixton Young Family Housing Aid Association, 75 Nursery Road, London SW2

Broadwater Farm Youth Association Co-op Ltd, 22 Tangmere, Willan Road, Tottenham, London N17 6NB
Tel: 01 808 0680/0665

Burhani Community Centre, 354 Lillie Road, London SW6

Campaign Against Racist Checks in Dole Offices, Contact . Hackney Centre For the Unemployed
Tel: 01 249 8994, or contact your local unemployment centre

Caribbean Craft Circle, c/o B.A.S.H.C., 7 Gayford Road, London W12
Tel: 01 749 0050

Caribbean Cultural International, 300 Westbourne Grove, London W11
Tel: 01 229 3086

Caribbean Development Foundation, 8 Penpoll Road, London E8
Tel: 01 986 5634

Caribbean Hindu Society, 16 Ostade Road, London SW2
Tel: 01 986 5634

Caribbean Housing Association Ltd, 122 Ashley Road, London SW1
Tel: 01 828 0905

Caribbean House Group, Caribbean House, Bridport Place, London N1 5DS
Tel: 01 729 0986

Caribbean Labour Solidarity, 138 Southgate Road, London N1
Tel: 01 249 8303

Caribbean Overseas Businessmen & Women Association, 36 Kings Wood Road, Tulse Hill, London SW2
Tel: 01 0671 1731

Caribbean Pastoral Centre, 416 Seven Sisters Road, Manor House, London N4 2LX

Caribbean Pastoral Service, Roman Catholic Organisation, 7 Henry Road, London N4
Tel: 01 809 3253

Caribbean Progressive Association, 316 Hoe Street, Walthamstow, London E17 9PX
Tel: 01 521 2334

Caribbean Teachers Association, 8 Camberwell Green, London SE5
Tel: 01 708 1293

Central Gurdwara of British Isles, 62 Queensdale Road, Shepherds Bush, London W11
Tel: 01 603 2789/ 01 603 01184

Centre for Information on Language Teaching & Research, 20 Carlton House Terrace, London NW5

Centuar Project, 313/315 Caledonian Road, London N1, (Tutorial Training)
Tel: 01 609 3328

Charisma Productions Ltd, TV Production/Variety Agent, 4A The Avenue, Highams Park, London E4
Tel: 01 531 3625/6

Chinese Information Advice Centre, 152-156 Shaftsbury Avenue, London WC2
Tel: 01 836 8291

Colebrooke Social Cultural and Welfare Association, 51 Huggon Road, London SW6 3ER
Tel: 01 736 8329

Commonwealth Resettlement Association, 61 Paddington Street, London WIM 3LB
Tel: 01 935 2980

Creation for Liberation, The Basement, 165 Railton Road, London SE24 0LU
Tel: 01 737 2268/2074

Croydon Race & Community Organisation, 47 Wellesley Road, Croydon Surrey CRO 2AJ
Director: Bishop M Ramsay

Dal Khalsa UK, 24 Farleigh Road, London N16
Tel: 01 249 8955

Deptford Community Supplementary School Community Centre, Pagnell Street, London SE8
Tel: 01 691 8935

Do Dil Group, Unit 11, Bridge Park Centre, Brentfield, Harrow Road, Stonebridge Park, London NW10 ORG

Dimbaleh Educational Centre, 334 Queens Bridge Road, London E8
Tel: 01 254-8642
Sat. School . 10am-1pm Age 5-16, (Additional Coaching) (African/ Westindian Culture Lesson)

East End Festival, c/o Half Moon Theatre, 231 Mile End Road, London E1
Tel: 01 791 1141

East London Westindian Association, 14 Denery Road, London E15 4HP

Ebony Community Project, Whiteholt Hall, Australia Road, London W12, Mail to: White City Community Centre, India Way W12
Tel: 01 743 0415

Elder Group Advice Centre & Youth Club & Health Project,Arts Activities, 322 Brixton Road, London SW9 7AA

Ethnic Minority Project, 91-115 Glenthorne Road, Hammersmith, London W6
Tel: 01 741 4220

Ethnographica, 19 Westbourne Road, London N7 8AN
Tel: 01 607 4074

European Calypsonian Association, 296 Amhurst Road, London N16 7UQ
Tel: 01 254 7245/01 263 6468

Federation of Bangladesh Youth Organisations, Montifiore Centre, Deal Street, London EC1 2SH
Tel: 01 247 8818

Federation of Black Housing Organisations (FBHO), 259a High Road, London N15 5BT, (Housing advice/info)
Tel; 01 802 7490

Friends of Bogle, 141 Coldershaw Road, Ealing, London W13
Tel: 01 579 4920

Friends of Mary Seacole, 57a Stowe Road, Shepherds Bush, London W12 8BE
Tel: 01 740 0427

Finsbury Park Action Group (for people living and working in Finsbury Park), Ground Floor, Alexandra National House, 330 Seven Sisters Road, London N4 2PJ
Tel: 01 802 2612/01 800 2630

Grass Roots Association, 7 Thorpe Close, London W10

Gurdwara Dasmesh Darbar, 97 Rosebery Avenue, Manor Park, London E12
Tel: 01 472 5248

Gurdwara Namdhari Sangat UK, 96 Upton Lane, Forest Gate, London E7
Tel: 01 471 6826

Gurdwara Guru Nanak Darbar, Old Mill Road, Plumstead, London SE18,

Gurdwara Nanak Darbar, 136 High Road, New Southgate, London N11 1PJ
Tel: 01 368 7104/01 361 0982

Gurdwara Singh Sabha, North East London, 68 Gloucester Drive, London N4
Tel: 01 800 9923

Gurdwara Sikh Sangat, 1a Campbell Road, London E8
Tel: 01 980 2281

Gurdwara Sikh Sangat, Francis Road, Leyton, London E10
Tel: 01 539 3818/01 556 4732

Hackney Asian Association, 17-19 Dalston Lane, London E8 3DF
Tel: 01 254 4898

Hackney Asian People's Association, 25 Allen Road, London N16 8SR
Tel: 01 249 6090

Hackney Black Peoples Association, 18 Stoke Newington Road, London N16
Tel: 01 254 1193

Hackney Chinese Community Service, 15 Pearson Street, London E2 8JD
Tel: 01 729 7145

Hammersmith & Fulham Asian Community Association Ltd, Asia Community Centre, 239 Uxbridge Road, London W12
Tel: 01 740 6940

Hammersmith & Fulham Asian Community Welfare Association, c/o 671a Fulham Road, London SW6
Tel: 01 731 5532

Hammersmith & Fulham Race Initiative Group, c/o 91-115 Glenthorne Road, Hammersmith, London W6
Tel: 01 741 4220

Haringey Asian Centre, 8 Caxton Road, Wood Green, London N22
Tel: 01 889 6938/9

Harold Road Ladies Club, Harold Road, London E13 OSE
Tel: 01 472 2785

Hindu Cultural Society, North London, 27 Dollis Avenue, London N3
Tel: 01 346 9976

H.I.T.E.C., Heritage International of Tamils for Education and Culture, 45 Avarn Road, Tooting, London SW17 9BH
Tel: 01 767 2585

The Hostel, 376 Uxbridge Road, Ealing Common, London W5

Imperial World Federation, 79 Chesterton Road, London W10

Indian Arts Council in the UK, (Sec.) 40 Priory Road, London N8

India Centre, 6 Thomas Street, London SE18

India Welfare Society, 11 Middle Row, North Kensington, London W10

Indian Muslim Federation (UK), Community Welfare Association, Trinity Close, Granleigh Road, London E11
Tel: 01 558 2247

Indian Student Hostel YMCA, 41 Fitzroy Square, London W1
Tel: 01 387 0411

Indo-Chinese Project, Greencoat House, 10 Francis Street, London SW1P 1DH
Tel: 01 834 5911

Jamaican Workers Support Group, c/o 7c North Hanger Road, Streatham, London SW16 5RX
Tel: 764 1458

Jenako Arts Centre, 49 Balls Pond Road, London N1
Tel: 01 249 6062

Kala Ujamaa Ltd, Research Centre, 340-343 Southbank House, Black Prince Road, London SE1 7SJ
Tel: 01 735 8669/01 587 0266

Kazimba Ijakadi Teta Dudu, Club of Dance and Self Defence, Paragon School, Searles Road, London SE1
Tel: 01 703 3360

Keskidee Arts Centre, Gifford Street, Islington, London N1 0DF
Tel: 01 226 4107

Khalistan Council, 12 Talbot Road, London W2
Tel: 01 221 3859

Khelaghor Project, 169 Cannon St. Road, London E1 2LX
Tel: 01 480 6760

Dr Martin Luther King Association, c/o B.A.S.H.C., 7 Gayford Road, London W12
Tel: 01 740 9580

Kurdish Cultural Centre, 13-15 Stockwell Road, London SW9
Tel: 01 247 6251

The Labour Black Sections, 39 Chippenham Mews, London W9
Tel: 01 286 9692

La Caye Housing Co-op, Tower Hamlets, Afro-Caribbean Association, (T.A.C.A.), 1 Brook Place, off Devons Place,
London E3
Tel: 01 729 2314 . Vince Philips, 01 515 8454/01 791 0501 . Secretary

Ladywell Action Centre, 135 Algernon Road, London SE13

Lajna Imaillah London, Ah Madiyya Muslim Women Association, 16 Gressenhall Road, London SW18 5QL
Tel: 01 870 8517

ASHA Lambeth Asian Women's Resource Centre, c/o 378 Coldharbour Lane, London SW9
Tel: 01 274 8854/01 737 5901

Lambeth Family Finders, 91 Clapham High Street, London SW4

Latin American and Caribbean Cultural Society, 20 Woodberry Crescent, London N10 1PH
Tel: 01 883 6959

Latin-American Cultural Centre, 140 Ladbroke Grove, London W10 5ND
Tel: 01 969 2433 ext. 285

Lignun Vite Club, 57a Stowe Road, Shepherds Road, London W12 8HE
Tel: 01 740 0427

Limers Sports and All Fours Club, c/o 41 Natal Road, Streatham, London SW16 6JA
Tel: 01 677 5130

MAAS (Minority Arts Advisory Service), 25-31 Tavistock Place, London WC1H 9SF
Tel: 01 383 4531

Maha Saba, 272 St. Johns Road, Walthamstow, London E17 4JN
Tel: 01 527 4738

Mangrove Community Association, 6/8 All Saints Road, London W11 1HH

Masimba Connection, P.O. Box 213, London W2 1UR
Tel: 01 723 2309

Masimba Uprising, 14 All Saints Road, London W11 1HH
Tel: 01 727 3063

Mauritius Association (Tooting Branch), 48 Huntspill Street, Tooting, London SW17 OAA
Tel: 01 946 7191

Melting Pot Foundation, 361 Clapham Road, London SW9
Tel: 01 274 9566

Memon Association UK, 7 Shakespeare Road, London N3
Tel: 01 346 4000

Migrants Resource Centre, 2 Denbigh Place, London SW1
Tel: 01 834 1152

Millan Asian Community Centre, 59 Trinity Road, London SW17 75D
Tel: 01 767 8718/9

Mohan (Tama), 239 Sumatra Road, London NW6
Tel: 01 435 0445

Mohyal Sabha, 85b Telephone Place, Lillie Road,
London SW6

Moonshine Community ArtsWorkshop, Victor Road, London NW10 5XQ
Tel: 01 969 7959

Mosque Committee, c/o 71 Sulgrave Road, London W6 7QF
Tel: 01 602 7388

Muhammad Ali Sports Development Association (MASDA), 403-405 Brixton Road, London SW9 7DS
Tel: 01 733 9145

Muslim Parents Association, 13e Hoe Street, Walthamstow, London E17 4SD

National Afro-Caribbean Libraries Association, Haringey Library, Haringey Park, London N8 9GA
Tel: 01 358 3351/888 1292
Chairperson: Ann Thompson

New Black Families Unit, 121/123 Camberwell Road, London SE5
Tel: 01 703 1089

Newham Community Renewal Programme, Harold Road Centre, Harold Road, London E13 OSE
Tel: 01 471 1024

Newham Immigration & Social Advice Service, 285 Romford Road, Forest Gate, London E7
Tel: 01 555 3331

North Kensington Family Centre, 73 St Charles Square, London W10
Tel: 01 969 6514
Mrs Ariadne Collier, Co-ordinator

North Kensington Moroccan Tarbia, 63 Golbourne Road, London W10

North London Bangladesh Welfare Association, 28 Caledonian Road, London N1
Tel: 01 278 0877

Nurses Association of Jamaica (UK), 74 Trevelyn Road, Tooting, London SW17 9LN
Tel: 01 767 4271

OBAALA, Organisation of Black Arts Advancement and Learning Activities, Obaala House, 225 Seven Sisters Road, London N4
Tel: 01 263 1918

October Gallery, (Cultural Centre/Art Gallery), 24 Old Gloucester Street, London WC1
Tel: 01 242 7367

Omnibus Theatre/Youth Group, 6 St Thomas Church Hall, East Row, London W10
Tel: 01 969 7135

One Love, 175 Upton Lane, Forest Gate, London E7
Tel: 01 471 4621

Overseas Indian Association G.B., 58 Hampstead Road, London NW1 2PY
Tel: 01 699 7508/01 387 1125

Pakistan Muslim Welfare Assoc., 30 Ransom Road, Charlton, London SE7

Pakistan Peoples Party, 30 Palmerston Road, London E17

Pakistan Society, 37 Sloane Street, London SW5
Tel: 01 235 6905

Pakistan Welfare Association, 95 Fernlea Road, London SW12 9RP

Pakistan Welfare Association, 181 Haydons Road, London SW19 8TB
Tel: 01 542 6176

Pakistan Youth & Community Centre, Station Parade, London NW2
Tel: 01 452 4103

Pakistan Youth Hostel, 5 Barkston Gdns, London SW5
Tel: 01 370 5859

Palestinian Community Centre, c/o Omayya Al-Masri, 8 Durweston Street, London W1

Peckham & Dulwich Caribbean, Association, c/o The Peckham Settlement, Staffordshire Street, Peckham, London SE15 5TF

Peoples Gallery, 71-73 Prince of Wales Road, London NW5 3LT
Tel: 01 267 0433

Project Fullemploy, 102 Park Village East, London NW1 3SP
Tel: 01 387 1222

Ramgarhia Sikh Gurdwara, 10-14 Neville Road, London E7
Tel: 01 472 3738/01 471 0335

Ramgarhia Sikh Temple, Willmont Street, Masons Hill, Woolwich, London SE18
Tel: 01 854 1786

Rastafarian Advisory Centre, 17a Netherwood Road, London W14
Tel: 01 602 3767

Rupert Morris Welfare & Advice Centre, 8 Bradbury Street, London N16
Tel: 01 254 0784/3726

Sam Morris Project, 1A Millers Way, Shepherd Bush Road, London W6
Tel: 01 743 3824

Sangam Association for Asian Women, 235/237 West Hendon, Broadway, London NW9

Sangat Bhatra Samparada UK, Gurdwara Sikh Sangat, Harley Grove, Bow, London E3
Tel: 01 980 8861

Senior Citizens Welfare Association, Family Day Centre, 49 Plashett Road, London E13
Tel: 01 472 6763

Sevashram Sangha, 17 Stanlake Villas, London W12
Tel: 01 749 2972

Sex, Race, Class, Black and Third World Women's Discussion and Study Group, Kings Cross Women's Centre, 71 Tonbridge Street, London WC1H 902
Tel: 01 833 4817

Shepherds Bush Social & Welfare Association, St. Thomas Hall, Thornfield Road, London W12

Shree Kutch Leva Patel Community (UK), 35 Heigham Road, East Ham, London E6 2JL

Sikh Association (Greenwich), 1 Calderwood Street, Woolwich, London SE18
Tel: 01 854 4233

Sikh Association (Southfields), 13 Kings Cliffe Gardens, London SW19

Sikh Gurdwara South London, 142 Merton Road, Southfields, London SW18
Tel: 01 874 3518

Sikh Sangat Gurdwara, Francis Road, London E10

The Sikh Temple, Cricklewood Road, London SE18

Sikh Temple, 62 Queensdale Road, London W11
Tel: 01 603 2789

Simba Community Project, 239 Uxbridge Road, London W12
Tel: 01 740 6879

Simba Project Centre, 48-50 Artillery Place, London SE18
Tel: 01 317 0451

Soca Baby Promotions, 71a Cathnor Road, London W10
Tel: 01 740 8016

Society of Black Lawyers, 11 Kings Bench Walk, Temple, London EC4 7EQ
Tel: 01 353 4931

St. Catherynes Westindian Rent Group, 124 Erlanger Road, New Cross, London SE14

St. Marks Youth Club, 22 Greenwich South Street, London SE10
Tel: 01 853 0563

Spitalfields Housing Co-op, 170 Brick Lane, London E1
Tel: 01 247 1040

Streetprints, 175 Kirkwood Road, London SE15 2BG
Tel: 01 639 4421 (Design & Publisher Black Imagery)

Sunshine Sport and Social Club, c/o 36 Bagleys Lane, Fulham, London SW6
Tel: 01 736 9512

Tamil Refuge & Immigrant Welfare Association, 68 Lymington Road, London NW6

Tamil Refugee Action Group, 23a Weston Park Road, London N8
Tel: 01 348 7611

The Pentonville Gallery, 7-9 Ferdinand Street, Chalk Farm, London NW1
Tel: 01 482 2948

The Pepper Pot Club, 140 Ladbroke Grove, London W10
Tel: 01 969 2433

The Roundhouse, Chalk Farm Road, London NW1 8PB
Tel: 01 482 1509

Theatre in Exile Ltd, (Theatre Co/ Charitable), 10 Eardley Crescent, London SW5
Tel: 01 373 3702

Theatre Workshops (Alternative Cultural Drama Training), New Promotheus Touring Co., (Cultural Theatre Organisation), c/o Housmans Bookshop, 5 Caledonian Road, London N1 9DX
Tel: 01 836 7071 Message 9am - 5pm only

Tower Hamlets Council For Racial Equality, School Keepers House,, Montifiore Centre, Hanbury Street, London E1

Uhuru Project, Gunthorpe Workshop, 3 Gunthorpe Street, London E1

Ujamaa Centre (Arts & Books), 14 Brixton Road, London SW9
Tel: 01 582 5590

Ujima Finsbury Park Project, 73-75 Lennox Road, London N4
Tel: 01 272 6586

Ujima Housing Association Ltd, 413-419 Harrow Road, London W9 3QJ
Tel: 01 960 5141

UK Caribbean Chamber of Commerce (UKCCC), 99 Stoke Newington Church Street, London N16
Tel: 01 254 4532

United Caribbean Association, 51 Denham Road, Peckham, London SE15

United Churches Welfare & Workers Association, 71 Hayter Road, Brixton, London SW2

Unity Association, 90/92 Lancaster Road, London W11

Upfront Enterprise, St Pauls Youth Centre, West London College, Gliddon Road, London W14
Tel: 01 741 1119 (Wednesdays, only)

Vietnamese Association Services, 3 Ravendale Gardens, London SE19
Tel: 01 771 5199

Vince Hines Foundation, 150 Townmead Road, London SW6
Tel: 01 731 4438

Vishva Hindi Parishad (UK), 20 Sprowston Road, London E7 9AD

Wadada Education Magazine (WEM), c/o Flat 6, 147 Conningham Road, London W12

Wandsworth Community Forum, Room 9, Battersea Town Hall, 66 Theatre Street, Lavender Hill, London SW11 5NF

WCCR Tooting Youth Project, 946 Garrett Lane, Tooting, London SW17
Tel: 01 960 1867

Westbourne Gallery, 453 Harrow Road, London W10
Tel: 01 960 1867

Westindian Community Association, 91 Tollington Park, London N7

Westindian Concern, Caribbean House,, Bridport Place, London N1
Tel: 01 729 0986

The Westindian Cultural Council
23 Hornsey Park Road, London N8
Tel: 01 889 3998
Chairman: Mr George Martin

Westindian Ex-Servicemen's Association (UK), (Community Service) (Everyone welcome), 165 Clapham Manor Street, London SW4
Tel: 01 627 0792

Westindian Leadership Council, 23 Hornsey Park Road, London N8
Tel: 01 889 3998

Westindian Parents Action Group (WIPAG), (Family Day Centre), 3-5 Gresham Road, London SW9 7PH
Tel: 01 733 7617

Westindian Standing Conference (WISC), 5a Westminster Bridge Road, London SW1 7XV
Tel: 01 928 7861

Westindies Cricket Supporters Association, 8 Hermitage Lane, London SW16
Tel: 01 679 5510

Women's Asian Cultural Organisation of Fulham, 3 Crookham Road, London SW6
Tel: 01 736 6672

Woolwich Simba Project, 40/50 Artillery Place, London SW18

Yaa Asantewa Arts Centre, 1 Chippenham Mews, London W9 2AN
Tel: 01 286 1656

Young Lewisham Project, 31 Manor Park, Lewisham, London SE13

Young Peoples Law Centre, 272 Willesden High Road, London NW10
Tel: 01 451 2428

Loughborough

Charnwood Baha'i Community, 106 Beacon Road, Loughborough
Tel: 0509 266130
Con. Les Woodfield

Charotar Patidar Samaj, Mr A Patel (President), 30 Garendon Road, Loughborough

The Garden Sports & Social Club, Kishor J Mistry, 11 Burder Street, Loughborough
Tel: 0509 261222

The Geeta Bhawan, Mr P.L. Tiwari (President), 5 Deenside Drive, Loughborough

Jansari Samaj, Mr S.S. Makwana (Chairman), 22 Howard Street, Loughborough

Kumbhar (Potters) Community, Mr Babubhai Savania, 112 Peopold Street, Loughborough

Limbachia Samaj, Mr J Sharma, 20 Royland Road, Loughborough

The Lohana Community, Mr J Davda, 61, Toothill Road, Loughborough

The Loughborough Mosque, The Secretary, Mr S.H. Ahmad, 81-83 King Street, Loughborough

Mativa Patidar Samaj, Mr N Patel (Secretary), 69 Ratcliffe Road, Loughborough

Mesuria Samaj, Mr H Mesuria, 47 Cambridge Street, Loughborough

Naya Jivan Youth Group, c/o The Garden, 43 Church Gate, Loughborough

Patel Surat District, Mr A.M. Patel, 24 Gt Central Road, Loughborough

The Raja Yoga Centre, Miss M Modwadhia, 25 Boyer Street, Loughborough

Shree Maher Samaj, B.S. Keshwala, 91 Beaumont Road, Loughborough

Shree Mandhata Hitwardhak Samaj, Mr V.L. Patel, 51 Russell Street, Loughborough

Shree Prajapati Samaj, Mohanbhai A Mistry, 11 Limehurst Avenue, Loughborough

The Shree Ram Krishna Centre, Mr K.D. Prinja (President), 34, Queens Road, Loughborough

The Sikh Temple, The Secretary, 33-34 Clarence Street, Loughborough

Soni Samaj, C. Vaitha, 11 Judges Street, Loughborough

Vanad (Barber) Community, Mr Bachubhai Vadia, 14 Wilmington Court, Loughborough

West Indian New Testament Pentecostal Assembly, Veronica Lewin, 86 Shelthorpe Road, Loughborough

Y.W.C.A., Mrs Premila Patel, Gt Central Road, Loughborough
Tel: 0509 212517

Luton

Bangladesh Welfare Association, 11 Conway Road, Luton, Beds. LU4 8JA

Gurdwara Guru Nanak Dev Ji, 12-16 Portland Road, Luton, Beds
Tel: 0582 571629

Luton Bharatiya Association, 288 Old Bedford Road, Luton, Beds. LU2 7EJ

One Foundation Organisation, Suite 6, Regent House, 50 New Bedford Road, Luton, Beds.

Pakistan Kashmir Welfare Association, 182 Dunstable Road, Luton, Beds.

Shree Sanatan Seva Samaj, Hereford Road, Lewsey Farm, Luton LU4 0PS

Sri Lanka Social & Sports, 30 Chester Avenue, Luton, Beds.

Lye

Ghausia Mosque and Welfare Association, c/o Lye Mosque, High Street, Lye, West Midlands
President: Mr R.G. Khan

Riverside Community Centre, Brunel St, Riverside , Cardiff,
Tel: 0222-20309

The Sikh Temple, 212a Pearl Street, Roath, Cardiff

United Caribbean Association, Grange Town, Cardiff
Tel: 0222 462858/0222 26349

Maidenhead

Asian Women's Association & 'Jankar' Asian Girls Club, 10 Gordon Rd, Maidenhead SL6 6BT, Berks
Tel: 0628 21890

Guru Nanak Sat Sang Gurdwara, 31 Rutland Road, Maidenhead, Berks.
Tel: 0628 23507

Manchester

Abasindi Co-op, Moss Side Peoples Centre, St Marys Street, Manchester
Tel: 061 226 6837

African Cultural Society, The Old Library, Cheetham Hill Road, Manchester 8
Tel: 061 740 9973

African Cultural Voluntary Organisation, 2 Crossbank Close, Longsight, Manchester M13 9AT
Tel: 061-273-1103

Asian Youth & Community Association, c/o Slade Lane, Neighbourhood Centre, Slade Lane, Longsight, Manchester
Tel: 061 225 6886

Bangladesh Association & Community Centre, c/o 63 Whitworth Street, Manchester M1 3NY

Bangladesh Women & Children Welfare Group, 64 Birch Lance, Longsight, Manchester M13 OWN

Black Arts Alliance, 111 Burton Road, Withington, Manchester M20 8HZ
Tel: 061 273 7964

Cheetham Asian Girls Project, Temple Junior School, Smedley Street, Cheetham, Manchester MG

Community Relations Housing Ltd, Elliott House, 3 Jackson Row, Manchester M2 5WD

Damesh Sikh Temple, c/o Woodlands Road, Crumpsall, Manchester 8

Friends of Asian Cultural Centre, 22 Ashlands, Sale, Manchester 33 5DP

Ghana Union of Manchester, 127
Leicester Road, Salford, Manchester M7 OHJ
Tel: 061 720 7448

Gurdwara Sri Guru Gobind Singh, 61 Upper Charlton Road, Brooksbar, Manchester 16
Tel: 061 226 7233

Jamaica-Caribbean Society, c/o Westindian Centre, 10 Carmoor Road, Chorlton-on-Medlock, Manchester 13

Manchester Pakistan Welfare & Information Centre, c/o Marfini, Dalton Street, (Off Rochdale Road), Manchester M10 7GG
Tel: 061 205 3341

Marassa Tadlimul Islam, 443 Cheetham Hill Road, Manchester M8 7PF
Tel: 061 740 3351

New Sikh Temple, Monton Street, Moss Side, Manchester 14

One Foundation Organisation, 28 Redgrave Gardens, Chorlton-on-Medlock, Manchester M13
Tel: 061 225 4724/061 224 3106
Secretary: Mrs G McKoy

Pakistan Society (Manchester), 292 Mauldeth Road, West Chorlton, Manchester M2L 2RF

Pakistan Welfare Aid Information Centre, Dalston Street, Manchester M10 7GG

Sikh Forum, North East, 5 Heathlands Road, Kersal, Salford M7 0GH, Manchester

Sikh Family History Project, North Hulme Centre, Jackson Crescent, Hulme, Manchester 15

Tadlimul Islam, 443 Cheetham Hill Road, Manchester M8 7PF

The Mosque, Barlow Moor Road, off Burton Road, Manchester 20

Westindian Sports & Social Club & Community Centre, Westwood Street, Moss Side, Manchester M14
Tel: 061 226 7236/226 8203
Secretary: Mr Aston Douglas

Middlesbrough

Council for Racial Equality Clevelands, 42 Gore Sands, Acklam, Middlesbrough, Cleveland TS5 8UJ
Tel: 0642 590880

Pakistan Welfare Association of Cleveland, 16 Warren Street, Middlesbrough
Tel: 0642 223108

Sikh Temple, 151 Southfield Road, Middlesbrough

New Barnet

Islamic Association of North London, 6 Crescent Rise, New Barnet, Herts.
Tel: 01 449 6346

Newcastle

Gurdwara Sri Guru Singh Sabha, Tindale Close, Newcastle-upon-Tyne
Tel: 0632 738011

Asian Women's Centre, 113-115 Farndale Rd, Benwell, Newcastle-Upon-Tyne NE4 8TX
Tel: 091 273 0972

Northampton

Al Jamatul Muslim of Bangladesh, 8 St George's Street, Northampton NN1 2TR
Tel: 0604 24930

Caribbean People's Association, 14 Bailiff Street, Northampton NN1 3DY,
Tel: 0604 30256
Con. Mr Roger Kirton

Islamic Academy of Manchester, (Northampton Branch(, 12 Keadale Road, Northampton
Con. Mr D.H. Khawaja

Islamic Centre, 66 Bostock Avenue, Northampton
Con. Mr D. H. Khawaja

Matta Fancanta Movement, (Afro-Caribbean), 34 Sheep Street, Northampton
Con. Mr H Cohen

Northampshire Asian, Advisory Panel, Norpak House, Harold Street, Northampton
Con. Dr F Makhani

Northampton Council for African and Caribbean Organisations, 14 Bailiff Street, Northampton NN1 3DY
Tel: 0604 30256

Pakistan Welfare Association, 22 Adams Avenue, Northampton
Con. Mr G. H. Khan

The Sikh Temple, 53 Queens Park Parade, Northampton

Sri Guru Singh Sabha (Sikh), 23/25 St George's Street, Northampton

United Social Club, 18 Regent Street, Northampton
Tel: 0604 21890
Con. Mr Ulric Gravesands

Vishwa Hindu Parishad, 10 South Paddock Court, Lings, Northampton

Westindian Parents Association, 43 Manning Road, Moulton, Northampton

Northfleet

Pakistan Association, 159 Dover Road, Northfleet, Kent
Tel: 0474 66220

Westindian Association, 110 Wallis Park, Northfleet, Kent
Tel: 0474 52951

Nottingham

Afro-Caribbean National Artistic Centre, 31-31a Hungerhill Road, St Anns, Nottingham NG3 4NB, Tel: 0602 608924

Guru Nanak Sat Sang, Gurdwara, (Sikh Temple), 62 Forest Road, Nottingham NG7 4EP
Tel: 0602 781394

Hindu Temple of Nottingham, 215 Carlton Road, Nottingham

Institute of Sikh Ideology, 193 Wollaton Road, Nottingham, NG8 IFU

Islamic Centre Nottingham, 18 Austen Avenue, Forest Field, Nottingham N67 6PE

Nottingham Catholic Racial Justice Association, 20 Leslie Road, Forest Fields, Nottingham 9G7 6PD
Tel: 0602 783889

Pakistan Friends League Centre, 163 Woodborough Road, Nottingham NG4 1AX
Tel: 0602 582973

Oxford

Neighbourhood Centre, 14 Turnagain Lane, St. Ebbes, Oxford OX1
Tel: 0865 728640

Sant Nirankarik Mandal, 76 Moorbank, Oxford OX4 5BH

Oldbury

West Bromwich Afro-Caribbean, Resource Centre, c/o Tolunka, 64a Birmingham Street, Oldbury, West Midlands B69 4EB

Oldham

Asian Muslim Welfare Association, 16 Brompton Street, Oldham OL4 1AB, Manchester

Bangladesh Association, Bangladesh Cultural Centre, Main Road, Oldham, Manchester
Tel: 061 652 2532

Clodwick Westindian, Association, Greenhill Community Centre, 115 Pitt Street, Oldham, Lancashire OL4 1AN

Pakistan Peoples Association, 30 Osborne Road, Coppice, Oldham, Manchester

Pakistan Society, 78 Wellington Road, Oldham, Manchester

Pakistan Welfare Association, 83 Queens Road, Oldham, Manchester

Pakistan Youth Society, 45 Worcester Street, Werneth, Oldham, Manchester

Peterborough

Marcus Garvey International, Community Assoc, 165 Cromwell Road, Peterborough

Pakistan Welfare Association, 115 Huntly Grove, Peterborough PE1 2QW
Tel: 0733 52014

Sikh Bhatra Temple, 186 Cromwell Road, Peterborough
Tel: 0733 65133

Portsmouth

Guru Nanak Sikh Temple, 5 Margate Road, Portsmouth, Hants.

Preston

Andhra Social & Cultural, Organisation, 221 Fletcher Road, Preston, Lancs. PR1 5HE

Bangladesh Association, 3 The Coombers, High Gate Park, Fulwood, Preston PR2 4LH

Bhatra Singh Sabha Sikh Temple, 2 Clarendon Street, Preston, Lancs.

Caribbean Sports & Social Club, 2 Emerson Road, Preston

Gujarati Hindu Society, Southmeade Lane, Fishgate Hill, Preston

Unity Centre, 3-4 Shepherd Street, Preston, Lancs.
Tel: 0772 25665

Reading

Federation of Black Housing Organisations, 82/84 Southampton Street, Reading
Tel: 0734 589 609

Indian Workers Association, 31 St Peters Road, Early, Reading

Reading Community Festival, Civic Offices, Civic Centre, Reading, Berks RG1 7TD
Tel: 0734 559111 Ext. 2318

The Sikh Temple, 30-32 Cumberland Road, Reading, Berkshire

UK Anglo-Asian Conservative Society, 26 Pitts Lane, Early, Reading

Walter Rodney House, 82/84 Southampton Street, Reading, Berks. RG1 2QR

Westindian Circle, 48 Old Town Hall, Blagrave Street, Reading RG1 1QL

Westindian Women's Circles, 27 Coley Place, Reading RG1 6AD
Tel: 0734 590525

Rochdale

Bangladesh Community Project, 5 Ramsay Place, Rochdale
Tel: 0706 343606

Society For The Advancement of British Asians, 39 King Street South, Rochdale

The Medway Towns Gurdwara, Sabha, Cossack Street, Rochester, Kent ME1 2EF
Tel: 063 49782

Rotherham

Pakistan Peoples Party, 15 St Johns Road, Eastwood, Rotherham

Rugby

Rugby Westindian Society, Westindian Centre, Chapel Street, Rugby, Warwickshire

Ruislip

India Society, 37 Stone Crescent, Ruislip, Middlesex HA4 7SR

Uxbridge

Islamic Educational Society, 10 Cowley Mill Road, Uxbridge, Middx

Scunthorpe

Guru Nanak Sikh Temple, 41 Normandy Road, Scunthorpe, S. Humberside

Gutunanak Sikh Temple, 22 Dale Street, Scunthorpe

Sheffield

Afro-Caribbean Education Trust, c/o Afro-Caribbean Society, Nelson Mandela Building, Students' Union, Pond Street, Sheffield 1

Afro-Caribbean Group, Broomspring Centre, Broomspring Lane, Sheffield 10

Anjuman-E-Haideriah, 166 Psalter Lane, Sheffield 11, Mr N Shevazi

Arabic Mosque, 275 Staniforth Road, Sheffield 9

Asian Welfare Association, Wesley House, Highfield Place, London Road, Sheffield 2
Tel: 0742 588207
Con. Mr M Nazir

Asian Women's Refuge Group, c/o Commonground, 87 The Wicker, Sheffield 3

Asian Women's Society, c/o Wesley House, Highfield Place, Sheffield 2
Tel: 0742 588207
Con. Mrs Z Kayani & Mrs K Asim

Asian Youth Movement, c/o Commonground, 87 The Wicker, Sheffield 3
Con. Mr Mukhtar Raj

Attercliffe Youth Club, Tinsley Park Road, Sheffield S9 5DL
Mr Mohammad Jamil and Mr M Younis

Bangladesh Allya Mosque, 16-18 Swarcliffe Road, Sheffield 8

Bangladesh Citizens Committee, 13 Convent Walk, Sheffield S3 4NA
Con. Dr P Majumdar

Bangladesh Women's, Association, c/o Roundel Street, Darnall, Sheffield S9 3LE, Con. Ms Khan

Bangladesh Youth League, Badsha Khandakel, 72 Sharrow Street, Sheffield 11
Tel: 0742 584722

Black Women's Group, c/o Mrs G Denis, 108 Upper Valley Road, Sheffield

Black Advisory Group, c/o The Hub Caribbean, Workshop, Mount Pleasant, Community Centre, Sharrow Lane, Sheffield 11,
Con. Mrs M Reid

British Muslims Association, (Sheffield), c/o 731 Ecclesail Road, Hunter's Bar, Sheffield 11
Con. Mr M Rashid or Mr K Campbell

Burngreave Child Care Centre Committee, 99 Mansfield Road, Aston, Sheffield S31 0BR, Miss L Blenman

Gausia Mosque Committee, 62 Andover Street, Sheffield 3
Tel: 0742 755508
Con. Mr Raja Tikka Khan . Chairman

Hindu Samaj, . Sheffield District, 25 Stumperlowe View, Sheffield S10 3QU
Con. Dr Shiv S Sharma

The Hub Caribbean Workshop, Mount Pleasant, Community Centre, Sharrow Lane, Sheffield S11 8AG

I an I Committee, 446 London Road, Sheffield S2 4HP

Industry Road Mosque Committee & Jaame Masjid, 91 Standon Crescent, Sheffield 9
Mr M Azim, 13 Industry Road, Mr Mohammed Hayat Khan
Tel: 0742 447686 & 441500

Islamic Centre, University of Sheffield, Western Bank, Sheffield S10 2TN

Islamic Centre/Madina Mosque, 24 Wolseley Road, Sheffield S8 0TU
Tel: 0742 588207 (day), 550391 (evening), Mr M Nazir, Secretary

Islamic Cultural Centre, 36 St Lawrence Road, Sheffield 9
Tel: 0742 441525
Con. Mr Mohammed Munshi

Ittehad Committee, 8 Briar Road, Sheffield 4
Con. Mr S Khan

Jamia Mosque Committee, 214 Darnall Road, Darnall, Sheffield S9 5AF
Tel: 0742 441500
Con. Mr Mohammed Siddique, President

Madni Islamic Community, Association & Mosque, 22 Wincobank Lane, Sheffield S4 8AA
Tel: 0742 611224/422998
Mr Qazi Mohammed Siddique, and Mr S Khan

Mary Seacole Women's Group, Ellesmere Community Centre, Buckenham Street, Sheffield 4
Con. Ms L Wenham

Mother and Baby Group, c/o The Hub, Mount Pleasant, Sharrow Lane, Sheffield 11

Owler Lane Mosque/Czhousia, Mosque, Owler Lane, Sheffield 4
Tel: 0742 387966, Mr Hafiz Wazir Ahmed

Pakistani Ladies Association, c/o Tinsley Community Centre, Ingfield Avenue, Sheffield 9
Con. Mrs S Rehman

Pakistan Muslim Welfare Association, 226 Darnall Road, Sheffield S9 5NA
Con. Mr M Walayat

Pakistan Students' Union, University of Sheffield, Students' Union, Western Bank, Sheffield S10 2TN

Pakistan Youth and Community Association, Vestry Hall, 2 Burngreave Road, Sheffield S3 9DD
Tel: 0742 754083
Con. Mr R Khan

Sahaja Yoga Group, 6 Clarkhouse Road, Sheffield 10
Tel: 0742 686583
Con. M I Harris

Sargam Indian Cultural Society, 21 Moorcroft Road, Fulwood, Sheffield S10 4GS
Tel: 0742 304148
Con. Dr Ajai Singh

Sheffield & District Afro-Caribbean Association, 13 Staindrop View, Chapeltown, Sheffield 30
Con. Mr H Franklin

Sheffield Caribbean Fortnight, Co-ordinating Committee, 42 Mona Road, Sheffield 10
Con. Mrs C Gordon

Sheffield & District Hindu Samaj, 25 Stumperlowe View, Fulwood, Sheffield 10
Con. Dr S Sharma

Sheffield & District Westindian Community Association, 83 Derbyshire Lane, Sheffield S8 9EN
Secretary: Mr R Johnson

Sheffield Sai Organisation, 22 Gardom Close, Dronfield, Woodhouse, Sheffield S18 5ZH
Con. Mr A Robinson

Sikh Temple, 113 Highcliffe Road, Sheffield 11
Con. Mr D S. Dhillon

South Yorkshire Indian Association, 692 Abbey Lane, Sheffield S11 9ND
Con. Mr M S Kalsy

Tantra Yoga Group, 36 Redcar Road, Sheffield 10
Tel: 0742 667321
Con. Dr I S Johnson

Westindian Women's Group, c/o Dorothy Dixon-Barrow, 53 Junction Road, Hunter's Bar, Sheffield 11

Sherwood

Sikh Temple, 26 Nottingham Road, Sherwood, Notts
Tel: 0602 622132

Slough

Asian Social Club, 58 Kendal Drive, Slough, Berks

Hindu Cultural Society, 2 Rowan Way, Slough, Berks SL1 3BG

Immigrants Information Bureau, 39 Warrington Avenue, Slough, Berks SL1 3BG

Pakistan Parents Society, 8 Gloucester Avenue, Slough, Berks SL 3AY

Pakistan Welfare Association, 16 Oakley Crescent, Slough, Berks

Rajasthan Welfare Society, 43 Boreshire, Slough, Berks SL2 5QY

Ramgarhia Sikh Temple, Baylis Road, Woodland Avenue, Slough
Tel: 0753 25458

Sri Guru Singh Sabha Gurdwara, Waxham Court, Sheehy Way, Slough
Tel: 0753 26828

Westindian Peoples Association, 3 Mendip Close, Slough, Berks SL3 89UB

Smethwick

Community Action Project, 8-10 Beechway, Smethwick, West Midlands
Tel: 021 565 3273

Southall

Afro-Caribbean Cultural & Educational Association, 192 Uxbridge Road, Southall, Middx UB1 3DX
Tel: 01 574 4879

Damesh Sat Sang Sabha, 6 Evelyn Grove, Southall, Middlesex
Tel: 01 843 1961

Elderley Asian Accommodation, 15 Western Road, Southall, Middlesex
Tel: 01 574 5439

Elderly Asian Day Centre, 20 Western Road, Southall, Middlesex
Tel: 01 574 0902

Gurdwara Guru Granth, Villiers Road, Southall, Middlesex
Tel: 01 574 7700/ 01 574 0037

Gurdwara Sri Guru Singh, Sabha, Havelock Road, Southall, Middlesex
Tel: 01 547 8476

Hindu Temple Trust, 22 King Street, Southall, Middlesex

India Youth Welfare Association, 32 Lyndhurst Avenue, Southall, Middlesex

Ramgarhia Sabha, 53-57 Oswald Road, Southall, Middlesex
Tel: 01 574 5635

Sharomani Akali Dal (UK), Head Office:, 15 Manor Way, Southall, Middlesex UB2 5JJ
Tel: 01 571 2842/01 578 7627

Sikh Missionary Society, Head Office:, 10 Featherstone Road, Southall, Middlesex UB2 5AA
Tel: 01 574 1902

Sri Guru Ravidass Sabha, 282 Western Road, Southall, Middlesex

Southall Youth Movement, 12 Featherstone Road, Southall, Middlesex

Southampton

Gurdwara Nanaksar, 3 Peterborough Road, Southampton

Gurdwara Singh Sabha, (The Indian Welfare &, Culture Association), 128-130 Northumberland Road, Southampton SO2 0ER
Tel: 0703 333016

Southampton Westindian Association, Trinity Road, Southampton
Secretary: Mr S Gullings

Sri Guru Tegh Bahadur, Sikh Temple, 8 Clovelly Road, Southampton
Tel: 0703 224744

Southshields

Gurdwara Khalsa Mero Roop Hai Khas 2 Dean Terrace, Southshields NE33 5LL
Tel: 0632 555 697

St. Albans

St. Albans Afro-Caribbean Association, 8 Bricket Road, St. Albans, Herts.
Tel: 0727 42470

Stafford

Caribbean Old Boy's Reunion,
176 Stone Road, Stafford
Secretary: Mr E.K. Beckford

Gurdwara Nanak Sar, Sikh Temple,
Bath Road, Stafford
Tel: 0785 58590

Guru Nanak Gurdwara, Tithe Barn Road, Stafford

Indian Cultural Association, 9 Willow Close, Walton-on-the-Hill, Stafford
Mrs D. H. Thanawala

Nanaksar Sikh Temple, 155 Westway, Stafford
President: J.S. Mahal, 8 Oxford Gardens, Stafford, Secretary: Mr K.S. Kang J.P.

Stafford Sikh Youth Organisation,
38 Penkvale Road, Stafford
Mr K.S. Takhar

Stevenage

Heights, 13B Middle Row, Stevenage, Herts. SG1 3AW
Tel: 0438 728 710

Stoke-On-Trent

Gurdwara Guru Nanak, Sikh Temple,
61 Liverpool Road, Stoke-on-Trent

Sikh Temple, Blackwells Row, Cobridge, Stoke-on-Trent

Surbiton

Sri Nankana Sahib Foundation, 19 Douglas Road, Surbiton, Surrey KT6 7RZ
Tel: 01 399 0942

Swindon

Asian Centre, 163 Cranmore Avenue, Park South, Swindon

Asian Youth Club, 61 William Street, Swindon, Wilts.
Tel: 0793 39317
Con. Mr W Masih

Hindu Samaj, 33 Okebourne Park, Liden, Swindon
Tel: 0793 694107
Con. Mr N.R. Patel

Indian Workers Association, 24 King Henry Drive, Grange Park, Swindon, Wilts.
Tel: 0793 874329
Con. Mr A.S. Tar

Jagriti Mandal, 11 Fosse Close, Rodbourne, Swindon
Tel: 0793 33338
Con. Mrs D.M. Clarke

Pakistan Muslim Association, 5 Irston Way, Blenheim Park, Freshbrook, Swindon, Wiltshire
Tel: 0793 481986
Con. Mr M.S. Khan,

Shree Lohana Mahajan, 12 Thackeray Close, Liden, Swindon
Tel: 0793 33884
Con. Mr N Amlani

Sikh Temple, 47 Graham Street, Swindon
Con. Mr P.S. Chana

The Sikh Temple, North Street, Swindon, Wiltshire

Swindon Ismaili Community, 27 Dawlish Road, Park North, Swindon

Swindon Westindian Community Association, 39 Faringdon Road, Swindon, Wiltshire
Tel: 0793 642140
Con. Mr Lloyd Smith

Thamesdown Islamic Association,
12 Don Close, Greenmeadow, Swindon, Wiltshire
Tel: 0793 693569
Con. Mr K.A. Nawaz

Telford

Guru Nanak Sikh Temple, Hadley Park Road, Hadley, Telford
Tel: 0952 51734

Telford Westindian Association, 1 High St, Hadley, Telford, Shropshire TF3 4LS
Tel: 0952 56840

Tipton

AACWA, 56 Leasowe Rd, Tipton, West Midland, DY4 8PJ,
Tel: 021-557-5441

Asian & Afro-Caribbean Welfare Association, (The Secretary), 56 Leasone Road, Tipton, West Midlands

Wakefield

Caribbean Cricket Club, 6 Ashwood Grove, Horbury, Nr. Wakefield

United Caribbean Association, Grange Town, Cardiff
Tel: 0222 462858/0222 26349
Secretary: Mr A White MBE

Walton-On-Thames

Caribbean Communications, 116 Queens Road, Hersham, Walton-on-Thames,
Tel: 0932 248 716

Walsall

Afro-Caribbean Youth Council, 42 Upper Rushall Street, Walsall, West Midlands,
Tel: 0922 21862

Guru Nanak Sikh Temple, West Bromwich Street, Walsall, Staffs.,
Tel: 0922 22199

Gurdwara Nanaksar, 4 Wellington Street, Walsall, Staffs.,
Tel: 0922 641040

International Sikh Youth Federation,
P.O. Box 63, Walsall WS1 4N, West Midlands,
Tel: 0922 36485

Muslim Community Information Centre,
62-64 Wednesbury Road, Walsall, West Midlands WS1 3RR,
Tel: 0922 20453

National Anti Racist Movement in Education, P.O. Box 9, Walsall, West Midlands WS1 3SF

Shree Hindu Mandir & Cultural Centre,
104 Kingsley Street, Walsall, West Midlands WS2 9Q8,
Tel: 0922 648595

Warley

Afro-Caribbean Teachers Support Unit,
Shirelands High School, Waterloo Rd, Smetwick, Warley, West Midlands,
Tel: 021 558 8086

Confederation of Sandwell Muslim Organisations, 194 Birmingham Street, Oldbury, Warley, West Midlands

Guru Nanak Gurdwara, 130 High Street, Smethwick, Warley, West Midlands B66 3AP, Tel: 021 558 2527

Watford

Indian Workers Association, (Watford), 18 Granville Road, Watford, Herts 13

The Sikh Temple, 18 Granville Road, Watford, Herts

Watford Afro-Caribbean Association, W I & Friends Organisation, 16 Florence Close, Garston, Herts WD2

Watford Afro-Caribbean Centre, 15 Harwoods Road, Watford, Tel: 0923 20810/679004

Waterdale

Gurdwara Guru Kalgidhar, 78 St James Street, Waterdale, Doncaster

Wellingborough

Carib Spicy Club, c/o 235 Kilnway, Wellingborough 6

Wellingborough Afro-Caribbean Association, 11 Fernie Way, Wellingborough

Wellingborough District Hindu Association, 133 Highfield Road, Wellingborough

Wembley

An-Nisa Society, 110 Thurlby Road, Wembley, Middlesex, Tel: 01 902 6074

Do Dil Group (for singles, divorced and separated), 36 Napier Road, Wembley, Middlesex HAO 2UA, Tel: 01 902 4660

West Bromwich

British Sikh Punjabi Literary Society, 29 Europa Avenue, Sandwell Valley, West Bromwich, West Midlands B70 6TL, Tel: 021 553 1192

Gurdwara Guru Har Rai Sahib, 126-128 High Street, West Bromwich, West Midlands, Tel: 021 525 3275

Guru Nanak Sikh Temple, 8 Edward Street, West Bromwich, West Midlands, Tel: 021 553 1242

Sadwica, 15 Lee Street, Hill Top, West Bromwich, West Midlands

West Bromwich Afro Caribbean Resource Centre, Thomas Street, West Bromwich, West Midlands, B70 6L7 Tel: 021 525 9177

Willenhall

Guru Nanak Gurdwara, 65/67 Walsall Road, Willenhall, West Midlands

Wirral

Wirral Support Group for Vietnamese Refugees, c/o Education Department, Metropolitan Borough of Wirral, Cleveland Street, Birkenhead

Wollaton

Institute of Sikh Ideology, (Sikh Youth, International), 193 Wollaton Road, Wollaton, Notts. NG8 1FU

Wolverhampton

Afro-Caribbean Cultural Centre, 2 Clarence Road, Wolverhampton WV1 4JH, Tel: 0902 20109 Secretary: Mrs W Downie

B.C.A.G., Black Community Action Group, 125 Waterloo Rd, Wolverhampton, West Midlands, Tel: 0902-712209

Guru Nanak Satsang, Sikh Temple, 204 Cannock Road, Wolverhampton, Tel: 0902 50453

Guru Nanak Sikh Temple, Vernon Street, Wolverhampton, Tel: 0902 26325

Guru Nanak Sikh Temple, Sedgley Street, Off Dudley Road, Wolverhampton, Tel: 0902 50285, 0902 870914

Guru Nanak Sikh Temple, 206 Lea Road, Wolverhampton

Hamarbee Association, 125 Waterloo Road, Whitmoreans, Wolverhampton WV1 4RB, Tel: 0902 712209 Con. G. Bandele

Marcus Garvey Advice Centre, 34 Hordern Road, Whitmoreans, Wolverhampton WV6 0HF, Tel: 0902 757641 Secretary: Mr E.C. Williams

Merridale Community & Youth Project, 49a Chapel Ash, Wolverhampton, Tel: 0902 713624 Con. Mr Brown

Nanaksar (Thath) Ishar Darbar, Mander Street, Wolverhampton, Tel: 0902 29379

Ramgarhia Sikh Temple, Westbury Street, Wolverhampton

West Midlands Caribbean & Friends Association 46 Arondale Road, Wolverhampton

West Midlands Caribbean Parents & Friends Association, 372 New Hampton Road West, Wolverhampton WV6 0RX, Tel: 0902 21783

Wolverhampton Afro-Caribbean Development Agency, 52-54 Worcester St, Wolverhampton, WV2 4LL, Tel: 0902 24005/6

Wolverhampton & District Commonwealth Citizen's Association, 34 Hordern Road, Whitmoreans Road, Wolverhampton WV6 0HF, Tel: 0902 757641 Mr Earlington C Williams

SCOTLAND

Dundee

Dundee International Womens Group, 49 Lyon St, Dundee

The Sikh Temple, 10 Tylors Lane, Dundee, Scotland, Tel: 0382 645770

Sri Guru Nanak Gurdwara, 1/3 Nilson Street, Dundee, Scotland, Tel: 0382 23383

East Kilbride

British Afroasian Sungum Kolet, 13 Aikman Place, East Kilbride G74 3JL Tel: 03552 26255

Edinburgh

Lothian Caribbean Association 95 Cluny Gardens, Edinburgh EH10 6BW

Mosque & Islamic Centre, The Iman, 12 Roxbury Street, Edinburgh EH8

Pakistan Association East of Scotland, 16 Marchmount Road, Edinburgh PH19 1ZH

Glasgow

Bangladesh Association, 18 Melville Gardens, Bishop Briggs, Glasgow G64 3DF

Bangladesh Association (Glasgow), c/o Dr. M.Z. Rahman, 'Lynedoch', Larch Avenue, Lenzie, Glasgow G66 4HT, Tel: 041 776 6428

Bengali Cultural Association, 15 Southview Drive, Bearsden, Glasgow G61

Central Gurdwara Singh Sabha, 142 Berkeley Street, Glasgow, Scotland Tel: 041 221 6698

Glasgow Language Teaching Centre, Napiershall Street, Glasgow G20, Tel: 041 339 0594

Gurdwara Singh Sabha, 32 St Andrews Drive, Glasgow, Scotland

Gurdwara Singh Sabha, 163 Nithsdale Road, Glasgow, Scotland, Tel: 041 423 8288

Guru Nanak Sikh Temple Ramgarhia Association, 27 Otago Street, Kelvinbridge, Glasgow G12 8JJ, Scotland, Tel: 041 334 9125

Minority Ethnic Teachers Association, c/o 115 Wellington Road, Glasgow G2 2XT

Pakistan Co-op Society, 172/174 Battlefield Road, Glasgow G42

Pakistan Social & Cultural Society, c/o Castle, 525 Crown Street, Glasgow

Scottish Asian Action Group, 537 Sauchiehall Street, Glasgow G3 7PQ, Scotland

Hamilton

Indian Graduates Association & Society, 49 Silvertonhill Avenue, Hamilton ML3, Scotland

Lanark

Indian Workers Association, Enfield Douglas Waterby, Lanark, Scotland

Eskdalemuir

Samye-Ling Tibetan Centre, Eskdalemuir, Nr Langholm, Dumfrieshire, Scotland DG13 0QL

WALES

Cardiff

Afro Caribbean Association, President: Mrs Ina C Douglas, 65 Plantaganet Street, Riverside, Cardiff CF1 8RQ, Tel: 0222-28508

Community Roots, 2nd floor, Duke St Arcade, Duke St, Cardiff, Tel: 0222-24039

Dasmesh Singh Sabha Bhatra, Gurdwara, 80-82 Ninian Park Road, Cardiff

Riverside Community Centre, Brunel St, Riverside , Cardiff, Tel: 0222-20309

The Sikh Temple, 212a Pearl Street, Roath, Cardiff

African Organisations in the UK

African Arts, Crafts and Culture, Alperton Youth Centre, Ealing Road, Wembley, Middlesex
Tel: 01-575 3814, (Zebby) 01-902 4250

Africa Arts in Education, Coburg Primary School, Coburg Road, London SE5
Tel: 01 703 1619

Africa Evangelical Fellowship, (SAGM), 30 Lingfield Road, London SW19
Tel: 01 946 1176

Africa Future Democrats, 1 Norris House, Trinity Estate, London SE8 5RF
Tel: 01 691 3253

Africa Inland Mission International (AIM), 2 Vorley Road, London N19 5HE
Tel: 01 281 1184

African Medical & Research Foundation, (Med. Charity), 68 Upper Richmond Road, London SW15
Tel: 01 874 0098

African National Congress (A.N.C.), P.O. Box 38 , 28 Penton Street, London N1
Tel: 01 837 4363

African Peoples Historical Monument Foundation, 378 Coldharbour Lane, Brixton, London SW9
Tel: 01 733 3044

African Peoples Movement Advice Centre, 226 Camberwell Rd, London SE5
Tel: 01 701 7121

African Peoples Movement (Vol. Organisation), 4 Offas Mead, Lindisfarne Way, London E9
Tel: 01 985 1139

African Refugee Housing Action Ltd, Head Office, 22-25 Leighton Road, London NW5
Tel: 01 482 3829

African Refuge Housing Action Ltd., 42 Albany Street, London NW1

African Study Programme, 82 Tynemouth Road, Tottenham, London N15 4AX
Tel: 01 885 5392

African Womens Association (AKOYA Project) P.O. Box 115 c/o Celestial Church of Christ, Stratford Parish Hall, Arcadia Street, London E14
Tel: 01 987 0371

African Womens Association (Community Services.), 135 Clarence Road, London E5
Tel: 01 985 0147

African Womens Collective, 2 Leighton Road, London NW5
Tel: 01 482 3829

African Womens Welfare Association, 12 Donovan Court, Exton Crescent, London NW10
Tel: 01 961 3337

Akina Mama Wa Afrika, c/o 38 King Street, London WC2E 8JT

Angola Information, 34 Percy Street, London W1P 9FG
Tel: 01 636 7108

Anti-Apartheid Movement, 13 Mandela Street, London NW1
Tel: 01 387 7966

Association of Zimbabwe Students, 207 Naish Court, Pembroke Street, London N1

Black Consciousness Movement, BCM A. BM Box 480, London WC1N 3XX

Britain-Zimbabwe Society, 5 Croham Park Avenue, Croydon CR2 7HN

Broad African Organisation, 28 Cordona Avenue, Thornley Park, Denton, Manchester MB4 2WP

Campaign for the Demilitarisation of the Indian Ocean, 139 Drakefell Road, London SE4

Campaign for Equal Opportunities in the Arts, 38 King Street, London WC2E 8JT
Tel: 01 379 6509

Committee for Human Rights in Cameroon, P.O. Box 551, London WC1N 3XX
Tel: 01 698 1017

Committee For the Release of Political Prisoners in Kenya, c/o 76 Stroud Green Road, London N4
Tel: 01 874 7802

East African Association c/o 120 Squires Lane, Finchley, London N3
Tel: 01 349 1412
Con. Mr P Pawar

East African Association, 8 Richmond Crescent, Slough SL1 LXD

Eritrean Relief Association, 391 City Road, London EC1

Eritrean Students Association, P.O. Box 7007, London WC1
Tel: 01 521 6404

The Ethiopian World Federation Inc., 28 Stagness Place, Kennington, London SE11 4BE
Tel: 01 735 0905
Con. K. Tskani

Foundation for African Arts, George Orwell School, Holland Walk, London N19 3EU
Tel: 01 263 8141

Ghana Union, 35 Westcott Way, Favell Green, Northampton
Con. Mr J. Arthur

Ghana Union Community Centre, St Andrew Church, Salisbury Road, London NW6
Tel: 01 624 0954

Ghana Union Of Greater Manchester, 127 Leicester Road, Salford M7 OHJ
Tel: 061 720 7448
Con. E.A. Djan

The Hackney African Organisation, 4/6 Dalston Lane, London E8
Tel: 01 241 2720/01 241 2740

The Greenwich African United Association, 3 Brookdene Road, London SE18 1EN, c/o Mrs R Williams

International Defense Aid Fund For Southern Africa, 64 Essex Road, Islington, London N1
Tel: 01 359 9181

Jenako Arts National Association of Development, Education Centre (NADEC), 6 Endsleigh Street, London WC1H 0DX

Malawi Support Committee, c/o 14B Grantbridge Street, London N1

Movement for Restoration of Democracy in Nigeria, 66 Gunton Road, Clapham, London E5 9JS

Mozambique Angola Committee, 35 Wellington Street, London WC2E 7BM

Mozambique Information Office, 34 Percy Street, London W1P 9FG
Tel: 01 636 7108

The Muslim Association of Nigeria (UK Branch), c/o Bro: Sadudeen, (Gen. Secretary), 46 Edge Hill House, Loughborough Rd Estate, London SW9
Tel: 01 326 0716

Namibia Support Committee, P.O. Box 16, Leverton Street, London NW5 2LW
Tel: 01 267 1941/2

Nigerian Community (UK), 276 Shirland Road, London W9, (Cultural/Legal)

Nigeria Social Centre & Club, 67 Upper Parliament Street, Liverpool 8
Tel: 051 709 4211

Nsutgman Association, Tim Ossei Berkon, 138 Durrington Road, Clapton, London E5 OHS
Tel: 01 985 2571

P.A.C. Movement Midlands Region, 104 Heathfield Road, Birmingham 21
Tel: 021 554 2747

Pan African Organisation, 540 Kingsland Road, Hackney, London E8
Tel: 01 241 2848

Chief Representative Pan Africanist Congress (PAC), 212 Church Road, Willesden, London NW10
Tel: 01 459 7392

Relief Society of Tigray (REST), UK Support Committee, 150 Hoe Street, London E17
Tel: 01 521 4712

School of Oriental and African Studies, (Extra Mural Division), Malet Street, London WC1E 7HP, (reference resource centre)
Tel: 01 637 2388

Sierra Leone Association, 145 Cramlington Road, Great Barr, Birmingham
Tel: 021 357 3429
Con. Mr R.A. Lisk-Carew

Sierra Leone Alliance Movement (SLAM), 31 Westerham House, Bayham Place, London NW1

Sierra Leone Social Club, 30 Alexandria Terrace, Liverpool 8
Tel: 051 709 1647

Somali Community Association, 16-17 Victoria Park Square, London E2
Tel: 01 521 4712

Somali Welfare Society, 584 Herries Road, Sheffield S5 8TR, Yorkshire.

Somali Association of Greater Manchester, 270 Great Western Street, Mosside, Manchester M14

Somali Community Association, Broomhill Community Centre, Broomspring Lane, Sheffield 10
Tel: 0742 25782
Mr Mohammed Ahmed

Somali Community Centre, Vestry Hall, Cemetary Road, Sheffield, Mrs A Deria

Somali London Community & Cultural Association (SLCCA), 17 Victoria Park Square, Bethnal Green, London E2
Tel: 01 981 6827

Somali Social Club, 45 Upper Parliament Street, Liverpool 8
Tel: 051 709 4710

South West Africa Peoples Organisation (SWAPO), P.O. Box 194, London N5 1LW
Tel: 01 359 9116/7

SWAPO – Womens Solidarity Campaign, P.O. Box 16, London NW5 2LW
Tel: 01 267 1941/2

Sudan Support Group, c/o 90 Union Road, London SW4 6JU
Tel: 01 622 3761

Uganda Community Relief Association, 391 City Road, London EC1V INE
Tel: 01 837 0993

Uganda Group for Human Rights, c/o Fellowship Foundation, Christian Alliance Centres Street, London SE1 8UF
Tel: 01 633 0128

Ugandan Human Rights Group, 1 Lodore Road, Fishponds, Bristol
Tel: 0272 659667
B. Ssebalij

West African Welfare Association, 27 Barnfield, Upper Park Road, London NW3 2OU

Zuriya African Performers, c/o 14 Brixton Road, London SW9 6BV
Tel: 01 582 5590

Caribbean Organisations in the UK

Antigua

Antigua and Barbuda Association, 8 Winstead Gardens, Dagenham, Essex RM10 7TL

Antigua and Barbuda Association, 214 East Park Road, Leicester

Barbados

Barbados Association, 83 Cannon Hill Road, Birmingham B30 2TD
Tel: 021 440 2016
Mr G Adamson

Barbados Caribbean and Friends Association, 11 Holton Road, Horfield, Bristol BS7 0EP, President and General Secretary: Mr U.F.G. Walcott, JP
Tel: 0272 691181

Barbados Community and Choir Association, 36 Duodale Road, Coventry
Tel: 0203 84799
Miss A. Riley

Alleyne School Old Scholars, Association, 336 Broadway, Gillingham, Kent
Tel: 01 897 1957
Secretary: Mr G Smith

Barbados Association, 27 Shepherd's Place, Leeds LS8 4LP
Secretary: Mrs J.V. White
Tel: 0532 622526

Barbados Association (Leicester), 51 Draper Street, Evington, Leicester LE2 1PQ, Secretary: Mrs E.V. Ishmael
Tel: 0533 738608

Barbados Merseyside Association, 1 Amberley Street, Liverpool 8
Con. Mr C. Brown

Barbados Overseas Citizens Association, 167 Boleyn Road, London E7
Secretary: Mr M Smith
Tel: 01 471 9378

The Foundation (UK) Association, 129B Ferhead Road, London N9 3ED
Tel: 01 829 3163
Con. Ken Braithwaite

Barbados Overseas Community and Friends Association, 'Caribbean House', Bridgport Place, London N1
Secretary: Ms O.L. Worrell
Tel: 01 263 9223

Cosmopolitan Association, 41 Amberwood, Finwood Park, Chadderton, Oldham OL9 9SJ
Secretary: Mrs L.L. Lynch
Tel: 061 626 7315

Barbados Overseas Association, 5 Cadum Walk, Manchester M13 9TR
Secretary: Mr Lauri Ford

Endeavour Group, 31 Waverley Cresenct, Plumstead, London SE18
Con. Ms Pauline Williams

Democratic Labour Party, 99 Stoke Newington Church Street, London N16

Dominica

Dominica Development Association (DDA), 96 Kingsgate Road, London NW6 2JG
Tel: 01 624 0635

Dominica (UK) Association, 4 Ridley Road, Forest Gate, London E7 OLT
Tel: 01 555 2548

Dominica Association (Bradford), 15 Swinton Place, Bradford, Yorkshire
Tel: 9274 571326
Chairman: Mr Murrey Celaire, JP

Dominica Carib Association, 22 Reginald Road, Forest Gate, London E7 9HS
Tel: 01 555 1348

Dominica Co-operative Relief Fund, 90 Trinity Road, Southall, Middlesex UB1 1EN

Dominica Freedom Party UK Organisation, PO Box 129, Maida Vale, London W9 2DL
Tel: 01 519 4255
Secretary/Treasurer: Mr A. Touissant

Dominican & Friends Association, c/o 18 Brenner Street, Eastville, Bristol BS5 6JB

Dominican Friendly Association, 39 Woodborough Street, Easton, Bristol 5
Tel: 0272 511794
Con. Mr C. Callion

Dominica Nationals Association (Preston), 2 Emerson Road, Preston, Lancashire PR1 5SN
Tel: 0772 792726

Dominica Overseas National Association, 11 Nemoure Road, Acton, London W3
Tel: 01 253 0245
Secretary: Miss Hazel Lecointe

Dominica Progressive National Charitable Association, 1-1a Henslowe Road, East Dulwich, London SE22 OAP
Tel: 01 693 7688
Secretary: Miss Yvette Samuel

Reading United Dominicans, Reading District Branch, 20 Grange Avenue, Reading, Berks

Grenada

Caribbean Social Charity Club, 58 Mendora Road, London SW6
Tel: 01 386 9267

The Caribbean Sporting Club, 73 Credon Road, London E13
Chairman: Mr Osban Phillips

Carriacou (Grenada) Association Bedford, 2 Chantry Road, Kempston, Bedfordshire
Tel: 0234 856206
Chairman: Mr Peter Gabriel

Carriacou (Grenada) Association Bedford, 30 Aylesbury Road, Bedford, Beds MK40 9RD
Secretary: Mrs Rita Scott

The Carriacou & Grenada Organisation, 70 Burrows Road, Kensal Rise, London NW10
Chairman: Mr Carlton Sylvester

Grenada Association (Reading), 2 Stanhope Road, Reading, Berks
Tel: 0734-65037
Secretary: Miss M. McGuire

Grenada Benevolent Society UK, c/o Mr Christopher Quashie, 22 Bradgate Road, Catford, London SE6 4TS

Grenada and Carriacou Benevolent Association, 77 Bromhill Road, London SE6
Con. Mr W. Simon

Grenada, Carriacou & PetitMartinique Health Workers Association, 206 Uxbridge Road, Southall, Middlesex
Asst. Secretary: Mrs T. Simon

Grenada & Carriacou Voluntary Aid Association, 58 The Links, Kempston, Bedford MK42 7LD
Con. Mr Rodrick Johnson

Grenada Charity Club, 44 Wesley Avenue, Park Royal, London NW10
Chairman: Mr C.J. Pennie

Grenada Cultural & Social Club, 114 Clonewell Road, London N17
Con. Mr B Fletcher

Grenada Ex-Police Officers Association, 6 Hemlock Road, London W12
Tel:01 743 6794
Con. Mr Roy McQuilkin

Grenada Invincible Seven
12 Ingersoll Road, Shepherd's Bush, London W12
Tel:01 385 7895
Secretary: Mr J.C. Ince

Grenada Nationals & Friends, 132 Elborough Street, Southfields, London SW18
Tel: 01 874 0877
Chairman: Mr Cosmos Wardally

Grenada Nationals & Friends,
23 Swan Court, Fulham Road, London SW6
Secretary: Ms Marie Thomas

Grenada Support Group (UK), 23 Longford Avenue, Southall, Middlesex UB1 3QW
Tel: 01 574 4647
Chairman: Mr McPherson Augustine

Grenada Support Group (UK), 23 Kingsmead Road, Tulse Hill, SW2
Tel: 01 674 6963

Grenada Overseas Association (Huddersfield), 64 Bankfield Road, Huddersfield, Yorks
Chairman: Mr Denis Lazarus

Grenada Overseas Association (Manchester), 29 Bridge Lane, Stockport SK7 3AB
Secretary: Mr A.M. Kaaba

Grenada Voluntary Hospital Fund-Raising Committee, 7 Robin Lane, Wellingborough, Northampton
Tel: Wellingborough 73731
Con. Mr Thomas Aberdeen

Grenada Voluntary Hospital Committee, 35 Georgia Road, Thornton Heath, Surrey
Acting Chairman: Thelma Mitchell

League of Friends of Grenada & The Grenadines, 88 Bordas Road, Hanwell, London W7
Chairperson: Mrs Mary Cruickshank

N.N.P. London Region, 145 Southampton Way, Camberwell, London SE5 5EW
Tel: 01 703 0469
Chairman: Mr Raymond La Touche

St John's Development Group, c/o Alex Sullivan, 140 Argyle Road, Ealing, London W13
Tel: 01 997 5825

Guyana

Association of Guyanese Nationals, 38 Mill Hill Road, Acton, London W3 7JH

Guylon Co-operation Society, 89 Broxholm Road, London SE27
Tel: 01 674 4090

Guyana Liberal Democratic Party, 1 Oxford Road, London N4
Tel: 01 263 5604/01 800 7714

Guyana Sports and Cultural Society, 125 Chubert Road, London SW15 2QS
Tel: 01 870 7209
Chairperson: H. Ishmael

Jamaica

Anglo Caribbean Conservative Association,
c/o 8 Turnpike Lane, London N8
Con. Mr Basil Lewis

Association of Caribbean Families & Friends, 28 Beaconsfield Street, Hyson Green, Nottingham
Con. Mr Eric Irons

Association of Jamaicans (UK), Trust, Mr Manley Coke, 104 Lodge Road, Croydon CRO 2PF
Tel: 01 657 5494

Association of Jamaicans (UK) Trust, 2A Temple Road, London NW2 6QB

Bristol Westindian Parents & Friends Association, 58 St. Paul's Road, St. Paul's, Bristol BS2
Con. Mr B. Dettering

British Caribbean Association, 65 Plantaganet Street, Riverside, Cardiff CF1 8RQ
Con. Mrs I. Douglas

Brixton Domino Club,
22 Coldharbour Lane, London SW9
Secretary: Mr A.U. Blair

Campaign Against Racial Discrimination, 42 Rucklidge Avenue, Harlesden, London NW10 4PS
Tel: 01 965 9635
Con. Mr Guy Elliston

The Caribbean Sunrise Social Club, 70 Fernhill Road, Cowley, Oxford
Vice Chairman: Mr T.S. Barrett

Croydon Association of Jamaicans, 557 Davidson Road, Croydon CRO 6DU
Con. Mrs M. Campbell

The Friends of the Heart Foundation of Jamaica,
205 Mitcham Lane, Streatham, London SW16 6PW
Tel: 01 769 1436
Hon. Secretary: Mrs Iris Gordon

Ipswich Caribbean Association,
15 Woodbridge Road, Ipswich, Suffolk IP1 2EA
Secretary: Mrs Roma Layne

Jamaica Association, 33 Dorchester Road, Upholland, Wigan Lancs.
Con. Mrs E. C. Robinson

Jamaica Aid Group, 166 Upper Allen Street, Sheffield S3
Con. Mr Martell Forrester

The Jamaica Caribbean Society, Headquarters – Westindian Centre, Carmoor Road, Chorlton-on-Medlock, Manchester 13
Tel: 061 225 4724/224 8203
Con. Mrs Cherry Byfield

Jamaica Community Service Group, 80 Churchill Road, Birmingham 20
Con. Miss N. Salmon, JP

Jamaica Community Service Group, Weld Community Centre, 35 Wilson Road, Handsworth, Birmingham 20
Co-ordinator: Mrs Joyce Powell

Jamaica Community Service Group, Mr L. Morris, 106 Copdale Road, Leicester
Tel: 0533 737799

Jamaican Freedom League (Westminister), 214 High Road, Harlesden, London NW10
Secretary: Mrs Elaine Spence

The Jamaica Labour Party (UK) Branch, 76 George V Way, Perivale, Middlesex
Secretary: Mrs E Wilson

The Jamaica Labour Party(Overseas), 338 Lower Addiscombe Road, Croydon, Surrey CRO 7AF
Tel: 01 654 2986
Secretary: Mrs N P Taylor

Jamaica Merseyside Association, 30 Osborne Road, Eccleston, St. Helens, Merseyside, Liverpool
Tel 051 709 3562
Mr Hugh White

Jamaica Mutual Association, 124 Cromwell Road, Peterborough
Tel: Mr G.E. Chin & Mr W. Haughton

The Jamaica Nationals Regional Committee (Northern), Huddersfield Branch, c/o New Arawak Club, 55 Brow Road, Paddock, Huddersfield, West Yorkshire
Tel: 0484 27211
Secretary: Mrs A Flowers

Jamaica National Association, 11 Sedberg Street, Preston PR2 3BP, Lancashire
Tel: 0772 717854
Chairman: Mr Lewish F. Walker

Jamaica Northern Committee, 21 Welford Avenu, Lawton, Warrington
Chairman: Mr A.A. Jackson

The Jamaica Nurses Association (UK), 5 Oak Drive, Erdington, Birmingham B23 5DQ
Con. Mrs F. Burnett

Jamaica Nurses Association (UK), c/o 12 Southway, Shirley, Croydon, Surrey CRO 8RP
Tel: 01 777 9246
Con. Mrs Dorothy Turner

Jamaica Society, c/o The Lodge, Harehill County Primary School, Roundhay Road, Leeds LS8 5AW
Tel: 0532 490045 (after 4pm)
Secretary: Mrs L. Powell

Lignum Vitae Club, c/o Jamaican High Commission, 63 St. James's Street, London SW1A 1LY
Tel: 01 499 8600
President: Mrs E. Walker

Mutual Protection Association, 140 Leonard Road, Birmingham 21
Con. Mr J. Hunte

Northampton Council of African and Caribbean Organisations, 9 Falcutt Way, Kingsthorpe, Northampton NN2 8NR
Tel: 0604 256119
Mr Bert Cuff

One Foundation Organisation, 28 Redgrave Gardens, Bramingham Wood, Luton, Beds.
Secretary: Mrs G. McKoy

Paul Bogle Foundation, 189 Kentish Town Road, London NW5
Con. Mr Bunny Barnett

People's National Party (UK), 285 Heeley Road, Selly Oak, Birmingham 29
Con. Mr R. Gayle

People's National Party (UK), 7 Castillion Road, Catford, London SE6
Tel: 01 461 0319

Society of Jamaicans, Mr Earle Robinson, 285 Catherine Street, Leicester LE4 6GG
Tel: 0533-666157 (home) 0533 539181 ext. 293 (office)

Spade, Hammer & Pen Friendly Society, 17 Minstead Road, Birmingham 24
Secretary: Mrs H. Tulloch

United Anglo Caribbean Society, Berrymede Middle School, Osborne Road, London W8 8ST
Chairman: Mr George Doyley

West Indian Cavaliers Club, Marcus Garvey Centre, Lenton Boulevard, Nottingham

West Indian League, 83 Pellat Road, London SE22
Tel: 01 693 0320/9
President: Mr George Crosdale

West Midlands Caribbean Association, 6 Merridale Road, Wolverhampton

West Indian Women's Circle, The Old Town Hall, Room 48, Blagrive Street, Reading, Berkshire
Chairperson: Mrs A. Adams

Montserrat

M.O.P.P.A., 46 Lydford Road, London W9 3LX
Con. Mr W.I. Trant

St. Kitts-Nevis

St Kitts-Nevis Association, 9 Morar Close, Castlevale, Birmingham B35
Con. Mr Albert David

St Kitts, Nevis & Anguilla Society, 146 Stratford Road, Sparkbrook, Birmingham B11 1AG
Secretary: Ms C Daniel

St Kitts, Nevis & Anguilla Society, 99 Third Avenue, Bordesley Green, Birmingham

St Kitts-Nevis Association, 163 Glyn Eiddew, Pentwyn, Cardiff CF 27 BS, South Glamorgan
Chairman: Mr Ronald Foster

St Kitts-Nevis Association, 7 Sycamore Avenue, Leeds LS8 4DZ
Con. Mrs Gertrude Paul

St Kitts-Nevis Association, 8 Rockingham Close, Leicester LE2 4EG
Con. Mr James Nisbett

St Kitts-Nevis Association, 79 Myrtle Road, Leicester LE2 1FU
Con. Miss Linda Herbert

St Kitts & Nevis Friendly Association, 44 Ledbury House, Pytchley Road, London SE22
Secretary: Ms Odette Bedford

St Kitts-Nevis Association, 155 Milkwood Road, Herne Hill, London SE24
Con. Mr D Moore

St Kitts-Nevis Association, 333 Mark House Road, Walthamstow, London E17
Con. Mr Neville Rawlins

St Kitts-Nevis Association, c/o Miss Butler, Flat 64, Compton House, 33 Parkham Street, London SW11 3JN

St Kitts-Nevis Association, 8 Beacontree Road, London E11 3AX
Con. Mr J.H. Phipps

St Kitts-Nevis Association, 30 Salisbury Street, Moss Side, Manchester M14 4ND
Con. Mrs Locita Brandy

St Kitts-Nevis Association, Christchurch Rectory, Montan Street, Moss Side, Manchester M14 4LT

St Kitts-Nevis Association, 155 Wilkinson Street, White Moore Estate, Nottingham
President: Mr O Harvey

St Kitts-Nevis & Friends Association, 62 Watermead Road, Simbury Mead, BEDS
Chairman: Mr George Richards

St Kitts-Nevis Association, 22 Hedley Road, St Albans, Herts.
Con. Mr Bob Liburd

The Combine Association, 51 Cavendish Road, St Albans, Herts. AL1 5ES
Chairman: Mr Peter Thomas

St Kitts & Nevis Development Fund, 54 Cornwall Avenue, Slough, Berks SL2 1A2
Secretary: Miss Janet Adams

St Kitts-Nevis-Anguilla Association, 28 Liverpool Road, Thornton Heath, Surrey, CR4 8LS

The Leeward Island People's Association, 52 Athol Road, Manchester M15 8QN
Con. Mr A.G Jones

St. Lucia

The St Lucia Association of Birmingham, 263 Hamstead Road, Great Barr, Birmingham B43 5TA
President: Mr C.E. Fessal

St Lucia Association, 91 Avondale Road, Liverpool L15 3HP
Con. Mr G Charlery

St Lucia Association of London, 375A Hornsey Road, London N19 4HF
Con. Miss Jessie Stephens

St Lucia Association, 8 Manfield Avenue, London N15
Con. Mr Burton Gajadhar

St. Vincent & The Grenadines

St Vincent & the Grenadines Association, 11 Chandos Road, London N17
Secretary: Mr S Patterson

St Vincent and the Grenadines Women's Association, 21 Forburg Road, Stamford Hill, London N16
Secretary: Miss St Hilaire

St Vincent Association (Rainham), 69 Monmouth Road, East Ham, London E6 3QU
Secretary: Mr V O'Garro

The Afro-Westindian Association, 82 Arnison Avenue, High Wycombe, Bucks.
Secretary: Mr S.H. Graham

Watford Caribbean Club, 7 Yewstone Court, Watford, Herts, WD 17HL
Con: Mrs M Wilson

Trinidad & Tobago

Trinidad & Tobago Association, 211 Pershore Road, Birmingham B5 7PF
Con. Mr L Malwah

Trinidad & Tobago Association, 79 Ponsonby Street, Liverpool L8 2TY

Trinidad and Tobago Association, 380 Green Lanes, London N4 1DW
Con. Mr I.P. Edwards

Trinidad & Tobago Association, 21 Faraday Avenue, Cheetham, Manchester 8
Con. Mr F Reece

Trinidad & Tobago Nationals and Friends Society, 16 Ebenezer Walk, Streatham Vale, London SW16 5SZ
Tel: 01 646 5507

Trinidad & Tobago Nationals Foundation, c/o 17 John Campbell Road, London N16 8JY
Tel: 985 0153

Trinidad and Tobago Nurses Association, 24 Godwin Road, Forest Gate, London E7

Latin America

Anglo Argentinean Society, Canning House, 2 Belgrave Square, London SW1 HPJ
Tel: 01 235 9505

Anglo . Brazillian Society, Canning House, 2 Belgrave Square, London SW1 HPJ
Tel: 01 235 3571

Anglo . Chilean Society, 12 Devonshire Street, London W1
Tel: 01 580 6392

Anglo . Colombian Society, Canning House, 2 Belgrave Square, London SW1 HPJ

Bolivan Working Group, 29 Islington Park Street, London N1
Tel: 01 359 2270

Brazilian Contemporary Arts, 1 Vaughan Avenue, London W6
Tel: 01 741 9579

(C.A.R.I.L.A.) Campaign Against Repression in Latin America, 29 Islington Park Street, London N1
Tel: 01 359 2270

Chilean Community for Human Rights, 23 Dunsmore Gardens, Dundee DD21 1PP

Chile Democratics, 95/97 Old Street, London EC1V 9JJ
Tel: 01 608 1920

Comunidad . Latin American Magazine (CLAM), Beauchamp Lodge, 2 Warwick Crescent, London W2

Friends of Bolivia, 57 Compton Road, London SW19
Tel: 01 947 1957

Institute of Latin-American Studies, 31 Tavistock Square, London WC1
Tel: 01 387 5671

Latin . American Advisory Committee (LAAC), Beauchamp Lodge, 2 Warwick Crescent, London W2

Latin American . Caribbean Cultural Society, No. 20 Woodberry Crescent, London N10 1PH
Tel: 01 883 6959

Latin American Community Project, 10 Bernays Grove, London SW9 8DF

Latin American Cultural Centre, 97 Caledonian Road, London N1 9JY
Tel: 01 837 2291

Latin American House Association, 97 Caledonian Road, London N1 9JY

Latin American Workers Association, 8 Southampton Row, London WC1
Tel: 01 403 0990

(CHRA) Committee for Human Rights in Argentine, (CHRU) Committee for Human Rights in Uruguay

(ELSSOC) El Salvador Solidarity Campaign

(CCHR) Colombian Committee for Human Rights

(BCRC) British-Cuba Resource Centre

The Peru Support Group

Paraguay Committee for Human Rights
21 Islington Park Street, London N1
Tel: 01 359 2270

Liberation Cuba Resource Centre, 313/315 Caledonian Road, London N1
Tel:01 607 0465

Nicaraguan Solidarity Campaign, 20-21 Compton Terrace, London N1
Tel: 01 359 8982

Commission for Racial Equality

The Commission for Racial Equality was set up by the Race Relations Act, 1976, for the purpose of working towards the elimination of discrimination and promoting equality of opportunity and good relations between different racial groups as well. The 1976 Race Relations Act replaces the whole of the 1965 and 1968 Acts. It became law on 24 November 1976 and took effect on 13 June 1977;

- to work towards the elimination of discrimination;

- to promote equality of opportunity, and good relations between persons of different racial groups; and

- to keep under review the Race Relations Act and to recommend amendments when necessary.

The Commission has broad powers to undertake investigations for any purpose connected with its duties. Where it finds discrimination, it may issue a non-discrimination notice requiring this to cease. It may bring proceedings against persistent discriminators and in cases concerning discriminatory advertisements and instructions, aid or pressure to discriminate. It undertakes advisory and educational work, and assists community relations councils, ethnic minority organisations, and other organisations in the promotion of equality of opportunity and good race relations.

Although the Commission is not obliged to investigate individual complaints, it has discretion to advise and assist complainants where there are special reasons for doing so.

- The Act provides that the Commission may issue codes of practices containing such guidelines as it thinks fit for either or both the following purposes: the elimination of discrimination in the field of employment; the promotion of equality of opportunity in that field between persons of different racial groups.

- The Act also provides that the Commission may give financial or other assistance to any organisation which, in its opinion, is concerned with the promotion of equality of opportunity and good relations between persons of different racial groups.

The nature of discrimination

The law, based on experience and common-sense, recognises two forms of discrimination: direct and indirect.

Direct discrimination is straightforwardly a matter of treating an individual less favourably than another on racial grounds. A direct discriminator can hardly fail to be aware of what he or she is doing and, so far as this is thought culpable, may well be upset if the charge of discrimination is brought.

Discrimination of this kind is widespread. At its worst, it is reflected in racial attacks, physical or verbal. At its most 'genial', it can be reflected in condescending forms of stereotyping.

Indirect discrimination resides in systems rather than in the head. It lies in requirements or conditions which, though they may apply generally, have a disproportionately adverse effect on one or more racial groups and cannot be justified. Word-of-mouth recruiting is an example of indirect discrimination, if the workforce is all white and internal recruits are sought, then the chances are that white people will fill the posts.

These two types of discrimination have to be tackled in different ways. Direct discrimination is ultimately dealt with by getting at people's head or hearts. Indirect discrimination is concerned with the structures over which they preside.

What can you do if you are discriminated against?

In the employment field

You may make a complaint to an industrial tribunal. Normally, you must make your complaint within three months of the act complained of (although a tribunal may accept complaints outside this time limit if there are very special reasons for doing so). If a hearing is held, and the tribunal upholds your case, it may award the following redress: a declaration of your rights; financial compensation (except where the case concerns indirect discrimination, and the respondent proves this was unintentional); recommendations to the respondent on action he should take to remedy the effects on the complainant of the discrimination.

Before a hearing is held, it may be possible to settle the complaint voluntarily. The complaint is referred to a conciliation officer of ACAS (the Advisory, Conciliation and Arbitration Service) whose duty is to try to secure a settlement without the need for a hearing.

The form for making a complaint to an industrial tribunal, and explanatory leaflets, are available from employment offices, job centres and unemployment benefit offices.

"A club may not discriminate in its treatment of members."

In housing, goods, facilities and services

You may bring proceedings in a designated county court or, in Scotland, a sheriff court. You must normally start proceedings within six months of the act complained of. It may be possible to settle the case out of court. If a court hearing is held, and the court upholds your case, it may grant the following redress: a declaration of your rights; damages (except where the case concerns indirect discrimination and the respondent proves this was unintentional); an injunction or order against the respondent. Costs are normally awarded against the losing party.

In education

If your complaint concerns the *private sector* of education, you may bring proceedings directly in a court, as above. If your complaint concerns the *public sector,* you must first refer it to the Department of Education and Science who must be allowed up to two months to deal with the matter before you may bring proceedings.

Note: only the Commission for Racial Equality may bring proceedings in cases concerning discriminatory advertising, or instructions, pressure or aid to discriminate.

Obtaining information from the respondent

In many cases, you may need further information about the treatment you received and the reasons for it, to help you decide whether to make a complaint, or how best to formulate or present your case. To help you get this information, you may, under the Act, put questions in writing to any person you think may have discriminated against you. You may use the questions and answers in evidence before an industrial tribunal or a court. A special questionnaire form is available from the Commission for Racial Equality, and from employment offices, job centres and unemployment benefit offices.

Who can advise and help?

In the employment field, you may be able to get help and advice from any trade union or professional body of which you are a member. ACAS will also be able to advise you of your rights.

You will also be able to get advice and help from local community relations councils. Ethnic minority organisations, legal advice centres, citizens advice bureaux, and other local bodies may also be able to advise you.

You may, of course, get advice from a solicitor. If your income is within certain limits you may be eligible for legal advice from a solicitor either free or at little cost. You may also have legal representation by a solicitor or barrister. This is not necessary (though it may sometimes be desirable) for industrial tribunals, where you may be represented or assisted by anyone you choose, or you may represent yourself.

Can the Commission for Racial Equality help?

The CRE may be able to help in a number of ways. It will be able to give general advice on your case. If you decide to go ahead with a complaint, it will be able to advise you on the procedures and how best to formulate and present your case. Or it may put you in touch with someone else who can assist or represent you. If there are special reasons for doing so, the CRE may be able itself to represent complainants and pay any costs.

The present Chairman of the CRE is Mr Michael Day OBE. He is 54 years old, married with two children. He was educated at University College School Hampstead, Selwyn College, Cambridge, and the London School of Economics. Since 1976 he has been the Chief Probation Officer for West Midlands Probation Service and was previously Chief Probation Officer of Surrey for eight years. From 1974-77 he was Chairman of the Conference of Chief Probation Officers and in 1982 became the first Chairman of the Association of Chief Officers of Probation which represents all Assistant, Deputy and Chief Probation Officers in England, Wales and Northern Ireland.

Mr Day's term of office commenced on 1 February 1988 and is initially for five years in the first instance.

Where do you contact the Commission for Racial Equality?

COMMISSION FOR RACIAL EQUALITY

Information Department
Elliot House
10-12 Allington Street
London SW1E 5EH

Tel: 01 828 7022

REGIONAL OFFICES

Birmingham

Alpha Tower (11th floor)
Suffolk Street Queensway
Birmingham B1 1TT
Tel: 021 632 4544

Leicester

Haymarket House (4th floor)
Haymarket Shopping Centre
Leicester LE1 3YG
Tel: 0533 517852

Manchester

Maybrook House (5th floor)
40 Blackfriars Street
Manchester M3 2EG
Tel: 061 831 7782/8

Leeds

Yorkshire Bank Chambers
(1st floor)
Infirmary Street
Leeds LS1 2JT
Tel: 0532 434413/4

Scotland

Royal Overseas League
100 Princes Street
Edinburgh EH2 3AA
Tel: 031 226 5186

Publications available from the Commission for Racial Equality

World Religions: A Handbook for Teachers £4.50
Home Tutor Handbook: Teaching English as a Second Language £3.50
Housing Choice and Ethnic Concentration: An Attitude Study £0.90
Unemployment and Homelessness: A Report £1.50
Urban Deprivation, Racial Inequality and Social Policy: A Report (HMSO) £1.75
Caring For Under-Fives in a Multi-racial Society £0.60
Fostering Black Children (Reprint) £1.60
Who Minds?: A Study of Working Mothers and Childminding in Ethnic Minority Communities £0.75
One Year On: A Report on the Resettlement of the Refugees from Uganda in Britain £0.75
Refuge or Home? : A Policy Statement on the Resettlement of Refugees £0.75
Five Views of Multi-racial Britain: Talks on Race Relations Broadcast by BBC TV £1.50
Muslim Burials: A Policy Paper – by Dr Muhammad Anwar (Reprint) £0.50
Who Tunes Into What? : A Report on Ethnic Minority Broadcasting – by Dr Muhammad Anwar £1.50
Votes and Policies: Ethnic Minorities and the General Election, 1979 – Dr Muhammad Anwar £1.50
Youth in Multi-racial Society: The Urgent Need for New Policies £1.50
Britain's New Art – by Naseem Khan £1.00
Probation and After-care in a Multi-racial Society: A Report Published Jointly by the CRE and the West Midlands County Probation and After-Care Service £2.00
Operation Interchange No. 1: Preparation for Work in a Multi-Racial Society £1.00
Public Awareness and the Media: A Study of Reporting on Race – by Barry Troyna £2.00
Administrative Guide for Self-Help Groups £1.00
Television in a Multi-racial Society: A Research Report £1.50
Loading the Law: A Study of Transmitted Deprivation, Ethnic Minorities and Affirmative Action by Prof. Alan Little and Diana Robbins £1.50
In Search of Employment and Training: Experience and Perceptions of Redundant Asian Textile Workers in Lancashire £1.00
CRE's Annual Report £1.00
Planning for a Multi-racial Britain: Report of the Royal Town Planning Institute/ CRE Working Party £1.50
Mother Tongue Teaching Conference Report: Conference Sponsored Jointly by the CRE and Bradford College, September 1980 .... £1.50
Towards a Black Perspective: Report of an Experimental Afro-Caribbean Training Project for Part-time Youth and Community Workers £1.00
Vietnamese Refugees in Britain £1.00
Ethnic Minority Broadcasting £1.00
Caribbean Connections : Six Programmes Broadcast by BBC Radio 4 .... £1.50
Code of Practice: for the elimination of racial discrimination and the promotion of equality of opportunity in employment *(Orders for more than one copy should be sent to the Employment Division)* £1.00
The Arts of Ethnic Minorities: Status and Funding. A Research Report £1.00
Overseas Doctors: Experience and Expectations – A Research Study £1.00
Employment of Graduates from Ethnic Minorities – A Research Study £1.00
Asian Links: Six Programmes Broadcast by BBC Radio 4 .... £1.50
Ethnic Minority School Teachers: A Survey in Eight Local Education Authorities £1.00
Training: The Implementation of Equal Opportunities at Work (Vols. I & II) £3.00

Free Publications

Racial Discrimination: A Guide to the Race Relations Act, 1976 (Prepared by the Home Office)
A Project on Race Relations
Racial Equality and Social Policies in London: A Discussion Paper Presented by the CRE to the London Boroughs Association
The Arts of Ethnic Minorities: A Role of the CRE
Working with Black Youth
Consultation with Bangladeshi Community
CRE's Evidence to GLC Police Committee Inquiry into Racial Harassment (November 1981)
Local Government and Racial Equality (April 1982)
Racial Attacks: A Survey in 8 Areas of Britain
The National Bus Company: An Enquiry into the Provision of Equal Opportunity in Employment
Review of Race Relations Act: Proposals for Change
Summary of Loading the Law
Employment Prospects of Chinese Youth in Britain: A Research Report
Asian Links Book List
Caribbean Connection Book List
Summary of Immigration Control Procedures
Ethnic Minorities in Britain: Statistical information on the pattern of settlement

General

A Guide to the Race Relations Act:
Advertising
Employment
Landlords and Accommodation Agencies
Your Rights to Equal Treatment Under the Race Relations Act 1976
A General Guide (English) Also available in: Bengali, Gujarati, Hindi, Punjabi, Urdu
Employment
Housing, Education and Services
List of Community Relations Councils
List of Ethnic Minority Press
Public Library Service for Multi-Cultural Society: A Report Produced by the Library Advisory Council and the former CRE Education Committee
Industrial Tribunal Applicants under the R.R. Act, 1976: A Research Report
Bengalis in Tower Hamlets – by Patrick Duffy
Poster: Fight Racism (two sizes)
Poster: We Can Help (two sizes)
Poster: You Have Rights, Use Them (two sizes)
Poster: Equal Rights
Poster: All Together Now
Poster: Racial Discrimination is Unlawful
Lapel Badges: Racial Equality (5 per order free of charge; 20 for £1.00; advance payment essential)
Leaflets:
Fight Racism: You Have Rights – Use Them

Formal Investigation Reports

Report of a Formal Investigation into Certain Activities of Genture Restaurants Ltd
Barlavington Manor Children's Home: Report of a Formal Investigation Into Certain Activities of the Proprietors
The Antwerp Arms Public House: Report of a Formal Investigation into Certain Activities of Mrs Geville-Walker, the Licensee
Mount Pleasant United Working Men's Club: Report of a Formal Investigation Into the Mount Pleasant United Working Men's Club, Edgbaston, Birmingham
The Woodhouse Recreation Club and Social Institute, Leeds: Report of a Formal Investigation
Cottrell & Rothon Estate Agent: Report of a Formal Investigation
(1) Mr G.D. Midda & D.S. Services Ltd. (2) Allens Accommodation Bureau: Reports of two Formal Investigations
(1) F. Broomfield Ltd. (2) London Drivers Supplied Services Ltd, Employment Agency: Reports of two Formal Investigations
Housing Discrimination Against Gypsies: Reports of Four Formal Investigations
B.L. Cars Ltd: Report of a Formal Investigation
Tottenham Trades Club
The Zone Insurance Co. Ltd.
The Allocation of Council Housing
Massey Ferguson Perkins Ltd.
Pembroke & Pembroke Professional Appointment Agents
Secondary School Allocation in Reading
Rank Leisure Service
The West Yorkshire Passenger Transport Executive ("Bradford Metro")
The Provision of Equal Opportunities within Operating Companies of Chubb & Sons PLC
Percy Ingle Bakeries Ltd.
Collingwood Housing Association Ltd.
Race and Council Housing in Hackney
Abbey National Building Society
Dunlop Ltd., Leicester
Hackney Carriage Drivers' and Vehicle Licenses in the City of Birmingham
St. Chad's Hospital
Amari Plastics
Immigration Control Procedures
Walsall Metropolitan Borough Council: Practices and Policies of Housing Allocation
Birmingham Local Education Authority & Schools: Referral & Suspension of pupils
Beaumont Shopping Centre
Race and Mortgage Lending
Teaching English as a Second Language: Report of a Formal Investigation
Chartered Accountancy Training Contracts
Medical School Admissions: Report of a Formal Investigation into St. George's Hospital Medical School

Employment

Equal Opportunity Employment: A Guide for Employers
Positive Action & Equal Opportunity in Employment
Monitoring an Equal Opportunity Policy: A Guide to Employers
Guidance Note on Sikh Men and Women and Employment
Religious Observance by Muslim Employees – A Framework for Discussion
Why Keep Ethnic Records?: Questions and Answers for Employers and Employees
Implementing Equal Employment Opportunity Policies
Equal Opportunity and the Youth Training Scheme
Report of Enquiries into the Recruitment Practices of Unigate Dairies Ltd.
A Study of Employment in the Metropolitan Borough of Kirklees
In Search of Skill: Ethnic Minoirty Youth and Apprenticeship
Racial Equality & Youth Training Scheme
Race Cases in Tribunals: A Guide to Presenting Cases
Guidelines for Advertisers and Publishers: Race Relations Act 1976 – Employment Advertisements (Situations Vacant)
Contract Compliance: Principles of Practice

Housing

A Selected Bibliography: General book on Race Relations Dealing with Housing Issues
Hackney Housing Investigated: Summary of a Formal Investigation Report
Racial Harassment on Local Housing Estates: A Report Prepared by the London Race and Housing Forum
Living in Terror
Race and Housing in Liverpool

Social Services

A Guide to Asian Diets: A background Paper
Counselling the Caribbean Family
Mental Health Among Minority Ethnic Group: Research Summaries and Bibliography
Rickets and Anaemia: Report of a Conference held on 5 December 1974
Sickle Cell Anaemia
Primary Health Care: An Agenda for Discussion
Children in Care: CRE's submission to the House of Commons Social Services Select Committee Inquiry into Children in Care

Education

Towards Genuine Consultation: Principles of Community Participation
Books and Periodicals in Asian Languages
Evidence on Education to the Select Committee: Enquiry on the West Indian Community (CRC November 1976)
Summary of Report on the West Indian Community Vol. 1
The EEC's Directive on the Education of Children of Migrant Workers: Its Implications for the Education of Children from Ethnic Minority Groups in the UK
Summary of the main issues of the Regional Consultations with voluntary classes on Mother Tongue Teaching in the UK, January to July 1981
Swann: A Response from the Commission for Racial Equality
Ethnic Minority Community Languages: A Statement

Reprints from Education and Community Relations

Teaching About the Caribbean (May 1973)
Teaching About India, Bangladesh and Pakistan (October 1973)
Teaching About Africa (March 1974)
Teaching in the Multi-Racial Primary School (April & June 1975)
Chinese Festivals (November/December 1975)
Teaching About Islam (May/June 1976)
Race in the Curriculum (March/June 1977)

Periodicals

NEW COMMUNITY – Three issues per annum. £4.00 per copy
(Index to volumes, 1, 2, 3, 4, 5, 6, 7, 8, 9, 10, 11 & 12 at 75p (each)
Annual Subscription: Individual £12.00
Institutions £16.00
NEW EMPLOYMENT REPORT – Three issues per annum .... Free

Please send your order to:
Information Department, COMMISSION FOR RACIAL EQUALITY
Elliot House, 10-12 Allington Street, London SW1E 5EH, Tel: 01 828 7022

Community Relations Councils

Greater London

Barking & Dagenham Council for Racial Equality, Methodist Church, London Road, Barking, Essex, 1G11 8AL
Tel: 01 594 2773
CRO: (in charge) Sheila Delaney

Barnet Community Relations Council, 1 Friern Park, North Finchley, London, N12 9DE
Tel: 01 445 6051
Senior CRO: Mr David Mayer

Bexley Council For Racial Equality, Riverside Baths, 3 Walnut Tree Road, Erith, Kent
Tel: 0322 340316
CRO: (in charge) Mr John Austin-Walker

Brent Community Relations Council, 194 High Road, Willesden, London NW10
Tel: 01 451 4499/4490
Principal CRO: Mr N. Mullings

Camden Committee for Community Relations, 58 Hampstead Road, London, NW1 2PY
Tel: 01 387 1125
Senior CRO: Mr Anthony Phillips

Croydon Council for Community Relations, 70 Park Lane, Croydon, CRO 1JE
Tel: 01 686 8014/8524
Senior CRO: Ms Diana Mukuma

Ealing Community Relations Council, 2 The Green, High Street, Ealing, London W5 5DA
Tel: 01 579 3861
Principal CRO: Mr Andrew Housley

London Borough of Enfield Community Relations Council, Enfield Highway Library, 258 Hertford Road, Enfield EN3 5BN
Tel: 01 805 6121
Senior CRO: Ms Chandra Bhatia

Greenwich Council for Racial Equality, 115-123 Powis Street (2nd Floor), Woolwich, London SE18
Tel: 01 855 7191/4
CRO: (in charge) Mr Makhan Singh Bajwa

Hackney Council for Racial Equality, 1 Crossway, London N16 8LA
Tel: 01 241 0097

Hammersmith & FulhamCouncil for Racial Equality, Palingswick House, 241 King St, Hammersmith, London W6
Tel: 01 741 5715
CRO: (in charge) Senior CRO: Mr John Rafferty

Haringey Community Relations Council, 14a Turnpike Lane, London N8 OPT
Tel: 01 888 6871/4

Harrow Community Relations Council, 64 Pinner Road, Harrow, Middlesex HA1 2AH
Tel: 01 427 6504
CRO: (in charge) Ms Rose-Marie Adams

Hillingdon Community Relations Council, Darren House, 65 High Street, Uxbridge, Middx. UB8 1JP
Tel: 0895-56536
CRO: (in charge) Mr Charan Singh Rai

Hounslow Community Relations Council, 51 Grove Road, Hounslow, Middlesex TW3 3PR
Tel: 01 570 1168
Senior CRO: Mr Inder Singh Uppal

Kingston Group for Racial Understanding, 107 Whitton Road, Hounslow, TW3 2EJ
Chairperson: Mr Ajit Singh

Lewisham Council for Community Relations, 48 Lewisham High Street, London SE13 5JH
Tel: 01 852 9808
Senior CRO: Mr Asquith Gibbes

Merton Community Relations Council, 36 High Street, Colliers Wood, London SW19 2AB
Tel: 01 540 7386
CRO: (in charge) Winston Moncrieff

Newham Race Relations Association, 175 Upton Lane, London E7
Tel: 01 471 4621
Senior CRO: Mr Z. A. Mirza

Redbridge Community Relations Council, Methodist Church Hall, Ilford Lane, Ilford, Essex IG1 2JZ
Tel: 01 514 0688
CRO: (in charge) Mr Mahtarr Samba

Southwark Council for Community Relations, 125 Camberwell Road, London SE5
Tel: 01 252 7033
Senior CRO: Ms Hyacinth Parsons

Sutton Community Relations Council (Three Borough Project), John Marshall House (Room 4), 246-254 High Street, Sutton SM1 1PA
Tel; 01 661 6385
Con. Ms Daphne Beaton

Tower Hamlets Association For Racial Equality, 347-349 Cambridge Heath Road, London E2 9RA
Tel: 01 729 5775
Senior CRO: Mr M.A. Sayed

Waltham Forest Community Relations Council, 25 Church Hill, Walthamstow, London E17 3AB
Tel: 01 521 8851/2/3
Senior CRO: Mr Choudhyry Anwar

Westminster Community Relations Council, 472 Harrow Road, London W9 3RU
Tel: 01 289 2277-8

South West England

Banbury Community Relations Council, Cedar Cottage, Wroxton, Banbury, Oxon OX15 6QE
Secretary: Ms Margaret Ferriman

Bath Council for Community Relations, Riverside Youth Centre, York Place, London Road, Bath
Con. Mrs B. Dixon

Bristol Council for Racial Equality, Colston House, Colston Street, Bristol BS1 5AQ
Tel: 0272 297899
Senior CRO: Peter Courtier

Gloucester Council for Community Relations, 15 Brunswick Road, Gloucester GL1 1HG
Tel: 0452 20483
CRO: Mr Ehsan-ul-Haq

Oxfordshire Committee for Community Relations, 44B Princes Street, Oxford OX4 1YP
Tel: 0865 240576
Chairperson: Mr Alam

Reading Council for Racial Equality, 2 Silver Street, Reading, Berks RG1 2ST
Tel: 0734 868755
CRO: Lester L. Lewis

Southampton Community Relations Council, 12 Palmerstone Road, Southampton SO1 1LL
Tel: 0703-29646
CRO: Mr Paul Hibbert

Thamesdown & District Council for Racial Equality, Farringdon House, 1 Farringdon Rd, Swindon, Wilts
Tel: 0793 28545
CRO: Mr Clive Norris

North & West Wiltshire Council for Racial Equality, Bridge House, Stallard Street, Trowbridge, Wilts
Tel: 02214 66439
CRO: Mr S. Foster

South East England

Aylesbury Vale Council for Racial Equality, 23A Walton Street, Aylesbury Bucks
Tel: 0296 25334
CRO: Mr B. Solanki

Bedford Community Relations Association, 36 Mill Street, Bedford MK40 3HD
Tel: 0234 50459/40728
CRO: Buddhdev Pandya

Chesham Committee for Community Relations, 35 Birch Way, Chesham, Bucks.
Tel: 0494 782820 (Home)
Hon. Secretary: Mr Ketteringham

Crawley Council for Community Relations, The Tree, 103 High Street, Crawley, Sussex
Tel: 0293-21058
CRO: Mr Erik Shopland

Eastbourne District Race Relations Council, 31 Ashburnham Place, Hailsham, East Sussex
Secretary: Mr Brian Burt

Essex Community Relations Council, Civic Centre (3rd floor), Victoria Avenue, Southend, Essex SS2 6EP
Tel: 0702 333351
CRO: Ms Marion Press
also
Gary Pryce
Church Walk House Church Walk, Basildon, Essex
Tel: 0268 22881

Gravesend & District Community Relations Council, 11 Parrock Street, Gravesend, Kent DA12 1BA
Tel: 0474 25885
CRO: Mr Gurdhev Singh Talwar

Ipswich & District Council for Community Relations, 17 Woodbridge Road, Ipswich, Suffolk
Tel: 0473 221954
CRO: Clive Sykes

Medway & Gillingham Community Relations Council, 114 Maidstone Road, Chatham, Kent ME4 6DQ
Tel: 0634 403001
CRO: (in charge) Ms Margot Kane

Milton Keynes Council for Racial Equality, Loughton Community House, 19/21 Speaklands, Loughton MK5 8DA
CRO: Ms L. Haq

Watford Community Relations Council, 16 Clarendon Road, Watford WD1 1JY
Tel: 0923 37005/56044
CRO: Mr Hemant Mistry

Wycombe & District CommunityRelations Council, 272 Desborough Road, High Wycombe, Bucks.
Tel: 0494 27616/0494 44339
CRO: Mr Alfred Webley

Wales

Pwyllgor Cyslltiadau Cymdeithas De Morgannwg, (South Glamorgan Committee for Community Relations), Room 10/11, 91 St Mary Street, Cardiff CF1 1NB
Tel: 0222 24097
CRO: H.S. Preet Ryatt

Gwent Community Relations Council, Gloucester Chambers (2nd floor), Skinner Street, Newport
Tel: 0633 50006
CRO: Mr M.M. Patel

West Glamorgan Community Relations Council, 1st Floor 23 Mansel Street, Swansea
Tel: 0792 42768
Chairman: Mr Ray Singh

West Midlands

Birmingham Community Relations Council, St Georges House, 32-34 Hill Street, Birmingham B5 4AN
Tel: 021-235 4097/2724
Principal CRO: Mr Leslie de Siriwardena

Coventry Community Relations Council, 58-64 Corporation Street, (Side entrance of Gibbs Elec. shop), Coventry, CV1 1GS
Tel: 0203 632236
Senior CRO: Mr A.J. Waugh

Dudley Community Relations Council, 16a Stone Street, Dudley, DY1 1NS, West Midlands
Tel: 0384 53167
CRO: Gurdial Singh Dhanjal

East Staffordshire Council for Racial Equality, Orchard House (formerly St. Modwen's Vicarage), Orchard Street, Burton-upon-Trent DE14 3SJ
Tel: 0283 53167
Chairman: Rev K. Channer

North Staffordshire Community Relations Council, Tontine Buildings (1st floor), Tontine Street, Hanley, Stoke-on-Trent, Staffs. ST1 1LY
Tel: 0782 24061
CRO: Mr M. Arshad

Redditch Community Relations Council, Town Hall, Alcester Street, Redditch, Worcestershire B98 8AH
Tel: 75 64252
Chairman: Mr Ernie E. Bond

Rugby Community Relations Council, 5 Pennington Street, Rugby CV21 1AZ
Tel: 0788 76424
CRO: Mr H.J. Hanoomansingh

Sandwell Council for Community Relations, 230A High Street (Arcade), West Bromwich, West Midlands B70 7QG
Tel: 021 525 1488
Senior CRO: Mr G.S. Sidhu

Stafford Community Relations Committee, SDVS Centre, Chell Road, Stafford ST£6 2QA
Tel; 0785 46471
Development Officer: Mrs A. Sinclair
Stoke and District Community Relations Council, 83 Stoke Road, Stoke-on-Trent

Walsall Council for Community Relations, The Advice Centre, 4-6 Lower Hall Lane, Walsall WS1 1RH
Tel: 0922 39090/0922 612448/
0922 21244 ext. 3263

Warwick District Community Relations Council, Mr Sarjit Singh Myrrpurey, 28 Hamilton Terrace, Leamington Spa, Warwicks, CV32 4LY
Tel: 0926 21447

Worcester Community Relations Council, The Old Palace, Deansway, Worcester WR1 2JE
Chairman: Rev. J. Quill

Wolverhampton Council for Community Relations, 2 Clarence Road, (off Clarence Street), Wolverhampton WV1 4HZ
Tel: 0902 27811 ext. 2304
0902 773589 & 773580
Senior CRO: Mr E.E. Warner

East Midlands

Cambridge Council for Racial Equality, 'The Bathhouse', Gwydir Street, Cambridge CB1 2LW
Tel: 0223 60333
Chairman: Hugh Carrington

Borough of Charnwood Community Relations Council, 43 Church Gate, Loughborough LE11 1UE
Tel: 0509-261651
CRO: Sandy Leong

Chesterfield Community Relations Steering Committee, 18 Dorset Drive, Brimington, Chesterfield, Derbyshire, S43 1DS
Tel: 0245 206711
Secretary: Mr Bernard Cummins

Derby Council for Racial Equality, 31 Mormanton Road, Derby DE1 2GJ
Tel: 0332 372428
CRO: Mr Tony Walsh

Leicestershire Steering Group for Racial Justice, 11 The Market Place 4th Floor, The Jetty, Leicester LE1 2ZL
Tel: 0533 549922 ext. 6074
Locum Worker: Mr Jagdep Singh Khahra

Northampton Council for Community Relations, 25 The Drapery Road, Northampton NN1 2ET
Tel: 0604 30722
CRO: Mr Richard Davis

Nottingham & District Community Relations Council, 67 Lower Parliament Street, Nottingham NG1 3BB
Tel: 0602 586515
Senior CRO: Mr Milton Crossdale

Peterborough Community Relations Council, 32 Russell Street, Peterborough PE1 2BQ
Tel: 0733 54630/0733 41061
CRO (Locum): Mr L.C. Simmons

Wellingborough District Community Relations Council, Victoria Community Centre, Palk Road, Wellingborough, Northants
Tel: 0933 78000
CRO: Mr Paul Crofts

North West England

Blackburn and District Community Relations Council, 11 Richmond Terrace, Blackburn BB1 7BD
Tel: 0254 61924
CRO: Mr Leonard Proos

Bolton Council for Community Relations, Room 39, Second Floor, Civic Centre, Le Mans Crescent, Bolton
Tel: 0204 28087/391567

Bury Metropolitan Borough Community Relations Council, 12 Tenterden Street, Bury
Tel: 061 761 4533
CRO: Mr H. Zaman

Hyndburn and Rossendale Community Relations Council, Regency House (2nd Floor), Blackburn Road, Accrington, Lancs. BB5 1HF
Tel: 0254 395719/395710
CRO: Mr Derek Loney

Manchester Council for Community Relations, Elliot House, 3 Jackson's Row, Deansgate, Manchester M2 5WD
Tel: 061 834 9153/4
Principal CRO: Mr Sayed Ahamed

Merseyside Community Relations Council, 64 Mount Pleasant, Liverpool L3 5SH
Tel: 051 709 0789/6858/6859
Senior CRO: Mr Alex Bennett

North East Lancashire Community Relations Council, 74 Manchester Road, Burnley, Lancs
Tel: 0282 54510
CRO: Mr Aziz A.Chaudhry

Oldham Council for Racial Equality, Cavendish House, 21 Union Street West, Oldham Lancs OL8 1DX
Tel: 061 678 4741/4
CRO: Mr Keith Bradford

Preston and Western Lancashire Council for Community Relations, Town Hall Annexe, P.O. Box No. 10, Birley Street, Preston PR1 2RL
Tel: 0772 266422
CRO: Mr M.F. Desai

Rochdale Community Relations Council, (All enquires to: Manchester Regional Office, CRE)
Tel: 061 831 7782

Tameside Council for Racial Equality, 35A Manchester Road, Denton, Manchester M34 3JU
Tel: 061 336 3359
CRO: Mr Dipak G. Chauhan, JP

Trafford Community Relations Sub-Committee, Trafford Borough Community and Family Advice Centre, 139 Stamford Street, Old Trafford, Manchester 16 9LT
Tel: 061-226 3206/7613

Yorkshire & North East England

Bradford Metropolitan District Community Relations Council, Mr Timothy Whitfield, Oakwell House, 8 Oak Avenue, Bradford BD8 7AQ
Tel: 0274 541358

Keighley Office: 2 North Queen Street, Keighley, BD21 3DL
Tel: 0535-607717

Calderdale Community Relations Council, 8 Wards End, Halifax HX1 1BX, West Yorkshire
Tel: 0422 60975/66804
CRO: Mr M.A. Bismil

Cleveland County Community Relations Council, 51A Kings Road, North Ormesby, Middlesbrough
Tel: 0642 222563
CRO: Mr Harbhajan Jagra

Doncaster Council for Racial Equality, 1 Chequer Road, Doncaster DN1 2AA
Tel: 0302 735201
CRO: Mr Lloyd Thomas

Kirklees Steering Committee for Community Relations
Dewsbury Office, Town Hall, Dewsbury WF12 8DG, West Yorkshire
Tel: 0924 465151 ext. 348
CRO: Mr Satish Malik

Huddersfield Office, 24 Westgate Huddersfield HD1 1NU
Tel: 0484 540225/6
ACRO: Mr Mohammed Aslam

Leeds Council for Community Relations, Centenary House, North Street, Leeds LS2 8JS
Tel: 0532 430696
Senior CRO: Mr John Roberts

Hull & District Council for Racial Equality, 2nd Floor, 79 Ferensway, Hull HU2
Tel: 0482 227601
CRO: Mr Steve Radford

Rotherham Community Relations Council, 11-13 Imperial Buildings, Corporation Street, Rotherham, South Yorkshire
Tel: 0709-373065
CRO: Mr Mohammed Almas Abbasi

Scunthorpe & District Community Relations Council, 106 Oswald Road, Scunthorpe, South Humberside DN15 7PA
Tel: 0724 281247

Sheffield Council for Racial Equality, 3 Surrey Place, Sheffield S1 2LP
Tel: 0742 727232/723951
Senior CRO: Dr Debjani Chatterjee

Tyne and Wear Community Relations Council, M.E.A. House, Ellison Place, Newcastle-upon-Tyne 1
Tel: 0632 327639
CRO: Mr Hariprasad M. Shukla

York & District for Community Relations, 10 Priory Street, York, North Yorks
Tel: 0904-610810
CRO: (Locum) Antonio DaSilva

Scotland

Lothian Community Relations Council, 12a Forth Street, Edinburgh EH1 3LH
Tel: 031 556 0441
Acting Senior CRO: Mrs Faroj Lal

Strathclyde Community Relations Council, 115 Wellington Street (2nd Floor), Glasgow G2
Tel: 041 227 6048
Senior CRO: Mrs Maggie Chetty

Tayside Community Relations Council, 20 Paterson Street, Dundee DD3 6QR
Tel: 0382 818806
CRO: (in charge) Andrew Jeffries

Grampian Community Relations Council, 74 College Street, Aberdeen AB1 2JP
Tel: 0224 57340
CRO: (in charge) Mrs Sabehia Mohamed

Central Region Community Relations Council, 12 Eastmains, Menstrie, Scotland FK11 7AW
CRO: (in charge) Mrs Pek Yeong Berry

Selected Addresses

Catholic Commission for Racial Justice, Church Hall, 1 Amwell Street, London EC1R 1UL
Tel: 01 278 5880

Commonwealth Foundation, Marlborough House, Pall Mall, London SW1
Tel: 01 930 1594

Community & Race Relations Unit, British Council of Churches, 2 Eaton Gate, London SW1W 9BT
Tel: 01 730 9611

Community Service Volunteers, 237 Pentonville Road, London N1
Tel: 01 278 6601

Friends Community Relations Committee, Friends House, Euston Road, London NW1 2BJ
Tel: 01 387 3601

Home Office, Immigration and Nationality Department, Lunar House, Wellesley Road, Croydon CR9 2BY
Tel: 01 686 0333/01 686 0688

Home Office, Community Programmes Department, 50 Queen Anne's Gate, London SW1H 9AT
Tel: 01 213 3000

Institute of Race Relations, 247/249 Pentonville Road, London N1
Tel: 01 837 0041

International Defense & Aid Fund for Southern Africa, Canon Collins House, 64 Essex Road, London N1 8LR
Tel: 01 359 9181

Joint Council for the Welfare of Immigrants, 115 Old Street, London EC1
Tel: 01 251 8706

London Voluntary Service Council, 68 Chalton Street, London NW1
Tel: 01 388 0241

Martin Luther King Foundation, 1-3 Hildreth Street, London SW12 9RQ
Tel: 01 673 6511/6512

Minority Rights Group, 36 Craven Street, London WC2N 5NG
Tel: 01 930 6659

National Council for Civil Liberties, 21 Tabard Street, London SE1
Tel: 01 403 3888

National Councl for Voluntary Organisations, 26 Bedford Square, London WC1
Tel: 01 636 4066

National Association of Citizens Advice Bureax, 110 Drury Lane, London WC2B 5SW
Tel: 01 836 9231

National Association of Community Relations Councils, 8-10 Coronet Street (lst floor), London N1 6HD
Tel: 01 739 6658

London Association of Community Relations Councils, Middlesex House, Room 505, 20 Vauxhall Bridge Road, London SW1V 2SB
Tel: 01 821 6449

The Runnymede Trust, 37A Gray's Inn Road, London WC1 8PS
Tel: 01 404 5266

UK Immigrants' Advisory Service, Brettenham House, 7th Floor, Savoy Street, Strand, London WC2E 7EN
Tel: 01 240 5176

Race Relations Employment Advisory Service, Department of Employment, Headquarters: Caxton House, Tothill Street, London SW1
Tel: 01 213 3000

Southern Division Race Relations Employment Advisory Service, Department of Employment, Red Lion Square, London WC1R 4NH
Tel: 01 405 8454

Northern Division Race Relations Advisory Service, Department of Employment, C/O Manpower Services Commission, 1 Moorfoot, Sheffield S1 4PQ
Tel: 0742-703745

Organisations involved in Race Relations

Anti-Apartheid Movement
13 Mandela Street, Camden, London NW1 ODW
Tel: 01 387 7966

All-Party Parliamentary Group on Race Relations
178 North Gower Street, London NW1 2NB
Tel: 01 387 9322

The Board of Deputies of British Jews
Woburn House (4th floor), Upper Woburn Place, London WC1H OEP
Tel: 01 387 3952

British Youth Council
57 Chalton Street, London NW1 1HU

Catholic Association for Racial Justice
St. Vincent's Community Centre, Talma Road, Brixton, London SW2 1AS
Tel: 01 274 0024

The Committee for Community Relations
39 Eccleston Square, London SW1V 1PD
Tel: 01 834 8692

Commonwealth Institute
Kensington High Street, London W8 6NQ
Tel: 01 603 4535 ext. 221, 226, 259

Community & Race Relations Unit
British Council of Churches
2 Eaton Gate, London SW1W 9BT
Tel: 01 730 9611

Community Service Volunteers
237 Pentonville Road, London N1
Tel: 01 278 6601

Evangelical Christian for Racial Justice
12 Bell Barn Shopping Centre, Cregoe Street, Birmingham B15 2DZ
Tel: 021 622 6807

Friends Community Relations Committee
Friends House, Euston Road, London NW1 2BJ
Tel: 01 387 3601

International Social Service of G.B.
Cranmer House, 39 Brixton Road, London SW9
Tel: 01 735 8941

Institute of Race Relations
2-6 Leeke Street, King's Cross Road, London WC1X 9HS
Tel: 01 837 0041

Joint Council for the Welfare of Immigrants
115 Old Street, Islington, London EC1
Tel: 01 251 8706

London Voluntary Service Council
68 Chalton Street, London NW1
Tel: 01 388 0241

Minority Rights Group
29 Craven Street, London WC2N 5NG
Tel: 01 930 6659

National Association of Citizens Advice Bureaux
Myddleton House, 115-123, Pentonville Road, London N1
Tel: 01 833 2181

National Association of Community Relations Council
8-16 Coronet Street (1st floor), London N1 6HD
Tel: 01 739 6658

National Council of Social Service (Incorp)
26 Bedford Square, London WC1
Tel: 01 636 4066

The Runnymede Trust
178 North Gower Street, London NW1 2NB
Tel: 01 387 8943

UK Immigrants' Advisory Service
County House, 190 Great Dover Street, London SE1
Tel: 01 397 6917

Embassies and High Commissions

Embassy of the Democratic Republic of Afghanistan, 31 Princes Gate, London SW7
Tel: 01 589 8891

United States of American Embassy, 24 Grosvenor Square, London W1
Tel: 01 499 9000

Angola Press Agency, The National News Agency, UK Office, 16 Maddox Street, London W1
Tel: 01 493 1611

Anguilla, General Enquiries, Windotel Ltd., Suite 19 College House, 29-31 Wrights Lane, London W8
Tel: 01 937 7725

Antigua and Barbuda, High Commission, 15 Thayer Street, London W1
Tel: 01 486 7073

Argentine Embassy, Economic Counsellor, 111 Cadogan Gardens, London SW3
Tel: 01 730 4388/7997

Australian High Commission, Australia House, Strand, London WC2
Tel: 01 438 8000

Bahamas High Commission, 39 Pall Mall, London SW1
Tel: 01 930 6967

Bangladesh High Commission, 28 Queens Gate, London SW7
Tel: 01 584 0081

Barbados High Commission, 1 Great Russell Street, London WC1B 3NH
Tel: 01 631 4975

Belize High Commission, 15 Thayer Street, London W1
Tel: 01 486 8381

Benin Consulate, 125 High Street, Edgware, Middlesex
Tel: 01 951 1234

Bolivian Embassy, 106 Eaton Square, London SW1
Tel: 01 235 4248

Botswana High Commission, 162 Buckingham Palace Road, London SW1
Tel: 01 703 5216

Brazilian Embassy, 32 Green Street, London W1
Tel: 01 499 0877

Brunei Government, 47 Cromwell Road, London SW7
Tel: 01 581 0521

Burmese Embassy, 19a Charles Street, London W1
Tel: 01 629 6966

Burundi, Embassy of the Republic, Square Marie Louis 46, 1040 Brussels
Tel: 230 45 35

Embassy of the United Republic of Cameroon, 84 Holland Park, London W11
Tel: 01 727 8436

Canadian High Commission, Macdonald House, 1 Grosvenor Square, London W1,
Tel: 01 629 9492

Cayman Island, 17b Curzon Street, London W1
Tel: 01 408 2482

Central African Republic, 29 Boulevard Montmorency, 75016 Paris, France

Chad, Embassy of the Republic, Boulevard Lambermount 52, 1030 Brussels, Belgium
Tel: 215 1975

Chilean Embassy, 12 Devonshire Street, London W1
Tel: 01 580 6392

Chinese Embassy, 31 Portland Place, London W1, Tel: 01 636 9939

Colombian Embassy, 3 Hans Crescent, London SW1
Tel: 01 589 9177

Congo, Embassy of the People's Republic, 37 bis Rue Paul Valery, 75116 Paris
Tel: 500 60 57

Costa Rican Embassy, 225 Cromwell Road, London SW5
Tel: 01 373 7050

Cyprus High Commission, 93 Park Street, London W1
Tel: 01 499 8272

Cuban Embassy, 167 High Holborn, London WC1
Tel: 01 240 2488

Dominican Republic Embassy, 4 Braemar Mansions, Cornwall Gardens, London SW7
Tel: 01 937 1921

Dominican High Commission, 1 Collingham Gardens, London SW5
Tel: 01 373 8751

Eastern Caribbean Commission, 10 Kensington Court, London W8
Tel: 01 937 9522

Ecuadorean Embassy, Flat 3b, 3 Hans Crescent, Knightsbridge, London SW1X OLS
Tel: 01 584 1367

Egypt Arab Republic, 75 South Audley Street, London W1
Tel: 01 499 2401

Embassy of El Salvador, 9 Welbeck House, 62 Welbeck Street, London W1
Tel: 01 486 8182

Ethiopian Embassy, 17 Princes Gate, London SW7
Tel: 01 589 7212

Fiji High Commission, 34 Hyde Park Gate, London SW7
Tel: 01 584 3661

Embassy of the Republic of Gabon, 48 Kensington Court, London W8
Tel: 01 937 5285

Gambia High Commission, 57 Kensington Close, London W8
Tel: 01 937 6316

Ghana High Commission, 13 Belgrave Square, London SW1
Tel: 01 937 6316

Grenada High Commission, 1 Collingham Gardens, London SW5
Tel: 01 373 7808

High Commission for Guyana, 3 Palace Court, London W2

Embassy of the Republic of Haiti, 36 Abbots House, St Mary Abbots Terrace, London W14 8NV
Tel: 01 602 3194

Honduras Republic Embassy, 47 Manchester Street, London W1
Tel: 01 486 3380

High Commission for India, India House, Aldwych, London WC2
Tel: 01 836 8484

Embassy of the Republic of Indonesia, 38 Grosvenor Square, London W1
Tel: 01 499 7661

Ivory Coast Embassy, 2 Upper Belgrave Street, London SW1
Tel: 01 235 6991

Jamaican High Commission. 63 St James, London SW1
Tel: 01 499 8600

Kenya High Commission, 45 Portland Place, London W1N 4AS
Tel: 01 636 2371/6

Kiribati Ministry of Foreign Affairs, P.O. Box 68, Bairiki, Kiribati Tarawa

Lesotho High Commission, 10 Collingham Road, London SW5
Tel: 01 373 8581

Liberian Embassy, 21 Princes Gate, London SW7
Tel: 01 589 9405

Malawi High Commission, 38 Grosvenor Street, London W1
Tel: 01 491 4172

Malaysia, Office of the High Commissioner, 45 Belgrave Square, London SW1
Tel: 01 235 8033

Maldives, , Info: Maldives Services Ltd, 50/52 Great Eastern Street, London EC2A 3EP
Tel: 01 729 5721

Malta High Commission, 16 Kensington Square, London W8
Tel: 01 938 1712

Mauritius High Commission, 32 Elvaston Place, London SW7
Tel: 01 581 0294

Mexican Embassy, 8 Halkin Street, London SW1
Tel: 01 235 6393

Mongolian Embassy, 7 Kensington Court, London W8
Tel: 01 937 5238

Moroccan Embassy, 49 Queen's Gate Garden, London W8
Tel: 01 581 5001

Mozambique Information Office, 34 Percy Street, London W1
Tel: 01 636 7108

Nauru Government, 11 Livingstone House, Carteret Street, London SW1
Tel: 01 222 3373

The Royal Embassy of Nepal, 12a Kensington Palace Gardens, London W8
Tel: 01 229 1594

New Zealand High Commission, New Zealand House, Haymarket, London SW1
Tel: 01 930 8422

Embassy of Nicaragua, 8 Gloucester Road, London SW7
Tel: 01 584 4365

Niger Embassy, 154 Rue de Longchamp, 75116 Paris, France
Tel: 567 61 89

Nigeria High Commission, Nigeria House, 9 Northumberland Avenue, London WC2
Tel: 01 839 1244

Embassy of Nicaragua, 8 Gloucester Road, London SW7 4PP
Tel: 01 584 4365

Embassy of Pakistan, 35 Lowndes Square, London SW1
Tel: 01 235 2044

Embassy of Panama, 2nd Floor, Eagle House, 109 Jermyn Street, London SW1
Tel: 01 930 1591/2

Papua New Guinea High Commission, 14 Waterloo Palace, London SW1
Tel: 01 930 0922

Paraguay Embassy, Braemar Lodge, Cornwall Gardens, London SW7
Tel: 01 937 1253

Peruvian Embassy, 52 Sloane Street, London SW1
Tel: 01 235 1917

Philippine Embassy, 9a Palace Gardens, London W8
Tel: 01 937 1609

Rwanda Embassy, Boulevards St Michel 101, 1040 Brussels, Belgium
Tel: 734 17 63

St. Lucia, St. Kitts-Nevis, St. Vincent & The Grenadines, Montserrat
Tel: 01 937 9522

Embassy of the Republic of Senegal, 11 Phillimore Gardens, London W8
Tel: 01 937 3139

Seychelles High Commission, Diplomatic Mission, 50 Conduit Street, London W1
Tel: 01 439 0405

High Commission for the Republic of Singapore, Chancery, 2 Wilton Crescent, London SW1
Tel: 01 235 8315

Sierra Leone High Commission, 33 Portland Place, London W1N 3AG
Tel: 01 636 6483/6

High Commission for Sri Lanka, 13 Hyde Park Gardens, London W2
Tel: 01 262 1841

Solomon Isles, Ministry of Foreign Affairs, Honiara, Solomon Islands

Somali Embassy, 60 Portland Place, London W1
Tel: 01 580 7140

Embassy of the Soviet Union, 18 Kensington Palace Gardens, London W8
Tel: 01 229 6412

Sudan Embassy, 3 Cleveland Road, St. James, London SW1A 1DD
Tel: 01 839 8080

Swaziland Kingdom, High Commissioner, 58 Pont Street, London SW1
Tel: 01 581 4976

Tanzania United Republic High Commission, 43 Hertford Street, London W1
Tel: 01 499 8951

Tonga High Commission, New Zealand House, Haymarket, London SW1Y 4TE
Tel: 01 839 3287

Trinidad and Tobago High Commission, 42 Belgrave Square, London SW1
Tel: 01 245 9351

Tunisian Embassy, 29 Princess Gate, London SW7 1QC
Tel: 01 584 8117

Tuvalu Minister of Foreign Affairs, Funa Futi, Tuvala

Uganda High Commission, Uganda House, Trafalgar Square, London WC2
Tel: 01 839 5783

Uruguay Embassy, 48 Lennox Gardens, London SW1
Tel: 01 589 8835

Vanuatu, Minister of Foreign Affairs, Port Vila, Vanuatu

Venezuelan Embassy, Cromwell Road, London SW7
Tel: 01 584 4206

Vietnam Embassy, 12 Victory Road, London W8
Tel: 01 937 1913

Western Samoa, Minister of Foreign Affairs, Apia, Western Samoa

Diplomatic Mission of the Republic of Zaire, 26 Chesham Place, London SW1
Tel: 01 235 7122

High Commission for the Republic of Zambia, 7-11 Cavendish Place, London WiN OHB
Tel: 01 580 0691

Zimbabwe High Commission, Zimbabwe House, 429 Strand, London WC2R OSA
Tel: 01 836 7755

Minority Women's Groups

African Refugee Women's, Group, c/o African Refugee Housing Action Ltd, 25 Leighton Road, London NW5 or 42 Albany Street, London NW1

Afro-Caribbean Mental Association, 48 East Lake Road, London SE5 9QL
Tel: 01 737 3604

African Women's Association, Mameisis Project (A.W.A.), 135 Clarence Road, London E5 8EE
Tel: 01 985 0147

Arab Women's Group, c/o Outwrite, Oxford House, Derbyshire Street, London E2 6HG

Asian Action Group, 30 Willoughby Road, Hornsey, London N8
Tel: 01-341 3802

Asian Women's Aid
Tel: 01 703 4319/4291

Asian Women's Association, 40 Argyle Road, Ilford, Essex
Tel: 01 518 0725

Asian Women Community Workers Group, 10 Bernays Grove, London SW9
Tel: 01-737 3617/8

Asian Women's Contact Network, Tindlemanor, 52-54 Featherstone Street, London EC1Y 8TR
Tel: 01 251 9276

Asian Women's Forum, c/o Asian Centre, 8 Caxton Road, London N22
Tel: 01 889 6938

Bangladesh Women's Association, 91 Highbury Hill, London N5

Battersea Black Women's Group, 248 Lavender Hill, London SW11
Tel: 01 228 8532
Open only Sundays 4pm onwards. Creche provided. Discussion meetings on general issues.

Bengali Women's Group, Thornhill Neighbourhood Centre, Orkney House, Caledonian Road, London N1

Berner Tenants Women's Centre, Philchurch Place, Pinchin Street, London E1
Tel: 01 481 2968

Black Women Conference, Mill Street Activity Centre, Mill Street, Derby
Tel: 0332 45538

Black Female Prisoners Scheme, 141 Stockwell Road, London SW9
Tel: 01 733 5520

Black Women's Radio Group, c/o Local Radio Workshop, 12 Praed Mews, London W2

Black Women for Wages for Housework, P.O. Box 287, King's Cross Women's Centre, London NW6
Tel: 01 837 7509

Black Women's Writing Workshop, c/o Women's Night Out, The Albany, Douglas Way, Deptford, London SE8 4AG
Tel: 01-692 0231

Black Women's Action Group, 30 Wolverton, Sedan Way, Walworth, London SE17
Tel: 01 708 4162

Brent Black Women's Group, 12 Donovan Court, Exton Crescent, London NW10
Tel: 01 961 3337/01 965 2477/01 965 0047

Brent Asian Women's Resource Centre, 134 Minet Avenue, London NW10
Tel: 01 961 5701

Brixton Black Women's Centre, Mary Seacole House, 41a Stockwell Green, London SW9
Tel: 01 274 9220

Camden & Islington Black Sisters, c/o Law Centre, 146 Kentishtown Road, London NW5
Tel: 01 485 6672

Centre for Black Women, 136 Kingsland High Road, PO Box 29, London E8

Claudia Jones Organisation, 103 Stoke Newington Church Street, London N16
Tel: 01 241 1646

Croydon Asian Womens Group, c/o Secretary, 9 Howden Road, London SE25
Tel: 01 653 1565

East London Black Women's Organisation, 747 Barking Road, Plaistow, London E13
Tel: 01 552 1169

Eleanor Street Women's Group, 8 Eleanor Street, Bow, London E3

Eritrean Women's Association, BCM Box 7007, London WC1
Tel: 01 794 6931

FAEERU Women's Group, 116 Ladbroke Grove, London W10
Tel: 01 221 2007

Grainne Mhaol Collective, 26 Boscombe Road, London W12

Greenwich Asian Women's Centre, c/o Macbean Centre, Macbean Street, London SE18
Tel: 01 854 1188

Greenwich Asian Women's Group, c/o Asian Resource Centre, LEB Buildings, Macbean Street, London SE18

Hackney Muslim Women's Council, 101 Clapton Common, London E5
Tel: 01 809 0993

Hackney Pakistan Women's Centre, 42 Stamford Hill, London N16
Tel: 01 806 3289

Haringey Black Women's Group/Centre, c/o Old Somerset School, Lordship Lane, London N1
Tel: 01 802 0912

Hounslow Asian Women's Community Centre, 126 Hanworth Road, Hanworth, Middlesex
Tel: 01 572 2484

Immigration Widows Campaign, c/o 131/132 Upper Street, London N1
Tel: 01 354 0133

Iranian Women's Support Group, c/o Spare Rib, 27 Clerkenwell Close, London EC1

Latin American Women's Group . CARILA, 29 Islington Park Street, London N1
Tel: 01 359 2270

Lewisham Asian Association Women's Section, 170 New Cross Road, London SE14

London Black Women's Health Project, Wickham House, 10 Cleaveland Way, London E1

Milap Ladies Group, Milap Day Centre, Town Hall Annexe, Southall, Middlesex
Tel: 01 843 1893

Millan Asian Centre, 59 Trinity Road, London SW17
Tel: 01 767 8628

Muslim Women's Welfare Association, 200 Capworth Street, London E10
Tel: 01 539 7478

National Union of Eritrean Women, BCM Box 7007, London WC1V 6XX

Pakistan Women's Welfare, Association, 20 Blackstock Road, London N4
Tel: 01 226 4427

Pakistan Women's Movement, Movement, 3 Downe Mansions, Gondal Gardens, London NW6

Peckham Black Women's Centre, c/o St Giles Parish Hall, Benhill Road, London SE5
Tel: 01 701 2651

Philippine Women's Centre, 1/2 Grangeway, London NW6 2BW
Tel: 01 624 0247

The Phoenix Womens Centre, c/o 226 Camberwell Road, London SE5
Tel: 01 701 7121

Pragati Asian Women's Association, 9-13 Nicoll Road, London NW10
Tel: 01 965 8643

Rights of Women, 52-54 Featherstone Street, London EC2
Tel: 01 251 6577

Shepherds Bush Black Women's Group, c/o 119 or 139 Becklow Road, London W12

Somali Women's Group, c/o 6 Oxford House, Derbyshire Street, London E2

Southall Black Women's Centre, 86 Northcote Avenue, Southall, Middlesex
Tel: 01 843 0578

Southwark Muslim Women's Association, Old Bellenden School, Bellenden, London SE15
Tel: 01 732 8053

SWAPO Women's Council, 96 Gillespie Road, London N5
Tel: 01 359 9116/7

Tamil Women's League, 42 Sickert Court, 3 Canonbury Street, London N1
Tel: 01-226 2367

Talawa Women's Collective, 19 Vernon Close, Hillfields, Coventry
Tel: 0203 23941

Theatre of Black Women, Box 6, 136 Kingsland Road, Dalston, London E8 2NS
Tel: 01 249 1660

United Black Women's Action Group, c/o Wood Green Community Centre, Stanley Road, London N15
Tel: 01 802 0911

Westindian Women's Organisation, 71 Pound Lane, London NW10
Tel: 01 451 4827/4961

Women & Employment Resource Centre, 179 Deptford High Street, London SE8

Woolwich Black Women's Group, c/o Simba Project, 48-50 Artillery Place, London SE15
Tel: 01 317 0451

Zimbabwe Womens Co-op (UK) Ltd., c/o 15 Sylvan Avenue, London N22 5HX
Tel: 01-346 2486/01-881 4246/5120

Projects and Resources based at 5a Westminster Bridge Road:
Asian Sheltered Residential Association Co. Ltd
Black Teens Magazine
Black Trades Union Solidarity Movemen
Multi-lingual Print Shop
Racism Awareness Programme Unit

Tanya, Latin American Women's Grou
Tel: 01 969 2433

Brazilian Women's Group
Tel: 01 928 8108

Sickle Cell Anaemia Research Organisations

Organisation for Sickle Cell Anaemia Research (O.S.C.A.R.) National Headquarters, 200a High Road, Wood Green, London N22 4HH
Tel: 01 889 4844/3300

Branches

OSCAR Birmingham, 12 Cregoe Street, Bell Barn Shopping Centre, Lee Bank, Birmingham B15 2DZ
Tel: 021-622 6806

OSCAR Bristol, c/o Homeland Travel, 58 St Nicholas Road, St Pauls, Bristol BS2
Tel: 0272-551917

OSCAR Lewisham, Forest Hill Youth Project, 2-4 Devonshire Road, Forest Hill, London SE23
Tel: 01 291 3976

OSCAR Nottingham, Ukaidi Centre, 9 Marple Square, off Woodborough Road, St Ann's, Nottingham
Tel: 0602-583173

OSCAR Reading, Appollo Youth Club, 24/26 Mount Pleasant, Reading
Tel: 0734-751 242

OSCAR Waltham Forest, 316 Hoe Street, London E17
Tel: 01 521 2334

Projects sponsored by OSCAR

Enfield Sickle Cell Project, Angel Community Centre, Raynham Road, Edmonton, London N18
Tel: 01 803 4222
Supervisor: Dr. S. Patel

Hackney Sickle Cell Project, 1 Kingsway Parade, Albion Road, Stoke Newington, London N16
Tel: 01 249 2924
Supervisor: Dr. K.O. Aseidu

Haringey Sickle Cell Project, 200a High Road, Wood Green, London N22 4HH
Tel: 01 881 0748
Supervisor: Mr Andrew Attfield,

Walthamstow Forest Sickle Cell Project, 316 Hoe Street, Walthamstow, London E17
Tel: 01 521 3709
Senior Supervisor: Mr O. Owen

Sickle Cell Society

Birmingham Branch, Lilieth Smith, Carnegie Centre for Health Promotion, Hunters Road, Hockley, Birmingham B19 1DE
Tel: 021 554 3899 ext. 236

Lambeth Sickle Cell Centre, 2 Stockwell Road, Stockwell, London SW9
Tel: 01 737 3588

Leeds Branch, Mrs L Powell, 66 Middleton Avenue, Burmantofts, Leeds LS9 7JM
Tel: 0532-488 8314

Main Branch, Ms Erica Powell, Office Manager/Secretary, Brent Sickle Cell Centre, Willesden Hospital, Harlesden Road, London NW10 3RY
Tel: 01 451 1292 ext. 4235

North & East London Branch, Mrs M. Rollins, c/o Durning Hall, Earlham Grove, Forest Gate, London E7
Tel: 01 478 5351/01 534 0085 (Day)
01 472 8998 (Evening),

Sickle Cell Centre, Moss Side Health Centre, Monton Street, Manchester M14 4GP
Tel: 061-226 8972

Slough Branch, Mrs Jeanetta Glasford, Secretary, 25 New Church Road, Slough, Berks
Tel: 75 26156

Southampton Sickle Cell Society, Ms Coleen Forbes/, Mr Saleen Gilliam, Social & Community Centre, Trinity Road, St Mary's, Southampton SO2 OBE
Tel: (0703) 2263388

Other Sickle Cell Centres

Sickle Cell Anaemia Research Foundation, Suite 4, 3 Bluefontein Avenue, London W12 7NX
Tel: 01 749 4934
Con. Melville Jones

Sheffield Sickle Cell Group, Ms M Reid, 48 The Wicker, Sheffield S3

List of NHS Sickle Cell Counselling Centres

Birmingham, Mrs Lillieth Smith, Birmingham Sickle Cell Centre, Community Service Unit, St Patricks, Highgate Street, Birmingham, B12 OYA
Tel: 021 440 6161

Brent, Ms Elizabeth N. Anionwu, Brent Sickle Cell Centre, Willesden Hospital, Harlesdon Road, London NW10 3RY
Tel: 01 459 1292 Ext. 4235

Cardiff, Mary Choiseul, Cardiff Sickle Cell & Thalassemia Centre, Bute Town Health Centre, Loundoun Square, Docks Cardiff
Tel: 0222 4888 026

City and Hackney, Mrs. Cora Woolcock, City and Hackney Sickle Cell Centre, St. Leonard Hospital, Nuttal Street, London N1 5LZ
Tel: 01 739 8484 ext. 369,

Haringey, Mrs Marjorie Ferguson, Prince of Wales Hospital, St. Leonards Hospital, Nuttal Street, London N1 5LZ

Islington, Lorna Bennett, Sickle Cell Centre, Royal Northern Hospital, Holloway Road, London N7
Tel: 01 272 7777 ext. 351

Lambeth, Christine William, Lambeth Sickle Cell Centre, Swan Mews, 2 Stockwell Road, London SW9 9EN
Tel: 01 737 3588/326 1495

Liverpool, Dorothy Zakwilliams, Liverpool Sickle Cell Centre, Abercomby Health Centre, Grove Street, Liverpool 8
Tel: 051 708 9370

Manchester, Verna Angus, Sickle Cell Centre, Moss Side Health Centre, Monton Street, Manchester 14
Tel: 061 226 8972/226 5031

Newham, Comfort Okolo, Shrewsbury Road Health Centre, Shrewsbury Road, Forest Gate, London E7 8QR
Tel: 01 470 1311 ext. 38

St Thomas Hospital, Rachael Ceilia, c/o Community Midwife's Office, St. Thomas's Hospital, London SE1 7EH
Tel: 01 928 9292 ext. 3123

Useful Addresses

Political Party Headquarters

The Communist Party of Great Britain, 16 St John Street, London EC1M 4AL
Tel: 01 251 4406

Conservative Party, 32 Smith Square, London SW1
Tel: 01 222 9000

The Co-operative Party, 158 Buckingham Palace Road, London SW1
Tel: 01 730 8187

Democratic Unionist Party, 1a Ava Avenue, Ormeau Road, Belfast BT7 3BN
Tel: 0232 691021

The Labour Party, 150 Walworth Road, London SE17
Tel: 01 703 0833

Plaid Cymru, 51 Cathedral Road, Cardiff
Tel: 0222 31944

Scottish National Party, 6 North Charlotte Street, Edinburgh
Tel: 031 336 3661

Sinn Fein, 51/55 Falls Road, Belfast BT12, Northern Ireland
Tel: 0232 323214

Social Liberal Democratic Party (SLDP), 4 Cowley Street, London SW1E 3NB
Tel: 01 222 4141

Ulster Unionist Party, 3 Glengall Street, Belfast
Tel: 0232 24601

National Organisations

Afro-Westindian United Council of Churches, Caribbean House, Bridport Place, Shoreditch Park, London N1 5DS
Tel: 01 729 0986

Federation of Bangladesh Youth Organisations, Montifiore Community Centre, Deal Street, London E1
Tel: 01 247 8818

National Adoption Society, Hooper Cottage, Kimberly Road, London NW6
Tel: 01 328 7786

National Anti-Racist Movement in Education (N.A.M.E.), P.O. Box 9, Walsall, West Midlands WS1 3SF
Tel: 0922 25124 ext. 298

National Association for Asians (Hqts), 46 High Street, Southall, Middx.
Tel: 01 574 1325

National Association of Black Businessmen, 44 Coventry Road, Small Heath, Birmingham
Tel: 021 771 0719

National Association of Community Relations Council, 8-16 Coronet Street, London N1 6HD
Tel: 01 739 6658/9

National Association of Community Relations Officers, Ethnic Minorities Development Unit, 169 Clapham Road, London SW9

National Association of Multi-Racial Education, 30 Lawrence Street, Glasgow G11

National Association of Patidar Samaj, 31 Bishops Park Road, Norbury, London SW16 5TX

National Association of Youth Clubs, 70 St Nicholas Circle, Leciester LE1 5NY
Tel: 0535 29514

National Committee on Racism in Children's Books, 6 Vernon Road, London N8
Con. Ms Ann Thompson

National Council for Civil Liberties, 21 Tabard Street, London SE1
Tel: 01 403 3888

National Council of Hindu Associations (NCHA), 41 Morris Avenue, Coventry CV2 5GU
Tel: 0203 445 044

National Council for One Parent Families, 255 Kentish Town Road, London NW5
Tel: 01 267 1361

National Council for Voluntary Organisations, 26 Bedford Square, London WC1B 3HU
Tel: 01 636 4066

National Convention of Black Teachers (NCT), P.O. Box 30, Pinner, Middlesex HA5 5EV
Tel: 01 866 1682

National Film Development Corporation of India, 42 Hertford Street, London W1
Tel: 01 499 7711

National Film Theatre, South Bank, London SE1
Tel: 01 928 3232

National Gallery, Trafalgar Square, London WC2
Tel: 01 839 3321

National Society for the Prevention of Cruelty to Children, (National Headquarters 24 hour service), 67 Saffron Hill, London EC1
Tel: 01 242 1626

National Union of Asian Students (NUAS), 32 Clarke Street, Shelton, Stoke-on-Trent, Staffordshire ST2 4PT

National Union of Students, 461 Holloway Road, London N7
Tel: 01 272 8900

National Union of Teachers, Hamilton House, Mabledon Place, London WC1
Tel: 01 388 6191

Royal Commonwealth Society, 18 Northumberland Avenue, London WC2
Tel: 01 930 6733

Royal Society for Asian Affairs, 42 Devonshire Street, London W1
Tel: 01 580 5728

Black Workshops

Black Audio Film Collective, 3rd Floor, 89 Ridley Road, Dalston, London E8 2NH
Tel: 01 254 9527/ 9536
Con. Ms L Gopaul

Black Film & Video Workshop Wales, 31 Hodges Square, Bute Town, Cardiff, Wales
Con. Mr C Thompson

Ceddo Film/Video Workshop, 1st Floor , South Tottenham Education & Training Centre, Braemar Road, London N15 5EU
Tel: 01 802 9034
Con. Ms J. Reid

Liverpool Black Media Group, 64 Mount Pleasant, Liverpool L3 5SH
Tel: 051 709 6858
Con. Mr M Greenidge

Macro Films, Holyhead School/ Community Centre, Florence Road, Handsworth, Birmingham B20
Tel: 021 523 7544
Con. Mr D Shaw

Retake . Film/Video, 25 Bayham Street, London NW1
Tel: 01 388 9031/2
Con. Mr M Jamal

Sankofa, Unit 5, Cockpit' Yard, Northington Street, London WC1
Tel: 01 831 0024/5
Con. Mr M Jamal

Star Productions, 61 Thistlewaite Road, London E5
Tel: 01 986 4470
Con. Mr R Patel

Other Useful Addresses

Aboriginal Land Rights Support Group (ALRSG), 19c Lancaster Road, London W11 1QL

Aid for India, 186 Cowley Road, Oxford DX4 1VE
Tel: 0865 728794

Alcohol Counselling Services, 34 Electric Lane, Brixton SW9
Tel: 737 3570/9
Con. Juliette Small

Anti-Apartheid Movement, 13 Mandela Street, London NW1

Amnesty International, Head of Press & Publicity, 1 Easton Street, London WC1X 8OJ
Tel: 01 833 1771

Artlaw, 358 Strand, London WC2
Tel: 01 240 0610

Association of Commonwealth Universities, 36 Gordon Square, London WC1
Tel: 01 387 8572

Bangladesh Womens Association, 91 Highbury Hills, London N5 1SX
Tel: 01 359 5836

British Academy of Film & TV Arts, 195 Piccadilly, London W1
Tel: 01 734 0022

British Defense and Aid Fund for Southern Africa (BDAF), Canon Collins House, 2nd Floor, 64 Essex Road, London N1 8LR
Tel: 01 359 9181

British & South Asian Trade Association, Centre Point, New Oxford Street, London WC1
Tel: 01 240 5903

British Commonwealth Ex-Services League, 48 Pall Mall, London SW1
Tel: 01 930 8131

British Council for Aid to Refugees, Bondway House, Bondway, London SW8
Tel: 01 582 6922

British Council of Churches, 2 Eaton Gate, London SW1
Tel: 01 730 9611

British Institute in Eastern Africa, Kensington Gore, London SW7
Tel: 01 584 4653

British Institute of Human Rights (Faculty of Laws), Kings College, Strand, London WC2R 2LS
Tel: 01 836 5454 ext. 2760

British Medical Association, BMA House, Tavistock Square, London WC1
Tel: 01 387 4499

British Museum, Bloomsbury, London WC1
Tel: 01 636 1555

British Museum (Natural History), Cromwell Road, London SW7
Tel: 01 589 6323

British Safety Council, 62 Chancellors Road, London W6
Tel: 01 741 1231

Caribbean Community Service, 416 Seven Sisters Road, London N4 2LX
Tel: 01 802 0550

Centre for World Development Education (CWDE), 128 Buckingham Palace Road, London SW1W 9SH
Tel: 01 730 8332

Central Office of Information (COI), Hercules Road, London SE1
Tel: 01 928 2345

Children First in Trans-Racial Fostering and Adoption, 662 High Road, London N12
Tel: 01 341 7190

Committee on South African War Resistance, BM Box 2190, London WC1N 3XX
Tel: 01 278 6928

Commonwealth Countries League, 14 Thistleworth Close, Isleworth, Middlesex TW7 4QQ
Tel: 01 568 9868

Commonwealth Human Ecology Council (CHEC), 63 Cromwell Road, London SW7
Tel: 01 373 6761

Commonwealth Institute, Kensington High Street, London W8
Tel: 01 602 3252, (Cultural/Educational)

Commonwealth Journalists Association, 3rd Floor, 8 Bouvier Street, London EC4Y 8BB
Tel: 01 583 0618

Commonwealth Secretariat, Marlborough House, Pall Mall, London SW1Y 5HX
Tel: 01 839 3411

Confederation of Indian Organisations (UK), 11 North Avenue, Harrow, Middlesex HA2 7AE
Tel 01 928 9889/836 9089

Duke of Edinburghs Award, 5 Prince of Wales Road, London W8
Tel: 01 937 5205

Equal Opportunities Commission, Overseas House, Quay Street, Manchester M3 3H
Tel: 061 833 9244

Equal Opportunities Commission, 1 Bedford Square, London WC2
Tel: 01 379 6323

Federation of the Commonwealth Chambers of Commerce, 69 Cannon Street, London EC4
Tel: 01 248 4444

Immigration Appeals, Thanet House, Strand, London WC2
Tel: 01 353 8060

Indian Welfare Society (IWS), 11 Middle Row, London W10 5AY
Tel: 01 969 9493

Indian Workers Association (IWA), Southall Town Hall, High Street, Southall, Middlesex UB1 3HA
Tel: 01 574 6019/7283

Indian Volunteers for Community Service (IVCS), 36 Headstone Road, Harrow HA1 1PE
Tel: 01 863 9544

Institute of Commonwealth Studies, 27 Russell Square, London WC1
Tel: 01 580 5876

Institute of Community Studies (Social Research), 18 Victoria Park Square, London E2
Tel: 01 980 6263

International African Institute, 38 King Street, London WC2
Tel: 01 379 7636

International Muslim Movement, 1 St Mary's Road, London E17
Tel: 01 520 4121

International Voluntary Service (National Office), 53 Regent Road, Leicester
Tel: 0533 541862

Islamic Arts Foundation, 5 Bathurst Street, London W2
Tel: 01 402 1451

Joint Council for the Welfare of Immigrants, 115 Old Street, London EC1
Tel: 01 251 8706

London Interpreting Project, 245a Coldharbour Lane, London SW9 8RR

Nottinghill Carnival & Arts Committee, 4/7 Thorpe Close, London W10
Tel: 01 960 5266

Nottinghill Carnival Industrial Project, 230 St Marks Road, (Under Westway), London W10

Ombudsman, 21 Queen Anne's Gate, London SW1H 9BU
Tel: 01 222 5622

Overseas Mauritian Aid Trust, 14 Birbeck Road, London SW19 8NZ

Overseas Student Trust, 117 Vauxhall Bridge Road, London SW1V 1ER

Oxfam, 274 Banbury Road, Oxford OX2 7DZ
Tel: 0865 56777

Pakistan Welfare Association, 181 Haydons Road, London SW19 8T8
Tel: 01 542 6176

Save the Children Fund, Mary Datchelor House, 17 Grove Lane, London SE5
Tel: 01 703 5400

Science Museum, Exhibition Road, London SW7
Tel: 01 589 3456

SHAC (The London Housing Aid Centre), 189A Old Brompton Road, London SW5
Tel: 01 373 7276

Shelter, The National Campaign for the Homeless Ltd, 157 Waterloo Road, London SE1
Tel: 01 633 9377

The Spastic Society (Head Office), 12 Park Crescent, London W1
Tel: 01 636 5020

Sports Council, 16 Upper Woburn Place, London WC1
Tel: 01 388 1277

Standing Conference of Ethnic Minority Senior Citizens, Ethnic Minority Research Centre, 5A Westminster Bridge Road, London SE1 7XW
Tel: 01 928 0095

Survival International, 29 Craven Street, London WC2N 5NT
Tel: 01 839 3267

Television Training Centre, 18 Grosvenor Street, London W1
Tel: 01 381 4412

Trade Union Congress, (TUC) Congress House, 23-38 Great Russell Street, London WC1B 3LS
Tel: 01 636 4030

Ujamaa Hostel, 5 Fern Grove, Liverpool 8

UK Immigrant Advisory Service, Refugee Unit, Brettenham House, Lancaster Place, London WC2
Tel: 01 379 7969

United Nations Information Centre, 20 Buckingham Gate, London SW1A 6LB
Tel: 01 630 1981

U.N.I.C.E.F., 55 Lincolns Inn, London WC2
Tel: 01 405 5592

Voluntary Work Advisory Service, 68 Eccleston Street, London SW1N 9NJ
Tel: 01 730 7212

War On Want (Head Office), 467 Caledonian Road, London N7
Tel: 01 609 0211

Westindian Standing Conference, 5 Westminster Bridge Road, London SE1 7XW
Tel: 01 928 7861/2

Coolie Odyssey – A Celebration of Survival

1988 marks the 150th Anniversary of the arrival of Indians to the Caribbean. They came as indentured labourers to work in the canefields which the African slaves had partially abandoned upon emancipation in 1834. Here they inherited both the arduous work and many of the conditions of servitude. Their history has been one of exploitation, violence and deprivation, but also of triumph in the face of adversity.

Despite the fact that Indians have played a significant role in the history and development of the Caribbean their history and culture have, until recently received scant scholarly attention, resulting in a primarily Afro-centric view of the Caribbean. It was to close this gap in knowledge that led Hansib Publishing to embark upon the publication of the "Coolie Odyssey" series. The popularity of this series has resulted in the addition of three extra titles to mark the occasion.

The series of six books published by Hansib could very aptly be described as a "Coolie Odyssey", taking the name from the poetry book by David Dabydeen, in which he evokes an odyssey from India to England. The odyssey is a journey of words and deeds rather than a chronicle of threaded events and it is this notion of "odyssey" which captures the experience of the Indian in the Caribbean.

As an expression of a "Coolie Odyssey" therefore, the need for the publication of this series is succinctly expressed by Dr Jeremy Poynting in his book *The Second Shipwreck: A Study of Indo-Caribbean Literature* (Hansib, 1988):

> 'If there is one overall pattern which Indo-Caribbean imaginative writing discovers in the history of Indians in the Caribbean it is the pattern of the journey, begun in ignorance, deception and blind necessity, seen initially as an accidental shipwreck, but coming to be recognised as an odyssey of survival and renewal, from "somewhere to somewhere".

Thus, the books in this series recognise and explore various parts of that odyssey.

In *Benevolent Neutrality* we are at the beginning of the journey, the 'accidental shipwreck' where the author explores the rationale for, experience and final plight of the indentured immigrants. The novel, *The Open Prison,* takes us a little further on in time to the early 20th century. This work takes its emotive source from slavery and indenture but plunges us into the tensions and conflicts of the aftermath as experienced by a mulatto child growing up in a society where black and white are trying to reassert their roles.

Indo-Westindian Cricket takes us into the next experiences of the odyssey, of survival and renewal, as we journey into the soul of the great Indo-Westindian cricketers, how their genius was shaped by the surrounding political and cultural context.

Web of Tradition examines in detail the writing of one of the most famous Caribbean authors, V.S. Naipaul. The author studies Naipaul's use of allusion as a response to cultural dislocation, a rootlessness embodied in the "somewhere to somewhere" of the odyssey.

The Second Shipwreck is an overall study of Indo-Caribbean literature, how it owes its character to its hybrid nature, how the writers and consequently their works have been shaped by the 150 year old odyssey.

India in the Caribbean, a collection of works by various Indo-Caribbean writers, ranges from the mastery of the cricket field to political leadership. It encapsulates the experience (the 'shipwreck'), the resistance (the 'survival') and the efforts and achievements (the 'renewal').

As an experience of an odyssey the publication of these six books marks an important point in the history of Indians from the Caribbean. From the 'Coolies' of the 19th century – the low paid 'jobbers' – the odyssey has surely brought us to a redefinition of that term.

As Marcus Garvey brought dignity and respect to the word 'Negro', thus the contribution of this series must in part be regarded as an affirmation of sacrifice and a celebration of survival. The term 'Coolie' must finally come to mean a word which embodies respect and pride born out of the suffering and experience of that 150 year old "Coolie Odyssey".

The publication of these titles inspired an addition of three extra titles to mark the occasion – *Coolie Odyssey*, the collection of poems by David Dabydeen, *Inseparable Humanity*, an anthology of reflections of Shridath Ramphal, one of today's most prominent thinkers whose roots lie in the Westindies and the indenture system, and *King of the Carnival and Other Stories*, a lively collection of Caribbean short stories by Willie Chen, a well known writer and personality from Trinidad.

Coolie Odyssey titles

INDIA IN THE CARIBBEAN
Ed Dr David Dabydeen
and Dr Brinsley Samaroo
A collection of essays, poems and prose by leading Indo-Caribbean scholars and writers on East Indian history and culture in the Caribbean.
ISBN: 1 870518 00 4 PB PRICE: £8.95
ISBN: 1 870518 05 5 HB PRICE: £11.95

INDO-WESTINDIAN CRICKET
By Professor Frank Birbalsingh
and Clem Shiwcharan
Two brilliant essays highlighting the sheer genius of cricketers like Kanhai, Kallicharan and Ramadhin and an exclusive interview with Ivan Madray. An insight into not only the cricketers but the game itself.
ISBN: 1 870518 20 9 HB PRICE: £7.95

THE SECOND SHIPWRECK: INDO-CARIBBEAN LITERATURE
By Dr Jeremy Poynting
A wholly original and pioneering study of Indo-Caribbean literature looking at both well known and lesser known writers – a book is a work of encyclopaedic scholarship.
ISBN: 1 870518 15 2 PB PRICE: £6.95

THE WEB OF TRADITION: USES OF ALLUSION IN V.S. NAIPAUL'S FICTION
By Dr John Thieme
A new and exciting study of one of the Caribbean's major and most controversial novelists.
ISBN: 1 870518 30 6 PB PRICE: £6.95

BENEVOLENT NEUTRALITY: INDIAN GOVERNMENT POLICY AND LABOUR MIGRATION TO BRITISH GUIANA 1854-1884
by Dr Basdeo Mangru
A detailed, scholarly essay on Indian migration, including a major, pioneering study of women migrants.
ISBN: 1 870518 10 1 HB PRICE: £12.95

THE OPEN PRISON
By Angus Richmond
A highly readable novel which explores the complex problem of colour from the point of view of a young mulatto girl growing up in early 20th century British Guiana.
ISBN: 1 870518 25 X PB PRICE: £4.95

COOLIE ODYSSEY
By Dr David Dabydeen
A collection of poems in which the experience of the diaspora, the journeying from India to the Caribbean then to Britain is probed with passion, energy and splendid emotion.
ISBN: 1 870518 01 2 PB PRICE: £3.95

THE KING OF THE CARNIVAL AND OTHER STORIES
By Willie Chen
Stories set in the Caribbean reflecting the colour and pace of local life giving an insight into the day to day drama of individuals and the community.
ISBN: 1 870518 12 8 PB PRICE: £6.95

INSEPARABLE HUMANITY: AN ANTHOLOGY OF REFLECTIONS OF SHRIDATH S. RAMPHAL
An anthology of reflections by one of today's leading thinkers, Shridath Ramphal the Commonwealth Secretary-General. Ramphal draws on the exploitation and inequities and abuse which exist in today's international economic and political system.
ISBN: 1 870518 14 4 HB PRICE: £14.95

Suggested reading on Third World issues

A LIGHT IN THE DARK TUNNEL
By Ashton Gibson with Charles Lewis
Described as "an invaluable contribution to race relations", this book responds to the urgency felt by professionals, doctors, social workers and probation officers to understand the needs of the Westindian community and their children.
ISBN: 0 906 890 683 HB PRICE £4.95

A LITTLE BIT OF PARADISE ANTIGUA AND BARBUDA
A Little Bit of Paradise is a magical pictorial journey through the history, geography and culture of the Caribbean's most natural twin-island state, Antigua and Barbuda.
The playground of the royals and the rich, the unspoilt charm of Antigua and Barbuda has been one of the best kept secrets of the world.
It is an ideal souvenir of Antigua and Barbuda, and a valuable contribution to literature on the Caribbean.
ISBN: 1 805718 09 8 HB PRICE £19.50

A READER'S GUIDE TO WEST INDIAN AND BLACK BRITISH LITERATURE
By Dr David Dabydeen
and Dr Nana Wilson-Tagoe
(Published jointly with the University of Warwick Centre for Caribbean Studies)
An invaluable aid to teachers seeking to expand and deepen the literature curriculum. Specially prepared for the new G.C.S.E. curriculum, the book is a lucid introduction to Westindian and Black British literature; it outlines their history and development, highlights their major themes, and suggests texts which best illustrate these themes for further reading.
ISBN: 1 870518 35 7 PB PRICE £6.95

BARRISTER FOR THE DEFENCE
By Rudy Narayan
For those who wish to look beyond the mystique of wig and gown Rudy Narayan, best known for his controversial confrontations with the British legal establishment, offers you the best chance of ever understanding the role and function of Barristers for the Defence.
ISBN: 09506664 2 4 PB PRICE: £6.95

BOOK OF COMMONSENSE
Compiled by Neil Prendergast
A collection of proverbs and quotations, old and new. Recommended as a coffee/bedside table manual which will give many pleasant hours of quiet browsing.
PB PRICE: £6.95 P&P £1.00

CROWNS OF EXILE
By K Andrew Herold
Set against a background of political turmoil this exciting novel traces Michael Alexander's return to Zambia after 10 years of living in London.
From the life of a drugs dealer, Michael finds himself becoming involved with the passion, the excitement and the conflict of life in Zambia.
ISBN 1 870518 11 X PB PRICE £6.95

ESSAYS ON RACE, CULTURE AND ENGLISH SOCIETY
By Dr Paul Rich (University of Warwick)
Dr Rich stresses the importance of the concept of race in the history of ideas, and traces its applications in the England of the nineteenth and twentieth centuries, as well as in a South African context. Writing of his previous work *(Race and Empire in British Politics,* Cambridge University Press, 1987), *The Times Higher Educational Supplement* stated: "The learning Paul Rich exhibits is not only voluminous but admirably diverse."
ISBN: 1 870518 40 3 PB PRICE £6.95

FROM WHERE I STAND
By Roy Sawh
A moving autobiography from one of Britain's leading black community spokesmen and a notable orator at Hyde Park. It is unique in being the first Indo-Caribbean autobiography published in Britain, a literary milestone.
ISBN: 0 9956664 9 1 PB PRICE: £5.95

GRASSROOTS IN VERSE
An extensive collection of poetry and verse submitted by the readers of *Caribbean Times, Asian Times* and *African Times.*
Lively, humorous, provocative and thoughtful – feelings experienced by young and old alike.
ISBN: 1 870518 13 6 PB PRICE £6.95

GREAT FIGURES FROM THE THIRD WORLD
by Elizabeth Mackie and Steve Garner
Biographical and illustrated essays on thirty eight great scientists, writers, politicians and thinkers from the Third World whose works have made a permanent impact on world civilisation. Meticulously researched and written in a popular, highly readable style, featuring Steve Biko, Mahatma Gandhi, Martin Luther King and Bob Marley.
ISBN: 1 870518 60 8 HB PRICE £11.95

HOGARTH, WALPOLE AND COMMERCIAL BRITAIN
By Dr David Dabydeen
Essential reading for students and teachers, this pioneering study of the politics of Hogarth's early work takes us beyond the conventional and obvious readings of his work with a perceptive and detailed eye.
ISBN: 1 870518 45 4 HB PRICE: £15.95

MY THOUGHTS
By Pamela Ali
A collection of verse and poems published in a delightfull presented 48-page paperback.
ISBN: 1 870518 11 X PB PRICE £2.40

MY TURN TO BARK
By Jennifer Muddle
Bengey is the type of dog who is loved by both children and adults. Shaggy, boisterous but with such winning ways, he has given the author many hours of happiness which he now invites you to share.
The illustrations by Jez Hill greatly enhance the tales of the true-life situations in which Bengey finds himself.
ISBN 1 870518 02 0 HB PRICE £5.95

PASSION AND EXILE
By Frank Birbalsingh
A collection of essays concerned mainly with the work of anglophone novelists and prose writers in Caribbean literature and reflecting the themes of passion and exile.
ISBN:1 870518 16 0 PB £8.95

RASTA AND RESISTANCE FROM MARCUS GARVEY TO WALTER RODNEY
By Dr Horace Campbell
A study of the Rastafarian Movement in all its manifestations, this book serves to break the intellectual traditions which placed the stamp of millenarianism on Rasta.
ISBN: 0 95066 645 5 PB PRICE: £6.95
ISBN: 0 95066 645 5 HB PRICE: £9.95

SPEECHES BY ERROL BARROW
Edited by Yussuff Haniff
A collection of speeches made by the late Barbadian Prime Minister, Errol Barrow, in which we see him as a true Caribbean man, fighting for the region's independent identity.
ISBN: 1 870518 70 5 HB PRICE: £10.95

THE CARIBBEAN: GUYANA, TRINIDAD & TOBAGO, BARBADOS, JAMAICA
By Steve Garner
Specially written for a general readership, and recommended to school teachers and students, this book is an excellent structured introduction to the history, politics and culture of four major Caribbean countries. It is lavishly illustrated, to bring alive the colour and vibrancy of Caribbean life.
ISBN: 1 870518 55 1 PB PRICE £6.95

THE GREAT MARCUS GARVEY
By Liz Mackie
A fitting tribute to a man who has inspired generations of black people. For anyone interested in the black struggle and the lessons of history this book should not be missed.
ISBN 1 870518 50 0 PB £4.95

THE IDEOLOGY OF RACISM
by Samuel Kennedy Yeboah
A well-researched analysis of the origin and development of Western racism, its ideology and the power which makes it operable.
ISBN: 1 870518 07 1 PB PRICE: £8.95
ISBN: 1 870518 08 X HB PRICE: £11.95

THE STATE OF BLACK BRITAIN
By Dr Aaron Haynes
This book is a major statement on the effects of public policy on black people in Britain. It directs attention to, and urges involvement in the decision making process of policy. An important reference source for practitioners, professionals and students seeking an understanding of the realities of the implications of various policies for black families.
ISBN:0 94645 00 7 HB PRICE £3.75
Hardback ISBN 0 946455 01 5 £5.95

THE REGGAE FILES: A BOOK OF INTERVIEWS
By Gordon C
A unique collection of inteviews with reggae stars from Jamaica and Britain which tells the story of their music in the words of those who play it.
ISBN 1 870518 03 9 PB PRICE: £6.95

THE UNEQUAL STRUGGLE
By Ashton Gibson with Jocelyn Barrow
A book aimed at examining the reasons behind the poor performances of Westindian children in British schools. For the first time a large-scale research project emanating from the Westindian community identifies the factors behind the plight of its own teenagers in Britain.
ISBN: 0948 477 032 HB PRICE £6.95

100 GREAT WESTINDIAN TEST CRICKETERS
By Bridgette Lawrence and Reg Scarlett
This lavishly illustrated and superb reference book is a must for all cricket enthusiasts.
ISBN: 1 870518 65 9 HB PRICE: £14.95

*** Please add £1.00 or US$2.00 post and packing per book.**

Hansib Book Club

The Hansib Book Club has been formed to make available to the widest possible audience a range of works covering all aspects of the life of Britain's visible minorities and the countries and peoples of the Third World as well as topics of general interest.

Through more than 15 years of publishing activity Hansib has become all too aware of the great range of useful works available and of the desire of members of the community to lay hands on them. At the same time the lack of proper distribution systems – even the absence of a good bookshop in many areas – has worked to the detriment of authors, publishers and the reading public alike.

It was in response to this short-coming that the Hansib Book Club was initiated. Although still in a relatively early stage it already offers a range of several hundred titles covering numerous subjects and designed to appeal to people of all ages.

Our regularly updated catalogue is available, free, from: Hansib Publishing Limited, Unit 8, Caxton Hill, Hertford, Herts., SNG 7NE. Tel: (0992) 501113
Credit cards accepted